1112

Discourse on Hamlet and HAMLET

A Psychoanalytic Inquiry

by

K. R. Eissler

23

p
INTERNATIONAL UNIVERSITIES PRESS, INC.
NEW YORK

Library of Congress Catalog Card Number: 73-125475

Manufactured in the United States of America

Table of Contents

SECTION II: SOME ANALYTIC INTERPRETATIONS

SECTION III: ON HAMLET'S MADNESS
AND HIS PROCRASTINATION

A) ways being killed
    1. Claudius
    2. Hamlet Sr
    3. Polonias
    4. R + G

B.) Deciet

C) Contradiction + Indecisiveness
    1. Ophelia - freely
    2. Ghost - listen
    3. solitaly - suicide

vii

God threw the dice
And they fell wrong.
That's all.

(Source unknown)

Il n'est point d'hostilité
excellente comme la chrétienne.

Michel de Montaigne

Gott will, dass die Gesetze
sich ändern.

Walter Hasenclever

Preface

A book on *Hamlet* has hardly any chance of arousing great interest in a public that has been, for years, saturated with the subject. All the greater is my indebtedness to Dr. A. Kagan for being kind enough to accept my manuscript for publication at its full length. This has also given me an opportunity to republish my paper "On *Hamlet*" of 1953, in an improved form. Since I had had no opportunity to correct the galley proofs of that version, the original publication should now be disregarded. Of the present volume, Appendix A and the essay on Fortinbras have recently been published in a slightly changed form.

The reader will no doubt discover some repetitions in the chapters that follow the original text. I want to assure him that I did try to spare him this inconvenience, but did not succeed, at least to the extent I had wished to.

I am deeply indebted to Mr. Harold Collins for the care and labor he expended on the production of a readable manuscript. His contribution was so extensive that I hesitate to add the customary assurance of the author's responsibility for possible faults. In this book, too, as on previous occasions, Mr. Collins' contribution went beyond that of an editor, since many a passage was changed in substance as the result of our discussion of his critical suggestions. I also owe Mr. Collins thanks for the index.

Mr. de Parmiter was kind enough to advise me on a point of Henry VIII's frequent marital irresponsibilities and to permit me to quote from his letter. Drs. Bertram D. Lewin and Harry Slochower were kind enough to comment upon the paragraphs on traumatophilia in the section on the doxaletheic function. I also owe thanks to Professor Leo Steinberg for advising me on those paragraphs in which I have drawn upon his lectures.

A word about the literature on *Hamlet,* the extent of which seems to confirm Montaigne's saying that "there are more books about books than about any other subject." Jan Kott says that the bibliography on *Hamlet* alone is twice as thick as the Warsaw telephone directory. He may be wrong; my impression is that it is double the size of New York's. It is evident that it is a hopeless task, at least for an outsider to literary criticism, even to try to undertake the bibliographic spade work that is necessary and customary in research. For that reason, I must state at the very beginning that I do not raise any claim to originality; any reviewer who knows the literature on the subject matter should not find it hard to quote historical predecessors, on questions about which I may have had the feeling of being original. Although the meanings of *Hamlet* may be in reality inexhaustible, nevertheless it has become rather difficult to discover in it any meaning that has not been set forth previously.

I should also like to emphasize something that, even though it will not be repeated in what follows, I would wish the reader to keep in mind —namely, that my intention has not been to offer a "solution" to the Hamlet problem. A solution to Hamlet is as little likely ever to be discovered as is a solution to life. In both instances, one deals with single sectors of an infinite universe. Still, there is a viewpoint that holds together my comments.

General Introduction

It is probably customary for an author to write the introduction to his book when he has finished the text. I wonder what this introduction would have sounded like, if I had started to write it before the rest.

The triangle formed by book, reader and author is not equilateral. Whereas in most instances the reader is likely to be somewhat unsure, in advance, about the gain he will receive from reading a particular book, an author should always be wiser after he has finished writing it than he was before. At least, this happened to me and most of this introduction is written in a spirit that I reached only when I began the concluding essay on *The Tempest*.

I. The effect achieved by Shakespeare's plays embraces many dimensions. The most puzzling effect, and yet possibly the most important one, can best be conveyed—if I may take on for a moment the role of storyteller—in the following fable.

It was the day of the Last Judgment, and God was holding court over mankind. One after the other, men came before his throne and tried to justify themselves. But listening to man and learning of what he had done on earth, the Lord became more and more angry. Everyone had done some mischief, had in some way betrayed His spirit—Pope, King and beggar. Finally, he became so angry that he did not want to listen any further, and He sent mankind—both saints and sinners—off to Hell.

At that moment, the Angel Gabriel pushed Shakespeare forward. "And what did you do?" God snapped at him. Thereupon Shakespeare started to recite his plays. The Lord listened with an attention that grew steadily deeper and more intense. He broke out in laughter while listening to *As You Like It* and wept as Shakespeare recited *King Lear*. And when Shakespeare was at last through with *The Tempest,* the Lord embraced him and said: "Indeed, what a fool I have been; now I understand what I have created on earth. You are all forgiven."

The less significant implication of this fable has to do with the service that the genius renders mankind in terms of exoneration, vindication, justification, or whatever we may choose to call it. Aside from the fact that we would probably still be living in caves if it were not for those unusual minds that have possessed the ability to dream of a world of an entirely new shape, as well as the urge and the courage to put their dreams into realistic forms, the sublime artistic achievements of the few to whom mankind has accorded the title of "genius" contain, in addition, an exceedingly great consolation.

Mankind's record—whether it is taken in its totality or in terms of individual man—is quite disheartening. The miracle of anthropogenesis —that transformation of the animal (an almost entirely stimulus-bound organism, devoid of both representational language and the oedipal conflict) into man, endowed as he is with the potential for constructing a variety of languages, as well as with conscience and the belief in a transcendental power, (a creature, in short, whose essence even now defies satisfactory explanation, so that it strikes one as being something of a miracle)—that marvel has not yet fulfilled what it must initially have seemed to promise.

I do not wish to burden these pages with a record of those abominations that have not only befouled the history of each nation, but stain as well the present existence of most of them. Nor will I go into the grave problem of whether it is possible at all—even under optimal conditions— for a human being to go through life without an inner and sometimes most skillfully denied and concealed treacherousness to standards, without a fundamental hypocrisy, both of which permit one to speak of the basic dishonesty that may be inherent in human existence, as soon as certain degrees of differentiation are reached. In moments of such awareness, no one could help turn away from the miracle of anthropogenesis, with the feeling that he would rather be the amoeba, from which organic development took its start, as against the present end-product of that development. That is, he might well feel that way, were it not for the creations of those geniuses who, despite the fact that they too have shared the pitfalls that beset the species, have yet brought forth such achievements as contain the beauty, harmony and perfection that one might have had the right to expect to come to pass in reality, yet which have been—over and over again—converted almost into their opposites by man's apparently unconquerable archaic heritage. Thus, one is inclined to muse, it is only the ontogenetic marvel of the genius that actually fulfills the phylogenetic miracle of anthropogenesis.

Yet the story I have suggested contains another implication. There is something eerie about the fact that what one encounters in Shakespeare's plays is a mind-created world—not just one aspect or one dimension, or even a series of moods, or of thoughts or structures of beauty—but a complete world, one that is parallel to the one we know, yet has a more concentrated, typical, indeed original shape. The vicissitudes of human life here appear to be compressed into such solid and meaningful forms that one might seriously wonder whether it were better to observe directly the history of mankind, by a study of man and his records, or by returning over and over again to the embodiments of Shakespeare's creative imagination. Be that as it may, it is only the rare occurrence of the achievements of genius that sustains the image of man's worth and vindicates mankind's unending sorrows. Without the luminosity of such achievements, many may feel prompted to agree with Hamlet that the world is a prison and, for that matter, rather a dungeon than a reformatory.

II. There is another dimension of Shakespeare's plays that I wish to set forth, in the form of a historical interpretation, which will hardly be likely to fall on willing ears.

The last word of Charles I—of whom the Puritans asserted that "Had he but studied Scripture half so much as *Ben Johnson or Shakspear* . . ." he would not have lost throne and life—was spoken to William Juxon before he stepped on to the scaffold: it was "Remember!" Historians ever since have been puzzled by its meaning. My own conjecture is that, since Charles was well versed in his Shakespeare, he was attempting to convey a world of meaning to the priest who had administered the last rites, since he must have meant, by that one word, to refer to the Ghost's departing words to his son on their first encounter.

As is well known, Charles V sent a full-length painting of himself, produced by the Styrian court painter, Jacob Seisenegger, to Titian, who then repainted it trait for trait. The new painting was quite different from the earlier one, although still the Emperor's portrait: now it was not only a painting of the man, but also the portrait of an Emperor, painted the way an Emperor ought to look. The great painter knew more about imperial appearance than nature and nurture combined were able to achieve. In the case of Charles I, the relation was reversed; it may well have been that here the King imitated the poet. A remarkable dignity, self-possession and resignation, we are told, characterized the King's last few hours, to the amazement of those who knew him; perhaps it had happened that, even though Charles I had not learned from Shakespeare how to govern his realm, he had learned from him how a King who was awaiting his execution ought to comport himself.

III. A third dimension is brought forth in a recollection reported by Strong (1954, p. 187): "I heard Yeats proclaim behind me, 'The moment Hamlet let pass the chance to stab his uncle, the modern psychological novel was born.' " This is a very remarkable comment; it needs only to be enlarged to include modern psychology as well. In Shakespeare's time, man had started to behave quite differently from his immediate ancestors, who had peopled the Middle Ages. New personality types arose, such as Pietro Aretino and Machiavelli; landscapes were painted differently; language changed, and many other things made it evident that mankind was in transition toward new goals. Shakespeare ripped open the curtain before the human world. Much as may be discovered in Shakespeare's plays about the medieval world, it was after all a brave *new* world that he put explicitly on the stage—brave in virtue and wisdom, but brave also in sin and crime. If we take the term "education" out of its usual academic context, and define it instead as the totality of those mental stimuli that change man's thinking and actions and behavior, then we may say that Shakespeare's educative influence on Western mankind has been and still is enormous.

Here for the first time—and never since to that same extent repeated—the *full spectrum of man's nature in conflict* was given recognition in a literary universe, not as it appears from a religious or philosophical point of view, but as it is. It was only after Shakespeare that man acquired the freedom to venture into the recesses of the mind, only after him that modern psychology became possible. Indeed, I believe that, with regard to some essentials, Freud may well have learned more from Shakespeare than he did from his patients.

It does not promise well for the future that the influence of Shakespeare's world is waning, even if it is true this has happened for no other reason than (as Mrs. Vera D. Owen once mentioned to me) that English-speaking youth has gradually lost its inner response to and become estranged from the language of the Bible—a language one has to have somewhat integrated, in order to be able to respond fully to Shakespeare's poetry.[1]

Although it is well to consider the linguistic aspect, the problem, I fear, goes deeper. To my horror, a youth in the streets of Moscow explained to me, in the following words, the superiority of Salinger over Dostoevski: "Dostoevski is too complex. One uses only straight lines in modern architecture." Thus it is quite possible that it may be not only the estrangement from the most important religious document written in the English language that has gradually led to the "debunking" of Shakespeare, but also the mechanization of life, which I assume is to be referred to here, as it so often is nowadays, as *the* scapegoat for all the ills of our time and an easy rationalization of our ignorance.

IV. Last but not least, Shakespeare's creative output should be, if only very briefly, considered in terms of its role as the builder of a nation —a function that Thomas Mann (1929, p. 355f) has claimed for the German classics. There is what I would call a sort of "vindictive vindication" that follows in the wake of great minds. The world of power—be it moneyed, military or political power—has usually looked down on the man whose life is centered in the mind, and who employs inner processes for the fulfillment of self. I am here thinking of those times, prior to the present and so different from ours, when the flight of a physicist may amount to a greater national catastrophe than the devaluation of the country's currency. Such hierarchical positions of intellectuals at the top have until now been practically unheard of in the record of social organizations, although there was a time, some three hundred years or so ago, when a Pope regarded a sculptor's service as so indispensable that he was ready to (ab)use his delegated power and to threaten excommunication if the artist dared to put himself into the service of another sovereign. Quite a compliment! Yet it still smacked of that overbearing despatch with which the man of intellect is treated by those in power.

[1] Rothe (1961) has made an interesting observation in this regard. Shakespeare's plays, written as they are in English, cannot be adapted to the requirements of modern English, since the text is safeguarded and hallowed by tradition. Hence the danger of the gradual estrangement precisely of his English-speaking heirs. For other nations Shakespeare can be integrated only by translation— which may paradoxically be an advantage, insofar as translations are not bound by tradition. Each new generation may therefore obtain a new translation, adapted to its particular linguistic spirit, and as a result it is possible that Shakespeare may remain alive for a longer time in the non-English-speaking nations than among the English and Americans.

The day of vindictive vindication arises sporadically in history, and ancient Rome, with all its secular power and glory, is conquered by the Cross. And that same sort of vindication occurred once again when the inspiring political pamphlets and dreary economic treatises of a penurious and fugitive scholar delivered the stuff with which to make a revolution and overthrow an empire and under whose sign Hitler's military machine came a cropper. At times, it seems as if the Word (or what one may also call *Geist* or *esprit)* in the long run conquered the secular power —enough of a happy illusion to warm the hearts of all intellectuals (unless, of course, they reflect upon the grievously corrupted state in which the pure text of their original finally obtains its vindication).

Shakespeare's text was also corrupted (this time in a literal sense) when it made its impact on mankind, but it was still pure enough to be of greater worth to England than India or the rest of her colonial Empire. Those she could lose without loss of identity; but what would England be without Shakespeare? Was it not *his* work that formed her into a nation as an indestructible spiritual structure? The reader will not hear anything further about the lofty subjects I have mentioned, however, for my own effort goes in an entirely different direction.

V. My concern here is with the application of psychoanalysis to *Hamlet.* As I shall indicate further on, Mr. Harold Collins has coined the useful terms *exopoietic* and *endopoietic* to distinguish two types of research. The first type undertakes to explain a literary work by seeking connections with factors outside the work itself, whether these be processes in the author's mind, or elements in the author's environment— economic, social or cultural. This approach has a greater appeal to the reader's imagination than does the endopoietic approach, which I am pursuing in this book. The latter type of research is more laborious, for both writer and reader, in that it does not leave much room to the imagination, but limits itself to the literary work under investigation.

Such interpretation tries deliberately to avoid the use of elements outside the work itself, but rather views each detail within it in the light shed by the whole play—that is to say, in terms of the aggregate of those details of which the work consists *and* their interpretation. This is indeed a painstaking and at times rather monotonous undertaking, and it tends to evoke the ridicule of the literary expert, so aptly put by Prof. Holland (1960), when he asked, "How many complexes had Lady Macbeth?" Prof. Holland himself, however, has traveled quite a distance, since it was he (1963, p. 101) who discovered in Romeo's dream an element that would illustrate Lewin's (1946, 1948, 1953) dream-screen.

Prof. Holland has the further merit of having found a methodological justification for the psychoanalytic interpretation of literary characters. The main phases in the history of Shakespeare criticism have been frequently set forth most satisfactorily by Prof. Holland (1966). Here it suffices to contrast two extremes. For the New Criticism, as laid down by L. C. Knights (1933, p. 20) "the only profitable approach to Shakespeare is a consideration of his plays as dramatic poems, of his use of language to obtain a total complex emotional response. . . . It is the main business of the critic to examine the words on the page." All abstractions are rejected "that have nothing to do with the unique arrangements of words that constitute these [Shakespeare's] plays" (p. 31). The New Criticism culminates in G. Wilson Knight (1930), in a work in which the *dramatis personae* are dealt with not as human beings, but rather as symbols of a poetic vision.

The other extreme is the psychoanalytic approach, which quite deliberately seeks to equate Shakespeare's characters with living human beings, in an attempt thereby to unearth the unconscious motivations of the former, as well as possible, by means of the data on hand.[2] For obvious reasons, this approach is unacceptable to the New Criticism.

VI. I shall start by attacking the latter's basic premise—namely, that Shakespeare's plays are primarily and exclusively dramatic poems, consisting of words, and that therefore only words may be considered. It is my conviction that this idea is fundamentally wrong. To be sure, the Folio does consist of words—as does, *per definitionem,* every other literary work; but these words are clues, directions, hints, keys as to how certain people, dressed in certain costumes (usually taken for granted and therefore not explicitly described) should talk, and how they should behave while talking in the prescribed way, during the time when they are on a stage and being watched by an audience for the limited span of time reserved for that particular purpose.

A play by Shakespeare may be looked at and it may be read as a dramatic poem, and an investigation of it along those lines may well lead to important insights. Nevertheless the play is primarily part of a corpus

---

[2] Whether or not this can be done satisfactorily from the psychoanalytic viewpoint is not here in question (cf. Kohut, 1960).

and as such contains innumerable bits of advice as to how people ought to act within a specific frame of reference. This guide to action is not, however, unequivocal, as a textbook of surgery would have to be, which cannot permit "alternative procedures." That is to say, from the corpus of Shakespeare's plays one cannot always learn whether a word should be spoken slowly or rapidly, with a smile or in tears. Yet, depending on such factors, the presentation of the action will evoke in the audience images of quite differing character. In *Hamlet,* the words of most *dramatis personae* are so cleverly chosen that at least two different characters can be evoked for each—characters that are not only not shades of a basic type, but are, in some instances, even diametrically opposed.

I do not see how this can be denied. But if it is so, then the scorn that has been expressed by the New Critics against the sort of Shakespearean criticism that does employ character interpretation is unwarranted. One should perhaps have argued that character interpretation is not sufficient, and that *other* modes of interpretation and criticism are necessary, or are methodologically justified; one might also have been able to reject some character analysis as erroneous, as has been done. But the methodological objection would seem, under the circumstances, to be untenable. This, of course, would not yet prove the methodological correctness of the psychoanalytic approach. Before we take up that question directly, however, it may be worthwhile to observe the New Criticism in practice.

VII. L. C. Knights (1933, p. 32f) starts what he calls "an essay in elucidation" of *Macbeth* by saying that the play "is a statement of evil." This assertion he connects with three themes that go through the play: the reversal of values, unnatural disorder and deceitful appearance. Curiously enough, these three themes can also be found in *Hamlet* and possibly in all of Shakespeare's great tragedies. We here run into the first objection, not to method, but to practice—namely, the high level of abstraction, so high that it cannot do anything resembling justice to the individual phenomenon under scrutiny.

Furthermore, there is one strange aspect of the history of the humanities that should be taken into consideration. Many who are engaged in their study start their particular pursuit by abjuring psychology: they are determined, it appears, to place their field on a genuine conceptual basis without borrowing from it. When the New Criticism turns so vigorously against character interpretation, that is what it really has in mind; the cry to examine words and nothing but words, to look at tragedy as a poem, basically means to avoid psychology. Yet in all such instances that

I have been able to observe, the investigator reaches a point at which he is forced to psychologize, even though this may happen against his will.

It happens with L. C. Knights. He very quickly finds himself in the midst of questions that are undoubtedly psychological in nature—for example, when he raises the question of whether or not Macduff is a traitor; if so, to whom; and was his flight due to wisdom or to fear (p. 41)? Knights himself seems here, at least, to be aware of his resorting to psychology. He writes: "It is no use discussing the effect [of Macbeth] in abstract terms at all. We can only discuss it in terms of the poet's concrete realization of certain emotions and attitudes" (p. 45). But surely this is a question of psychology, although of a very limited psychology, and despite the fact that the method he suggests at one particular point is wholly unsatisfactory: "We have to . . . define our impressions in terms of our response to the play" (p. 49). This is crude intuitivism, and as such it is unverifiable by empirical methods; it can only lead to a variety of interpretations standing side by side, each "correct" in its own terms —namely, those of the particular interpreter's idiosyncrasies.

Knights' criticism of psychological interpretation is often well taken, in that he selects instances in which that method has failed. This does not, however, negate the value of the method per se. In trying to show that details that are meaningless to the critic who does character analysis serve as the carrier of the poetical meaning of the work of art as a whole, he seems to admit only those interpretations that take us back to the work's *Gestalt*. This is arbitrary (an axiom that Holland (1963, p. 102) repeats in a different form), for an interpretation of detail may be quite correct and yet still be wholly separate from a comprehensive view of the total configuration.[3]

Nevertheless, the reader will find in this book instances in which character analysis has tied subplots all the more firmly to the play—to cite one example, the Reynaldo scene, which even the great T. S. Eliot regarded as a foreign body, is demonstrated to be an indispensable part of the tragedy. To be sure, the New Criticism and the school of symbolism, so close to it, do sometimes discover meaning in episodes that had been

---

[3] Method ought never to choke off the richness of science's potentialities. Freud (1916-1917, p. 37) was able to prove incontrovertibly the correctness of his basic model of parapraxia, by making use of a slip of the tongue that Schiller had a character make in one of his tragedies. The fact that major parts of Freud's theories lay embedded, like a kind of Aristotelian entelechy, within a detail of a literary production—that is to say, that some psychoanalytic theories could have been deduced from a playwright's creation—is far-reaching and essential to a discussion of the question of art versus life.

bypassed by content research. It is difficult on such occasions to decide whether this was due to the narrowness of the previous researchers, their lack of astuteness, or the shortcomings of the method per se.

Here is how Knights divides critics into good and bad (p. 32): the good critic "points to something that is actually contained in the work of art," the bad one "points away from the work in question; he introduces extraneous elements into his appreciation and smudges the canvas with his own paint." The key word here is, of course, "actually." For the New Criticism words alone possess actuality and, beyond them, the poetry that they create. The locus of its inquiry is therefore that thin plane on which the playwright's words intersect with the listener's emotional antennae, his sense organs. Knights says, for example, that "*Macbeth* has greater affinity with *The Waste Land* than with *The Doll's House*" (p. 33). But on the strength of what comparison can this be asserted?

Difficult as it may be to determine what Shakespeare's intentions might have been in writing the tragedies, I can well imagine that, if he thought of the audience at all, it was *that* intersection that was his only concern. If he succeeded in arousing strong emotions when the words of the play impinged upon the listener's sense organs, then he could be sure that he had done what needed to be done if he wanted to "stay in business." Whether or not the audience penetrated into the universe that he had *actually* created, whether its sights reached the horizons that this new universe contained, may have been of little concern to him, so long as no interference arose from that quarter with the creation of his universe.[4]

Why should a critic, however, stop his inquiries with the listener's immediate response, at the moment when the latter is overwhelmed by the beauty of language and is therefore hardly in a position to penetrate in depth? No matter how fruitful it may be to focus on that intersectional area, it can never comprise the *entire* area of necessary and well-founded criticism. Moreover, the goal of the New Criticism can be reached, if reliability is to serve as a criterion, only when the psychological spadework has already been completed.

I believe it to be altogether impossible, by using the methods of the

[4] By this comment I by no means want to assign the poetry of Shakespeare's works to a secondary place or to suggest that Shakespeare's interest in poetry was nothing but a desire to create a bait for the audience. I only conjecture that, if Shakespeare was indeed concerned with audience responses in any practical context, then he *might* have been anxious whether the audience would respond to his poetry.

New Criticism, to delineate the psychological variety of personages that Shakespeare has often created in one and the same character. In what follows, I shall try to show, without ever being able to do so exhaustively, the ambiguity in the creation of a single character. The dual, triple, even quadruple meanings that are involved in his presentation of single characters become completely lost when reliance is placed on the immediate impact of words.

For several reasons it is necessary for the psychologist first to stake out the full scope of that universe of discourse that is contained in the tragedy, in terms of the human psyche. What is due to stage convention, to allusion to the playwright's own world, to the effect on him of his particular society—all that is quickly lost in the progress of generations, and remains explicit only in the footnotes of editors. Only that remains universally effective that has its roots in the universals of the human world. Nevertheless, it has to be considered whether or not that which the historically-minded critic knows to be stage convention, or topical allusion, is at the same time imbued with a human factor and can also be interpreted in terms of psychology, for one and the same element that is no more than stage convention in one playwright will become the carrier of a particular and important meaning in Shakespeare's hands.

In one regard, the New Criticism, if it should consider the matter, would be all too correct. Even if psychology were successful in discovering the last ounce of content meaning, we would still not be able to say very much about why it is that the clothes in which the psychological facts are placed before us have the power to move us so profoundly. It is not possible to speculate at this point what in the totality of this effect is to be attributed to content and what to form. But there is no doubt that attempts at changing either of them have up to now done nothing but *reduce* the effect of Shakespeare's creations.

VIII. Analysis along the lines of psychological content can produce its best results when it treats Shakespeare's plays as if they were full-fledged human reality. Among the many problems of literary criticism, the relationship between real and created reality seems to have puzzled the critic most.[5] How can we apply the yardstick of reality—the laws that govern living people—to characters that owe their creation to a literary

---

[5] The problem has been discussed frequently; see, for example, Jones (1949) or Holland (1964a), where an extensive bibliography is to be found and the psychoanalytic method constitutes the point of departure.

genius? Even though there is indeed a paradox (to be dealt with later) involved in the relationship between the two worlds, it still is not quite clear why this question has so severely troubled the critic's mind. When we look at a landscape painted by Rembrandt, we perceive mountains, skies, trees—all the ingredients of a landscape. If we disregard ornamental and abstract works, we see that for the most part art has been the presentation of some portion of external reality. In the field of art there are also those who want to convince us that we should disregard content analysis and limit the evaluation of our artistic experience to its purely visual qualities. They do not accept the charge that we thereby lose the real profundities that a great painting may contain.

In 1636 Rembrandt painted *Samson Made Prisoner by the Philistines,* selecting for that purpose the moment of Samson's being blinded. It is a superb painting. If it is interpreted in terms of visual qualities, one would emphasize the light-dark distribution, the direction of light from the right toward the center, which finds its maximum in the left middleground, and further the parallel movement in oblique direction from the right front to the left back. The vividness of movement is enhanced by Delilah's rushing away from Samson in that very direction, yet turning her head back to her lover, who lies prostrate in the foreground and is being subjected to a kind of brutishness the delineation of which was perhaps surpassed only by Goya.[6] Here the content must become visually relevant, since it is a running figure that is the carrier of movement.

It is remarkable that in the same year Rembrandt painted a canvas about Danae that is visually structured in a similar way. I have not seen the two paintings side by side and may therefore be mistaken when I assert that there is a great similarity between them in regard to color tone. The direction of movement is certainly the same—from the right foreground obliquely to the left background. The amazing thing—the reason why I introduce the two canvases at this point—is that the contents of the two paintings are diametrically opposed. The Samson painting shows the castrating woman in triumph over the male; in the *Danae,* the woman appears in a state of unambivalent abandonment to the male, whom she expects or whom she may have already perceived, although he is invisible to the beholder. The superb visual accomplishment, independent of any content, is unquestionable. But the true greatness, the incomparable

---

[6] Rilke (1914) was deeply impressed by the painting. He marvelled how it was possible that "the most insane violence" can be made "innocent" by art.

beauty and depth of the canvas become recognizable, in this instance as well, only after one has acknowledged the presentation of emotions.

I do not hesitate to describe Delilah's face as a kind of miracle. No other face has been painted, to my knowledge, that reflects at one and the same time so many emotions, some of them contradictory: triumph over, revenge against, and sheer hatred of the ugly old man, whose caresses this beautiful girl, evidently just awakened from childhood, had had unwillingly to bear. But there is also visible sexual excitement and sensuality, in addition to terror and pity, as the man cringes in exquisite pain.

Danae's face is by contrast filled with one and only one emotion, which can hardly be described, perhaps, because it is a superhuman emotion: it is the epitome of love, and yet at the same time it has been purified of passion and perhaps even of sensuality. It has nothing to do with chastity, even though the woman depicted may be chaste; the emotion represented is beyond sexual passion and sensuality, purity and chasteness, it is the total abandonment of self, an almost devotional surrender to the male object, without any search or desire or even thought of the woman's own pleasure. Yet one knows that, perhaps without becoming aware, she will be filled with the highest pleasure, merely through the presence of the male god, and will experience with him the peak of self-fulfillment.

Mystics have often described just such experiences and sensations; but here the experience is realized in wholly secular, worldly terms, without that admixture of hysteria, frenzy or agitation that, however remote it may be, can be felt in the ecstasy of the mystically possessed. Some critics have asserted that in the visual arts form and content become fused, and that to differentiate them is therefore an error. To my mind, the two Rembrandt paintings prove that form and content must often, if not always be kept separate, for while the visual, formal similarity of the two canvases is quite marked, in content they could not be further apart. In great literary art, superb form is combined with great content; only this makes up the perfect work. When I try in what follows to convey some of the richness of *Hamlet's* content, this is never done without the knowledge that all that wealth of content, if it were to be divorced from the perfection of form that marks the tragedy, might make an interesting story, but it would never account for the great tragedy that is *Hamlet*.

IX. Critics often object to the psychoanalyst's viewing literary characters in terms of living people, on the grounds that this approach implies that Shakespeare copied nature. Before discussing this supposed implication, I feel that I have to dispel another confusion, which also occurs frequently and blurs the issue. The analyst's discovery in Shakespeare's plays of "the laws of nature" is quite different from the fact that, in the aesthetic experience, literary reality often gives the impression of being real reality. From this effect alone one may not, however, conclude that one will find in such a literary work a confirmation of psychoanalytic findings. The impression that a work of art leaves in the aesthetic experience must be kept sharply separated from the findings that one arrives at by way of reflection and scientific scrutiny.

To be sure, after the two types of phenomena have been attained (by two different methods), their relevance to each other will have to be investigated. Up to now, however, it has not been proven empirically that what the analyst finds in a literary work by his special technique actually plays a role in the aesthetic experience of the bulk of the audience. Some of the subtler psychoanalytic meanings may be neutral in their effect on an audience.

Let us now return to the mistaken implication that Shakespeare copied nature. Perhaps it is this very absence of copying or imitation that may seem to gainsay the application of psychoanalysis to Shakespeare's characters. Nor is the matter greatly improved when we say that it is not a question of copying or imitating, but rather of "recreating" nature. In my opinion, nature is not recreated in Shakespeare's plays; instead, the Shakespearean corpus constitutes a universe in itself. It is not nature *re*-created, but a newly *created* universe.

I spoke earlier of a paradox, and here we have it. Hamlet, Horatio and the rest have never lived and never will live, although it is true that Hamlet has been "discovered" time and again in living people. Wulf Sachs (1947), in selecting *Black Hamlet* as the title of his book, made a good choice of title, qua title, but the protagonist of his book has little to do with Shakespeare's Hamlet. If there were any person for whom an identity with Shakespeare's Hamlet could be found, that would speak against Shakespeare, not for him. This is true as well of the great works that have been created in other media. Never will a landscape be found that looks like any one of those few that Rembrandt created (cf. Gombrich, 1960), although we can identify each single object by its similarity with natural objects.

To return to Shakespeare, one would have to say that his characters are more human than living people. If there were not the danger that the term might easily be misunderstood in this context, I would say they are "ideal-types," in the sense in which Max Weber used the term. They are intensifications of what nature has produced, just as Charles V in Titian's portrait is more imperial than he was in actual appearance.

Titian did not have to resort to external trappings or symbols to bring forth the imperial status; he used purely human data, such as the beholder needs no prior historical knowledge to grasp.

In order to understand more fully the process of creating a universe, one has to think in terms of such theories as have been evolved by writers like Wilde and others. They have asserted that art is *superior to* life, that it *creates* life (cf. Edel, 1957, p. 59); their theory is that life follows art and not the other way round. Such theories sound mystical, yet it is not impossible that they may be true. An adequate discussion of such propositions would require a greater digression than this Introduction can accommodate, but at least the following may be said.

At a certain point, the organic aspect of evolution came to a standstill and the process switched over to psychobiological equivalents. If organic mutation had succeeded in leading to an even higher degree of differentiation, that might have endangered survival. Moreover, mutations work in one direction: the same organic structure cannot function at one and the same time like a telescope and like a microscope. Finally, either such differentiation would have made it impossible for the organism to cope with the objects that are encountered in everyday life—objects that are necessary for the gratification of everyday needs.

In the "best-of-all-possible-worlds" context, therefore, one has to say that the best thing is to leave the organic structure of the eye as it is and to provide instruments that, when the need arises, can make the eye capable of penetrating both the world of the most minute things and that of the most distant things. The history of technology is the history of that psychobiological evolution that our sense organs and muscular system underwent without organic mutations. Similarly, the history of science is the history of the evolution of knowledge about and insight into the external world, which have been gathered on the basis of sense data gained by way of psychobiological evolution. Colossal as the effect of such evolutionary processes has been, they still cover only areas that have to be described as peripheral in relation to man's evolution qua man.

The direction of man's evolution was, prior to the advent of scientific psychology, in the hands of priests, philosophers and artists. The great founders of religion, like Moses, Buddha, Christ (I believe this to be less true of Mohammed), represent *new types of man,* which do not occur in reality, just as there is actually no human eye that can perceive microscopic particles. In Shakespeare, the process of man's evolution was taken over by the secular power, in accordance with the spirit of the times. Many others also did the same thing, but I think that in no one else is it to be seen in as broad an area and with such intensity as it is in Shakespeare's corpus. He formed categories and types of life that went far beyond what was accessible to him by direct observation.

The historical literature that examines the many strands connecting Shakespeare's plays both with his own time and with the past, indispensable as it is, is overlooking the real issue—his connections with the future. This concept has not yet been generally accepted, even though it has been brought out by many, and I shall therefore be coming back to the point again and again. However, as soon as it is acknowledged that Shakespeare was the creator of new forms of life, that he created his own original universe rather than put on the stage one that was the product of imitation or recreation, it then becomes understandable that "the laws of human nature" can be discovered in his characters—without that assertion implying that his universe was, after all, lacking in originality. Biologists may one day be able to construct an organic eye that will be capable of perceiving microscopic details. That will indeed be an original creation; yet it will still follow the organic laws that are embodied in the "natural" eye.

The psychoanalytic investigation of Shakespeare's characters has probably been lagging in setting forth what it is that the "newness" of life embodied in his plays consists of. For that purpose, such historical knowledge may be necessary as does not properly belong within the scope of the analyst's *métier.* But it *is* within the scope of his *métier* to draw out of Shakespeare's characters the maximum of psychological insight. In the last analysis these characters more readily and truthfully reveal to the audience their unconscious than do the living subjects of the customary psychoanalytic investigation. If, nevertheless, Hamlet has so far continued to defy any completely satisfactory unraveling of the mystery that he embodies, it is not because the playwright has made him reticent or reluctant to communicate with the world. He says everything he knows; it is *our* knowledge of the psyche that is still quite limited.

If so many characters in *Hamlet* are ambiguous, it is only because life as created by Shakespeare is ambiguous. Another Renaissance genius also succeeded in portraying ambiguity; the *Mona Lisa* has rightly become the symbol of the Western art of portrait-painting. When Eliot describes Hamlet as the Mona Lisa of literature, he is verbalizing a deep insight, even though in other respects his genius faltered vis-à-vis *Hamlet*. In the *Mona Lisa*, Leonardo succeeded in creating a portrait into which almost any type of beholder can project himself. (I believe that he took up in it the challenge that had been posed by Cusanus.) This is also true of Hamlet, as many a critic has observed.

Here again, however, one discovers an aspect that goes far beyond life as it is embodied in real, living people. Since the latter are limited by their own narrowness, they generally attract and are loved by few, whereas Hamlet attracts everyone, with few, even though notable, exceptions. Had Shakespeare achieved this by drawing a character who did not follow the laws of nature, it would undoubtedly have diminished the value of his achievement. From this vantage point two variables would be the determinants of artistic value: ambiguity and clarity of presentation. The highest value would be attained when maximum ambiguity had been reached in combination with maximum clarity of detail and composition.

This same criterion can be applied to visual representation. The portraits painted by Picasso after his blue period are also characterized by ambiguity, yet it is produced by willful deviation from the laws of nature. It is quite likely that the future critic will classify such portraits as inferior to anything that Leonardo painted, insofar as they were created by departing from the laws of nature. Ambiguity despite clarity of detail and of the entire composition—that is what makes up a great work of art such as *Hamlet*!

Of the many intricate ways in which Prof. Holland (1964a, 1966) justifies psychoanalytic literary criticism, I shall select one more. He writes (1966, p. 123): "The characters are real or not real only as we make them so, only insofar as we endow the character with our wishes and defenses. We are, in effect, partners with the artist. . . . His [Shakespeare's] real medium is surely the most difficult, intractable of all—our minds—and therefore all the greater an artist is he—or any writer—because he creates us into creators" and (p. 122): "The [Shakespeare's eighteenth and nineteenth-century] critics have been looking at the characters when we should look instead into ourselves, for it is we who recreate the characters and give them a sense of reality." This is, of course, correct; yet I believe that it too bypasses the real issue.

If generalized, this approach dissolves the whole of the humanities into pure psychology. In the instance at hand, what it would mean, in simplified terms, is this: "If you want to know what the psychological content of a play is, study what is going on in the mind (conscious or unconscious) of the audience." Whatever can then be said about a cultural product is to take in nothing but the nature of the human mind's response to it. While I am here vulgarizing a highly sophisticated view, I am trying to defend the eighteenth- and the nineteenth-century critic. Their misfortune was that they did not have an appropriate psychology at their disposal; methodologically, however, I think that they were right.

Audience response is an important and highly promising field of research. My contention is, however, that, even if it could be shown that a psychoanalytic interpretation of a character has never yet found an equivalent process in a member of the audience, that interpretation could still be correct. Prof. Holland himself rightly states that what he experiences as a spectator of a play by Shakespeare is quite different from what he finds out about it when he approaches it as a critic. One may conjecture that nevertheless, during the heat of actual artistic participation, something becomes at least unconsciously relevant in the audience— something of the sort that is set forth explicitly during the course of the psychoanalytic examination.

Would we have to conclude that psychoanalytic interpretations are wrong, if empirical testing were not able to show that any of the contents claimed by psychoanalysis have ever become relevant in audience response? Would Wölfflin's statements about Renaissance and baroque art be proven wrong, if no beholder were shown to have responded to the qualities he set forth? For me, psychoanalytic interpretations of Shakespeare's characters are valid statements about something objectively given (cf. Holland, 1964a, pp. 314-317). They are given to error, as any kind of interpretation may be; in this context, however, it is only the principle that matters.

The question of why man is able to experience Shakespeare's characters as real is a problem of a different sort; it has nothing to do with the primary aim of endopoietic research, which attempts to reach clarification of the meaning of a tragedy as it is.[7]

---

[7] Prof. Holland (1966, p. 119f), in order to prove or perhaps merely to exemplify his methodological position, refers to perceptual experiments that have demonstrated the animistic responses of subjects to moving triangles and other shapes that are experienced by them as live—that is, as expressing or being motivated by feelings and intents. The context in which Prof. Holland cites these experiments makes them equivalent to Tinbergen's (1951) experiments, in which the minimal

I further cannot agree with Prof. Holland (1964a, p. 347) that "any criticism worth the ink to write it must have a place in the living theater." Such considerations can do nothing but distract from the single goal of fathoming the full depth of a uniquely created universe.

Nietzsche (1875-1876, p. 364) knew of this universe. He spoke of "those hidden mysteries of the mind [soul] . . . in which the work of art is born" [*jene verborgenen Seelen-Mysterien. . . . in denen das Kunstwerk geboren wird*]. Even though he was at that time speaking of the mysteries in the artist's mind, every great literary work also contains a mystery of the mind. The area of mystery has been reduced by the application of psychoanalysis; yet it is still considerable, and one cannot yet assert that psychoanalytic research into Shakespeare's characters has been finished.[8]

---

physical configurations (patterns of stimuli) were determined to which an animal will respond in the same way as it does vis-à-vis live animals.

The animation of triangles and squares may well be a core experiment in the psychology of art experience, but to make it the starting point of an understanding of the psychological content of works of art, in whatever medium, is methodologically wrong. The confusion in methodology becomes apparent when Prof. Holland (1966, p. 122) writes of the spectator's identification with a literary character as an act "of taking in from the character certain drives and defenses that are really objectively 'out there,' and of putting into him feelings that are really our own, 'in here.' "

Along these lines, Prof. Holland gives a splendid analysis of Mercutio; but then he seems to regret that in principle he acted like a nineteenth-century romantic and adds (1966, p. 122): "We need him, and we take him in—re-create him from our own feelings—because he acts out for us in an objective way solutions to the danger we feel from the tragedy. . . . We make Mercutio part of us because he helps us deal with our fears for the tragic victims." Prof. Holland may be right or wrong in his assumption about my fears. Quite independently of what these may be, however, I and any other critic can follow his analysis of Mercutio's character, and agree or disagree with his findings, by reference to objective data embodied in Shakespeare's corpus.

The psychoanalyst, unless he is to shift his focus from the literary work to the spectator's perceptive apparatus and his unconscious, has to approach that work with an attitude that is almost equivalent to the one he employs in the analysis of a patient. To be sure, when we examine the processes by which the analyst arrives at his conclusions, we discover all sorts of patterns; but this is, methodologically speaking, a different question from: "What is going on in the patient, and how did it happen that he became what he is?" Whatever the way in which he may have reached his conclusions, the critic's final psychological statement about a literary character's structure should not carry any traces of personal wishes, inhibitions or defenses; it should instead be testable—as are the investigations that are involved in any scientific pursuit—by empirical yardsticks designed to fit the subject matter.

[8] Although the appropriate use and the limits of Coleridge's famous "suspension of disbelief" have been variously discussed, I want to add that it does not seem suitable to Shakespeare's tragedies. One aspect of the greatness of dramatic works (and perhaps of art in general) may well be measurable in terms of its ability to overcome resistance and to set in motion some grasp of reality even when the viewer's disbelief is at its height. There are, of course, "fair" and "unfair" means of overcoming disbelief, and it is often the product of inferior quality—such as the detective story—that absorbs the reader, whether he feels so inclined or not. Thus it is also a question of what sort of reality is conveyed, once suspension of disbelief has been established. It is my belief that, while Shakespeare's great tragedies require a minimum of "willingness" in order to have a full effect, they also have the dramatic capability of piercing barriers and *forcing* the reader and spectator, not into a suspension of disbelief, but into assent and submission, despite any attempt on his part to maintain his disbelief.

X. In the corpus of Shakespeare's work, there are depths of the human universe that scientific psychology has not yet come to understand. I want to make a point here on which I shall speak further in the text—namely, that it was probably during his contact with Shakespeare's plays that Freud developed his conception of a death instinct. It is the privilege of the playwright-genius to make palpable—no matter how dim it may still be under the veil of poetry—what may remain inaccessible to direct clinical observation. If my guess is correct, Freud did not do what so many psychologists do—that is, consistently use literary works merely as *confirmatory evidence* for established psychological theory. It was the privilege of the genius in psychology to learn from the genius of drama.

But can one say that Shakespeare depicted reality? He did it just as much as did Goya, who is supposed to have been the first to paint the legs of running horses in their correct position, as was proven much later by slow-motion cinematography. Yet although something about "natural laws" can be learned from Goya's paintings, the latter nevertheless represent a uniquely created universe.

Science has since then, of course, moved away from surface observation and has penetrated to minutiae to which the artist's eye is no longer able to penetrate. Psychology is on the verge of doing the same thing. Within a few decades, psychologists will be studying chemical compounds instead of memory, and electric brainwaves instead of dreams. Will the corpus that Shakespeare has left then still have the power to stimulate the production of comprehensive constructs about the human mind?

It is very likely that Freud too was far ahead of his time with his construct of a death instinct. Here we come upon a rather engrossing problem. Kraus (p. viii), in scrutinizing some texts of the French nineteenth-century literary avant-garde, observed that chronological comparison of the results produced by art and science shows that the insights of the former anticipate those of the latter by three to four decades.[9] Similar sequences have been shown with regard to Renaissance art and science.

In Shakespeare, art outran science by centuries. That he was a

---

[9] Sarton (1948, pp. 61-64) distinguishes history as presented in textbooks from what he calls "secret history." The latter is concerned with "the development of the activities which are most specifically human, the development of all that is best in humanity." Within this secret history is enclosed another secret history, comprising those minds who prepared the way for those who were later to become renowned in "the development of all that is best in humanity."

master in the presentation of human passion, character and destiny has been readily acknowledged, but the full depth and scope of his universe could be asserted explicitly only after psychology had even half-way caught up with his insights. To what extent he was aware of these insights, to what extent he himself would have been able to explain in determinate and discursive terms the psychology of the characters he created is as open to question as what Leonardo da Vinci would have answered had he been asked whether he believed in the heliocentric theory.

All we know is that Leonardo once wrote "The sun does not move." Sarton (1957, p. 220f) quite rightly asserts that this is not sufficient evidence to call Leonardo a predecessor of Copernicus, for "a man of science must prove, or at least explain clearly, what he has in mind."[10] Leonardo was also one of those minds that outrun their own century. In his instance, a judgment about the interrelationship between science and art is far more difficult to make than it is in Shakespeare's case. If we think of science as a system of determinate and discursive terms, then Shakespeare had no scientific aims and made no contribution to science. Yet in an artist's work there may be "science" present, without his aspiring to produce it.

To give a trivial example: In one of Botticelli's paintings there are 30 different species of plants represented, and in one by Holbein one finds a variety of plant that has since become a rarity (Sarton, 1953, p. 88). A painter may, *merely by devoting himself to his vocation,* make an important contribution to science. Transposing this observation to Shakespeare's corpus, one may say that Shakespeare responded to an indeterminate number of psychological facts that were not yet known to his contemporaries, and some of which it took 300 years to set forth in a scientific way. Thus even if Shakespeare's work could be reduced to an imitation of nature, it would still be stupendous, inasmuch as what he "imitated" was unknown to his contemporaries and required several centuries to be discovered by others.

XI. Here then is the paradox: Shakespeare's plays reflect an external, objectively existing reality and yet one that is as removed as one could conceive from imitation. It is the fact that his world is a reflection

---

[10] Oddly enough, Sarton, who was probably the greatest of all historians of science, almost equates Leonardo's single statement about the sun with Freud's basing his contribution to Leonardo's psychology on a single childhood screen-memory. What he overlooks is that in the former we have either the end-result of a long chain of deliberations or a momentary intuitive flash, while in the latter we have a piece of historical evidence the explanation of which calls for a maze of verifiable theories. In his essay on Leonardo, Freud certainly explained "what he had in mind."

of something objective, in which we too can participate, that makes it possible for us to understand that world at all. But it is precisely this area that is the area of concern in this present study.

If psychology were sufficiently advanced, we should be able to obtain a psychological interpretation from each line, as we should be able to with each association on the part of a patient. Needless to say, we are lucky if we can do as much with even extended portions of a play by Shakespeare. But, in order to forestall misunderstanding, let me say here that, even with such refined interpretations, we will not have exhausted his meaning. By and large, one can say that every element in Shakespeare's plays serves "multiple functions," as Waelder (1930), following Freud, maintained with regard to the functioning of the psychic apparatus. Applied to Shakespeare's plays, this principle takes on an even broader meaning.

Particularly in *Hamlet,* Shakespeare has made supreme use of poetic ambiguity: under ideal circumstances several different psychological interpretations, some of which may be quite contradictory, may be given with regard to one and the same line. This multiplicity of possible interpretations is the direct consequence of the psychological principle of multiple function. Yet Shakespeare's lines serve not only to convey something psychic in the narrower sense of the word, but also poetry, philosophical ideas, politics, historical material, topical views, and many more things. In other words, there is a variety of multiple functions; in the present context, of course, it is the multiple psychological interpretations that are the main concern.

Objectively speaking, these various functions have equal status; partiality sets in when, as the result of the critic's particular interest, the existence of other aspects is minimized or denied. Equality of status, however, does not exclude hierarchy (a word so often used nowadays to cover our ignorance of the exact structure of patterns). I, too, do not know how these multiple functions are patterned in Shakespeare's plays. One can certainly say that, whatever the actual theme may be, the function of poetry is constantly active; even themes that are per se dry and tiresome become inspiring under the magic of Shakespeare's language. I also believe that something psychic is being conveyed throughout the play.

The rest takes place in a field whose abscissa is the psyche, and whose ordinate is poetry. Yet psychology holds a special place, in that it refers to a tangible world, and its conclusions can be checked by reference to an objective framework. I am not certain that interpretations based on poetry can be submitted to objective checks. Perhaps, when poetic and psychological interpretation diverge, it may, after all, be the latter that is decisive.

In my opinion, true psychoanalytic interpretation exhausts itself in what is called "motivational research." It is directed toward unconscious forces, whose interplay leads to data that do become, unlike these forces themselves, accessible to direct observation. Yet I wish to emphasize that the high probability in Shakespeare's plays—it is by no means a certainty—that practically every line (even when it can be dealt with as a stage convention, a topical allusion or a poetical necessity) requires or is accessible, in addition, to a psychological interpretation, is not to be expected in the creations of other writers. If it is true, it is something that is true and characteristic of Shakespeare and constitutes one aspect of his creative greatness. Freud, of course, was aware that in general there is a limit to psychological (what I have here called endopoietic) research: there are elements in a literary work that may be due to poetic license (1907, p. 41), and whose full meaning can be established without one's having to find in them any correlation to or reflection of a psychological reality.

Furthermore, in examining Ibsen's characters, Freud found one example of where psychology and the playwright's presentation did not "click." Freud (1916, p. 329) explained this in terms of "laws of poetic economy," which necessitate the avoidance of the explicit presentation of deeper motives, since these would arouse "serious resistances, based on the most distressing emotions" in the spectator. Earlier Freud (1905, p. 59f) had pointed out one significant difference between a case history and a short story: the writer "simplifies and abstracts."

Poetic license, poetic economy, and simplification are three strong elements limiting the application of psychoanalysis to works of literature. There is much in such works that may be in general correlated with these and similar factors, but it is my conviction that this precaution is scarcely necessary with regard to Shakespeare's universe. In his writing, every line is fused with the spirit of intensified life, which does require for its explication the tools of psychology. The fact is, after all, that most case histories that have yet been written appear to be simpler than any one of his great tragedies.[11]

XII. My study is directed toward motivational research, therefore,

[11] In one tragedy by Shakespeare, Freud (1916, pp. 316-324) did discover a psychologically "blind spot." I am not certain whether there really exists here what one might call a blind spot, but I shall not pursue further the challenging problem of Macbeth and his Lady, the explanation for whom seems to require the assumption of mutual complementation.

even though it often leads to problems of psychological structure. I use the term "motivational research" here in a broader sense than the one in which it is usually used. At some points, however, I shall step outside this area and deal with problems that are nonmotivational.

(a) Lesser (1957) deals with the discrepancy between those contents in a novel or short story that are manifest (conscious) and those that are imperceptible (unconscious), yet have significant effects. They are quite different. Lesser's *law of contradictory series* can be confirmed in *Hamlet*. I give it a somewhat different turn by not proceeding in terms of conscious and subliminal perception, but rather, by disregarding audience responses, I remain within the limits of inquiry into an objectively existing entity. Following Pfister, I therefore speak of the "manifest" and "unconscious" content of the play. They are, in accordance with Lesser's law, diametrically opposed in *Hamlet*.

(b) At another point in what follows, I shall try to uncover the rhythm of the subplots. The pattern of their beginnings and endings, and the points at which they become relevant to the main plot, imply an organic structure. It may be that, in discussing the formalism of retroactive effect, I shall also be touching upon a subject that is outside motivational research.

(c) In a few instances I do refer to constructs that have been based on audience responses. This happens especially when critics have tried to explain *Hamlet* by reference to the historical particulars of Shakespeare's times. Then it becomes necessary to object by appeal to the fact that audiences that are in all other respects totally divorced from those particulars have also succumbed to the impact of the play—which proves that more must be contained in the play than those critics seem to recognize as being there.

(d) In one of the appendices, I was unable to resist the temper of the times and so hypothesized the presence of a special ego function in the literary genius. Giving in even further to a personal predilection for linguistic oddities, I then baptized that function as *doxaletheic*.

(e) At various points, I have gone beyond the narrow assignment in which the psychoanalyst does have an obligation to be expert, and have discussed problems that belong rather to the sociologist. On one such occasion, I have indulged in critical remarks about Prof. Erikson's theories, which have achieved some fame. I hope that in my own endeavors I have greater luck than he is appearing to have, and have not replaced old pitfalls with new ones. My excursions into sociology are maximal in the

Appendix on *The Tempest,* in which perhaps I stray furthest from the *Hamlet*-problem. Nevertheless, I am confident that excursion is not a foreign body in the totality of this venture into literary criticism.

(f) The issue of religion and Christianity is given great stress in the sections written in 1967 and thereafter. It takes no great astuteness to discover that I am an atheist, whatever my personal religious feelings may be. (Oddly enough, one has to be, it seems, almost a religionist at heart in order to be an intellectually convinced atheist, whereas the writings of the religious zealots almost regularly make you sense their doubts and scruples.) I do hope that my strong conviction has not led my inquiry astray. A more detailed discussion of Shakespeare's relation to Montaigne, a truly fascinating topic, would have added considerable weight to some of my assertions. There is no doubt that those two minds stand like towering sentinels at the beginning of that historical process that in the end led to the doom of Christianity—a process whose final paroxysms have greatly contributed to the pains of the present epoch.

(g) I did become involved in two discussions which may perhaps strike the reader as needless: the one with Grebanier, most of whose comments must strike anyone familiar with *Hamlet* as simply absurd and therefore not requiring the spelling out of criticism; the other with Professor Holland, whose merits in furthering psychoanalytic literary criticism deserve more praise than censure. I trust he will be magnanimous enough to excuse my focusing in this context on the latter.

XIII. Regrettably it was only after I had written the main sections of this book that I had the opportunity to attend a lecture by Professor Leo Steinberg, in which he set forth a method of art criticism that can be used most profitably in literary criticism as well. Professor Steinberg suggests that, instead of discussing the correctness or incorrectness of an interpretation or criticism of a work of art, one should examine what it was that gave rise to that interpretation or criticism. The advantages of this approach are evident: it sharpens one's analytic capabilities, it also serves to shift criticism from negative debate to a constructive synthesis of theories that at first glance may even appear to be incompatible. The effort to ascertain the particularity that gave rise to an interpretation or theory forestalls premature rejection or dismissal on insufficient grounds, and assures the broadening of that basis on which new theories are actually built. The reader may notice that, in discussing ambiguity in *Hamlet,* I came close to using such an approach as Prof. Steinberg has set forth. However, since I did not have Prof. Steinberg's explicitly formulated method at my command, the result was not set forth with that degree of precision nor was the inquiry carried out with that consistency that might otherwise have been achieved.

XIV. I have to apologize for having quoted the German *Der bestrafte Brudermord* consistently as *Ur-Hamlet*, although the two are certainly not identical. If I had read Gundolf's (1911) essay on *Shakespeare and the German Spirit* earlier, I would have evaluated the German play quite differently. I fear that at times I overrated its usefulness as ancillary to a correct interpretation of *Hamlet*.

XV. Initially my intention was to use the opportunity presented by the current work to refute the criticism published sometime ago in the official *Journal of the American Psychoanalytic Association* with regard to my study of a decade in Goethe's life. However, I have decided against this and will instead add a short comment on the reviewing policies that now prevail within the group that identifies itself with the preservation and further development of Freud's heritage.

Differences of opinion between author and reviewer have become a part of the traditional pattern of intellectual life of the West; occasionally, this even goes so far as to lead to unbending personal enmities. I know an editor of one leading psychoanalytic journal who has avoided the snares of his perilous assignment by asking each author to indicate whom *he* would like to have assigned as the reviewer of his book. By means of this ingenious device, the author himself is made responsible for any frustrations he may suffer on reading the review of his work; yet one may be certain that, since that policy was instituted, such frustrations have occurred only rarely. Notwithstanding the gain in friendship and popularity that this technique yields to its clever inventor, for obvious reasons it is in fact a serious disservice to psychoanalysis.

It is clear that the problem of healthy criticism starts with the choice of reviewer. *The Psychoanalytic Quarterly* indulges sporadically in the pleasure of giving forth with a venomous attack against any author who has suffered the misfortune of having his theories accepted by the bulk of analysts and of being regarded as having made an original contribution of some consequence. Such periodic warnings against the acceptance of additions to psychoanalytic theories may be quite wholesome per se, whether one agrees or disagrees with their substance. Moreover, the *Psychoanalytic Quarterly* is a private undertaking and therefore has no obligation to the official group of psychoanalysts. Such a periodical has the right, if it should wish to do so, to place its facilities at the service even of a crank.

The situation is quite different with respect to an official organ of the American Psychoanalytic Association, whose editors do have an obligation—I might even say, a responsibility—toward the members of the Association. Criticism appearing in its columns, under assignment by editors, carries great weight. Some of the critical essays that have been published in the pages of the *Journal of the American Psychoanalytic Association* have lived up to the requirements of high critical standards. Occasionally, however, the *Journal* is remiss in that regard, and a word of caution to apply discretion in each instance in its choice of official critical essayists may not be out of place. One ought to make sure at least that the person selected possesses some minimal knowledge of the sheer facts of the subject-matter of his essay, that he has at least read the entire text he has been called upon to evaluate, and that he has at his disposal that minimal discipline of thinking that differentiates science from sciolism.

I am aware of the sensitivities that are active—even though sometimes they lie dormant—in every author, whether he is arrogant or pretends humility. As long as criticism remains the accepted way of dealing with the output of scientific papers, there will be hurt feelings, even if such criticism is fairly and adequately presented in all instances. But that fact should not lead to the conclusion that it is invariably an author's narcissistic vulnerability that has made him lodge a complaint. If the pseudo-critical comment that provided the occasion for these remarks had been published in a journal without official standing, I would almost certainly have forgotten it by now.

XVI. In Murry (1936, p. x) one finds a piece of good counsel, which is worthy of full quotation and some discussion.

> Best of all perhaps would be that a critic who, early in life, determined to try to say something of permanent value about Shakespeare, should write a book once every ten years or so based on a sudden and complete rereading of Shakespeare, careless each time of what he had said before, discarding his note-books, with a plain text in front of him, concerned with only what he, at that moment, understood and felt and conjectured. *Si jeunesse savait, si vieillesse pouvait.*

For the practicing analyst, Shakespeare studies can, unfortunately, assume only a secondary place; he remains, with rare exceptions, as Freud (cf. also Edel, 1957, p. 57) stressed, a dilettante in the field to which he applies the tools of his profession. It is open to question, therefore, to what extent he may indulge in the belief that he has said "something of permanent value." The ultimate judges on that question will be those who make literary criticism their central activity. The analyst remains at the periphery; only from there does he peer toward the center, where the decisive battles in the history of ideas are being fought out. When I now look back at the paper I wrote in 1953, there is not much I have to take back. (That may be, paradoxically, one of its weaknesses.) In adding the other sections, which were written during 1967 and 1968, I was not able to follow Murry's advice. A German wit once observed that a deeper meaning "falls out" of a German proverb when one "turns it upside down." Perhaps it is truer, then, to say: *Si jeunesse pouvait, si vieillesse savait.*

As behooves age, experience may arouse doubts in what one once believed with full conviction. I read in Euripides:

"How then can man distinguish man, what test can he use?
We can only toss our judgments random on the wind."

(Electra 373, 378)

Here I find fully developed Hamlet's conflict about appearance and reality. Further:

"A polluted demon spoke it in the shape of god."

(Electra 979)

Here I find Hamlet's doubt about "honest" ghosts. Still further:

"All men are flawed" *(Heracles* 1314) and "No man on earth is truly free. All are slaves of money or necessity" *(Hecuba* 864f).

These lines sound almost as though they were straight out of *Hamlet.* And Polymestor's "neither earth nor ocean produces a creature as savage and monstrous as woman" *(Hecuba* 1181) really "out-Hamlets" Hamlet in its brutality.

Thus lines to which the psychoanalyst has attached a specific psychological interpretation were spoken in an essentially different (literary) universe two millennia previously. It is not a matter of myth, which one has to expect to find in various places; it has rather to do with lines that sound rather personal. Does this cast any justified doubts on the analytic conviction that Shakespeare's corpus represents an individual universe, which has to be examined for its unique psychological content? Does it suggest that what is after all unique is only Shakespeare's *poetry,* that the psychological content is of secondary importance—the unavoidable stuff, so to speak, that one needs in order to create poetry? Is this not a principle akin to those of the New Criticism?

Be that as it may, Euripides' and Shakespeare's universes are totally different and one may look at the verses that I have quoted as not at all surprising coincidences, due only to the fact that not only Shakespeare, but perhaps Euripides as well, placed at the heart of his universe man in conflict.

XVII. I do not know whether one is here facing a true dilemma, or whether there might not be a simple solution at hand. In either case, it may be worthwhile listening to what a great writer had to say about the subject.

In 1890 Knut Hamsun gave three lectures, of which the second—on psychological literature—is of considerable interest in this context. In turning against the accepted Scandinavian literature of that time, Hamsun raises the demand for a new type of literature. Modern times have produced a mind, he says, that is of higher differentiation than that of Shakespeare's times, yet "we still drone the three or four basic emotions —which Shakespeare ground out. We know them by heart . . . . they are love, anger, fear and awe" (p. 38). [*Wir leiern noch immer die drei, vier Grundempfindungen ab, die Shakespeare ableierte, wir kennen sie auswendig . . . es sind Liebe, Zorn, Furcht und Erstaunen*] (p. 38).[12]

We enjoy Shakespeare, Hamsun continues, particularly when he is interpreted for us by an actor—that is to say, a modern person; but that is not enough to prove that Shakespeare is a modern psychologist (p. 39). Shakespeare's plays belong to that literature in which human beings appear and are represented as types [*Typendichtung*], and such literary creations are capable of satisfying many people throughout all epochs. To such literature belong Plato's *Dialogues,* David's *Psalms,* Dante's *Commedia,* Defoe's *Robinson Crusoe,* Goethe's *Faust.*

Hamsun offers one example of the new literature he would like to see realized. He and a writer were once watching a child playing with his blind grandfather; the child was rather rough and hurt the old man, who bore the torment patiently. Hamsun asked his companion how he would

---

[12] This reminds me of a remark I once heard a discussant make. He asserted that only a genius can make a valid statement about another genius—meaning, of course, that what a person of average endowment says about a genius is not valid. At first hearing the objection sounds quite convincing, but the above quotation is one of the numerous examples one can adduce of one genius' being totally in error in his judgment of another one.

use the episode they had just observed, and the latter answered that they were witnessing an outstanding example of human kindliness. Hamsun, however, having observed the family for quite a while, knew that the grandfather had been bearing the grandchild's harassment mainly out of the need to humiliate himself. Hamsun had described the old man stealthily edging up to a pot of cheese in order to filch from it, and being surprised by his daughter, who had reserved this tidbit for her husband. We are suddenly in the midst of a story that sounds very much like a psychoanalytic case history; yet it was written at a time when Freud was still three to four decades away from attaining his insight into moral masochism and the need for punishment.

This lecture, as well as the paper *Vom unbewussten Seelenleben* ("About the unconscious life of the mind") of the following year, are truly astonishing, in that both read as if they had been composed by the most committed psychoanalyst.

In the example just mentioned, Hamsun takes a firm stand against behavioral psychology, and demonstrates that an act does not necessarily have the meaning it seems to have, as the manifestation of character or as a simple, commonsense event; *all* its antecedents must be known, if one wishes to fathom its meaning. An act is the end-result of *chains* of thoughts, experiences and emotions. Furthermore, to judge from Hamsun's example, he was apparently aware that acts that appear to the observer to be merely one-dimensional and self-evident outgrowths of the present situation are in fact based on internal conflicts. Here is a strong statement with regard to the dichotomy of appearance and reality, whose differences do not create confusion in this instance, since insight makes such differences understandable.

Hamsun speaks of emotional states that seemingly arise from nowhere, yet lead to actions of great consequence for the individual: the unfolding of thoughts brought about by "these almost unnoticeable mimosa-like movements of the soul" [*diese beinahe unmerklichen Mimosenbewegungen der Seele*] (p. 91). He asks that books be written in which we can learn something about the unconscious life of the soul (p. 92). Indeed, he came quite close to Freud's technique of free association, since he had observed in himself series of associations that had been precipitated by seemingly neutral perceptions, such as a by no means unusual word in a newspaper (p. 87). Having discovered the psychologically meaningful in the seemingly trivial, he clearly defended what Freud years later was to call the "dynamic" point of view—the coming into being of psychic phenomena as a result of the action and interaction of a number of psychic forces.

At the same time, he asserted the full reality of fantasy. Philosophers have their doubt about external reality, "but even *if* reality exists, is a fantasy that is actually spelled out then less real than an overcoat that actually exists?" [*Aber selbst wenn es die Wirklichkeit gibt, ist eine tatsächlich vollzogene Phantasie dann weniger wirklich als ein tatsächlich existierender Überzieher?*] (author's italics) (p. 57). He was ready to pursue fantasies with uncompromising consistency, even though he was well aware that the result of such journeys might lead to serious conflicts with what contemporary natural science was asserting about reality. It seems quite probable that he was aware of the fact that these fantasies were the derivatives of something that itself remained unconscious.

In Hamsun's lecture and article we find once again an instance of art being ahead of science by a few decades. To be sure, Hamsun's manifesto had in mind only the novel. He proposed that "literary presentation of character[13] should be rooted out from all non-dramatic literature; in dramatic literature it must continue to exist; for there it is indispensable. Yet in the psychological novel, literary presentation of character should be done away with, for as a *modern canvas of psychic life it is untrue*—that is to say, it does not penetrate sufficiently, and is therefore too superficial and an all too cheap piece of merchandise" [*die Charakterdichtung aus aller nicht dramatischen Dichtung ausmerzen sollte; in der dramatischen Dichtung dagegen muss sie weiterleben, denn dort ist sie unentbehrlich. Doch im psychologischen Roman sollte die Charakterdichtung abgeschaft werden, denn als modernes Seelengemälde ist sie unwahr, das heisst, sie dringt zu wenig ein, ist also zu oberflächlich und zu billige Ware*] (author's italics) (p. 52). Knut Hamsun was mainly a novelist, and we shall not pursue any further his interesting denial of psychological drama; nor shall we inquire about why he was ready to reduce Shakespeare to a psychologist of the "four humors," although, as we shall see, at one point, at least, Shakespeare ridiculed this kind of simplistic psychology.[14]

[13]Hamsun means by "character" here something quite different from what is understood at present by the term.

[14] There is a distinct irony in the fact that Hamsun propounds a task for literature, in terms of a "new" psychology that psychoanalysts will later prove to have been fulfilled centuries earlier—and by the very same playwright whom he had cited as an example of the defect he was seeking to overcome.

The point of interest here is that a writer of Hamsun's eminence avers that he has drawn, or will draw into the composition of his characters large areas of precisely that psychic territory of which the psychoanalyst finds so many clues in Shakespeare's creations. There is, of course, one difference, which I trust will not disturb us unduly—namely, that the analyst puts much emphasis on genetic interpretations, while these are lacking in Hamsun's literary manifesto. Here is an area where the genius-scientist was ahead of the genius-novelist, at least in his function as a critic.

Nevertheless, I am almost certain that the novelist would not have objected had someone in 1891 called his attention to the fact that many, if not all, of the puzzling emotional states that he was refusing to ignore by denial are linked with forgotten experiences of bygone years.

Knut Hamsun's literary manifesto may be used as a document to justify the analytic application to literature. For a moment, it raises the curtain on the novelist's workshop. In conformity with the new *Zeitgeist*, Hamsun was given to setting forth, quite differently from what had been done in previous centuries, as much as possible in explicit terms; this relieves us of the need to resort to interpretations that customarily give rise to disagreements. Whether Shakespeare proceeded, consciously or unconsciously, in the way Hamsun suggests here, is of secondary importance. I take Hamsun's manifesto solely as documentary proof that the most intimate psychic processes—processes that are very close to the unconscious—may enter explicitly into the consideration of a literary work and that it is therefore legitimate to trace them and to explicate them in terms that are suitable to the source from which they stem. The principle is not applicable to all literary works. Hamsun is right in differentiating between what he calls literary presentation of character and psychological literary work.

In the first part of Marlowe's *Tamburlaine the Great* one meets with a hypermasculine, hypervirile type of man. There are two passages here that call for a psychoanalytic interpretation. Tamburlaine hurls at one of his many victims, who is bewailing his impending annihilation, the following:

> The thirst of reign and sweetness of a crown
> That caused the eldest son of heavenly Ops
> To thrust his doting father from his chair
> And place himself in the imperial heaven,

Moved me to manage arms against thy state.
What better president [precedent] than mighty Jove?
(II.7)

A few lines later, one of Tamburlaine's aides confirms this:

For, as when Jove did thrust old Saturn down,
Neptune and Dis gained each of them a crown,
So do we hope to reign in Asia,
If Tamburlaine be placed in Persia.

The mythological parallel refers to a typical son-father relationship. In it there is no ambivalence, only unmitigated hatred. The father is nothing but a disturber of the son's relationship to his mother, just as he himself sees in his son nothing but a rival. He is not the bearer of a tradition nor does he function as a subject of identification. This is the preoedipal father; with Zeus, a more advanced type of father ascends to the Olympic throne. To recognize this, the two mythological references are not necessary; Tamburlaine's actions and ranges per se testify to it.

I believe that the character is built around a straight axis. It is even questionable to what extent the introduction of the unconscious is necessary in order to make his actions more understandable. I can well imagine that this will be disputed by many analysts, and perhaps rightly so; but the comparison with any of Shakespeare's characters will lead to the conclusion that each of his dramatic characters after *Titus Andronicus*— or, to be more cautious, after his chronicle plays—is a psychological enigma that cannot be solved (at least, in part) without the help of psychoanalysis.

The difference one will encounter in applying psychoanalysis to literature of character and to psychological literature is a challenging task, which I shall not pursue further. I started with the problem of the close similarity between some of Euripides' lines and some of Shakespeare's. We can now see that the question raised may have been put wrongly. A closer examination, in accordance with Hamsun's propositions, may make it open to question whether Euripides' universe should be approached at all in the way that proved so productive with Shakespeare. Perhaps the coincidences we encounter in mythological man and in psychological man ought not to perturb us at all.

However that may be, the excursion into Hamsun's literary manifesto will permit us to return all the more certain that the analyst's tendency to look at Shakespeare's characters as living persons is not a matter of confusion or of misapplied methodology.

· 33 ·

XVIII. It would have been gratifying if the outcome of my inquiry had been something that would have deserved some such title as *The Anatomy of Tragedy*. The psychological content of a play may be compared with the bones and muscles of the body, which are uncovered only through dissection. The articulation of plot and subplots would then act as the joints, while the skin and the visible form, which are the carriers of the body's beauty, would be the poetry of the play. Lesser (1957) has done that much for the novel and *his* book might have deserved such a title. If ever the anatomy of modern tragedy is written, I am certain that it will be accomplished by a dissection of *Hamlet*, although I cannot say that my own attempt at dissection succeeded in carrying me to any such depth and completeness as a treatise on the anatomy of the play would produce. Still I think I have pierced the epidermis at places and obtained a view of some of the bone and muscle underneath it.

I have purposely chosen a crudely concrete metaphor; it harbors a challenge. Much as I am in general opposed to psychology's borrowing its conceptual frame from other, more advanced and sophisticated sciences, I shall myself do so here.[15] Heisenberg (1953, p. 182), following Weizsäcker, speaks of various levels of language: "One level refers to the objects. . . . A second level refers to statements about objects. A third level may refer to statements about statements about objects, etc. It would then be possible to have different logical patterns at the different levels."

Psychoanalysis has faced and is still facing a basic language crisis, insofar as it is still forced to describe unconscious processes in a language that is adapted to the description of conscious experiences. A statement that is true when it refers to the conscious may be wrong when it is made with regard to the unconscious. As in quantum physics, the basis of classical logic—*"tertium non datur"*—no longer holds true for psychoanalysis. A man has either done or not done an action; no third possibility exists. But it is incorrect to say: "A either hates or does not hate B." Ambivalence makes it possible, in such a case, to say truly that *"tertium datur."*

Quite aside from this dilemma in the application of psychoanalysis to literature, the idea that there are levels of language takes on great relevance. In the clinical situation, the psychoanalytic interpretation has to

---

[15] The history of fashions with regard to use in psychoanalysis of terms borrowed from other disciplines would be a suitable subject of examination. The danger is that authors, in using these terms, may believe that they have lived up to the requirements implied by them. Whether an approach is dynamic or structural is not decided by the frequency of the occurrence of those terms in the discourse in question.

do with the *world of facts*. But when it is applied to literature, interpretation has to do with *statements about facts*. The discussion with the New Critics, finally, has taken place at the third level—the level at which statements are made about statements about objects. Whether these three different levels require three different languages, as seems to be true in physics, has certainly not yet been decided.

Heisenberg's conclusion to his chapter on "Language and Reality in Modern Physics" may, when applied to our discourse, introduce a decisive new factor. He writes (p. 180):

"In the experiments about atomic events we have to do with things and facts, with phenomena that are just as real as any phenomena in daily life. But the atoms or the elementary particles themselves are not as real; they form a world of potentialities or possibilities rather than one of things or facts."

The clinical situation is to the psychoanalyst what the experimental situation is to the physicist. There he meets phenomena that are just as real as those one encounters in real life. But is Hamlet the equivalent of the physicist's potentiality or possibility? According to the New Criticism, *Hamlet* is nothing but words read or spoken on a stage. Yet these words harbor the power to become embodiments of a living person's words, gestures and actions. If the words are investigated not as words but as *potentialities of life*, then new insights may be gained that might bring the New Criticism and psychoanalysis closer together. This may also lead to a more sophisticated psychoanalytic approach to literature. It might, finally, eliminate the possibility of ever talking about an *Anatomy of Tragedy*.

As a potentiality, *Hamlet* also brings us closer to ambiguity and in part reduces its enigmatic character. If it is a potentiality, then we have something that may grow into one shape or another. Although it may be true of all literary characters that to a certain degree they are potentialities, it is nevertheless not as true as it is of Shakespeare's. The greatness of some literary creations may lie in the degree to which they are potentialities or, as Borges (1952, p. 5) says: "that imminence of a revelation that is not yet produced is, perhaps, the aesthetic reality."

All of us have come upon books the reading of which was undoubtedly impressive, absorbing, moving; and yet we would not feel impelled to read those books once again, for we know that this would lead to little more than a repetition of the previous experience. From the rereading of such books, we cannot anticipate new impressions or insights. The events and characters, however skillfully they may be presented, admit of one and only one interpretation. In such cases, "potentiality" is almost zero.

With Shakespeare's plays it is essentially different. One could hardly imagine anyone with a sense of literature rereading one of Shakespeare's mature plays—no matter how often he may have read it previously—without discovering some new nuances, such as might lead to the recognition of a new aspect, and from there to a new interpretation, with regard to one of the main characters. Anyone who says that he has no need to reread a play by Shakespeare because he knows "everything there is to know about it" can rightly be suspected of not having grasped anything of the fundamentals.

This inexhaustibility of meaning, which makes Shakespearean criticism a matter for a lifetime, proves, in a sense, that his literary characters are potentialities of practically inexhaustible complexities. This makes it also understandable why critics disagree (and will never find agreement) about even some seemingly simple traits of Shakespearean protagonists. The literature about such subordinate characters as Marcellus, Bernardo, and Francisco is not inconsiderable, and every so often they become the subjects of a new interpretation. Tempting, however, as it has been to view Hamlet as a potentiality, the course I shall pursue in what follows is an old one. Hamlet is for me a living person, whom we know better—and about whom we knew more—than we do most people in our environment. It is his full-blooded psychic reality that seems to me to render legitimate the application to him of the classic psychoanalytic approach.

(New Year's Day, 1969)

PART ONE

PART ONE

1. Introduction

Someone living in the twentieth century can hardly imagine the sense of momentousness that surrounded a journey to Italy in earlier centuries—to be more specific, what that journey meant to a Central European during the eighteenth century. I have in mind the cultural élite, in whose eyes Italy appeared to be the haven of culture, beauty and civilization—that is to say, of antiquity. A journey there certainly meant more than any such journey could mean to a traveler in our own times. Indeed, I dare say that it meant even more than the Ph.D. means at present to the recipient of it, for the significance of the degree gradually recedes from the memory of the graduate, whose initial pride often gives way with time to a sense of its being an almost routine matter.

Not so with the memories of an Italian journey, two centuries ago, which remained in the lucky traveler's mind for the rest of his days, providing ample material for narratives and *causeries*, no matter how long he lived on afterwards. The happy man who had seen Italy knew that nothing he would ever again encounter could possibly match his Italian experience. Once he had spent some time in Italy, that person possessed the feeling of being culturally "respectable": he could now put in his claim for membership in the cultural élite.

To be sure, such an almost institutionalized journey (it was called *Kavalierstour*) may have been—in many, perhaps most instances—a cloak for merely routine behavior. Of one instance, however, it is known that the journey to Italy became the traveler's preoccupation, in one form or another, for the rest of his life. This was Johann Kaspar Goethe (1710-1782).[1]

Appreciable wealth had been accumulated by the Goethe family through wise marriages and the industriousness of their ancestors; but their social standing in Frankfurt-am-Main was not commensurate with their financial means. Kaspar was therefore chosen by his father to remove this blemish. First, he was sent to the finest *Gymnasium*. Even his father's death, in 1730, did not interfere with the role that had been assigned to him. He then went on to the University of Leipzig, which his famous son was to attend 35 years later. Following this, he enriched his knowledge of jurisprudence at the Imperial High Court of Justice in Wetzlar where, 37 years later, his son (ostensibly serving the same purpose) was to absorb the various impressions that were later developed into *Werther*.

In 1738, Johann Kaspar Goethe acquired a law degree; then he devoted the following two years to professional training. At last, on December 30, 1739, accompanied by a servant, he left Vienna to begin his journey to Italy. By contrast with his son, who 46 years later would also start on his journey to Italy—to retrace his father's trek to a surprising degree, and yet to turn back North only after having visited Sicily—the father headed back after a sojourn in Naples.

He arrived in Frankfurt with a collection of notes so copious that for 28 years he was kept occupied with the composition of his *Viaggio in Italia*. An Italian teacher was engaged to assure stylistic elegance. Goethe's childhood was heavily colored by his father's literary labors, and Piranesi's magnificent etchings, which filled many a room in the house, had already made Rome a living entity to the boy, decades before he was to experience that thrilling moment of entering the city, for which he had felt a passionate longing from his childhood on.

It is apparent that the father wished to recapitulate his own development through his son, as can be seen first from Goethe's attendance at the University of Leipzig and then from his court year at Wetzlar. The relationship between father and son was intense and somewhat peculiar. Often, a son will hide his own identity behind paternal trappings, but in Kaspar's relationship to his son, this situation was occasionally reversed. The father had been prevented from entering the profession for which he

[1] For a history of recorded Italian journeys and attitudes toward Italy see von Klenze (1907). Unfortunately, the author did not sufficiently delve into Johann Kaspar Goethe's report on his journey to Italy.

had laboriously prepared himself, but when his son, who was at that time in the middle of his own *Sturm-und-Drang* period, and hence entirely unprepared to endure the rigor and discipline of a law practice, settled down in his native city in order to engage in that very profession, it was the father who did most of the work. Thus, it was the son who served the father, in this instance, as a kind of chrysalis.

Under such circumstances, it can be readily understood why Kaspar Goethe so ardently wished his son to go to Italy. Since the event had been an apogee in his own life, how could it fail to take place in the life of his son, whose superiority he had early acknowledged? But, as though by an invisible vise, Goethe was held back, even though Italy had been the subject of his phantasies ever since his childhood. Twice he stood on the St. Gotthard (once he even sketched a "Parting Glance toward Italy"), and twice he turned North. Indeed, a third instance is known in 1775, when he already sat in a carriage that was filled with a small library of Italian guidebooks that his father, passionately desiring his son's trip, had assembled for him. Interestingly, even though the traveler had already gone through part of the itinerary that his father had mapped out for him, he turned around, and was led by his demon back to Weimar.

Many years later—when, as an old man, he would write his life story—he would refer to his father's pressure to make him go to Italy as "a passionate error of [old] age" (*ein leidenschaftlicher Irrtum des Alters*). Why so? Why was it such a "passionate" error, if the 26-year-old man, who was apparently feeling restless, unhappy and deeply disappointed within the narrow confines of Frankfurt, might have found liberation, pleasure, possibly even new poetic inspiration, in the bewitching atmosphere of Italy?

And why then was he capable of going to Italy a decade later (September 1786)? It had been for him a decade of frustration, of hard service in the administration of a small Dukedom. The man who for years prior to that had been unwilling to bear the shackles of a well-ordered bourgeois community, at his new abode had been spending his nights poring over briefs and accounts, and scheming how to get the state budget balanced. For a time, even the artistic production that had made him a famous man all over Europe came to a standstill.

Even this prodigally teeming mind, which could effortlessly produce verse after verse, while its possessor was aimlessly taking a pleasure stroll through nature, and which could wake up from sleep with poems already perfectly formed—even such a mind was incapable of doing two such things at the same time, as solving such sober problems as those that are involved in the building of roads, the organization of the army and what not, and also writing poetry and tragedies. For Goethe, at his own request, took on duties for which several civil servants are ordinarily needed. Indeed, he became what would now be called a "trouble-shooter"; wherever problems had to be solved, he was called in.

Thus, he felt himself to be responsible for the taming of the reigning prince's extravagant passions. Karl August (1757-1829) was himself in the throes of his own *Sturm-und-Drang* period, which was sweeping the entire nation, and there was many an ominous prediction of lean years for a Dukedom whose sovereign had barely come of age and who was already enthralled by the poet who had created *Werther*. As the symbol of a disorderly life, of abysmal weakness, of a degenerate psychopathy that must necessarily lead to suicide (Goethe was accused of having caused a wave of suicides among the young in Central Europe), that book had become anathema to those who stood in favor of law and order.

Yet not a single one of those forebodings turned out to be true. Scarcely a meeting of the State Council did the poet miss: he became an exemplary civil servant. He had changed, there can be no doubt of that—had changed more profoundly and in a more essential way than other human beings change, when advancing age begins to encrust the plasma of youth.

But why was he now—after such years as those—able to go to Italy? Why had he first had to undergo this stupendous change—and what was its actual nature? Why did he now have to execute his plan furtively, using a pseudonym and confiding in no one but his servant—not his sovereign, not even the woman whom he loved beyond all measure and with whom he had shared the most intimate secrets of his heart—that he would be absent from Weimar for almost two years. I have tried elsewhere to answer that question, in an all too ponderous manner that made the inclusion of this essay on *Hamlet* inadvisable. Yet the reader will rightly ask what Shakespeare's tragedy could possibly have had to do with Goethe's journey to Italy. As I shall try to show, the tragedy is altogether germane to it.

Hamlet comes to the attention of a psychoanalytic biographer of Goethe, for one reason because the latter, during the period before his departure for Italy, occupied himself intensively with the play. Other preoccupations, such as that with Spinoza, for example, can be brought into a meaningful context with the dominant psychic trend of that period.

But why should *Hamlet* have aroused Goethe's interest so preponderantly at that time? What was there in the history of that unhappy prince—who cursed the moment of his birth, who (so it would seem) by his own ineptitude brought on the annihilation of the royal family—to excite the interest of the poet, who was, by contrast, approaching a moment of triumph, who stood at the brink of the fulfillment of a wish (both infantile and mature) that had long been overcathected, but the fulfillment of which he had, for unknown reasons, until then inhibited?

T. S. Eliot criticizes Goethe for interpreting Hamlet as a kind of Werther; but when he asserts that, in so doing, Goethe was projecting himself into Hamlet, he is wrong. For when Goethe wrote about Hamlet he had already outgrown (at least temporarily) his own Werther period.[2]

Goethe's preoccupation with *Hamlet* is all the more remarkable (and in need of a psychological explanation), since one does not find in his writings a comparable analytic scrutiny devoted to any other of Shakespeare's tragedies. Moreover, Goethe's interest in Shakespeare had, for obvious reasons, been greatest during his *Sturm-und-Drang* period; but at the time of his renewed interest in *Hamlet*, he had left that period far behind him. He was now quite close in time and in inner readiness to the classical period of his artistic output—which is not at all consonant with Shakespearean idiosyncrasies.

It seems highly probable that *Hamlet* had, in Goethe's unconscious, a quite different meaning from that which is contained in the current psychoanalytic interpretation of Hamlet as someone who constantly seeks to put things off till some later time. Indeed, Goethe was similarly a "delayer" in relation to his Italian journey, which had been imposed upon him by his father, perhaps with the same passion with which the task of revenge had been imposed on Hamlet by his father. At first glance, one might say that scarcely anything could be more discouraging to a man who was on the verge of overcoming an inhibition of his

---

[2] To be sure, even in old age Goethe was seized by Werther moods, but these became quite infrequent after his *Sturm-und-Drang* period. Moreover, Eliot is wrong, to begin with, when he asserts that Goethe did interpret Hamlet as a kind of Werther figure. Werther's tragedy in his inability to cope with life—*in whatever form*. To illustrate this by one instance: the idea that he will inevitably be destroying some life merely by taking a walk drives him to despair. Yet he himself is destined for voluntary death—whatever it is, until that moment, that fate may have in store for him. By contrast, Hamlet is crushed by an extraordinary fate, which he could do no more than hold at bay. In Goethe's view, the core of Hamlet's tragedy was the encounter between an intrinsically unheroic man and a task that destiny has placed on him and which requires, for its carrying out, the hardihood and courage of nothing less than an authentic hero.

obedience toward a paternal command than the intensive reading of *Hamlet.* Yet the record leaves no doubt that it was *Hamlet*, from among all of Shakespeare's tragedies, to which Goethe returned, over and over again, during the crucial time of preparing for his Italian journey.

From the sixth chapter of his quasi-autobiographical novel *Wilhelm Meisters theatralische Sendung* (the first version of the famous novel, discovered only in 1909), we can get a fair idea of some of what was then going through Goethe's mind, since the chapter was finished only 10 months prior to Goethe's departure. The specific psychological meaning that *Hamlet* held for Goethe becomes unquestionable when we read in the novel that Wilhelm and Hamlet had begun to merge into one person. Thus the biographer of Goethe is forced to turn to *Hamlet* and to search for a new interpretation of it, unless he prefers to let Goethe's interest in the play remain no more than a puzzle, an accident.

And indeed, it has been worthwhile to go through *Hamlet* with this question in mind since, after long examination, I have found a key that fits the problem perfectly. As it has turned out, the key is not as original as I had thought it was, for a similar proposition had already been made more than a half-century earlier (Türck, 1890). Aside from the rather peripheral question of originality, it is worthy of note that the interpretation I suggest is conceptualized for the most part within the framework of ego psychology, whereas Freud's and Jones' interpretations aim predominantly at the uncovering of repressed content and its effect upon the ego's potential activity. It is, of course, unnecessary to say that the two approaches are not at loggerheads but instead complement each other.

I shall now give up any further reference to the initial problem I encountered in Goethe's life story and shall take up again in the Epilogue the affinity between *Hamlet* and Goethe, at the time of his preparations for setting out to Italy. In the essay proper, I shall present other observations that I made during the course of my examination of the problem, without claiming any originality for them, either.

2. Discourse on "Hamlet"[1]

Hamlet has, to a greater extent than most literary works, challenged critical acumen. So often has this play been interpreted and reinterpreted (Williamson, 1950) with regard to the psychological structure of its main character, its broad context, and the minute details of its plot, that little in the way of essentially new insights can be expected from yet another study. Nevertheless, it may be worthwhile to approach this time-honored subject once again from the standpoint of Freud's ego psychology.[2]

I

In interpreting the tragedy that Elton (1922, p. 26) has called "the greatest melodrama in the world," one encounters many difficulties: the text is in places unreliable, and entire parts of it may actually be missing; the meaning of many words is doubtful, inasmuch as English has changed since Shakespeare's time; the sequence of scenes is not without question; and details of great import with regard to the staging of the play are open to speculation.[3]

---

[1] This is a revised version of a paper published in *Samiksa* 7, Nos. 2 and 3, 1953. Later additions are bracketed.

[2] As mentioned earlier, and as will be seen below, the point of my thesis has been in some measure anticipated by Türck (1890, p. 48). See also Alexander (1933, pp. 592-606) and Kanzer (1948, pp. 131-134).

[3] The reader need only be reminded of the still unresolved question of whether or not Claudius does witness the dumb show of the subplay.

Furthermore, in addition to the presently identifiable allusions to contemporary events, there are no doubt many others that would be of great service to the scholar—if he knew them—in his work of deciphering the general meaning of the tragedy. It is not even known for certain which passages aroused laughter in Shakespeare's audience, or which ones were written for that purpose. Even more, we know that a tragedy by another poet hides behind the present form of *Hamlet,* yet we do not know how this now lost text influenced Shakespeare. Nor do we know exactly when Shakespeare wrote *Hamlet,* any more than we know for certain about any other circumstance of his life.

It is well to be mindful of all these factors, for it almost seems as though fate had plotted against our ever finding out what is at the bottom of this tragedy, which has puzzled so many illustrious minds. Most puzzling, perhaps, is the great effect the play has had, and still continues to have, on those peoples who have had some share in the developments of Western culture.

Mutilated at times by rewriting, even desecrated at other times by being supplied with a "happy ending," the play has, nevertheless, always moved the spectator deeply. And this is all the more surprising when one considers that, under analysis by the expert, the play is seen to have so many faults, inconsistencies, even glaring contradictions, that some critics have bluntly declared it to be an artistic failure.

Nothing of all this, however, has dimmed the enthusiasm of either audiences or readers of the play. In view of the bitter criticism to which this tragedy has been at times subjected, however, we are faced with the question: how has it happened that a genius of both tragedy and comedy should be regarded by some critics as having failed in precisely that play that has, during the course of time, most enhanced his fame, and on the widest scale?

One must often concede, indeed, that neither reflection nor reasoning seems to be of much help in providing a satisfactory explanation of the play's elements. Not infrequently one discovers to one's astonishment that some marvel of subtle and logical reasoning has resolved one problem, only to reveal all the more clearly new contradictions in other parts of the tragedy. Shakespeare apparently succeeded, with uncanny mastery, in constructing such a plot, and in giving its main personages such characters, as to make the play altogether inaccessible to a finally satisfactory analysis.

Ambiguity,[4] in other words, would seem to be a fundamentally inescapable characteristic of the play. It is my contention that it is also the ultimate source of *Hamlet's* power—that, if the tragedy had indeed been explicable in any consistent fashion, it would never have had the penetrating effect it has demonstrated ever since the days of its first performance.

Now it is not really very difficult to write a play that is inaccessible to explanation; in fact, many a piece of literature has fallen into oblivion precisely because it did not make sense. The marvel of *Hamlet* is that absolute consistency prevails as long as one is content merely to follow the playwright; this changes to inconsistency, however, as soon as one begins to reflect on what one has gone along with. That is, so long as the spectator or reader keeps to the path laid out, and looks upon the events of the tragedy as if they were a segment of life, he can hardly escape being impressed by the absolute necessity inherent in their sequence. When once he begins to analyze this seemingly necessary sequence, however, what would appear to be ineluctable decisions, reflections and feelings on the part of the personages break up into almost disconnected episodes, however beautiful they may each remain even then.

One instance will serve to illustrate how even a well thought out explanation of a seeming inconsistency may create so many new contradictions that one is forced to forgo it. John Dover Wilson tackled the inconsistency that lies in Hamlet's speaking, after having held discourse with his father's ghost, of "the undiscovered country, from whose bourn no traveler returns." Wilson felt that he had resolved this contradiction: "the true explanation . . . is that in this mood of deep dejection Hamlet has given up all belief in the 'honesty' of the ghost, and that Shakespeare wrote the lines to make this clear to the audience."[5]

An intriguing explanation, indeed. But why then does Hamlet, in the discourse with Ophelia that follows immediately, take all precautions against the eavesdroppers whom he suspects or knows to be listening? If he had really given up all belief in the Ghost and his message, one should instead expect a considerably lighter mood and the complete abandon-

---

[4] I use here a term that has become firmly rooted in literary analysis and criticism. See Empson (1930) and further, Kaplan and Kris (1948). The ambiguity I speak of in regard to the plot of *Hamlet* is roughly of the type that these writers have designated as "integrative ambiguity." An analysis of the conception of ambiguity would, however, lead far afield and is not necessary in this context [cf. Bowers, 1959].

[5] See *Hamlet*, Cambridge edition, 1948, p. 192. For a powerful rebuttal of this scarcely tenable opinion, see Robertson (1931, pp. 35-39).

ment of any plans for revenge. Such a keen investigator as Loening (1893)[6] believed that the soliloquy has "no or at least no direct connection with the vengeance incumbent upon Hamlet"; it is, for Loening, merely the expression of Hamlet's mood, which is depressed as a result of the tragic events that have befallen him.

It is of interest to note that the opinion that this passage expressed Hamlet's disbelief in the Ghost had been voiced as early as 1865 (Loening, 1893, p. 166). Other early attempts to explain the contradiction were that the ghost is nothing but a phantasmic image of Hamlet's (Greg, 1917); that purgatory is not, after all, a place of the next world; that Hamlet is speaking here of man in general and without reference to his personal experiences; that Hamlet had in mind a corporeal, not a spiritual, return.

Now I must admit that, although I have read the play a number of times, the passage in question has never struck me as involving a contradiction. This might, of course, simply bespeak inadequacy of astuteness or of analytic capacity on my part; but I would venture to guess that thousands of others have also followed the tragedy attentively, and have been deeply moved by this soliloquy, without sensing any contradiction in it.

In view of the apparent impossibility of reaching agreement on the point in question, one might be tempted to wish that Shakespeare had either left out that line altogether or else had resolved the contradiction by the addition of some other words. But, strangely enough, it is just this line about the "undiscovered country" that has become quite meaningful for a great many, and no one will seriously believe that it would improve the play to leave it out. Further, I am convinced that any attempt to clear up the contradiction that seems to lurk here can only result in producing a vastly decreased effect on the reader.[7]

Wilson believes that the point can be clarified, even readily explained, as soon as one becomes acquainted with Elizabethan demonology, and he has done much to familiarize us with the main beliefs of Shakespeare's century in regard to ghosts (Lavater, 1928). Yet, in his

---

[6] See pp. 164-175 for Loening's analysis of the soliloquy, and particularly p. 166 and fn. 36 for a review of the many explanations offered for this contradiction.

[7] Wilson's explanation presupposes that the reader, or spectator, upon learning that Hamlet believes that no man returns from the beyond, must at once conclude that Hamlet has now been convinced of the devilish origin of his father's ghost. I very much doubt that anyone who has been moved by this play has concerned himself with such questions.

imagery of the ghost of Hamlet's father, Shakespeare does not follow those beliefs. The fact that the Ghost comes out of purgatory, for example, is in contradiction to the ideas of the new Protestantism on the subject. Wilson may have been right in saying, "The ghost in *Hamlet* was a far more arresting and prominent figure to the Elizabethan audience than he can ever be to us."[8] Yet he should have been aware that a contradiction with regard to the point under consideration might not have been felt either by Shakespeare's audience or by Shakespeare.[9]

At this point, it is appropriate to say a word about the general role of contradictions in tragedy. When Stoll, referring to the passage noted, calls it "an unguarded word, such as we find not in Ibsen," (Stoll, 1919, p. 35)[10] he is partly right; but he has at the same time furnished one of the reasons why the number of people who find inspiration and artistic enjoyment in Ibsen's plays has been decreasing, while *Hamlet* has remained as fascinating as ever. It is just such "unguarded words" that infuse lifeblood into the picture of Hamlet, and the absence of them that makes Ibsen's personages, despite his marvelous dramaturgy, relatively bloodless.

It would scarcely appear contradictory to a twentieth-century audience for the hero of a play to express belief in the omnipotence and omniscience of God and then, a few moments later, to hold a criminal responsible for his misdeeds. A few centuries hence, reflective spectators may regard these two statements as irreconcilable, or else may believe

[8] Throughout his analysis, Wilson underestimates not only the unconscious of Shakespeare's character, but also that of the audience. Presumably, if the play is well acted, many twentieth-century spectators may watch the ghost scenes with feelings as intense as those we may suppose to have prevailed among Shakespeare's audience. Cf. Freud (1907, p. 71): "A man who has grown rational and sceptical, even, may be ashamed to discover how easily he may for a moment return to a belief in spirits under the combined impact of strong emotion and perplexity." He then goes on to report an instance of the sort that happened to him personally [Cf. Heilman (1965, p. 29f)], and speaks of "an inclination for, and a sense of, mystery that does not quite surrender to the commanding patterns of rationalistic life."

[9] The stronger the feelings involved in an intellectual issue, the greater is the likelihood that contradictory statements will be made about it. Is it not obvious that to all known civilizations such contradictions as these, and even grosser ones, have proven to be quite acceptable? (See Feis, 1844, p. 89), where it is rightly pointed out that the presence of such contradictions is quite legitimate.) An age considers itself to be superior to those that came before it: it regards itself as free from contradictory beliefs that it belittlingly assumes to have been rampant earlier—only to be victimized in turn by a different set. The contradictions of one's own age are in general not perceived, but condoned. The eternal separation of the living from the dead was a subject of controversy in Shakespeare's times, and there can be little doubt that, if a contradiction had been sensed at all at this point in the play, Shakespeare would have felt it necessary to remove it or explain it away.

[10] Cf. also Archer (1923) about imitation and passion as sources of drama, and his statement on modern realistic drama as a pure and logical art form (p. 5).

that the author meant to indicate to the audience that the hero had at that particular moment given up his belief in the omnipotence and omniscience of God.

Man's ability to endure contradictions is indeed one of the most characteristic aspects of the human condition. The purely logical—that is to say, that which is purified of intrinsic contradictions—is often quite difficult to assimilate, or else quite without savor. What has become most meaningful to large segments of mankind has often harbored the crassest contradictions. The most outstanding example, of course, is the Bible; purging it of its contradictions would only make it that much less valuable to man as a source of edification, spiritual elevation, or poetic enjoyment.

This is not to say that it is a matter of indifference *what sort* of contradictions find their way into great spiritual and artistic achievements. An examination of literary history will show, I think, that only a certain, as yet unknown, combination of contradictions or of the internal structures within those contradictions themselves, is capable of exerting a profound effect on a wide scale. But while little is known about the laws that govern this class of phenomena, we may be certain that they do govern, with full and unimpeded sway, in the tragedy of Hamlet. This is evident from the fact that no effort to eliminate some of the many contradictions in the play by new plot construction has so far been able to compete for very long with the original. One can only conclude that Shakespeare—unconsciously or consciously—endowed both plot and the chief personages in it with a set of contradictions that, in the given circumstances, have been able to elicit the maximal artistic response in the audience. Hence, literary analysis of the tragedy should not aim at eliminating these contradictions but must instead try to comprehend their meaning.

Much controversy can indeed by avoided if it is clearly understood that a tragedy like *Hamlet* cannot be considered in relation to a single group of factors; often it is a plurality of causative factors that has to be correlated, in any effort to explain a detail. For example, Wilson writes (1936a, p. 34): "The usurpation [of the throne by Claudius] is one of the main factors in the plot of *Hamlet* and it is vital that we moderns should not lose sight of it." The evidence he brings to bear will undoubtedly enrich the reader's understanding of *Hamlet;* but one may still take issue with his specific proposition that the usurpation is "one of the main factors." If this were so, then how could audiences without any understanding of or feeling for the laws governing the succession to the English crown be deeply affected by a performance of the tragedy?

A real *Hamlet* craze ran through Germany in the last quarter of the eighteenth century, even though the German public could have had only a smattering of knowledge of English constitutional law and no real feeling for English institutions. In this connection, it is worthwhile to read an account written by a German in 1776 after he had seen *Hamlet:*

> As many-headed and many-tongued as an assembly in a theater may be, as varied as the individual opinions about performance and play usually are, yet each crowded audience present at the three performances of *Hamlet* in Hamburg . . . was so attentive, so enraptured, that they seemed to be one person only, one pair of eyes only and one pair of hands—so universal was the silence, awe, amazement, weeping and applause . . . . Anyone that is not stirred and enraptured by the mighty spirit of Shakespeare, who can make cold indolence cry and laugh, such a person must be lifeless matter [Loening, 1893, p. 5].

I would interpret such a reaction as proof that the question of succession cannot be one of the main factors in the plot of *Hamlet*, even though it is quite likely that Shakespeare himself, as well as some among his audience, had such a question in mind.[11]

A similar problem of provenance arises in the study of neuroses. Among the factors that lead to neurosis one finds a frustration of the individual's desire to obtain prestige. In order to understand this facet of the neurotic symptom, one has to know what, in that particular society, confers prestige. But just as a frustrated desire for prestige will never of itself produce a neurotic symptom, so the conflict of a wronged prince who wishes to assert his rightful claim to the throne will never of itself yield a great tragedy.[12]

Similar considerations hold for such controversial issues as the nature of the ghost of Hamlet's father. The Ghost per se is quite understandable, and will remain understandable so long as man retains any traces of his fear of the supernatural. Flatter (1949) has provided a searching analysis of the bearing the Ghost has on the whole tragedy,

---

[11] Cf. Freud (1916-1917), "Shakespeare's *Macbeth* . . . was a *pièce d'occasion,* composed to celebrate the accession of the King who first united the crowns of the three Kingdoms. *But does this immediate historical occasion cover the content of the tragedy?*" (p. 96, *S.E.,* Vol. 15; italics mine)

[12] That is to say, knowledge of the laws of succession to the English crown will contribute as much or as little to an understanding of *Hamlet* as knowledge of the societal sources of a patient's prestige values contributes to an understanding of the neurotic symptom.

without once referring to Elizabethan demonology; he has thus proved that, even for this configuration, understanding can be obtained without reference to the historical framework.[13]

It is indeed true that nearly every personage in *Hamlet*, every detail of the plot, perhaps every individual thought, shows some reflection of historical factors of the time in which Shakespeare lived. But I would suggest that each of them is also much more than that. A work like *Hamlet* has an incredible breadth, far greater than we are able to fathom. Shakespeare himself may not necessarily have been aware—he was probably not aware—of the full meaning inherent in his tragedy. Even Shakespeare's more perceptive contemporaries may have been overwhelmed by the wealth of references to facts of their own historical period that were integrated into the play.

A single dream, Freud stressed, is for all practical purposes infinite in its depth of meaning, and the analysis of it can never safely be regarded as having been concluded. A good many dreams must have gone into *Hamlet*. I cannot, therefore, agree with J. Dover Wilson when he objects "on principle" to Jones's analysis of Hamlet's character.[14] Wilson asserts that "apart from the play, apart from his actions, from what he tells us about himself and what other characters tell us about him, there is no Hamlet." Yet Wilson himself, despite his attempt to narrow most stringently the area from which to derive his explanations, does not live up to his own principle, as Jones so rightly shows (1949, p. 19). In practice, he seems to admit speculation only about conscious motives. But in a previous publication (Wilson, 1918, pp. 129-154) he had said that Hamlet's hesitation "is a problem of character, not of circumstances"—which would seem to me to imply the necessity of paying attention to unconscious factors as well, if one wishes to deal seriously with the problem.

If we agree that Hamlet is a potential structure within the human world, then it is correct to say that Hamlet is quite as "real" as any person we have ever known or learned about through oral or historical report.[15] In the person of Hamlet, Shakespeare created someone who corresponds to the actual personages of human life—primarily by telling us about what is going on in Hamlet's conscious mind. Yet it must not be

---

[13] And yet this would seem to be a preeminent example of those configurations for which much historical spadework is needed as a prerequisite to understanding.

[14] *Hamlet*, Cambridge edition, 1948, p. xliv ff.

[15] With a living person, the unconscious elements can be ferreted out only when there become available to the analyst many conscious manifestations of these elements.

forgotten that each of the large number of conscious manifestations with which we are presented in the play itself is resonant with the implications of unconscious factors and, no less than in the case of a living person, the skilled analyst is able to deduce these unconscious factors from their conscious manifestations.

What we must ask ourselves is whether it is possible for such a man as the one described by Shakespeare to have acted and spoken in that way, had he actually lived within that historical and physical context. In other words, if someone were to write in the form of chronicles everything that we know about Hannibal and everything that Shakespeare lets us know about Hamlet, could anyone decide from those two chronicles alone which was the historical figure and which the fictitious character? It seems not unreasonable to challenge in this fashion anyone's ability to distinguish between the historical record of a person who actually lived and [the sort of psychological record that Shakespeare has left us in this tragedy.[16] Moreover, a careful analysis may well show that the imaginary heroes of the great poets have left deeper marks on history than have those heroes who did actually at one time live in history.

Just as some of the great historical figures are interpreted anew by each generation (Gundolf, 1925), so do the poet's heroes undergo reinterpretation. But we must ask: are these new interpretations improvements over the old, or are new and old mutually contradictory? A study of the great variety of previous *Hamlet* interpretations might well show that the majority of them have been valid, even though the full claims of their authors would have to be disputed. The probability is that, while the historical figure is ultimately exhaustible by interpretation, the personage created by the poet is an infinite cosmos, so that each generation is able to unfold only one of its many meanings.

If one could measure essentials of human life quantitatively, it might even be permissible to suggest that one can find more of them in *Hamlet* than in any record we have of a historical person. Moreover, the latter usually attracts our attention only insofar as that person himself had entered into the sequence of historical events—a small segment of

---

[16] [A discussion of Aristotle's distinction between historian and poet ("the one describes the thing that has been, the other a kind of thing that might be") would lead too far afield. I want only to refer to Peter Alexander's *Introductions* (1964, p. 82), in one of which he so ably discusses what makes Shakespeare's histories and tragedies distinctive. In my statement above, I did not intend to refer to any problem of that kind, but had in mind only a comparison between abstractions: one produced from chronicles and the other from plays of any *genre*.]

him, indeed, when measured against his whole personality. We may not be able to decipher the riddle of Hamlet, but the material on which an interpretation can be based is amply given, and it is therefore with justice that one can say that implicitly we know—or can know—more about Hamlet than about Hannibal.[17]

Some plays require for their understanding only historical knowledge: if the reader is familiar with the times, then he can follow the play quite easily. There are also plays in which knowledge of the author's life and times can be helpful, and yet the context will itself be sufficient to convey consistent meaning. Finally, there are plays—and it is only these, I believe, that have acquired lasting eminence—in which, after these two groups of factors have played their explanatory role, there will still remain a gap that can be filled only by factors drawn from an entirely different source—namely, the unconscious.

It is clear what one means when one asserts that the neurotic symptom is a derivative of the unconscious; it is less clear what is meant by the assertion that the unconscious must be considered in an explanation of *Hamlet*. Freud and Jones have explained that Hamlet's hesitation in avenging his father's death is the result of his own childhood wishes—wishes that are regularly repressed, yet still leave their imprint on the adult's character and behavior. The rationale underlying their thinking can be formulated as follows: Observation of a number of similar situations in the lives of subjects has shown regularly that such inhibitions are the consequence of repressed childhood wishes. Any man who, like Hamlet, behaves in this way must therefore have had certain wishes in his childhood and developed certain character traits during the course of repressing these wishes.[18]

[17] [I have chosen Hannibal, because the vengeance motive played such a significant role in his life too; but no offense should be taken by my statement that our biographical knowledge of this particular historical personage is scanty. In the great creations of literary art (at least within the last four centuries in the West) life has been captured with such forcefulness and pregnancy that the stuff required for a reconstruction of a major character's personality structure and even of the relevant unconscious elements can be found at least as extensively as in well-documented biographies of historical personages. Considering the scantiness of our knowledge about Shakespeare, we are able to assert more about Hamlet's personality structure—and with greater reliability—than we can about that of his creator. (1966)]

[18] This is one point at which the unconscious finds its rightful place in literary analysis. The question that is raised in conjunction with such problems usually has to do with the author's own personality: Was Shakespeare expressing his own conflicts by having Hamlet act as he does in the tragedy? This question is of a different order of relevance. It is theoretically conceivable that a poet could create such personages without deriving the stuff for them from his own life history. Instead, the stuff of his personages could be derived mainly from his observation of others about him. Since it is known, however, that the process of observation also depends on the observer's unconscious, one

II

In what follows, I wish to go further. I believe that the full depth of a tragedy like *Hamlet* can be grasped *only* if one investigates it in the way in which the analyst is accustomed to investigating dreams.[19] This may appear to be in contradiction to my earlier comparison of *Hamlet* with a record of historically real events. Yet I believe that we are here face to face with the outstanding characteristic of great tragedy—that it is the equivalent both of a historical record of real events and, at the same time, of a dream.

Interestingly enough, when we witness a play on the stage, we tend to display attitudes that are comparable to those we show toward dreams. In a dream, we usually accept the product of our nocturnal mental life as true reality. Similarly, under optimal conditions we accept the events on the stage as being just as valid as those of reality, and we are moved by these events as if they did involve real life. In most dreams, of course, we are not able to shake off dream reality in favor of the actual reality; in the theater, however, we are generally able to switch back instantaneously to the realness of actuality.[20]

During the dream, our critical functions are asleep, and we permit ourselves—or are forced—to accept the illogical as valid. The spectator at a play behaves in the same way. The merely illusory reality of the stage world—such as the speaking in verse, the singing, the aside, the soliloquy, inconsistencies of the plot, the fact that the performance will be repeated—all this is accepted with the same seriousness with which reality in general is approached. This seemingly uncritical attitude is extended to orientation in time and space, as well as to plot content. When the action that takes place before our eyes is supposed to be taking place in bygone times, we accept that apparent illogicality; when the same stage

---

feels inclined to assume, in this instance too, that the poet's own unconscious has been deeply involved. But this is an entirely different question from the earlier one, as to whether we must assume that only an unconscious reason could have delayed Hamlet from embarking at the earliest possible moment upon the avenging of his father. [The Freud-Jones theory has been held up to ridicule by many literary critics. For a recent criticism, as vitriolic as it is devoid of any knowledge of the workings of the mind, see Grebanier (1960), who avers that he found only one explanation that is sillier than "even the Freudian" (p. 90).]

[19] For a similar approach, see Sharpe (1946, p. 219f). See also Rickmann (1940, pp. 294-313). For an extensive discussion of the application of psychoanalytic methods to the interpretation of works of art, see Kris (1950). Bonaparte (1933, p. 654f) has traced dream mechanisms in literary works.

[20] There are some situations, rare as they may be, that leave us in doubt as to whether an event has to do with the world of the stage or of actual life.

space is occupied in succession by scenes with altogether different locations, we accept that, too.

Another noteworthy similarity between dreamer and spectator is the passivity of the two of them. Dream reality and stage reality are both incompatible with active interference, by either dreamer or spectator; in both situations, a basic condition of "participation" is that access to the motor system has been blocked off. The analogy can be carried even further. Anyone who has been compelled for personal reasons—that is, for reasons that are not connected with the artistic requirements of the play—to remain aware of the artificiality of the theatrical illusion will generally, as a consequence, show a disturbance comparable to that of the dreamer who is incapable of experiencing the illusion of the dream as if it were reality. [21]

Most people are more inclined to compare seeing a stage play with daydreaming. [22] Breuer's famous patient, for example, called the world of her daydreams her private theater. [23] Evidence can undoubtedly be adduced to justify such a comparison, but I think that it does not go to the heart of the matter. In daydreaming the course of the entire fantasy is usually anticipated: the chain of daydreams is a gradual unfolding of a more comprehensive structure, of which the daydreamer is, from the first, somewhat aware. It is true that daydreams sometimes do take an unforeseen turn, to the surprise of the daydreamer, but this is the exception rather than the rule.

Furthermore, daydreams are usually restricted in their choice of topics and in their concomitant affects (cf. Freud, 1908). They are generally concerned with ambitious or erotic wishes and are therefore accompanied by the corresponding feelings. Again, this is not an absolute. During periods of mourning, or in situations of impending danger or of depression, daydreams may take on an entirely different emotional coloring. Under such pathological conditions, however, I think one comes close to compulsive daydreaming.

The affects of dreams, on the contrary, comprise the whole gamut of emotions, while the sequence of events is usually unforeseen by the dreamer. When the dream becomes too unpleasant, the dreamer may remind himself that this is, after all, only a dream, just as the spectator, if

---

[21] For a discussion of the aesthetic illusion and its disturbances, see Kris (1941, pp. 13-63).

[22] For a profound comparative analysis of the work of art and the daydream, see Sachs (1924, pp. 11-54).

[23] See Breuer and Freud (1893-95, pp. 22, 218).

a play is intolerably depressing, may take refuge in the idea that reality can never be so desperate. A deepgoing analysis will show, I surmise, that there are other, and also more concrete, parallels between the phenomenology of stage plays and that of dreams.[24] I wish to point out only one more such correspondence.

The audience usually knows more about the plot than does any individual person in the play. Some of the stage persons are, of course, presumed to have knowledge that the onlooker does not yet possess, and that will unfold only during the course of the play. Soon after the play has begun, however, the onlooker is already in possession of knowledge that he cannot rightly assume to be shared by all the persons in the play, unless it happens to be, by way of exception, a play in which all the characters are on the stage at the same time, and nothing is said or done that does not come to the attention of all of them.

A careful scrutiny of dream phenomenology will show that this factor of superior knowledge is implicitly given in the dream. In some dreams it becomes, so to speak, the center, as in the following: "His father was dead, but had been exhumed and looked bad. He had been living since then and the dreamer was doing all he could to prevent his noticing it" (Freud, 1916-1917, p. 188). Here the element of knowing more than the other person in the dream is outspoken. Yet I am not referring here to those dreams in which the superiority of the dreamer's knowledge is the content of the manifest dream, but rather to a tacit quality that is inherent in most dreams and is indirectly connected with the ego's infantile sense of omnipotence, on which, in the end, every dream is based.[25]

I should like now to extend my hypothesis by introducing a genetic viewpoint. As is well known, members of some primitive societies are incapable of distinguishing between dream and reality (cf. Lincoln, 1935, pp. 27-29), and the assumption is that, during the early phases of its development, the child is likewise unable to make that distinction.[26] The discovery that dreams are not reality may constitute a narcissistic blow,

---

[24] See, for such parallels, Sharpe (1946, p. 219).

[25] A narcissistic component in the enjoyment of stage performances also comes to the fore in the fact that the spectator at a play usually feels as if the actors were playing for him. This narcissistic affinity between subject and observed event is less pronounced at the cinema, and usually altogether absent when one is reading a book. Yet these factors show such a great personal variation that no general statement can yet be made with safety.

[26] [See Piaget (1929, p. 91). In view of recent research into the physiology of dreaming and the discovery that the physiological mechanism of the dream is fully developed in the new-born (see, e.g. E. Hartmann, 1967), this can now be restated with greater certainty.]

later compensated for by the conviction that it is a supernatural power that makes its appearance in dreams. The question I wish to raise here has to do with the possibility that the effect of stage plays, in particular, and perhaps of art in general, has one genetic root in the narcissistic frustration that follows upon the discovery that dreams are only a product of man's imagination and that reality is something apart from the events that occurred in the dream.

This discovery results in the setting up of an ego boundary that restricts the archaic ego's feeling of limitlessness. The stage play then restores the imaginary to the place of "real" reality. The dreamer's consciousness is wholly occupied with the perceptive material of the dream, all other stimuli being excluded that would enforce an orientation in accordance with reality. Similarly, the spectator at a play surrenders himself to the stage reality and excludes the time- and space-orientation of his real environment. What he thereafter perceives, however, is not the product of his own repressed; instead, it is the playwright and the actors who furnish the content of his dream.

> We are such stuff
> As dreams are made on, and our little life
> Is rounded with a sleep.

These remarks may suffice as a theoretical justification for my occasionally dealing with *Hamlet* as if it were the manifest content of a dream.[27] There are differences, of course. The dream can usually be interpreted only if we know the dreamer's associations, whereas these are missing in the analysis of a play.[28] More crucial is the difference arising from the fact that, in order to fulfill its function, the dream must not make its meaning patent. While instances are known in which the dream has become so well-organized and structured that only a minimum of the subject's associations have been needed for the interpretation (cf. Rank, 1910, pp. 465-540), as a rule the manifest dream content hides more than it shows.

If a play were under the necessity of doing the same thing, it would

---

[27] The application of dream analysis, when applied to esthetic analysis, makes for great freedom of approach. The literary scholar may well reject this approach on the grounds of the method—which may easily lead to abuse, of course, if conclusions are not checked by the direct study of man, as is done in the clinical application of psychoanalysis.

[28] I am not considering in this context biographical data about the author, which can sometimes be used in the same way as one uses a patient's associations.

become incomprehensible to the spectator. While we find brevity—particularly the brevity that is achieved by means of condensation—to be an essential tool of dreams and jokes, it is to be noted that novels and plays, even though they do not dispense entirely with condensation, have to elaborate extensively on their inherent, latent themes. Here we encounter equivalents of the secondary revisions in the dreamwork (cf. Freud, 1900, pp. 488-508). These elaborations, which have the task of making certain that the spectator will receive the message contained in the play's latent content, may be regarded as taking the place of the free association with which the patient supplements his dreams. The latent content, of course, must be set forth in a tragedy with as little distinctness as it is in the dream; otherwise esthetic enjoyment would be converted into displeasure.

I would like to stress, however, that up to this point no reference has been made to the author's own psychology. The content that is obtained by the interpretation of a tragedy does not necessarily reflect—or even imply the existence of—corresponding processes in the author. The analyst does well to put off making any inferences about the author's psychology until material can be adduced from sources other than the play. As soon as a literary work has taken shape, it has become an objective structure, which exists independently of its author and can therefore be interpreted independently of him. It has a manifest content that must be carefully studied and understood; it also has a latent content that is different from what the author has directly formulated or may even have consciously intended to formulate. I have called this latent content "the unconscious," in correlation with the terminology derived from the analysis of dreams and neurotic symptoms.[29]

I should like now to raise a few points derived from a study of the play's manifest content, which make inescapable certain assumptions about its underlying unconscious.

Although in terms of the manifest content of the play Hamlet, Ophelia and Laertes are not all three the offspring of the same father, their relationships nevertheless have the character of that of siblings. At some crucial points during the course of the tragedy, conflicts arise among the three that seem to point to a brothers-and-sister relationship

---

[29] The concept of a latent or unconscious content of a literary work is the self-evident consequence of the psychoanalytic approach. It seems to me that the first one to formulate the concept explicitly was Pfister (1913). That cultural structures, such as the joke, have latent meanings had already been demonstrated by Freud and used by him for purposes of explanation as early as 1905.

among them. Some of Hamlet's problems are those that typically show up in the lives of the older brothers, while some of Laertes' problems are those that generally make their appearance in the lives of younger brothers.

The difficulty that a "crown prince" generally faces lies in the conflict between his assurance that he will *one day* carry out the functions of head of state (the father), and his lack of any assurance about *when* he will be permitted (or required) to assume these functions. The ambiguity in the position of the oldest son is not limited to princely families; it is as old as the system of primogeniture, if not older, and can be observed even in modern societies, where each son expects to acquire an equal share of independence. Oldest sons are often conservative; they demand privileges for themselves, however, that they then deny to other children. Among the younger siblings, the hatred that has its origin in rebellious impulses against the father is thus displaced onto the eldest brother.[30]

The aging father, knowing that his death will bring the greatest advantage to his oldest son, turns with affection and tenderness toward the youngest son, finding in him an ally who detests the impending yoke of the brother even more than he does the present yoke of the aged father. The father's authority has been a constant feature of the past and is therefore legitimate in his eyes; the oldest brother's ascendancy, however, smacks of usurpation and is regarded as accidental. "It is just by chance that *I* am not in the position of the oldest" sums up one aspect of the younger brother's feeling. The aging father, being somewhat afraid of his oldest son, does not really mind discord between the brothers; an irreconcilable feud between siblings may even be a heritage that he leaves almost with secret satisfaction, as a sort of punishment for his successor.

These aspects are clearly present in the relationship between Hamlet and Laertes. What Hamlet strives for is the establishment of law and order, insofar as he is trying to carry out the avenging of his father's murder. In this regard, he behaves like the oldest son, who already acts as king even though he has not yet taken over the reins of government. Laertes, by contrast, shows all the earmarks of the younger brother. With the freedom of one who is not destined for any important state func-

[30] In Greek mythology, it is often the youngest son who commits the oedipal crime; it is he who survives the father's wrath and is, so to speak, the only one who is left to take over for the aged father. The pattern of the fairy tale is analogous; it is the youngest son, long the victim of the eldest brother's oppression, who is triumphant in the end. In a society in which children are protected against paternal ambivalence, however, it is the oldest son who takes the father's place, and the younger brothers are thereupon thrust into a position of increased rivalry with the oldest.

tion, he is permitted to go off to Paris, whereas, from the beginning of the tragedy, Hamlet has to make the sort of sacrifice that members of a royal family must often make, through having to disregard personal desires in favor of a societal function, without reaping any immediate benefit therefrom for themselves.

With particular subtlety, Shakespeare has Claudius, following his speech from the throne, address first Laertes and then Hamlet. External factors, such as Claudius's gratitude to Polonius for having helped him obtain the throne, have been adduced in order to explain Claudius's demonstration of affection toward Laertes in this scene; but, as has been remarked before, the same event can be read within the context of different levels, and the psychological purpose is far more effectively achieved if it can be hidden behind or within an action that seems to be well justified in terms of purely realistic motives.[31]

In the relationship of the two brothers to Ophelia, however, the roles are reversed. It is the oldest son who lays claim to the sister, while the younger brother upholds the moral principle, demanding punishment and revenge. There is a remarkable precedent for this in the Old Testament, where there is a similar but more outspoken sibling relationship—namely, among Jacob's children. Jacob has six sons and one daughter by his first (but unloved) wife, Leah. Reuben, his oldest son, acts throughout the narrative as his father's representative in his efforts to uphold the law. He objects to his brothers' murderous plans against Joseph; he organizes the expedition to Egypt; he vouches for Benjamin's safe return to Jacob by pledging the lives of two of his own sons. It is he, in short, who fulfills the social functions that his aging father is incapable of carrying out. Strangely enough, he also commits incest. Reuben "went and lay with Bilhah, his father's consort," who had borne children to Jacob. Bilhah had taken the place of Rachel, Jacob's favorite wife, who was stricken by long-lasting barrenness.

Although the Old Testament is more outspoken than Shakespeare, the traces of repression are also visible here, insofar as the incestual act takes place only after Rachel's death. Yet the incest motive had already been anticipated symbolically when Rachel bartered with Leah for Reuben's mandrakes, in return for which Leah was promised renewal of intercourse with Jacob. The context makes inescapable the inference that

---

[31] Those modern plays that attempt an explicit psychology and the verbalization of unconscious trains of thought are incomparably less effective than are plays in which the deepest psychological meaning is hidden, encapsulated within what seems overtly to be psychologically neutral.

"mandrake" here stands for semen, and that Rachel was buying permission to have intercourse with Reuben, Leah's oldest son. Significantly, Rachel, previously barren, became pregnant soon after she received the mandrakes.

In another context—this one more obscure—Reuben's affinity for incest is intimated. When his sister, Dinah, was violated by Shechem, it was not Reuben but her other brothers, Simeon and Levi, who killed Shechem and his father, in order to avenge their sister's dishonor. True, the vengeance was accomplished through a crafty ruse. Shechem and his father had agreed to circumcision in order to make Shechem's marriage with Dinah possible, and the avengers took advantage of the men's "soreness" to attack and kill them.

It might be argued that Reuben, the conservative upholder of the law, did not wish to participate in such a breach of law. Still the question can be asked why he did not, at the very least, admonish his brothers to avenge their sister's honor in open battle. Reuben's name is conspicuously absent in this episode; it is the younger brothers who fulfill the role that ancient society would by custom assign to the oldest.[32] It may be that the latent thought was that it was he who had ravished Dinah and was killed by the younger brothers.

In all these circumstances, Reuben's relative freedom from punishment raises many questions. The Biblical story is usually explicit as to the punishment meted out to evildoers. Onan had to die for an action that could hardly be regarded as criminal: he had refused to make his older brother's widow pregnant. Reuben, by contrast, had committed incest. Yet, of the judgment against Reuben, we know only what can be inferred from the words spoken by Jacob shortly before his death: "Reuben, thou art my firstborn, my might, and the beginning of my strength, the excellence of dignity and the excellence of power: Unstable as water, thou shalt not excel; because thou wentest up to thy father's bed; then defiledst thou it: he went up to my couch."

The comparison between Hamlet and Reuben is inconclusive, chiefly because the information we have about the latter is somewhat scanty, whereas in *Hamlet* the tragedy of the oldest son is put into a central position. The main figure among Jacob's sons is of course Joseph; he is of interest here because his victory over his brothers is linked to Reuben, who saved Joseph's life when it was being threatened by the jealousy of the

[32] For a different interpretation of the meaning of absence in a play, see Kris (1948).

older brothers. Thus Joseph's life is inextricably intertwined with that of Reuben, and an interpretation of the Joseph story would have to give Reuben far greater prominence in it than the manifest content might lead one to believe.

Another Biblical episode must be mentioned here: the rape of Tamar by her half brother Amnon, the oldest son of David. Again the father does not punish the misdeed; but Absalom, the younger brother, does take revenge by killing Amnon, while Solomon plays a role that is roughly comparable to that of Joseph. It is interesting to compare the two Biblical sets of sibling relations and to observe what has been distorted in one and expressed clearly in the other.

Dinah's and Tamar's further vicissitudes are not mentioned. They vanish, just as Ophelia must vanish. To be sure, the characteristic misogyny of the Old Testament is considerably mitigated in *Hamlet*, and Ophelia's tragedy is more fully spelled out. Nonetheless, parallels can be dimly perceived. Shechem is deeply in love with Dinah, but outside interference separates them; Amnon turns in unspeakable hatred against Tamar, following his rape of her. The attitudes of both Shechem and Amnon can be discovered in *Hamlet*.

If the relationship of Hamlet, Ophelia, and Laertes *is* that of siblings, who, then, is the father? Suppose a patient were to report a dream that followed the outline of Shakespeare's *Hamlet*, or during a certain period of his analysis, were to have dreams that piecemeal revealed occurrences equivalent to the gross events presented in the tragedy. One would, of course, then point out to him that the dream or sequence of dreams referred, on the one hand, to *three* fathers (the Ghost, Polonius and Old Fortinbras) and *two* uncles—that is to say, two father substitutes, Claudius and Old Fortinbras' Brother—and on the other to three sons (Hamlet, Laertes, and Young Fortinbras).

It is of interest to compare briefly these father figures and their substitutes. The Ghost, we learn, was an absolute ideal; Polonius is a dotard; Fortinbras was killed in a duel; Fortinbras' brother is sick and bedridden; Claudius is a criminal. The five men of the older generation thus represent various kinds of fathers that sons may have:[33] ideal, senile, dead, sick, and criminal. The play includes, by and large, all the major variations, the Ghost and Claudius being at the opposite ends of the spectrum.

[33] Kris (1948) has pointed out "three versions of the father-son conflict" in *King Henry IV* and ingeniously revealed Falstaff to be a depreciated father figure (p. 278).

Now in analysis one finds with astounding frequency a parallel, or even identical, series of pictures referring to one and the same father. It is true that often other men are used by the patient's unconscious as substitute bearers of images that are incompatible with the real image of the father, or are unacceptable for emotional reasons. Not all these images, of course, have the same relevance in all patients. Some images may make their appearance in only a few of the patient's remarks; others may constitute the hub of highly charged complexes. In general, however, one will find references to or fantasies about the ideal, the savage or criminal, the senile, and the sick father, as well as about the father's death— whether or not that has actually occurred.

In view of the clinical finding that these images are standard fantasies, at least in almost all analyses of men, the conclusion is permissible that what the poet has done here, in creating these five personages, is to split up the comprehensive image of the father into a number of different persons. While each must be studied for his own personality and for his destiny in the play, the five fathers must also be viewed as five different aspects of one and the same father personality.[34]

It is of importance that there is only one mother in the play and not a single reference whatsoever to the wives of the other fathers.[35] If it were not general knowledge that every human being must have a mother as well as a father, one would almost be tempted to think of Ophelia and Laertes as the offspring of a single parent.

As a counterplayer to these five fathers, there stands Gertrude, the queen, who is the only mother in the entire tragedy. One of Shakespeare's greatest achievements,[36] Gertrude is, I believe, the product of an immense condensation. She has to contend, so to speak, with five men, yet she fills the tragedy. Flatter (1949) asserts that Hamlet's father is the cornerstone and the true mover of the play; an equal claim can be made for Gertrude, who is "mother" to Hamlet, Ophelia, and Laertes.

Why Shakespeare chose to use decomposition in the creation of father

[34] See Jones (1949, p. 131) on decomposition as a mechanism of myth-formation. This mechanism is found typically in paranoid psychoses; see Freud (1911). There can be no doubt of the contribution that this mechanism has made to the greatest works of art; it is the counterpart of condensation. For a different kind of splitting, see Jekels (1917-19, pp. 170-195), and Freud (1916).

[35] This is true with only one exception: Laertes (*IV.5.117*) says that, if he remained calm in the face of his father's death, it would impugn the honor of his mother (cf. later).

[36] I cannot agree at all with Rothe (1961, p. 282) who characterizes Gertrude as "insufficiently anchored" in the play and "unclear" in her intentions. He is certain that the figure reached us in a mutilated form at the hands of later editors and that the final form in which Shakespeare conceived her was quite different (1968).

images, and condensation (Rank, 1912, p. 49) in creating the mother image, I do not know. I myself would surmise that the one mechanism is closer to a masculine principle, the other to a feminine one.[37] Yet such speculations do not get us very far. We may move closer to the empirical level by pointing out that decomposition is likely to be closer to destructiveness then it is to love, while with condensation it is just the other way around. The degree of aggressiveness that is correlated with a given mechanism[38] may have a bearing on its utilization for aesthetic purposes.

One of the chief problems, of course, is the relationship of these sons to the various father figures. One outstanding feature, which has been noted by others, has to do with Hamlet's ambivalence toward the Ghost (cf. Symons, 1928, pp. 96-119; Sharpe, 1946, pp. 242-65, p. 254). In a scarcely noticeable way, this is intimated from the very beginning. It is worth considering at what point Hamlet encounters the Ghost for the first time. He has been pondering upon the corruption that men, despite "their virtues else—be they as pure as grace," may suffer "for some vicious mole of nature" in them. These thoughts had been precipitated by his revulsion against Claudius's revels and drinking feasts, yet Hamlet seems to imply that in this behavior the new king is actually following the habits of the late king, Hamlet's father *(I.4.13)*. The latter, as the audience is later informed, then comes to him from purgatory, where he has been suffering unspeakable tortures, and there are indications that these were the punishment for his intemperance in food and drink *(I.5.11)*.[39]

By musing about the evil consequences that intemperate drinking can have for an otherwise perfect character, Hamlet suggests an associative connection with his father. I believe that the words Hamlet is speaking at the moment of the ghost's appearance[40] have a significance that is more than coincidental. It may be that Shakespeare is here making use of sequence to express a causal connection—once again a formal characteristic of dreams. Hamlet's speech begins with a reference to Claudius's reveling and ends with the appearance of the Ghost; thus the speech

---

[37] Of course, a very realistic factor must be considered—namely, that Shakespeare wrote for a theater in which no actress was permitted to perform. The effect upon Shakespeare's plays of the necessity of employing boy-actors in female roles has been discussed by many authors.

[38] For the problem of ego mechanism and aggressive energy, see Hartmann (1950).

[39] Cf. J. D. Wilson in the Cambridge edition of *Hamlet*, pp. 157, 160.

[40] . . . the dram of eale
Doth all the noble substance of a doubt
To his own scandal.

(about the vicious mole[41]) becomes a gesture, connecting Claudius with Hamlet's father. The unconscious underlying thought would seem to be: "My father was no better that Claudius," and the listener's unconscious may possibly be receiving at this point the first hint of the conflict that lies ahead.

The ambivalence is more clearly expressed in the cellarage scene, after the ghost's disappearance. Wilson has explained Hamlet's strange replies to the Ghost, who is following him about underground, by reference to certain superstitions prevalent in the Elizabethan age, as well as by Hamlet's need to withhold the truth from Marcellus, who had joined him with Horatio. While this may be valid, Hamlet's brusqueness with the Ghost must also be regarded as a derivative of his own ambiguous feeling. It is true that there was a belief that a threefold oath in the presence of a powerful devil is binding, and it is also true that it might well have been necessary for Hamlet to prevent Marcellus from telling anybody about his meeting with the Ghost.[42] Yet would it not have been better to inform the two witnesses of the Ghost's report while they were still under the full impact of the eerie encounter, and then to rush with them to the palace in order to execute the culprit on the spot?

Trench (1913) sees as early as in Hamlet's first reply to the Ghost an anticipation of the inhibition that will later cause him so much unhappiness. Hamlet promises the Ghost to sweep to his revenge "with wings as swift/ As meditation or the thoughts of love." Such thoughts, Trench believes, signify "the exact reverse" of speed—a subtle point of interpretation, although not exactly valid, if one thinks in terms of magical thinking. There can be no doubt, however, that Hamlet's ambivalence is expressed in his soliloquy following the Ghost's disappearance, when he declares that he will banish from his memory everything except the Ghost's commandment—only to set down in his notebook immediately thereafter "that one may smile, and smile, and be a villain." I see in the difference between what Hamlet may have intended to and what he actually did set down, an example of the effect of the "counter-will," which plays a major role in all kinds of neuroses (Freud, 1892-93; Breuer and Freud, 1893-95, pp. 91-93).

[41] There is a punning connection between this and one of the derogatory epithets with which Hamlet addresses the Ghost in the ensuing cellarage scene: "old mole."

[42] In the *Ur-Hamlet* the Ghost repeats *"Wir schwören"* four times until Hamlet exclaims: "It seems that the ghost of my father is not satisfied that I should reveal it. Gentlemen, I beg you, leave me. I want to reveal everything to you tomorrow" *(I.6).* Here the ambivalence is brought out quite openly.

The way in which the counter-impulse manifests itself in Hamlet's soliloquy is reminiscent also of the sequence of doing and undoing that is characteristic of the compulsive-obsessional neurosis (Freud 1926a, p. 119f). The content of the undoing action, however, shows that we are dealing here with something more than a compulsive symptom, even though in its formal structure it does resemble such a symptom. As will be shown later, it does contain a reference to a valid problem (cf. Ichheiser, 1949), which has been suggested to Hamlet by reality. Yet the content of the undoing action betrays, as it usually does, the true meaning of the action against which it is directed. The doubt Hamlet expresses with regard to the genuineness of a smile is, in brief, the result of an internally perceived doubt regarding the genuineness of his own intention to think of nothing but the Ghost's message.

Upon reflection, it will be seen that the Ghost behaves towards Hamlet in a way that must necessarily provoke ambivalence.[43] When he alludes to his torments and Hamlet expresses pity, the Ghost rejects the pity and instead demands attention. Although he has just complained that there is not much time left for him to tell his tale, he continues to recount in the most pitiful terms the sufferings to which he is being exposed in purgatory. When he says that his tale is not to be revealed to men, one wonders why he started telling it at all. After he has spoken of having been murdered and Hamlet promises revenge, the Ghost then replies with the kind of irony one uses to a child—"If I find thee apt"— and adds that Hamlet would indeed be dull if this news did not enrage him. Then he reveals the name of the murderer, who, he asserts, "won to his shameful lust/The will of my most seeming-virtuous queen."

The meaning of this multi-layered recital has long confounded literary analysts. Did the Ghost mean that Gertrude had committed adultery during his lifetime, or was it her subsequent marriage to his brother that he referred to as incest and adultery? I shall postpone discussion of this question until later; here I wish only to emphasize that, by painting his brother as a "beast," "a wretch, whose natural gifts were poor/To those of mine," the Ghost puts himself—either directly or indirectly, as the case may be—in an exceedingly poor light. A man may be treacherously murdered by his brother while taking a nap in his orchard, and still remain a hero; but to be made a cuckold, particularly when the competitor is a weakling, is quite incompatible with the image of a hero.

[43] Rank (1912, p. 229) emphasized the point of the Ghost's provocative aggressive behavior toward the son.

The Ghost seems to imply that witchcraft was the causative agent in the seduction; if that were indeed so, then his demand upon Hamlet ought, out of consistency, to have been to liberate the queen from the spell. It is quite clear that he regards his queen as guilty, a victim of her own lust, even though she is "a radiant angel." If we look behind the impression that the Ghost gives at first, of being the voice of truth from the other world, then we see that his speech reeks rather of weakness.

The conscious memory Hamlet had of his father was of the man who had defeated Fortinbras and slain the Poles, who tenderly loved his wife and was an ideal husband; yet now Hamlet hears that this idealized father had not been able to keep his wife faithful, had been cuckolded, all the while that he himself had lived up to all the restrictions traditionally imposed on man's sexual life. Moreover, the heretofore omnipotent parent is now smarting in purgatory and lamenting his fate. Hamlet is suddenly face to face with a castrated, weak, and defeated father, who treats him harshly, who neither expresses the slightest sign of pity, love, or affection for his son nor mentions the son's claim to the throne, but rather imposes on him a demand that is couched exclusively in terms of the father's own self-interest.

The Ghost's demand has two parts: two commands and an injunction. The commands are that Hamlet avenge his father's murder and that he undo the intolerable situation of the incestuous marriage. In practice, these two commands are of course one, since to kill Claudius is to put an end to the marriage. There can be little doubt that Hamlet accepted the fulfillment of these behests as his duty, and that he was not troubled by any scruples about "Thou shalt not kill." But it is the injunction: "Taint not thy mind, nor let thy soul contrive/Against thy mother aught"—it is this, along with the idea that he should leave his mother's punishment to heaven and her own feelings of guilt, that makes Hamlet's task immeasurably complicated.

This division of a command into "you must do this" and "you must not do that" reminds one of Freud's formulation of the child's basic relationship to his father (Freud, 1923, p. 34). The child is supposed to be like the father, yet he is not permitted to do everything the father does—a moral and ethical antinomy that goes through the whole superstructure of society and even extends to religious systems. [44]

---

[44] The faithful are supposed to identify with Christ and achieve maximum charity and self-sacrifice—but they must not punish their enemies. "Vengeance is mine, saith the Lord."

As is to be expected in a compulsive personality, Hamlet thereupon breaks out with "O most pernicious woman," even before his wrath turns against his uncle with "O villain, villain, smiling damnèd villain." The Ghost's injunction does seem to offer Hamlet protection against the possibility of his committing matricide, but one wonders whether the prohibition has not increased that danger rather than eliminating it. (Orestes seems, after all, to have fared better in that respect than Hamlet.) Furthermore, it creates an especial burden for Hamlet, insofar as he is called upon to let his mother suffer: he must not even help her regain her salvation.

The Ghost thus really re-erects, or, better, re-emphasizes, the taboo of the oedipal situation, by telling Hamlet, in effect, that the mother is none of his concern. He pushes Hamlet into a particularly infantile and helpless situation; at the same time, by destroying the ideal picture of the dead father, he denies Hamlet identification with a strong father image at the very time when Hamlet needs such identification most urgently.

From Hamlet's point of view, a psychological impasse had thus been created. If the Ghost had simply said, "Revenge my murder," the way to action would have been opened up; similarly, if he had said, "Rescue thy mother from the spell the devil has cast over her," Hamlet could have proceeded at once to action. But the combination of "Thou must revenge thy father's death" with "Thou must leave thy mother to heaven" [that is, to me and to her own conscience] is a cruel and humiliating one.[45] It disregards Hamlet's individuality and renders him a simple tool in his father's hands. To bring this dilemma into full relief, one has only to consider the preceding scene, in which Polonius bids farewell to his son Laertes. He showers him with good advice, which culminates in: "This above all: to thine own self be true,/And it must follow, as the night the day/Thou canst not then be false to any man."[46] Yet this is the one thing that it is impossible for Hamlet to do after his talk with the Ghost. He cannot be true to himself, precisely because he has become inescapably intangled in an acute oedipal situation, which forces him to be false to every one, including himself.

The implications are far-reaching. For purposes of comparison, one may imagine Polonius appearing as a ghost to Laertes and demanding

---

[45] For a discussion of other implications of the Ghost's two-pronged demand, see Flatter (1949, pp. 60-64).

[46] The two parallel scenes also mark the difference of paternal attitudes toward the younger and the older son.

vengeance. Would such conflicts as beset Hamlet be possible then? Is it conceivable that Polonius would express his appeal for vengeance in such terms as the Ghost uses? Can one conceive of Polonius ever being content with merely issuing an uncompromising dictatorial demand? Would he not rather advise Laertes on how to go about fulfilling his task, in order to escape harm?

On the other hand, we also have evidence of how Laertes would act in such a situation. When Laertes wants to take revenge for his father's death, he acts in a way diametrically opposed to the way Hamlet acts. He assumes without scruple or further investigation that Claudius is the culprit, and when the queen tried to calm him, he replies: "That drop of blood that's calm proclaims me bastard;/Cries cuckold to my father; brands the harlot/Even here, between the chaste unsmirched brows/of my true mother" *(IV.5. 117)*. (But Hamlet's father *had been* a cuckold, and his mother may have been a harlot.)

Hamlet's attitude toward Polonius, a father substitute, is of great importance. Only one point need be raised here: while Hamlet's manifest relationship to Polonius appears to be a uniformly negative one, there is, nevertheless, a secret affinity between them. Polonius is a man who must forever play second fiddle and who, for all his scheming and intriguing and planning and plotting, ultimately needs the permission of his master, the king. While it is only temporarily that Hamlet is condemned to a secondary place, his role during the interval of his waiting for the inception of his reign is comparable to that of Polonius. The opportunity to identify with Polonius is thereby implied.

Once again, a reality situation stands for a deep psychological, subjective problem—namely, the conflict that arises in the oldest son (whose childhood took place during the father's most manly years) when he must deal with the aging father, whom Polonius represents. In his own maturity, everything in the son fights against the renewal of an old pathway of identification, since he would now derive from it not succor but weakness, the original object of his identification having become by this time a dotard. On the other hand, the youngest son (whose childhood falls in a period of the father's life when affection has come to prevail over superego demand) is drawn even closer to his father by the latter's infirmity. Thus we see that Laertes is not in the least disturbed by Polonius's garrulity, whereas Hamlet finds it unbearable. The matrix of *his* identification is derived from a true king, a strong father, and he therefore repudiates even temporary empathy with the weak and aging father.

Although Laertes is somewhat injured through the necessity for identification with a degraded father image, he has nevertheless relatively free access to action, whereas Hamlet, who is burdened by an excessively strong superego, shows what amounts at times to a definite block to action. As is well known, of course, such blocking is not always successful: there are situations in which Hamlet resorts to rash actions of far-reaching consequence (a seeming contradiction, which has caused much critical perplexity).

In analyzing these environmental factors, I may have given the impression that I regard Hamlet's plight as merely the reflection of his father's ambivalence. Such a trend of thought is now current in many quarters; it holds that the psychopathology that is observed in an individual is merely a reflection of the psychopathology of his environment, or a reaction to the unwisdom of his elders. Leaving aside at this time the question of whether or not this point of view is valid for the clinical psychopathology of the living, it surely cannot be applied to the central figure in Shakespeare's play.

It is always Hamlet in his full individuality who acts, doubts, fears and curses. What unfolds on the stage is a series of events that suggests a certain past, and outlines certain possibilities of future conduct—such as how Hamlet might act if he were the youngest, or if his father had been different, or if his mother had not done this or that. Of course, in the effort to express in explicit terms what the poet only suggests, one has to resort to the barren stimulus-reaction diagram; poor though it is as an auxiliary tool for the purpose of coming to grips with any type of individuality, it is still helpful—provided we do not fall into the wrong belief that the stimulus *creates* the reaction.

Stimuli offer to individual *possibilities* of expression and action: each stimulus evokes a specific fantasy that makes that particular act of stimulation an individual event. This comes to the fore impressively if we once again compare Hamlet with Laertes. As was noted above, after the scene with the Ghost, Laertes would have acted entirely differently from the way Hamlet acted; he would have rushed to the palace, with the intention of killing the king. But would he actually have done so? Perhaps not. With a few friendly words, a pat on the back, a little offer of passive homosexual gratification, Claudius would probably have been able to talk him out of his intention. Laertes is the man of good will who neither sees into the future, nor considers the past. He is history's misfortune, because he is gullible; addicted as he is to the present, he is incapable of acting, except on the spur of the moment. Hence, his changes of mind are not signposts on the path of a development, but rather on-the-spot responses to accidental changes in his immediate surroundings.

Even when Laertes brings about Hamlet's downfall he is merely, on the one hand, an instrument of the scheming king and, on the other, an accident in the unfolding of Hamlet's destiny.[47] For Hamlet must die. But the sequence of action by which he brings about that fall (despite its dependence on Laertes' unconscious hatred and envy of his older "brother") does not follow as the necessary result of his past; it is once again only an accident. Laertes' life story is not essentially enriched by the event. After he has killed Hamlet, we do not know anything about his character that we did not in essence already know previously. The act depended more on the king than on any tragic seriousness of Laertes' own conflicts.[48] Laertes is a tool, and his final treachery acquires significance rather by the impact it has on Hamlet than by any meaning it may have in terms of his own individuality.[49]

Thus far in the present attempt to describe some of the external conditions that contributed to Hamlet's ambivalence, I have followed but one path. One may also look at the problem of ambivalence, however, from the standpoint of Hamlet's fantasies. As was pointed out earlier, Hamlet's criticism of his father is implied in his remarks about the national custom of reveling—remarks that precede the Ghost's appearance. When he exclaims "O my prophetic soul!" upon hearing that Claudius had murdered his father, he refers indirectly to fantasies of the sort that the child inevitably forms in conjunction with the death of a beloved person.[50]

[47]On the accidental in Shakespeare's tragedy, see Spengler (1918, p. 143).

[48] [To my way of feeling, Ribner (1960, p. 85) exaggerates when he discovers in Laertes a particular "evilness." It is true that, on the spur of the moment, he mouths formidably blasphemous oratory, but it disappears as quickly as it came. The responsibility for his final misdeed lies clearly at Claudius' doorstep. Laertes' confession and turn toward Hamlet during the final moments of his life places the final stamp of goodness upon his personality. We cannot ascribe any particular intelligence to him and this alone prevents the critic, unless he sees in *Hamlet* a morality play, from associating Laertes with evilness per se. After all, these almost super-human evildoers of Shakespeare's imagination, like Iago and Macbeth, are all endowed with an extremely high I. Q., which no doubt their Rorschachs would bear out. (1968)]

[49] [Since the emphasis in the tragedy is on the fate of the oldest son, Laertes takes an inferior place. This contributes to the fact that the playwright leaves us in relative ignorance of his character; enough is said about him, however, to make a delineation of his character possible. Shakespeare himself was born when he was 16 years old; two sisters had died before his birth. His youngest brother was born when he was 16 years old, and had the name of Edmund—the name of one of the vilest characters the poet ever created—and a bastard, to boot (1966).]

[50] [Grebanier (1960, p. 110n), however, believes it to be absurd to interpret the line as express-

Death by natural causes is alien to unconscious thinking, and the Ghost therefore elicits from Hamlet only what had already existed in him as a preformed fantasy. Since Claudius was the beneficiary of the king's death, he must also have been, in accordance with certain equations that prevail in unconscious thinking, the king's murderer. But the Ghost brings another message, of even greater importance: he speaks of the queen's unfaithfulness. This reference to unfaithfulness and incest may refer, however, either to the queen's marriage to her brother-in-law or to adultery, and it therefore becomes necessary to discuss some of the reasons why Shakespeare maintained ambiguity about a point so crucial to his plot.

III

The discussion that follows may seem to go far afield; nevertheless, the question of ambiguity in the plot construction of *Hamlet* seems to me to be a sufficiently significant one to approach from various angles.

During the Middle Ages, the marriage of a brother to his widowed sister-in-law was regarded as incest by the Catholic Church. But since the Church sometimes granted a dispensation permitting such a marriage, the relationship must have been looked at differently from an incestuous marriage between blood relatives, for which a dispensation was almost never granted. Moreover, there were instances when the former type of incest was committed with impunity. Trench (1913, pp. 257-260) discusses briefly the historical implications of this problem in England. (I have not been able, however, to determine what the average Briton's reaction was to marriages of this sort in Shakespeare's times.)

It is striking that, in Shakespeare's play, no one but Hamlet or the Ghost speaks of incest. Horatio, before he is informed of Claudius's crime, concedes only that the haste of Gertrude's second marriage is worthy of censure. There would have been ample opportunity, within the play as it stands, for others to make some reference to the irregularity of the union, if they thought it such. When Marcellus and Horatio, who know about the Ghost's visit, discuss the possible motivations for it at the beginning of the play, they could easily have surmised that it must have

---

ing Hamlet's prior suspicion of Claudius' crime. "The line means merely that he feels now [that] his old hatred of his uncle has a real basis." And did it not have any "real" basis before the Ghost revealed the crime? Does not Hamlet later seek to convince his mother of her second husband's contemptibility without any reference to murder, merely by describing his external appearance and his character, and without making any reference to special events?

been the commission of a grave offense of that sort that had forced the dead king to return to earth. Incest in the royal family, as the occasion for punishment being visited upon the community, is a frequent theme in mythology and folklore. The gravedigger scene also offered an excellent opportunity for reference to the alleged crime of incest. It would be curious, indeed, for Hamlet to be haunted by the image of a "crime" that has supposedly been committed quite openly, yet is not recognized as such by anyone in the play but the Ghost.

The effect is reminiscent of the typical dream of nakedness, in which the dreamer is overwhelmed by the shame of his nakedness, while others in the dream appear to be completely oblivious to his offense (Freud, 1900, pp. 236-242). Dreams of this sort are generally concerned with a pleasure that is forbidden to the adult, even though it is enjoyed without punishment by the infant or child. Nakedness was the infant's privilege, the latter's enjoyment of it being shared by the adult, who tenderly caressed the baby's naked body. All of us are, so to speak, guilty of actual incest, committed prior to the oedipal phase, which in turn is significant for its oedipal fantasies rather than for incestuous actions. The early years of childhood are, indeed, replete with actions that, if they were performed by an adult, would unquestionably be regarded as incestuous.

The dream of nakedness may perhaps stand for a variety of physical pleasures such as the child could enjoy without guilt, but the memory of which and the longing for which arouse in the adult feelings of shame, horror, guilt and fear. We do not know, however, why so few dreams are structured as the typical dream of nakedness is. In spite of the taboo put upon it, nudity is less offensive to the adult, even in our society, than are the incestuous gratifications of which the child has unwittingly made himself guilty. This may well be the reason why perhaps other infantile gratifications can hide behind the typical dream of nudity, and why that dream does not lead to an outbreak of anxiety in the adult, but stops instead with the feeling of severe embarrassment.

Shakespeare had the good fortune to hit upon historical circumstances that made it possible for him to present pathology by means of a reality situation. If Hamlet's story had taken place in a society that permitted without question the union of Claudius and Gertrude, we should then have to regard Hamlet as a mentally deranged person; whenever he spoke of the "incest" of his mother and uncle, we should know that he was in the grip of a delusion. In Shakespeare's society, however, there was a tacit understanding that such unions were not commendable, just as we agree with the dreamer that it is not commendable to appear in public disrobed.

Yet, if the dream is taken at its face value, we do not blame the dreamer for feeling so strongly embarrassed in his dream (this does not, of course, touch upon the question of *why* he dreams about an embarrassing occurrence at all), but are instead surprised that other people in the dream are, as a rule, unaware of the dreamer's offending nakedness. In the same way, it is understandable that Hamlet should suffer over the possibility of his mother's having committed incest; yet what still remains a problem is why no one else except the Ghost has taken cognizance of that crime.

Some writers have seen in Hamlet's sadness over the queen's hasty marriage, even before he is apprised of his father's murder, a sign of a "predisposition to actual unsoundness."[51] I am not certain that we are entitled to draw any such conclusions. Hamlet is the son of a king. It will be his social function to fill the place once held by his father; the welfare and fate of the state will depend on what he does. The narcissistic overvaluation of his own ego, so characteristic of the neurotic, is here quite justified by the social setting. In a different social milieu, a son's indifference to questions of his parents' morality might be taken to be a sign of healthy independence. But a behavior pattern that, in a bourgeois environment, would strike us as particularly unsound, may well appear in a different light if it is viewed against the background of a court and a royal family.

As a matter of social reality, the king enjoys those privileges that the child in his fantasy attributes to the father. The crown prince is duty bound to perform certain actions that may well coincide with some that a child carries out in his fantasies. That is one reason why the feudal-aristocratic, royal background serves so extraordinarily well for representing as real what we find in the repressed part of the modern adult's neurotic personality.

I would guess, therefore, that Hamlet's initial reaction of mourning over his mother's hasty second marriage was not intended by Shakespeare to indicate a deviated or pathological reaction. It strikes me from this viewpoint rather as being a justifiable reaction by the king's son, following the discovery that his mother has not lived up to the highest moral standards. When we translate that same situation, however, into one that

[51] Connolly, quoted after Jones (1949, p. 64).

is consistent with our own experiences, we touch upon the repressed part of the personality. In other words, to the extent that we ourselves might act like Hamlets, we are neurotic, and it is because neurosis is a universal part of civilization that we understand Hamlet.

That does not necessarily mean, however, that Hamlet is a neurotic, in the ordinary sense of the term. He has all the privileges of the child, which we readily grant him because he is the prince we dreamed of being when we were young. If a child were to grieve because his mother fell in love with a stranger shortly after his father's sudden death, we would not call this reaction a neurosis, however much the child's grief might be connected with his erotic feeling toward his mother.

This is not to say, of course, that Hamlet is a child. He certainly has the intellect of an adult; yet Shakespeare's plot is so subtly constructed that what, under ordinary conditions, would be regarded as neurosis or psychosis, appears here as the valid response of an extremely sensitive adult, who has preserved the privileges and the emotional genuineness of a child. The direct implication of childhood may be seen in the fact that no other adult in the play seems to share Hamlet's horror at his mother's supposed incest.

Nevertheless, the spectator does not regard Hamlet's reaction as a psychotic one. Instead, he concedes this reaction to Hamlet, just as he would concede a similar reaction to a child, if the latter had witnessed parental intercourse. Moreover, Horatio—the enlightened scholar, the humanist, the unprejudiced friend to whom Hamlet reveals his inner life, although not in its entirety—understands Hamlet's behavior and does not regard it as contradictory.

The suggestion that Hamlet represents not an adult neurotic but a combination of the soul of a child with the intellect and body of an adult should, I think, help us to understand quite a few problems in the play. On what other basis are we able to share the feelings that prompt Horatio's farewell: "Good night, sweet prince,/And flights of angels sing thee to thy rest"? Hamlet has caused the death of three people without seeking to find out whether they have indeed deserved it; he has been responsible for the suicide of a girl who loved him tenderly. Why should flights of angels sing *him* to his rest? Nevertheless, the spectator is likely to agree, on the basis of only *prima facie* evidence, that Horatio could not have spoken truer words at that moment. With Hamlet's death, our own childhood vanishes[52] and Fortinbras, the man of action, appears and takes over.

The ambiguity in plot construction persists throughout the play; it is, as was suggested earlier, Shakespeare's principal device. There is the very important question, already touched upon, of whether or not the queen had actually committed adultery prior to the king's death. If she was truly guilty of adultery, then she probably conspired in the murderous plot against Hamlet's father; if she was faithful to him, however, then the suspicion of her conspiring to murder the King can be dismissed. As outstanding and conscientious an interpreter as J. Dover Wilson (1936a, Appendix A., p. 292) is convinced that the Ghost's report leaves no doubt about Gertrude's adultery; he refers to the Ghost's use of the words "adulterate" and "traitorous" when he is speaking to Hamlet. Yet Van Dam has shown that "Shakespeare used the word adulterate more in the meaning of unchaste, lewd, than of unfaithful to the marriage bed,"[53] thus throwing serious doubt on Wilson's assertions (Cf. also Keller, 1919, p. 152).

One could also refer to the Ghost's statement that he was "at once" deprived "of life, of crown, of queen" *(I.5.75)*. If he had earlier meant adultery in the ordinary modern sense, he must have believed that he had actually lost his queen far earlier than he lost his life and his crown. I think it is needless to argue the point. What is more important is to note that Shakespeare has suggested the one idea as much as he had the other, and I am certain that most readers can adduce evidence from the play for either.

The same situation holds true for the question of the queen's participation in the murder of Hamlet's father. In a hypothetical jury trial, Flatter reaches this conclusion: "a verdict of 'not proven,' that is all a jury could arrive at. But even if, for lack of evidence, I am compelled to say 'not guilty' as a juror, as a private individual I may still be convinced

---

[52] See Webster (1948, p. 137), a paper with whose basic idea, however, I disagree.

[53] [See Van Dam (1924, p. 56). Draper (1939, p. 112) points out that the term "adulterate" retained in Elizabethan times "something of its wide etymological meaning, as appears in its uses in the New Testament and in Canon Law." Draper also cites a most remarkable error of Bradley, who adduced as allegedly a most convincing proof of Gertrude's adultery the Ghost's reporting on it *(I.5.42f)* before telling of the murder (Bradley, 1904, p. 166), whereas in reality the sequence is just the reverse (Draper, 1939, p. 113). Elton (1922, p. 26) calls Gertrude's portrait "unfinished"— which I think, a quite misleading way of characterizing what I would call an ambiguous portrait. He admits that some passages may strengthen the idea of adultery, yet these same passages "can be taken as merely referring to a too hasty second marriage." (1967)]

that the acquitted person had done the deed" (1949, p. 80). Van Dam points out that in the first quarto version (Van Dam, 1956, p. 54, referring to line 1533) the queen declares openly: "I never knew of this most horrid murder."[54]

The queen may be lying, of course, but I think that the deletion of this line in later versions suggests that Shakespeare deliberately tried to establish a situation that would leave the broadest possible margin of ambiguity with regard to the motives and occurrences that lay behind the events presented on the stage. This descrepancy between the reality of the events on stage and the ambiguity about those events that do not take place before the spectator's eyes is one of the techniques by means of which Shakespeare succeeds in producing the overwhelming effect of the tragedy.

It is at this point that we must consider the relationship between the appearance of reality and its interpretation in the minds of children, for it is this very relationship, in my opinion, that is so basic in *Hamlet*. The appearance of reality has as its basis the data that are conveyed by the various perceptive systems. The older a man becomes, however, the less is he inclined to place full value on data that are delivered directly by sense perception and the more does he take to living in a world of meanings and symbols.[55] The perceivable aspect of reality then becomes a somewhat routine matter.

In the child's life, by contrast, the physical appearance of the world is a matter of daily surprise; it retains for many years an unchanging quality of newness. That is why children are apt to respond to perceptions to which the adult makes no response.[56] The sense of newness and surprise makes reality appear oversharp to the child, and I have the impression that in *Hamlet* too reality is presented almost as poignantly and

[54] Was this line at one time part of Shakespeare's play and later omitted? The first quarto was a "bad" quarto.

[55] Cf. Goethe's remark (April 28, 1819) that "now he could weep only at the perception of something of rare ethical or aesthetic value, no longer from pity or from his own need." [. . . wie er nur noch bei Gewahrung seltener, sittlicher oder aesthetischer Trefflichkeiten weinen könne, nie mehr aus Mitleid oder aus eigener Not.] Burckhardt (1870, p. 32).

[56] Cf. Goethe (March 28, 1824): "In my experience the ablest discoverers are not the people with the profoundest knowledge. The child is closer to the earth with his nose; he often sees sooner than do all others the insect that is crawling about on its surface. . . ." [Nach meiner Erfahrung sind die tüchtigsten Entdecker nicht die Leute mit den tiefgründigsten Kenntnissen. Das Kind ist mit seiner Nase der Erde näher, es sieht oft früher als alle andern das Insekt, das auf ihrer Oberfläche herumkriecht. . . .] (Houben, 1929, p. 115).

penetratingly as it may be perceived to be by the child when he discovers a new sector of it.[57]

Yet sense perception is for the child an inspirer of fantasies as well, and all too often the child fuses the two into an imagery in which they are inseparably united. This may be the chief reason why sense perception contains such buoyancy in childhood. The child is not prepared to make the distinction between sense data and their interpretation—the distinction that rules, or ought to rule, adult life. The child's sense of wonder about each new sense-perception and his quick inclusion of it in a fantasy constitute one source of the charming effect that his mental life has upon the adult, who has gradually lost both these "childlike" faculties, as a result of their being crowded out by the secondary processes. However, it is just because of the readiness with which the child fuses perception and fantasy—which is, in itself, a source of pleasure, making the world all the more enjoyable to be in—that the world becomes a troubling one to him.

For as apt as pleasurable stimuli are to elicit excessive joy, just so likely are unpleasant ones to lead to excessive anxiety and panic. Further, the child's fantasies may change rapidly, and fantasies that are, in terms of logic, mutually contradictory may become attached to one and the same external stimulus at the very same time.[58] The child is convinced of the veracity and the real existence of the imagery he himself has formed out of stimulus and fantasy; in that way, he creates a view of the world that is consistent with his needs, wishes and experiences. In spite of the great advantages otherwise offered by this way of reacting, it does make the child's orientation in the world quite difficult. When a harsh external reality proves the content of the fantasy to be nonexistent, then the imagery falls apart and in its place bewilderment sets in.

[57] Since stage decoration can scarcely convey this oversharp quality of the childhood representation of reality, a fuller impression can be obtained from reading the play than from seeing it staged.

[58] [Years after I has speculated about this mode of early experience of sense perception, I had the sad opportunity of observing it clinically in the reports of patients who had taken LSD. The fascination of the LSD experience (unless the subject responds with anxiety) is rooted in the reexperience of an infantile pleasure from which the adult is forever enjoined. A fusion of self and perception, a complete absorption into the perception, and a modification of perception in accordance with archaic laws of the unconscious—all these, taken together, provide a pleasure that cannot be matched by any source of pleasure in "real" reality. Tannhäuser did not visit the *Venusberg* unpunished, and LSD, even if taken only once, insidiously undermines an adequate evaluation of reality. In some respects Shakespeare's dramas have a comparable effect. An immersion into his work leaves the sentiment, not necessarily explicit, that there life is more concentrated, more real, exists in a purer form than one has ever encountered in "real" reality. (1967)]

But this is the very difficulty that is also encountered in *Hamlet*. The plot is so constructed as to give the reader an impression of consistency. Yet this consistency is not identical for every spectator, the plot being ambiguous enough to permit a variety of interpretations, each of which is consistent in itself (just as each child forms, by virtue of its imaginative capacity, a picture of the world that is consistent in its own right). As little as the child is aware that the reality stimulus per se permits alternative interpretations—that is to say, may be fused with a variety of quite different fantasies—so little is the adult reader likely to notice that the plot in *Hamlet* also permits a variety of interpretations, each consistent in itself.

Further, as little as the child is aware that his image of the world was born out of fantasy—that *he himself* has added to the bare content of the sense perception—so little is the reader likely to be aware that the poet has held back just enough information [to permit a variety of consistent interpretations, and indeed has structured what he presents in such a way as to force the reader to synthesize disparate details into a consistent whole, without noticing that this has been accomplished by the addition of his own fantasy. Ambiguity and consequent variability of interpretation may be produced by looseness of presentation or vagueness, and is then a serious fault and defect. Shakespeare makes himself guilty in *Hamlet* of neither. That is what I would call "the miracle of *Hamlet*," when the formal aspects of the tragedy are considered.

The fact is that it is not at all vagueness of presentation in this case that makes it possible for an unusually wide scope of variability to be proven from the writings of the various critics of the play. Each of them is certain that he can set forth indubitable evidence to prove the correctness of his particular report of "What happened in *Hamlet*" and equally indubitable evidence to prove the incorrectness of his colleagues' conclusion. It is really the same situation as one encounters with witnesses at court whose testimonies are contradictory to the extent of being mutually exclusive, despite the fact that all of them had been present when the action under investigation occurred and they are all certain that it took place in the very way in which they are bringing it to the judge's attention.]

When one listens, therefore, to the subtle reasoning of scholars about "what happens in *Hamlet*," one is quite properly reminded of children arguing about whether a piece of wood is a knight or a devil. The irreconcilable disagreements among scholars about the "bare facts" of the content of the tragedy are the direct consequence of Shakespeare's ingenuity in constructing a plot that cannot do anything else but make for almost diametrically different interpretations.[59]

Wilson suggests that all the inconsistencies except those that are "due to historical causes"—that is to say, those that arise out of later revision—are the necessary consequences of *Hamlet's* being a stage play. "Verisimilitude and not consistency or historical accuracy is the business of drama, and its Elizabethan artists, working in a theatre without drop-curtain or act-pauses, knew that the audience could not ponder or check the coherence of events or character as a reader can."[60] The suggestion is tempting and might be acceptable were it not for these reasons:

(1) Hamlet is more than a theatrical masterpiece, cleverly put together for stage effects.

(2) The effect of the play is, if anything, even greater when it is read than when it is seen on a stage.

(3) It is possible by thorough analysis to reveal the paradoxical consistency underlying the hidden inconsistencies—a consistency that is far beyond and altogether extrinsic to problems of stage effects.[61]

---

[59] Bridges (1927, p. 16) writes: ". . . but to sustain surprise in a worthy hero, he had sometimes had recourse to devices which are intended to balk analysis. In order to attain the surprising, he will risk, or even sacrifice, the logical and consistent; and as such a flaw, if it were perceived, must ruin the interest, he is ready with abundant means to obscure the inconsistency. It seems to me that one method was to take advantage of uncertainty or confusion in motives or matters of fact lying partly or wholly outside the drama."

[60] *Hamlet*, Cambridge edition (1948, pp. xlvii-xlviii).

[61] [Moreover, neither Quarto 2 nor Folio 1 was ever presented on the stage and could not possibly have been written for the sake of being performed, since they are both far too long to be acted within the time limits allocated to stage performances by law in Elizabethan times. This is one of the many reasons why Rothe (1961, 277f) seems to be so certain that the *Hamlet* versions (Quarto 2, Folio1) in our possession are not Shakespeare's final product, but a misunderstood composite of *different stages* through which Shakespeare's work on the play had gone. Rothe writes (p. 281): "What other authors destroy as soon as the work is finished, has been preserved in the text of *Hamlet*—it is as if one wanted to look at that which Goethe had thought about the subject of Faust in the course of a long life, not as phases but as a unified work [einheitliches Werk]." I can well imagine that 400 years from now a critic will raise Rothe's arguments against the two parts of Goethe's *Faust*.

What speaks so strongly against Rothe's claim is the outstanding interpretability of *Hamlet*. If Quarto 2 and Folio 1 were really the sort of product that he conceives of them as being, psychological penetration would have to run into nonsense situations—which it never actually does. The argument that no human documentation ever completely loses the character of interpretability would not hold ground as an objection since, in this instance, psychological investigation confirms the eminent quality of a creation that attracts in equal measure the psychologically unbiased reader, the literary critic and the psychologist. The fact that Quarto 2 and Folio 1 do contain an *oeuvre* that was quite apparently more than a text designed to be staged may be taken as proof that Shakespeare's vision aimed here at something greater than a play with which to impress his contemporary audience. In this respect, *Hamlet* may be compared with Goethe's *Faust*, in which play too the theatrical form is used as a medium, but with the natural bounds inherent in this literary category being rent asunder in the process. (1968)]

· 81 ·

This opinion does not challenge the validity of an attempt to view *Hamlet*, if that is possible, from the standpoint of stage-effect and stage requirements. It is the distinction of great art that, in detail as well as on the whole, the masterpiece is multifunctional (See Waelder, 1930; Kris, 1936, pp. 87-117, and 1950, pp. 303-318). A love poem may fit perfectly the personal situation of a poet and thus win the heart of his beloved; it may also express his sentiment in general terms, well enough to provide deep meaning for a large number of people who have no idea whatsoever of the particular circumstances under which it was written. At the same time, the poem may clearly reveal an unconscious conflict on the poet's part—a conflict of which the poet himself is probably unaware. That is why it is believed that multifunctional perfection is one of the essential properties of great art.

It is important to learn, as we can from John Dover Wilson, how many features of the play were enforced by theatrical necessities—that is to say, out of consideration for the effect upon the spectator, arising out of the limitations and potentialities of a specific physical, historically determined environment. Stage necessity would correspond, in my comparison, to the reality that the world appears to present to the child. And, as I have tried to point out, in both cases this seeming consistency covers a maze of problems and alternatives.

Once his belief in the consistency of reality has been shaken, the child is bewildered. We know that he cannot tolerate this state of bewilderment for a long time but instead tries to arrive at an alternative, to which he may then cling with great stubbornness. Something similar may happen to an interpreter of Hamlet. Once he comes upon that one among the alternatives offered by the tragedy that has satisfied him, he may maintain it thereafter as "the" correct explanation, while overlooking other alternatives that are equally valid. [62]

[62] [I am moving here within a paradox that may be easily misunderstood and may therefore arouse the objections of the literary critic. On the one hand, I am asserting that Shakespeare created in *Hamlet* an over-intruding reality and, on the other, that the action is so constructed that ambiguity may permit contradictory interpretations, which could—but quite wrongly—be regarded as a defect. The over-intruding reality, however, can be proven by the insistence of most critics that their interpretation is correct and indeed the *only* correct one. The ambiguity is clearly proven by the undeniable fact that, despite all efforts, the divergence of views has not become closed during the course of time. One may safely say that, as long as critics write about *Hamlet*, there will be disagreement. But can that not be said about almost all subjects on which man ponders? Irreconcilable disagreements usually arise from the application of divergent frames of reference, whereas literary critics usually work within the same one. Furthermore, the irreconcilable disagreement in this instance already starts at the level of bare facts—namely, "What happens in *Hamlet?*—a question about which one might·expect that a group of intelligent and well-trained critics would be able to find half-way

In reading *Hamlet*, one is struck by how full it is of components that, not only in their formal properties, but also in their content, are characteristic of the mental and emotional life of pre-adult developmental stages. For example, the queen is drawn in such a way that most of the typical fantasies about the mother that one finds in children and in the repressed part of the adult personality are compounded in this single personage. Gertrude is the bad, sexual, seducing mother, who kills the father and lives only for the gratification of her needs and her ambitions. She has rebelled against the hero father, disposed of him, and married a self-indulgent lecher who fawns upon her.

Yet Gertrude is at the same time the weak, tender, innocent woman who has been trapped by a monster and unwittingly connived at his crime. She is also the good mother who loves her only son above all. As Claudius says, she "lives by his looks": whenever both Hamlet and Claudius are present, she is concerned almost exclusively with Hamlet. The preference she shows toward Hamlet over all the father-figures coincides with those wishful fantasies with which a boy is unendingly preoccupied. She condones the killing of Polonius at once and then successfully covers up for Hamlet, in order to allay the king's suspicions. She will even go so far as to give Hamlet up to Ophelia if by her love he can be restored to health.

Gertrude's closeness to Hamlet is brought to the spectator's attention very forcefully. Of the 18 times she speaks prior to the closet scene, 15 are to address Hamlet or to express her concern about him. It is as if Shakespeare were trying by these means to counteract the image of the bad mother that he has so effectively put into the spectator's mind by what has been revealed about her from other sources. Her death by the poison intended for Hamlet can be correlated with a barely camouflaged fantasy of mother and son dying together in voluntary suicide.[63]

Every element of that finale is drenched in unverbalized meaning.

---

agreement. It is worthwhile reading, with the above paradox in mind, Grebanier's (1960) text. The scorn, ridicule and contempt he heaps upon all previous critics, with the exception of perhaps three, is remarkable; in all seriousness he claims to be the first one who has ever discovered the correct events in Shakespeare's play. (1967)]

[63] See Jones (1911, pp. 9-15). Sharpe (1946, p. 210f) sees in this scene a manifestation of libidinal regression to the oral zone. If the scene is taken literally, its manifest content does permit this suggestion. On the other hand, if a poet wanted to refer to his hero's adult, genital strivings toward the mother, how better could he do it than by using socially acceptable orality as a symbolic medium of expression? The restrictions imposed in our society on references to genitality facilitate pregenital interpretations; a consideration of the dominant context is necessary in order to decide whether the seemingly pregenital form is to be taken literally.

First Gertrude expresses her worry for Hamlet's health and provides him with a napkin with which to wipe his brow. Then she toasts his good fortune and drinks from the cup that was meant for him, thus shielding her son from the father's aggression by substituting herself as victim. But then she offers the cup to Hamlet, who significantly answers: "I dare not drink yet, madam," as if he were aware, unconsciously, of the full implications of the situation, yet still had a task to fulfill before sharing her fate. Thereupon, as the last favor she will ever do for him, she herself wipes his face.

Here the closeness between mother and son is presented symbolically through the regressive form of the mother's care of the infant. After that gesture of affectionate care, only one task still remains for her—namely, to denounce the king and thus to remove the last obstacle that could possibly stand in the way of Hamlet's carrying out his decision. When the king tries to conceal the fact that it was he who had caused the queen to be poisoned, she belies his words and turns toward her son with words that are again amazingly ambiguous.

In order for it to remain possible for Gertrude to be viewed under quite opposite aspects, she has to be allowed to speak very little. Except for the closet scene, it is extraordinary how rarely she does speak while she is on stage. Moreover, it is a question not only of how few her speeches are, but also of the paucity of the words that she utters each time. The spectator, of course, hears a great deal about her from others. I believe that Shakespeare is here using a technique of intimation, so that the spectator should be free to project onto the queen a large number of opposing images.

This same technique of intimation is also, by the way, employed in his handling of the Ghost. He is described by others as a great hero, and when he speaks, he speaks ponderously; yet, as has been pointed out above, many elements make him out to be an image of the castrated, weakened father. This aspect of the Ghost reaches its climax in his final appearance in the queen's closet. That will be discussed more fully later; here I wish only to emphasize that Hamlet's father too is presented in such a way as to leave open the possibility of projecting at least two opposed fantasies onto one stage figure.

Here I want to add a third aspect of the father that is most subtly introduced. I believe that Yorick is a thinly disguised father image.[64] He

---

[64] See Sharpe (1946, p. 260); Symons (1928, p. 101) believes that Yorick is a father-substitute. [A. Dührssen (1956, p. 307) thinks that Hamlet faced "confusing double influence" inasmuch as he

is the tenderly loving, affectionate father, with "those lips that I have kissed I know not how oft," who "hath borne me on his back a thousand times." He is the only person in the entire play of whom Hamlet speaks with unreserved tenderness. He died when Hamlet was seven—which suggests when the repression of that relationship occurred. It had indeed been a fateful relationship: Hamlet had thereafter become a great jester, too. The identification with Yorick seems to have been quite strong. Hamlet's feminine passive relationship to his father[65] is of course the most dangerous of all, and he remembers it only in connection with a substitute figure and within the context of death.

Yet despite the great importance of the father and of father-substitutes, in the background there looms, with even greater importance, the queen. If Hamlet's narcissistic and object-libidinal wishes are considered, one must concede that Hamlet was right in procrastinating and that no other way of proceeding could have provided him with so many and such thoroughgoing wish-fulfillments.

Had he rushed to the palace and killed Claudius, Laertes-fashion, one thing would certainly have happened: he would have lost his mother's affection, possibly forever; from that moment on, Gertrude and he would have been irreconcilable enemies. In the search for reasons why Hamlet postponed the avenging of his father's death, some writers have maintained that it was because the Ghost's command could not actually be carried out.

Some, indeed, have invoked external reasons; these, however, must be regarded as invalid. The whole climate of the tragedy is such that no one can doubt whether, all along, Hamlet actually does have free access to Claudius. The execution of revenge depended simply on Hamlet's pulling out a dagger and thrusting it into Claudius. The poet strongly emphasizes this by having Hamlet stab Claudius at the end, without any particular preparation. What Hamlet does after Gertrude's death he could just as easily have done at the beginning of the duel, were they merely external hurdles that were involved.

Other critics have maintained that Hamlet did not proceed because he was unable to prove the veracity of the Ghost's message, since he had no witnesses to its contents. This objection is not supported by the play.

---

was exposed to the "feudalistic-primitive royal father and the humiliated fool filled by deep emotions." Although she also refers Hamlet's "fooling" to an identification with Yorick, she seems to interpret the childhood experience as representing not a phase of the son-father relationship but rather, sociologically, the source of Hamlet's empathy with the underprivileged. (1968)]

[65] See, for the problem of Hamlet's femininity, Jones (1948).

Hamlet had witnesses to the Ghost's appearance and to the Ghost's having spoken to him. As the king's son he had, of course, all the prerogatives of an elevated court position and his word counted for more than did that of others.[66]

Flatter (1949, p. 98) believes that it was the double command of the Ghost that made compliance impossible: how *could* Hamlet kill Claudius without hurting his mother? According to Loening, Tschischwitz had proposed this last suggestion as early as 1868 (Loening, 1893, p. 122), and it must be said that Loening's efforts to refute it are not quite convincing. I myself feel inclined to agree with Flatter when he says that the Ghost's behest does seem to contain some singular difficulty, such as has the effect of making the taking of revenge well-nigh impossible for Hamlet.

Yet, if that difficulty is the admonition about Gertrude, Hamlet does not seem to heed that part of his father's command very scrupulously. He certainly does "taint" his mind, and let his "soul contrive aught" against his mother. It is noteworthy, however, that what he does against his mother he does in such a way as to draw her nearer and nearer to him, until she actually allies herself with him against Claudius.[67] It must not be forgotten that, despite her affection for Hamlet, she still protects Claudius.

This becomes clear when Laertes threatens the King. In that situation, she interposes herself without hesitation between the threatened King and Laertes (the "younger son"). My guess is that if Gertrude had

---

[66] For an excellent discussion of these political and juridical aspects, see Loening (1893, pp. 81-107).

[67] [Whitaker (1964, p. 260f) writes that in Quarto 2 and Folio 1 no understanding is reached between Hamlet and the Queen in the closet scene, and he sees in this one of the main differences with Quarto 1. I think he goes too far in this respect. In Quarto 2 enough is intimated to suggest an alliance, the extent of which is left to the reader's imagination. The victory of Hamlet over Claudius in the last scene is manifest and definitive. Also, when Whitaker thinks that the Queen "must have been ten times as miserable as Hamlet accused her of being" (p. 345), because she allegedly overlooked Hamlet's remark, in the closet scene, insinuating the murder of his father, one may refer to Shakespeare's consistent ambiguity. Whitaker's interpretation is well taken, but it is not the only one possible. Since Hamlet is clearly in a state of overexcitement when he makes the remark, and shortly thereafter claims to see his father, whom the Queen is unable to perceive, it would not necessarily be a sign of insensitivity on Gertrude's part to infer from Hamlet's remark nothing more than a high state of tension on his part. Further, with his relentless badgering of his mother, Hamlet left her little opportunity to inquire into the meaning of her son's puzzling remark. Lastly, one may say that she is following the example of Jocasta, who was not reproached for insensibility and knew well indeed that persistent inquiry could lead to the downfall of a great house. What from one standpoint may have the appearance of insensibility from another standpoint would appear to be sagacity and even the intuitive divination of mysteries, to state which explicitly can do nothing but bring injury upon man's mind.]

been brought to the point of being forced to choose between Claudius's welfare and Hamlet's, she would under all circumstances have decided in favor of the latter. But Hamlet does not see this clearly, and his prolonged delay may thus be viewed as a manifestation of the unexpressed question: "How can I revenge my father and nevertheless preserve or acquire, as the case may be, my mother's love?"

Thus the external difficulty imposed by the Ghost's complicated demand has an internal counterpart in Hamlet's unconscious desires: the desire for vengeance on the one hand, and the longing for his mother's love on the other. In the language of the archaic oedipal complex, his desire could be worded thus: "If I do eliminate my rival (father), will mother then accept me as a substitute? Will I find out that I am her first choice anyway, or will she reject me because I am too weak to replace father?" If this was the problem that Hamlet had to cope with, he could hardly have acted differently from the way in which he actually did.

In the end, he did succeed in winning the undivided affection of his mother, not to speak of that of the younger brother (Laertes), who turned toward him, confessed his hostility, repented his envy and rivalry, and decided in favor of Hamlet against the king. In this sense, Hamlet was the real victor in the tragedy: had he pursued a different path, he might never have gained so much in the end.

If, however, only the manifest content of the play is considered, then the final estimate of the effect of Hamlet's procrastination will have to be different: Hamlet must then be regarded, as he has been by many interpreters, as an ineffectual person who has bungled the whole situation, and thereby brought the greatest disaster upon his entire family. This is another instance of how Shakespeare has constructed the plot in such a way as to make at least two readings possible, and at that, two quite opposite ones.

An additional hypothesis would seem to be necessary, however, if my thesis that Hamlet was in essence successful is to stand up to critical examination—namely, that in certain contexts of the tragedy, death or killing is identified with intercourse.[68] As is well known, intercourse is imagined by nearly every child at certain times as being an aggressive, destructive act, and it rarely loses this connotation altogether in the adult. This fantasy pictures intercourse as something dreadful that is

---

[68] Jones (1911, pp. 326-327) describes the erotic components that make their appearance in Claudius's story of his brother's death as well as in the Ghost's account of the event.

happening either to the father or the mother or to both. At that level, the whole problem has already found a rich elaboration, but there is a more archaic state in which it may be that love means the loss of one's own ego and, consequently, a transformation into the beloved person—a process that later becomes identified with death.

In schizophrenic patients, one occasionally finds some of the symptoms tied to this level: "Contact with human beings results in a loss of self." It is as if the flow of libido toward the object took with it the person from whom the libido stems. This is of course a painful symptom; it is a little like being an observer of one's own execution. The patient knows that he is alive, yet he cannot feel so, because his life has, in effect, gone into his partner. Some patients of this sort protect themselves by counteracting any interest they may feel in others or else limiting their object relations exclusively to aggressive ones. My own opinion is that the schizophrenic patient's withdrawal, for example, is often a defense against this painful loss of ego.

Such a loss may perhaps be a normal and even a necessary consequence in intercourse, as is suggested by the French expression *petit mort,* as well as by the fact that seventeenth-century English poets often use the word "die" to refer to the loss of identity they believe one experiences in love. There may be an early level at which love and death are regarded as identical. One may think of the infant falling asleep while being held in its mother's arms or, quite generally, of falling asleep after satiation. (Cf. Lewin, 1950, pp. 103, 150f)

Be that as it may, when Hamlet prepares himself to join his mother before the closet scene, he is quite close to that level *(III.2.391).* The words he speaks at that point have been variously interpreted. He refers to "the very witching time of night," to hell's "contagion to this world"; he could "drink hot blood,/And do such bitter business as the day/Would quake to look on"; he warns his heart not to lose its nature; "let not ever/The soul of Nero enter this firm bosom." Although the reference to Nero strongly bespeaks a struggle with matricidal impulses (Jones, 1949, p. 100), the archaic identity between intercourse and death must not be forgotten.[69]

---

[69] See, for the various interpretations of this soliloquy of Hamlet's, *A New Variorum Edition* of Shakespeare, Vol. III, ed. by Horace Howard Furness, *Hamlet,* Vol. I, p. 273. One of the commentators (Hunter) thought it strange that Shakespeare found it necessary to have Hamlet say that he would not use a dagger against his mother. "That the thought should arise detracts from our admiration of his [Hamlet's] character, as much as it precludes approbation or silent admission of the moral taste discovered in this play by its author." Furness, loc. cit., pp. 273-74. [Ingeniously

Hamlet's frenzy sets in after he has proved to his satisfaction, by watching Claudius's reaction to the subplay, that the latter is guilty. He seems to be in a state of deep regression, to a level at which incest and matricide can stand for each other and where he himself does not really know which he wants; what he does know is that he must master himself if he is not to become entangled in irreparable guilt. Hunter[70] rightly says that matricide at this point would delay, if not entirely frustrate, the execution of the Ghost's behest. To Hamlet, the king's reaction during the subplay is evidence by way of self-confession; it has all the more weight because it occurs in the queen's presence. The father-substitute is still more discredited through having shown anxiety, and now the way is open to Hamlet's complete regression to a preoedipal level.

The reduction of the father progresses even further, however, as can be seen from the Polonius incident in the closet scene, when Hamlet does not hesitate to kill the person who has disturbed his discourse with his mother. The evaluation of this episode by various interpreters is again contradictory, some contending that Hamlet really thought the king was behind the arras, others arguing on equally good grounds that he could not possibly have thought so.

Jones (1949, p. 32) adopts the latter view, following the arguments of Loening (1893, pp. 242f and 362f), who refers to a physical circumstance: Hamlet had just left the king praying, and the latter could not have reached the queen's closet before him. I do not like arguments that depend on such questions as whether the queen's closet had one or two doors, since Claudius might, after all, have easily entered the room after Hamlet did (or he might have walked faster, for that matter). Furthermore, I do not think that Hamlet, who is at this moment in a state of extreme excitement and acting impulsively on the spur of the moment, can be supposed to have engaged in ratiocination in the manner of a detective.

Loening asserts that Hamlet did not know the identity of the man who was hiding behind the arras; that the eavesdropper had to be killed

---

Dührssen (1956, p. 305) points out that Nero had an uncle and stepfather with the name of Claudius, who was ridiculed because of his physical imperfection of stuttering. He was betrayed and poisoned by his wife Agrippina. Oddly enough, the appraisals he has received in history are twofold: that of a cruel man and that of a wise, liberal statesman. Ribner (1960) tries to soften the implication of matricide by interpreting part of the passage as referring to Hamlet's intention of killing the King. It seems to me, however, that here Shakespeare did not leave any room for a variety of interpretations. (1968)]

[70] Quoted after *Variorum Edition*, Vol. 1, p. 274.

whoever he was, because he had heard Hamlet's offensive statements about the queen's marriage; and that only after the deed, when the queen broke out into lamentations, did he hazard the guess that it was the king who was hiding in the room. However, this thesis contradicts Loening's earlier reasoning that Hamlet could never have believed that the king had reached the closet before him. Loening reasons here in a self-contradictory way—a further illustration of my point that Shakespeare constructed the play in such a way that we can assume any one of two or more alternatives about almost any episode in it.

It would be of interest to discuss the consequences of adopting some of these alternatives. If Hamlet really did think that the eavesdropper was the king, then his action would imply that he had at that time the desire to take revenge but could do so only after being overpowered by a sudden emotion—impulsively, and not as the consequence of deliberation. If, on the other hand, Hamlet unconsciously knew that it was Polonius who was listening, then one must attribute to him more aggression and destructiveness than one customarily does. There were many reasons for Hamlet to hold a grudge against Polonius, and his "error" would thus be one of convenience, a way of getting even with a personal adversary. But this would be to introduce a criminal tendency into Hamlet's character. Nor would the picture necessarily be changed if we assumed that Hamlet did not know at all who was behind the arras. Yet the evidence Shakespeare presents allows any and all of these interpretations.

In terms of the unconscious conflict of the tragedy, still another possibility suggests itself. If we take up the previous thread of Hamlet's wanting to win over his mother, then the killing of Polonius is a kind of rehearsal, designed to test the queen's reaction. It is a provocation of sorts when Hamlet asks whether the eavesdropper is the king and then later asserts that he took Polonius for his better. More remarkable, however, is the queen's reaction. She seems not to be as perturbed as might have been expected by Hamlet's wish to kill her husband, thus furnishing Hamlet for the first time with evidence that he may count on her and that it is he, after all, who can consider himself closest to her heart.

Actually, the queen does change her attitude toward Hamlet after he has killed Polonius. At the beginning of the scene, she is not ready to listen. To be sure, Hamlet has launched a terrible attack against her, culminating in a statement that sounds as though he laments the fact that she is his mother. The lines that cause her to want to leave are significantly ambiguous:

You are the queen, your husband's brother's wife,
And would it were not so, you are my mother.[71]

In this version it is left to the reader to apply the words "And would it were not so" either to the preceding line or to the statement that follows. The *Variorum Edition* gives the line as follows:

And—would it were not so!—you are my mother.

The Folios, however, read:

But would you were not so. You are my mother. (*Variorum Edition*, Vol. I, p. 286).

Again the choice of interpretation is left to us. If Hamlet's intent was to express the wish that Gertrude was not his mother, then her desire to break off the conversation would be understandable. But then Hamlet's killing of Polonius, together with his assertion that he thought the victim was Claudius, may be understood by Gertrude as a sign of his intense love for her. From that moment on, Hamlet seems to have grown in stature in her eyes: she thereafter accepts him in the role that he arrogates to himself during the course of the closet scene—that of a sort of moral tutor. He seems, in her eyes, to have become a man as soon as he has manifested not only the intention to eliminate his opponent, but also the ability to do so.[72]

This, I think, brings us closer to an understanding of the Ghost's behavior in his last appearance. Hamlet is understandably frightened, and the Ghost rightly justifies his return as necessary to whet Hamlet's almost blunted purpose. To Hamlet, his father's murderer has become for the time less important than his mother. Perceiving the change in the situation, the Ghost no longer speaks in a harsh and commanding way to Hamlet, but instead begs his son to take care of his mother. With this he admits defeat, acknowledging the fact that Hamlet has grown in stature, has indeed become an adult.

Hamlet's appeal to the Ghost not to arouse pity in him, lest the sternness of his purpose become weakened—though seemingly

---

[71] This is Wilson's version, in the Cambridge edition.

[72] [There is still another interpretation possible within the framework of the unconscious, as outlined previously. The King's self-revelation in public, as contrived by Hamlet, his falling into the "mousetrap," is a triumph of almost unimaginable significance for the son. The first consequence is that Hamlet can now eliminate any identification with the senile father. The killing of Polonius, then, would stand for the termination of the psychological effect that a certain form of paternal imagery has had on the son. It is also to be considered that, as will be shown later, the killing of Polonius makes reconciliation with Ophelia impossible. Once Claudius has been shown to be criminal, the way to the return to the mother is open, and the need of the sister as a substitute for the mother has become superfluous. (1966)]

paradoxical, for such pity might even be expected to be one of the pre-requisites of his revenge—reveals some of the most important unconscious processes. Here he almost equates his father with Claudius, so far as his own emotional responses go, as if he could not be aggressive toward the latter while still feeling pity for the former. It has also been demonstrated that his decisions and actions are still dependent on the kind of images he forms about his father's character.

Moreover, the two ways in which the Ghost has now made his appearance signify different stages of Hamlet's development during the oedipal phase. His first appearance is correlated with a Hamlet who is meek and does not dare to rebel. When the Ghost appears to Hamlet for the second and last time, in the closet scene, Hamlet is in process of demanding justification from his mother for her actions: he is reprimanding her openly and trying to impose his will on her. Now the harsh, commanding, heroic ghost of the first appearance becomes a suppliant.

As Hamlet grows, then, endeavoring to overcome internally the childhood picture of the father, the Ghost loses in stature and magnificence—a loss that is expressed symbolically in the change of costume explicitly prescribed by the stage direction.[73] By this subtle correlation of the Ghost's appearance and behavior with phases of Hamlet's oedipal development, it is indirectly intimated that the Ghost is a projection of Hamlet.

The extent to which Hamlet has grown can be seen when, following the Ghost's "stealing away," he issues precepts to his mother as to how and why to avoid sexual relations with Claudius. This inner freedom from the father, which is seen blossoming in the closet scene, finds its culmination in the final scene; Hamlet, having stabbed the king, forces him to drink the cup of poison: "Drink off this potion. Is thy union here? Follow my mother." The passage is reminiscent of the end of Hamlet's speech about Yorick: "Now get you to my lady's chamber, and tell her..."

I would suggest that these similarly constructed passages are both unambivalent. If Yorick goes to the lady's chamber, he will be rejected and Hamlet can have sole possession of him. Although the sentence sounds hostile, it is the result of a deep affection for the father.[74] After the

[73] In *I. 1* the Ghost appears "clad in armour from head to foot, and bears a marchal's truncheon." In the closet scene, the Ghost appears "in his nightgown."

[74] [Symons (1928, p. 101) interprets Hamlet's addressing Yorick's skull with these words as an expression of ambivalence. This passage does, to be sure, sound like derision. However, in my opinion it is at the same time the strongest expression of Hamlet's unswerving love for his father beyond

queen has drunk from the cup and offered it to Hamlet, and after Hamlet has been poisoned by Laertes' stab, he has reached a physical state identical with that of his mother. When he forces the king to drink, and then hurls the bitter words, he has reached the zenith of his hatred for a father-image. There is no longer any ambivalence; this is unambivalent hatred. Fear of the father and the guilt feelings caused by aggressive impulses have both vanished; Hamlet has become instead the hero who commits the oedipal crime, fearlessly and deliberately.

IV

A study of Hamlet's six soliloquies[75] now follows. By means of them, an imposing portrayal of character development is presented, in broad but incisive strokes.[76] They seem to be arranged in three pairs: The first soliloquy *(I.2.129),* in which Hamlet describes his melancholy mood, can be paired with Hamlet's decision *(I.5.91)*, after the Ghost has vanished, to devote his future to revenge. The Hecuba monologue *(II.2.552)*, goes with "To be, or not to be" *(III.1.56)*. The fifth soliloquy *(III.3.72)*, in which Hamlet wrestles with his impulse to kill the praying king, has a particular affinity with the Fortinbras soliloquy *(IV.4.32)*, when Hamlet discards the last barrier to action.[77] A careful

---

the grave, insofar as it asserts that only he continues steadfast in this love, whereas the mother would reject the father once he was reduced to a skeleton. It is as if he were saying, "Mother's love for father may have reservations, but my love is unqualified."

[This is true only for the transitional period, however, shortly after the repression of the oedipal tie to the mother and the formation of a superego have both begun—a time when the superego has not yet grown into a solid, semiautonomous structure that would make the youngster independent of the father and prepare him for that rebellion against the father that is already foreshadowed in prepuberty. In the early stage of the latency period, the ambivalence toward the father is reduced and a warm, good relationship to him favors the growth of the superego, which will in turn provide the latency child with relative independence. (1966)]

[75] The short soliloquy at the end of III-2, mentioned above, has not been included in this discussion. It is not a landmark in Hamlet's character development, but rather the explosive expression of an unconquerable feeling.

[76] Cf. for an opposite view, Oliver Goldsmith's pungent criticism of one of them: "The soliloquy in *Hamlet* which we have so often heard extolled in terms of admiration, is, in our opinion, a heap of absurdities." (Quoted by Williamson, 1950, p. 10.)

[An equivalent devaluation of the soliloquies reappears in the writings of some modern critics in the form of doubts with regard to their relevance. See, for example, Grebanier, 1960, p. 194: "the tragic impact of the plot in no way depends upon any of the soliloquies." For a somewhat different view, see Braddy (1964, p. 63): "It is significant that only in Act V does Hamlet forgo his ubiquitous soliloquies. Their absence points up the transformation wrought in the Prince." (1968)]

[77] Flatter (1949, pp. 174-79) has expressed doubts that the final soliloquy is now in its right place. He believes that if it is to be included at all in the final version, it belongs before the Mousetrap play. Since this soliloquy is omitted from the Folio text, it has given rise to various speculations about what its function is in the play.

review of these three pairs of monologues will reveal certain facets of the development of Hamlet's character that might otherwise be missed.

The content of the first soliloquy includes expository information, an evaluation of facts, and a description of Hamlet's emotional state. These three are intimately connected, of course, the facts that Hamlet selects and the way in which he evaluates them being reflections of his emotional state. The information that Hamlet conveys in 30 lines is already well known; it has to do with his father's death and his mother's speedy marriage to his uncle. The evaluation consists chiefly of judgments of the key people involved: Hamlet's father was to be compared with Hyperion; he was exceedingly tender with the queen, and she loved him ever more and more, as if her loving generated new love. After her husband's death the queen had grieved like Niobe; her speedy marriage to an unworthy person is therefore beyond comprehension. The situation is intensified, however, by Hamlet's adding the quite separate reproach of incest. The description of Hamlet's own state of mind—the real subject of the soliloquy—is condensed into the narrowest possible space: in his desire to die, he wished that God had not forbidden suicide; the "uses of the world" do not yield any pleasure; Claudius is as little comparable to his father as he, Hamlet, is to Hercules; he must be silent even if to do so breaks his heart.

Over nearly every line of this soliloquy hovers the fact that Hamlet's belief in the trustworthiness of human emotions has been shaken. The conflict has arisen out of a series of observations he has made of his mother: there can be no doubt that she loved his father, and that she showed all the signs of supreme grief upon his death; nevertheless, subsequent events have made it impossible for Hamlet to continue to regard as existing any longer that which his earlier observations had presented as existing, and beyond any doubt. The impact of this discrepancy must necessarily lead to grave conflict, for once one's emotions have lost their function as reliable guides in one's contact with and behavior toward other human beings, confusion is bound to ensue. Hamlet finds himself here in a situation analogous to that of a pilot who one night discovers that the points on the compass had been secretly interchanged.

In the strict sense of the term, Hamlet's conflict cannot be called a neurotic one, since it takes place between him and external reality. His confusion is the result of correct but obviously discordant observations.[78]

---

[78] However, according to an interpretation made by one of my patients, it is this aspect alone that would prove the existence of an internal, neurotic conflict. According to the patient's interpretation,

The resulting dissonance with reference to a vital problem has involved all layers of his psychic apparatus and therefore has some bearing on the reality principle.

A quite different constellation is to be seen in his relationships with his father and his uncle. When he compares the distance between the two with that which lies between himself and Hercules, his self-evaluation represents a neurotic attitude (Cf. Slochower, 1950, p. 218). In putting his father into a divine position, he is asserting indirectly that he himself is no better than Claudius—that is to say, that he is as unworthy of taking his father's place as was his uncle. The Hercules simile is also a subtle reference to the unconscious conflict that Freud described in Hamlet; it hints at a situation of temptation. What Hamlet seems to imply is: "I always thought that, since mother was accustomed to the love of a sublime person, she would never accept me, a miserable wretch [but now that she loves a satyr, inferior to my father, there is some doubt, after all, whether or not she might have granted my wish-fulfillments even at the price of violating the taboo of incest]." Thus the way has been opened to the gratification of a repressed oedipal desire, which is tantamount to a temptation. I believe that this conclusion is unavoidable if one thinks the Hercules simile through to its logical end.

It is true, of course, that Hamlet's simile sounds quite innocuous, and the objection could be made that grave conclusions are here being

---

there is no problem at all involved in Gertrude's speedy marriage— what has prompted her to marry so quickly is her sexual appetites; she "cannot stay for long without a man." From this viewpoint, Hamlet's conflict has arisen from enforced acknowledgment of the fact that his mother is a sexual, passionate being, rather than from confusion that has been brought about by mutually contradictory observations. (It seems needless to add that this patient was a woman.) Hamlet's quest for motives beyond the sexual urge in order to explain the queen's second marriage may very well be the reflection of certain male prejudices. [In favor of the patient's concept, it may be stated that, indeed, Hamlet's description of what he had observed in his mother prior to her marriage with Claudius did not rule out her being a woman who, as long as her sexual appetites are satiated, abandons herself totally to her lover, but who, once deprived of this particular set of circumstances, is compelled to reestablish the *status quo* after a short while with another. To a certain extent one may say that Hamlet responds to Gertrude's second marriage the way the Mariolatrist would if it were proved that the Holy Spirit was a mythical cover-up for the biological force; or more generally, the way in which the child who believes in his mother's purity responds, upon finding out about parental intercourse. This, indeed, is the infantile conflict, which is present in the development of most children; it is presented in an adult form in the first soliloquy.]

On the other hand, I think that my patient rather oversimplified Gertrude's personality structure. In this instance, Hamlet must be granted the benefit of the doubt; the queen's behavior seems, after all, to have been contradictory.

drawn from something that is itself small and inconsequential.[79] Yet if one considers that Gertrude played in the life of Hamlet's father, a role almost identical with the role played by Deianira in Hercules' life, this seemingly innocuous reference to Greek mythology is revealed as the carrier of an extremely far-reaching suggestion—namely, that, even before being apprised by the ghost of what had actually happened, Hamlet had unconsciously divined the events that led to his father's death.

Moreover, in *I.4.83* Hamlet again uses an element of the Hercules myth. At that point, when his friends want to hold him back from following the ghost, he compares himself to the Nemean lion, in order to symbolize the strength with which he will defend himself against their interference. The Nemean lion was, of course, slain by Hercules, and his skin became one of the hero's traditional appurtenances. Thus, in connection with Hercules, even a symbol that is ostensibly used to signify strength turns out to contain a reference to defeat. It therefore seems all the more justifiable to take seriously the fact that Hamlet completes his figure of speech by making a pejorative comparison between himself and Hercules. The low estimate of himself thereby expressed is less an outgrowth of what has been called Hamlet's depression or melancholia than it is the derivative of his unconscious wish, which is identical with what Claudius has accomplished in actuality by marrying Gertrude.

The secret identification with the bad father does not militate against the strong reproaches that Hamlet repeatedly hurls against Claudius. The identification with the hero-father has not succeeded in taking place; the ego feels itself small in comparison with the powerful and radiant image of that ideal, and the tormented ego diverts its self-reproaches into reproaches against the rivals. Thus what Hamlet is entangled in would seem to be an intricate and neurotic father-conflict; up to this

---

[79] Such a simile as that of Hercules is certainly not without consequence in a search for the hidden meaning of the play. From the aesthetic point of view, not much would be changed if the comparison were expressed in terms of a different set of gods, such as Hyperion and a satyr—which we actually do find in the same soliloquy, before the Hercules simile is introduced. If, however, the question can be raised why Shakespeare selected from the many possibilities available to him precisely this one, then the simile does become crucial. Does such a choice have an effect on the listener, who has no time for thinking analogies through to their logical ends? Experimental dream studies (See Poetzl, 1917; cf. Malamud and Linder, 1931) have confirmed Freud's theory of the great importance that trivial day residues may have for dream formation, and it seems well proved that it is precisely the perception that does not reach the level of awareness that is important for unconscious processes. Since no equivalent experimental studies have been made in the matter of artistic effect, it is a moot question whether the simile of Hercules has an effect on the spectator's unconscious. [Dührssen's (1956, p. 299) interpretation seems to confirm my speculation about the simile. (1968)]

point of our discussion, at least, the conflict with the mother has been chiefly an external one.

Yet Hamlet employs another surprising simile in this same initial soliloquy. He says of his mother that she was "Like Niobe, all tears" when "she followed my poor father's body." But Niobe is the symbol of the narcissistic, maternal woman, who is all mother and very little wife, who is able to ignore her husband's suicide and yet becomes a weeping rock because she cannot survive the loss of her children. Niobe is also the vain mother, for whom the possession of children is a reason for bragging and boasting, whose narcissistic pride therefore turns into her children's downfall. Whatever aspect of the Niobe myth is considered, it remains a strange simile to select in order to signify grief following a husband's death.

There are no clues, however, that might guide the reader in the selection of the correct implication among the several that are suggested by the introduction of the Niobe myth at this point; the unconscious does not reveal itself here in a distinctive way. It may be that for a moment Hamlet has indeed identified himself with his dead father, and believes that, if *he* had died, his mother would have wept for her son as Niobe did (even though she would nevertheless have found new sources of pleasure, without turning into a weeping stone, the symbol of eternal melancholy). Thus Hamlet's own tendency toward melancholy may constitute an effort to do what he thinks his mother should be doing, a demonstration to her of how a faithful wife ought to be behaving after the loss of a beloved husband.

The reference to Niobe may also be an expression of jealousy, as if Hamlet wanted to say: "When mother cried so heartbreakingly after father's death, she was behaving the way a mother ought to after a child's death." This would point to the possibility of an erotic excitement in Hamlet as he watched his mother's outbursts of grief when she withdrew all interest from her son and engaged only in mourning for her husband. At that point, the son may have had the fantasy that he would like to be in the place of his dead father, to hear his mother weep so heartbreakingly for himself, thereby making sure that her concern was exclusively for him. When he was shocked by the discovery that this grief may not have been genuine, however, his jealousy was revealed to have been possibly quite unnecessary. Thus the Niobe simile indicates a neurotic conflict about the mother, too.

Yet this conflict is concealed in the manifest content of the soliloquy, and it is Hamlet's disorientation and confusion about the unreliability of human emotion that is put into the foreground instead. Hamlet's complaint is not a rationalization but rather a valid description of his external reality. An early hint of this, which precedes the soliloquy, can be found in his lecture about human emotions *(I.2.76)*. The queen, in Jocasta fashion, has begged Hamlet to stop mourning for his father; she has appealed to the reality principle: since all who live must die, "Why seems it so particular with thee?" It is that word "seems" that elicits Hamlet's tirade about human emotions; around that one word revolve all his qualms, scruples, suspicions and fears ("Seems, Madam? Nay, 'tis!").

Like a psychosomaticist, he spells out the physiological manifestations of grief and sorrow, and as if he were an experienced anthropologist, he then goes on to enumerate the varied customs of mourning. Yet he is wiser than both these figures when he then says: "These indeed seem"/ [they may be feigned] "But I have that within which passeth show." He even speaks disparagingly of "the trappings and the suits of woe," without letting us know why, if he does indeed have "that within which passeth show," he nevertheless needs all those external manifestations of his own. For Hamlet is not only sad; he shows his sadness in a profuse way, making himself conspicuous to those about him.

To some extent, he is himself "like Niobe, all tears," and his reminder to his mother that behind the external trappings there ought to be true feeling sounds once again like an appeal to her—namely that, in spite of her gay clothes, she should be mourning. Hamlet's need for his external trappings may have another root: it may be that his general doubt with regard to human emotion extends to his own emotions. It is as if he can no longer rely on his own feelings, now that his mother's have proved to be so unreliable; he therefore needs all the reassurances he can muster that he is really sad.

The beginning of this first soliloquy ("O that this too too solid flesh would melt") is ambiguous. It is usually thought of as referring to Hamlet's wish to die—which is later implicit, supposedly, in the wish that God had not forbidden suicide. It could, however, refer equally to the wish that another person should die—Gertrude or Claudius. Then it would mean: My mother, who disgraces my father's memory, ought to vanish; if this does not happen, *then* I wish I could be permitted to commit suicide. If this interpretation is accepted as a possibility, then an important point of identity would be established between Hamlet and his mother: both of them should suffer the same fate. Since this "solid flesh" could also mean Claudius, the end of the tragedy—in which all three do die—would thus be anticipated in this very first line of Hamlet's first soliloquy.[80]

The greatest incongruity in the soliloquy, however, appears in the passage in which Hamlet, in a rage about his mother's recent wedding, first hurls the reproach of "wicked speed" at her and then adds the accusation of incest. The charge of speed, at most a transgression of custom, pales to insignificance alongside the great crime of incest. Yet it is precisely the speed of Gertrude's marriage that seems to have made the situation intolerable to Hamlet at this point, since that is the factor that has aroused Hamlet's suspicion of Gertrude's sincerity in her show of love and grief.

It is as if Hamlet were indicating at this point that he could forgive his mother all her alleged misdeeds, if only he were able to continue to believe in the genuineness of her emotions. In other words, if Gertrude had married an unworthy man—but many years later—then Hamlet would not have been compelled to conclude that her previous manifestations of feeling had been spurious. On the other hand, the combination of speed and incest into one reproach, with special stress on the speed, intimates early in the play an unconscious equation of incest and adultery, an equation that plays an important part in establishing the ambiguity of the plot. If, soon after her divorce, a woman marries a man whom she has known earlier, the divorced husband may easily suspect that there had been adultery before then. Hamlet's unconscious is here reacting in much the same way as his father's might well have, if he had lost Gertrude yet remained alive.

I have not yet mentioned an emotion that must surely have been rampant in Hamlet—namely, rage (see Sharpe, 1929, pp. 203-213). With all his beliefs and hopes disappointed, and being aware of the dishonor that has been visited upon his father's memory (the last thing in which he can still believe), he finds himself in a helpless position, as a result of which he may suddenly break out into extreme anger. Nevertheless, he conceals his anger at this point and instead goes along with Clau-

---

[80] [As is well known, Bowers (1956) brought Shakespeare's original "sallied," (meaning "sullied,") to new honors, and "solid," indeed, may have been an unnecessary and even misleading emendation. "Sullied" would establish a particularly close affinity between Hamlet and Gertrude, since her allegedly immoral conduct would have sullied his flesh. Bowers' reading would not necessitate many changes in the above interpretation. (1968)]

dius's request not to leave the country. I wonder how far the exhibitionistic tendency and the conspicuousness of his attire are also derivatives of suppressed anger, as if his elaborate signs of grief were meant to be an indirect reproach to the court for not mourning his father's death in an appropriate manner (and, of course, even more so to his mother).

The immediate result of this complex situation is Hamlet's decision to hold his tongue, even if his heart should break. In these words he expresses his readiness to accept the world as it now appears to him—at least in the form of its external behavior—despite his many objections to it. His actions will henceforth be in conformity with societal requirements, in spite of his possessing a rich and highly structured internal cosmos of his own, in which criticism and independence of judgment prevail. Hamlet's internal independence is from this point forward to be in marked contrast to his external conformity. The bridge between internal independence and independence of action—which are linked, if at all, by the full force of the emotional world—has suffered profound harm in Hamlet.[81]

[81] [The problem of appearance and reality has been discussed by many interpreters as central in *Hamlet*. It is not always clear whether the discussion has been approving or disapproving. The question of the discrepancy between appearance and reality, or of the general relation of the two, is of course basic in philosophy and may never find a conclusive solution among the philosophers. But Hamlet does not place the question within that context. He is involved solely in the human world of emotions; for him, the problem is under what conditions an observable emotion is valid—that is to say, in correspondence to psychic reality (in Freud's terminology)—and when it is a mere ripple on the surface and therefore capable of being replaced by another one that is, in fact, irreconcilable with it.

If Hamlet had conceived the idea that the period following his father's death had brought to the surface a previously repressed emotion in his mother—that is to say, that both ranges of emotion are genuine and belonged within his mother's full spectrum of emotions (as a sophisticated contemporary person may judge)—then he would have been able to maintain a rational view of the human world. That step, however, he was not able to take. Curiously enough, Hamlet's confusion about human emotions is central to many subjects who are suffering from a schizophrenic disorder. By no means do I want to hint by this last remark that Hamlet is suffering in any way from a psychotic disorder. The reference is justified, however, since the schizophrenic subject in particular wrestles openly with issues that are or should be our concern but are repressed, denied or minimized, whichever the case may be, precisely because existence would be otherwise intolerable, as it is, in fact, for the schizophrenic.

The truth is that neither any of our own emotions nor any of our fellow man's are anywhere nearly as absolutely dependable and reliable as is the presence and effect of gravitational forces. The persistence of an emotion or of an attitude that is grounded in strong emotions can be weighed only in terms of probability; it never becomes a matter of certainty. Under favorable conditions, the child believes in the certainty of his mother's love. If he discovers at too early a stage, however, that this is an illusion, as well as if that conviction persists and is not weakened, rendered obsolete, or abolished—in both these instances, grave psychopathology is the consequence, outside of a few exceptional situations. Doubt about the reliability of human emotions is closely connected with the reproach of hypocrisy, and in Hamlet's first soliloquy, one can find the root of his later general conflict about hypocrisy. The central question of Hamlet's first soliloquy, then, is a problem that actually cuts across all dimensions of human existence. (1969)]

The second soliloquy, which follows the disappearance of the Ghost *(I.5.91)*, has only 20 lines, yet it substantially confirms the psychological conclusions one can derive from the first soliloquy. Here Hamlet makes himself the instrument for the realization of the Ghost's demand for vengeance. The soliloquy is replete with expressions of the strong feelings that have been aroused in him by the news the Ghost has conveyed. The ambivalence that comes to the fore in these emotional outbreaks, which has already been mentioned, may be better understood now.

The two opposing thoughts are as follows: On the one side, Hamlet decides and faithfully intends that "thy commandment all alone shall live/Within the book and volume of my brain." That intention, however, is short-circuited by the idea: "O most pernicious woman!" which immediately obtrudes, distracting Hamlet from his initial devotion to carrying out his father's command. It is from this second idea that we are able to learn one of the reasons why Hamlet cannot devote himself completely to the single goal of taking revenge: it is once again the question of the unreliability of human emotions. After the emotions of his most important love object have proven to be capable of being sham, can Hamlet any longer trust his own emotions?[82]

When Hamlet adds: "That one may smile, and smile, and be a villain," we see him extending to Claudius his doubts concerning the reliability of expressions of emotion. In the first soliloquy, an intimation was already given of Hamlet's identification with Claudius, and in the fact that Claudius is now included in this disorientation with regard to emotions further proof is presented that Hamlet's conflict actually rages about his own emotions. As soon as he has finished making certain that the observations he has made about his mother in this regard are also applicable to Claudius, he returns to his initial idea of concentrating, from now on, on his father's command.

The closing words of this soliloquy, however, show that, from a psychological point of view, Hamlet is still in essentially the same position as he was at the end of the first soliloquy. Both "But break my heart, for I must hold my tongue" and "Now to my word; It is/'Adieu, adieu! remember me,' "—which is a mere repetition of the Ghost's last words— both these statements are expressions of surrender to an external force,

---

[82] It still remains undetermined whether his doubt concerning his own emotions was merely precipitated by the traumatic experience he had just suffered; or was it the traumatic experience itself that caused the doubt? I think that the latter alternative comes closer to the meaning of the tragedy than does the former, which has the character of a scientific opinion based on clinical observation.

without the involvement of his own individuality. To be sure, the social consequences, if followed up, would be quite different: in the one instance, the result would be complete passivity; in the other, even though the underlying psychological passivity (in the form of obedience) would still be great, outwardly there would be activity. Yet Hamlet is really not ready to tread either path. No sooner has he acknowledged the necessity of having to hold his tongue than he makes the most sarcastic remarks to his friends about his mother, while his inability to pursue the revenge to which he is committed quickly becomes evident. Thus, despite the difference in the social consequences of Hamlet's following each of these attitudes, what underlies them both is the identical psychological disposition to conform to something external, or something enforced by external reality—which disposition is not, however, translated into action, since something in Hamlet opposes such surrender. Since Hamlet cannot yet evolve a purely personal motivation, he is confronted at this point with two alternatives, both of which would force him into the position of acting as a tool.

The attitude to which Hamlet's ego tries to cling is that of obedience to his father. He had already avowed obedience to his mother, as well as to his uncle, in the very first soliloquy, when he expressed his determination to remain silent about his moral rejection of his mother. This is the basic position that most children take: they assert their intention of being obedient, yet, in devious ways, they reveal their actual ambivalence toward the demand that has been placed on them. The child's expressed determination to maintain a surface of obedience, while concealing the rebellion that lies behind it, creates tension; occasionally, this tension leads to explosive reactions.

Such an explosion follows immediately after Hamlet's second soliloquy, when, in the cellarage scene, he is joined by Horatio and Marcellus, while the Ghost roams underground. Wilson believes the crux of Hamlet's problem to be "the burden which fate lays upon his shoulders" (Wilson, 1936a, p. 217), and he therefore explains Hamlet's emotional outbreak—his madness in the cellarage scene—as resulting from the discrepancy between the weight of that burden and Hamlet's strength to bear up under it. I think that this view oversimplifies the problem.

Hamlet is at least as strong as Laertes. Instead of swearing to silence Marcellus and Horatio, who knew of his conversation with the Ghost, he could have rushed into immediate action: Laertes would surely have acted unhesitatingly—and possibly effectively. But Laertes[83] could never function as the principal character in a tragedy because he does not rise above the level of effective obedience, which is per se no theme for tragedy. In order to act at that moment in Laertes' fashion, Hamlet would have had to renounce forever his own individuality.

To have performed the deed at that moment would have been to perform it in a spirit of submission and obedience, as a mere tool in his father's hands, and without any regard for his own feelings, whatever they might have been. Since this duty that has been put on his shoulders is the most consequential of his entire life, delay is necessary if he is not to forgo forever the opportunity he still has of being able to outgrow the narrow shell of the obedient son. There is always some element of rebellion implied in individuality; in its formation, both the integration and the rejection of reality are involved at one and the same time. Hamlet's horror of acting as a tool is a token of his rebellion against his father (his ambivalence is expressed in the way he addresses the Ghost in the cellarage scene), yet there is more to it than mere rebellion. The violence of this outbreak is due to Hamlet's frantic effort to establish an entirely personal, individual frame of reference for action.

He could also have engaged his friends to assist him. Historically, this solution would have been favored; there are many examples of such action by the coterie that surrounds the Renaissance prince. Yet he definitely wants to perform this deed as his own, prepared and executed by his own individual efforts. Furthermore, the cellarage scene revolves around Hamlet's insistence on his friends' swearing silence. Wilson puts forward valid and quite realistic arguments to explain Hamlet's insistence on that oath. I should like to add another, purely psychological, one. Since he had dedicated himself to the Ghost by an oath, there must be a particular meaning to the fact that Hamlet now forces his friends into a situation that duplicates what he himself had just been exposed to.

An archaic technique for overcoming a trauma consists in visiting upon others what one has been made to suffer (Freud, 1920). When Hamlet swore to his father, he was passive. Since his life's mission has now become little more than a reflection of his father's command, he has been pushed still deeper into the position of obedience, of serving as a mere appendage of paternal authority. The parting words of the Ghost,

---

[83] Laertes is a foil: one of his functions in the play is to throw Hamlet's problem into relief.

"Remember me," contain implicitly Hamlet's spiritual death sentence—unless he defends himself.

His immediate defense against the Ghost's intrusion into his life is symbolically represented by Hamlet's constantly moving away from the place where he is able to hear the Ghost's voice (see Türck, 1930, p. 142f). And when Hamlet, half-ironically, half-plaintively, says of the Ghost: "*Hic et ubique*," he is pointing to the very danger that he fears—namely, that the Ghost may actually become the "*hic et ubique*" of his life.[84]

His further defense against domination by the Ghost is to maneuver his friends into the same passive situation that he has been placed in. *He* has had to take an oath: "Now to my word; . . . I have sworn't," and now he forces his friends into a similar situation. Hamlet's insistence on his friends' swearing thus impresses me as being born of the deepest anxiety, an archaic attempt to overcome a terrific danger—namely, that of being permanently devoured by the magic power of an archaic father-image.

The scene ends with the famous exclamation: "The time is out of joint: O cursed spite,/That ever I was born to set it right!" This has often been interpreted as a sign that Hamlet is weak.[85] Yet such a conclusion is not entirely warranted. In this outcry, Hamlet does not repudiate his mission. "I was born" definitely emphasizes the passive element that is involved in the situation. Here he seems to be preoccupied with his having been selected for a task that is not of his individual choosing, but instead requires his surrender to an external power. He is in despair over having been chosen for the task, yet he does not refuse to accept the challenge. In short, he does not use any of those subterfuges with which an ego may attempt to escape having to carry through a task that has been assigned to it.[86]

---

[84] The cellarage scene shows rivalry between Hamlet and the Ghost: the Ghost repeats Hamlet's injunction as if he cannot stand that it should be Hamlet that is giving the order, while Hamlet runs off to another place where he can get away from the Ghost's voice and then addresses to his father's spirit disrespectful names of all sorts.

[85] Much has been made out of the suicidal tendencies that Hamlet expresses in his first monologue, but little attention has been paid to the question of why he did not commit suicide. This I think is more important. While his ego perceives and acknowledges the desire to die, it is strong enough to master the impulse; suicide occupies him only as a wish, not as a procedure that is actually accessible to him. If anything, he proves himself to be strong in that situation, even if his rejection of suicide is asserted at this point out of obedience to a divine command.

[86] [Hamlet's outcry of regret about having been chosen for a mission has an old history. It is a frequent mythological theme. Moses was reluctant to accept the Lord's call, and in the story of

He will struggle intensely for inner justification of the deed—not so much in the sense of moral justification, which, I think, he takes for granted, but rather in the sense of individualizing the doing of it. While one finds such conflicts in an outspoken form in some schizophrenic patients, they are also to be found generally. These patients rage about their quest for full participation of the ego, as well as about their struggle against those actions that men perform merely as tools. While some schizophrenics are extremely sensitive even to the most trivial situations in which their egos cannot participate fully, this is a sensitivity that also exists, although to a far lesser degree, among normal people. Hamlet's ensuing struggle seems to me to be a struggle for the right activation. He is incapable of hypocrisy, as a result of his having that truly touching craving for genuineness that is at the bottom of his "antic disposition."

When the Ghost informs Hamlet of what has happened, he imparts to him at the same time all the justification that Hamlet may need (in terms of *external* reality) in order for him to take revenge. Yet the external and internal justification still remain quite far apart, and it is this discrepancy that lies behind the wild and whirling words that Hamlet hurls at his friends, rather than any supposed infirmity that marks him as being close to madness at this point.

If he had been able to lie (the word "lie" is used here in a generalized, purely ethical sense), he could have proceeded at once to carry out the ghost's command; his "inhibition" at this point does not prove that he is a weak person, but rather one who is not willing to adapt himself to the severe injury his ego suffered when it was assaulted by the father's expectation of total surrender. He must go on struggling to attain the

---

Jonah the fate of a disobedient prophet becomes a leading element. Bickerman (1967, p. 10) calls this element "the unwilling Prophet" and adduces pertinent illustrations. Indeed, Hamlet is one who belongs to the group of unwilling prophets.

Of course, in *Hamlet* the issue is put on stage in modern vestments and the reappearance of an old mythical element is not readily detectable. But the mythologist might find in the "unwilling prophet" theme the central issue of the play, couched in terms of psychological conflicts. I do not know the mythologists' explanation for the prophets' unwillingness. It seems that carrying the message of a superior power constitutes a danger to the bearer, in the same way as does a projectile that may explode and destroy the crew that carries it. The underlying idea of the psychology of magic might have been that to carry a divine message means to have part of God's all-consuming power in one's own entrails; the danger of contact with such powers, either by touch or through sense perception, is a frequent motive. In *Hamlet*, this animistic psychology is only vestigial: Hamlet's repugnance to being made his father's tool still echoes the Biblical prophet's unwillingness. Yet it is no longer the magical dread of carrying part of God's (father's) spirit, but the demand for independence. A new fear has arisen—that of the "stunted personality," which leads ultimately to Nietzsche's vision of the Superman] (1968).

supremacy of his ego over the necessities of reality, as well as over the subservience that had taken possession of him at the time when his father's ghost put on his shoulders the great task of revenge. [Whatever progression has taken place from the first to the second soliloquy may be found in the replacement of the initial determination to preserve silence and to go through the motions of conforming, by the newly acquired determination to resort to action in the future. The initial conformity, which called for passivity, is now replaced by a conformity of a different sort, which will lead to social action. (1968)]

A further step in this struggle can be discerned in the third (Hecuba) soliloquy, which comes at the end of the second act; the events preceding it are clear. Hamlet has witnessed the spectacle of an actor's being overwhelmed by his own emotions, as he is reciting Hecuba's misfortunes. Both the actor's recital and its content are of psychological significance. Hamlet has not left the selection of the topic to the actor, but has asked for the story of Priam's slaughter; further, he himself has recited the introduction to the story, dealing with the description of the dreadful Pyrrhus, who is about to commit the nefarious deed of killing an awe-inspiring yet essentially defenseless old man, whose fatherhood is actually his most outstanding feature.[87]

Thus Hamlet has selected an incident in the killing of an innocent father, in which Pyrrhus—young, uninhibited, and destructive—stands as a son-substitute. In that light, Hamlet's recital of the introduction sounds like an attempt on his part to identify with a purely destructive person, one who transgresses without scruple all barriers of tradition and ethics. It could also be taken, however, as a warning of the evil consequences of rash action, taken under the impact of blind wrath.

The point at which Hamlet stops in his recitation is the moment when the narration turns toward the slaughter of Priam—as if he were inhibited even about describing such a dreadful deed. His gradual buildup toward the actor's recital thus sounds as though Hamlet were trying to seduce someone else into picturing all the details of the murder of a father figure. On a more archaic level, the recital may fulfill the function

---

[87] [Prosser (1967) points out that Pyrrhus too had the obligation of avenging the death of his father, Achilles. This had escaped my attention. The element of obligation, of course, enriches the meaningfulness of the episode in the play and, in addition, proves the profundity of psychological meaning that is implied in each of Shakespeare's choices of symbols. See also Dührssen (1956, p. 305f), who was perhaps the first to point out the meaning of the Pyrrhus-choice. Shakespeare enlarged it by also tying in the Polyxena part of the myth with the tragedy. (1968)]

that Freud attributed to thinking processes in general—namely, that of "trial actions" (*Probehandeln*) (See Freud, 1911, p. 221). The actor then takes over at the point at which Hamlet leaves off, and goes on to give what could be a full account of Priam's slaughter, except that he is interrupted by Polonius, who seems to have an aversion to the whole procedure, almost as if he intuitively understood Hamlet's unconscious purpose.

Yet, since Hamlet wants to hear about the effect of the slaughter on Hecuba, Priam's wife, the actor proceeds, only to be once again interrupted by Polonius, who has noticed that the actor is himself overwhelmed by Hecuba's indescribable suffering over the death of Priam. To be more precise, the player is apparently unable to bear the thought that the gods do not seem to be moved at all by "things mortal"—thereby alluding to a situation that is close to Hamlet's heart and pushing the son's relationship to his mother into the foreground. This time Hamlet also agrees that the recitation should be stopped, as if his own thinking has become blocked at the point at which the mother's despair reaches its peak.[88] Nevertheless, he makes it clear that he intends to carry the "rehearsal" further: "I'll have thee speak out the rest of this soon."

There is still another important link between the scene with the strolling players and the central conflict in Hamlet. The speech that Hamlet has asked the actor to recite is part of the tale that Aeneas relates to Dido, and this constitutes a free elaboration on one portion of Vergil's *Aeneid*. Aeneas is a typical example of the good, obedient son, who respects weak father figures and achieves his greatest success through his devotion to established authority—that is to say, he is a son who has overcome the aggressive component of the oedipal situation. We can now understand why Hamlet "chiefly loved" this tale: it is an indirect, but important, allusion to the Fortinbras subplot, which will be, as we shall see, interwoven with the main plot.

As soon as he is alone, however, Hamlet turns upon himself with fury, lashing himself with the contrast between the player's ready emotionality and his own absence of any. The player "could force his soul" in accordance with his own imagination, so that the emotions that accompanied what he imagined burst forth into outward signs in his phy-

---

[88] It is worthwhile recalling here that Pyrrhus marries Andromache, Hecuba's daughter-in-law, an allusion to the consummation of the oedipal crime. Andromache was, of course, the wife of Pyrrhus' father's most dangerous rival.

siognomy. Here again Hamlet is involved in the conflict over observable physiognomic data and the genuineness of the underlying emotion. In the case of his mother, while there had been a great cause and a physiognomic outburst, there had been no true feeling, he believes, as subsequent events had since proven. In the player's case, the cause was only a fictitious one, yet he was able to produce the physiognomic display that was to be expected in a person who had actually been overcome by strong feeling.

It is not that the player's manner and facial expression do not suit what he is imagining *(II.2.579f)*; what Hamlet seems to be shaken by is primarily how perfectly suited they are, despite the fact that the cause is fictitious, and as Hamlet describes it, "all for nothing." What would the player do if he were in *his* place? asks Hamlet. His own answer to his question contains a strange inconsistency: "He would drown the stage with tears." Yet this is just the sort of behavior that the player has shown for Hecuba's sake—that is, behavior of which Hamlet himself is, after all, quite capable, as Trench (1913, pp. 111-117) rightly points out. Logically, if Hamlet is truly to prefer the actor's behavior to his own, one would expect him to assume that, upon being confronted with Hamlet's task, the player would leave the stage and proceed at once to action. Yet this seeming inconsistency vanishes if one considers the problem in which Hamlet's ego is entangled; it even becomes an important clue to the nature of that problem.

We are concerned here with the unreliability of emotion as the motor of action. While a great cause may induce strong emotion, a fictitious cause may also have the same effect; and even if a person does feel strongly, nevertheless his subsequent actions may give him the lie. Thus all the admiration that Hamlet spends on the player and all the envy he professes to have with regard to the player's strong emotionality constitute in reality nothing more than a refusal to accept feelings, including his own, as an adequate starting point for planned action. Whether emotions are genuine or false, is in that context irrelevant; in either case, they cannot be used as a justification for action. At the beginning of the play, Hamlet was seen to be in a state of confusion about human emotions; here he is trying to dispel their effects altogether, by exposing them as unreliable incentives to action in general, whether the goals they serve are real or fictitious.

When an interpretation of Hamlet's character goes beyond the manifest content of the tragedy, the question is sometimes raised as to why Shakespeare did not have Hamlet verbalize the point at issue. Freud's interpretation (1900, pp. 264-266) has, in addition to many other merits, the great advantage of referring to Hamlet's childhood conflict, which he *cannot* verbalize. Since his erotic childhood impulses for his mother and his childhood desire to see his father absent are repressed, they cannot find their way to his conscious mind. This constellation in the repressed, however, does not rule out a multiplicity of ego problems that depend on factors extraneous to the one that is repressed.

After all, the Hamlet we see at the end of the tragedy is not the same person he was at the beginning. We may well ask in what way and why he developed, so that in the end he was able to perform the task. It is often asserted that, since he had only a short while to live, it was the nearness of death that compelled him to accomplish what he had set out to do. This, however, would mean that the final accomplishment depended on accidental events (see Spengler, 1918, Vol. I., p. 143). According to my thesis, at the end of the play Hamlet has acquired the ability to mold an impulse into an action without surrendering to an external command, so that he would have taken revenge even if the poisoning by Laertes had not taken place.

Still, if Hamlet's problem at the stage of the Hecuba monologue is that of searching for a reliable motivation, and if he is now rejecting emotions as acceptable motives, why is all this not stated explicitly? Why does Hamlet instead put the actor and his emotions in a place superior to his own? This question has to do with a ticklish problem of ego psychology. It is clear—one almost feels inclined to say it is self-evident—why the repressed must remain unconscious and cannot be verbalized. It is not as clear why the ego has to remain so profoundly ignorant of itself.

The fact is that those parts of the ego that border on the repressed cannot come into consciousness without thereby endangering their efficacy, for awareness of the defense mechanisms may serve to bring the ego dangerously close to awareness of those contents against which the defenses are directed. It is the automatic activity of the defense, unimpeded by the meddling of the conscious ego, that guarantees its primary goal—namely, to keep offensive contents away from the conscious mind. Is Hamlet's repudiation of emotions such a defense, of which the ego must not become conscious, for the sake of safety? I believe that, to a certain extent, this is so. The question is whether the aspect of defense is a sufficient explanation of why the whole problem remains unconscious, and this may become clearer once we know against what the defense is directed in this soliloquy.

In our study of the development of Hamlet's distrust of the reliability of emotions, we must remember that this distrust was already present before the Hecuba soliloquy, in the form of doubt about the reliability of others' emotions. The problem with which he wrestled in the first soliloquy was "How is it possible that a woman like my mother—who loved my father affectionately and wept so heartbrokenly at his death—could marry an unworthy person at all and, what is more, so quickly?" He found a tentative explanation in the ghost's message—a fantasy of Hamlet's, if we examine it psychologically—the answer that this message suggested being: "Mother never loved father. Her affection was feigned: She must already have loved her second husband while his predecessor, my father, was still alive."

His mother's behavior, according to what is verbalized in the tragedy, is the primary root of Hamlet's distrust of emotionality, which is then extended from there to his own emotions. From the psychoanalytic point of view, one must draw the conclusion that, in the Hecuba soliloquy, Hamlet performs a full identification with his mother in this respect. The terms he uses for himself actually imply homosexuality: he calls himself a whore, a drab, a male prostitute ("stallion") (See *Hamlet,* Cambridge edition, notes to 591, p. 188). Yet this identification with the mother is so offensive to him that it is impossible for him to verbalize his basic conflict directly. The belief that feelings are not sufficient per se as motivating forces is riveted to his accusation that his own strong feelings are as unreliable as those of his mother, who, had she sincerely loved his father, would have died like Niobe. The apparent admiration for the actor's skill at play-acting therefore implies derision of the mother: "Your weeping is like mother's: you weep for Hecuba—for nothing; she too wept—and that too was a lie."

Hamlet rightly doubts whether it is really cowardice that prevents him from taking action, for cowardice could, after all, be overcome by willpower. He quite correctly describes his difficulty as that of being in a state in which he is "unpregnant of his cause." Yet it should not be overlooked that it is during the course of the soliloquy in which feelings are identified as unreliable incentives that he forms the plan to test his adversary's conscience. It is interesting indeed to note that it is this particular soliloquy that leads to action: his devaluation of feelings per se was what seemed to liberate some strivings in him for an active role. It is as if Hamlet came to believe that, even if he was no better than his mother, he could nevertheless proceed to act: since emotions in general are unreliable, he is permitted to disregard his own emotional state and pass on to action.

Significantly, he is here following a mechanism that we observed previously in the cellarage scene. Having been shaken himself by the player's recital, he now devises a plan in which he will shake his antagonist by a theatrical performance.[89] Since he had been trapped by his own emotions, he will now undertake to lead his enemy into misfortune by entangling *him* in an emotional conflict. Once again he will do to someone else what has been done to him.

He has also succeeded in putting a certain distance between himself and his father by entertaining for the first time the possibility that the Ghost's message may have been false. Analytically, this would constitute a doubt with regard to his own fantasy—which would be in fact the logical consequence after a general devaluation of emotions.

The fourth soliloquy, beginning "To be, or not to be," *(III.1.56)* follows closely after the recital of Hecuba's story. Wilson, like Trench, believes that in this soliloquy Hamlet returns to the position he had held before the ghost apprised him of what had happened. In Loening's view the soliloquy has no connection with Hamlet's chief task of revenge, but is rather a theoretical deliberation, meant to be valid for man in general.[90] I do not agree with these views but would rather regard this soliloquy as the psychological continuation of the Hecuba monologue.

If emotion is an unreliable guide, and if an action should not be undertaken for the sake of emotional gratification, then what is it, Hamlet seems to ask, that does make man act? Death is sleep; therefore, according to the pleasure principle, man ought to seek sleep, especially in view of the unbearable burden of reality. But the fact is that he does *not*

---

[89] This mechanism can be seen again in Hamlet's arranging the death of Rosencrantz and Guildenstern, after he has discovered that they had been assigned the task of doing that to him. [The tendency in Hamlet to identify with what has been just perceived or experienced is indicated early by Shakespeare in an eminently subtle way. As soon as the Ghost has left and Hamlet has discharged at least a portion of his excitement by some general exclamations ("Oh all you host of Heaven, etc.") he continues: "And you, my sinews, grow not instant old, But bear me stiffly up." He has just faced an old and deceased father and apparently has sensations that would be more suitable to his father than to him, a young man. The fact that he feels suddenly close to a state of muscular collapse may be interpreted as the effect of a short-lasting identification with the father's corpse, of which the Ghost has reminded him.]

[90] Loening (1893, p. 164) tries to prove his hypothesis by referring to the First Quarto, in which this soliloquy is spoken by Hamlet at his first appearance in the second act.

seek eternal sleep. He prefers certainty, painful as it may be, to uncertainty and the fear of a pain of unknown kind and intensity. This train of thought alone reflects the development that Hamlet has made since the first soliloquy, where the religious prohibition (now not mentioned at all) was held to be the principal factor militating against suicide.

Hamlet has discovered, significantly enough, an emotion that functions as an efficient barrier against suicide, and he uses this discovery for a magnificent attack against morality in general. Man's action is now seen as not based on his strivings towards an ideal. No ethical principle is at the bottom of history; one finds there only man's fear, or, as we might say today, his instinct of self-preservation. Take away fear, and the history of the human species would soon be at an end, because man would no longer be able to resist his longing for sleep. Yet this fear, while it ties man to life, also prevents him at times from being willing to take risks when he *ought* to act.

These thoughts are usually interpreted as a manifestation of Hamlet's deep pessimism. Yet one should not forget that it is after this soliloquy that his behavior becomes audacious, at times even reckless. He breaks with Ophelia, he insults Claudius in front of the court, he kills Polonius. He even seems at times to approach hyperactivity (see Sharpe, 1929, p. 203), no traces of which are to be seen in the earlier part of the tragedy.[91]

Hamlet has often been called a philosopher; but if he did indeed have any pretensions to being one, many a flaw could be discovered in the philosophy he gives voice to in the play. He might perhaps have become a philosopher later on—had death spared him. In the phase of his development that one observes in the tragedy, there is nothing of the philosopher to be found, unless we are to give the name of "philosophy" to any endeavor toward orientation in the world. Hamlet is a man who is struggling intensely with life. He is a sharp observer of others and of himself, and he is not ready to waste his energy in sporadic outbursts, as Laertes is, although he is capable of immediate action if it fits into an overall scheme. Yet he is too sensitive a man and too self-observant to take existing goals for granted.

It is all too easy to read some of his soliloquies as if they were the disputations of a philosopher, for the general tone in which his thoughts are couched seems to suggest such an approach. To my mind, however,

[91] For the heedlessness one may discover in his following the Ghost, see later.

all that Hamlet speaks and does has direct reference to him not as a philosopher but as a human being in conflict.[92]

Hamlet has now discovered the fear of death to be the obstacle to taking action. According to Freud, it is castration anxiety that is at the bottom of the fear of death, and it is significant that the problem of castration anxiety appears at this point. Inasmuch as Hamlet is grappling in this soliloquy with his fear of his father, one may say that he has made a significant step forward. "Th' oppressor's wrong, the proud man's contumely. . . . The insolence of office," in the tragic world of the grown-ups, correspond to the humiliation and injustice that the little boy finds himself suffering because of his strong father's authority. The great role that castration fear plays in that relationship is too well known to need elaboration here. The point of interest is that it is his own admission of the prevalence of fear that apparently enables Hamlet to overcome that very fear.

The whole structure of the soliloquy is reminiscent of the Hecuba soliloquy. There, under the pretense of extolling strong emotions, Hamlet has shown that he has reached the point of being able to dispense with them; here, he seems to accept fear as the exclusive regulator of action, yet it is because of this discovery that he is now able to take the first step toward overcoming his own fear.[93]

The action that follows the soliloquy must now be considered; it reaches its first climax in the final break with Ophelia. Wilson (1936a, p. 129f) has contributed greatly to our understanding of this scene, in the context of the tragedy, by proving that most of what Hamlet tells Ophelia is meant for the ears of eavesdroppers, of whose presence Hamlet has soon come to know. Important as this may be in terms of textual understanding, it nevertheless seems evident that, under the guise of using a ruse, Hamlet is expressing what he actually does believe to be necessary.[94]

[92] As Flatter says (1949, p. 156), "But conflict there must be. Nothing is permitted to exist on the stage . . . that does not owe its existence to emotions, tendencies, politics, clashing with each other. Conflict is the life of drama. . . ." I think it is wrong to view such an important soliloquy as a kind of philosophical manifesto rather than as a focus in which a number of conflicting psychic tendencies come together.

[93] [The meaning of this soliloquy will be taken up later more extensively.]

[94] [On further consideration, I have reached the conclusion that Hamlet's discourse with Ophelia becomes even more significant when it is assumed that Hamlet is unaware of the eavesdroppers. (See later.) (1967)]

There has been much speculation about Hamlet's relationship to Ophelia. Most writers have emphasized the fact that Ophelia's desertion of Hamlet at her father's behest has given her lover just cause to be dejected and angry with her. Notwithstanding the validity of this view, it does not do full justice either to the depth of the tragedy or to Hamlet's character. He is man enough, and passionate, too, to parry Polonius's intrigues. His decision to break with Ophelia therefore derives from reasons that lie, not outside of but within himself.

It is based partly on the archaic belief that women tend to have a weakening influence upon men. One may mention in passing the taboo in many primitive tribes against intercourse by warriors for a certain length of time before they go into battle, and the necessity for many men during the Middle Ages to spend their lives in celibacy, in order not to be disturbed in their contemplations and meditations. Hamlet is at this point the hero who is preparing himself for a great deed and must therefore separate himself from what he loves. (That he loves Ophelia, I do not doubt, although it is also evident that his feelings about her are ambivalent.)

In order to understand his discourse with Ophelia, one must consider the misogyny that pervades the tragedy to a rather frightening degree. It cannot be a coincidence that the only two principal personages who survive in the end—Horatio and Fortinbras[95]—never address a woman during the play. By means of this technique, Shakespeare seems to have expressed indirectly the belief that contact with a woman must necessarily lead to man's weakening or destruction. The primary root of this supreme misogyny lies in castration fear, and it is impressive how, by an incredibly skillful technique, an emotional climate is created that conveys a feeling about women such as could not have been easily reproduced by direct verbalization.

Wilson was the first interpreter, I think, to point out that the famous line, "Get thee to a nunnery," which Hamlet hurls at Ophelia immediately after this monologue, has a double meaning, inasmuch as "nunnery" was a common expression in Shakespeare's times for a brothel. This is an important suggestion, in that it provides a clue to an understanding of Hamlet's attitude toward women: they are acceptable only as

---

[95] There may be a slight doubt regarding Horatio in *IV.5.14.* It was of interest to me to notice that E. K. Chambers does not hesitate to call the Horatio-Queen scene in Quarto One un-Shakespearean, although he does not give any reason for the certainty of his opinion. (See Chambers (1930), Vol. 1, pp. 417, 419.)

saints or as prostitutes. Either way, a personal tie is avoided: the female is kept away from the strictly personal world of the man, who thus preserves his freedom of action. (However, it must be added that thereby the way is also kept open for regression to the mother.)

When Hamlet, at the beginning of this fourth soliloquy, sets forth the alternative ways of coping with the world—either to suffer or to rebel (by contrast with the first soliloquy, where silence is envisaged as the *only* way)—he puts into words a problem that plays an enormous role in modern mental science, although it has not yet found adequate treatment. Hamlet himself seems in the end to come closer to accepting rebellion—that is, action—as the valid and correct way. Again, this is not directly stated. What Hamlet has come to see is that it is reflection[96]—or, as I should interpret it, self-observation—that blocks free access to the motor system.

In that way, Hamlet devaluates his anxieties. It is as if he were to say: "It is not the fear of danger but only my incessant self-reflection that makes me fearful." In so doing, he has shifted the source of his anxiety from the outside into his own person—which is to some extent correct, inasmuch as the castration anxieties of the adult (even though they have originated in fears of reality; see S. Freud [1926a]) become integrated and therefore more and more divorced from external realities. By ferreting out the true source of anxiety, Hamlet has come one step closer to finding a way toward taking the action that he is committed to take.

It is understandable, therefore, that in the fifth soliloquy *(III.3.72)* we encounter Hamlet in an entirely different mood. On his way to his mother's closet, he is arrested by the sight of the praying king and the impulse seizes him to thrust his sword through his adversary. Yet Hamlet does not use the opportunity to do so, and his failure to kill Claudius then is frequently interpreted as a sign of renewed procrastination on his part.

Notwithstanding his indubitable delay in consummating his revenge, Hamlet is *almost* ready at this point to carry out the deed. As will be seen later, he has not yet achieved the internal development that is prerequisite to ego-syntonic action—if the action is to be the outgrowth of his own individual decision and not the consequence of an external

---

[96] See Glossary in the Cambridge edition of *Hamlet* (1948): "reflection" is equivalent to "conscience."

command.[97] Hamlet's expressed reason for his delay in taking revenge at this point is that Claudius is praying—a circumstance that would bring him forgiveness in heaven. That is when Hamlet decides to kill the king at a time when he is in a state of sin. Modern man all too readily overlooks the seriousness of this argument, for what Hamlet has contemplated is actually the worst revenge that a Christian can take. As Samuel Johnson rightly says, from the standpoint of Christian moral theology Hamlet's speech is too horrible either to read or to utter.[98]

Whatever the rationalization that Hamlet may still put forward for delay, his inner readiness and his capacity to carry out the necessary action have clearly grown immensely. A new element has appeared, one that Wilson chooses to attribute to Hamlet's character in general but which is actually, I believe, the result of the development that has taken place in Hamlet during the course of the play itself. Wilson speaks of Hamlet's "malicious delight in hoodwinking, fooling and tripping up his enemies" and further of the fact that "his love of such employment accounts in part for his delay in killing the king. He wants to play with him as a cat plays with a mouse."[99] What we are concerned with here is Hamlet's sadistic pleasure in torturing his prospective victim, whom he seems to take a devilish delight in lulling into security just before the "kill." This moment of enjoying the revenge is an additional sign of his having appersonated the entire action. In the Hamlet whom we met at the beginning of the play, such a feeling would scarcely have made any sense at all, even after the fateful command by the Ghost.

Furthermore, a sneak attack, one that did not bring the victor face to face with the enemy, would deprive the former of an important narcissistic gratification. Whereas, at the beginning of the play, the killing of the king was a necessity only in the sense of its satisfying a superego command, it has grown more and more into a task that the ego now poses for itself, or rather into a desire that the ego itself now craves to

---

[97] [Although Hamlet appears to be ready to carry out the deed, the residue of dependence in him on the external command is subtly disclosed by the fact that Hamlet still measures Claudius' punishment in terms of his father's sufferings. (1968)]

[98] Quoted after *Variorum Edition*, 1877, Vol. I, p. 283.

[99] Wilson, 1936a, p. 176; cf. also Montaigne, in the essay "Cowardice, the Mother of Cruelty": "Just vengeance is to be pitied when its object loses the means of feeling it. For, as the avenger wants to be aware of it, in order to derive pleasure from it, the one on whom he takes revenge must be aware of it, also in order to suffer pain and repentance. . . And we do him the greatest favor of life, which is to make him die suddenly and insensibly. . . . If we thought that by valor we would always be masters of our enemy and triumph over him at our pleasure, we would be very sorry for him to escape us, as he does by dying" (1580, p. 524f.).

have fulfilled, quite independently of any sanction, either from (internal) conscience or from (external) authority. In this soliloquy, therefore, the full sadistic impulse breaks through: the "native hue of resolution" has been restored and "the pale cast of thought" has vanished. Hamlet is full of rage and malice, determined not to lose one ounce of the pleasure that can be derived from gratification of the desire for revenge. Now that doubt about his own emotions is gone, the consummation of revenge has become feasible, inasmuch as the passionate desire for it has taken hold of him.

In the sixth and final soliloquy *(IV.4.32),* we witness the dissolution of the last barrier that has until then prevented Hamlet from integrating his task. This soliloquy takes place in the midst of a military expedition by Fortinbras, Prince of Norway, against Poland. The bone of contention between these two countries, as Hamlet is informed by a captain of Fortinbras' army, is a patch of land without value. When he is speaking to the captain, Hamlet characterizes such action as the product of degenerative disease; when he is left to himself, however, Hamlet expresses ideas that are the opposite of those he has just conveyed to the captain. Under the impact of another's willingness to go to death for a trifle, Hamlet's immediate outcry is: "Now all occasions do inform against me,/And spur my dull revenge!" At first glance this may seem like a return to the very point of development at which Hamlet stood on the occasion of the Hecuba monologue. Such a conclusion would be valid, however, only with regard to the structure of his complaint, not with regard to its content. The center of the problem has shifted quite significantly— from the authenticity of emotions to the worthwhileness and actuality of goals.

Hamlet has now raised the question of what sense there is to action in the universe. After the last (fifth) soliloquy we left Hamlet in a state in which at least one thing was clear: that he was at last able to perform the deed of revenge—provided he did so under the impact of an acute, intense, passionate breakthrough. Rightly he now raises the question of what it is that makes the difference between man and beast. The latter, he answers himself, is compelled by its nature to do nothing but gratify physical urges, as he has just observed in those thousands of soldiers who are readily marching toward their graves. Here Hamlet is groping for an intellectual frame of reference into which he can fit the deed that he is now ready to perform.

In achieving this clarification, Hamlet employs a mechanism that is reminiscent of the one we encounter in the Hecuba soliloquy but which is now set forth without ambiguity. This mechanism is expressed in the following seeming contradiction: when he is informed by the captain of the purpose of his expedition, he condemns such military actions in very strong terms; yet later, in his soliloquy, he approves of them. To be sure, he has often feigned agreement, as with Polonius or with Rosencrantz and Guildenstern, but in those cases his pretense was adopted for reasons of planned intrigue and purposeful concealment. No such motive is evident in his discourse with the captain, and moreover, the captain's disapproval of the military action is not brought forward strongly but rather lies between the lines. I can only conclude that, in his own disapproval, Hamlet was expressing his true feelings about the matter.

If we now turn to the extravagant glorification of honor, a peculiar ambivalence is to be noted in Hamlet's words. The viewpoint that Hamlet propounds is actually couched in such terms as to persuade the listener *against* honor rather than to win him to favor it. While he seems to be granting full honors to the concept of honor, Hamlet actually does so in such a way as to succeed in belittling it. "A fantasy and trick of fame" cannot possibly justify the killing of so many soldiers that they could not all be buried in the piece of land for which they had fought. Such a justification will not elicit agreement even from someone who already believes honor to be one of the highest values. Thus, in his very seeming to agree, Hamlet is seriously calling into question the validity of what is under discussion.

A complicated mechanism is to be observed in action here. While it is related to the mechanism described by Freud in his essay on Negation (1925, pp. 235-239), it is in some respects the opposite of negation. What negation does is to make the ego partly independent of repression, in that, in its negative form, a repressed content can find access to it. While repression obtains its due, insofar as the content is not acknowledged as existent, the act of negation still allows the ego to take hold of it—at least in its negated form. In Hamlet's soliloquy a judgment is seemingly accepted as valid, yet both the context and the way in which it is brought forward make it clear that the statement is actually being negated. Such a mechanism does not lead to a repression but rather to a dismissal or repudiation *(Verwerfung)* of the content: the judgment that has been seemingly accepted simply loses its power over the ego. A similar process can be observed in psychoanalysis when a repressed thought returns to consciousness and is accepted as valid; from that moment on, it often loses its power. Repression has here become replaced, not by negation but by dismissal.

The unconscious meaning of the Fortinbras soliloquy can be understood only in terms of the place that the whole Fortinbras story holds in the tragedy. It is sufficient here to recall that Hamlet's father was a man of pride who fought a duel the night his son was born. The encounter with Fortinbras's army is thus linked to Hamlet's father, who represented the ideology to which Hamlet is here paying such extravagant (and false) homage. Thus his dismissal of the point of honor by way of seeming acceptance is a reflection of his repudiation of his father: Hamlet has at last freed himself from the tutelage of his father.[100]

In dealing with this mechanism one is reminded of apophasis, a literary device that was used by Shakespeare quite successfully in the speech by Antony following Caesar's death. In apophasis the speaker insinuates the very thing that he denies he is saying. This is a working tool of the conscious ego, just as negation is. It is not certain which serves the ego better, repression or negation; it may be that the answer depends on a quantitative factor. Apophasis is not, however, a mechanism that belongs among the tools that the ego uses in coming to terms with the repressed. It comes into play only when an ego-syntonic tendency has to find expression in the face of some opposition. In Antony's funeral speech this opposition is an external one; the ego circumvents this barrier and finally removes it altogether, by professing agreement and at the same time insinuating belief in the opposite of what it appears to agree with.

The opposition need not be based, however, on external reality; it may stem instead from an internal force, such as the superego. Particularly when the superego is not fully integrated but is still represented in part by external objects, the ego may achieve the goal of taking those parts of the superego that continue to be represented by external equivalents and discrediting them through exaggerated submission, as well as by subsequently showing up the superego demands as absurd—which is exactly what Hamlet does in this monologue.

The ego-syntonic striving in Hamlet is his desire to free himself from his father as a representative of the superego and to evolve in himself a fully integrated superego—that is to say, one that is independent of

---

[100] Flatter (1949, pp. 102-107 and Appendix F) tries to prove that the Fortinbras soliloquy has no logical place in the action and offers that as the reason why it was omitted from the Folio text. He thinks that it was included in the Quarto by mistake. To my way of thinking, however, it is the logical and necessary prelude to the graveyard scene.

his relationship to his father, as a love object or an ideal. Concomitantly with such a step, the last remnants of the Oedipus complex are dissolved, and the deed against Claudius can be carried out as the consequence of Hamlet's freely choosing to do so.[101]

The process of freeing oneself internally is difficult when agreement already exists between subject and external authority, as in the case of the necessity of wreaking revenge upon Claudius. When he is talking to the captain, therefore, Hamlet expresses for a brief moment his true feelings. What he says then implies, in my opinion, an indirect criticism of his father's behavior toward the old Fortinbras, a behavior that was dictated by honor. After this brief, open frank criticism of his father, the rebellion is buried and it would seem that the father is reinstated into his position of authority.

The fact is, however, that the father's ideology is then pushed to its ultimate limits, at which point it reaches absurdity and can be dismissed without further effort. The ego thus maintains the rightfulness of obedience to the father of the childhood period, but without thereby accepting the obligation of obeying him any longer. Hamlet has thus accomplished the objective of freeing himself from his father, and with an immense saving of guilt feelings.

In this particular instance, I can lend some weight to my interpretation by referring to a detail in the life of Shakespeare himself—namely, his relationship to Montaigne, which has been the subject of literary research.[102]

Interestingly enough, some early writers, such as Stedefeld and Feis, regarded the core of the tragedy of Hamlet as a kind of anti-Montaigne manifesto. Modern research does not follow that course, but instead believes that Shakespeare remained greatly under Montaigne's positive influence.[103] The parallels in the writings of the two are really astounding, particularly at times in *Hamlet*. One can easily imagine how much Shakespeare must have been struck by the *Essays*, which have not failed to affect deeply each generation since their first appearance, and one may be reminded in this connection of Schiller's relationship to

---

[101] Hamlet has by now become capable of disagreeing with his father, as has already been noted with regard to his refusal to carry out the second part of his father's command. The closet scene was therefore a successful partial rebellion against the father.

[102] See Stedefeld (1871), Feis (1884), Robertson (1897), Taylor (1925), Türck (1930). Cf. also the two short remarks of Wilhelm Dilthey (1887, Vol. VI, pp. 128, 212).

[103] [This point has been made the very center of Rothe's (1961 passim) comment on the profound changes that Shakespeare's plays show in his second period of creativity, starting with *Hamlet*.]

Kant. Great art has often found inspiration in a great philosopher.

Be that as it may, it is difficult for anyone who is familiar with modern research to see how earlier scholars evolved their theory that *Hamlet* was a polemic against Montaigne. The fact that *Hamlet* can be interpreted in two contradictory ways, with regard to even its plainly expressed ideology, strengthens my belief in the amphibole that is I think, carried consistently throughout the play. Perhaps what Feis sensed in *Hamlet* may have been Shakespeare's desire to lift himself beyond Montaigne. After all, a man may be convinced of the correctness of someone else's opinion and nevertheless grope for a truth that will go beyond it. May Shakespeare perhaps have had a conflict about Montaigne, comparable to that of Hamlet about his father?[104]

Since *Hamlet* in particular, among all Shakespeare's plays, contains so many parallels with the *Essays*, it is all the more astonishing to find in the Fortinbras soliloquy a pointed deviation from one of Montaigne's basic views. Montaigne strongly opposed war, and in the *Apology for Raimond Sebond*, during the course of analyzing the differences between man and animal, he writes:

> As for war, which is the greatest and most pompous of human actions, I should be glad to know whether we want to use it as an argument for some preeminence, or, on the contrary, as testimony of our imbecility and imperfection; as indeed the science of undoing and killing one another, of ruining and destroying our own species, seems to have little to make it alluring to the beasts who do not have it. . . .
>
> For those warlike movements that ravish us with their horror and terror, this tempest of sounds and shouts . . . this frightful array of so many thousands of armed men, so much fury, ardor, and courage—it is comical to consider by what inane causes it is stirred up and by what trivial causes extinguished. . . .
>
> All Asia was ruined and consumed in wars for Paris' lechery. . . .
>
> The souls of emperors and cobblers are cast in the same mould. Considering the importance of the actions of princes and their weightiness, we persuade ourselves that they are produced by some causes equally weighty and important. We are wrong: they are led to and fro in their movements by the same springs as we are in ours. The same reason that makes us bicker with a neighbor creates a war between princes . . . like appetites move a mite and an elephant [Montaigne, 1580, pp. 347f, 350.] [105]

[104] It is idle perhaps to raise such questions, in view of our ignorance of any of the particulars of Shakespeare's life, yet it is difficult to resist the temptation to make a guess of that sort.

[105] [Since the mechanism I have postulated to be at work in the Fortinbras soliloquy may appear far-fetched, I was happy to discover that, according to Theodore Spencer, precisely the same mechanism underlay Montaigne's *Essays*, from which I have just quoted. Montaigne had translated Raimond Sebond's (d. 1437) *Natural Theology* from bad Latin into French at the request of his father, who greatly admired the book. The translation was therefore "an act of filial piety" and not the

And in his essay "Of Diversion," in which he deals with the question of why men participate with fury in battle, Montaigne reaches this conclusion: "Why a cause? None is needed to stir our souls; any idle fancy, without body or object, will rule and stir them" (Montaigne, 1580, p. 732).

Thus, if one takes the Fortinbras soliloquy literally, one encounters a significant deviation from Montaigne's philosophy. It strikes me as meaningful to find such a deviation in just that monologue, since from the psychological viewpoint, the latter can be regarded as being a negation by means of exaggerated affirmation; the net outcome would thus be an expression of agreement with Montaigne also on the subject of war.[106]

The effect of the step taken by Hamlet in the Fortinbras soliloquy is comparable to the effect of the step he takes in the Hecuba soliloquy. There Hamlet overcame his doubts regarding his emotions; here he vanquishes his uncertainties regarding the intellectual frame of reference of action. When we meet him again in the graveyard scene, he is at a peak of freely moving contemplation, quite reminiscent of the spirit that pervades Montaigne's *Essays*. Worldly power and worldly accomplishment are here recognized as transitory and evanescent: what remains of Alexander is the stopper of a bunghole. The ego may cringe in pain and feel nauseated ("My gorge rises at it") by the sight of the senselessness of life; yet it is strong enough to bear the impact of reality without resorting to new illusions.

Many a society has made death the central issue of its civilization, but never, I believe, has that been done without the offer of some hope or compensation. Shakespeare himself stood at a threshold. Behind him lay the medieval period, with its addiction to death and its fear of hell and

---

result of Montaigne's interest. Sebond's book was of late scholastic vintage. "Montaigne's pretended defense of it smashes the whole structure to pieces. Stimulated by his recent reading of skeptical philosophy, and irritated, perhaps, by the boredom of translating the naïve and monotonous ideas of Sebond, he proceeds to demolish Sebond by launching an elaborate attack on the arrogance and vanity of man" (Spencer, 1942, p. 34). "Smashing by pretended defense" —what could better express my own interpretation of Hamlet's final soliloquy? If my hunch is correct, we may discover a truly remarkable coincidence (so far not noticed)—namely, that Shakespeare had Hamlet carry out the last step in his freeing himself from his father in the same way as a similar freeing had been accomplished by the philosopher whom he evidently greatly admired, when the latter had to deal with his own father's beliefs, which the philosopher did not dare to refute openly. The fact that Montaigne's *Apology* proved that man is by no means superior to the beast, while in the soliloquy, Hamlet stresses man's superiority, may warrant further speculation (1968).]

[106] My interpretation of the Fortinbras soliloquy was made prior to my reading the two essays by Montaigne that I have quoted here. I now feel surer of the correctness of my interpretation than I should otherwise have been.

craving for heaven; ahead of him rose a new era, which was to lose its belief in the immortality of the soul, only to replace it with an equally unverifiable belief in the endless progress and the omnipotence of man.

The graveyard scene is a reflection of the brief moment between these two eras. Death is perceived in all its finality, as the end of all ends, and man is perceived as being no more than a senseless particle, once he is separated from his illusions. How much he would like to believe in chivalry and art, in honor and poetry, in the beauty or the excitement and commotion with which he fills his busy days! But no, the ego elevates itself beyond all that; no longer is frailty's name woman, it is Man.

The riddle propounded by the ancient Sphinx had to do with man's life: man himself was its central issue. Whoever proved to be able to solve the riddle could then return to the fountainhead of life, to have intercourse with his mother. In *Hamlet,* the Sphinx reappears in the form of the gravedigger, whose riddle is: "What is he that builds stronger than either the mason, the shipwright, or the carpenter?" His friend, being optimistic, believes that it is the gallowsmaker. If it were the gallowsmaker, man's illusion would be no illusion but rather truth; the great hope of man's redemption, brought about by the continuous pacification of his destructiveness, would at some time in the future make this world a haven, for a world without gallows is not at all unthinkable. The sphinx of the sixteenth century knew better, however, and Hamlet does solve the riddle. He knows that it is death that is the meaning of life, not man, and that there is no life after death; he too is given Oedipus's reward, after he has solved the gravedigger's riddle—the reward of incest.

In both riddles—that of the ancient Sphinx and that of the gravedigger—there is hidden a reference to the powerlessness of the father: in the former, it is in the theme of man's being subject to aging; in the latter, it is in the idea of death's being the ultimate force. Thus, in order to be able to solve either riddle, one has to know that the father is not omnipotent but instead liable to weakening by old age and finally by death. One interpretation is therefore valid for both riddles: it is that the man who has made the discovery that the omnipotent father of childhood will (or has) become infirm, will rally enough courage therefrom to be able to carry out his incestuous desire.

By the time of the graveyard scene, Hamlet is free both of his fear of death and of his fear of incest. He has reached a stage that lies beyond the question of action or inaction, since neither of these is any longer decisive: if there is an opportunity to act, then he will most certainly act; if there is none, then he will not.

The Western world had changed much in the two thousand years since Sophocles. Whereas Oedipus was permitted to perform actual incest, Hamlet's incestuous consummation takes the form of the dying-together.[107] One may object that, since Claudius and Laertes also die at the same time, I am in error in assigning this meaning to the death of Gertrude and Hamlet. One could, of course, take the content of the tragedy literally, as we so often do, and in that light regard Hamlet's acceptance of the challenge of the fencing match as a disguised suicide (Flatter, 1949, p. 117), his mother's death as the consequence of his clumsiness (Trench, 1913, p. 230), and the final consummation of his revenge as having been made possible only by his knowledge that he has been fatally wounded. One could similarly interpret the graveyard scene as the outcome of Hamlet's extreme pessimism and of his fear of death, to which, driven by anxiety, he has finally surrendered. The poet has stacked the frame so wide that many pictures can find their place in it. But I think that my interpretation also belongs in the picture, because I believe that it comes close to the area in which we are so deeply affected when we read or see *Hamlet.*

Claudius's death means something entirely different to us, once we compare it with that of Laertes; Hamlet's death is meaningful to us in a way that is different from these two, as well as being different from Gertrude's. Taken literally, all four were subject to the same biological process of dying; if death means no more than that to us, then Hamlet was a blundering amateur, inferior to any modern gangster. Yet the psychology behind an individual's death varies as much as that of the individual himself. In one instance death may be the revenger, in another the redeemer; then again, it may constitute either accident or defeat (See Sharpe, 1946, p. 246).

The fact that the queen turns towards Hamlet with all her maternal affection and that she drinks the cup that was intended for him is sufficient to convey, by means of outward signs, the close connection between her death and that of Hamlet. Moreover, there is an undeniable similarity between the ways in which Hamlet and his father die: both deaths are arranged by Claudius; in both, treachery, perfidy and poison are at work; in both, a younger brother is the instrument of the misdeed. In the

---

[107] What Romeo and Juliet were denied, Hamlet obtains. Friar Laurence's "greater power than we can contradict" which "hath thwarted our intents," does not exist in *Hamlet.*

final scene, the queen behaves as (interpreting the action on the symbolic level) she should have behaved when Hamlet's father was in danger. Thus in his death Hamlet triumphs over his father and is united with his mother.[108]

A psychological analysis of Hamlet's soliloquies was published by Arthur G. Davies in 1964. The work contains many profound observations, one of the best of which has seemed to me to be the remark that Hamlet thinks so much *because* he is prevented from acting ("He cannot act; therefore he thinks," p. 110), and not the other way around, as was assumed by Coleridge. Indeed, when he does act, there is little thinking, either before or after; if anything, one might wish he had spent more thought on preparing for the act and, once it has been performed, on its consequences.

Although Davies does have a fine feeling for the dynamics of ego psychology, and despite the fact that his deductions are based on the same basic assumptions as mine—namely, that Hamlet was neither prevented from carrying out his father's command by any external obstacles, nor did he himself ever doubt his obligation or the moral justification for killing Claudius—nevertheless he comes to quite different conclusions. He sees the crux of the matter as lying in Hamlet's shirking his duty (p. 73): "It was a difficult and painful duty to pursue. . . . This failure is consistent with his character, but not consistent with right and wrong. Whatever is consistent with his character is simply the logic of character portrayal. But what is not consistent with duty cannot be justified." And later (p. 97), Hamlet is described as being unfit for his "arena of life," by virtue of his innate goodness.

These concepts then lead to such statements as "Hamlet's idealism [lies] in the fact that he is more desirous of the rewards of idealism than its unpleasant duties" (p. 198)—an idea that, in my opinion, is untenable. Aside from the fact that Davies omits any explanation of Hamlet's weakness, I cannot imagine why a character of the sort he delineates would succeed in leaving such a deep impression on Western thinking, even if the author were correct in his assertion that Hamlet has an angelic character.

For me, as I have indicated in my examination of the sequence of the

[108] Flatter's interpretation (1949, pp. 128-29) comes close to mine in certain respects. Yet I think he overestimates Hamlet's concern over the queen's reputation. Hamlet had forgiven the queen a long time before that, and the tragedy moves at this point on a far deeper level than Flatter envisages. Still, the merits of his interpretation are unquestionable.

soliloquies, Hamlet introduces a new ethical dimension, a new ethical demand: Moral and ethical commands should not be fulfilled solely because of the respect one accords to their source, nor should tenets and principles be adhered to solely because of their objective correctness. The man who does the right thing because he was ordered to do it is less ethical than the one who has appersonated (see later on, for the full meaning of this term) the ethical demand, who has made it his own and who acts ethically because ethics has become part of himself, his personal conviction, and not dependent on what authorities have to say on these questions.

By way of this self-imposed demand, Hamlet makes his life infinitely *more* difficult; he does not act, as Davies seems to assume, in conformity with the pleasure principle, in the sense of his seeking to avoid displeasure.

In the analysis of the soliloquies, I have so far ignored an argument that speaks strongly in favor of this latter viewpoint. Hamlet has been characterized as naïve and unskilled; he has been described as being impractical in his seeking to test the veracity of the Ghost by organizing the Mouse-trap, since the test itself serves to intensify the difficulties inherent in his mission and even to endanger his life, by virtue of the fact that Claudius now knows that the secret of the murder is shared by his nephew. Yet, so long as no open warfare has been declared between Hamlet and Claudius, so long as Hamlet is plotting secretly against his uncle, waiting for the most suitable moment to stab him, he remains a hired assassin; he is still no more than his father's emissary, and in that regard shares the status of the character who is paid by Macbeth to kill Banquo.

Hamlet's growth into an ethically and morally independent person —that is to say, an *adult,* in terms of modern psychology and philosophy —calls for not only internal processes but also at least a minimum of external changes. One of these is the necessity of telling Claudius that in Hamlet he is face to face with the man who will restore to the state the order that has been disrupted by the King's crime. Although I do not believe that Hamlet is making use of a rationalization when he abstains from killing Claudius while the latter is praying, my belief is that his stated motive, terrible as it is, is not complete.

If he were to fulfill his mission by stabbing a defenseless victim in the back, he would, after all, be acting like any person who has to shun the open daylight, so as to conceal his actions. Such secrecy alone would be incompatible with ethical conduct, in the way in which Hamlet conceives it, for it is only when the emphasis is put on the Royal *command* that the circumstances under which the deed is performed become immaterial. If Old Hamlet had survived or if he were to come to life, it is hardly likely that he would take his revenge stealthily. Why then should stealth be the proper backdrop for his son's actions, unless the latter has been reduced to the position of a mere emissary, who has the obligation solely of seeing to it that the deed is carried out, no matter under what circumstances?

Although I myself have at certain points spoken of Hamlet's plight, as if it were universal and representative of the plight of mankind at large, I believe that, in the last analysis, the title that Davies chose—"Hamlet and the Eternal Problem of Man"—is inappropriate. To be sure, some of Hamlet's problems do deserve to be regarded as universal; but by and large, the tragedy could not have been understood by ancient or medieval man, neither of whom would have been able to empathize with the moral demand that makes an act of mere obedience to external demand a basically immoral one.

Further, my analysis is wrong if Rothe (1961) is right in his conception of *Hamlet*. Although his book introduces most refreshing viewpoints and does bring one aspect of Shakespeare's work close to our hearts, I think that, in the last analysis, Shakespeare would not have been that overpowering genius that Rothe consistently claims him to be, if Rothe's were the reasons for such a claim. According to him, Shakespeare wanted to produce, in *Hamlet,* nothing but a theatrical stunt *(Reisser)* (p. 287); the play was received as nothing else by his Elizabethan audience.

I would not be surprised to find that the latter were indeed true; but what has that to do with what the play meant to Shakespeare himself? The erroneous evaluations made by geniuses of their own creations are so well known that I can safely proceed without citing examples at this point. Even if it were proved that, in writing *Hamlet,* Shakespeare was interested solely in producing a great theatrical success, I still would not take this as proof that the play itself is no more than that.

Is it not more probable that at this point Shakespeare took the theatrical effect of his creations for granted, that he had acquired sufficient self-assurance with regard to his great gifts for the practical success or failure of one of his plays not to mean too much to him? Rothe quite rightly places the effect that Montaigne had upon Shakespeare at the center of the ideational backgound out of which *Hamlet* was born. But if it is true that *Hamlet* is the outcome of a new view of man, which must have lain dormant in Shakespeare until it was brought out explicitly by his acquaintance with Montaigne's philosophy, then Shakespeare must have embraced, at least preconsciously, visions that went far beyond anything that could be understood as aiming solely at the maximal theatrical effect.

In order to avoid misunderstanding, however, I want to emphasize that no one would be more astonished than I if it were ever to become established that Shakespeare consciously pursued a psychological development of the play's chief character, along the lines I have suggested in outline. This notion is so improbable that it does not even deserve consideration. Hamlet shows no signs of having been constructed, or even evolved intellectually. He breathes human life—so much that the end-result forces me to assume that Shakespeare saw *Hamlet* in a wholly visionary way.

It is quite possible that Shakespeare would have been unable to answer, had he been asked why Hamlet's soliloquies succeed each other in just the way they do, rather than in some other order. There must be some reason for the sequence, however, and by chance my guess may be the right one. I only want to add that the fact that my proposition may not—and very likely does not—coincide with Shakespeare's conscious intentions is not sufficient to determine either its correctness or its incorrectness.

According to Rothe (1961), the shape of *Hamlet,* as it has reached us (Second Quarto and Folio), is a compound of different phases through which Shakespeare's play had gone. The huge variety of interpretations is allegedly caused by the fact that the text does not contain Shakespeare's *final* version but rather, side by side, the entire host of conceptualizations he had formed. The ambiguity that to my mind is the epitome of Shakespeare's genius becomes, under Rothe's searching inquiry, the token of Shakespeare's defeat.

If the "final" version of *Hamlet* is indeed as Rothe represents it, my interpretation would undoubtedly be wrong. According to him, the play opened with the council chamber scene; "to be or not to be" occurred at a different place; Hamlet reached a full reconciliation with the Queen and therefore became incapable of carrying out vengeance upon his mother's lover (p. 283); and the problem in *Hamlet* then was "How shall I pass up [*versäumen*] taking vengeance for my father's murder?" (p. 282). Rothe possesses an intuitive mind and I am in no position to dispute his conclusions. But if he is right, I can only express my own personal satisfaction that Shakespeare's "final" version of *Hamlet* never reached us.

V

The last scene of the tragedy rests on deep layers of archaic symbolism; in it death, incest and rebirth form an identity.[109] The theme of rebirth is expressed through Fortinbras's sudden appearance; he is Hamlet reborn. No sooner has Hamlet died than he reappears as the hero, no longer divided by conflicts.[110] Fortinbras exemplifies also the man whose father was defeated when he was young, and who therefore did not have to struggle with stern paternal authority; even his uncle is sick and weak, and about his mother nothing is heard. He has been spared the effect of an oedipal conflict that, under extreme conditions, can be devastating; and he takes over, in effect, where Hamlet has left off.

One aspect of *Hamlet* is a presentation of those processes that, during the course of his development, occur in man's unconscious, as well as in his preconscious. If a man is to become an adult he must, in his unconscious, kill his father and accept incest.[111] The path is tortuous and painful. Hamlet succeeds in slaying the father and in reducing the good father to a memory of something that he has now outgrown; he loses his horror of incest and commits the oedipal crime, albeit symbolically. Psychologically, he has now reached something akin to the stage that Fortinbras had been given by circumstances. Thus the finale symbolizes at once death, incest and rebirth (See Slochower, 1950, pp. 200 and 228).

But Fortinbras has played still another role throughout the play. In the graveyard scene it is revealed that, on the day Hamlet was born, his father fought a duel that might easily have cost the infant his heritage, or part of it. The combat between the older Hamlet and the older Fortinbras is either a derivative of ambivalent fantasies that Hamlet has about his father, or an expression of the king's ambivalence toward Hamlet, or both. It is the earliest biographical information Hamlet possesses about himself; it is his earliest recollection, so to speak. It can be paraphrased thus: "The day I was born, my father gambled with my heritage and slew a man."

The aggressive character and the ambivalence of this recollection

---

[109] The identity of killing and incest has been mentioned above. (See also Geza Róheim, who offers parallels in many of his papers and books.)

[110] For a different interpretation of Fortinbras, see Sharpe (1946, p. 256f).

[111] The clinical validity of this statement will not be discussed here. It should be taken only as reflecting the tragedy's frame of reference.

are both evident. In the play, this recollection holds the place that, in the analyses of neuroses, is held by the recollection of primal scenes. I would suggest that it is the record of a distorted primal scene, and that in it conception and birth are fused. The father's ambivalence with regard to the mother, the paternal aggression against the mother, both of which are found in the primal scene—these are expressed in the father's desertion of the mother when she is in childbirth. The recollection of the primal scene is fantasied back to the time of conception and birth.[112]

The deepest roots of feelings of guilt are attached to this complex: "A crime was committed. Mother was made to suffer and I issued from this." In addition, traces of wish-fulfillment are discernible here, such as: "I was alone with my mother when I was born, undisturbed by father, who was a hero and fought in order to aggrandize my heritage." Nevertheless, one little boy had to be damaged in the combat, and seemingly it was young Fortinbras, who lost part of his heritage. Yet it is that same Fortinbras who reappears at the end of the play, having regained his birthright.

With incredible finesse Shakespeare set the Fortinbras story as a frame around the tragedy of Hamlet, placing it distinctly at the beginning and then again at the end of the play, letting it appear sporadically throughout the play, and finally riveting it firmly to the base of the entire story by revealing toward the end of the play that the combat between Fortinbras' father and Hamlet's father took place on the very night when Hamlet was born. The casualness with which this significant bit of information is conveyed is reminiscent of the casual way in which a patient may disgorge, toward the end of his analytic treatment, a most important infantile recollection, which suddenly focuses the scattered material upon one episode, showing thereby that what have until then seemed to be disconnected bits of recollections and fantasies are in fact derivatives of one event, whether that event be real or fantasied.[113] In short, Fortinbras' arrival at the moment of Hamlet's dying symbolizes the undoing of the damage of the primal scene.

[112] The slaying of the man, the staking of possessions and wealth, the mother's isolation with the child—all these insinuate a maze of mythical and folklore motives, as well as fantasies that are well known from the analysis of neurotics. Possession stands here for penis, and the primal scene is pictured as one in which someone is deprived of a penis, out of which a child is made; the mother protects the child against the father's aggression. Thus motives are referred to that are well known from the group of myths about the birth of the hero (See Rank, 1909).

[113] The last period of Freud's analysis of the Wolf-man may serve as a paradigmatic clinical example thereof (Freud, 1918).

In the foregoing discussion, I have tried to demonstrate that Hamlet's six soliloquies show the development of a man who, by stages, integrates a task that had been imposed on him from the outside.[114] In the final analysis, this is the task that, at least in the West, every man in his growth from childhood to manhood must face and accomplish. By shedding one illusion after another, by integrating the task that has been imposed upon him, Hamlet makes it possible for his individuality to grow; he attains a degree of independence far transcending what his father had originally demanded of him.[115]

My thesis is cognate with that of Türck (1890, p. 48). His analysis finds the center of the psychological problem to lie in Hamlet's transition from an optimistic outlook on life through pessimism to serenity. I should describe it rather as the development of one member of Western society—or at least of one member of its elite—from childhood through puberty to mature adulthood. In keeping with the external framework of the tragedy, the childhood and puberty phases of this process are not differentiated, yet the hero is presented as going through a developmental process that aims at working through the reaction to his father's death and freeing him from a strong erotic tie to his mother.[116] Türck's stress on the differences between Hamlet as he must have been prior to his father's death, the Hamlet whom we meet at the beginning of the tragedy, and the Hamlet he finally becomes toward the end of the play was an important contribution.[117]

Because of the ambiguities of meaning that prevailed at Shakespeare's particular historical moment—which allows for an interpretation of the word "adulterate" either as being a literal reference to unfaithfulness on the part of the queen, or as characterizing a forbidden second marriage, or finally as the expression of male sensitivity—the whole oedipal situation is kept in flux for the spectator or reader, who can interpret the most important events in the play in a variety of ways,

[114] Sharpe (1946, p. 258) writes: "Hamlet's soliloquies are a part of his defense against action: they belong to the period of procrastination and are finally replaced by action." I myself believe the soliloquies to be the landmarks of an extensive process of reorganizing the defensive apparatus and bringing it into the proper relationship with a changed internal milieu.

[115] This is why I disagree strongly with Moloney and Rockelein's interpretation. To believe that Hamlet is afraid of becoming king and averse to assuming responsibility is to miss the whole point of the tragedy. The authors could just as easily have reduced the entire Hamlet problem to his "laziness." (See Moloney and Rockelein, 1949.)

[116] [While this may sound contradictory to my earlier symbolic interpretation of Hamlet's consummation of incest, it is in keeping with psychoanalytic theory. (1968)]

[117] This differentiation is also found in Goethe's analysis in *Wilhelm Meister*.

or even as fantasy. This ambiguity made it possible for Shakespeare to present the most crucial unconscious processes in a realistic form, without being limited to the unambiguous exactness of a scientific psychology, or restricted by the limitations imposed by the nature of symbolic presentation. While the action that takes place on the stage is extremely realistic, it is nevertheless so loose and wide-framed that nearly all of man's major, typical unconscious fantasies can be projected onto it.[118]

To give one further example of this: It would not be going beyond the bounds of the play to surmise that the queen may have conspired with Claudius to murder Hamlet's father, after all, but to have done this in order to secure the throne for her beloved son; and that, having been frustrated by Claudius's own ambitions, in her efforts to achieve her goal she thereafter sided with Hamlet and showed an unmistakable coolness toward her second husband. As a matter of fact, one sometimes finds among the fantasies of children, upon the death of one parent, the notion that that death was brought about by the other parent for the sake of the child.

The multiplicity, and even more the paradoxical character, of the unconscious fantasies whose traces one discovers in *Hamlet* is one of the chief reasons for the appeal that this tragedy has had for nearly every type of personality and during nearly every historical period. It seems scarcely possible that there is anybody who cannot find some aspect of himself in *Hamlet*. One of the many questions of the psychology of art and of aesthetics that present knowledge is so far unprepared to answer is how Shakespeare was able to achieve the fusion of a multidimensional unconscious content with a stage plot and with actions that were, after all, ostensibly meant to have but one meaning—that is, with a stage content that is concisely constructed, and that never, aside from the appearance of the Ghost, goes outside the bounds of realism.

VI

One cannot become seriously concerned about the well-nigh fathomless content of *Hamlet*, however, without feeling tempted to speculate upon the meaning of the play-within-the-play, which holds the exact center of the tragedy. The subplay is, as is well known, introduced by a dumb show, a fact that remained the insoluble enigma for all Shake-

---

[118] Cf. Eliot (1919, p. 131f): "It would be hard to say in what the clarity and sharpness and simplicity of *Hamlet* consists."

speare interpreters until Wilson (1936a, pp. 143-153) and Flatter (1949, pp. 49-50).

The enigma lay in the fact that, while Claudius does not react to the direct presentation of the Ghost's story by pantomime in the prefatory dumb show, he is suddenly perturbed when Lucianus, the nephew in the subplay proper, pours poison into the king's ear. Wilson and Flatter both bring forth a reason for this that at least contributes to an explanation—namely, that Claudius does not actually see the dumb-show. Flatter believes that the dumb-show took place on the upper stage—a customary part of the Elizabethan theater—and was therefore not visible to Claudius.[119]

No doubts remain about the literal meaning of the subplay, however, when it is viewed within the context of the stage action. Hamlet's motive for staging the play is altogether evident: he wants to use Claudius' reaction as a test of the veracity of the Ghost's story.

Significantly, the plan to proceed in this way comes to him during the course of the Hecuba monologue,[120] in which, let us remember, the key idea is the validity of emotions, in relation to the external events with which they are linked.

If, however, the subplay is psychologically evaluated in itself, then one is impelled toward conclusions that may at first seem far-fetched. In a footnote (1949, p. 89, fn. 3) Jones compares the play-within-a-play to

---

[119] [The explanations suggested by Wilson and Flatter, which impressed me in 1953 as being ingenious, now seem to me to be considerably less telling than I had thought, after reading Grebanier's proposal of a far simpler and convincing course of events. According to Grebanier (1960, pp. 228-231), Claudius "starts" as soon as the dumb-show reaches the point of the poisoning, but masters his nervousness at that point, telling himself that "it is fantastic that I should allow myself to find a special meaning in the play." Only later under Hamlet's repeated attacks and innuendoes does he lose his nerve. Berry, in his sensitive and notable study *The Shakespeare Inset* (1965, p. 136) writes: "Poor Claudius is obliged to suffer the reenactment of his villainy twice—once without words and once with. He finds the play past enduring when for the second time he is made to witness poison being poured into ears—but that is *because* it is the second time" (author's italics). Berry finds in the dumb-show the equivalent of a slow-motion film by which Claudius is "softened up."

It is impressive how, in this instance, the application of a well-chosen commonsense psychology has solved a matter that seemed for a long time hopelessly entangled. If Claudius had asked for light as early as during the dumb-show, this would certainly not have reduced Hamlet's assurance of the King's guilt and vulnerability. If we assume that Hamlet staged the entire performance, he certainly planned it with great insight and cunning, in having the King exposed to a series of shocks that would make it impossible for him—in full view of the Court—to find a subterfuge in the assumption of a coincidence. (1968)]

[120] See Trench (1913, p. 125), however; he adduces strong arguments to prove that, contrary to the usual supposition in this regard, Hamlet did not decide upon the play until the very end of the Hecuba soliloquy, which cannot therefore be spoken of as "leading" to that decision.

the dream-within-a-dream, and attaches to it the sort of meaning that is usually found when a patient reports such an experience.[121]

Before we "analyze" this dream, however, another problem needs to be dealt with. After the puzzle of the dumb-show—or "the argument," as it is called in *Hamlet*—which introduces the subplay, the interpreter is confronted with a new riddle, which poses a perhaps even more difficult critical task. The subplay proper consists chiefly of dialogue between the Player King and the Player Queen, the subject of their discourse being the Player King's premonitory feeling of imminent death and his fear that after he has died, the Player Queen will marry again. The Player Queen protests, and then, after she has left, Lucianus, whom Hamlet identifies as "nephew to the king," enters and kills the Player King by pouring poison into his ear, whereupon Hamlet adds to the text the observation that the nephew will win the love of the Player Queen *(III.2.267f)*. That is all the spectator is told in the subplay.

The puzzle is, of course, why Hamlet has a *nephew* commit the murder, since it was a father's brother who had been the culprit in the actual event. It seems illogical that the play that Hamlet designed, by his own admission, to test Claudius should make himself—he was, after all, the king's nephew—appear guilty.

Wilson's (1936a, pp. 176-183) contribution to the clearing up of this puzzle is as follows: he believes that the dumb-show, which was not noticed by Claudius because he was engaged in conversation with Gertrude and Polonius, was put in by Shakespeare in order to remind the spectator of the nature of the original crime. As proof thereof, he reports the observation that the modern idea of staging *Hamlet* without the dumb-show tends to puzzle those unsophisticated spectators who have not become familiar with the contents of *Hamlet* by way of repeated readings. Since poisoning by ear is used in the dumb-show as the method of murder, the mere fact that it is used at all understandably makes the king realize that his crime has become known to Hamlet, while the spectator, having been reminded by the dumb-show of the original crime (about which he has already been told) can readily understand why it is that Claudius reacts so strongly to the subplay. Hamlet, however, who

---

[121] For Freud's interpretation of the dream-within-the-dream see Freud (1900, p. 338). Jones' proposition gains in significance in the light of Trench's belief that Hamlet wrote the entire play, and not only one part of it as most interpreters assume. (For another psychoanalytic study of the subplay, see Rank, 1915.) [Since the initial publication of this essay, Grinstein (1956) has published a paper on the same topic. His interpretation of the dream-within-the-dream, as presented in this subplay, is, however, different from mine. (1968)]

does not want either to disavow his mother or to compromise her, allows the court to believe that the reason for his wanting to kill Claudius is his own ambition.

Wilson here proposes a purely utilitarian nonpsychological explanation for Hamlet's making Lucianus be the one to kill the Player King. As has been mentioned before, Hamlet made Polonius believe that his madness was due to his infatuation with Ophelia, while he talked with Rosencrantz and Guildenstern as if it was frustrated ambition that was at the bottom of his bizarre behavior. At these times, he is apparently trying, by one or another means, to shield his mother. While I agree with Wilson that that motive does play a role in Hamlet's actions, nevertheless I do not find his explanation entirely satisfactory. For the fact is that the subplay contains many innuendoes that must be embarrassing precisely for the queen.

The psychological explanation, of course, goes in an entirely different direction. The subplay—that is to say, the dream-within-the-dream—falls into two parts: first, the dumb show, which depicts what, according to the ghost, actually happened; and second, the play as written by Hamlet. A dream that falls into two parts often has the meaning of two sentences (See Freud, 1900, p. 315, pp. 347-348). Since the first part of the dream (the dumb-show) is quite short, it constitutes, according to Freud, a subordinate clause. The problem that faces us is to find the right conjunction in this case, since the representation of conjunctions is beyond achievement by the dreamwork and therefore must be guessed at by the interpreter.

It could be "because"—in which case the subplay would mean: "It is because my uncle killed my father that I will kill—or want to kill—him, in the same way as he killed my father." Such a dream thought might be correct; yet its very correctness would mean the vitiation of the interpretation. In order to express this thought, Hamlet would have no need to dream; this is something of which he is already convinced, as a conscious person.

If we introduce a different conjunction, however, then the dream is shown to express something extremely important. Suppose we were to substitute, for the "because" we have spoken of, a "whether or not," (see Freud, 1900, pp. 316-318); then the dream would mean: "Whether or not my uncle killed my father, I will kill him." Since Claudius is a father-substitute, and since Lucianus kills the queen's loving and beloved first husband, the dream subplay now means: "True, Claudius killed my

· 135 ·

father and married my mother; but whatever had happened, I would still have killed my father, or [in the words of preconscious thinking] I would have wanted to kill my father and marry my mother.'' The distortion that this dream thought has suffered in the manifest content of the dream-subplay follows well-known laws of the dreamwork: since in the subplay, it is not a son but a nephew who does the killing, the dream content thereby becomes acceptable to the dreamer's conscious mind.

According to Freud, the content of the dream within the dream is what the dreamer most strongly wishes *had not ever happened.* In terms of the specific dream under discussion, Hamlet wants his own parricidal wish and the wish to marry his mother to be the least likely to come true, yet in the subplay-dream he confirms (at least from the clinical point of view, when applied to literary interpretation) the indisputable reality of these wishes.

The subplay is therefore direct proof of the fact that Freud's interpretation of Hamlet's unconscious was correct. (See Slochower, 1950, p. 221.) It supplies clinical evidence that the content against which Hamlet's defenses are directed is the positive Oedipus complex,[122] and thus disproves the assertion that Hamlet's main defenses are directed against a matricidal impulse (see Moloney and Rockelein, 1949, p. 106). That impulse does have its importance, of course, but it is not on *this* conflict that the tragedy hinges.

Moreover, a property of dream psychology can be discovered here, in the realm of aesthetics. The tendency of the ego to keep the offensive unconscious content away from consciousness is well known from the psychoanalytic investigation of dreams. The "mousetrap," while ostensibly designed to unmask Claudius's true character, is in fact used by Hamlet to reveal his own unconscious. Just as the dreamer would never think of looking for indisputable reality in the dream within the dream, so the spectator would not ever look for Hamlet's unconscious in the "mousetrap" that he has set to catch Claudius. In this respect too, the subplay follows the laws of the dream-within-the-dream.

[Whatever the meaning of the subplay is in the light of a psychoanalytic interpretation, the manifest meaning of this part of the stage action requires some further comment. First, it is constructed in a way that makes the Player-Queen (and thereby Gertrude) the ostensible center of a vituperative attack. This contributes all the more to the shocking effect

---

[122] See also Horatio's comparison *(I.1.112)* of the Ghost's appearance with the events preceding Caesar's murder; thus the play alludes from the very start to parricide.

upon Claudius who, until Lucianus' appearance, may have gladly let himself believe that Hamlet's indiscreet behavior was aimed at his mother. Second, the fact that the Queen shows no sign of perturbation although the manifest content of the subplay centers in the theme of female fickleness and, further, that she does not respond to the Player-King's death by murder, suggests that she acted in the past in good faith and was, moreover, ignorant of what had really happened to her husband. Yet, as usual, one may surmise the opposite, and those critics whose concept of the Queen is unfavorable may regard her insouciance either as renewed proof of her lack of sensitivity or as the poise of an iron will that is immune to feelings of guilt after the crime.]

VII

The profoundest problem in the tragedy, and the one that is also the most challenging, from the standpoint of the central present-day interests and research of psychoanalysis, is the question of Hamlet's madness, his "antic disposition." There will have to be much more clinical investigation before we shall be able to explain such a complicated structure of psychopathology; I shall offer here only a few observations.

Three types of mental involvement are presented in the play: that of Hamlet, that of Polonius, and that of Ophelia. While I agree with Jones (1949, p. 87, ftn. 1) that behind Polonius's garrulity there is much worldly wisdom, I nevertheless believe that he is representative of a certain type of disorder, referred to in the play simply as "old age." Ophelia's disorder is a masterfully drawn psychosis, following exactly the lines that Freud suggested for those disorders that were formerly called "amentia." With her father's murder by Hamlet, reality took a turn that was too painful to be borne by the ego, and Hamlet became inacceptable to her as a love object. Where she loves is precisely where she ought to hate; where she hates is where she would wish to love. Reality has been rent asunder, and the ego is swamped by the archaic. The relevant issue in Ophelia's disturbance is not that her father has died, but rather that it was the man whom she loves who killed him. Furthermore, from her point of view, it must look to her as if Polonius had been killed as a consequence of her rejection of Hamlet. Thus it was she who had caused her father's death—and by her very obedience to him.

Here is the point at which Hamlet's and Ophelia's life-stories become riveted together: while Hamlet is struggling to obtain internal sovereignty, in order to be able to renounce the state of obedience and thus to make his reason for destruction not the demand of another but his own, Ophelia, who has never—explicitly at least—aspired to sovereignty, has unwittingly caused destruction, or so she believes, by her very act of submitting to the powers that be.

I think one could say that, from the point of view of antiquity, it would be Ophelia who was the tragic figure, not Hamlet. Sophocles' Oedipus and Ophelia are nearly identical, so far as the ego's entanglement with reality is concerned.[123] By contrast, it is Ophelia's fate that brings the central issue of Hamlet's fate into full relief (Cf. Jekels, 1933).

Hamlet's "antic disposition" cannot be clinically diagnosed because it lies essentially outside psychiatric typology (Cf. Slochower, 1950, p. 216). If single mechanisms are dealt with out of context, one finds some that belong to melancholia,[124] some to schizophrenia and some to hysteria. Hamlet's own assertion that his antic disposition and his strange behavior have both been intentionally arranged by him in order for him to be able to attain external goals is of the sort, as Freud discovered, that one encounters in hysterics. His behavior is actually a compromise: the ego must suffer the imposition of forces that stem from outside its realm; yet it is "brave" and says: "I want this to happen." One cannot call such behavior neurotic, in the narrower sense of the word, because in so doing the ego does not turn against the invader; it does not condemn it, but rather justifies it.

Unless the term "neurosis" is to be applied to *any* conflict in which the unconscious is involved, Hamlet cannot be called a neurotic, despite the presence in him of mechanisms that one encounters in neurotics. The mere fact that his seeming procrastinations do at last end in action militates against emphasizing this aspect of his behavior, or looking to the neuroses for the key to the problem. Shortly before the resolution of the tragedy, in fact, Hamlet admits his madness—that is to say, he distinguishes between Hamlet and Hamlet's madness, thereby acknowledging that certain of his past acts were due to madness and not to Hamlet.

One may here be reminded of Nietzsche's (1886, p. 90) famous

---

[123] That is why I do not agree with Miss Sharpe (1946, p. 207), when she asserts that Ophelia presents the same problem as Hamlet, or that she "is an epitome of the elaborated dramatized suicidal theme of the whole play." If one sees in her fate no more than "a narcissistic withdrawal after the father's death, the incorporation of the lost love-object, the reproaches against this loved one directed to the self," one has lost sight, I fear, of the specific reality problem that Ophelia is called upon to face.

[124] See Freud (1917); Sharpe (1929, p. 204). For a detailed discussion of the diagnosis of Hamlet's disorder see Jones (1949, pp. 65-70).

saying;[125] it is as if Hamlet wanted to deny the congruousness between his past actions and his *persona*. Yet what Nietzsche was describing epigrammatically was the act of repression, and Hamlet is far removed at this point from undergoing a new wave of repression. As he himself describes it, he has won for himself full freedom to *turn against* his madness: "Hamlet is of the faction that is wronged; His madness is poor Hamlet's enemy."[126]

This last statement, in order to be evaluated correctly, has to be looked at alongside the first statement that Hamlet makes in the play, when he answers Claudius's address: "My cousin Hamlet, and my son" with the aside: "A little more than kin, and less than kind." That is a statement of far-reaching implications, and it has found a wide variety of interpretations (see *Variorum Edition*, 1877, Vol. I, p. 33f), one of which I shall refer to at this point. There was a jingle current in Shakespeare's times: "The nearer we are in blood, the further we must be from love; the greater the kindred is, the less the kindness must be."[127] This jingle reveals with surprising frankness the fundamental conflict inherent in kinship relationships that are inescapably marred by ambivalence. To a certain extent, one could say that these two verses contain the salient point that has made psychoanalysis unpalatable to so many.

If one considers this from the standpoint of the ego's development, however, one can describe the single line of Shakespeare's as going straight to the heart of the fundamental issue involved in the ego's whole relationship to the external world—namely, the necessity of its assimilating and integrating a world that is essentially distant, cold and foreign to the ego. In that one line is summed up the problem of transforming the ego-alien into the ego-syntonic—a process that lies unalterably beyond the strength of the schizophrenic; its accomplishment overtaxes his capacity for reality-testing, which is as a result shattered in the struggle.

This general statement, of course, calls for a more extensive elaboration, which would carry us well beyond the scope of this paper. I would like at this point to discuss only one of the objections that might be raised to it. The healthy infant does not experience the world as ego-alien, and such catastrophes as would completely overdraw on the child's funds of

---

[125] " 'This is what I have done,' says my memory. 'I could not have done this,' says my pride and remains unyielding. Finally—memory gives in."

[126] See Bradley (1904, p. 120f) for a discussion of the pros and cons of whether Hamlet had a psychosis.

[127] Stevens, quoted after *Variorum Edition*, 1877, Vol I, p. 33.

energy are rather the exception. In view of that observation, I do not agree with those who would place the greatest emphasis, in their discussion of Hamlet, on early pregenital processes (see Sharpe, 1929; 1946 quoted earlier), but believe rather that Hamlet's problem revolves around those conflicts that are so often encountered in the latency period and in puberty—problems that the adult never completely outgrows, but which, at best, he sometimes learns to master. These problems have to do with the great issues of man's living in a culture-community.

In regard to these issues, I think that the conflict that rages is of the sort that Hamlet refers to by implication in the very first line he speaks. Kinship here would stand for all those "given" relationships into which we are born; all the irreversible decisions that history made before we ourselves became active members of the community; all those values, prohibitions and standards that have been set up as constants—of which the most representative and consequential is kinship in its literal meaning. *All* of this has to be accepted by the ego and made part of it; it must become of the ego's "kind." Yet the ego would like instead to set up its own scheme of selection and therefore tries from the outset to accept as kin only that which is "of its own kind."[128]

This struggle between the ego-alien and the ego-syntonic becomes of paramount importance—unless a person makes himself a tool of the world and thereby surrenders his privilege (in Shakespeare's time, it was not yet a right) of deciding for himself what he will integrate and what he will reject. It is this, I think, that is at the basis of Hamlet's confrontation of "kin" and "kind," aside from all the implications in the word "kind" of the idea of friendliness.

The very first line that Hamlet speaks, then, is conceived so masterfully that it seems, in itself, to connote almost an infinity. As a result, the contrast between the "more" of kinship and the "less" of kind characterizes the entire background of Hamlet's emotional state at that moment (just as it conveys, in a broad sense, the emotional tone that generally colors man's undaunted grappling with the culture of his time).

By rights, Hamlet ought to have gone along with events and accepted Claudius as uncle, stepfather, even king (which is really more than kin); yet he could not for a moment, at this point, regard Claudius as having anything in common with himself. At the end of the tragedy, however, Hamlet has succeeded in converting the ego-alien into the ego-

[128] See Freud's remarks about the pleasure-ego (1925b, p. 237).

syntonic. He has integrated what has become his mission in life; he has accepted and integrated death as the ultimate meaning of life, without however denying his responsibility to posterity (he assigns to Horatio, at the end, the task of telling his story); and—most difficult of all—he has reconciled himself with his mother and accepted her in all her frailty. Childhood illusions having been abandoned, the ego bows in tolerance and humility, asking pardon for all the destruction that that long process caused—a process in which the alien world became synthesized at length into the ego's frail framework.

That too is the meaning of Hamlet's madness. Hamlet is as little a malingerer as he is insane—whatever meaning that word may have had for the past or may have now.[129] Hamlet's madness is a composite of all the thrusts toward the world, as well as all the retreats from it, with which a healthy ego duels on its way to finding its self-assertion in a bewildering world. Anatole France put the problem of Hamlet's madness into the most concise statement possible: "He is a man; he is man; he is all of man. . . . You are quick and slow, bold and timid, benevolent and cruel, you believe and you doubt, you are wise and above all you are mad. In a word, you are alive. Which of us does not resemble you in something? Which of us thinks without contradiction and acts without inconsistency? Which of us is not mad?"[130]

One other question ought to be added: "Which of us has never been believed by others to be mad?" For this is what has happened to Hamlet. The poet of course leads us astray, and we follow him willingly, just as we ourselves often level the judgment of "madness' when our friends try to assert themselves, to throw off the thin skin of conformity. Yet there is another aspect to Hamlet's madness: he himself predicts his "antic disposition." At one point *(III.2.88),* he tells Horatio frankly that he must now act as if he were out of his mind, and from then on he does act as if he were really a malingerer. Yet truly Hamlet malingers as little as any human being can.[131]

---

[129] When Claudius calls Hamlet "most generous, and free from all contriving" *(IV.7.134),* the characterization is not an *ad hoc* construction, but rather an important clue to the effect that is created by Hamlet's personality, even on his enemy.

[130] "C'est un homme, c'est l'homme, c'est tout l'homme. . . . vous êtes prompt et lent, audacieux et timide, bienveillant et cruel, vous croyez et vous doutez, vous êtes sage et par-dessus tout vous êtes fou. En un mot, vous vivez. Qui de nous ne vous ressemble, en quelque chose? Qui de nous pense sans contradiction et agit sans incohérence? Qui de nous n'est fou?" (France, 1888, Vol. I, pp. 1, 8).

[131] See, however, Alexander (1929). This paper sounds like a travesty, the result of a student-like application of textbook psychiatry to a work of art.

This is the puzzling thing about man: that he can never lie nor can he ever speak the truth; what he says is always "in between." When he tries to lie, there is always some truth in what he says, and usually far more than he is aware of; when he tries to be truthful, there is more contrivance and cunning in his words than he himself knows. Only by persistently overlooking the fact that human life always moves in the area between antinomies, and that mental health can be measured only in *degrees* of inconsistency and not by either its absence or presence, could writers such as Wilson or Bradley come to the conclusion that Hamlet is laboring under a mental disorder.[132] When Coleridge (1836-1839) contends that "Hamlet's wildness is but half-false. O that subtle trick, to pretend the *acting* only when we are very near to *being* what we act" (author's italics), one cannot but agree.

In order to preserve a feeling of integrity, an ego may pretend, or even wish, that some horrible event—which will in any case unavoidably take its course within the ego's boundaries—is one that *ought* to occur. Thus it may try to spare itself the horror that becomes its constant companion when it finds itself being coerced by internal, irrational forces.

In his farewell speech to the world, when he apologizes to Laertes and regrets his previous destructiveness, Hamlet repudiates those destructive acts of his as not being expressions of his true self. It was not Hamlet who wronged Laertes, but his madness.

> Then Hamlet does it not; Hamlet denies it.
> Who does it then? His madness. If't be so,
> Hamlet is of the faction that is wrong'd;
> His madness is poor Hamlet's enemy.

(V.2.240-243)

The ego is now capable of admitting that the antic disposition was after all not pretense, but forced upon it.

Yet the integration of the past into the present, the fortitude to affirm that past madness is as true of Hamlet as past good deeds—such deep insights into human nature as Shakespeare, here far ahead of his times, set forth poetically have not yet been generally accepted even by present culture and must still wait for later generations in order to be

---

[132] See Wilson (1936a, p. 217): "We are driven to conclude . . . that Shakespeare meant us to imagine Hamlet suffering from some kind of mental disorder throughout the play." This statement is later qualified (p. 222): "A man who can describe his own mental symptoms in rational fashion is still one of ourselves." Yet Wilson seems to identify the psychologically explicable with the consistent (p. 220).

generally acknowledged. Hamlet's ego, at last recovered, can enter its new phase only by sequestration of those parts of the past that have aroused its shame. This act of sequestration is equivalent to the repression of the childhood phase by the adult.

During the course of the tragedy, Hamlet's real ego-ideal has become evident. It is represented in Horatio and clearly defined in the scene preceding the dumb-show, when Hamlet describes Horatio as "one, in suff'ring all, that suffers nothing" *(III.2.64)*. If a man can accomplish this, then he is "not a pipe for Fortune's finger," he is no longer "passion's slave" (See Sharpe, 1929, p. 212). The ego's relative independence of both external and internal stimulation is here symbolically described with particular subtlety; it is correctly correlated with the capacity for vanquishing masochistic propensities.

Whether Hamlet ever reaches that ideal we are not told, but my guess would be that he does not do so any more than man is generally able to. It is Horatio, unruffled by passions and the whims of fortune, who will write down Hamlet's story, and in so doing symbolize the victory of the superego over the ego's eternal attachment to the world.

VIII

I would like, by way of conclusion, to make a few hypothetical statements about Shakespeare's personal involvement in the writing of *Hamlet*. It is always tempting to guess at the personal background out of which a great work of art grew; such attempts form a good part of the psychoanalytic literature on art and artists. In Shakespeare's instance, where not even the "rough-hewn" data of his life are known, the matter is certainly hopeless. But following Miss Sharpe's technique of reconstructing from the text of *King Lear* a childhood event that may have underlain the plot of that tragedy, one can make certain surmises about *Hamlet*.

Since the center of the play is a dream that refers to Hamlet's aggression against his father and his libidinal impulses toward his mother, and since Hamlet, after the presentation of the subplay suddenly breaks off (as in a nightmare?[133]), goes to his mother in great excitement, and in so doing passes by the praying Claudius, one may surmise that the little boy was once awakened from a dream of similar content; that he felt frightened and ran to his parents' bed, and that there his mother consoled

---

[133] [If this reconstruction is correct, the playwright's presentation would contain a reversal. In the play, it is the bad father, not the son, who jumps up jolted by fright and asks for "some light," as a dreamer does when rudely awakened by anxiety. (1968)]

him, while his father lay asleep; that his father woke up after a while and scolded the little intruder.

How the little boy reacted to his father's admonitions cannot be guessed, but he must have been very angry, since in the story plot that is devised by the adult, Polonius is instantaneously stabbed when he disturbs Hamlet's discourse with his mother. The hidden aim of *pavor nocturnus*—to interfere with parental lovemaking—may be discovered in Hamlet's subsequent advice to his mother on how to escape Claudius's advances. I am certain that the derivatives of many more, and quite different, childhood episodes can be discovered in this tragedy.

The value of such reconstructions must not, however, be overestimated. The impossibilty of verifying them, for one thing, gives rise to danger. They are valuable only insofar as they remind us how close artistic production may lie to instinctual processes.[134]

The period to which the writing of *Hamlet* is assigned is usually placed between the years 1596 and 1601.[135] The only events that occurred during that period whose chronology is certain, and which can therefore be put into a meaningful connection, are (as far as I know) the burial of Shakespeare's son, Hamnet, on August 11, 1595, at the age of 11 years, and the burial of his father, John Shakespeare, on February 8, 1601.

There is one event in between those two dates, however, that should be mentioned here. In 1597 Shakespeare bought the freehold house of New Place in his native town. "William Underhill, the vendor, was poisoned by his son, Fulke, and Shakespeare had to secure warranty through a fresh fine with another son, Hercules, to whom the felon's estate had been granted" (See Chambers, 1930, Vol. I, p. 74f, and Vol. II, p. 98).

Out of these three facts one can make either much or little. If one goes as far as Chambers does, when he says in reference to the name of Shakespeare's son, that "the resemblance of the name to that of the hero of Shakespeare's tragedy, which has a different Scandinavian ori-

---

[134] Yet they also lead the analyst to assume manic-depressive cycles where they may not all exist, instead of observing the actual change in the interplay and selection of ego mechanisms. Miss Sharpe tries to differentiate between "the manic-depressive cycle in so-called normal people and clinical people and clinical cases" (Sharpe, 1946, p. 264); my own thinking on this is that processes that lead to a higher differentiation and individualization should not be subsumed at all under the rubric of the manic-depressive cycle.

[135] For an extensive discussion of the question of dating *Hamlet*, see Jones (1949, pp. 108-13) and the Cambridge edition of *Hamlet*, pp. xvi-xxii.

gin, can hardly be more than a coincidence" (Chambers, 1930, Vol. II, p. 4), then of course these facts can never be meaningfully connected with the play.[136] Even if we do concede that there is a danger, during a psychoanalytic investigation, that details may be loaded with unwarranted meaning, it is hard to understand why there should be any doubt as to the meaningfulness of these names.

There are a few psychic patterns of which we can be certain that, whenever and wherever they have occurred, they have followed the same laws. Whenever a slip is made or a dream is dreamed, one is entitled to assume that the laws that Freud proved to govern slips and dreams apply, whatever the culture or whatever the historical period in which they may have occurred.[137] It is also reasonable to assert that, whatever the period of history in which a poet worked, if he wrote a tragedy about a hero whose name is similar to or identical with that of his dead son, this cannot have been a coincidence, that the poet's conscious and unconscious imagery concerning his son must have had some bearing on the creation of that work of art.

What sort of bearing it had we can, of course, scarcely guess at. Whether he expressed what he wished his son might have become, or what he feared might have happened, or what actually did happen—among many other possible variations—will not become discoverable, unless rich biographical material comes down to posterity.[138]

Concerning the other date—namely, that of Shakespeare's father's death—the following is to be considered. Usually the death of a father is stressed in psychoanalytic biographical writings; in some instances, however, the events that led to it are as important as the event itself, if not more so. A son's unconscious often begins to react to the first signs that the event may take place. Unfortunately, nothing is known about the circumstances under which John Shakespeare died; we do not know, for

[136] In his first reference to Hamlet, Freud pointed to the identity of names; he also connected the writing of the play with the death of Shakespeare's father. Jones elaborates extensively upon these two factors.

[137] [This, of course, holds true only if Freud's findings are accepted as a kind of anatomy of the mind, if such an allegory is permissible. I would then compare the assumptions one is permitted to make with regard to the mind of a person whose biographical record is scanty, with the tacit assumptions we make regarding the body of a deceased historical person. No one will doubt that Socrates had a heart, although the actual proof thereof is bound to fail. However, questions such as whether Socrates had a dexterocardia and what his average pulse rate was, are not likely to be made a matter of either speculation or inquiry. (1968)]

[138] [I want to add two remarks here. A most surprising (if not embarrassing to the psychoanalyst) feature is that the choice of the name of Hamnet for the son and of Judith for his twin did not apparently grow out of unconscious determinants, as happens most often nowadays in the selection by

example, whether he was sick for a long time or whether his was a sudden death.

It is my belief that the main work on *Hamlet* was done by Shakespeare at a time when the death of his son lay behind him and his father's death was yet to come. There is a peculiar "inhibition of death" in *Hamlet*. Hamlet's father is kept from his rest and stalks the world for a long time before he at last disappears forever. Hamlet's hesitation in killing Claudius is faintly reminiscent, in a distorted way, of the impulses that someone may have who has witnessed the protracted final illness of a beloved person.[139]

The third event, the poisoning of the owner of New Place by his son, seems to me also to be meaningful.[140] It reminds me of other instances in which an event in an author's environment serves as a point of crystallization for fantasies that must have been evolving preconsciously or unconsciously for a long time. Living in a house (actually or in fantasy) whose owner had been poisoned by his son may make identification well-nigh unavoidable,[141] and thus this event in reality might have become the point of crystallization that precipitated the writing of *Hamlet*. If a man loses a son whose twin sister survives, and if his father dies at a time when his mother is still in good health, a horrible fear of women may evolve. Hamlet's impending death may have been one root of the almost eerie misogyny that one can feel throughout *Hamlet*.

---

parents of their children's names. It seems that, in the case of Hamnet and Judith, accidental factors were at play, since the children were named after their godparents Hamnet Sadler (d. 1624) and Judith (d. 1614). Here then would be one of the oddest and most meaningful coincidences in world literature. Further, I want to recall Goddard's (1951, Vol. 1, p. 332) most engaging observation when writing about little Hamnet's possible effect on the play "that Dostoevsky had a son, Alyosha (Alexey), whom he loved dearly and who died before he was three, and that the father began writing *The Brothers Karamazov* that same year." It is always moving to discover patterns that at first glance appear to be accidental but later may take on the dignity of leitmotifs within the biographies of some geniuses. (1968)]

[139] It should be unnecessary for me to say that this is pure hypothesis, since there is no record of John Shakespeare's disease, or even of the extent and frequency of Shakespeare's contacts with his father.

[140] If we were to assume that the Underhill episode and the writing of *Hamlet* really fit together in a biographical context, then some interesting speculations could be added. In the reality event the son poisoned the father; in the tragedy it is the father-substitute who poisons the son. This looks like a defense against the fantasy of the potential destructiveness of children against their parents. At the last minute, so to speak, the content that is apparently to be denied breaks through, and Hamlet almost literally showers Claudius with poison: the stabbing with the poisoned sword is not sufficient; he forces the king to drink poison. It sounds as if the repressed or denied paranoid idea (children want to kill their parents) has belatedly spilled over the defense, and now in orgy-like fashion it is making up for the damming-up it has previously had to suffer.

[141] I wish also to point out that the culprit's brother was called Hercules. Might this have been a factor precipitating the Hercules imagery in the final tragedy?

In that sense, the writing of the tragedy may have had the function of a great consolation. Poor Hamnet was buried, but Hamlet would live forever; and the fact is that Shakespeare did succeed in erecting an indestructible monument for his son. Here we encounter a realistic root of the theme of rebirth with which the tragedy ends.

There may also have been consolation, however, in another respect. Was not Hamnet happier than Hamlet? He was spared Hamlet's execrable sufferings; flights of angels sang him to his rest before he was even able to become ensnared in the world's temptations. Thus Horatio's sudden impulse to commit suicide, upon seeing Hamlet dying, may be very intimately related to an impulse that Shakespeare himself had felt, and Hamlet's final words to Horatio may have been, in the end, the voice of the poet's superego:

Absent thee from felicity awhile,
And in this harsh world draw thy breath in pain
To tell my story. . . .

If only we knew the compass of that "my"!

3. *Epilogue*

Perhaps the reader will now be able to grasp the answer to the question I raised in the Introduction, as to why Goethe became so intensely immersed in the tragedy of Prince Hamlet at the time when he was preparing himself secretly for his journey to Italy. The reason was that the structure of Hamlet's conflict was closely similar to that of his own.

Hamlet labored under the necessity of coming to grips with a task that had been placed upon him by his father. While he was willing to carry out that task, he was held back for a long time, to his own surprise, by inner forces of whose nature he was ignorant. As soon as, by way of developmental change—that is, through his maturation—he had "appersonated" (as I would like to call the process) the external demand, he became capable of performing the deed.

He had earlier made his father's command his own; he had internalized it, and in that sense he was ready to respond to it. Yet, as long as this internalized command still carried the marks of its external origin— that is to say, was still represented internally as having come from the outside—he remained unable to act. Indeed, if he had acted only in terms of what would have meant to him conformity with his father's demand, he would never have become an adult, in the psychological meaning of the term.

Goethe faced the same problem. His father had requested that he undertake a journey to Italy, and he had acknowledged both the necessity and the desirability of the undertaking. Despite several attempts, however, he had recoiled from carrying it into effect, and had rationalized his putting it off by all sorts of reasons. If one concedes that Hamlet, by turning at once to action, in accordance with the paternal command, would have left a permanent roadblock standing in his way toward maturation, one must also say of Goethe that too early compliance with his father's request might well have been followed by psychological disaster.

The journey would have taken place before Goethe had shed all traces of his *Sturm und Drang* period—that is to say, at a time when he was by no means internally prepared to integrate direct contact with the South and with antiquity. These would have remained foreign bodies and, even worse, would have disarranged and disorganized, by their sheer presence, the serene development of his art. One can hardly overestimate the infelicitous consequences that a premature voyage would have produced with regard to his mental and artistic growth, through the disorder created in the interrelationship among very important mental structures. Both Hamlet and Goethe acted wisely when they put off fulfilling the demands of their fathers.

Now, when Goethe was approaching the moment of making the plan his own—that is, of wishing to go to Italy on his own—and was in process of becoming capable of doing so in response to an inner call, so to speak, he experienced his inner conflict and its solution, in empathy and possibly even in identification with Hamlet. By immersing himself in *Hamlet*, he may well have accelerated the solution of his own conflict: he may have derived reassurance, or borrowed strength from his poetic model; or he may have consoled himself by setting the dread command under which Hamlet labored against the relative lightness of his own task. The specific character of the tragedy's effect on him cannot be deciphered from the extant biographical record, but I am compelled to assume that it was this aspect of the tragedy that aroused and held fast Goethe's interest at that particular moment in his own life.

However, there are many critics who assert that Goethe saw Hamlet as young Werther; if this were so, it would of course mean the death knell of my theory. One could try to explain Goethe's preoccupation with a Werther type at that particular time, by suggesting that he wanted to impress upon himself the evil consequences of Werther-like behavior and in that way to prevent himself from regressing to a previous juncture, now that reality was demanding of him activity and a masculine forging-ahead. This would be, however, a rather forced explanation.

In addition, it would postulate a pattern that is quite un-Goethe-like. To frighten oneself in order to keep oneself from behaving in a certain way would be more like a neurasthenic obsessive than the Goethe who had developed during that magnificent decade at Weimar, before leaving for Italy. Moreover, there is a good deal of evidence that he had shed quite completely the previous Werther chrysalis, and nothing could have been more alien to his mind at that time than absorption in any character type that was even remotely associated with Werther.

When T. S. Eliot ascribes to Goethe a Werther-interpretation of Hamlet, he does so not only without presenting convincing evidence but also in a bewildering fashion. He first writes of "that most dangerous type of critic: the critic with a mind which is naturally of the creative order, but which through *some weakness in creative power* exercises itself in criticism instead," and then goes on to say, "These minds often find in Hamlet a vicarious existence for their own artistic realization. Such a mind had Goethe, who made of Hamlet a Werther" (1920, p. 95) (my italics). I cannot think of any other instance in which Goethe is reproached for "some weakness in creative power."

The essential characterization that Goethe gives of Hamlet definitely does not contain Werther-like features.[1] Goethe describes Hamlet as a normal fine human being who suddenly faces a task that is beyond his strength. This is not Werther, who was bound from the start to perish tragically because of his oversensitivity. Whatever the circumstances that may surround him, he is unable to endure the least strain that life puts on man. This characterization is indirectly denied by Goethe with regard to Hamlet, in his specific reference to the *magnitude* and *quality* of the specific conflict that cruel fate had decreed for the prince. Werther would lose his incomparable pathos if there were any imaginable life circumstances under which he could thrive. It was the very denial that life is in any way livable for one whose psychic apparatus is excessively delicate in structure, that assured the novel its unmatched suc-

---

[1] The erroneous assertion that Goethe saw in Hamlet a Werther-like personality can be traced far back into the nineteenth century. I have not been able, however, to ascertain who was the first to make this error. One may think that Goethe himself was responsible for this misinterpretation when, in describing the background of the Werther phase in the 13th book of his autobiographical novel, he gave this exposition of the influence of English literature: "Everyone thought he was permitted to be as melancholic as the prince of Denmark, although he had not seen a ghost and did not have to revenge a royal father." Goethe is here referring to years far earlier than those in which he was to put forward his analysis of Hamlet's character, which later became so famous. How little satisfied Goethe was with that analysis in later years can be seen in a remark he made to Eckermann (25 December, 1825) about it: "Shakespeare gives us golden apples in silver bowls. From the study of his plays, we obtain the silver bowls; we, however, have only potatoes to put in them, and that is the distressing thing [*das Schlimme*]."

cess and made the accusation plausible that many a youth committed suicide after reading it, as Goethe was indeed reproached for a long time.

It would be quite surprising to find suicidal ideas being incited in any youth through the force of Shakespeare's play. Surely Goethe would have been grossly mistaken, if he had perceived in the prince a Werther type; he was certainly discriminating enough not to be reminded—by a hero who in the end comes to terms quite actively with his fate—of his own creation, who suffered tragically, primarily because of his very low threshold of stimulation. How could Werther ever have carried into effect the equivalent of Hamlet's rough handling of Polonius and of his former friends, or of his aggressive organization of the mouse-trap—to cite at random two of the many un-Wertherlike traits in Hamlet?

Thus Eliot's judgment was faulty in two respects. Goethe's concept of Hamlet was not, to begin with, Werther-like; and at the time when Goethe was forming his image of Hamlet, as it is described in the novel, he had already outgrown his own Werther phase: his image of himself no longer included the shadow of Werther. Perhaps T. S. Eliot had taken over, without questioning, a German tradition. He might perhaps have been impressed by Gundolf's comment: "Hamlet is a heroically pathetic man [endowed] with all the specifically modern dangers and anguishes. From him a straight line leads to Brutus, the hero of antiquity, and a no less straight one to the sentimental middle-class child, Werther." [Hamlet ist ein heroisch pathetischer Mensch mit allen spezifisch modernen Gefahren und Qualen. Von ihm aus führt ein gerader Weg zum antiken Helden Brutus und ein nicht minder gerader zum sentimentalen Bürgerkind Werther.] (Gundolf, 1916, p. 95)[2]

When I equate the motivational power of the Ghost's command to his son with Kaspar Goethe's wish to know that his son was in Italy, these two may at first impress the reader as incommensurate; yet the equation can be checked by historical and biographical research. The evidence at hand certainly seems to favor my proposition. In addition,

[2]For a comment on Hamlet's spiritual kinship with Brutus cf. Gundolf (1928), Vol. 2, p. 74. It is of interest that what Gundolf did was to reformulate Goethe's concept in a more modern and acceptable form, thereby anticipating Peter Alexander. He wrote: "The old argument whether or not Hamlet is a weakling may thus be settled: an elevated personality, strong enough for the regular course of life, comes face to face with a task that overpowers him, as the result of his abundance of spirit and soul. . . . It is not a flaw, but his virtue that brings him to grief." [Der alte Streit ob Hamlet ein Schwächling ist oder nicht mag dahin geschlichtet werden: ein hoher Mensch, stark genug für jeden gesetzlichen Lauf, gerät vor eine Aufgabe die aus seinem eigenen Überschuss an Geist und Seele . . . ihn überwältigt. Nicht seine Schwäche, sondern seine Tugend bringt ihn zu Fall" (ibid.).]

one may perhaps surmise that I am overestimating the importance of Goethe's Hamlet studies *qua* his preparations for the Italian journey. In this respect, I would like to report that, as far as the biographical record permits any conclusion, Goethe spent more time on *Hamlet* before leaving Weimar than he did on the study of the current travel literature. Another aspect of that preparatory period is directly reminiscent of Hamlet's behavior, in that Goethe really acted with Hamlet's secrecy in preparing for the journey. His servant was the only one whom he permitted to know of his intent and Goethe pleaded with him to keep the secret to himself, with no less passion than the prince employed with Horatio and Marcellus, in the cellarage scene, when he pleaded with them never to let anyone know of the Ghost's visitation.

To be sure, it may seem somewhat far-fetched to attempt to explain Goethe's secrecy, which he himself could rationalize only lamely, solely by way of identification with Hamlet; yet I would not overlook this aspect in considering the great stress he put on secrecy. The objection may also be raised that I am putting too much emphasis on the personal-subjective aspect of Goethe's Italian journey, to the neglect of the many other factors that were involved, with regard to both historical tradition and his own artistic needs. I am not unaware of those factors and I do not underestimate their importance for Goethe's development as a creative artist, and particularly with regard to the content and form of his later productions.

That is to say, I do not minimize Goethe's motives or the intensity of his conscious desire to establish direct contact with the world of antiquity. But many a man has gone to Italy motivated in the main by cultural and artistic factors, and yet has not done so with the fervor, passion, drive and secrecy that characterized Goethe's voyage. Further, it cannot have happened too often that a man from the North enters southern lushness at the age of 37 and there has sexual intercourse for the first time, as can be proved with almost documentary certainty in Goethe's case (Bode, 1921). He really rushed to Italy, when he did go, like a kind of Fortinbras, to set many a problem right that Hamlet had left unresolved.

When one also considers that Hamlet was the only one among Shakespeare's dramatis personae into whose character structure Goethe made an elaborate and original inquiry, we are entitled to feel all the more certain that the psychological specificity of the time and content of his interest in Hamlet can hardly be overestimated.

PART TWO

4. General Remarks

As befits a psychoanalyst, I have focused upon the psychological content of *Hamlet* and have therefore tended to see in the play the development of a personality, the conflicts and griefs and the other inner processes that a man has to go through until he attains a state of maturity, in the form of conflict-free and independent action. In order to unearth that content, some elements in the play have to be understood realistically, others symbolically. It is likely that almost every element needs to be interpreted at both levels, although there are also complementary series to be expected here, in which one element is closer to the symbol and another closer to reality, two poles that Fergusson (1949, p. 127) would probably conceptualize as ritual and improvisational entertainment.

At this point I would like to raise the question of whether *Hamlet* is a psychological tragedy, or something more. As one consequence of what I would call the "psychological bias," I am inclined to assume that it is the psychological content that has moved the spectator and guaranteed the play's artistic effectiveness, throughout the generations and at almost any place that has evolved great art of any sort.

As a work of art, however, it is undoubtedly more than a psychological tragedy. Its sociological content, for example, is quite striking, and the root of its great effectiveness may very well be the fact that it is a synthesis of many of the aspects or forms in which man's nature, so baffling in its arcana, finds expression. Although some of the other channels may be somewhat far-removed from those that are familiar to the psychologically minded, in what follows I shall attempt to venture into them.

To begin with, *Hamlet* is, in addition to being a psychological tragedy, the tragedy of a cankerous society. Its sociological framework, like its psychological one, seems indeterminate, wide enough for the projection of many facets of a wide spectrum. Kott (1964, p. 81f), for example, after witnessing the 1956 performance of *Hamlet* in Crakow, was able to regard the play as a drama of political crime. He therefore speaks of a specifically Polish *Hamlet,* such as would be of relevance only after the famous 20th Congress of the Communist Party of the Soviet Union, apparently finding the play to be a reflection of one particular contemporary event, whose repercussions, as profound as Kott believes them to be, were primarily political.

On the other hand, Fergusson's predominantly socioanthropological frame is wider and, for that reason, far more appealing in a general sense. He does not overlook the psychological angle and even makes an attempt to give Jones' Oedipus theory of *Hamlet* its due (1949, p. 122ff). I do not think, however, that any enlargement of the oedipal theory to include the ego-psychological parallel would remove Fergusson's objection, which reads as follows: "The Oedipus complex does not account for the fact that Hamlet, besides being a son, is also a dispossessed prince, nor that Claudius, besides being a father symbol, is also the actual ruler of the state" (1949, p. 123). To be sure, the one does not account for the other; but the fact is that Hamlet talks surprisingly little about his having been dispossessed[1] and, at least in terms of the way in which he expresses himself, sometimes sounds as if he were ready to become reconciled to Claudius' wearing the crown—if only the new king were not so vastly inferior to the image of his father.

Now, it may be that Shakespeare took the prince's political frustrations so much for granted that he regarded it as superfluous to have Hamlet verbalize them. It may also be considered that the oedipal entanglements in Hamlet's relationship to Claudius are only pretended, in order to cover up the former's secret or unconscious intent to arrogate power to himself. Man may have been quite different three hundred odd years ago. Present-day clinical observations strongly suggest that such power motives are secondary derivatives of infantile conflicts, yet the last

---

[1] The one point that remains with the audience in this regard, and perhaps not always then, is Hamlet's statement, ". . . I lack advancement." Even then, he seems to be pretending madness—which would not, of course, rule out the psychological truth of this statement.

word has not yet been spoken in that regard. In clinical practice, frustrations often become tolerable and lose their conflict-arousing power, once the patient comes to understand their infantile matrix.

Even if one assumes that the power issue, being self-evident, did not need explicit elaboration, I must conclude that it was not actually Shakespeare's primary interest. That it was not would seem to be shown by the fact that he points so often, without fully verbalizing it, to what Freud has explicitly and fully—beyond conscious derivatives—set forth as a positive and negative Oedipus complex and its implications. And, if dispossession is one of the main factors or even *the* main factor, why then does Fortinbras not fall into a comparable network of conflicts? His "legal" situation is, after all, almost identical, yet the structure of their oedipal conflicts is sufficiently different to account for the differences in their political behavior.

Be that as it may, Fergusson follows Kernodle (1944) in placing *Hamlet* right at the midpoint of the Occidental development from the Greek theater on, and thus sees in *Hamlet* "a species of ritual drama" (p. 128). This takes him, just as it does the psychoanalyst, to Sophocles' *Oedipus*. But, by contrast with the analyst, he finds the elements shared by both in "the royal sufferer . . . associated with pollution, in its very sources, of an entire social order"; in the initial "invocation of the well-being of the endangered body politic"; in the close intertwining of the individual and of society; in the purgation and renewal that become possible only after the suffering of the royal victim (Fergusson, 1949, p. 130). Hamlet is thus an Oedipus "elaborated by a process of critical analysis," yet still showing "the stages of the ancient ritual sacrifice."

Fergusson's mode of examination is rich, imaginative and highly stimulating, and it would be a pleasure to report the details of his analysis of the play, from prologue to epiphany. Indeed, the psychoanalytic discovery of the oedipal complex as the play's core appears somewhat poor alongside the richness of details that find explanation in his panoramic view. That may be one of the reasons why he lays stress on the "reduction" in Jones' perspective. Yet the objection of "reduction" would be warranted only if Freud had attempted to explain more than Hamlet's hesitation by reference to the Oedipus complex. Moreover, I do not believe that Freud himself would have objected to Fergusson's anthropological interpretation, so long as it does not amount to denying that Hamlet's hesitation is a facet of his Oedipus complex.

For the complex per se may either make a man kill his father (or a substitute), as Oedipus inadvertently does, or else make him hesitate to carry out such a deed; it may even prevent action in a situation in which action is permissible, necessary or highly commendable. The ritual, anthropological, historical forms change; but what is it that remains as the perennial core? Even the psychological surface of that perennial psychological core, to be sure, can take on some quite surprising forms.

The following incident may demonstrate what bizarre forms the psychology of the Hamlet complex, if I may call it that, can take. I would like to refer briefly here to an instance of political assassination in our century, in order to show one strange course along which the oedipus complex has traveled. In October 1916, Friedrich Adler (1879-1960)[2] assassinated Count Stürgkh (b. 1859), who had been, since 1911, the Prime Minister of the Austrian Monarchy. Friedrich was the son of Victor Adler (1852-1918), founder and leader of Austria's Social-Democratic Party, who was widely beloved as a man of the highest idealism, devotion and self-sacrifice.[3]

That fateful October afternoon actually brought about an immediate turn in Austria's inner politics and later an awakening of the population from its political lethargy, such as Victor Adler was either unable or unwilling to accomplish in this critical period.

By contrast with Hamlet, Friedrich Adler did not aim his attack at a contemptible, infamous victim. Initially, he had thought of assassinating the Chief Censor, who was suppressing a free press; but this man was, in his eyes, "a rather inferior object." Then he thought of selecting the Secretary of Justice, in retaliation for the execrable crimes that had been committed during the war in the name of justice. But he did not want to take as the center of his drama a man for whom he felt nothing but contempt. His final decision therefore fell on Count Stürgkh, who was the key figure in the reigning absolutism and who had been responsible for the wartime suspension of Parliament.

Friedrich Adler respected him chiefly because he was not diseased by "Austrian immorality," but instead working, consciously and energetically, toward Austria's transformation into an absolute state. "He was a man whom one had to remove, yet whom I did not want to hurt [*kränken*]." In the hour during which he contemplated his victim, who was sitting not far from him in a restaurant, Adler did not think of the

---

[2] For the facts in what follows, see Braunthal, 1960.

[3] Father and son deserve a thorough psychoanalytic study; the intimate and as yet unravelled connection between individual psychology and history could be well studied in this instance.

life he was getting ready to destroy, nor of wife, children, parents, but only "of the sacrifice of my own life."

At one point he wanted to back out, yet he rejected the idea: "You will have reason to feel ashamed, if you leave so close to your target, without achieving anything." He had the distinct feeling of a state of mind that would be incompatible with self-respect, "if I did not carry out what I knew my duty was." The similarity with *Hamlet,* particularly with the prayer scene, is really striking. After the deed, Adler recovered his equilibrium, but he was now disquieted by the possibility that his victim might not have been mortally wounded, after all. When he was apprised of the truth, a state of complete peace of mind and even of contentment took hold if him.

From all this, one would hardly be able to guess the psychological background of the deed. Until the outbreak of the war, father and son had lived together in exceptional harmony. The son admired the father's genius; although he himself was a promising physicist, he decided to follow in his father's footsteps and to devote himself to full-time political work. A serious political conflict developed, however, between Friedrich and his father during the war, with regard to what political course the Social-Democratic Party should take. Contrary to their previously accepted principles, the German and Austrian parties both took a favorable view of the World War, once it had broken out. "Worse than the war would be a victory of the Allies"—that view may summarize the change from their previous basic anti-militarism to their support of the national war effort.

Victor Adler by no means stood at the extreme right, and he was free of outright imperialistic aspirations; yet he too supported the war as a defense against the Allies. The son, by contrast, consistently upheld the accepted prewar principles of international solidarity against war, and thus became his father's reproof. Here, interestingly enough, one encounters the reversal of what one meets with in *Hamlet:* it is the son who has here become the father's bad conscience. Although they remained personally attached by great affection, explosions between them during political meetings became the rule. Three days prior to the assassination, the father had shouted at him, during one session: "You are provocative; apparently, you want to be expelled."

The murder, it is reasonable to assume, was supposed to have the function of showing the father that he was in error, as well as of demonstrating how a socialist ought to act, if he is aware of his responsibilities. Spiritually, therefore, the deed was directed against Adler's father. The victim, who was free of "Austrian immorality"—a man of clear intention and firm will, in the son's words—apparently possessed those qualities that the son found missing in his father. Half of the victim's image was that of an idealized father; the other half was a reflection of the reprehensible aims toward which his misguided energy was at that time vigorously striving, and which had led to his constant breaches of the constitution. Yet the father had also violated an unwritten constitution of socialist principles, for whose pursuit the son had admired him, up to the point when World War I broke out.

It is not surprising to learn that Friedrich Adler read *Hamlet* in prison, while awaiting trial, and that the father insisted that his son's crime was the result of madness. But it was not only this that Friedrich Adler shared with his literary ancestor. A friend of the family described Friedrich as follows: "Nothing will wipe out the impression which the youth and then the man made upon me—that silent greatness, that relentless wrestling for truth, that mercilessness of criticism which is strangely mixed with extreme delicacy, almost bashfulness of feeling." It was not only Hamlet who was a bundle of contradictions in the eyes of the critics; so too was Friedrich Adler, for his friends.

When Fergusson places at the center of his study the cankerous state of Denmark, and the various ways in which this affected the protagonists, as well as the ways in which they, in turn, dealt with the canker, he is apparently not aware to what extent he partly confirms Freud's sociohistorical findings and partly extends them even beyond Freud's vision. For it cannot be just accidental that this canker is the oedipal crime. I follow Fergusson in his beautiful elaborations about ritual and epiphany, yet what he says could be applied to any kind of canker, and I do not find an explanation in his book of how it happens that in Sophocles' *Oedipus*, as well as in Shakespeare's *Hamlet*, the canker from which the body politic is suffering consists of this unique and well-defined deed. The socioanthropologically minded historian may object that Claudius' deed is not oedipal, when the latter term is taken literally, since the equation of fratricide and patricide is arbitrary. The objection does not strike me as valid any more than if someone were to reject the idea that the oedipal complex is the center of *The Brothers Karamazov*, on the grounds that Grushenka is not the brothers' natural mother but merely old Karamazov's bride.

Claudius has killed his brother because he was driven by the urge to have carnal relations with the latter's wife, and to arrogate to himself the powers that the brother had until then exercised. We are not informed either of his age relation to his victim—or for that matter, of his spouse's. The context leaves no doubt that he is the younger brother, but there is no way of knowing whether he is older or younger than Gertrude. The impression that one obtains is that they are coeval. However, Gertrude occasionally takes the initiative and acts in a protective way, and Claudius talks to Laertes about her in a way that permits an interpretation of dependence. Thus maternal features can be discovered in the direct relations between King and Queen. If one adds to this the fact that Claudius is also jealous of Hamlet, one discovers the usual elements of a positive Oedipus complex. And if all these factors are considered collectively, there can really be no doubt that the canker in Denmark's state is the oedipal crime, just as it is in Sophocles' *Oedipus*.

I am quite convinced that one can find in the works of literary geniuses objective truths about human nature (see Freud, 1930, p. 133). The difficulty lies, of course, in knowing when the artist is correct and when he is not. Since he does not use and certainly does not rely upon empiricism and experimentation, some of his claims about man may be—even though they are impressive, beautiful and esthetically pleasing—wrong, in what has to do with the real structure of the mind. Therefore, the artistic claim always has to be taken with a grain of salt and scrutinized in the light of science. Yet this observation should not be taken as anything more than a warning; it does not ignore the fact that the artistic genius often has the ability to bring to the surface a truth that is still hidden from the empiricist.

Was Shakespeare responding to an objective context, when he made the content of Hamlet's personal conflict coincide with the content of the state's corruption? The directions that negative answers to the question will take are obvious. It may be said that aesthetic reasons—that is, those that are rooted in literary techniques having to do with the structure of a play—necessitate the fusion of the two contents, since Hamlet is a prince. In such a situation, it would be particularly awkward to have two parallel actions: Hamlet's conflict and social conditions. It might be further pointed out that, for long periods of history, the personal conflicts of the man at the top of the hierarchy were decisive for the entire state. The "top man" was more than, and quite different from, what we call nowadays a "representative" of a state. War and peace, freedom and restraint, and many more such questions depended on the personal and wholly arbitrary decisions of the King or his equivalent. I do not need to go into all the qualifications that this statement—which is certainly incorrect, if it is taken out of context—requires. Yet the idea was that the sovereign held his power by divine command.

When *L'Etat c'est moi* had to be verbalized, this was no longer true; but the political world in which Prince Hamlet moves is one in which King and Community are still coterminous, even though unruly citizens may at times take a threatening attitude and the Church may try to impose its own demands on the Royal prerogative.[4] Thus it may be conceded that, in the imagery surrounding the mythological-absolutistic-apostolic-monolithic-hierarchical kingdom, the myth that forms the basis of the Oedipus complex may have a place.

Yet in the world that Shakespeare created in *Hamlet*, the oedipal crime is more than a myth; it is a deed that shakes the very foundation of the state—not only by virtue of the fact that it was perpetrated on the King, but even more importantly because it is the source of hypocrisy. Here Shakespeare really went beyond Freud, in making the complex the fountainhead of a poison that has pervaded the whole fabric of society.

What incenses Hamlet almost to the breaking point is Claudius' insolence in offering the face of honesty to perfection, *after* he has committed the oedipal crime. Since the perpetration of the crime in social reality is rather rare, Hamlet's resentment and indignation have to be understood as reactions to the older generation's persistent denial that at one time it was itself no better than the generation of its sons, that it had ever felt the patricidal impulse. It is this denial of "I, too, wanted to do it and have actually done it—in a dream, in fantasy, symbolically—when I was as young as you are," that separates the generations and deepens the younger generation's feeling of guilt to the point where that feeling becomes insufferable.

Hamlet has found out by chance that the older generation is also guilty. He does not deny his own guilt: "I could accuse me of such things that it were better my mother had not borne me" *(III-1-123f)*. It is interesting to compare Hamlet's self-accusations with what Freud (1917b,

---

[4] It would be necessary to determine exactly the sociological type of the political structure that is realized in *Hamlet*. Brunner (1956) has set forth the main categories that would have to be considered, I anticipate ambiguity, however, even within the sociopolitical framework. The question of the consequences of this looseness within this dimension of the play's structure is beyond the scope of the present investigation. It poses a challenging problem for aesthetics, as well as with regard to the psychology of man's relationship to his society.

p. 246) has to say about the melancholic patient: "He . . . seems to us justified in certain . . . self-accusations; it is merely that he has a keener eye for the truth than other people who are not melancholic. When in his heightened self-criticism he describes himself as petty, egoistic, dishonest, lacking in independence . . . it may be, so far as we know, that he has come pretty near to understanding himself; we only wonder why a man has to be ill before he can be accessible to a truth of this kind." Freud quotes *Hamlet* on this occasion and asserts that such reduction of self-esteem, whether it is based on fact or on delusion, is a sign of illness.

This is very true in clinical reality, where the melancholic exhausts his self-reproaches nonconstructively in exhibitionistic masochism; but when we observe Hamlet's gigantic struggle against societal hypocrisy, it becomes understandable that he should feel that he first has to cleanse himself of hypocrisy by voluntary admission of his own wickedness. No doubt, the self-observational function has been heightened in Hamlet at this point; yet he is different, in one major respect, from the melancholic patient. The latter, having been disappointed by a beloved person, turns against himself the aggression that has thus been aroused. Hamlet, too, has been disappointed by a beloved person, but in his case a substantial part of his aggression continues to flow not against himself, but against the enemy who has brought unhappiness upon him.[5] This is, I believe, an important difference. Hamlet's confession of guilt—which does not seem like neurotic mortification, but rather the result of correct self-scrutiny—represents an inner purification.

Oddly enough, Freud had found himself in a situation similar to Hamlet's when he was writing his book on dreams. In his letters to Fliess (1887-1902), one finds moving lines, which express his pain and grief about the fact that he has to bring to public attention some reprehensible impulses and wishes of his own (see letter of 21/9/1899).[6] Freud too combated societal hypocrisy; in his work, however, this takes a secondary place. The process of self-revelation and self-confession—even though it served a process of self-cleansing after his father's death—is lifted to a more sublimated level than it reaches in *Hamlet*. Freud's scientific background and his theoretical goals provide a more solid platform

---

[5] The disappointment brought about by his own father, of course, would set off in a character of different sort a drift toward melancholia.

[6] The sentence in question is as follows: "ist es nicht arg, so etwas andeuten, für jeden Wissenden also heraussagen zu müssen." [isn't it awful to have to hint at something of that sort, and in that way to spell it out to anyone who is in the know?] (my own translation). (For a possible identification by Freud with Hamlet, see later.)

than Hamlet's having to "set his time right." Thus, I do not see Hamlet's self-accusations as a sign of melancholia, but rather as an important step in his process of ridding himself of the poison within, which he is also trying to fight in social reality.

It is strange, perhaps, to see hypocrisy closely connected with the Oedipus complex. As a social phenomenon, hypocrisy actually deserves a great deal of attention, because of its pervasiveness, its existence in all societies. It is such a regular occurrence that one can be almost certain to detect it as an indispensable prerequisite of societal existence. Indeed, even the relationship of two people may become intolerable without some of its admixture. From what I have seen, at least, when two people have determined to be uncompromisingly honest and sincere to each other, that decision has amounted to hell-fire.

Truth can be extremely destructive. Hamlet's farewell speech to Laertes (or to his mother) implies the acknowledgment on his part of the fact that evil is necessary and thus hypocrisy must be forgiven. This is the most difficult step for an idealist to take; yet the acknowledgment of necessity does not preclude forceful opposition to it. Such acknowledgments may even sharpen the weapons employed against it, in that they include insight into the nature of what is being opposed.

Although the ubiquity of hypocrisy is widely acknowledged, strangely enough almost everyone feels deeply offended by a charge of hypocrisy and bigotry; many a person who would be able to tolerate the reproach of error or even of misdeed will nevertheless resent the other reproach.

Psychoanalysts are inclined to seek uniform explanations for phenomena that may actually be brought about by highly diverse causes. Myer Mendelson (1960) has tried to demonstrate this by a scrutiny of the psychoanalytic literature on depression. Am I now falling into the same mistake, of treating hypocrisy as if it were a uniform phenomenon? Is the hypocrisy of two lovers, of parent and child, of the Churches, the State, society at large the same phenomenon? I do not know, although to me Shakespeare seems to follow that line of thinking. Freud (1913d) placed the oedipal deed and the Oedipus complex at the center of his reconstruction of the dawn of civilization, and all occidental religions have their center in man's relationship to God, to whom qualities and traits of a plainly paternal nature are attributed. The family, which is the cell of society, certainly functions under the aegis of that psychic structure.

According to Shakespeare, at least in *Hamlet*, the connection of warfare with the Oedipus complex is quite striking. The ambition of young Fortinbras to invade Denmark is the direct consequence of his legacy from his father, and his war on the Poles is undertaken at his uncle's instigation. Fathers may thus be said to incite wars so that their sons are forced to deflect their aggressions, which they turned originally against their own fathers. Can it be, after all, that the artistic genius has intuited the truth again, as has so often happened in other instances, and are all those sociologists and anthropologists wrong who "prove" the "fallaciousness" of *Totem and Taboo?*

Hamlet is the tragedy of man and, at the same time, the tragedy of society. Whether, as Fergusson claims, the latter is the center and the former periphery, I will not debate here. We find the same uncertainty in the discussions of scientists and philosophers, when these discussions turn toward such questions as "nature vs. nurture," "constitution vs. environment," "the individual vs. society." Society presupposes individuals, individuals presuppose society. The relevant point in this context is the overlapping of the two areas in the Oedipus complex.

And the tragedy will go on. Fortinbras is symbolic of that future for which each generation fights, with the conviction that it will prove to be better than the past. For suffering in the present and the possession of illusions about the future seem to be intimately connected. We are dealing here with the *great promise* that is so typical of the human condition: parents allegedly sacrificing themselves for the sake of their progeny, and that progeny, when it has itself grown up, repeating the same cycle.

Christ and his early followers really believed that "glad tidings" would eventually ameliorate the human condition; instead, that condition actually reached its worst under the devastations of the religious wars. Enlightenment announces the reign of reason and science—and then brings into the world the horror of almost praeternatural destruction. Socialism has found the key to most of all human evils: a new man, less destructive and charitable, will arise once societal conditions have been established in accordance with its precepts. But no country has yet succeeded in satisfying the stipulations of socialism; and, while this may be no more than a coincidence, where they are approximated, the incidence of suicide is significantly heightened.

Thus Fortinbras serves in the end as a coda, to send the spectator away in less despondent spirits. We can be certain no new millennium will start with Fortinbras, however, since he is, after all, fictitious. No one escapes the oedipal conflict; each succeeding generation is weighed down by the curses of the generation that preceded it.

Yet here we may catch the fringe of another dimension that is embodied in the play—namely, its mythical aspects. One may be reminded of a God or semi-God who descends into the world in order to cleanse it, and in so doing is initially wounded but later resurrected to Heaven. Elements of the Christ and Hercules myths appear here. But is not the tenor of the fairy tale also heard from afar: "Once upon a time there was a prince, handsome and sweet to behold, who was melancholic. . . . " Myth, fairy tale, chronicle, legend, ritual—are these perhaps the ingredients that are condensed and synthesized in all those great plays that, once they have been created, persist in haunting man's imagination? I do not know, and I must leave it to others to decide.

Hamlet strikes me as being far more than what one ordinarily means when one speaks of "great tragedy." Still, it is foremost and manifestly a tragedy—which forces me to put down a few words in general about the nature of tragedy.

Western thought about tragedy centers about Aristotle's definition of it as the "imitation of an action." Since the word "imitation" has acquired a slightly pejorative shade, Aristotle would not object, I assume, if we replaced it with "presentation" or "representation." But is what one finds in *Hamlet* the representation of an action? It would rather seem to be the retardation of an action. This is, of course, a well-known and legitimate part of the technique of playwriting, but the legitimate use of retardation involves one step forward and a half-step backward, and that is by no means the rhythm of retardation in *Hamlet,* as I shall presently demonstrate. It may also be said that "retardation of action" can be subsumed under "action," and in that sense *Hamlet,* too, falls within the scope of Aristotle's definition. Yet—and this would strike me as a spurious argument—not only is it highly improbable that Aristotle's definition of action also included, let us say, passivity; quite independently of Aristotle, and the way in which he might have defined action on logical grounds, the plot of *Hamlet* cannot be described, it seems to me, as the representation of an action.

The following stages have to be distinguished: (a) Hamlet forms an intent, under the pressure from his father, to kill his father's murderer; (b) the first "action" he undertakes is the organization of the subplay, in order to verify the Ghost's report; (c) the realization of this plan and its inherent revelation of Hamlet's knowledge of Claudius' misdeed, as well as the implicit warning it gives to the prospective victim of his revenge, then generate a new series of external complexities, which make the fulfillment of Hamlet's primary aim far more difficult; (d) the next active step, the killing of Polonius (an active step, even though possibly an involuntary one), in turn, enlarges these external complexities, which now, in terms of Hamlet's enforced exile, make the realization of his mission not only infinitely more difficult but even improbable; (e) after his return, he accepts the challenge to a duel, although he is warned and himself has a foreboding that he is being lured into a trap. He goes into the trap and is poisoned; according to all external evidence, his last chance to obtain his goal has been lost.

Only at the moment when there are no chances left is that action carried out toward which almost the whole of the preceding play has pointed—but not until after the hero has caused one obstacle after the other to be piled up on its way. The depth and profundity of this conspicuous and often discussed disproportion between Hamlet's inner (psychologic) readiness and the external (psysical and social) barrier to his action is perceived—retroactively by the less astute spectator, but immediately by the reader—when it becomes clear that all the formidable external obstacles, which accumulate progressively and relentlessly, have in turn their stimulating effect upon Hamlet's internal growth. Even though one cannot attribute to those obstacles the character of being indispensable to Hamlet's growth—the play itself leaves that question open—their intertwining with Hamlet's internal growth is the key to the dramatic tension and creates in the spectator the inner conviction that Hamlet will consummate the final deed.

The extent to which *Hamlet* violates Aristotle's canon can be seen when one considers the following sentence in the *Poetics*: "The worst situation is when the personage is with full knowledge on the point of doing the deed, and leaves it undone. It is odious and also (through the absence of suffering) untragic; hence it is that no one is made to act thus, except in some few instances." The only example that Aristotle cites is an incident between Haemon and Creon from Sophocles' *Antigone*.

It is worthwhile examining more closely Aristotle's example of what is, in this context, "odious." Haemon, Creon's son, has left his father in despair, since the latter has decided on Antigone's death, even though she is to be his son's bride. When the repentant King, in order to free her, approaches the cave in which he has ordered that Antigone be enclosed so that she may starve to death, he hears his son's voice. Upon entering the cave, he perceives Antigone hanging, with Haemon embracing her. When the King pleads with him to come out, as the Messenger later tells the story, "The boy looked at him with his angry eyes, spat in his face and spoke no further word. He drew his sword, but as his father ran, he missed his aim. Then the unhappy boy, in anger at himself, leant on the blade."

If this was "odious" to Aristotle, what would he have said about Hamlet's behavior in the prayer scene? He would have regarded it as unimaginable that any such play should be considered a work of art at all. Viewed from any of a number of angles, *Hamlet* must be regarded as an abomination, in the light of the Aristotelian conceptual framework of tragedy. Consider, for example, Aristotle's insistence that in tragedy either happiness should go to misery or misery to happiness; yet in *Hamlet* the plot proceeds from one misery to another. Indeed, if we did not interpret the plot but merely took it literally, it would be hard to decide whether or not Hamlet was more miserable at the beginning of the play than he was at the end of it. [7]

 Peter Alexander, in an admirably profound study (1955), has reconciled Hamlet with the Aristotelian canon by means of an ingenious interpretation of *hamartia*—the "tragic flaw," the error of judgment in the hero that brings him to his fall. In so doing, he has also smashed to smithereens Campbell's (1930) and Anderson's (1927) views that Shakespeare put on the stage the psychological theories of his times. Without knowing Alexander's work, I had already tried to show in 1953 that, from the point of view of psychoanalytic ego-psychology, Hamlet's alleged *hamartia* (whether this *hamartia* is reflected in his unnecessary delay or in his rash killing of Polonius) was not at all a tragic flaw, but rather an index of a positive, constructive psychological process. I therefore welcome Alexander's reinterpretation of *hamartia*. Yet here is the point at which one can demonstrate the broad advantage that literature may be able to obtain from depth psychology, for despite the correctness (in my opinion, at least) of Alexander's

---

[7] One could perhaps say that *Hamlet* is a tragedy of suffering, like *Ajax*. There are, it is true, some similarities between *Hamlet* and *Ajax*; the madness, the unhappiness brought on the family, the conflict about disgracing the father. Odysseus' rescue, at the end, of both Ajax's prestige and his body may be equated with Horatio's final eulogy of Hamlet. But *Ajax* is not a tragedy of Peripaties and Discoveries, such as abound in *Hamlet*. The fact that Hamlet makes his first appearance in a state of conflict and grief makes him, as is to be discussed later, exceptional among Shakespeare's tragic heroes.

analysis, the traditional view of *hamartia* as a tragic flaw is also correct.

The *hamartia* that Hamlet suffers from is the living presence of a repressed Oedipus complex. If he had been truly adult at the beginning of the play, he would have responded to his father's story, as well as to his demand, quite differently from the way in which he did respond. Instead, his personal conflict and the relative unpreparedness of his ego to meet the demands of a task that has been imposed upon him by social reality make delay necessary for him.

Here is *hamartia* in the manifest sense in which Aristotle meant it to be understood. It does not make Hamlet a "bad" man, since he wants to be good; yet he arouses our pity because he is, despite the actuality of his good intentions, not yet ready to fulfill them. When he reaches the zenith of his preparedness and signifies that fact by saying "The readiness is all" *(V-2-224f)* we know that he has fought bravely and has overcome his particular *hamartia*. At that point, he deserves not our pity but our admiration.

The different views and evaluations one arrives at, depending upon whether one views Hamlet from the vantage point of the repressed or from that of the ego, make an exciting contrast, which is true to life. The imposition of reality on the self forces the ego to engage actively in a reorganization or further structurization of the self, in order to make ego-syntonic action possible. Hamlet's initial statement that he feels "spited" by the necessity of carrying out a task imposed upon him by reality *(I-5-189f)* (a confession that is more often interpreted wrongly than rightly) is a comment on his conscious willingness to follow up the demand that has been placed before him, and at the same time a confession of the fact that, for him, that paternal demand is ego-dystonic.[8]

We are dealing here with a category of conflicts to which H. Hartmann (1950, pp. 138-140, 145f) has called special attention—the intrasystemic conflict. We know that this is not the full area of conflict in Hamlet; behind the intrasystemic conflict, or engulfing it, rises the intersystemic conflict—the paralysis of the ego because it has been called on to avenge what was once and may be still an unconscious, repressed wish on the part of the avenger himself.

The interplay between intersystemic and intrasystemic conflicts in Hamlet heightens the sense of life that breathes through the play. It is

---

[8] I shall come back to this point later, when I discuss the function of retroactivity in Shakespeare.

plainly not enough to place the concept of conflict at the center of one's analysis of the play; one can follow up the quality of the various conflicts in the finest details of the play's fabric.

We shall now also be able to understand better the dynamic flow of the plot. The correlative of the delay in external action is the progress of inner action, and it is by just this disproportion between external and internal action that the unmatched dramatic tension of the play is created. Throughout the play the distance between Hamlet and the attainment of his goal increases, in terms of the reality that is depicted on the stage. The Mousetrap play, despite its success, makes its attainment less probable; the murder of Polonius, the exile to England, Claudius' plot and Laertes' willingness to cooperate—all these events cooperate to produce a final situation, in which it appears to be well-nigh impossible for Hamlet to attain his goal. Yet, parallel with this, we feel Hamlet's growth, his coming closer and closer *internally* to goal attainment.

That is why I find the key to the play's dynamic tension to be in the *disproportion* between external and internal reality, the flow and counterflow in external events and internal processes, the fact that the change in magnitude of distance goes in opposite directions, depending on whether one measures it in terms of external events or internal processes. There is the possibility, I admit, that a cynical mind may describe the plot as dealing with an habitual bungler, whose history is made presentable by the fact that the playwright artificially adds an inorganic ending of the *deus-ex-machina* type, through combining a lot of quite improbable, if not altogether impossible factors, so as to create a closing tableau that will conform to contemporary fashion, with as many corpses as possible and one conquering hero. While I myself would never agree with that opinion, I would like to note that, despite its seeming correctness, it does not explain why the play has preserved its dramatic effectiveness through several centuries and laid down a challenge for adequate explanation to the most illustrious minds.

Nevertheless, the role of *accidents* in *Hamlet*, and particularly their accumulation at the end, permits one to ignore that the end of the play is the organic outgrowth of what has preceded, and to assert instead that it (the end) is an artificial and aggregatelike addition. It is just here that we can observe how much of a challenge *Hamlet* is to the Aristotelian canon—almost, indeed as if Shakespeare wanted to prove its inadequacy. For, aside from his adherence to peripaty and discovery, without which drama is impossible, he did almost consistently the opposite of what Aristotle had advised playwrights to do.[9] There should be one action, says Aristotle, which forms a complete whole; its incidents must be so closely connected that the withdrawal of any one of them will disjoin the whole. And he offers us a method of verification with regard to this: if an incident makes no perceptible difference either by its presence or by its absence, then it is no real part of the whole. This measure has been applied, particularly by Robertson (1930), to many incidents in *Hamlet*—a fact that would seem to prove the play's lack of complete wholeness.

Aristotle also criticizes, at least indirectly, incidents that occur of themselves or by mere chance. Such incidents, of course, abound in *Hamlet*; in fact, they increase in frequency the closer the drama comes to its end. At least, Aristotle demands, the incident should not be without meaning, as happened when the statue of Mitys fell down during a performance and killed the author of a play whose subject was Mitys' death. In other words, incidents of an animistic nature are meaningful, even when they seem to occur by mere chance. And when Aristotle says that there should be nothing improbable among the actual incidents, it is clear that he would give Shakespeare a bad mark for *Hamlet,* which is surely, at the literal level, an accumulation of improbable incidents.

Here one may also recall Aristotle's definition of "episodic" plots as being those in which there is neither probability nor necessity in the sequence of episodes—something that could be said about most of *Hamlet*. If, by contrast, one looks closely at a play like *Ajax*, which I have mentioned before, one is struck by its infallible logic. Ajax's rage over having been cheated out of a prize he deserved; his killing cattle and sheep instead of Kings and counselors, because a goddess had blinded and deluded him; his shame and subsequent suicide; his brother's dispute with Menelaus and Agamemnon over the body's interment; Odysseus' intervention—all these episodes evolve from what has preceded them, with stringent necessity. They are almost predictable in their cold logical sequence.

Thus we have to discuss the difficult problem of *accident* in *Hamlet*. A mind that in my opinion looked deeply and profoundly into the chaos that surrounds us, yet had to be severely criticized for its own errors and

---

[9] Shakespeare did not know Aristotle's *Poetics* (Whitaker, 1965, pp. 50, 54, 61), and therefore his massive differences from Aristotle cannot be reckoned as intentional.

inconsistencies, wrote the following about the accidental in Shakespeare: "Hitherto, neither our research nor our speculation has hit upon this in him—that he is *the Dramatist of the Incidental* . . . It is incidental that the political situation of *Hamlet,* the murder of the King and the succession question impinge upon just that character that Hamlet is . . . " (Spengler, 1918, Vol. 1, p. 143, author's italics). And he continues, to use my own translation: "The fact that Shakespeare takes the anecdote as he finds it and in so doing fills it with the impulsion [that is inherent in] the innermost necessity . . . this one has not yet been able to understand." I must add that Spengler uses—for what was translated as incident—the term *Zufall,* which is actually closer in meaning to the co-incidental and the accidental. In Shakespeare's plays, the accidental really plays an enormous role. With incredible ingenuity he goes about finding solutions for seemingly unresolvable complications.

Now we know that there are no "accidents," in any real sense, in the universe: each event is determined by an infinitely long series of causes. Yet the factor of accident is part and parcel of the way in which the world is experienced. We call it an "accident" if an event whose occurrence does not impress us as being necessary, simply because it takes place at a certain time and place, has effects that are out of proportion with those the same event would have had, if it had not coincided with a specific other event. When a tile falls from a roof and kills a passer-by, we say that the tragedy was brought about "by accident," although the event is as strictly determined as it would have been if the tile had dropped a second later and not killed anyone.

What we deny is the strict causality that has brought together the tile's fall at this particular time and the killed man's presence at that same moment and in that same place. We say the man might just as well have been at this time a yard ahead or a yard behind. The tile's fall is not therefore experienced as a meaningful event that is fully connected with the man's death. We do not perceive a strict determination in the coincidence. We will probably be inclined to conclude that the tile could not have dropped at a later time, because of the physical wear and tear that has been superimposed upon the mason's sloppiness or his inefficiency, but at the same time that the passerby's presence at the time of the accident depended on a variety of factors that were not either relevant or meaningful to his personality. If he had met a friend at the corner and been delayed, if he had received a telephone call before leaving, then nothing would have happened to him. Indeed, he would not have had the slightest inkling of how close to death he had been or of the fact that the call had saved his life.

Yet when such accidents take place, gradually a transformation by psychologizing sets in. Such reactions may occur as: "Who would ever have thought it?" or "He only recently spoke of his forebodings of an early death." In brief, the event now takes on the coloring of destiny. For certain, those who were close to the man who was killed will henceforth refer to the event as an act of destiny. The widow and the children will incorporate it into their own life experience, as one that has been ordained by the profound mystery of destiny. Indeed, modern psychology may come close to viewing the course of individual lives as the compound of effects brought about by forces that stem in part from the momentary state of the subject's unconscious, in part from the general tendencies of the individual compulsion to repeat, and in part from the repetition compulsion that governs the history of groups.

Repetition compulsion is intimated in *Hamlet* at two levels. Hamlet repeats his father's "destiny": he, too, is poisoned (my belief is that this was also at the hands of a younger "brother"). Fortinbras does to Denmark what Denmark had done to old Fortinbras. Passivity is turned into activity: what old Fortinbras has suffered, the Crown of Denmark has to suffer at the hands of Norway.

Yet this does not touch on the heart of the problem. The improbable pirates of mercy and Hamlet's sudden, and equally improbable, return to Elsinore; the exchange of rapiers; Gertrude's death and many more such events in the play are, if looked at from the ordinary point of view, no more than accidental coincidences. Critics have even accused Hamlet of being so irresponsible as to have wound up making the consummation of the final deed dependent on coincidences that were outside his sphere of volition and actually determined by Claudius' plotting—as if, even at the end, Hamlet were no more than a plaything of happenings that were external to him and, in the long run, mere accidents. It is questionable to what extent such an interpretation is at all legitimate; it sounds to me more like a travesty than an adequate description of the universe that Shakespeare created.

The pirates of mercy constitute the medium that was operative in the direction of Hamlet's return, but the return itself was his destiny. His absence from Elsinore has been enforced by a number of different factors. (In terms of plot presentation, one additional factor was the necessity for Shakespeare to get him out of the way, temporarily, so as to make possible the unimpeded unfolding of Ophelia's fate.) The accumulation of external obstacles, along with the increasing improbability of Hamlet's attaining his goal—all these continued under the pressure of a dynamism that was inherent in the tragedy itself. Their flow was not to be interrupted. We are dealing here with a paradox: the more the obstacles seem to be accidental—mere aggregates of events, when viewed in isolation—the more they nevertheless leave the impression of being part of a sequence, interlocked by an internal pressure that is invisible yet relentless.

But I would also compare Hamlet's absence with what is known in the psychoanalytic process as a period of "working through." When we last saw him before his departure for England, he was in a state of excitement as the result of the most consequential experiences, which had certainly widened his horizon and made him more adult. When we meet him again in the graveyard scene, he has become quieter. Gains in terms of the growth of his personality have become integrated, and he now conducts himself with admirable serenity—at least up to the point of renewed traumatization by Ophelia's funeral, or of provocation by Laertes. He behaves in the way one can observe a patient behaving after a period of "working through," and between two phases, in the latter of which new material will emerge that will call for new interpretations.

The choice of the particular agent, pirates of mercy, may require specific interpretation, but that is a question without relevance to the fact of Hamlet's return: it was his *destiny* to reappear. Similar thinking can be applied to the complications of Gertrude's death and the exchange of the rapiers. Whether Gertrude's death is really determined by destiny is questionable. It is perhaps Claudius' destiny to destroy her, since she would have been the only one who could have rescued him. Just as Ophelia's destiny is determined by the vicissitudes of her father and her lover, so perhaps is Gertrude's by the ferocious combat between two men, one of whom is her son.

Perhaps these two women have no fate of their own; their fate is imposed on them. By contrast, Hamlet, Claudius, Laertes do have a fate, and they actively involve themselves in its fulfillment. In any case, Gertrude's drinking poison, while ostensibly this takes place by "accident," is in actuality an organic part of the total situation. There are intimations of suicide, of flight from the world before she has to suffer supreme grief, of retribution for foibles and sins, but there is certainly nothing of the coincidence of two events brought about by mechanical forces.

The exchange of rapiers is to a greater extent determined by

Laertes' destiny, and carries with it the implication of retribution and salvation, leading to Hamlet's final apotheosis. Yet whatever Shakespeare's choices of accident might have been, what is essential is that Hamlet's consummation of the deed has by this time become a certainty. The *deus ex machina* in ancient tragedy is an addition—"free for the asking"—since the Gods pursue opposites and it was only question of which one of the many available Gods to call in. In *Hamlet* the physical obstacles have almost made the deed impossible—or so it appears to the spectator—yet the latter is certain that it will come to pass, because Hamlet is now ready and it is his destiny. The accidental character of the agents only stresses the fatefulness of the event as arising out of inner necessity; for the greater the external obstacles, the greater becomes Hamlet's inner determination.

To my mind, Alexander's (1955) Northcliffe Lectures of 1953 constitute a great step forward in the understanding of Hamlet: he has defeated for good, and with enviable persuasiveness, any theory that attempts to see in Shakespeare an exponent or mouthpiece (not to say puppet) of contemporaneous psychology or morality, an idea that had previously drawn a thick curtain before any possibility of really understanding a work like *Hamlet,* or even of coming close to it. He has purified the air of many a prejudice that had long stood in the way of efforts to grasp the depth of Shakespeare's work. He has, finally, brought delivery from these burdens by demonstrating that what critics had always previously regarded as inconsistencies in Hamlet are not flaws in literary creation but rather opposites that form a union.

Union of opposites—this is, indeed, the key to many seeming riddles in Hamlet, and Alexander traces the history of the concept in the history of Western thought. Union of opposites is also the hallmark of Freud's work; in Alexander's essays there are thus traces of the *Zeitgeist* to be found. Yet, despite the excellence of his literary analysis—or better, precisely because of this excellence—the opportunity has been created to demonstrate just how far literary criticism alone is able to penetrate into the secrets of a great literary work, and at what point psychological knowledge also becomes necessary.

I cannot see the literary critics as being able to explain the opposites, their function and origin, or why the one lies at the surface, while the other is not fully observable. Alexander illustrates opposites by using examples from antiquity, such as that of Epaminondas, in whom courage and humaneness were equally present and to a maximal degree. Yet courage and humaneness do not any longer strike us as opposites, even though, to be sure, the type of pseudo-masculine man who equates consideration with weakness, who must constantly prove his freedom from fear by exposing himself to danger, is clinically well known. For him, of course, courage does per se exclude humaneness.

Alexander applies the principle of the union of opposites, for example, to the prayer scene. As is well known, many a critic has drawn consequences unfavorable to Hamlet from his not making full use of the opportunity. The author asks: "Might not Hamlet also be sufficiently a man to refrain without loss of face from stabbing a villain in the back?" and he compares this internal check with Romeo's self-discipline, when he is challenged by Tybalt. Yet Hamlet himself assures us that he is not restrained by any consideration of humaneness, but solely by the enormity of his revenge and by his inability to endure the thought of his enemy's going to Heaven while his poor father must continue to suffer in Purgatory. I fear that the principle of the union of opposites has here led to an idealization of motivation. Likewise, I do not believe that Alexander's explanation of Hamlet's madness does full justice to the problem. If I understand him correctly, he assigns to that madness primarily the function of letting the victim know what is coming, without at the same time betraying to anyone else the secret that he and Claudius share (p. 180). Yet for this purpose the mousetrap play would suffice.

That there is a union of opposites in Hamlet I do not doubt; but I find these opposites in areas that are quite different from those in which Alexander finds them. It is my opinion that in *Hamlet*, we have a union of opposites not only in the tragic main character, but in the dynamic flow of the action. The fact that there is an action imposed on the protagonist that consistently goes in opposite directions is, in the long run, what provides the extraordinary aesthetic tension of the play.

This is the disproportion I have already referred to between external obstacles and inner inhibition: when, initially, one is zero, the other is maximal; at the end, the former is at maximum and the latter zero. It is this that endows the structure of the plot with an inner tension and strain that are scarcely endurable. To have been able to keep the two consistently balanced against each other, as Shakespeare did, testifies to incomparable skills.

In this, the play achieves an anti-Machiavellian flavor. One aspect of Machiavellian philosophy can, I believe, be epitomized as the justification of practicality in state matters, in complete disregard of ethical considerations.[10] Machiavelli would have advised Hamlet against the mouse-trap play, against offending Rosencrantz and Guildenstern, against a break with Ophelia; instead, he would have been in favor of a quick marriage with Ophelia, as one way of bringing Polonius onto Hamlet's side, and he would have thought it a fatal mistake on Hamlet's part to accept the proposition of the voyage to England. Thus Hamlet acts throughout the play against the precepts of Machiavelli. If he had only relied on the latter's policy, it is very likely that he would have obtained the crown.

Hamlet is the very proto-type of impracticality, and yet he does attain his goal: the state emerges healthy and rejuvenated, after the evil in it has been destroyed by someone whom most critics describe as a political bungler. The general meaning of *Hamlet*, I believe, is that it is not the *action* that necessarily counts; the *state of mind*, the *motive*, is at least as relevant. This is an idea that is not at all compatible with Machiavelli's politico-psychological theories. *Hamlet* represents, indeed, an extreme point of view. Even if the deed is in conformity with societal standards, even if it is compellingly necessitated by them and at the same time demanded by one's own conscience, nevertheless it should be carried out only when the entire personality is able to accept it without inner conflict and doubt, and in that way can truly carry it out. Ethical standards are here dissolved into psychological realities—a feat in which Shakespeare was several centuries ahead of the Elizabethan psychologists, moral philosophers and theologians—not to speak of some of our own time.

I would like now to turn to a purely psychoanalytic question, which may have little direct bearing on the structure of the play. Freud's interpretation of the central conflict in Hamlet revolved around the clash between a repressed wish and a task that is demanded by external reality. In trying to express that conflict in detail, one may say that, while the ego accepts the task, the superego interferes with its execution by saying: You, of all people, to punish a culprit for a crime that you yourself desired to carry out! The feeling of guilt about the past wish then paralyzes the ego, which is thereby prevented from carrying out what it knows to be its duty. If it merely accepted the role of the avenger without itself changing, it would make itself guilty of hypocrisy—which is probably one of the unconscious reasons for Hamlet's sometimes exasperated accusations against hypocrisy, as well as for his fight against it.

[10] See Spencer (1942) for Machiavelli on Shakespeare.

With the development of ego psychology by Freud, however, it has become challenging to look once again into the Hamlet problem. As I have already suggested, a sequence is discoverable in the soliloquies that speaks strongly in favor of a meaningful development in terms of ego change. My interpretation along these lines may have sounded strained and at times even far-fetched, but I can only hope that it did not go beyond the possible, even though it did not always follow the probable. Be that as it may, this viewpoint would refer the play's excitement to an intrasystemic conflict: the battle between repressed and superego, fought out within the ego's territory, would then be replaced by a strife between two factions, both of which, however, reside legitimately in the ego.

The question then arises, of course, as to why the ego does not know of this strife. In our examination of various interpretations by critics, we found ourselves raising the question: "If what is claimed by the critics does go on inside Hamlet, why doesn't he tell us so?" In the soliloquies he confesses to the existence of feelings and problems that live in him unhampered by external considerations. When one suggests a motive that is not verbalized by the protagonist, therefore, one should be expected to add an explanation of why the protagonist is not aware of that motive. That is what it now behooves me to attempt.

After all, the self-imposed demand that one carry out the deed in the name of personal conviction and not merely because one has been told to do so by authority is egosyntonic, and it is not clear what could prevent it from becoming conscious. Indeed, if the repressed and the ego were kept strictly separate, this problem would also grow to full awareness in Hamlet. There are patients who seek treatment because they feel like automata, incapable of experiencing work and love as *their* work and love.

If I have given the impression (and I fear I may have) that Hamlet's problem is the integration of a task, I have made the same mistake as Beres (1965), who does not differentiate between integration and what I call here appersonation. The degree of psychic integration is by no means correlated with whether a duty is fulfilled because it was ordered by secular or divine authority, or is carried through out of personal conviction, and quite independently of any external power. The external demand may be fully integrated as a demand, while still preserving its representation in the self as an external demand.

There are religions that demand of the believer that he bow to divine authority and accept God's word as it is set forth in the revealed texts. Such a demand having been fully integrated by the believer, the request to make the content of what the divinity demands a matter of personal conviction would be quite unacceptable to the orthodox. As we can see in the story of Abraham, it is the unconditional and unquestioning submission to Divine commands that is the sign of true piety, and only he who has integrated this attitude has fulfilled the principles that are embodied in his superego. Integration is, so to speak, of a different dimension from the modality of representation of superego demands as having their source either in external demands or entirely in internal ones.

Hamlet's problem is the *transformation of modality*. He demands of himself that a duty that he accepts as valid and correct, and which he has integrated *qua duty*, should be carried out only when it is represented in him as a *dictate of his own conscience*, quite independently of what his father has commanded him to do and, in the end, even quite independently of what happened to his father. In both these versions, however, there is the seed of rebellion against the father.

This self-imposed request for a fully appersonated modality is subterraneously connected with infantile aggressive drives against the father, and for that reason Hamlet's self-reproaches are quite correct. It is not only the repressed oedipal wishes that Hamlet must avenge in Claudius that are neither permitted nor able to become conscious; the intrasystemic struggle for appersonation of the motive also suffers this fate.

Such a request for appersonation, it seems, can be as strong as it is in Hamlet only when a strong ambivalence toward the father, stemming from infancy, lurks behind it. The effect on creative productivity that arises from ambivalence toward the father during the course of male development comes to the fore here. Hamlet's striving toward full appersonation is, indeed, a striving toward an ego state that must be evaluated as being of a higher order than one in which external demands are integrated in the form of authoritative commands. This sector of Hamlet's psychopathology cannot, therefore, be regarded as neurotic; it is that psychopathology that is involved in growth and development into independent adulthood. While it carries within it the seed of neurotic conflict, in Hamlet, as the final deed shows, it has led to fully integrated and appersonated male adulthood.

* * *

I will close this section with the discussion of two problems for which I cannot find an answer and will therefore leave in the form of questions.

A play-within-a-play should arouse our particular curiosity when it occurs in a play by Shakespeare, whose principal purpose and function was, after all, to write plays. I shall not here consider other instances of the sort in Shakespeare's plays. In *Hamlet*, the play-within-a-play holds a central place. I have tried, by judging it to be the equivalent of a dream-within-a-dream, to show what the repressed wish was to which Hamlet gave expression by his staging of this play. But I have neglected the fact that the primary function of the play was, after all, to find out whether or not the ghost was right. The play-within-a-play in this case is a question that the playwright poses, a question that is directed toward external reality.

This is strange. We usually think of a work of art as an attempt to suggest or propose an answer, an attempt to *solve a problem*. Yet here the play is a big question mark, and the answer to the question it poses will be given by a force outside of itself, the King, who is in this sense the most important member of the play's audience. I have the feeling that in this a profound secret is revealed, a mystery that ties the artist to the world. Were all the plays that Shakespeare created, in the end, also questions? Is there in every play, unbeknownst to us, a buried question, which the creator hoped would be answered from without? From what force did he expect the answer to come?

In *Hamlet* it is the King who will answer. We cannot equate him with an ordinary audience: he is at the head of the state, and the mouse-trap was created indirectly at his instigation. It is his response that will decide whether or not the whole state is on sound foundations, whether it will continue or perish. The place he holds is that of a quasi-divine power. It is of interest that the mouse-trap per se is a frequent symbol of time and death. Can it be, then, that every great masterwork is a question posed to the Divinity, which the artist hopes will be answered by some transcendental force?

The other problem is Shakespeare's evident predilection for choosing the subjects of his dramatic works from other sources and not being as original in setting up the plot as one would expect from such an eminently productive original mind.

5. Limitations of the Historical View

Modes of Interpretation of Literary Works.

The many different strands that connect Shakespeare's tragedies with Elizabethan moral philosophy and psychology have been amply documented. One result has been that Shakespeare has now been made to appear as no more than a child of his century, bound in the end within the limits of the historical age that he lived in. What may have been lost through this approach, however, is the way in which Shakespeare actually did transcend the discursive, explicit knowledge of his contemporaries.

True, he seems to have been familiar with Elizabethan tracts, and many a passage of his can indeed be connected with passages in the writings of the moral philosophers. The same thing can also be said about the language Shakespeare used. It was, after all, Elizabethan language, even though he did enrich it by original coinage. What is most important in this regard, however, is that he used the language in a new and unique way, forming out of the Elizabethan language a tool such as no one either before or after him has wielded.

One has to make some comment at this point on the *Zeitgeist* of this particular historical period. As Boring (1955) has so penetratingly shown, the *Zeitgeist* will either favor or obstruct certain cultural pursuits. What the *Zeitgeist* of the Elizabethan age did favor was psychological inquiry into the nature of the human mind and its functioning. The tradition in this respect was strong, but not uniform. Aristotle,

Plato, Augustine, the medieval figures, Thomas Aquinas—these were all quite alive, in terms of the influence of what they had said about virtue, sin and Man. The theory of "humors," "spirits" and "passions" was quite flexible and had therefore produced a never-ending mulling-over of topics that were by their nature essentially psychological. Curiously enough, the Elizabethan concept of man was not entirely dissimilar to wide areas now covered by psychoanalysis; there is not only a psychological reason, therefore, but an historical facet as well, involved in Shakespeare's deep influence on Freud.

In the Elizabethan notion of a variety of humors one can see the antecedents of the current idea of a variety of forms of libido; already at that time man was viewed as being constantly engaged in a conflict between reason and the passions. Indeed one might say that, at least in one sense, the Elizabethan age was richer than ours in aliveness to the human world: it was a world in which God—certainly one of the most human of all concepts that have sprung from the human brain—was still endowed with full reality; a world in which the Devil still set traps, and ghosts stalked the land, in which honor was still regarded as a positive value, and people spoke earnestly of virtue and true love. While the medieval world had maintained these attitudes and beliefs, however, they no longer constituted, by the time of Elizabeth, shackles upon observation and adventure.

Thus the *Zeitgeist* reflected a strong impetus toward adventurous inquiry into the world of the human mind—not yet in terms of scientific, that is, quantitative inquiries, but rather as inquiries that were to be carried through by direct observation, having been born primarily of curiosity and empathy. Although the human mind had not yet been completely reduced to something quantifiable or explainable, it was no longer viewed as quasi one-dimensional in its relationship to God. Thus the time was most propitious for the emergence of such a genius as Shakespeare. The eye was free to look at man, in all dimensions, as he was; there was no theological or any other such barrier to the satisfaction of passionate curiosity; and the new abstractions offered in books by the erudite laid out a frame that was sufficiently broad not to hamper the curious but rather to provoke them into tackling deeper and deeper mysteries.

In that sense, the historical approach doubtless enriches our understanding of Shakespeare's tragedies. Yet a firm line of demarcation must be made between those literary works that can be understood and enjoyed only under the guidance and through the mediation of historical knowledge, and those works that by and large stand on their own, because of the richness of life that they contain or create.

In reconstructing the historical background of these latter works, one has to be very careful not to misconstrue the core of the work—which is what happened, in my opinion, with one author who has made, in terms of the reconstruction of the historical background, a meritorious contribution to the literature on Shakespeare (Campbell, 1930). Miss Campbell really did bring to life the psychology of the Elizabethan age. Despite differences of opinion among the moral philosophers, she was able to draw quite precisely the framework of the psychology of that period, as well as to indicate the problems that became the center of inquiry, and the main answers to these problesm that were set forth by Shakespeare's contemporaries.

How was this extraordinary feat of erudition applied, however, to the *Hamlet* tragedy, which, according to Miss Campbell, was a tragedy of grief? "Persons of different temperament are shown under the influence of the same passion, so that we may see the passion variously manifested." Quite correctly she goes on to observe: "The play of Hamlet is concerned with the story of three young men—Hamlet, Fortinbras, and Laertes—each called upon to mourn the death of a father." Following the desire for revenge, "each must act according to the dictates of his own temperament and his own humour." Hamlet summed up in a psychology of temperament and humour? Our interest in Shakespeare's plays would have waned long since, if there were no more than that in them. Perhaps his contemporaries may have seen no more in his characters, and it is even possible that Shakespeare himself might have agreed with Miss Campbell's analysis. Yet once we turn back to the text itself, we meet on every hand a far more complex and profounder world than that of temperaments and humours.

Hamlet's father had been at one and the same time heroic and unaffectionate toward his son; his mother had made herself guilty—in his eyes, even enormously guilty; and he himself had been put under a yoke of what he called a "dread command." While Laertes was younger than Hamlet, however, his father was considerably older than Hamlet's father had been when he died. Thus Laertes was born late, at a time when the father's image is characterized rather by the traits of a grandfather than by those of an authoritarian father.

This difference in the way in which Hamlet and Laertes were treated by their fathers is most penetratingly presented by Shakespeare. There is only one reference to Laertes' mother—a fact that is most significant. If *he* remained calm in response to his father's murder, says Laertes, that would prove that he was not his father's son: "cries cuckold to my father, brands the harlot/Even here, between the chaste unsmirched brows/ Of my true mother" *(IV.5.117-120)*. That is to say, the mother had not herself given any cause for doubt; it would be only the failure of the son that besmirched her.

Fortinbras did not grow up under the tutelage of a father at all. Moreover, he had to cope with an uncle who was merely an infirm and apparently nonauthoritarian guardian. And once again, very pointedly, not one word is said about his mother. In psychoanalytic parlance, fate— the accident of circumstances—has spared him the oedipal conflict. He can therefore be brave, uninhibited, masterful—and victorious.

What Miss Campbell and perhaps Shakespeare's contemporaries thought of as differences in temperament and humour was in reality differences among personages who, according to the text itself, had lived up to that point under essentially different psychological-environmental conditions. The structures of their respective Oedipus complexes were essentially different, which was why their behavior and reaction to identical, almost identical, or at least very similar stimuli were essentially different. Shakespeare went far beyond the limits set for his contemporaries by their own blinders. His characters are therefore by no means the product of temperament and humour; they are organisms growing out of a living matrix. They have temperament, it is true; yet this is presented not as a static factor, but rather as intimately connected with a variety of environmental variables.[1]

At one point, it seems to me, Shakespeare proffers a hidden yet unmistakable criticism of the psychology of his own time. I have in mind two speeches by Claudius at the beginning of the play: his speech from the throne *(I.2.1ff)*, and his consolatory address to Hamlet *(I.2.87ff)*. In the former, says Miss Campbell, the sort of wisdom is exalted by the

---

[1] It is interesting to view here the most elaborate "study" of oedipal reactions. In *The Brothers Karamazov* Dostoevski portrays four types: Dmitri, who plans and wishes to commit the oedipal crime but recoils at the last moment; Ivan, who opposes it while secretly favoring it; Aliosha, who is beyond it, and Smerdiakov, who talks little about it but carries it out. It is noteworthy that Dostoevski does not drop hints about the childhood histories of his characters, but presents them in breadth by most subtle psychological details, taking the view that only someone who is mentally deranged— which probably meant to him brain-injured—could become a patricide. Lastly, I believe one would have to regard Shakespeare as the greater psychologist of the two.

King that consists of trying to find the mean between the extremes by mixing them (*one auspicious and one dropping eye; mirth in funeral, and dirge in marriage*), and Plutarch is cited, the wisdom of the former being taken back to Seneca. What the King is supposedly offering here is the consolation of philosophy. Thus what we are here encountering, it would seem, is a poetic exposition of that philosophical and psychological knowledge with which the Elizabethan elite was already quite familiar.

Yet one cannot overlook the fact that this knowledge is used, within the context of the play, by a criminal, who is attempting to rationalize his own offensive behavior of marrying his former sister-in-law, after she had been widowed through his own poisonous deed. What is more, Claudius' consolation is misplaced, in that it is directed toward a son who only *seems* to be grieving unduly about the loss of a father, when in reality he is heartbroken because of his mother's offensive behavior. Yet it is in this very scene that Hamlet turns his back upon appearances and instead exalts "that within which passeth show."

It is in this scene, then, that Shakespeare, to my mind, turns against the psychology of his times, which depended on outward signs, thereby disregarding the true issue, which is really conflict. Shakespeare's own psychology—as we see it expressed in *Hamlet* among other plays—is that of conflict. Elizabethan psychology, while it was rich in observations of detail that were astute and, for the most part, valid, did not penetrate to the core of the personality; instead, it got itself caught in surface observations that, in accordance with the contemporary bias, were explained in terms of humour and temperament. The speech from the throne sounds to my ear like a highly sophisticated and rather subtle parody of Elizabethan common-sense psychology.

Tamerlane may be humour and temperament; Hamlet is certainly far more. Shakespeare could never have created his great tragedies, if the inner representation of the characters he gave birth to had had its roots in what appears somewhat impoverished, when compared with the psychology that can be abstracted from the soil of Elizabethan moral philosophy. He must, of course, have been familiar with the common-sense psychology of his times but the question is *what he created* out of that common sense—that is, what universe he left in his plays. And I think I could prove, point by point, for all of Miss Campbell's examples, that what he created went far beyond what he created it out of. Shakespeare's tragedies are not studies in affect, even though affect stands at their center, just as affects do with regard to human life.

A brief digression on this theme may not be out of place at this point. Every age develops its own psychological common sense, the origin of which is not our concern here. In the Victorian age, "common sense" told you that a "normal" woman was either chaste or had no sexual appetites; those instances that did not follow this common-sense rule were regarded as deviations, or else as that famous "exception to the rule," which is, in fact, supposed to prove the rule. In our own age, common sense has become more and more inclined to tell us that the little boy has incestuous wishes and that he will be fighting them throughout the rest of his life. As has often been noted, the past discovery of the genius becomes the common sense of the present.

This has its bearing on the problem of artistic creation. When an age gains new insight, that insight usually makes its appearance in a variety of different fields. Some of the discoveries that go to Freud's credit can also be traced back historically to the works of the Austrian dramatist and novelist, Arthur Schnitzler, whose novels, short stories, and plays are scarcely known in this country—and quite undeservedly so. I have the impression that, initially, the poet might have been ahead of the scientist, at least for a few years. Yet, by and large, although mutual fertilization cannot be ruled out, one could say on good grounds that neither Schnitzler's artistic output nor Freud's scientific output would probably have been very much different from what each actually was, if either of the two had not been active. One can therefore assume that it was a common historical matrix, or the identity of the *Zeitgeist,* that led these two geniuses to create comparable values—in different media, of course —in accordance with the specific endowments of each.

In addition, there is the historical constellation of a genius who is making revolutionary discoveries that will upset most of his contemporaries and provoke their rejection, and yet will be picked up by at least one other congenial mind which, under their influence, will then create the unusual in his own area. To select arbitrarily one example among many, one could mention Jean-Jacques Rousseau's influence on the German *Sturm und Drang* movement, which culminated in Goethe's *Werther.* At that time, at least in Germany, J.-J. Rousseau's philosophy had not yet been reduced to a common-sense level. It was still marked by its earlier *coup de foudre* flavor, with its provocative appeal and ensuing strong emotions.

Psychoanalysis, on the other hand, has come more and more to be in this country a common-sense psychology. Its effect on literature, I believe, has much to do with that fact. The public has become accustomed, primarily by way of the artistic media, to the idea that children evolve strong and forbidden emotions toward their parents and therefore become later involved in strange conflicts, bizarre sexual patterns, murder, and what not. Yet when any psychology becomes a common-sense one, it loses its artistically inspiring effect. The genius is the arch-enemy of common sense; again and again he upsets it. Without the genius, we might all still be squatting in caves.

The relationship between common sense and artistic production is only one aspect of a problem that has not yet been solved. There are artists who do succeed in freeing their thinking from the bounds of contemporary common sense, and thereafter produce works whose meaning seems to pierce through the walls of the *Zeitgeist*, and yet which are not endowed with that undefinable quality that is needed to make them enduring masterpieces. Instead, they strike us as being rather bizarre; their content has not been matched by their form.

However great Shakespeare may have been psychologically, he would not have been able to create his tragedies if he had not possessed the linguistic genius to make his characters speak in a way that stirs us. The formal element should therefore not be forgotten; in the master, the two are united and equally superb: the conception of life and the form in which that conception becomes transmitted. It may even be—although I have my doubts about this—that the one is not possible without the other, and that those people are right who assert that, in general, content and form cannot be separated or ought not to be separated.

Be that as it may, those who like to see in Shakespeare the mouthpiece of Elizabethan moral philosophy, and in his works the form in which that age's psychology can be studied, thereby do a grave injustice to his genius and to the scope of his work, even though a study of the psychology of his times is no doubt an integral and justified part of Shakespearean research.[2]

It now becomes necessary to tackle a problem of some consequence to literary criticism. In every work of art, whether it be literary or visual, there is something explicitly or implicitly represented. While the opinions of different interpreters may differ widely concerning a literary work of *Hamlet's* scope, an unsophisticated viewer may be tempted to

---

[2] Grebanier (1960, p. 197) expressed this most succinctly when he called on us to "think of Hamlet as a human being, instead of as an automaton operating exclusively according to Elizabethan conventions."

respond that *Hamlet* is, after all, nothing more than the representation of an historical event. For the psychologically minded, however, it may be the study of an affect—a representation of all the different forms that a certain affect may take in different personality types. To the analyst, on the other hand, it may mean the representation of one particular way of reacting to the Oedipus complex.

This diversity of approaches (and there are many more) need not disquiet us, not only because we find an equal variety of approaches behind the reactions (both scientific and nonscientific) to human life, but also because it would speak against the excellence of the work if its interpretative scope were really a narrow one. When we cut up the tragedy into its elements or single parts, however, we do so in the expectation of ultimately obtaining a *rapprochement* with regard to the vexing question of what it is that is being represented. Let us see what happens when we try this with one of the highlights of the tragedy—the graveyard scene, with its discourse between Hamlet and Horatio on the subject of death.

In Hamlet's first soliloquy, it is clear beyond any doubt that the subject of his discourse is Hamlet's emotional reaction to an event that he has experienced as tragic. It is true that, during the course of his emotional outbursts, the spectator also learns some so far unknown details of real events. Yet these are clearly not the primary contents of the representation. Hamlet's speech on the transience, frailty, evanescence of human existence leads Miss Campbell to comment that in the grave-diggers' scene "Hamlet exhibits another accepted manifestation of his being the victim of melancholy *adust* as it is derived from the sanguine humour, for the sanguine *adust* turns tragedies into comedies, as does Hamlet here, while he jests with horror" (p. 141).

Is the content of the representation in this scene really Hamlet's temperament? I shall have more to say about Hamlet's discourse on death when I discuss his madness; I want to limit myself here to commenting that that discourse is not in any sense an illustration of temperament, that the content of the representation is rather a general statement of human life or existence. It is, in fact, an objective statement—logical, flawless and irrefutable. One could perhaps raise the question of what it was that had enabled Hamlet to reach such heights of philosophical serenity, at least qua content; but it is little more than a *lapsus* to find in his discourse nothing more than a representation of one single "temperament," when it is an aspect of objective reality that is clearly its content.[3]

As I shall demonstrate later, however, even today Hamlet's discourse would be regarded by some as the efflorescence of disease; we can thus see that not only the tragedy as a whole, but even its single elements, provide the opportunity for an impressively large scope of interpretation, just as both real life and its elements do.[4]

I cannot refrain here from discussing another approach to Shakespeare's Hamlet and its results, for it might otherwise readily cast doubt upon my principal conclusions. Robertson, that delightfully pugnacious "disintegrator" of the canon, who fought his literary battles with admirable candor and whose work is perhaps not altogether adequately appreciated, propounded the following thesis: In its present form, the tragedy is the end-product of two trends, whose directions were incompatible, in fact so disparate that even Shakespeare's genius could not synthesize them into an organic whole. "Hamlet is an adaptation of an older play, which laid down the main action, embodying a counter-sense which the adaptation could not transmute" (Robertson, 1930, p. 11).

The critics who try to explain Hamlet's procrastination by subjective theories do not take into account his capability for prompt action, according to Robertson, while those who attempt to explain his delay by referring to objective obstacles ignore Hamlet's self-accusation.[5] Yet both subjective and objective theories have to be rejected, the former because Hamlet repeatedly acts rashly, the latter because Hamlet himself never refers to objective hindrances standing in his way. All such discourses are likely to be miscarriages since the only proper way to speak is "of Hamlet the *dramatis persona*" and not "of Hamlet the man, that God created," as Poe in his *Marginalia,* as well as others before him, had already demanded (p. 25).

Shakespeare transformed into a new character the Hamlet whom he had found in a play by Kyd, yet he still had to fit that new character into the plot of the old play. Because of the play's popularity, among other reasons, he could not merely adapt it to the demands put on it by the new

---

[3] If Hamlet is really shown in a state of "melancholy adust" (which I must categorically deny), it could be only a matter of demonstrating that, in a state of severe psychopathology, truth can be attained that is ordinarily not at man's command. The situation here is comparable to Plato's "sacred madness" of the great poet.

[4] Those who object to the reduction of Shakespeare's work to a compendium of Elizabethan conventions, morals, psychology and what not are not few in number. Cf., for example, Goddard, 1951, vol. I, p. 9.

[5] For a short survey of the grouping of critics, see Muir (1963), pp. 11-13.

protagonist. "He retained all the archaic machinery," says Robertson (1930), "while transfiguring all the characters" (p. 67). In the old play, there *were* external obstacles, such as the guards who surrounded the King; for that reason, the delay was in fact physically enforced, with the result that Hamlet did not accuse himself, if the German version (*Der bestrafte Brudermord*) can be relied on. When Shakespeare had to leave out the guards (since guards were not the custom at the Elizabethan court), he was forced to replace an external obstacle by an internal one, without, however, being able to do so altogether satisfactorily.

In this view, Robertson agrees in principle with the German author, Bendix, who, during the seventies of the last century, took strong issue with Germany's Shakespeare mania, asserting that such episodes as those of the embassies, Reynaldo's mission, and Fortinbras' campaign were superfluous, because they were no longer relevant to the new conception of the Hamlet story. "To suppose that Shakespeare invented them is to impute to him a kind of gratuitous mismanagement . . . Rather we must assume that they too were given him; and pronounce that his error lay in retaining them" (1930, p. 51). Robertson even asserted that "Hamlet pretends madness because Kyd's Hamlet did so before him" (p. 66).

When Dover Wilson tried to justify the Reynaldo episode for dramatic reasons, such as its being a way to convey the passage of time, it was easy enough for Robertson to attack that argument on the grounds that there is no time-relation indicated in the episode, the worried father having easily sent a spy after his son very soon after the latter's departure to Paris (Robertson, 1930, p. 27 et sequ.). Robertson's notion was given new standing by T. S. Eliot's verdict of artistic failure in *Hamlet*—a view that was based in part on Robertson's initially very convincing historical spadework.

A question of principle can be raised when one sees literary critics grappling in vain with such episodes as this, unable to detect any justification for them—aesthetic, dramatic or otherwise—if they cannot find a historical one. Speaking psychologically, one has to regard the Polonius-Reynaldo discourse as a particularly subtle and fine-webbed elaboration on one of the play's leitmotifs.

The Ghost is, after all, an emissary from the nether world, as well as a kind of spy who interposes himself in his son's life, to boot; the emissary whom Polonius sends after his son, however, is benign and the meshes of morality are far wider, in terms of paternal permissiveness with regard to Laertes, than they are in the case of the Ghost's demands upon Hamlet. The Polonius-Reynaldo scene is thus one of relevance and meaning, an indispensable part of a broad canvas, whose dimensions do not, however, fit in with the hustle and bustle of twentieth-century speed and singlemindedness.

Mr. Robertson also regards the embassy to Norway as being a mere carryover from the original *Hamlet*, which cast an unresolvable burden on the playwright's task of revision. The psychologist will once again appraise that episode differently: to be sure, Shakespeare could easily have omitted it; but with what uncanny genius it is interwoven into the main streams of action! Fortinbras is the subject of the first political action of the new King, and it is he who has the last word in the tragedy—itself a remarkable piece of symmetry. Further, it is precisely the three-layered structure of the tragedy—the Hamlet-arc, the Laertes-arc and the Fortinbras-arc, with their proportionately diminishing diameters—that makes Hamlet a tragedy which encompasses all of mankind. By putting Fortinbras at the very beginning of Claudius's speech from the throne, Shakespeare has prevented us from forgetting him—which might all too easily happen, since his later transactions only rarely cause more than a ripple during the course of events being presented on stage. Yet without Fortinbras' appearance at the end, the entire play would have an entirely different drift. Thus, the sequence of subjects in the speech from the throne—Fortinbras, Laertes, Hamlet—is not accidental, but follows a deep-rooted dramatic intention.

Likewise, my guess is that Shakespeare's leaving out the guards who, in the original play, formed around Claudius a wall that was impenetrable by Hamlet—even though they were, according to Robertson, an integral part of that play—is not at all explainable by reference to contemporary court procedure, but must rather be seen as one of the indispensable prerequisites to transforming *Hamlet* into an "interesting" play. With one stroke, a detective story ("how shall I bring a criminal to bay?") is converted into a psychological tragedy. Here too one can observe that it has not become futile or out of style to raise the question of whether Hamlet does or does not have the physical opportunity to carry out the revenge. In my opinion, the essential meaning of the entire play depends precisely on there being no mechanical obstacle to the deed, with the possible exception of a few instances—for example, when Hamlet is abducted to England. One may say, in short, that the raw plot, as Shakespeare found it, underwent at his hands a process of *internalization*: what was earlier an outer impediment has now become an inner structure.

It is one of those most infelicitous accidents that the original Hamlet play has been lost. If the German version has any similarity to Kyd's play, one could indeed say that the preservation of the original would have served to demonstrate the full glory of Shakespeare's genius. Robertson's thesis of the presence of "fracturelines" in Shakespeare's play— as the result of his putting a new *Hamlet* into a preformed plot, the two of which could not be harmonized (as may indeed happen when the earlier seams of an altered garment remain visible in some spots)—cannot find any confirmation in a psychological analysis.

If a purely impressionistic remark may be permitted here, however, I would say that the tension between old plot and newly created characters may well reflect the tension between the world as it is and the individual. The two never seem to fit; what appears in a life story as a "fractureline" is revealed, upon deeper psychological analysis, to be a reflection of the basic precondition of human existence—namely, conflict. Who is it that does live in a state of harmony with the world? None but the idiot, as he squats before fattening dishes, or the old sage who has turned away from the world and patiently waits for death.

A Statement of Principle.

It is precisely in connection with the vast literature on *Hamlet* that certain arguments that have been used as objections to philosophical, psychological and literary interpretations have come up over and over again. Notwithstanding their partial usefulness, such interpretations would (if accepted at face value) impede research into and understanding of all forms of art, rather than stimulate them.

One of these objections in principle has been formulated quite clearly by Draper (1939, p. 5):

> Only by making himself over into an Elizabethan, if that be possible, and seeing the play given complete, on an Elizabethan stage and in Elizabethan fashion, could the subjective critic achieve a result that would approximate Shakespeare's meaning; and Shakespeare's meaning, insofar as it can be learned, is the only true or important meaning, the only meaning that a teacher has any right to ask his class to spend their time in learning or that a critic has any right to present before his readers.

In the previous section, I have tried to demonstrate that it would be folly to measure Shakespeare's psychology in terms of Elizabethan psychology, as if a genius were not able (or permitted?) to outgrow the limits of his age. We speak of "The Age of Shakespeare," indicating by that very phrase that it was *he* who gave the stamp to his time and set those bounds beyond which none of his contemporaries had the ability to step. Why then should we measure the giant with the yardstick that we employ for measuring dwarfs?

Yet Draper goes one step further when he insists that interpretation, if it is to be accepted as valid, *must not* go beyond the horizons and the modes of thinking of the "average man" of the year 1600, as he was witnessing a performance of *Hamlet*. He does not even consider the highly probable possibility that *Hamlet* may not have been performed—even in Shakespeare's time—in the way in which Shakespeare perceived it in his spiritual eye. His assumption is rather that what Shakespeare felt, saw, conjured up in his mind while he was creating *Hamlet* could be fully realized by human means, in the Elizabethan or any other age.

Since Shakespeare was a practical man, he may of course have anticipated how his troupe would realize his play on the stage; yet, even granting this, it is a mere *petitio principii* to deduce that this realistic ("adjusted") estimate was identical with his inner vision. Do playwrights in general ever agree with the way their plays are put on the stage? Nowadays they are grateful to the producer, if only their plays are staged in such a way as to ensure their success; but even harmony of that sort between author and producer would be no proof of the identity between theatrical reality and inner vision. The demand that interpretation be reduced to the horizons of the Elizabethan audience, and the assertion that only such an interpretation is valid, seems to me to be a piece of particular methodological nonsense, capable of producing particularly shrunken results.

It is a legitimate goal, of course, to attempt to achieve even a half-reliable reconstruction of the meaning that *Hamlet* might have had to the Elizabethan audience, just as it is legitimate to try to reconstruct the meaning that it might have had to a Restoration audience or to any other historical audience. But to imply that Shakespeare's own audience came closer than could any other to the truth of *Hamlet*'s meaning is an arbitrary and rather far-fetched assertion. Audiences have probably never grasped the full meaning of a creation by a genius of their own time. To be sure, most of the great ones did make an impression upon their contemporaries (Van Gogh is among the exceptions); yet these same contemporaries were rarely aware of the superabundant greatness of those great ones whom they were privileged to see in the flesh.

It is precisely Shakespeare of whom one can feel certain that his audience did *not* grasp his play's full meaning. If it had, the play could not possibly have pleased and impressed such a wide variety of audiences as it actually has since then. Those works of art whose beauty and meaning is *fully* grasped by their own contemporary audience cannot, by definition, have that surplus of meaning that may make them even more meaningful to later generations than they were to their own.

It is one of the secrets of a very few geniuses that they are able to please their contemporaries and all subsequent generations. I have been told that, among painters, it is only Leonardo da Vinci whose greatness was acknowledged as supreme by his contemporaries as well as by all subsequent ages. What happens more frequently is that appreciation of greatness varies during the course of time, although it is sometimes surprising to discover how many of the truly great were already recognized as great by a significant number of their contemporaries. From all this it can be safely deduced that it would be an error to regard the contemporary standard as being ultimately the only valid one.

In no other field of the arts is this done. No musicologist, for example, would think for a moment that determining or reconstructing the effect of Mozart's music on his eighteenth-century audience is the only valid aim of attempting to interpret it. It is the essence of the great work of art that its meaning is many-layered, multidimensional and, in some few instances, possibly inexhaustible in meaning.

Since there is apparently no cogent reason, therefore, for equating audience response with Shakespeare's meaning, we now have to turn to the meaning that *Hamlet* may have had to Shakespeare himself. What, to begin with, do we mean when we speak of what a play by Shakespeare "meant" to him? Are we to reconstruct what Shakespeare *intended* when he created *Hamlet,* or to estimate the meaning he *attributed* to it after it was written?

The grave errors that authors have made in the evaluation of their own works are well known. Goethe thought that his greatest achievement was his theory of colors, yet we know today that that theory was incorrect. Rousseau thought that his operas, or his methods of musical recording, constituted his greatest achievements. Furthermore, authors have been known to change their opinions about their own works, to interpret them in different ways, which really reflect different stages of their own development. Goethe included among his works an article that he had never written. At times, painters cannot say with certainty whether a painting that has been attributed to them is one they themselves actually did or a forgery.

Nothing is more subject to change than the meaning that the creator of a work of art attributes to his own creations. And, in any event, which meaning is the real one—the author's conscious evaluation, or the meaning that the work of art he has created has for his unconscious? What of the artist who attributes to his creation a far-reaching meaning that is probably not contained in it at all? Most creative people either overestimate or underestimate their achievements, and there is no indication that their own views, intentions, interpretations—at least, as far as the conscious ones are concerned—are reflections of an accurate estimate. Great art is often created in a fugue state, when the creator is somnambulistic; if we follow Draper, then such achievements would have no meaning, since their creators may themselves look at them as if they were the product of someone else's mind.

Draper quite candidly rejects some interpretations solely on the grounds that they would not have been acceptable to Shakespeare: "In short, these statements are in effect admissions that their interpretations are not Shakespeare's *and so have no critical validity*" (p. 166; my italics). It would constitute an enormous enrichment of the study of the creative process if we knew what had gone on in Shakespeare's mind while he was writing *Hamlet,* or if we knew his psychic processes during the period when *Hamlet* was still growing in him, and before he turned to its actual creation. Yet it is quite possible that, if we did come to know these things, we would be greatly disappointed. We might find a wealth of imagery side by side with a state of frenzy, in which the creation gradually took shape before the creator's inner eye with an unbearable vividness, forcing him to put down line after line without fully knowing what the next moment would bring forward.

The great creations also have value as symbols. To be sure, *Hamlet* is not a symbolic play, and I myself feel altogether averse to efforts to dissolve it into an allegory. But Osric is more than an Italianized court flunky; while he is that too, the exact place at which he is introduced, ostensibly in order to give us comic relief, taken together with other details, warrants Flatter's profound interpretation of him as a messenger of death. Only when we grasp an idea of this sort do we become aware of Shakespeare's full greatness. But was Shakespeare himself aware of the fact that, with Osric, he was introducing a symbol whose function was to announce Hamlet's impending death? I can easily imagine him scoffing at that idea, and my guess would be that what his own audience saw in Osric was solely a comic figure. Would this then refute Flatter's interpretation? I myself do not see that it does.

A work of art, once created, is a structure that has become entirely separated from its creator, that has started to live its own life. Its value is now utterly independent of its originator's intentions. There are minds whose ratiocination is so subtle and extensive that what they have created has, long before the moment of creation, already gone through innumerable processes of well-controlled refinement. Leonardo da Vinci was probably such a mind; as Professor Leo Steinberg has suggested, a wealth of conscious and deliberate meanings and subtleties may have gone into the "Last Supper" that critical analysis has nowhere near exhausted by this point.

In others' minds, a work of art *grows*. It is there; yet they themselves do not know where it came from. The best part of it was formed in the unconscious, from which it entered into the volitional sphere in perfect shape, and the creators would truly serve quite poorly if they were to be called in as interpreters of their own creations.

Draper's book, even though it serves a useful and necessary purpose, and has enriched the literature on *Hamlet,* at the same time shows the limitations of the historical approach, when the latter is set up as the final arbiter of a literary work's meaning. His reconstruction of the meaning that *Hamlet* had to Shakespeare and to his audience is ingenious and sounds convincing. Although the meaning that the play had to Shakespeare will remain forever unknown, Draper may actually have grasped correctly the way in which the Elizabethan-Jacobean interpreted it. But even if he is right when he says that *Hamlet* is "a drama of diplomacy and intrigue" (p. 229), at whose center stands the problem of regicide (p. 237f), is that the essence of *Hamlet?* Why should a drama of Renaissance diplomacy and intrigue, why should the problem of regicide, arouse deep emotions in a spectator of the twentieth century—particularly, let's say, one with an American background?

Without indicating in so many words that he is doing so, at the end of his treatise Draper broadens the vista of his vision. Then *Hamlet* becomes "the struggle of a single champion of right and vengeance against a social order founded on the evil of regicide" and, even more, "*Athanasius contra mundum,* a play of the vindication of right by the individual against society" (p. 242). Now Hamlet is "the knight-errant, the champion of right in a corrupt society" (p. 243).

There is no objection to be raised against this interpretation, and many a spectator may have been absorbed by this aspect of the play, without ever going beyond it. But I seriously doubt that it is *this* human value that makes *Hamlet* the enigma that has so stirred man's curiosity as to cause him to attempt, over and over again, to penetrate it.

For Draper, the protagonist's conflicts fall into two parts. The first part of the tragedy following the prolepsis has to do with Hamlet's doubt about the truthfulness of the ghost's message. Once this doubt has been removed by Claudius' indirect confession, the play becomes a matter of "frustrated purpose" (p. 201), with the frustration being overcome in the finale. But, according to Draper, and hence (in his conception) to Shakespeare's audience, this delay in execution was enforced by external circumstances. "Hamlet grows more and more proficient in the technique of court-intrigue," says Draper, but this education in diplomacy "was particularly exasperating to a man of Hamlet's open, impulsive nature."

We are asked, in all seriousness, to view Hamlet's development, during the course of the tragedy, as that of a man who "grows from a courtier in mere outward form of etiquette and charming manners to a manipulator of the weapons of intrigue" (p. 200). As if these were not merely the outer trappings behind which lurk some formidable human problems!

We are, further, to believe that "he envies the actors who may give even their fictitious feelings free expression . . . and . . . envies Fortinbras . . . and the Captain who can express their honorable designs in terms of instant action," whereas he "will not risk an unpropitious time, whatever the strain of waiting" (p. 200f). Does Shakespeare really present Hamlet, after the play-within-the-play, as a man who "is guarded and must bide his time until the fencing match sets him before the King with a weapon in his hand" (ibid.)—that is to say, *Hamlet* as the tragedy of a man who for some time lacks the external opportunity to carry out a duty of revenge? If this were all there was to Hamlet's conflict, the play would surely have long since fallen into oblivion; in that case, it would be no more than a murder mystery or a detective story.

Why should Hamlet curse himself in the vilest language and call himself "unpregnant of my cause" *(II-2-572)*, if the key to his problem were a matter either of doubt about the Ghost or of external circumstances? The fact is that Draper exaggerates Hamlet's doubts about the Ghost. There is nothing in the play that justifies Draper's assertion that, "Day and night, his doubt of the Ghost's message throbs through his brain" (p. 202). The doubt comes to his mind quite casually and, despite all that we now know to be true of the complexities of Elizabethan demonology, Hamlet's doubt is also an expression of his ambivalence toward his natural father and a well-rationalized cause for further delay.

The tragedy is a true masterpiece only if we accept the situation as one in which a son, who is perhaps the most well-adjusted model of his times, is informed of his father's murder; accepts his duty to avenge the crime against his father, which was committed by his stepfather; has the physical opportunity to carry out the vengeance at his own chosen time, and yet refrains from doing so, as the result of internal conflicts whose causes are unconscious.

In the play is shown the son's development into a man who in the end carries out the very act that has been the pivot of conflict, yet without either conflict or feeling of guilt, but rather in harmony with himself. He sees the vengeance no longer as a duty imposed upon him from the outside, but rather as something that involves the participation of his whole personality; or, to put it more simply, the ego-dystonic has been converted into the ego-syntonic.

This is, indeed, a general problem of Western man in modern times. Medieval man would never have understood Hamlet; but ever since man's obligation to take spiritual authority for granted has become the subject of doubt, and he has instead had to fall back on his own resources, as the only guide by which to decide what is right and what is wrong, this problem has become an unsettling one for him.

Whether Draper has overemphasized the problem of regicide, I do not know; to me, Hamlet does not seem to be very sorely troubled by this aspect of the situation. It may be valid enough for Laertes; but since Hamlet was the next in line of succession after Old Hamlet's death, as well as the heir presumptive to Claudius—that is to say, the potential King—his killing of Claudius would not mean depriving a King of his Divine Rights, or the State of its duly anointed King, but rather removing an obstacle to giving the State its rightful head.

Yet Draper does correctly point out some deficiencies in Hamlet criticism, with regard to the proper characterization of Claudius and Polonius. The critic usually sees only Claudius' villainy and Polonius' foolishness, but Claudius and Polonius are actually delineated in a quite different fashion by Shakespeare. Draper offers all the details that are needed to prove that Polonius "was an Elizabethan courtier, an Elizabethan father, an Elizabethan noble in high office . . . not far removed from the Elizabethan ideal of what a courtier, what a father, what a 'Worthie Priuie Counceller' should be" (p. 53), and he is critical of Hamlet's harsh judgment of him. "Hamlet, in his interpretation, stands out single *contra mundum* . . . Shakespeare then intended the spectators to see Polonius both in himself and through the Prince's eyes" (p. 51). The same contrast also surrounds the characterization of Claudius: Draper enumerates all the engaging qualities of the King, his statesmanship, his love of Gertrude, his diplomacy, his skill in handling people, and many more such.

Two comments need to be made here. Not only does Hamlet change during the course of the play, but neither was Polonius quite the same person at the beginning of the play as he is at the time of his death. I have the impression that his mental failings increase, the culmination coming in the short exchange between him and Hamlet about the shape of the cloud *(III-2-11, 381-387).* I would therefore suggest that Draper's characterization has to do with what Polonius had *once been*; what the play shows, in his case, is the gradual disintegration of an erstwhile efficient personage. Claudius' change during the course of the play is less visible, yet there are indications that, as the play progresses, he moves further and further away from being, as he was at the start, in full control of his feelings of guilt. He is even presented, when the play begins, as someone who is quite free of remorse and devoid of any conflicts about his past misdeeds. Yet, during the course of the play, he becomes a person whose feelings of guilt are gradually able to catch up with him, and he ends as someone who is no longer in control of self. The only immutable characters are Horatio (the embodiment of ethos, morality, conscience and superego), and Rosencrantz and Guildenstern (the burnt-out, counterfeit victims of surrender).

Yet the two versions of Claudius and Polonius—the way in which they actually behave and the way in which Hamlet sees them—belong together: the one is their phenotype, their mode of societal appearance; the other, their genotype, what they really are. A statesman of Polonius' caliber and loyalty who unwittingly served a regicide must be counted a fool. Anyone who possessed real statecraft, of course, would have been able to see through Claudius' *bonhomie*. Indeed, were Polonius less efficient, we could probably forgive his misjudgment more easily.

Somewhat the same thing is true of Claudius. His affectionate behavior toward Gertrude, his suavity, his statesmanship, his kindness to his subordinates—all these fine qualities of his predispose us *against* him, perhaps even more than do the crimes that Macbeth perpetrates, once he has seized the kingship. While these latter crimes revolt us, they are consistent with Macbeth's regicide; we may even feel pity for him for being as incapable as he is of extricating himself from guilt, once he has committed the initial crime. For Claudius, however, one can scarcely feel pity, despite a temporary flicker of this that may be evoked by the Prayer Scene. His very smoothness makes him as character and person even more detestable—only to someone, to be sure, who has discovered how he came into power.

What Draper overlooks—and, I can well imagine, the Jacobean audience as well—is that it is Shakespeare's positive presentation of Polonius and Claudius that contains his worst accusation against society; it amounts, in fact, to a total condemnation of power hierarchy. One must never trust, say these presentations, even legally established kingship; efficient statecraft may mask a fool. The most ghastly fact is Claudius' ability, throughout his reign, to make himself respected and loyally served by his people. While Macbeth was known, from the start of his accession, for what he was, Denmark was duped by Claudius.

Here arises a question that Draper astutely asks: If Hamlet was right in condemning Polonius, Claudius, Rosencrantz, Guildenstern and Gertrude, what of the court of his father? Since all these personages had been integral parts of the earlier society, Draper's assumption is that Hamlet's views are distorted and that he is ignoring those assets that these people must surely have had. I believe the contrary to be true, and I agree with Alexander (1955) that, in the background, one perceives— and not too dimly, at that—a grave accusation against the old King. Though it is not spoken, Hamlet's reproachful question to the father-King is clearly implied: "Is *this* the society that you have left on my hands to repair?"

Indeed, do we not perceive here the eternal conflict between generations: the older generation reproaching the younger for not living up to the standards of their forefathers, and the younger generation chafing and fretting under the disorder that has been left them as a crushing heritage?

In the foregoing I have discussed what has been pointed out by others repeatedly, perhaps in less detail, but certainly without more success. Over and over again, historical studies are carried out with great knowledge and understanding of the culture in which Shakespeare lived. It cannot be sufficiently stressed how important such studies are. They reveal the baseline above which Shakespeare's works rise. Further, it cannot be doubted that such studies are indispensable for the understanding of some aspects of Shakespeare's works. But when the attempt is made to present the baseline as if it crossed the highest point of the curve—that is to say, to reduce the meaning of a Shakespeare play to something that did not go beyond what would be completely appreciated by an Elizabethan, or to reduce the cosmos created by Shakespeare to one that is no more than the poetic and dramatic realization of what has reached us of Elizabethan writings—then one has to protest vigorously.

It is a valid task, after all, to aim at a reconstruction of the meaning, the laws, the processes that are discoverable by interpretation, since the universe created by Shakespeare stands as a self-contained world, in independence of any historical implication. This is a difficult task to carry out in a scientifically acceptable way and many failures are strewn along the arduous path—failures that testify in many instances to the difficulties of the task rather than to the incompetence of the researcher. For the historian to scoff at such endeavors is not only out of order, it is methodologically untenable.

6. Two Consistent Character Profiles

In any attempt to obtain a clear conception of Hamlet's character, one faces a dilemma similar to the one I have presented above, with regard to the interpretation of plot details. This can perhaps be seen best in a comparison of two consistent character-analyses of Hamlet—one by Huhner and the other by Madariaga.

Max Huhner (1873-1947), a urologist, who is famous for devising a sterility test, which is named after him, also published several essays on literary subjects. His Hamlet study was published posthumously. For Huhner, Hamlet was "a student, inexperienced in the ways of the world, very conscientious, very loath to shed blood, in fact almost a coward in that regard, and his insanity was feigned" (p. 1). Hamlet, he felt, was unable to play the hypocrite or "do anything underhanded. It was contrary to his very nature as a man of honor, a scholar and philosopher" (p. 31). Moreover, his character was sluggish and he suffered from "an enormous amount of inertia in his make-up" (p. 71).

Huhner seems to take this last aspect of Hamlet's character as given, yet he might have deduced it both from Hamlet's conscientiousness and from his primary avocation as a scholar. Hamlet knows that he will get into difficulty, Huhner reasons, and he needs to feign madness for the purpose of carrying out his mission. He rehearses his pretended madness first with Ophelia, for even if he should fail there in his act of simulation, that failure will not cause him any real harm. The manifestations of insanity that Hamlet will show become predictable—which is, to Huhn-

er's mind, a sure sign that it is a simulated and not a real insanity.

When Hamlet is with a trustworthy friend, he is rational and sy
tom-free; as soon as those persons appear, however, whom he want
convince that he is mad, he changes his behavior so as to implant dif
ent explanations in their minds for his noticeably irrational behav
With Rosencrantz and Guildenstern, he makes believe that the rea
for it is frustrated ambition; with the Queen and the King, that it is th
marriage that has upset him; and with Polonius and Ophelia, that i
frustrated love that has driven him mad (p. 105f). "These rapid a
clumsy changes from rational speech with those he trusts to irration
conversation with those whom he wishes to impress are strong eviden
of fraud" (p. 104).

Huhner reduces the problem of Hamlet to one factor, of the sort th
Freud conceptualized as "secondary gain in mental disease." Hamle
says Huhner, "could not hold his tongue or keep a secret, and was ther
fore entirely unfitted for diplomatic work. In a sense his feigning insanit
was his sole avenue of safety" (p. 110). It is along these same lines tha
Huhner tries to prove the reasonableness of Hamlet's cruel dealings wit
Rosencrantz and Guildenstern, justifying on grounds of practical necessi
ty and the desire to avoid risks the fact that Hamlet arranged their execu
tion without their having had a chance to receive the assistance of the
Church.

It would take too long to reproduce here the details of Huhner's rea
soning. One can summarize his character analysis of Hamlet as essential
ly a picture of an impractical man, who has nevertheless proceeded with
optimal effect under existing external and internal conditions. Since
Hamlet's initial character structure is taken as a matter of course, no
psychological problem remains. All his enigmatic utterances, his crude
and harsh behavior toward Ophelia, and other such passages are explained as being, in effect, part and parcel of his feigned madness, which
in turn allegedly lives up to the requirements of reality-adequate behavior—that is to say, such behavior as is necessary under the prevailing
conditions for the achievement of a specific goal.

Madariaga's (1948) principal thesis is, by contrast, that the present-day concept of Hamlet is essentially falsified, un-Shakespearean,
romanticized, and adapted to suit Victorian biases. "Hamlet, the man
born in an era of no gentleness whatever, must become a gentleman" (p.
2.). "Hamlet was bearded like Drake and not clean-shaven like Mr.
Winston Churchill" (p. 1.). Shakespeare's Hamlet did indeed wear a

beard, as is clear from the text; it is equally clear that a Hamlet with a beard would probably lead to theatrical failure on a modern stage, although more recently this has become questionable. This detail alone may provide a strong argument in favor of the author's contention that the modern view of Hamlet is based on a historical misunderstanding. By deromanticizing Hamlet, Madariaga obtains a portrayal that is entirely different from Huhner's.

For Madariaga, Hamlet is the very incarnation of self-centeredness; all the seeming peculiarities he shows can be derived, he believes, from this one factor. Once Hamlet's extreme self-centeredness is acknowledged, his character loses all those contradictions that have puzzled previous investigators and have never been explained satisfactorily. The author asserts that Hamlet never really intended to avenge his father; what inhibits him is really "an essential and primal indifference or lovelessness" (p. 83). "In his innermost being he is not interested in avenging his father; he only reacts sword in hand when he *thinks himself* in danger in the arras scene, and when he *knows himself* betrayed at the end" (p. 139, author's italics). In the end "he has avenged himself—the only person he cares for" *(ibid.)*.

He is, in Madariaga's eyes, devoid of any capacity to love. With Ophelia he "had strayed into intimacy without much depth of love" (p. 59). It is the suspicion that she had been "using him as an instrument of her ambition or whatever it was she was using him for" ("the sacrilege an egocentric man never can forgive") that leads him to violence against her (p. 64f). There is neither love of his mother ("not even in the carnal way an extravagant theory would have us believe") nor hatred toward her. "He just *thinks* her" (p. 74). Rosencrantz and Guildenstern's cruel fate at Hamlet's hands provides Madariaga, of course, with rich opportunities to demonstrate his callousness, his terrible cruelty, his egotism. "It means: 'you are welcome to do anything you like in the world, but you must not touch ME' " (p. 19f).

The true tragedy of Hamlet is, therefore, according to Madariaga, that he can only think Hamlet, while still remaining unable "to be Hamlet" (p. 95). "Action requires an outgoing, and his was an incoming heart" (p. 78). In view of all this, the reader will not be surprised that some of the author's critics "interpreted my views on Hamlet as if I saw in him a kind of gangster" (p. 144). Madariaga denies this, however. He has described Hamlet as being "amoral to a point," he admits, but in two ways Hamlet's attitude is different from that of ordinary gangsters:

"It recognized liberty from common standards only to the great; and it expected greatness from the great thus exempted from the rules" (p. 144). Yet this, in my opinion, comes very close to the attitude of the gangster—who is likely, after all, to equate gangster-ism with greatness.

To be sure, in the last paragraph of the epilogue that he added to the second edition, the author sees Hamlet as being "the most powerful incarnation ever conceived of the struggle of the spirit of man with the ego that fetters it." This is, in my opinion, in contradiction to the au-thor's earlier thesis, which he nevertheless did not abandon or reject at this later date. A struggle of the spirit with the ego transcends by far the realm of self-centeredness. For my purposes I shall disregard this later comment, since it strikes me as being little more than a change of heart, and I shall stay with the character analysis originally presented by the author.

It is a *tour de force*, brilliantly and convincingly written, indeed as convincingly as was Huhner's study. Like the latter, it is one-di-mensional: it explains Hamlet solely in terms of the narcissistic com-ponent, in the sense of a pathological overcathexis of self. If one does not become diverted by details, it is possible to accept both studies as valid, although, as will be shown presently, Madariaga's interpretation does violence to even more details than Huhner's does.

The two studies are based on quite different conceptions of Ham-let's madness. Huhner denies that it is real, and instead explains Ham-let's strange behavior as being consistently a matter of pretense, dictated by compliance with reality needs and therefore consisting of "feats of adjustment," so to speak. Madariaga also negates Hamlet's madness, but takes his strange behavior to be the clue to his true character. When Hamlet goes into antics, is brutal, talks foul language, Huhner says, "See how cleverly he pretends!" What Madariaga exclaims is, by con-trast, "See how self-centered and crude he actually is!" In one thing only do they agree—namely, that Ophelia had had intercourse with Hamlet; and the inventor of the sterility test even adds to this his belief that she was pregnant.

Huhner's analysis is quite patently vulnerable at one point, as Madariaga cleverly points out: Although Hamlet confesses to his mother that "I essentially am not in madness, But mad in craft" *(III.4.187f)*, he nevertheless does not change his behavior in any way. "Therefore, this heartless exhibition of callousness and cynicism has nothing to do with madness" (Madariaga, p. 23). Nor with feigned madness, either, one has to add, since Huhner denies that Hamlet ever was mad. It is a small point, one that can easily be overlooked, yet it is still a point that does not fit in with Huhner's thesis.

Madariaga, on the other hand, has to do violence to more than one point. He does not put much trust in psychoanalysis ("psychoanalysts and other fanciful commentators" p. 74), and therefore does not deign to take seriously Freud's theory that Hamlet is grappling with an oedipal complex ("Strange that an attempt should have been made to explain his case as an Oedipus complex," p. 74). Yet, oddly enough, at one point Hamlet does express this conflict openly, and does so at the psychologically appropriate point, besides—namely, after he has succeeded in showing up a father-substitute as a coward, when Claudius takes flight after the mouse-trap. Then he breaks out into the towering lines: "This is now the very witching time of night" *(III.2.393)* [1] with their gruesome reference to Nero.

Now, whether one believes that at this point Hamlet is facing a genuine impulse to kill the mother or that killing stands in this instance for raping, it can hardly be denied that Nero was in the throes of an oedipal complex. How does Madariaga interpret these lines? "No one in his senses can maintain that Shakespeare did not realize that he was writing sheer nonsense in these lines and marring the style and figure of the Prince for the judicious" (p. 127). The author may be judicious enough in general, but here he is facing a state of human affairs that is too terrible for him to face up to and, as happens so often with others, he uses laughter as a defense (Kris, 1939) against the horror that the terrible might otherwise provoke in him.

It seems strange for a critic to reject a theory by arbitrarily describing as "nonsense" the fact on which it is based. While some writers simply do not take cognizance of certain lines and by way of such omission safeguard the "purity" of their theories about *Hamlet,* Madariaga is unique in that he quotes the very lines that stand in the way of his theory, and then declares them, without any justification, to be nonsense. The fact is that he could acknowledge the Oedipus complex without having to give up his proposition that it is Hamlet's self-centeredness that is central to the play.

It is different when he accepts all of Hamlet's statements as *bona*

---

[1] This line has been interpreted by some critics as referring to Claudius. I do not think that the context permits this.

fide clues to his character. Here he owes a proof, for Hamlet's announcement that he will "put on an antic disposition" remains unexplained, while Huhner is able to find in this announcement a strong argument in his favor. Whereas Huhner sees in the scene that takes place in Ophelia's closet—when Hamlet puts on this "antic disposition" perhaps for the first time—the initial rehearsal of feigned madness, Madariaga takes it to be a sincere expression of Hamlet's actual sadness. "It is evident that in this scene Hamlet is in deep distress, that he is not feigning" (p. 59). It is of interest to note that, in this instance, it is an event that does not take place on the stage but is described by one of the participants in it, that permits of diametrically opposite interpretations. It is, so to speak, "free for the asking" whether one is to accept one or the other.

Gerald Bullit, who took a critical view of Madariaga's character analysis, asserted ". . . that is what makes *Hamlet* the unique masterpiece it is—it can equally bear quite other interpretations" (quoted after Madariaga, p. 142). Unfortunately, he then added a sentence that nullified the correctness of his previous statement. "By careful selection you can prove almost anything from the text of Hamlet, as you can from the Bible" (*ibid.*). Madariaga, of course, picked up this unreasonable extension immediately, and rightly said that, if *Hamlet* were such a "village-common for minds to play any cricket...they pleased, it would not be a masterpiece at all. A masterpiece is gloriously positive." He admits that there is room for diverse interpretations "of many spiritual developments," but rejects the idea "of many interpretations as to who is who and what is what in it." "A minimum of unity" is indispensable; without it, "many a vision of him in the realms of the mind" would not be possible (p. 142f).

That Hamlet does bear different interpretations, none of which can be shown to be exclusively valid, I have already tried to prove. This does not imply, however, that almost anything can be proved from it as can in truth be done from the Bible. With that enlargement, an impression is created that psychological data are kept so vague in the play that any assumption, even the scurrilous and the bizarre, may fit. The fact is that the unity is quite compact; but the miracle of *Hamlet* is that, within that unity, diametrically opposed views can be put forth, depending on where one places the focus.

A comparison is suitable at this point that is drawn from the realm of visual perception. I refer the reader to such visual illusions as Necker's cube or Rubin's ambiguous configurations. In the former, there is reversible perspective; in the latter the effect varies, depending on what is taken as figure and what as ground (Graham, 1951, p. 894)—that is to say, a shift in focus is sufficient to provide quite different pictures, without any change in the external pattern.

In *Hamlet* the matter is, of course, infinitely more complicated; more is needed than a mere shift of focus in order to permit a new image of Hamlet's character to arise, more or less suddenly. Yet it is not without point to mention that our perceptive apparatus is already constructed in such a way that identical patterns of external stimuli may provide quite different images (*Gestalten*) from one moment to another, merely by shifts of our attention. It is not difficult therefore to devise a large number of such patterns, once one knows the underlying principle. But it is indeed an almost frighteningly extraordinary achievement to create a character that allows a plurality of readings, each in a fairly consistent and almost convincing way.

There is no need for me to point out, I hope, that I do not agree with either Huhner's or Madariaga's analysis of Hamlet. Any one-dimensional and unchanging analysis of Hamlet is bound from the start to be incomplete, since the Hamlet of the graveyard scene is quite different from the Hamlet of the first soliloquy. The formulation of his character must be a dynamic one, such as will indicate both the starting and the end points, and sets forth the series of turning points that link them.

It is neglect of insight into the essential nature of Shakespeare's play as the *development of a personality* that has made literary critics try over and over again to place all of Hamlet's peculiarities over one single denominator. Freud's thesis too had to do with only one factor—namely, Hamlet's procrastination—which he contrasted with Hamlet's vigilance and aggression against both Polonius and Rosencrantz and Guildenstern.[2]

In contrasting two such mutually exclusive profiles as those devised by Huhner and Madariaga, one can hardly escape the impression that the cultural backgrounds of the two authors were highly relevant to the end-result of their speculations. Huhner, apparently a very practical man, grew up in an all-too-practical civilization; for him, everything that Hamlet does is of indisputable practicality. Madariaga, I assume, integrated the monolithic, all-inclusive, awe-inspiring edifice of Catholic

---

[2] Freud's thesis, however, does not suffice by itself to explain the totality of Hamlet's conduct, for it does not provide any explanation for Hamlet's final ability to carry out the deed that he has all along been unable to perform.

dogma and moral theology, to which the faithful bow, trusting fully in the wisdom of the Church. Yet, to my mind, Hamlet is a Protestant, a heretic, even an unbeliever, who goes through a gigantic struggle to convert dogma into a personal conviction that has been born out of the self.[3]

Hamlet's anti-authoritarianism must be a thorn in the flesh of a traditionalist, even when he himself is liberal and generous. He could hardly forgive a son's audacity in carrying out, at last, the "dread command" that his father had laid upon him—and doing so without any profession of filial obedience, but rather in full conviction that he was acting on his own accord. That Hamlet does *not* proclaim himself, after Claudius' death, to be his father's avenger is for me the clear assertion of his new dignity and the consummation of a new spirituality on his part. It is no less than a break with the medieval sense of glory, a portentous refusal to identify with Christianity.

Yet the fact that the same play permits two different interpretations, which are both convincing and consistent, as well as being *almost* in full harmony with the facts as they appear on the stage, and yet are actually antithetical, miles apart in their implications, basically irreconcilable— that fact alone is an incomparable testimony to Shakespeare's greatness.

---

[3] It is questionable whether or not one is justified here in saying that Hamlet did this in disregard of the "wisdom" that sacred institutions have accumulated during the course of centuries.

7. Hamlet and Revenge
(The Christian View)

In the present analysis of *Hamlet*, I have begun with two assumptions: (1) that throughout most of the play Hamlet has access to the King, so that the physical possibility of his murdering Claudius is given from the start; and (2) that, having accepted his father's command to revenge the crime, Hamlet is thereafter inhibited from obeying that command for a reason of which he is not himself conscious.

A book (Prosser, 1967) was recently published in which the author attempts to just refute such assumptions. Her assertion is that Hamlet was in conflict because he was torn between opposing and therefore irreconcilable value systems: obedience to his father and the consequent desire to kill Claudius *versus* obedience to the Christian prohibition of revenge which, if he follows it, makes him a coward in the eyes of the majority, if not of all members of his society.[1] The proof of this thesis is undertaken by the author with an enviable command of Elizabethan moral,

[1] Farnham (1936, p. 345), while acknowledging that, according to Elizabethan moral philosophy, revenge belongs to God, nevertheless writes (p. 441): "It deserves all possible emphasis that Shakespeare does not make Hamlet struggle with the inconsistency between a barbaric tribal code and the Christian code of morals in the matter of revenge, as a Christian Aeschylus might have made him struggle. There is never a sign that Hamlet or anybody else in the play recognizes this inconsistency, however much we may recognize it and be tempted to read the tragedy accordingly, or however much an Elizabethan auditor may have recognized it in the light of the current condemnation of revenge. *Shakespeare is dramatically about other business*" (my italics). More recently Boklund (1965, p. 119f) in full acknowledgement that stage tradition, if anything, pointed in the opposite direction insists that Hamlet "feels that he is under an absolute obligation to revenge his father's death" and he seems to advise the reader that, if we want to understand the play, we "should accept his [Hamlet's] feelings as genuine, irrespective of our own opinions."

theological, philosophical and dramatic literature. She leaves hardly any source untouched in her effort to prove that the Ghost was an evil spirit, and that the Elizabethan spectator, even though he may have sympathized with Hamlet, disapproved of most of his "immoral" talk and regarded Hamlet as a callous murderer.

For roughly the first 150 pages, any reader will be deeply impressed by the multitude of proofs that Miss Prosser adduces, of the most striking sort, and embracing almost the entire realm of the Elizabethan printed word. Only at one place will a glimmer of doubt possibly arise.

In the arguments that Miss Prosser employs, in her effort to disprove the widely accepted view "that Shakespeare unquestioningly accepted the morality of revenge" (1967, p. 90), she uses Macbeth as a test case. She says that "only one passage can be offered in support of a revenge ethic," the one in which Macduff says that "My wife and children's ghosts will haunt me still" *(V.7.16)* if he does not slay the tyrant. She seems to me to be wrong, however, when she says that "in the light of the rest of the play, I find the speech a contradiction" and that "the denial of personal revenge motives by Macduff is explicit" (1967, p. 91). I myself find what amounts to even an explicit request for and approval of personal revenge in Malcolm's exhortation of Macduff: "Let grief/Convert to anger; blunt not the heart, enrage it" *(IV.3.229f)*. Menteith reports that "Revenge burn in them" *(V.2.3)*, when he speaks of Siward and Macduff. I also find an acceptance of the revenge motive in Macduff's "Th' usurper's cursed head" *(V.8.55)*, with which words he holds Macbeth's head up for Malcolm to see. [2]

Be that as it may, the portion of the book that is capable of convincing the reader comes to an end when Prosser analyzes the "To be" monologue *(III.1)* (pp. 158-171). [3] According to her, Hamlet defines "being" and "non-being" in terms of enduring evil passively, on the one hand, as Church, State and society demand that an individual do, and on the other hand of actively fighting to defeat it. Hamlet is here facing, she maintains, the dilemma of medieval theology and Florentine humanism—of metaphysical wisdom, which is attained by contemplation, and humanist wisdom, which is based on action in temporal matters (p. 162). For one

---

[2] I have no doubt that there are other instances in the plays that could raise some question in the reader's mind about Prosser's certainty that personal revenge was always looked at askance in Shakespeare.

[3] For an excellent historical presentation of the varied criticism to which this soliloquy has been subjected, see Richards (1933). I shall limit myself here to Miss Prosser's interpretation, which has, incidentally, many historical antecedents.

man cannot truly "be" if he retreats into passive resignation, while another finds his self-identity, his "being," precisely in obedience. In the eyes of the latter, therefore, obedience to the Divine injunction against private revenge would be an act of the highest nobility.

As a secondary consideration, Hamlet raises the question of his own death, insofar as it is highly probable that he will be killed in his effort to take revenge (p. 164). In lingering over that theme, he recalls his nightmares and concludes that it is only out of fear of the unknown terrors of Hell that man is willing to endure evil. It is conscience, the inner voice of moral judgment, that warns against a damnable action and thus makes a man a coward (p. 167f). Every instinct in Hamlet cries out for action; his conflict is brought about by "a metaphysic that defines man in terms of . . . surrender of his will, in terms of passivity and resignation" (p. 170f).

Miss Prosser is not the only one whose interpretation leans in that direction, and at first reading her reasoning appears to be irreproachable. Yet a careful study reveals some inconsistencies that make the end-product dubious, even though she may be right in saying that many of Shakespeare's contemporaries understood the soliloquy in the way she would have us understand it.

Her conception of the first five and one half lines of the "To be" soliloquy is convincing. Hamlet poses the question of what man's existence is: Does he find his true being in suffering or in acting? Indeed, that question did puzzle philosophers of yore, and it is a very real problem in our own times.

Her conception of "To be" finds much support at first in Macbeth's "Nothing is/ But what is not" *(I.3. 140-142).* But then the soliloquy continues, surprisingly: "To die, to sleep." This is not a likely continuation of the primary universe of discourse, as Miss Prosser sees it. She herself is aware of that fact and therefore introduces a supplementary hypothesis, which it is worthwhile to reproduce in full.

"Although the opening question of the soliloquy is concerned only with the morality of taking aggressive action, the terms in which Hamlet has phrased the alternative choices now suggest to Hamlet a secondary consideration. In striking out at Claudius, it is highly probable that he himself would be killed" (p. 164).

This interpretation is unwarranted for several reasons; for one thing, it is an *argumentum ad hominem.*[4] There is not even any evidence

---

[4] Richards (1933, pp. 149-151) and many others use the same train of thought.

of Hamlet's ever abstaining from action because of fear for his life. Such fear would be, in fact, out of keeping with the personality profile that is presented in the play. He was a soldier (and an exemplary one, to boot) before he returned from Wittenberg, and on various occasions he has no hesitation about risking his life. If anything, he is presented in such a way as to make one wish sometimes that he would take fewer chances. Nor does the opportunity to take his revenge without risking his own life, while Claudius is praying, arouse in him in the least any greater willingness to do so at that time.

For the natural and widespread fear for one's own life to break forth merely at the thought of carrying out the revenge that is so dear to his heart makes no sense at all. If Shakespeare had intended to picture the protagonist as laboring under a fear of that kind (unless what he was fearful of was his being prevented from fulfilling his mission because of his premature death), he would surely have had to let us know about it at a different point and in a different way, for at that moment the spectator is more likely to assume quite the opposite, in view of Hamlet's express intention to let Claudius know that he is in possession of the latter's secret.

There is, moreover, a formal point that, in my opinion, disproves Miss Prosser's interpretation even more fully. The "To be" soliloquy is a typical Shakespeare "inset," of the kind that Berry (1965) has described.[5] It belongs to the type of inset Berry has found in Mercutio's "Queen Mab" speech. The stage action comes to a complete standstill, while the speaker presents a train of thought that is very meaningful in the light of the play as a whole, yet makes no immediate contribution to the plot action at that moment. It is an imaginative device, designed to create atmosphere—to add, if possible, a new dimension of meaning to the play, and much more; yet, for all that, it is to be taken out of the events that surround it.

Preceding the soliloquy, the stage action has been pushing ahead quite forcefully. Within the space of 55 lines we are informed of the effect of Rosencrantz and Guildenstern's spying mission, the King's delight that Hamlet wants to entertain the court with a play (a master stroke of irony!), the King's and Polonius' plan of watching Hamlet "affront

---

[5] An inset, according to Berry (1965, p. 31) is "a kind of episode [in a play], where the imagined spectacle is at odds with 'the actual spectacle.' Insets may have varying depth, temporal range and function" (p. 11). What they have in common is that "they all demand a break from the dramatic now, a shift of tense accompanied by a vocal change in their rendering to suit that shift."

Ophelia," Ophelia's agreement to cooperate, the Queen's affectionate hopes for Ophelia, and finally, the King's aside, in which he admits his guilt for the first time. All this is, indeed, even in the light of *Hamlet's* generally tight-packed action, a supercharge of events. The inset lasts 33 lines, and is followed by the rapid crescendo of 63 lines of discourse between Hamlet and Ophelia. Before the inset, a concentration on action of immediate importance; after the inset, passionate discourse of great future impact; in between, timeless, abstract metaphysics: no reference to the speaker himself or to any persons in the play. And yet the abstract interval, for all that it completely modifies the time dimension that is inherent in dramatic action, is thoroughly immersed in the play's content and momentum and significantly illuminates it.

If Shakespeare had smuggled into this context a particular fear that Hamlet feels with regard to a particular event in the stage action that he anticipates, he would have committed an aesthetic blunder and spoiled the special beauty of these magnificent lines. This is quite aside from the fact that he would be posing for the spectator a task of divination that he cannot possibly fulfill.

Miss Prosser's interpretation of the initial five and one half lines is, nevertheless, of great help in our efforts to grasp the inset's full dramatic impact. In view of her documentation, it is highly probable that the question of "To be or not to be" was indeed introduced as an existential one, as the audience is made to believe by the subsequent explication of "Is it nobler to suffer or to take up arms?" Yet by the unexpected throwing in of "to die, to sleep," the spectator is informed that he has let himself be misled and that the universe of discourse is in fact the question of life and death. The logical structure of what the spectator has until then been led to regard as the main proposition is thus retroactively changed:

At the risk of repetition, I want to summarize this point, which seems to me to be of decisive importance. The first five and one half lines represent, in accordance with Miss Prosser's interpretation, the existential view:

A (to be) and B (not to be) form the same ratio as (a) (to accept evil passively) and (b) (to meet evil actively).

By the apposition of death, this ratio is then changed to the following:

A (to be) and B (not to be) are in the ratio of a^1 (to accept evil passively) and a² (to meet evil actively) and b (to die).⁶ I do not see in what other way the apposition of the death theme in the 6th line can be understood, particularly since Hamlet ends the existential proposition on the note of the successful conquest of evil ("And by opposing end them"), which precludes the imagery of defeat and death. If he was worried about the possibility of losing his life in the process of opposing evil, he would never be able to end those evils. The sequence of thoughts alone therefore disproves the explanation that Miss Prosser offers.

The soliloquy has been taken by many to be a meditation on suicide (Richards, p. 745f), as if Hamlet had to fight off a suicidal impulse; but that is a viewpoint that Miss Prosser strongly rejects, and in that one has to agree with her. Preoccupation with suicide would make no sense at this point in the Hamlet who is in process of testing the Ghost; furthermore, it would be out of place in that he had already rejected suicide peremptorily in his first soliloquy.

When Hamlet introduces the theme of death, it is in the form of natural death, which is aptly symbolized by sleep. Hamlet reflects first on the question of whether life in either its active or passive form is preferable to death. A man may regard death as preferable to life and yet not contemplate or even approve of suicide. When Hamlet says that death is "a consummation devoutly to be wish'd," therefore, he is not speaking of suicide but only offering an evaluation of life's tribulations in terms of the summary statement: *"cela ne vaut pas la peine."* In his considering the desirability of eternal sleep, he comes upon man's uncertainty about the afterlife. Miss Prosser is sure that by this "rub," he means the fear of hell. While that may be a possibility, Hamlet is keeping his ratiocination outside any religious framework; he is merely stressing the fact of *uncertainty.*⁷ If he had in mind, or went along with the Christian prohibition of personal revenge, as Miss Prosser confidently asserts, there should be no doubt in his mind, since moral theology leaves no doubt about that

---

⁶ Although the origin of the First Quarto has not yet been resolved, I shall nevertheless quote the beginning lines of this soliloquy, as they appear there:

"To be, or not to be—ay, there's the point:
To die, to sleep—is that all? ay, all. No."

According to Weiner (1962), the First Quarto is a version of *Hamlet* as it was once actually performed. If only we could be sure of that! It would prove that the soliloquy made sense to an Elizabethan audience (according to Weiner, it was a provincial audience), without the necessity for any initial reference to the difference between an active and a passive life.

⁷ Although Richards also understands Hamlet to refer to a fear of punishment in hell, he finds "the two pivots" upon which the soliloquy turns in: (1) the uncertainty of dreams and (2) the dread of something after death, both of which paralyze action (1933, p. 763).

point: hellfire awaits the vengeful murderer. Under these circumstances damnation is certain, and it is precisely that certainty which enforces self-restraint.

Hamlet then goes through a long list of the forms in which man has to suffer pain, and it is only at this point that he introduces the possibility of suicide, which man does not make use of, mainly because of "the dread of something after death." Here the second point of culmination is reached. Whereas in the first soliloquy suicide is rejected out of hand and without reflection, solely on the grounds of the Divine injunction against it, here it is discussed within a psychological framework and without any reference to moral or religious or Christian deliberation. At this point Hamlet says simply: the reason why man does not commit suicide is that he is afraid that worse pains may await him after death than those he now has to bear. That is why he tries to postpone the moment of dying as long as he possibly can.

There is no reasoning here about the question of whether the pain of afterlife depends on the way in which a man had died—as, for example, by suicide—or on the state of his soul—as, for example, in mortal sin. There is only a weighing of the question in terms of the pleasure-pain principle, which Freud described as the dominant principle of psychic life. Under all circumstances man remains in fear of uncertainty. In Hamlet's ceasing to employ any moral or religious standard at this point, I perceive the seed of an eminently non-Christian conception of life, although—as Miss Prosser rightly points out—there is in this soliloquy no expression of disbelief in a life after death.

Here too a glance at the First Quarto may prove useful. In that Quarto, one does not find in the first soliloquy any reference to suicide and its prohibition by the canon, such as appears in later and better known versions of that soliloquy. Nevertheless, the key position with regard to suicide in the "to be" soliloquy is held there by the "everlasting judge . . . at whose sight the happy smile and the accursed damn'd." By contrast, in the later version of the play, in which the "canon 'gainst self-slaughter" does appear in the first soliloquy, and there holds the key to thoughts about suicide, in the subsequent "to be" soliloquy it is "the dread of something after death," and not God, that keeps man from taking his own life.

Why was any explicit reference to God deleted in the "to be" soliloquy of the final version, despite the fact that a specific reference to God is already to be found in the first soliloquy of that very version? Surely the imagery of "And borne before an everlasting judge" (First Quarto) cannot have been felt to be offensive for poetic reasons. Since aesthetic reasons fall aside, it is plain that deep determinants of a personal nature are responsible for Hamlet's conspicuously turning away from any direct reference to a Divinity at the moment when he reaches this crucial point.[8]

The remainder of the inset deals with the consequences for man's initiative when dread of the future has become predominant in him. It not only makes him prefer to endure present pain, thereby keeping him from suicide, but it also casts a pallor over spontaneity and the immediate pleasure that is to be gained from forceful action. The word "conscience," which occupies the nodal position here, has a variety of meanings; each interpreter is permitted to select the one that confirms the drift of his particular interpretation. Shakespeare thus makes full use of his art of ambiguity.

I think I have delimited fairly accurately the universe of discourse of this soliloquy. Its meaning, as representing a certain stage in Hamlet's development, has been discussed previously. This meaning has no primary bearing on the soliloquy as an inset. It is a piece that stands on its own ground, by contrast with the other soliloquies, which are insets of a different type.[9]

Miss Prosser looks at this soliloquy in a static way and thus misses the movement: (1) from the starting point—the contrast between activity and passivity—to the contrast between life and death; (2) from there to the question of what is it that, in the last analysis, binds man to life, and keeps him from hastening to the end that awaits him in any case; and (3) from there to the final reflection upon the general effect that this tie has on man's ability to take forceful action.

It is up to the historian to demonstrate the antecedents to each successive element of this discourse, as he finds them in the treatises of philosophers and moralists (Miss Prosser does this admirably); but it is

---

[8] Richards, whose reconstruction anticipates the bulk of Miss Prosser's interpretation, is aware that Hamlet's thoughts are not expressed at this point "with extreme clarity" (p. 757). The reason for this can be found, he thinks, in the drama itself: the King and Polonius, he asserts, overhear Hamlet and "the playwright could not permit him to reveal his secret to his enemies thus early." Miss Prosser does not resort to this argument, which is shared by others. I believe that any assumption that there is some stage character listening to Hamlet's soliloquies is, for a number of reasons, wholly out of the question. (See also Whitaker, 1965, p. 189, for a comment on the soliloquies as documentation of what is going through Hamlet's mind.)

[9] For types of insets, see Berry 1965, p. 22.

up to the critic to demonstrate, aside from poetical analysis, the unique features of this discourse (Miss Prosser does not do this at all), insofar as a problem that may have a rather long history seems to be presented here in a quite new fashion.[10]

From Miss Prosser's analysis, most importantly, it does not become clear why it is that, after the soliloquy, Hamlet gains freedom of action. If fear of damnation and conflict about the morality of revenge are the relevant elements, why then do not his scruples increase after such meditations? She writes: "The Ghost's challenge has fallen on receptive ears . . . He has decided to act" (p. 171). Against this, one has to say that Hamlet's ears were far more receptive to the Ghost's challenge at the time of the first meeting with him than they are now; furthermore in the soliloquy he certainly does not arrive at any decision to act, but merely reaches the conclusion that it is a *psychic* factor (an emotion) and *not* "His canon 'gainst self-slaughter," as he had previously put it, that stands between man and death.[11] For Miss Prosser, the soliloquy poses an existential question, not the question of life or death.

If Shakespeare had written his plays in present-day Russia, I might feel more inclined to agree with Miss Prosser. If a contemporary Russian playwright desired to present a conflict of Christian morality in a non-pejorative way, he might have to be extremely careful, since the State power there is averse to using the public stage for Christian indoctrination. But the problem that, as Miss Prosser sees it, is dealt with in the soliloquy was officially quite acceptable in Shakespeare's time; it was one about which there might not have been any agreement but in regard

[10] Proser (1965, p. 87) quoting from G. B. Harrison, *Shakespeare's Tragedies* (London, 1951) writes: " . . . the introductory words of the soliloquy, 'To be or not to be,' [is] a traditional medieval formula appropriate to such 'a common topic for philosophic discussion' . . . " The historical antecedents of the "to be" soliloquy have been brought to public attention recently in the *New York Times* in an interview with Professor William Heckscher. I was not successful in my attempt to familiarize myself with the medieval texts. An exact comparison of the medieval models with Shakespeare's final product, and a psychological analysis of their differences constitute promising ways of ascertaining what the *punctum saliens* of the soliloquy is. If it should turn out—which is highly improbable—that the soliloquy amounts to a versified translation of the Latin prose the critic would face a challenge, for certain, no less baffling than it is subtle and stimulating.

[11] A final argument against Richards' interpretation may be raised. He reaches the conclusion that "it is not his [Hamlet's] life but his soul that he is chiefly concerned to preserve" (p. 759). If this is correct, how then does one explain the fact that, after a meditation upon activity and passivity, Hamlet comes upon the idea of death? His initial reaction is in favor of death, as preferable to life. Since he is not afraid of losing his life, why does a meditation upon activity and passivity conjure up the imagery of death at all? That question, it seems to me, remains unanswered in Richards' essay.

to which, as far as I know, no danger of censure or prosecution was involved. Why then should Shakespeare have presented this problem in such a circumspect way, speaking of "the dread of something after death" when he meant Hell, a word he has already used quite freely on other occasions?

I would not be at all surprised if someone were to prove that Shakespeare preferred to be understood by his contemporaries in precisely the way Miss Prosser suggests, in order to escape the stir the soliloquy would have caused if its full implications were grasped. While the soliloquy is couched in words that make it possible to proceed in the way Miss Prosser suggests, it reveals a far more formidable truth when it is taken as it stands: the world is a terrible place to *be* in, and it is only the fear that something even more terrible than we can now imagine will follow, that interferes with man's ability to say farewell on his own to the place that God has created for his enjoyment.

Some critics have spoken of Hamlet's pessimism (Walker, 1948, p. 58), even of his "very nihilism" on this occasion; in so doing, however, they have conveyed their own personal evaluation, for what Hamlet sets forth here is for him a fact (and, by the way, not too far from some of the theories of modern psychology). Statements of pessimism are essentially evaluations or interpretations, as with Gloucester's "wanton boys" and the Gods, that require further testing or examination. Hamlet does not deny the possibility of pleasure in the temporal world; he merely refers to the difficulty one experiences in attempting to obtain it.

If the central problem in Hamlet's soliloquy really were the conflict between the natural drive to take revenge and kill and the Divine demand of forbearance, forgiveness, and charity, how would it thereafter be possible for him to endure, almost without conflict, the killing of Polonius and Rosencrantz and Guildenstern? Indeed, we would have every right to charge the playwright with harboring a rather tragic flaw in his genius, when he invites us to identify with a protagonist who is torn by conflict about taking revenge by killing, and then, following that, fails to convey to us any reaction of guilt, on that same hero's part (or, at least, only a mild one in the case of Polonius), when he has actually committed a conflict-arousing violation of an ethical system that allegedly had possession of half his mind. Hamlet is not, after all, Iago; even in Macbeth, the arch-killer, one can observe the pressure of guilt feelings.

According to Miss Prosser, *Hamlet* is, in effect, a play about Satan's taking gradual possession of a young man's more or less innocent soul, and leading him to damnation by way of conflict-free kill-ing. But Miss Prosser ignores Hamlet's peculiar position, in that there was no court through which he could seek redress.[12] Both his being the next in succession and his having had a claim to the throne after his father's death make him the only one in the State of Denmark into whose hands the welfare of the state has actually been entrusted. In this respect, Laertes finds himself in a situation quite different from Hamlet's: *he* can turn to Claudius and ask for the punishment of a culprit.

From the beginning, the audience is reminded that this is, as far as Hamlet is concerned, more than a play about personal motives and in-volvements. Horatio's immediate response of "This bodes some strange eruption to our state"; a disinterested outsider's "Something is rotten in the state of Denmark"; Hamlet's "The time is out of joint"—these are pointed statements, which stress the concomitance of the personal and the politic. Even if Hamlet were to renounce personal vengeance, he still would not escape his obligation to restore the purity of the State (cf. Spencer, 1942, p. 103; Fergusson, 1949; Holmes, 1964, p. 81).

The correlation between subjective spheres and spheres of State was not only an Elizabethan axiom; it also amply pervades Shakespeare's plays, as many a writer has pointed out. I do not believe one can contra-dict the proposition: "The State of Denmark is in danger as long as Claudius sits on the throne." If this is so, then it is all the more signifi-cant that Claudius is presented, in his overt acts, as a superior adminis-trator and statesman, as well as a paragon of a husband.

The whole atmosphere of the tragedy would be profoundly changed if Claudius were to make himself guilty, in Macbeth-like fashion, of open tyranny. In that case, Hamlet would not carry his responsibility alone, for it would have been spread over a plurality of people. Hamlet does not find himself in Macduff's situation, which is experienced by the audience as conflict-free; Malcolm, says Miss Prosser, is "the divinely appointed agent of God's punishment" (Prosser, 1967, p. 91). Yet Malcolm's mis-sion is Hamlet's as well; Hamlet's last act is a political one: he assures Fortinbras' accession, therewith making known his temporary royal sta-

[12] It is worthwhile to quote Holmes (1964) at this point. He tried to reconstruct what might have been known about the Danish Court in England and writes: "The nobility were a powerful force in Denmark. They could not be condemned to death for any offense unless they were convicted by a public assembly of the State . . . Capital crimes against the person were settled out of court by private revenge, which was looked upon as more decorous and unobtrusive than the scandal of an official prosecution" (p. 50).

tus. But was he not the rightful King *throughout* the play, since Claudius's royal status, despite its external legality, has been the consequence of a crime he has himself committed? From this viewpoint as well, there would be no great possibility of Hamlet's being regarded by the audience as culpable of a merely "destructive" act.

Miss Prosser is definitely biased against Hamlet. When she interprets Fortinbras': "This quarry cries on havoc" as implying that "Hamlet's revenge has led him to wanton and meaningless slaughter" (p. 235f), she is following the opinion of many another commentator. (Objectively, of course, one does have to hold Claudius responsible for Gertrude's death, as well as for that of Laertes.) Yet she goes one step further: "I, for one, see no hope for Denmark in the fact that Fortinbras is now at the helm." The state has been abandoned to a foreign adventurer, she says (p. 236); it sounds almost as if she would have preferred to see Claudius on the throne. The character profile that she devises of Fortinbras is not a promising one, and here too she finds a failure on Hamlet's part.

As I shall note later, it is essentially an illusion to believe in the hero's power to regenerate the state; yet it is a fact that the note on which the tragedy ends nourishes that illusion. Fortinbras, free of guilt (specifically of oedipal guilt), will succeed to the throne that has been besmirched by Claudius' misdeeds. Since Fortinbras is guiltless, the State will be rejuvenated, if not actually regenerated.[13] Hypocrisy will no longer reign, because the head of the state no longer needs to camouflage any past act of evil.

Miss Prosser raises some very fine points, it is true, in her effort to depreciate Fortinbras, and one has to admit that he too is drawn, in the end, in a somewhat ambiguous way. He does not act as Denmark's guest, but instead, by greeting the ambassador of England with a volley even before he has been apprised of his succession, he gives reason to be suspected of having entered as a conqueror (p. 236). Yet further arguments can be raised in his favor. He is the guiltless one, who, because of his freedom from malice, must wait until destiny provides him with the opportunity to use the abundance of his energy constructively. Until then, he is forced to use it in a playfully annoying way, even though this sometimes leads him into useless battle. But the fact that Miss Prosser holds

---

[13] Walker (1948, p. 108) suggests the possibility that Shakespeare anticipated in Fortinbras the young Ironsides.

amlet responsible even for the character of his successor makes me be-
ve that perhaps what she was irritated by was the fact that Hamlet
derived the decisive measure of his action from his own inner and subjective quality, and in independence of the objective canon of a Divine law.

Here I must refer to the posthumous Hamlet analysis by Goddard,
that sagest and after Murry certainly friendliest among all the Shakespeare critics (as long as he is not dealing with psychoanalysis), for he too
presents a view that is the opposite of mine. He says that Shakespeare
"expected his audience to assume that Hamlet should kill the King"
(1951, Vol. 1, p. 336), and that "only on the assumption that Hamlet
ought not to have killed the King can the play be fitted into what then
becomes the unbroken progression of Shakespeare's spiritual development" (Vol. 1, p. 336). Very engagingly Goddard writes: "We have an
advantage over Shakespeare. The author of *Hamlet,* when he wrote it,
had not had the privilege of reading *King Lear* and other post-Hamletian
masterpieces. But we have had it, and can read *Hamlet* in their light"
(Vol. 1, p. 338).

Yet, unfortunately for his analysis, tragedies can always be interpreted in two quite different directions. They may provide the occasion
for contemplation of the "tragic flaw" in the hero, or they may be recognized as containing the gravest accusations against the forces to which
human destiny is destined to submit. So much has been written about the
tragic flaws in Macbeth and Lear; yet one may focus instead on the evil
intent of the supernatural, which is in the end responsible for Macbeth's
misdeeds, and on the ingratitude of children, which ultimately causes the
downfall of a kindly King. It is a hazardous undertaking to reproject
from later works onto earlier ones, for many reasons, not the least of
which is the genius' freedom to create a work that is, in terms of the general drift of his total output, atypical.

The moral question is rather complex in *Hamlet.* "Honor they father and thy mother" stands in close proximity to "Thou shalt not kill"
among the Commandments, and certainly for Hamlet to have abided by
the latter would have amounted to a diminution of the former's effect. All
the while that there was no court of justice from which Hamlet could
have obtained redress, an evil king was endangering the entire community. Such points seem to have been neglected by those who deny Hamlet's
duty to kill Claudius—an act that was, in this case, equivalent to a criminal's execution.

I wish to summarize my point of view as vigorously as possible. If the morality of Hamlet's "vengeance" is to be disputed, then one has to consider that Claudius was not the rightful King, that Hamlet was the only person (except Horatio) who was in possession of that secret, that there was no court of law above the ostensibly de jure King for Hamlet to turn to, and that Hamlet was the only one existing who had the duty and the capacity to restore justice. Thus it is more appropriate to speak of Hamlet's "execution" of the King than of "revenge." But if Shakespeare had made that explicit prior to, and more strongly than Hamlet's final political act of surrendering the Royal authority to Fortinbras (cf. my later remark about Shakespeare's device of retroactivity), he would have destroyed the psychological fabric of the whole play.

Be that as it may, when Goddard writes: "Loyalty to his father and the desire to grow unto himself—thirst for revenge and thirst for creation —are in Hamlet almost in equilibrium, though of course he does not know it," and "Hamlet's delay shows his soul is still alive and will not submit to the demands of the father without a struggle" (Vol. 1, p. 341), it becomes apparent that psychoanalytic interpretations (on the grounds of ego-psychology, at least) and Goddard's are in some places not too far apart, even though he rejects—on insufficient grounds, I believe— Freud's interpretation. [14]

Prosser's argumentation takes a new turn when she tries to prove that the Ghost was an evil spirit, which tempted Hamlet to commit sin. [15] In her collection of the data that can be culled from contemporary literature, to be used for that purpose, she establishes an impressive list. The Ghost appears at night, and must vanish with the first crow of the cock; he is pale; he relies on exclusively sensual imagery (as Iago does) when he is speaking to Hamlet, and tells him only what he wants to hear; he

---

[14] Goddard writes as if Freud's discovery of the Oedipus complex in Hamlet aimed at explaining the whole tragedy, whereas it was meant only to reveal the unconscious motive for Hamlet's delay. Goddard denies the bearing of the Oedipus complex on this particular situation, in view of its ubiquity. He looks at the impulses involved in the oedipal situation as per se pathological, as if Freud had ever equated the oedipal impulse with pathology, or had been unaware that an intense and positive affection for the mother could, under propitious circumstances, provide the foundations for creativity (cf. Freud, 1917).

[15] It is interesting to compare Miss Prosser's view with that of Lings (1966), who also interprets the play in a Christian spirit, yet reaches the conclusion that Claudius, being the equivalent of the Devil, has to be destroyed under all circumstances. "The Ghost initiates Hamlet," he writes (p. 29) "into the Mysteries by conveying to him the truth of the Fall not as a remote historical fact but as an immediate life-permeating reality, an acute pain which will not allow his soul a moment's rest." Lings evidently feels that it would have been unchristian if Hamlet had not carried out the deed. When Miss Prosser says that Augustine would be in complete accord that "one should fight the good fight against Satan" (p. 162f), she comes close to Lings' view. She does not elaborate this point further, however, because "emphasis on action contains an implicit rationale for rebellion" (p. 163).

never refers to God and he speaks from below, in the cellarage scene, in which Hamlet indeed treats him as a devil; the *hic et ubique,* for example, "cannot refer to an 'honest ghost', for only God and the Devil can be both here and everywhere at the same time" (p. 140).

Miss Prosser adduces a wealth of data, which seem to prove that many, almost all, of the Ghost's characteristics coincide with those that are attributed to an evil ghost, in terms of Elizabethan beliefs. Even the fact that he tells the truth speaks against him, because many an evil ghost tells the truth, in order to deceive his victim. Here the author herself detects a weakness in her reasoning. For Horatio does not warn Hamlet that his test of the truthfulness of the Ghost's account is not reliable. "Admittedly, the argument of this study would be strengthened immeasurably if Horatio countered with the warning that the instruments of darkness can tell us truth in order to betray us" (p. 178). [16]

The author even goes so far as to assert that the Ghost's second appearance "has served only one purpose: not to lead Gertrude to Heaven but to leave her to Hell" (p. 198). This conclusion she derives from the Ghost's being invisible to the Queen. Had he shown himself to her: "she would know that Hamlet is sane, she would learn the truth about Claudius, and she would have to face herself honestly. Of course, she would be put through torture, but out of such painful self-knowledge comes salvation" (p. 197f). Indeed, the fact that the Ghost makes the Queen believe that her son is insane affords further proof to Miss Prosser that he cannot be a spirit of grace. The greater love, after all, would have been to warn her about Claudius rather than to let her trust him and thereby to cause her own death. Rightly, Miss Prosser admits that her view leaves Hamlet's reference to the Ghost's "piteous action" *(III.4.127)* ("the major objection to the present interpretation") unexplained.

The reader may recall at this point my initial statement that many an interpretation of *Hamlet* has a great appeal because of its explanatory value with regard to many details, only to turn out to be disappointing in that it allows other details to remain unexplained, details that were in fact well covered by the interpretation that the author is trying to displace. Here is a typical example. Up to a certain point, Miss Prosser's conception of the Ghost as a devil carries much conviction, particularly when the reader has to submit to the thumbscrew of medieval and Re-

---

[16] I wonder also whether there is any precedent for an evil ghost being equipped to reveal an important truth—the only truth in this instance that was of importance to a bereaved son and to the welfare of the commonwealth.

naissance moral theology; but then a point is reached at which one suddenly gets the feeling that the questions answered by the new theory are outweighed by the unsolved problems created by its introduction. Besides, Miss Prosser had in her hands the possibility of an adequate solution. It becomes clear from her book that the way in which the Ghost is described and presented in *Hamlet* does not follow exactly either Catholic or Protestant pneumatology.

It is evident that Shakespeare employed imagery and knowledge about ghosts that, even though they were contradictory in detail, were current in his time, and out of them he created a new and formidable figure that—because it was, after all, a figure created by Shakespeare—is beyond any pneumatology. Since the Protestants denied the existence of purgatory, it must be a Catholic ghost.[17] According to Catholic pneumatology, however, no corpse could be moved, ergo he must be a devil.[18]

Conclusions of that sort have no bearing on the Ghost of Old Hamlet. Ghosts are part of human life and there was never a ghost created who was so telling and so much alive. Of course, he comes from Purgatory, and he is the person whom Hamlet knew as his father. Even if Claudius had not admitted his guilt in an aside, I doubt that many would have been dubious beforehand about the chances of the mouse-trap test confirming the Ghost's story. Finally, there is no indication of any doubt—unless the spectator is either overeducated or obsessional—about the Ghost's arrival from Purgatory.

If the impression that Miss Prosser's comment leaves with the reader is intended to be that pneumatological subtleties were alive in Shakespeare's audience (which I seriously doubt), then I can draw only one conclusion—namely, that Shakespeare was trying to lead current theories *ad absurdum*. But I doubt that Shakespeare was at all concerned with pneumatology. The Ghost's "phenotype" is not devilish. His

[17] Cf. Prosser, p. 123: Shakespeare wisely drew from both Catholic and Protestant beliefs in order to encourage the widest possible response." Imagine Shakespeare reading up on the literature about ghosts, in order to spread the appeal of the play among the largest possible audience! Here the author seems to be greatly mistaken, indeed: if Shakespeare was motivated primarily by a striving for success among contemporary audiences, his play would of necessity have had to lose its effect on subsequent generations rather rapidly.

[18] The author does not indulge in any such crude conclusions; instead, her reasoning is quite subtle. She discusses, for example, "the true Catholic position as spelled out in the two works written in direct answer to Lavater" (p. 106), thus admitting that one had to be quite a specialist in order to grasp what the "true" belief was in any Church. Has Shakespeare ever been preoccupied with what the "true" theory of ghosts was—and who in his audience, unless he was a specialist on pneumatology, would know what the "true" position was?

harshness in his conduct with Hamlet is quite conspicuous, and there is in him no lure, no devilish seduction. He speaks with the voice that has been in all men for thousands of years. It is the archaic father's harsh voice, which is found at the basis of the superego, by anyone who identifies with his father. It is also the voice in which a Royal father who was forceful enough to defeat the enemy on the battlefield will talk to his son, when great injustice has brought him secretly to his end.

Shakespeare's Ghost is the product of his unconscious imagination, just as all his characters go far beyond the Chronicles, morality tracts, books of history and the other sources he used to stimulate and channelize his imagination. The theological preoccupation here seems to stand in the way of psychological understanding, which Miss Prosser seems at one point even to warn against.

In discussing the closet episode, that landmark in Hamlet's relationship to Ophelia, she writes: "If we must inquire closely into Hamlet's motives—and I am not at all sure that we should, for the audience simply does not have time for conjectures. . . ."[19] (p. 146). This, I would guess, is even more true with regard to pneumatologic subtleties. Yet there is one difference between pneumatological and psychological subtleties. Unconscious imagery about motivation is stored in every human being; subliminally, it is constantly being stirred and stimulated during a play of *Hamlet's* dimensions. The effect that is made by the presentation of problems of pneumatology, by contrast, depends on the previous existence of special knowledge. Therefore it is reasonable to conjecture that a psychological analysis of the play may make explicit what may be going on subliminally in the spectator.

The state of helpessness into which an inquirer is thrown who would like to extract the secret of *Hamlet,* yet wants to avoid psychology, can be learned from Miss Prosser's comment on Hamlet's madness. To begin with, she states categorically that "Hamlet is not mad. He never is" (p. 147); and she holds "sentimental critics in the eighteenth century" (p. 148) responsible for this interpretation ever having come up at all. Then she describes Hamlet's behavior as contradictory; he surrenders to instinct, while suffering a loss of rational control (p. 190f); he suffers "most of his truly emotional outbursts" at the moments when he approaches the breaking point (p. 149f*;* "he rises to a state of hysteria,

---

[19] I must repeat that a great play must not only grip the spectator, but must also prove its eminence when it is subjected to critical analysis in the calmness of the study. The stage alone is not decisive with regard to the perennial value of a dramatic work.

incoherently raving" (p. 201); he revels "in the license of his feigned lunacy," he indulges in "grotesque nonsense" (p. 203), etc.—all of them characteristics about which it would be hard to say just why else they are applicable to a man, if not because he is mad. The author's way out is to assert that Shakespeare drew "real insanity" in Titus, Lear, and Ophelia (p. 148), in a way that is quite different from his handling of Hamlet.

That is quite true, but why should Shakespeare have had to confine himself to the limited views of the medicine of his times, which still persist in some circles in our own day, and to accept only the classical psychoses as "real insanity"? Does not Hamlet in the end say himself that he has been mad? And how does the author solve this dilemma? "Even though Samuel Johnson and others have wished, and with good warrant, that Hamlet had not offered his *nonexistent madness* as a defense, the apology to Laertes somehow [sic!] has the ring of honesty. The curious wording of the speech may, of course, be simply a *lapse* on Shakespeare's part" (p. 234, my italics).

With this last haughty remark, Prosser has lost, in my opinion, some of the trust we might otherwise have placed in her. In Grebanier (1960) we encounter the assumption of an utterly un-Shakespearean stage trick, in order for him to be able to get around Hamlet's insight into his own past madness, which seems to be a veritable embarrassment for a certain brand of Shakespeare critics; now we are told to put our reliance in the really scurrilous idea that Shakespeare was "simply" absentminded when he was writing a crucial passage of the tragedy.[20]

Modern psychology, which has such a bad name with most critics, has led to the insight that in addition to "real" insanity, there is still another insanity, some of which lies dormant (at times not altogether dormant) in everyone of us. Freud even ventured to say that a dream is a temporary psychosis; Shakespeare would have understood him, perhaps even agreed. Here, in Hamlet's farewell speech, Shakespeare proves his real genius and rushes several centuries ahead of his time, by enunciating the deepest insights into the fundamental fabric of man's mind; yet he is still refuted by the spiritually cowardly, who are reluctant to enter an ideology that is new to them and about the consequences of which they are fearful. For in this farewell speech, whatever ambiguity there may be

[20] One is almost reminded, by the attitude that certain critics show with regard to Hamlet's madness, of those resistances that Freud postulated as existing in some critics of psychoanalysis. Of course, it must be expected to arouse fear in the timid and the frightened to learn that the hero with whom one has identified was at times mad.

with regard to the stage action, there is no ambiguity in terms of the content.

It is the proclamation of the great humanitarian who no longer lets the madman stand naked and freezing, chained to a dank wall, but instead leads him back into human company, by solemnly declaring that madness is part and parcel of the human mind. Anyone who wants to utilize his potential to the fullest, and to make his way along the myriad avenues life opens up to him will more than likely at one or another time have to pass through a siege of madness. While the "really" insane remain there, Hamlet—like most of us—succeeds in grappling his way out of it. Yet once it is made clear that we (the "rest of us") are not separated from the "madman" by a wall, but that there is rather overlap, then insanity loses its quality of "foreign body" and becomes humanized. And is this momentous message, prolific in its consequences—which it took 300 years to realize, at least *in spiritu*—now to be reduced to mere absentmindedness?[21]

Prosser herself admits that "it may have seemed that I was putting Hamlet into a straightjacket of Christian morality" (p. 249). While she says that was far from her intention, nevertheless all the while I was reading her book, I kept thinking exactly of that term, only to find it spoken out, in the end, in the form of a denial. At one point, however, it even looks as if Miss Prosser were acknowledging the ambiguity of the play, in terms of the message it indirectly conveys. She believes that "this long study has led for the first time to an awareness that many strikingly diverse and even contradictory views of *Hamlet* can be illuminating" (p. 251), and she spells out the Christian, the existentialist, the Freudian and the Nietzschean views, asserting that "every sensitive analysis of the tragic experience can lend new insight." And this can be done, she alleges, not in spite of but because of "our recognition that the orientation of *Hamlet* is explicitly Christian" (ibid). That may be so; it all depends on how broad an area we delineate as that ill-defined country "Christian."

I wonder whether the author is not somewhat biased. For some, wars and famine and capital punishment, even physical torture, have been quite compatible with a profoundly Christian attitude. But I do not

---

[21] Many other statements from Prosser's pen might be reviewed critically, such as her assertion that Gertrude remains loyal to Claudius (p. 196), and that Hamlet's "tirade" against her "has no effect on her whatsoever" (p. 193); but all that would be anticlimactic, as compared with what has been said so far.

want to repeat outworn arguments, and would only cite Oskar Pfister (1913), who made an effort to demonstrate that Freud was a "real" Christian, whose works realize the "true" spirit of the Savior's message, far beyond what the Churches have ever taught. Of course, almost everything that has been created since Christ's incarnation (and some historians claim that much of His message had already appeared before His coming) can be connected with the spirit of Christianity. Karl Marx's message contains in part the spirit of the early Christians, with its promise of happiness and the ending of sufferings, etc. A diabolical mind may even see in Hitler's destructiveness the coming about of the providential end of the Jews who, according to some prominent Christians, lost their *raison d'être* after His coming.

But what is it that Miss Prosser means by "explicitly Christian"? "The consensus of civilized man, therefore, is that discipline of emotions, obedience to established law, and love (or, at least respect) for one's fellow man are moral goods, whereas surrender to emotions, defiance of law and hatred of (or, at least, indifference to) one's fellow man are moral ills. By recognizing the Christian perspective of *Hamlet,* we thus do not narrow the ethical base of the play, we broaden it" (p. 249f). I doubt that these are exclusively Christian principles.[22] Some oriental philosophies, moral systems and religions—not to speak of the ancient Stoa— have, it seems to me, preached such principles, and even more penetratingly than Christianity.

Be that as it may, if *Hamlet*'s message were really confined within the spirit of antiseptic homilies, we should quickly lose our interest in the play. Yet we may be reassured by the conviction that Miss Prosser must have come to her conclusion as the result of having studied a different version of *Hamlet* from the one that is on my desk. In the latter, Hamlet kills Claudius in a state of passion, and without any trace of "discipline of emotions." Miss Prosser tries to excuse this passion, on the grounds that Shakespeare does everything in his power to make Hamlet's killing of Claudius "as sympathetic as possible" (p. 233).[23] "Hamlet is guilty of manslaughter, not premeditated murder. He would undoubtedly have

[22] Frye (1963) warns over and over again against appraising as typically Christian what could already be found in the writings of the ancients and was never regarded as being characteristic of Christian morality by the great Protestant innovators.

[23] It is interesting to quote Braddy (1964, p. 69) here, for he perceives just the opposite development: ". . . a wily victim of injustice divests his heart of sorrow to invest it with vengeance. The wry wit-snapper ends by waking to violence; the tristful thinker ends by unsheathing a wrathful sword."

received a royal pardon in the Elizabethan courts and even today would be treated with leniency"[24] (p. 234).

Miss Prosser is apparently aware that Hamlet, when he is killing Claudius, "is enraged and savage. . . . He is still a terribly human being who has had his new armor of patience all but ripped from him." It is therefore difficult to see how she can reconcile rage, savagery and "terribly human" with her idea of Shakespeare's doing "everything in his power" to make Hamlet's final deed appear sympathetic, unless the Christian playwright did not let his left hand know what the right hand was doing.

I should now like to discuss Miss Prosser's Christian interpretation within a broader context. The fact that the play does take place *within a Christian frame* is clear from many details. Elton (1922, p. 18f) is correct when he says that Shakespeare's Denmark "is a Christian land and under the old faith." There is talk of Purgatory, angels, nunneries; a Christian funeral takes place. In brief, what I would call the Christian machinery is quite well represented. When Elton calls Hamlet, watching Claudius at prayer, "a theologian, and presumably a correct one" (ibid.), he may be right or wrong. But at this point Hamlet is certainly not a good Christian; unless, as many do, one takes his reasoning as a mere excuse for further delays, one can hardly disagree with Samuel Johnson that this speech is too horrible to be read or listened to.[25]

I do not think that Hamlet is much of a theologian, although he may have known some theology, which would not after all be surprising. His initial rejection of suicide on the grounds that the canon forbids it, is done without further reflection. A similar rejection is also reached in the later "to be" soliloquy when he deals with the problem along the lines of personal deliberation, pursuing this, it should be noted, with an intensity that contrasts with the flatness of his previous reference to the canon.

And then there is the augury passage, as famous as it is beautiful, and drenched in the New Testament atmosphere. This Johnson (1952, p. 204) stresses—through a clever, although by no means obligatory inter-

---

[24] I am not as sure of either of these two propositions as Miss Prosser seems to be. Would it not have depended upon who Claudius' successor was; and as for the "even today," again, one has to ask, "In which country, and under what government?"

[25] The imagery of hell has lost its hold on the Western mind; this is true at least for the élite, but also for a large part of the uneducated. For that reason, the full brunt of Hamlet's outburst cannot be felt by the modern reader. It will be, however, if he substitutes for hell its modern equivalent, and imagines a modern Hamlet who not only wished but also used his wits to see to it that somebody was actually carried away to a concentration camp.

pretation of "We defy augury"—as meaning literally a rejection of divination from the flight of birds, in accordance with *Lev. XIX.26* and *Deut. XVIII.10*. The injunction against divination, through the reference to Providence, is set side by side with the admonition in the New Testament to see the hand of Providence in a bird's fall *(Matt. X.29-31* and *Luke XII.6-7)*. Miss Prosser interprets the sparrow passage as meaning: "The only terror is the death of the soul" (p. 230).

In the *Ur-Hamlet (V.3)*, at the equivalent point, Hamlet has a nosebleed and faints. He says upon awakening: "When I thought of going to court, a quick fainting fit overtook me. What this will mean is known to the gods." When Horatio expresses the hope that Heaven will cause this omen not to portend anything bad, Hamlet replies: "Be it as it will, I'll none the less go to court, and even should it cost me my life." As with the rest of the play, here too Shakespeare makes out of the physical-crude something psychological-ambiguous. The defiance of augury may, after all, also mean the decision not to respond to fear and sadness ("How ill all's here about my heart")—that is to say, to those emotional factors that threaten to interfere with necessary reality pursuits.

Miss Prosser is certain that Shakespeare intended "his audience to leave the theater believing that somehow Hamlet has been granted salvation" (p. 235). Although Frye (1963) reminds us that Shakespeare was primarily interested in the temporal and this-worldly lives of his protagonists and not at all concerned with their salvation, I agree with Miss Prosser that Horatio's eulogy is germane to the play; it is indeed a focal point, if one tries to decipher what the message is that is inherent in the tragedy, even though it is never set forth explicitly.

The salvation that Miss Prosser speaks of depends, of course, on her interpretation of "special providence," "the fall of a sparrow," and "readiness." For Miss Prosser it can mean only one thing: " 'God's will be done. Amen.' . . . Hamlet has surrendered his will to Divine Providence." She finds here the echo of a New Testament passage, which says that God in his infinite love has ordained a plan for every man, a plan that cannot nevertheless be known to man, who "can only by an act of faith lay hold of the promise that God knows the plan to be good. And the plan includes his own death" (p. 229f). Miss Prosser's suggestion that Hamlet is here asserting his integration of the idea of death makes it probable that she is on the wrong track. She interprets the graveyard scene as a meditation on the death of the body, which she takes to mean "a preparation for meditating on the more important truth: the eternal life of the soul" (p. 223). But there is really no indication at all of such a meaning.

To my way of thinking, the greatness and the powerful effectiveness of the graveyard scene lie precisely in its finality, in the fact that there is no loophole through which one may steal a glance at a life thereafter. Yorick's and Alexander's destinies are both, as Hamlet seems to present his case, completely and conclusively ended in their skulls and bones. After this exposition, death seems to be no problem any longer for him. It would therefore mean a regression to a problem that the spectator has the right to assume that Hamlet has already solved, if with the augury passage he once again takes up the problem of death.

What remains after the graveyard scene is the consummation of a deed. Yet the passage that is quoted by most critics as convincing evidence that the augury passage refers to death is Hamlet's saying: "The readiness is all." "For Hamlet," writes Frye (1963, p. 138) "the context of readiness is essentially and explicitly Christian. . . . With Hamlet, the 'readiness' is not only linked to but even seems to summarize the declaration of his reliance upon New Testament promises," and he invokes Luther's, Calvin's and Hooker's authority as final proof.

It may seem somewhat brazen if, in view of all this, I suggest still another interpretation of the passage in question. Miss Prosser reasons that Shakespeare would not "have used the familiar language of Christian doctrine and specific references to a familiar Biblical passage" (p. 229) had he not wanted to convey beliefs that he knew to be expressed by this vocabulary. "To argue otherwise is to assume that Shakespeare did not know the meaning of his own words" (ibid.). Arguments such as this should not exercise a restrictive force on interpretation, for they are not quite as valid as they may appear to be at first glance, if the following two considerations are taken into account.

It may be that Shakespeare preferred an audience to believe that he was an adherent of current Christian doctrine; it may be that he was not fully aware of the consequences of what he was writing (many geniuses are not aware of them). I regard both questions as moot and unanswerable, although we do have the text and we can check on its objective structure. What I object to is that critics take their authority solely from the Scriptures, that they really believe that man does not ever pour new wine into old bottles.

It is, of course, important to know the connection between Shakespeare's words and thoughts and past tradition, but it is more important to discover what he created out of them. Does his genius lie solely in his poetry, his ability to form and manage words? Does not the universe he created contain people that have never lived before, that were altogether beyond the scope of imagination of his by-and-large mediocre environment? He certainly did not imitate life; he observed and absorbed it and then created something perfectly new out of the cliché, if one is permitted to use that pejorative term for the chronicles and histories and the other materials that were readily accessible to others as well as to himself. Is it probable that moral values remained altogether untouched in the giant's brain? It is indeed highly improbable that the creative process in Shakespeare stopped short at the limits set for it by hallowed principles of moral theology.

It would be quite out of keeping to attempt to evaluate Hamlet's killing of Polonius in terms of Christian morality. Hamlet, as created by Shakespeare, is a man such as the world had not previously known, moving through a society that Shakespeare devised for him, with thoughts, demands, wishes, solutions, motives that are all new, specific, original. Nevertheless—and that is the mystery of the genius—all that was done in such a way that we are able to find ourselves in it. The psychotic is also very original at times; yet the fact remains that he has broken away from our world and for that reason has become basically incomprehensible to us. The overlapping of the creative, clinically psychotic patient and the genius is all too well known, and I bring it up now only because the originality of the genius is still underestimated. Because he presents his own, original cosmos in a way that enables us to share it, many believe that he *reflects* reality, and that his work is a sort of "mirror of the world."

To be sure, the conflicts that have shattered and disjoined man ever since his emergence as man also enter into this new world. Goddard was wrong when he chided Freud for discovering the Oedipus conflict in *Hamlet*—thereby, or so he thought, reducing to something regressive a masterpiece that points into the future. What Freud did was to extend one dimension of the play into the shadowy realm of the prehistorical past, which has been alive in every man born since then, and in Shakespeare as well; without it, he could never have become the most human of all playwrights. He was not a dadaist or an abstractionist, someone who is generally more interesting for what he is suppressing and *not* creating than for what he does create. The greatness of minds such as Shakespeare's lies in the specific cosmos they create; Janus-like, it contains both the world we know and their own, amalgamated into a new original specific cosmos that is still indubitably recognizable as their own. The pusillanimous, of course, will see only the first mentioned component.

The Christian morality to which Prosser subjects *Hamlet,* along with its modern equivalent, mental hygiene, bears the odor of antiseptics, which deprive life of its beauty, its greatness, its infinity. The Shakespearean cosmos does not keep itself within the limits of either of these. Shakespeare created no character who would fit exactly Christian morality or would satisfy the principles of mental hygiene—not even Portia or Paulina do. That is why every critic finds something to rail against in Shakespeare; the fact that he pleased everyone and no one is one proof of his greatness.

That Miss Prosser and others have been able to present *Hamlet's* morality as essentially Christian, in the narrower sense of the meaning, ought to increase our admiration for the play. It shows that the masterful ambiguity in plot construction and characterization also holds for the moral, ethical and philosophical abstractions that lie buried in the play.[26]

What then is the ethical message in *Hamlet?* I do not believe that *Hamlet* carries a particular message, as so much drama of the reform movement and the period of realism does; instead, by the introduction of a new character it becomes, so to speak, unintentionally, the carrier of a new ethics. It seems to me that such critics as Knight misinterpret those steps by which Hamlet transcends Christian ethics, in that they regard these steps as being essentially negative. Apparently, it is difficult for the symbolist, too, to evaluate objectively. Christ is free of conflict since he is free of sexual impurity, and any ethics that is begotten for the sexless is a metaphysical ethics—that is to say, no ethics at all, but an abstraction.

---

[26] I believe that Prosser belongs to the large group of critics whom Braddy has wittily called "the detractors of Hamlet" and against whom he wrote, in order "to restore to Hamlet his good name" (1964, p. 2). He could not have found a better title for his book than *Hamlet's Wounded Name.* It would be worthwhile to investigate what the reason is for the enmity of so many critics toward Hamlet. I would guess that it is the increasing decay of religious sentiment and the consequent fear, the heightening inner conflicts, the vanishing trust in the future that sharpens the critics' ears for the implicit—at times, desperate—atheism that one feels in some passages in *Hamlet.* It is this that makes them turn with resentment against the first dramatic embodiment of the new European spirit. If Shakespeare had overtly shaped Hamlet as an atheist, he would surely have aroused wholesale resistance and rejection from the start. It may be that Shakespeare himself was not aware of how atheistic or, at least, anti-Christian (in the narrower sense of the word) his play really was. He himself may have been consciously a devoted believer. But it may well be alarming to the religious mind to discover that here the spirit of atheism is insidiously poured into the spectator's mind by way of inviting him to identify with the protagonist, yet without spelling out the message sufficiently to arouse his objections. One defensive weapon may then be to cry out: "Hamlet was a murderer; do not identify with him!"

Christian morality holds at best an inferior place in *Hamlet*. With the secularization of ethics that takes place in the play, the cornerstone of a new ethical movement was laid—a movement that, notwithstanding some of its consequences, is intellectually superior to any system that man had thus far been exhorted to follow solely because it was revealed.

To be sure, the tragedy could have been written only by a Christian, someone who had grown up in a Christian community and had integrated Christian ethics; yet one can also say that it could have been written only by someone who was deeply dissatisfied, indeed desperate, about the state of the world, and who, one can be sure, did not expect to find salvation through the potentiation of Christianity or of the Churches. The tragedy's end may be interpreted—as I have tried to show—as Hamlet's having attained a state in which he acts, ethically speaking, irreproachably, in a state of ego autonomy. This interpretation depends, of course, on the significance one accords to the factor of accidents in Shakespeare's plays. Knight's (1930, p. 45) concept of the final action being *forced* upon Hamlet by circumstances (fate)—which is almost no interpretation at all, but merely the result of a literal reading of the text—is permissible; but it reduces some of Shakespeare's plays to the level of slapstick comedies. Yet it is precisely the interpretation of the final scene that has a retroactive effect upon the understanding of some preceding passage.

When Johnson writes that Hamlet "has arrived at an attitude that bridges the gap between the real and the ideal and transcends the conflict between appearance and reality, as well as that between passion and reason" (1952, p. 206f), I follow him. But when he calls this Christian Stoicism and finds in Hamlet obedience to Providence, I must object. This would mean that Hamlet gave up being the agent of a paternal command in order to become the agent of a divine one; yet it seems to me that the play's ending speaks against just such a concept. Johnson's idea amounts to an infringement on the subject's autonomy, sublimated as this would be when compared with Hamlet's initial state.

Of all the societal restraints Shakespeare had to labor under, I most regret "An Acte to Restraine Abuses of Players" (Halliday, 1952, p. 13) which, although it was in fact promulgated (27 May 1606) after the creation of *Hamlet*, still brings to our attention some of the dangers of which the genius had to beware. In it a strong stand was taken against the "abuse of the Holy Name of God," and a fine levied against those who "jestingly or prophanely speake or use the holy Name of God or of Christ, Jesus, or of the Holy Ghoste or of the Trinitie, which are not to be spoken but with fear and reverence, etc." Whatever the effect may have been on Shakespeare's subsequent writings, one consequence seems clear enough: he had to tread carefully in religious matters (cf. Seibel, 1924, p. 38). The quandary for the historian, however, is that he is in no position, at least in my opinion, to draw any reliable conclusions as to whether Shakespeare's plays did as a result contain more or less of Christian ethics, morals—or, more generally, of the Christian spirit, in the narrower meaning of the term—for either way the playwright would have run the risk of arousing the interdiction of secular as well as Church powers.

We know that in every society the genius finds himself in a position similar to that of the dreamer. The dream too is not permitted to state the whole truth. It is forced to revamp its original meaning, in order to circumvent the ever-watchful inner censoring agent. In the same way, the genius produces within the limits set by society's pressures on him. Curiously enough, this pressure frequently stands him in good stead. It is often a prognostically bad sign when the dream censor breaks down and the tendencies to obscure no longer have any effect on dreams. A society that did not, even indirectly, set any limits upon the artist in terms of what he might or might not bring to a stage, might well introduce thereby a phase of artistic decline.

Shakespeare wrote in a society that permitted its writers a far broader leeway than they had enjoyed during preceding centuries; yet there were definite limits and expectations, in part codified and in part taken for granted, without their being stated explicitly.[27] I do not mean here such things as the use of certain words. From some of the differences between the Folios and the Quartos, we do know that certain expressions were not welcome and the Valladolid folio, as censored by the Jesuit Father Sankey, is an important source for the study of Catholic sensibilities (Frye, 1963, pp. 275-293).

What I have in mind here is rather views about the world, man, religion—views that may have lain dormant in the playwright or been subjects of his meditation and contemplation; rebellious ideas that may have presented themselves explicitly to him and been rejected by him, and yet may have found their way into such a play as *Hamlet*. I would guess that it may be precisely the tension between the Christian garb and a hidden

---

[27] Of course, there must have been a middle area, in which the author was uncertain as to whether or not he was going beyond what was permitted.

message of a quite different character that is one (a very important one) of the many factors that make the play so very effective, as well as the eternal riddle of critics. Something of that sort has been suggested by Verrall (1895, pp. 232-235) with regard to Euripides' tragedies. He propounds the idea that "without harmony and without discrimination, upon contradictory hypotheses" Euripides proceeded to present on the one hand the gods and miracles of anthropomorphic religion and on the other "incidents and language pointing directly to the opposite conclusion, stimulating an adverse sentiment, consistent only with disbelief in the traditional religion and rejection of the anthropomorphic gods."

One might feel inclined to make almost the same statement with regard to Shakespeare's tragedies. He has actually been claimed as one of their own by opposing ideologies. In Shakespeare, however, it seems to me, the matter is even more complicated, since the two ideologies cannot be neatly kept apart, and sometimes the same line in the play may be cited as proof by diametrically opposed views. In Shakespeare, artistic harmony is preserved. *Hamlet,* when taken as a whole, has the sort of unity we may find in plants or other organisms. Only by a careful analysis, which takes one out of a primarily aesthetic experience—only after the careful weighing of microscopic details—does one become aware of currents and counter-currents. One then sees the whirlpools that, in addition to giving Shakespeare's tragedies the momentum and profundity of life that contribute so greatly to their aesthetic effect, also enable one to arrive at conclusions with regard to the particular attitudes and beliefs by which his characters are motivated.

Whatever the outcome of such microscopic analysis may be, however, it is not a stringent conclusion that by dint of it we will have gained insight into Shakespeare's own attitudes and beliefs. The literary creation of new worlds, I would assume, was more important for him than the exposition of religious or ethical truths. The creative impulse might have been of such intensity that, even if he had been a devout Catholic or Protestant or any other form of believer, he might nevertheless have infused a substantial portion of atheism or theism or whatever into a character about whom he had intense feelings, when the artistic conception of that particular embodiment of life, as he saw it, called for it within this new cosmos.

Be that as it may, in my opinion, once we go to the bottom of *Hamlet,* we discover there something that is very unchristian. There is, for example, the problem of Hamlet's last words "The rest is silence." Stevenson (1958, p. 30) sees in it a denial of belief in a life after death; Seibel (1924, p. 24) describes it as if it were, according to Stevenson, "the epitaph of an agnostic," and Levin (1959, p. 99) associates it with a prospect of nonexistence. Frye (1963, p. 53), however, points out that "the reference to death as silence is common in Scripture and was interpreted by orthodox commentators as referring to the faithful man's inability to continue his vocation in this world after his death." He acknowledges that, in the light of the twentieth-century connotations of words, the agnostic interpretation is natural; yet, he says, this would result in "a foreign meaning to the characterization of Hamlet," if it were applied back to Shakespeare's own period.

Here we seem to face the typical dilemma of the modern Hamlet critic. An interpretation that would now appear to be unassailable vanishes into thin air, when viewed under the historical perspective. In the First Quarto, Hamlet's dying words are: "Heaven receive my soul"; but with all the reasons we have for doubting the authenticity of the Quarto, can we be certain that these were the original lines? Miss Prosser believes so, and it is interesting to consider her explanation for Shakespeare's change, which should be compared with Seibel (p. 24): "To have Hamlet presume on Heaven's reception . . . would inevitably make an audience uneasy . . . following so closely on his savage outburst as he kills Claudius" (p. 235). But does Hamlet presume or wish? And should not the audience become far more uneasy when Horatio, the ideal type of Chorus, who is always expressing the balanced, the rational, the "correct" view, calls Hamlet in the next line "a noble heart," and gives voice to imagery that causes us to see Hamlet on his way to Heaven?

It cannot be an accident, after all, that in *Hamlet*, on three occasions and in quite prominent places in the play, reference is made to the state of the soul at the moment of dying. The question of this state contributed the chief motive for Hamlet's postponing the taking of revenge in the prayer scene, and the audience is (purposefully?) reminded of it again toward the end of the play, when Hamlet makes the (almost gratuitous) remark "Not shriving-time allow'd" *(V.2.47)* about the deaths of Rosencrantz and Guildenstern. As a matter of fact, his sardonic remark about the death of the two courtiers and his own last words are only 315 lines apart. This should not be overlooked, I believe, particularly in view of the change from "Heaven receive my soul" to "The rest is silence." (I must admit, of course, that *Hamlet* would mean to me something quite different from what it now means, if the First Quarto version had been maintained.)

A discussion of the Old Testament references that Frye cites, in order to make Hamlet's parting words Christian in character, would show the possible pitfalls of the historical approach for the interpretation of these passages. Aside from the fact that they occur in the Old Testament, in which the afterlife does not play a prominent role, they do not at all justify a Christian's parting from this world with the very categorical dictum and apparent conviction that all he now had to expect was silence.[28] Furthermore—and it is difficult to say which is of greater import— when Hamlet is apprised of his impending death, at that very moment he carries out what was in the eyes of the Church a mortal sin: killing in rage. We are reminded, of course, of the mitigating circumstances, yet no apology can be found for his action if, at the very moment of his death, he is devoid of any concern about the future, and instead pointedly expresses concern only about what posterity will have to say about him and his cause.

Laertes' death is different. He asks Hamlet for forgiveness; he wishes that Hamlet will not be punished for Polonius' death and his own, and he dies repentant for his having been instrumental in the killing of Hamlet. To be sure, at this point Hamlet also speaks of Heaven and wishes that Laertes may be freed from any guilt. The addition of "I follow thee" is one of these superb ambiguities with which the play is replete; it allows the believer to assert that it can mean only: "I follow thee to Heaven" and the skeptic that it could just as well mean: "Soon I too will die, just as is happening to you now." Yet there is no doubt that, from that moment on, Hamlet has turned away from all eschatological thought. But what else was to be expected if one recalls the deep impression that was made on him by the Ghost's story of his sufferings in Purgatory, which he hears at the very start of the play? Considering the light in which he was presented initially, would he have been capable, if death had befallen him *at that time*, of parting with words such as "The rest is silence," and of being primarily concerned with the image that posterity would form of him?

In his farewell, there is even a striking parallel with his father's story. In that initial account, the father aroused curiosity and horror by say-

---

[28] Curiously enough, the psychoanalyst may be able to help the theologian at this point, by offering for his use the supposition that Hamlet was indeed so afraid of what would happen to him after death that he had to deny his soul's imperishable existence.

ing: "I could a tale unfold" *(I.5.15);* the tale referred, of course, to the "eternal blazon" of purgatory that Hamlet—if his thinking were at this point confined within the bounds of Christian eschatology— would have had to expect. But when Hamlet himself is stricken and looks around, he sees the "audience to this act . . . pale and tremble," as he himself was pale and trembled when he was the audience; like his father, he too says at this moment: "O! I could tell you!' . . ."

Yet nowhere did his father employ the sort of imagery that would permit such an association as "The rest is silence." Thus Hamlet's parting words acquire, by their very context and position, a special meaning, which is not at all exhausted by the testimony of tradition. Here indeed is new wine in old bottles! Moreover, it makes the augury statement appear, retroactively, in a new light.

If the augury passage does not contain anything different from the equivalent New Testament passages whose vocabulary it uses, then the death scene is indeed absurd. Absurdity, which can be brought to light only by logical analysis, is, to be sure, permissible in a literary masterpiece—so long as it is in the service of poetry and the production of dramatic tension, and so long as its character remains unnoticed as such by the audience. But I must re-emphasize that, in a play like *Hamlet,* one discovers, over and over again, the concurrence of many dimensions without that fact ever leading to the absurd. The dramatic effect that the play has made on the spectator in performance still holds its ground when, in the quiet of the study, the play falls under the scalpel of logical analysis.

Surely the dramatic effect of that last scene can hardly be overestimated. Horatio's attempt to die together with his friend, and Hamlet's plea to Horatio to abstain, along with his appeal instead to "Absent thee from felicity awhile," is perfectly structured and written in well-nigh perfect language. Furthermore, it is so moving that no spectator should be expected to reason that all this is contradictory to the augury passage, which he may have understood till then as most commentators have, as being a clear-cut Christian pronouncement of belief in Providence and eternal life.

Hamlet has to his record, on the face of it, two manslaughters, the purposeful abetment of the murder of two former friends and, shortly before his death, the passionate killing of his uncle, committed in full and conscious hatred. In three separate instances, therefore, he has killed with the avowed purpose of assuring the victims' eternal damnation—

that is to say, he has done so with an intention for which there is no Christian pardon. Moreover, there has never at any time been any reaction of true remorse forthcoming from him.

For, even when he confesses to his own madness, he expresses regret *only* for his having caused Laertes pain and not at all for having performed the deeds that caused that pain. Is it conceivable that a man of that intellectual stature would express whole-hearted acknowledgment of an all-powerful Divinity, and this in what is clearly meant to be the position he finally arrives at after a quite tortuous and painful development—and then let it go again and fly in the face of it all, *at the moment of his death*? Even if such a sequence could be justified by that area of illogicality that must be conceded to the art of playwriting, it is not really to be expected in such a play as *Hamlet*, which contains so much psychological insight and of a very subtle sort, at that.

When Hamlet comes to terms with death in the graveyard scene, and integrates dying as that unavoidable part of life with which it ends, he becomes capable thereby of reshaping his attitude toward the future. His acknowledgment of a Providence, and his reference to the sparrow, with its orphic coda, may stand for a new synthesis between the vaguely defined future into which we are irrevocably drawn at each moment and the self's well-defined purposes. The future is constantly realizing itself in a form that is different from cherished personal purposes. "I will accept it," says Hamlet, at this point, "as determined and inevitable."

Before this, he has been enraged and even rendered desperate by the discrepancy he has discovered between anticipation and realization. Yet his acceptance of a Providence does not lead him to abandon his striving to give the present the form he would wish it to have. It was in fact his recognition of a Providence—of an order in the future—which realizes itself constantly at each moment, that made it possible for Hamlet to act.

At the moment of his initial traumatization, the world that Hamlet had until then taken for granted, without inquiring into it, became "out of joint"—that is to say, chaotic. But in a chaotic world, which does not abide by *any* rules or order, action becomes impossible. Actual chaos can be met only with chaotic movement, which is no action at all but a "threshing around"; this is precisely what all of us would be doing if we were living in a chaotic world; and under the pressure of severe traumata, such as occurs on a battle line, that is just what can be observed. The traumatized patient either becomes stricken to mutism, or else he is driven to senseless motions. This did not happen to Hamlet, of course, since he was not suffering from a traumatic neurosis. But he did lose a stable frame of reference—which was one of the many reasons why he could not get himself to the point of carrying out the one deed that he knew he had to do. [29]

In the passage about Providence, Hamlet announces that he has reached a new plateau—and indeed a higher one than the one he had stood on when he was still acting while taking the world for granted and without reflecting upon it. It is a new plateau, from which he is capable of viewing as "necessary" whatever may happen. He thereby acknowledges retroactively that past events too—which at one time had also been lying in the future, and which, when they did occur, had impressed him as being chaotic—that even those events had been providential, and not, as he had originally thought, arbitrary and avoidable. In other words, he is here presenting, even if only obliquely, a world view that is in essence the modern scientific view—namely, that what may at first impress us as irregular and chaotic is in reality determined, caused, inevitable. But how else could this new understanding have been presented, if not in the archaic language of visual imagery, derived from sacred texts?

I am not trying to say that Shakespeare anticipated Newton or explicitly conveyed a scientific outlook with regard to the world and its events. I want only to say that, after coming to terms with death, Hamlet succeeded—this is, from the psychologic point of view, quite tenable—in organizing his outlook on the future in such a way as to make action possible. I do not think that a Christian interpretation can be reconciled with what follows thereafter in the play. [30] Only if the new wine is found that Shakespeare poured into the old bottles are we able to see into the deeper meaning of the tragedy. And if we acknowledge the validity of this interpretation, then we also thereby grasp the character of the new ethics.

[29] According to Bradley's (1904, pp. 113, 118-120) "shock" theory, Hamlet was a person whose character traits made it impossible for him to react in a healthy way to a trauma. These character traits were, as Bradley saw them, assets and not deficiencies. However, I would disagree with his conception of Hamlet's pre-traumatic personality. In discussing Bradley's theory, one must keep in mind that he uses the term "shock" where at present one would speak of trauma.

[30] Bush (1956) has given a careful and sensitive analysis of what appears to the modern reader as an inconsistency, but seems in Shakespeare to be the representation of contradictions in a unified action. "In *Hamlet*," he writes (p. 117), "Shakespeare's vision expresses itself through contradiction; the variety and incongruities of *Hamlet* are what make it seem more than a play; *Hamlet* is 'the way things are.' It is inconsistent that grace comes in violence, that revenge is a remedy; the contradiction of action lies in its involvement both in time and in what is outside of time."

Hamlet's lack of concern about the future of his soul can be understood as the introduction of a new and essential function into man's life. It is no longer sufficient, and surely not decisive, to determine whether or not he has lived in harmony with the Canon. A new frame of reference has been introduced: his own individuality. Conformism in whatever form—the adaptation of one's actions to an outward frame of reference, in whatever way or for whatever purpose—is superseded by the necessity of living up to an inner demand that goes beyond the bounds of externally-imposed duty. That is how modern man's dilemma begins. At one time, it is the quest for a distinct identity, and then later on the search for a feeling of belonging; but it has throughout the quality of an *inner* experience.

Alexander (1955, p. 184) has expressed it somewhat differently: "To what may be called *the instinctive wisdom of antiquity and her heroic passions,* represented so impressively by Hamlet's father, Shakespeare has united *the meditative wisdom of later ages* in Hamlet himself." (author's italics) I find the addition to be in a category somewhat different from Alexander's, yet he reminds us that it is an addition to, and not a break with the past. Hamlet is not a delinquent, shunning his obligations and duties; rather, he extends these later to include service to the whole community, which here stands for mankind. What the play depicts is a struggle to obtain the right motivation—which is possible only when the subject has inner freedom of choice.

When Hamlet departs with: "The rest is silence," I take that as an expression of his being reconciled with whatever the Divinity may have decided with regard to his soul. He has fulfilled his duty toward the world *and* toward himself. If he has displeased God, he will have to suffer; yet he could not have acted otherwise than he did, and he therefore dies with a minimum of regret and no plea for a happy future. He has become more concerned—and rightly so—about how mankind will judge him than he is with the Heavenly Judge who, in any case, had made up his mind from the beginning.

Horatio's eulogy, with its certainty of Hamlet's welcome in Heaven, whatever the evaluation of his actions may be in terms of the religious canon, thus expresses the idea that this man will be forgiven his sins and go to Heaven—if there is a Heaven—not because he has lived up to the demands of the Canon, but because he had valiantly struggled for the fulfilment of his individual destiny in terms of his best individual judgment. Thus the whole religious issue, though still present, moves to a secondary place. Man has moved into the center that up to then had been held by the Canon.

No doubt all this may sound quite atheistic, yet it is not at all likely that, even in his most secret thoughts, Shakespeare was an atheist.[31] The solution to this discrepancy between the Christian and non-Christian interpretation may be found in the following. If we try to trace back the present flowering of atheism, the steady lessening of the hold that the Christian religion and the Churches have on man's mind and on the conduct of his affairs, we shall find one root of this in Protestantism. As soon as Protestantism encouraged the study of science and the liberal arts and declared this study to be *necessary* in order to prevent man's degeneration into a wild beast, as soon as it no longer insisted that meditation upon God, or striving toward salvation, is the *sole* function of man's stay on earth, then the fate of Christianity was indeed sealed. From then on man became more and more involved in the pursuit of temporal truth, rather than, as he had been, in seeking the truth of the Heavenly Kingdom.

To put the matter in a nutshell, one can draw on two quotations. Thomas à Kempis (1441, p. 28f) wrote:

> A humble countryman who serves God is more pleasing to Him than a conceited intellectual who knows the course of the stars, but neglects his own soul . . . Restrain an inordinate desire for knowledge, in which is found much anxiety and deception . . . Indeed, a man is unwise if he occupies himself with any things save those that further his salvation.

In Frye (1963, p. 72f) we read: "In his sermon 'On the Duty of

---

[31] Who knows, really? What he has left in his plays is probably only an infinitesimal part of what crossed his mind during the course of the 52 years of his life. In turn, what crossed his mind was an infinitesimal part of the mental processes that went on in him subliminally, either preconsciously or unconsciously. One thing we may be certain of is that a mind like his did not take much for granted, but was in constant movement, observing, watching and thinking (I omit the emotional responses). The notion that, in the innermost recesses of his heart, he "followed the beaten path" with regard to any content that occupied his mind is so improbable that one feels inclined to dismiss it as absurd. It is, to be sure, conceivable that what we observe in *Hamlet* is an echo of a remote, secret, profound doubt in Christian eschatology. Yet as far as the critics are concerned, it is striking that I found Seibel's quite remarkable work (1924) rarely even cited, not to speak of its being reprinted. Seibel accumulated and summarized quite surprising material, which introduces the reader to a Shakespeare who stands quite aloof from Christianity, who deals with the Christian faith as an unbiased outsider, who treats the faith like any other peculiarity he has had an opportunity to observe in his fellow-men. Is it possible that most critics are limited by an inner restraint, which makes it impossible for them to associate Shakespeare's hallowed name with a mind that viewed the Christian faith from outside, so that it did not truly live in his heart? Apparently, to judge from the fact that *Shakespeare's Bawdy* has been reprinted, while Seibel has not, there is greater leniency toward Shakespeare's obscenities, as much uneasiness as these may arouse, than toward his implicit atheism.

Sending Children to School', Luther met head-on the objection that a child may, through his exposure to education, become a heretic and responded forthrightly: 'Well, you must run the risk.' "

Two different worlds face each other in these two quotations, although both of them live in the minds of good Christians. Once the West was ready "to run the risk," which would have been unthinkable to Thomas à Kempis, the Christian system was indeed doomed. If Luther had had the slightest inkling what all the consequences would be of the spread of science and knowledge, he would probably have preached in the same vein as Thomas à Kempis had before him. Knowing as we do the end-product of the gigantic drama that followed after the breakdown of the religious system that had dominated the West for over one and a half millennia, we can perhaps perceive in magnified form those atheistic ingredients that were embedded in the cultural productions which stand at the beginning of that process whose end we are now witnessing.

The imagery that Shakespeare uses is Christian, to be sure, but the new wine was already fermenting in the old bottles, as *Hamlet* proves, perhaps more than in any other of Shakespeare's plays. The Christian interpretation of *Hamlet,* as set forth by Miss Prosser and Knight, might well have obtained Shakespeare's approval. He may not have been aware how eminently un-Christian the foundation of his play was, just as Newton was apparently unaware that his genius had struck a deadly blow to the Christian system—for there is just no place left for a Divinity in Newton's space, despite all reassurances that one still hears to the contrary. If Augustine or Luther or Calvin were to share our lives for only one day, they would surely tell us that Christianity has been irrevocably lost. And this extraordinary play, *Hamlet,* has contributed its share to that loss, for "the readiness is all" cannot possibly mean the readiness to die and to appear before one's Creator, but the readiness to *act.* When Hamlet died, he was certainly *not* ready to appear before his Creator, for his soul was immersed in sin; yet he had reached a state of mind in which he was ready to *act,* whether or not it was at the cost of his life, or even of his hope of eternal bliss.

Horatio's eulogy frees Shakespeare from the accusation of atheism, but it also says that, whether or not man has sinned, as long as he has struggled forcefully toward the realization of his individual potentiality, he will be forgiven. What counts is not the act per se, but rather the motive for the act. Hamlet's father, Rosencrantz and Guildenstern, and perhaps Polonius as well (he, too, died without proper preparation of his soul) do not go to Heaven—not only in our imagination, but also in terms of what we are made to believe about them in the play. Hamlet is the *only* one of whom we are explicitly assured that he has gained salvation, even though no doubt is left in our minds by the end of the play that he has sinned more than any other of the major figures, aside from Claudius.[32]

He is the only one in the play who does not take society and the world for granted. He is least concerned about action as such, and most concerned about the motive for it; he never expresses feelings of guilt of a religious nature, and he never asks Heaven for forgiveness. Indeed, if we were to go by the Canon, Claudius would seem to have a better chance of being admitted to Heaven than Hamlet, as many a commentator has pointed out; yet, despite all that, it is Hamlet and only Hamlet, according to the play, of whose privilege in that regard we are explicitly assured. All this gives me at least a modicum of certainty that in *Hamlet* a profoundly new ethos was placed on the stage within the husk of hallowed language; whether or not this was Shakespeare's intention, indeed whether or not he was even aware of doing so, I too feel a burning desire to know, yet also the certainty that no one will ever know.

Miss Prosser does not stand alone with her Christian conception of *Hamlet*. The difference between her and others who think the same way in their interpretation of detail is often considerable, however. There seems to be no consensus among this group, even about the nature of the Ghost. To what contradictions the Christian view may lead can best be studied in Ribner (1960). If he were right, then Shakespeare would not have transcended the level of the problems one finds in morality plays, notwithstanding the author's protestations to the contrary: "Shakespeare framed the role of Hamlet to represent the life-journey of everyman in an ordered universe ruled by a benevolent God" (Ribner, 1960, p. 82).

"At the end of the play," writes Ribner, "Hamlet learns to accept the order of the universe and to become a passive instrument in the hands of a purposive and benevolent God" (p. 66). And this, despite Hamlet's magnificent outbreak of rage at the end, which is manifested, among other ways, in the very fact of his using more means than were needed in order to kill Claudius. This surely shows no traces of passivity and is incompatible with the tenets of the New Testament.

[32] Clutton-Brock sees in *Hamlet* "a prophecy of a higher state of being" (quoted from Walker (1948, p. 3).

Hamlet's initial "excessive grief . . . represents the state of man . . . before he has learned the lesson of faith in the perfection of God's universal order" (p. 71). "The ghost . . . imposes on him the duty of every Christian soul" (ibid.). "What Hamlet must learn is that man frustrates evil merely by his faith in God and by the cultivation of his own goodness" (p. 72). One can hardly understand how Ribner can make such claims, in view of the fact that Hamlet does not ever leave the punishment of evil to God's hands, nor does he carry out a single act that can be interpreted as Christian charity. His speech about brotherly love to Laertes is directed not toward someone who has done something malicious to him, but rather to someone whom *he* has grievously hurt.

Hamlet's not killing Claudius in the prayer scene, says Ribner, "is not designed to depict psychological truth, but to underscore dramatically the inability of man to execute the justice of God" (p. 77). In the end, the validity of such claims evaporates into thin air. According to Ribner, the whole act of regeneration in Hamlet allegedly occurs miraculously during the sea voyage. The internal maturation, the psychological progress during the course of the mouse-trap play and the liberating consequences that follow from it—all these are ignored. ("The ineffective schemer of the first three acts is no more. Hamlet has become a passive instrument in the hands of divine providence," p. 81.)

I could go on presenting many more such examples of contradiction and misinterpretation, but I shall instead finish this section by discussing a theme that has a directly religious bearing.

I have again and again stressed the masterly way in which Shakespeare used ambiguity in *Hamlet;* it may now be time to set forth one example of an unambiguous position, brought forward by way of a sequence of ideas about an identical theme. It seems to me that there is in the play only one well-circumscribed subject of objective validity about which Hamlet makes three distinctive statements. That is the question of suicide.

In his first soliloquy, there is a brief, perfunctory statement, which amounts to: "It is forbidden by God's laws, and therefore I shall not commit that sin, even though I should like to do it." No reflection is devoted to the prohibition; it is accepted without question.

In the "To be" soliloquy, the question of suicide appears for the second time. Whatever may be the principal meaning of this inset, suicide is one of its themes. But this time there is no direct reference to any law imposed upon man by a force outside him; instead, the matter is discussed in clearly secular terms, even if those critics are right who maintain that Hamlet is here referring to the fear of Hell. The main point, to repeat, is that it is no longer an external injunction that Hamlet invokes in order to prove why suicide—in general, or in his instance—does not or ought not to take place. It is solely *fear* that makes man abstain from the act, whatever the content of this fear may be.

The third time the subject of suicide appears is close to the end, when Horatio decides, upon a sudden and unexpected impulse, to commit suicide and is prevented therefrom only by Hamlet's swift interference. Horatio, who unquestionably represents an ideal in the play, expresses this desire in open defiance of Christian teaching, by recourse to ancient morality, which is more permissive in this area, as it is in so many others:

> I am more an antique Roman than a Dane.[33]

Hamlet does not object to the intended deed on Christian grounds, however, although he does say that "By heaven" he will prevent it. He appeals explicitly to Horatio's bravery: "As thou'rt a man." The "By heaven," as well as the subsequent "O God, Horatio," serve as expletives; they are used for the sake of emphasis, not as specific references with religious content.

In Hamlet's appeal to Horatio, which follows, there is a statement of extraordinary importance in this regard. He asks Horatio, as a sign that he has ever loved him, to:

> Absent thee from felicity awhile.

I have always interpreted this as being Hamlet's request to Horatio that he forgo for a while the pursuits he cherishes most and subject himself to the burden of writing his friend's history. Some critics, however, have suggested that "felicity" here means the Heavenly bliss to be expected after death. Indeed, the context does make it clear that Hamlet is asking Horatio to postpone his death. This becomes evident in the setting

---

[33] At this point the bias of authors like Ribner (1960) becomes conspicuous. He writes of Horatio's *Christian* stoicism (p. 68), even though Horatio refers *expressis verbis* to that of ancient philosophy and despite the fact that suicide is incompatable with Christian teachings.

of "felicity" against breathing in pain "in this harsh world." The lines, in full, run as follows:

Absent thee from felicity awhile,
And in this harsh world draw thy breath in pain,
To tell my story.[34]

If one considers Horatio's character picture, as Hamlet has previously traced it (III.2.64 sequ.), it is hardly conceivable that Horatio actually finds "felicity" in his secular pursuits. The assignment to function as historiographer for his beloved friend could hardly amount to such a toilsome labor as to justify a request that, in order to carry it through, Horatio absent himself from felicity in this sense. If anything, such a task would necessarily involve deep fulfillment of self.

Hamlet's words make sense only if one keeps in mind that they are directed toward a man who has chosen death over life. For such a man, even breathing becomes pain, and Hamlet's appeal can be understood best as a request that he bear the pain of life for a limited time—at least until he has finished his apology for Prince Hamlet.

Even though Hamlet does not here give his approval to Horatio's suicide, he comes close to it, for he begs him only for temporary postponement and does not by any means appeal for total rejection of the deed, as he did of himself at the beginning of the play. It is also remarkable that Hamlet's plea presupposes the certainty that a man of Horatio's greatness would under all circumstances obtain eternal bliss after death ("felicity")—even when he has died burdened with a deed that the Church has declared to be an unpardonable sin.

Be that as it may, Hamlet clearly is not turning against suicide any longer as a matter of principle, but is instead pleading only for postponement. Furthermore, the mere fact of Horatio's attempt at suicide is an extraordinary event. He is set up as Hamlet's ideal and critics have accepted him as such. What then does it mean that Shakespeare takes a man who was till then depicted as being ideally suited for living and immune to life's tribulations, and now makes him attempt to commit

---

[34] There is in this context an interesting ambiguity attached to the verb absent in its reflexive use. Does "to absent oneself" imply a previous spatial contact with the area from which one absents oneself? Can one absent oneself from an area in which one has never been before? Present usage would favor a negative reply to the last question—which would make it impossible for felicity to mean heavenly bliss in this context. But the OED gives two meanings: "To keep away or withdraw (oneself) away," thus leaving the question open. At least as the matter stands, the verb alone does not rule out the possibility that "felicity" here means "heavenly bliss."

suicide? And by invoking ancient philosophy, to boot? Since Horatio has all along held a sort of moral superiority over Hamlet, does not this alone demonstrate that the final focus of the tragedy cannot lie in Christian stoicism or in any form of Christian morality?

We are thus confronted with a three-step development in the attitude toward suicide: first we see literal and unquestioning adherence to the religious canon; next, the problem loses its link with morality, having been lifted out of the context of religion to become a personal, subjective one, to be dealt with in terms of pleasure and pain, so that suicide is now rejected solely because it may not serve its primary purpose of ending man's anguish; finally, it is indirectly approved, or at least man is now set up as the final judge, entitled to decide for himself whether or not he ought to continue bearing life's pain. The fear of punishment in the nether world has disappeared altogether.

In view of this clearly stated sequence, one may also describe Hamlet as a play of moral development, by way of reversal of the motivational framework: from fear of hell and purgatory to the inner freedom of choice in matters of existence. A detailed inquiry into the development of the suicide theme in *Hamlet* does not confirm the idea proposed by many critics that a Christian regeneration is at the heart of the play.

Murry (1936, p. 250) so very correctly wrote: "From 'But that the dread of something after death' to 'Absent thee from felicity awhile' is the utmost progress of which the human soul is capable."

A Note on the Technical Device of "Retroactive Effect."

I have referred in several places to a literary device that Shakespeare uses quite often, which I have called the "retroactive effect." I do not know how widely this effect was used before Shakespeare. It often occurs in jokes and humor, as when—following a statement that is presented as though it were a statement of fact—at the end, and without any advance notice, the negation is added. It denies, without warning, the content of the previous statement—the very statement that the listener had all along been induced to accept as true. This is, of course, the most primitive form of retroactive effect. It is the technique that is generally used in mystery stories. When the reader is informed at the end who the culprit was, all preceding events are retroactively made to appear in a different light.

There are many more instances of this in *Hamlet* than the one I have mentioned. With his full mastery of poetic ambiguity, Shakespeare could, of course, induce the spectator to go in a variety of different direc-

tions, only to inform him later that he had led him astray, thereby anticipating the rather crude technique of the mystery story.

> 'There's a divinity that shapes our ends,
> Rough-hew them how we will'   *(V.3.9f)*

sounds very Christian; over and over again it is quoted by the critics as a
sure sign of Hamlet's turn toward a Christian religious outlook. Yet it is
always taken out of context and it is that enforced isolation, rather than
its own content, that permits the critic to hold on to the primary association that it was evidently intended to bring to mind.

Yet, when the retroactive effect of the total context is taken into account, an entirely different aspect is revealed. That context has led to the
murder of two men; the two lines are only 37 lines away from the providential disaster of the "Not shriving-time allow'd." Retroactively, of
course, this "divinity" then appears in a totally different light. True, it
had saved Hamlet; but in doing so it had caused the damnation of two
other Christians who, had the divinity let Hamlet fall into the trap that
Claudius had laid out, might have been given a chance for their salvation. Retroactively, then, it thus becomes a divinity that symbolizes—just
as the "Providence" does, of which Hamlet speaks later—Hamlet's view
of the future. The traditional concept of Providence lays its stress on a
different aspect; this is the future that constantly comes *to* man, *whether
he wishes it or not,* and to which man must be ever ready to respond.
With Hamlet, however, the stress is on a future on which man exercises
an active influence, a future that he does not wait for until it reaches him.

The retroactive effect has already been mentioned in connection
with my interpretation of the "To be" soliloquy. Another instance of
this effect is Hamlet's initially appearing in an extraordinary state of
mind, which is then followed by his peculiar behavior, and still later by
the information the audience obtains from Ophelia, a sequence that
appears suddenly in a different light when we hear from Ophelia that
Hamlet had earlier been the very ideal type of his time. One can also
discover this effect when Hamlet's strong reaction to the Ghost's story
is first presented as a personal reaction to a paternal demand, yet only a
short while later is expressed in the famous lines:

> 'The time is out of joint; O cursed spite
> That ever I was born to set it right!'

This transforms a family conflict into a universal mission, and retroactively makes Hamlet's mission a matter of destiny, a sign, so to speak, under which he had been born.

Once again everything that had been witnessed up to then is retroactively endowed with new and unforeseen meaning. Fortinbras' emergence in the end is, of course, a brilliant device, which throws a new light, retroactively, on all the previous events related to him. Although the end of the tragedy is an organic one, so that the spectator may be made to feel that the tragedy could not have ended in any other way, nevertheless there has been no previous indication that a subordinate character who, if anything, may well annoy some by the delays in the dramatic development that he has seemed to cause without any apparent necessity, would suddenly end the dramatic tension by becoming the central figure in the resolution.

8. Internalization and Appersonation

On the Rereading of Great Literary Works.

Many have said that literary or any other criticism of Shakespeare's writings must keep in mind, above all, the fact that Shakespeare wrote his plays for the theater. In terms of this emphasis on the character of the medium, many of the peculiarities that have in fact evoked some rather far-fetched interpretations on the part of literary critics are supposedly to be explained simply by reference to Shakespeare's outstanding stagecraft —that is to say, his understanding of what will create the most intense impression in the audience.

I myself have occasionally used the argument, in the text of this study, that the explanation offered by some critic cannot be valid, inasmuch as it does not take into account what actually comes to the attention of the spectator. I now wish to qualify that argument; it is not valid in the way in which it has been stated, if for no other reason than that it neglects the possible effects of subliminal perception.

I doubt that Shakespeare was very much concerned with questions of stagecraft when he was writing his great tragedies. (This is an assumption about which I shall have more to say later.)[1] It can be said with

---

[1] In his early attempts, no doubt, written at a time when Shakespeare was still a tyro of the dramatic craft, his experimenting with stage effects can be noted rather readily, as well as his delight in making full use of the possibilities offered him by various aspects of stage mechanics. But by the time he reached the heights of his creative power, he seems to have integrated the mechanics of stage effects so completely that he was able to take their possibilities for granted and instead to focus his attention on values that far transcended the narrow framework of stage effects. The mere perusal of

safety that such truly great masterworks as *Hamlet* and the subsequent tragedies approach perfection at all levels. While their stage effect is unquestionable, details that seem to be adequately enough explained by mere reference to stage necessities reveal meanings of far greater profundity when they are placed in their proper context. These are the meanings one usually becomes aware of only after one has witnessed the play repeatedly—indeed, only after repeated readings.

What is perhaps more important, certain meanings become evident only during the course of history. New generations—more sophisticated, more sensitive, endowed with the ability to take in a wider range of questions—gain insights that carry them far beyond the horizons of earlier decades, not to speak of those of centuries past. It takes many generations before the full meaning of a great masterwork is even approximately acknowledged, inasmuch as each historical period seems to discover new meanings in it. Indeed, it may be one of the characteristics of truly great art that it has inexhaustible depths, so that the process of valid interpretation can *never* find a natural end.

The greatness of a work of art can be decided only in terms of the effect that repeated experiences of it provide. I have myself observed that the effect of a single artistic experience is not decisive. There are even actors who produce an overwhelming impression when one witnesses their performance for the first time. Yet, with each repetition, the effect is weakened, and the emptiness of what was fascinating upon first encounter becomes in the end painfully noticeable. Similarly, there are works of art that spell out the totality of their effect in one generation or perhaps two, and thereafter decline until they become structures that possess merely historical value. Only what is not destroyed by a series of repetitions—which may even increase the intensity of effect, during the course of generations—falls into the category of truly great art.

It is not difficult to explain at least one element that will determine whether the effect of repetition is to intensify the artistic effect or to weaken it. Since a detail, or a group of details, or even the entity as a whole can have one or several meanings, it is (to express the matter

---

the great tragedies is able to elicit, in many an astute reader, a deeper impression than even that which is achieved by the best productions of contemporary companies.

Hale (1964, p. 13) expressed this succinctly for any artistic medium, as follows: "I am inclined to think that *no* artist can be called an accomplished craftsman until all matters of technique are so well learnt that they are part of his subconscious equipment. I know it is very difficult for an artist to express himself adequately unless this has been done. . . . Technique is but a means to an end, and should never be confused with the end itself" (italics by the author).

quantitatively) the number of meanings that are condensed into a work of art that determines the number of repetitions one can experience without any slackening of the original effect. The great work of art shares with the dream the character of being overdetermined. Just as one never knows for certain whether all possible meanings of a dream have been unearthed in analysis, so the meanings of great art works may well be inexhaustible. Laying aside for the time the question of the correctness of any given interpretation, one can say that the danger in this connection is not of over-interpretation, but precisely its opposite.

It is in that sense that a great play bears interpretation at all levels. Any detail will be explicable, at one level, in terms of its immediate stage effect; it will also, however, warrant philosophical, psychological, dramatic and poetic interpretation, and it may even have topical meaning. Whenever interpretation is actually reducible to one facet alone, to the exclusion of all others, one has an instance of artistic weakness. The crowning effect is achieved, of course, when elements in the play are able to bear several different interpretations within the same dimension of meaning.

The question of Hamlet's age may serve as one detail, selected quite at random, in which some of this can be exemplified. There are a number of references in the first third of the play that force the spectator to see in Hamlet a youth of about twenty. On equally good grounds in each case, ages have been suggested that include all the years from 17 to 25. In the graveyard scene, however, Hamlet's age is given as 30. This discrepancy has been explained in a number of ways. (See *Variorum Edition*, Vol. 1, pp. 391-394.)

One may easily think here of dramaturgic sloppiness—or even reject the problem as essentially meaningless—since from the standpoint of stagecraft what is involved is a detail that will very likely not arouse the suspicion of a single spectator, so rapidly is one carried from one scene to another without being given the time to ponder on such small matters as this. The age of 30 is certainly suited to the tragic view of things that Hamlet takes at the latter point. It simply would not fit well if the spectator were to have to think of Hamlet, in this particular context, as a youth of about 20; for that reason, Shakespeare's reference to an older age may be regarded as a contrivance (probably effective on a subliminal level) with which to create the proper mood.

So much we can take as correct, whether Shakespeare did it intentionally, or as a kind of unthinking legerdemain. There is far more contained in a detail of this sort, however, that many may judge to be trivial. With enviable ingenuity and subtlety, Granville-Barker (1946, p. 43) writes: "Why does Shakespeare take the trouble, thus late in the day, to establish Hamlet's age so exactly? To counteract the impression of the youthful prince, which circumstance . . . will have made on us . . . Hamlet is inevitably a maturer figure than was the morbid young rebel at its beginning. . . . The play is nearing its end and it must be . . . a tragic end." When the time concept of Elizabethan tragedy is considered, the detail appears in its essential flawlessness (contrary as it may be to logical—that is to say, inartistic—deliberations). Hamlet *is* now 30 years old, even though, according to Newton's time concept, he should be only one-half a year or so older than he was at the beginning of the play. Moreover, the audience itself has aged more than the three hours that have elapsed since the play's beginning—if it has permitted the full impact of the tragedy to penetrate into its unconscious.

Hamlet has traveled a path of many years' value (if not duration) from Wittenberg to the graveyard, in terms of the process of life; as Granville-Barker intimates, the "falsification" of age becomes also the carrier, the harbinger of an impending event. It is this synthesis into one seemingly insignificant detail, of stagecraft, time acceleration and signpost of the future, that reveals Shakespeare's genius.

In the world that Shakespeare puts on the stage in *Hamlet*, the intensity of condensation is extreme. It is an intensity that can otherwise be found only in dreams. In the dream, however, this is accomplished at the price of intelligibility, so that the variety of meanings that have been thus compounded into single elements can be extracted only through the subject's associations. In the tragedy, by contrast, the meanings are explicit—that is to say, the mass of details in the manifest content admit a great variety of explanatory schemes.

It is through the interpretation of details, of course, that these explanatory schemes come into being; but here interpretation signifies a procedure that is different from the one used in the psychoanalysis of dreams. The latter is possible only by reference to elements *outside* the dream, whereas the explanatory schemes in the interpretation of a literary work remain *within the bounds of the work itself.*

In the interpretation of dreams, the interpreter faces at the start an infinity of interpretative possibilities, which then become fewer and fewer with each of the subject's associations. In literary works, the range of choice is limited from the start; what the interpreter does is to shuffle and reshuffle elements that per se are well defined. The element "age of 30 years" in a dream may refer to an infinity of contents, aside from years—for example, the figure 30 may mean "three plus zero" and stand for a synthesis of male and female. In the graveyard scene, however, no such possibilities are open to the interpreter. The element "Hamlet is now 30 years old" does not bear any other interpretation. From that starting point, however, a huge area is opened out that ranges from "the poet's sloppiness" (that is to say, "no significance in meaning") to "a mark of Hamlet's development" (that is to say, "a hallmark of the drama's essential process").

Enigma of Old Hamlet.

I want now to discuss one of the more significant explanatory schemes that one encounters in the literature on *Hamlet*. Among the modern critics, Flatter's conception of the play is most remarkable for its originality, consistency and logic. Yet what is most striking is that his interpretation breaks down precisely because of its consistency and logic. For Flatter the center of the play is not Hamlet, but Hamlet's father.

Among the many arguments he raises in favor of his interpretation, I find his comment on the tragedy's protasis most convincing. As a rule, Shakespeare introduces in his delightful protatic scenes a partial delineation of the protagonist whose fate will become from then on the center of our empathic sensibilities. In *Hamlet* it is the ghost who takes up this position, and Flatter concludes that Shakespeare is abiding, even in this instance, by his own rule, so that it is the ghost who is to be considered the tragedy's true protagonist.

Be that as it may, it is difficult for me to imagine Shakespeare abiding by anybody's "rules"—his own included. One can certainly note the presence of habits or routines, but the fact that the ghost holds the protatic center must not be taken as proof with regard to the meaning of the play as a whole. I am inclined to derive a different meaning from this protatic shift (cf. Walker, 1948, p. 2). What might otherwise have been created would have been a confusing—that is to say, an inartistic—imbalance with regard to the conflict that Hamlet was destined to suffer.

Let us suppose that the play had started with what is now the second scene, in the Council Chamber. The spectator would then have been moved into the area of Hamlet's conflict with the mother, and this conflict would have remained uppermost in the spectator's mind. The introduction of the Ghost prior to the spectator's being apprised of that conflict arouses in him an expectation of new knowledge that will give an additional dimension to the state of conflict in which Hamlet is introduced, quite aside from the tension that is built in the spectator by his knowing something about Hamlet of which Hamlet himself is still ignorant, when we meet him for the first time. As the result of the protatic position of the Ghost, there is a balance between the two sources of conflict in man: father and mother. With a mere 75 lines (not reckoning the four-time outcry "Swear!" in the cellarage scene) at the foot of the castle wall, and only six lines in the closet scene, Shakespeare was able to build up a formidable structure under whose shadow the events proceed to the final climax.

Still another "irregularity" warrants attention at this point. The fact that in *Hamlet* the protagonist is introduced in a state of acute conflict is of greater dynamic significance than the seeming irregularity from which Flatter draws such far-reaching conclusions. Neither Richard the Third, Romeo, Caesar, Othello, Lear, Coriolanus, nor Leontes is in a state of conflict at the time when he is first introduced. While these characters may feel frustrated or angered, they know what they want; they have a firm position from which they feel able to approach the world and to tackle hopefully the particular problem they are facing at that moment. Only Hamlet (as far as I can see) among Shakespeare's tragic heroes is in conflict with himself, in a condition of helpless suspense, at the very moment when the audience first becomes acquainted with him.

Conflict, to be sure, is the heart of Shakespeare's world, yet in *Hamlet* conflict seems to hold an intensified and all-embracing position; it is brought at once to the spectator's attention by Hamlet's initial state of mind. Lear would have spared himself his break with the world, had he not sought to relinquish his kingly station; and Othello is, in the end, himself ultimately responsible for the fact that he is able to be alienated from his beloved. Hamlet, however, is in conflict because man and world are in conflict. In *Hamlet* man's destiny is revealed as unavoidably, and in that sense inherently, conflicted. This may be one of the reasons why the protagonist is introduced in a state of grave imbalance, rather than in a state of initial relative equilibrium—short as such an initial state may be, once the action of the play unfolds (as for example in *Macbeth).*

I am here introducing the comparison with *Macbeth* because, in both tragedies, a leading role is played by the supernatural. It may be worthwhile to consider for a moment the difference in the way in which the supernatural is introduced in the two plays. In *Macbeth*, it appears in the very first scene, and only Macbeth's name is mentioned. In the second scene (which, according to Flatter's rule, ought to be the first one) Macbeth's solidly formed, reliable character is introduced by conversation about him. This is a relatively short scene, followed immediately by Macbeth's ominous meeting with the supernatural. Yet Macbeth is supposed to be conflict-free right up to the second before the supernatural interferes so cruelly with his life.

From what we know about Macbeth, at our first encounter with him, we have no reason to expect the play to unfold a life that is increasingly besmirched with abominable crimes. This is in contrast with Hamlet (1) about whom we are told nothing, prior to our first encounter with him; (2) whom we observe in conflict, from the first sentence that he speaks; and (3) of whose previous life we only later come to know about, for example, such conflict-free episodes as his happy times with Yorick and his love letter to Ophelia. It may be that Macbeth would have done in any case what he was bound to do, that the supernatural functioned in his case as nothing but a catalyst. At any rate, in *Macbeth* the supernatural swoops into human reality with weird rapidity, only to dart out of it once again with equal speed.

In *Hamlet*, the introduction of the supernatural is far more weighty and, I think, more consequential. Without it the tragedy, if it developed at all, would develop in entirely different directions, just as civilization, culture and human fate would be essentially different from what they are, if Man's oedipal complex encompassed no more than the relationship to mother. It is interesting to note that in both tragedies the supernatural, which is highly relevant to the development of the tragedy, enters before anything has yet been learned about the protagonist.[2] This in itself speaks against one of Flatter's arguments.

Another difference in the structure of the two tragedies is that in *Macbeth* the protatic delay caused by the introduction of the supernatural is minimal, while the supernatural itself is divorced from the past or present, its function being exclusively to push the action into the future. In *Hamlet*, by contrast, the intervention of the supernatural has its effect both on the conception of the past and on the action of the future.

In no other of Shakespeare's tragedies, I believe, is man's fated ensnarement by his own past brought forth so penetratingly as it is in *Hamlet*. The Ghost is the symbol of the never-silent voice of the past,

---

[2] This is also true of *The Tempest*.

which lays its hands on every man who fights—although in vain —against invisible and unrecognized forces. Yet the Ghost is, at the same time, the representative of the future, in the sense of its being the never-silent demand upon man, with regard to what it is his duty to do and not to do. With scarcely noticeable finesse, Shakespeare lets us know first about Hamlet's conflict with his mother and only later about that with the father, thereby repeating the actual sequences of man's development.

The protasis, consequently, is divided into three factors: (1) the ominously silent appearance of the Ghost; (2) the surface of Hamlet's acute conflict, brought about by the father's death and the mother's hasty marriage (the delay in the succession to the throne being only adumbrated); (3) an acute internal conflict, caused by the mother's gravely offensive acts following the death of her husband.

Only in the light of these three components is the full extent revealed of that past under which Hamlet will have to smart. Thus the Ghost's appearance in silence, taken together with his departure after having delivered his "dread command," surrounds the protasis as a frame does the painting that it contains.

According to Flatter, Hamlet's actions, following the Ghost's revelations, were reasonable, wise, and extremely well adjusted to his goals.[3] First he ascertained the truth of the Ghost's claim and then he carried out the revenge demanded by the Ghost, without committing any offense against his mother. Any other choice of action would have, in one way or another, compromised his mother, and that, according to Flatter, had to be avoided under all circumstances, in view of the way in which Hamlet's father had worded his command. The sequence of events may indeed be read in that way and Flatter's reasoning does carry conviction. Yet it bypasses the crux of the matter and bears the marks of an essential misunderstanding, at least as far as the psychological context is concerned, in view of Hamlet's persistent self-accusations.

If Flatter were right, then Hamlet would have to be regarded as an out-and-out neurotic, even perhaps as a psychotic. Why should a man who consistently acts in accordance with reality feel mortified by his own behavior, even to the extent of giving voice to the wildest self-castigations? We do, after all, have to proceed on the assumption that what we learn from Hamlet's soliloquies is the true nature of his conscious feelings. This is the one certain and indisputable point in the

---

[3] I have taken up the question of Hamlet's supposed adjustment to reality already when I discussed Huhner's character profile of Hamlet.

play's fabric, which otherwise is quite loose. If this one certainty is disputed or eliminated, then the whole tragedy collapses, for with it the only certain foothold the spectator has is lost.

There are only very few elements in this vast structure whose authenticity is undisputed. One of them is Hamlet's emotional state, which is intermittently revealed in some of the soliloquies: the feeling that he has not been sufficiently active in either the deed or the preparation for it, in response to his father's command, and his consequent self-condemnation. It would amount to a rather paradoxical state of affairs, if it really did turn out that throughout this time he had indeed been making a maximum contribution in the service of his father's revenge.

I have, however, exaggerated Flatter's position. He describes Hamlet as acting in a reality-adequate fashion only in the first half of the play. Hamlet's ostensible failure, which Flatter discovers in the second half, is not based on any "disobedience to his creator, nor unwillingness to carry out his duty, nor any physical or psychological weakness," but solely to the fact that the Ghost is demanding something that Hamlet *cannot* fulfill, so long as he is hemmed in by the added injunction regarding Gertrude. When Hamlet seeks to ascertain his mother's share in the crime, the Ghost, in his second appearance, prevents him from doing so (Flatter, p. 90).[4]

Although I do not agree with Flatter's explanatory schema, its originality and, more importantly, its practicability are to be recognized. It is interesting to compare Flatter's conception with the development of neo-Freudian psychoanalysis. The theory of the mother's all-inclusive responsibility for her children's later neuroses and psychoses is at present one of the most widely accepted deviations from Freud's classical theory. In the end, Flatter adheres to the same theory. According to him, Gertrude had an adulterous relationship with Claudius during the King's

---

[4] If Hamlet is indeed driven by such curiosity as Flatter alleges, he must be totally unconscious of it, for he makes no direct statement or allusion to any such curiosity. It would appear to be reasonable to say that he had to suppress such curiosity, since it was part of his forbidden oedipal strivings. Yet it would not fit the dramatic context if Hamlet, shortly after one aspect of his curiosity had been satisfied by the triumphant success of the mouse-trap play, were driven by a new bout of curiosity. The "association" he makes to Nero, with its double innuendo, on his way to his mother's closet, has to do with the deepest layer of the oedipal conflict—that is to say, with the part that is most forbidden and therefore most repressed. When such archaic impulses are stirred up by the triumph over a father-substitute, it does not ring true for a far less forbidden impulse not only to be in the center of attention, but also to be repressed. Hamlet enters his mother's closet as master of the situation. What he wants is not to learn anything from his mother, but to rouse her feelings of guilt, to make her mend her ways, and, as he says openly, to prevent her from having any further intimacy with a hated father-substitute.

lifetime, and it is even very probable, though not provable, that she knew of Claudius' fratricide. One is therefore justified in regarding her as the real malefactor in her son's tragedy. She would then be the symbolic representation of the "bad" mother, irresponsible and entirely neglectful of her obligations toward her offspring.

But then Flatter introduces the "bungling" father who, by his perversity and authoritarian stubbornness, forever destroys his son's potential happiness, forcing him into passivity—that is to say, making it impossible for him ever to become an adult. It is a matter of the greatest interest that *Hamlet* can be interpreted in this respect in two ways, each of which coincides with trends in present psychological research: the responsibility for Hamlet's tragic situation can be attributed either to insensitive paternal authoritarianism or to maternal seductiveness, guile and neglect. In both instances, Hamlet is passive, molded by the contingencies of accidental environmental (cultural) complications. Life is so superbly recreated in this tragedy that, in the critic's responses to it, the same pitfalls can be detected as those into which the scientist is lured when he is studying life itself.

There are, however, episodes in the interpretation with regard to which critic and psychologist will not see eye to eye. One of these is Hamlet's plan to check on the reliability of the Ghost's report. For the most part, this has been discussed as a valid step of adjustment, particularly in the light of sixteenth-century beliefs about the nature of ghosts. Contemporary literature has been amply adduced to prove that the belief prevailed that ghosts were at times the emissaries of the devil, and if only for that reason, it is asserted, Hamlet was justified in checking upon the veracity of the Ghost's report. I do not dispute the historical statement, but I do wonder whether Shakespeare actually read the particular treatises in which those views were set forth, and whether he was at all concerned with the metaphysics of erudite theologians, or instead adhered to familiar and widespread beliefs.

I can well imagine the literary critic of three hundred years hence combing twentieth-century Western drama from the viewpoint of psychoanalysis, in the belief that this system of psychology was generally accepted in that epoch. Notwithstanding the effect that psychoanalysis has had upon literature, it is a fact that in some countries psychoanalysis is still an "outsider," with little actual influence, and it would be wrong to attempt to establish any direct causal relation, whenever some detail in a play is in accordance with psychoanalytic theories of man's mind.

Be that as it may, even if the connections between contemporary theory and Hamlet's "test" of the Ghost could be established with certainty, I think that Hamlet's plan of verification nevertheless calls for psychological explanation. Hamlet's doubt is the consequence of his own ambivalence. Some have taken note of signs of ambivalence prior to the mousetrap play, yet although these signs were interwoven with positive expressions, they were implied on the emotional level, rather than being explicit and discursive. The mousetrap play is an intellectual conception. Hamlet's new position, "Is the Ghost's story true?" is the first step that he takes toward putting a distance between himself and his deceased father. A manifest critical attitude has begun to emerge. If the idea of the mousetrap play is conceived exclusively in terms of problems associated with Elizabethan demonology, Hamlet's subsequent triumph in dealing with his mother makes no sense. After all, the verification of the Ghost's story brings in no new element, when it is viewed rationally, for Hamlet still faces the same issues as he did before.

Psychologically, however, the situation before the mousetrap is quite different from what it is after the play. Hamlet has now proceeded on his own: his action is divorced from the Ghost's command, with the possibility implied that that command may even have to be ignored. His ego-syntonic, self-conceived action has led to success in two respects: (1) From this point on, when he takes revenge it will not be because the Ghost has told him to do so, but because he himself has discovered the truth of Claudius' crime. (2) He has seen Claudius in a state of weakness and fright. This debasement of the father-substitute, in my opinion, also colors the image of the real one.

If this observation is correct, then what we are dealing with is something irrational—which can, however, be observed again and again. It has to do with the peculiarity of unconscious thinking, which makes inferences from categories to individuals, and vice versa. If a man is cheated by a Jew, a Negro or a Catholic, he may draw the conclusion that all Jews, Negroes or Catholics are bad, unless his own membership in one of these minorities protects him (and not always so, at that) against that sort of generalization. If a man has a bad relationship with his father, there is a great likelihood that he will have a critical attitude toward all carriers of authority. When the authority of the State is compromised, the chance of the rebellion of youth against their fathers setting in manifestly is vastly increased. Thus Claudius' openly compromising himself leads, in Hamlet's mind, to a devaluation of *all* representations that carry the mark of "authority."

It cannot be sufficiently emphasized (if we wish to avoid hopeless confusion) that, prior to the plan of the mousetrap and its realization, Hamlet is observed in only one episode of outright activity—namely, when he is resisting his friends who try to prevent him from following the ghost. Yet this activity is carried out in the spirit of the obedient son, for his insistence on forcefully counteracting his friends is an action that is wholly in keeping with the Ghost's request. In the same way I would regard his break with Ophelia, if one can call that a sign of activity, as being expressive of an obedient attitude toward the father. To be sure, this break is caused by a plurality of motives, only one of which is obviously the desire or necessity to revenge his father.

The psychology of activity and passivity is quite difficult to put on a sound footing, precisely because of the gap between externally observable indices and meaning. I can hardly imagine symbols more expressive of tranquillity, repose, and utter lack of movement than the statues of Pharaoh. Any sort of observable activity would be irreconcilable with the image those ancient sculptures convey. Unperturbed by the movements around them, they appear destined eternally to gaze into space and eternity. Thus one could look at them as captives of unending passivity.

And yet this interpretation seems quite insufficient: notwithstanding their passive appearance, they appear to be the foci of concentrated energy, centers of gigantic power, which dominate the universe by their mere existence. Indeed, if they were forced to move by necessity, that itself would amount to weakness, a sign of decline from supreme power. External inactivity may therefore be a form of expression of supreme activity. In turn, the hustle and bustle of the slaves who, with great effort, erected those gigantic figures, may have seemed to the observer to be an indicator of great activity, whereas in reality it was a matter of enforced actions, on the part of people who were in fact passively submitting to forces outside themselves.[5]

With this caution against the acceptance of activity solely on the grounds of external manifestations (cf. Rapaport, 1953), there may be less objection when Hamlet's early outbreak of activity, directed toward

---

[5] It may be that this paradox with regard to activity and inactivity has its roots in a paradox of the psychology of infancy. In the earliest stages of development, when the infant is objectively in a state of passivity, its "state of mind" is probably marked by a feeling of limitless omnipotence, yet it is precisely in growing up and becoming objectively more active that it becomes aware of its own limitations, and experiences itself, more often than not, as dependent and passive.

his friends, is not accepted at face value but is rather interpreted as a sign of obedience (and passivity) toward the father. Actually, reality would have required him to show toward the Ghost that same suspiciousness that caused his friends to worry about his safety. His determination to follow the Ghost may therefore be taken to be the result of his loyalty, obedience, and to a certain extent, dependence on his father, at least as far as his conscious feelings are concerned. The idea of the mousetrap, and his desire to check on the Ghost's veracity and reliability, must therefore be understood as a signal step toward independence and self-determination—a step that presupposes an increase in or, at least, a new and constructive use of ambivalence.

If the explanations drawn from contemporary sources had the validity that literary critics like to assign to them, the whole mousetrap episode would have to remain without meaning to the modern spectator, who is likely to be completely ignorant of Elizabethan demonology. Yet the mousetrap play remains one of the peaks in the unfolding of the dramatic action, and neither the reader nor the spectator encounters difficulty, in modern times, in grasping fully the meaning of that episode. Only psychological analysis unearths the meaning that persists throughout the cultural and societal changes that have been brought about during the course of centuries, and makes it possible for a play to be enjoyed and admired even by later generations, which may have no inkling whatsoever of the historical time that gave birth to the creator.

In accordance with Freud's basic scheme of male development, Hamlet harbors ambivalent feelings against his father, even when, in the first soliloquy, he extols his father and demeans himself by denying any value of his own by comparison with his progenitor. Such demeaning of self per se cannot be described as an outright pathological formation in the clinical sense, in view of the acute mourning reaction which regularly leads to diminution of self-value. In Hamlet's instance, however, this self-depreciation is excessive and a sure index of ambivalence, precisely in that it goes beyond what would be *justified and necessary under the circumstances.*

From the analytic point of view, one might think of such an excessive reaction as a barrier against the narcissistic triumph entailed in recognition of the fact that the father is now dead and the son has at last achieved freedom. For obvious reasons, such a feeling of triumph is highly objectionable to the civilized; yet when the defeated father appeals to the son for help and the son is in danger of shaping the rest of his existence under the yoke of a paternal demand, the whole psychological constellation changes. The possibility that the Ghost is telling falsehoods is thus used as a rationalization for ambivalent feelings, as can be seen from the triumphant outbreak that follows.[6]

When Hamlet obtains *prima facie* evidence of his father's deplorable end, one might have expected a new wave of melancholia to ensue. His focus of interest at this point shifts, however, from his natural father to his stepfather; now his awareness of the terror and anxiety that lie behind the smooth, well-organized, unperturbed surface that Claudius so effectively offers to the court, becomes a stimulus to him. Authority has become further compromised. At this moment the hierarchical barrier that separates the son from his mother crumbles, and Hamlet assumes an authoritarian attitude toward her that would indeed have been more appropriate to his father.

The Enigma of the Queen.

In reviewing the character-analyses that have been devoted to Hamlet's mother, I get the impression increasingly that the literary critics have not been sufficiently aware of the multitude of interpretations that Shakespeare made possible by his way of handling this character. As one reads the play, Gertrude arises as a solid, massive personage, comparable in its reality to those voluminous female figures that Michelangelo created in the Medici Chapel (a comparison I suggest only for the purpose of characterizing the degree of reality that Shakespeare succeeded in giving to this character). Yet, in contrast with this global impression, one discovers from detailed analysis that, except for one trait (which is usually neglected by critics), nothing can be stated about her character with any degree of certainty.

The prevailing interpretation of the Queen's sinfulness, arising from her illicit relationship with Claudius, may serve as one example. To be sure, the entire atmosphere of the play may easily lead to the impression that the Queen did entertain a sexual relationship with Claudius, prior to her husband's death. No one can reject such an interpretation out of hand as being completely far-fetched or inadmissible. Both Hamlet's father and Hamlet himself, it is true, speak of her as a sexually de-

---

[6] In a purely unpremeditated way, Hamlet decides to test the Ghost and does so about two months after their meeting. As will later be discussed, the outcome of the mousetrap play did not, after all, prove anything in terms of Elizabethan pneumatology. All such difficulties are dissolved when one takes into account the ambivalence conflict, which generally takes on an ever clearer manifestation as time progresses following the death of a beloved person.

praved person, yet neither of them is, of course, a disinterested party, the accuracy of whose judgment on this score is to be taken for granted.

There is many a husband to whom the idea that his wife might remarry after his death is highly offensive, and who would therefore regard such a consummation as a breach of marriage vows. The times when widows were given to retiring to convents were not too far from Shakespeare's own times, and the widow's loss of the right to continue enjoying life in any form has found embodiment in one of the world's most ancient civilizations. The fantasy that a widow's remarriage is somehow incompatible with chastity may be recognized as being almost universal, at least as far as male expectations are concerned, and has to be almost expected from the son.

Even under optimal conditions, it is regarded as embarrassing, as late as in our own time, for a son to witness his mother's wedding. The inclination to deny the existence of parental intercourse, which is observed clinically almost with regularity, is by no means an overlay of past Victorian sensitivities, as is so convincingly proven by the myth of impregnation through the Holy Spirit and its extension to the Immaculate Conception.

The remarriage of a widowed mother brings most painfully to the son's attention evidence of the fact that she too experiences carnal wishes and carnal satisfactions, which is reason enough to call her a whore, inasmuch as unconscious ideation admits nothing but extremes (cf. Freud, 1910). Yet it may be pointed out that Hamlet uses this extreme, sexually derogatory language only after being apprised by his father of the reason for his death. Until then, as far as sexual conduct is concerned, he accuses his mother only of incest—which may serve as an objection to the claim that remarriage as such is interpreted in the unconscious as adultery. This objection, in turn, may be adduced as proof that the Queen's opprobrious conduct extended back to a time that was prior to her husband's death.

To be sure, the word "adultery" is not used in Hamlet's first soliloquy, yet the comparisons and the symbolic expressions he uses are extreme, and refer to nothing but sexual depravity. If a patient spoke that way about his mother, the analyst would be pretty certain that the unconscious reproach went beyond incest. Unconscious imagery often needs reality events, in order to unfold itself fully in the conscious mind. What Hamlet's father and Hamlet, no doubt, hold against the Queen is not only that she married at all, and in particular that she married her husband's brother, but also that she married her husband's murderer. This is characteristic solely of unconscious ideation, which somehow holds beloved objects responsible for every event that occurs.

Curiously enough, the Ghost's reference to witchcraft *(I-5-43)* could serve as a potent argument in defense of the Queen. Moreover, the King's words, if taken literally, never do state unmistakably that the Queen's moral downfall occurred prior to his death. In the end, he demands of his son that he not bear "luxury and damned incest" *(I-5-83)*, without making any reference to adultery, and—what is to my mind quite decisive—he declares that he was deprived of his queen *only* by death. Adultery would certainly have deprived him of the queen much earlier. The citation of all these arguments does not aim to prove wrong the claim of adultery, for which the King's calling Claudius an "adulterate beast" *(I-5-42)* may be taken as sufficient proof. Yet in disregard of the hardly deniable fact that a man may burst out, without proper justification, into the use of such a term, merely upon observing that his brother (the rival of his infantile days) has succeeded in taking possession of his erstwhile wife (not to speak of this very same rival having deprived him as well of life and crown), I want only to point out that there is no clearcut evidence of the Queen's having committed adultery.

In my opinion, one encounters a similar ambiguity with regard to incest in the Queen's second marriage. Here, however, the critics seem to agree that, in the light of Catholic as well as Protestant prohibitions, the Queen's relationship to Claudius is to be looked at as incestuous.

It may at this point be worthwhile to cast a glance at the way in which the Queen is presented in the so-called *Ur-Hamlet*. There it is explicitly stated in the prologue that the Queen did not know of her husband's violent death nor had she cohabited with Erico (Claudius) prior to their wedding. Moreover, the Queen expressly states that she had received dispensation from the Pope to marry her brother-in-law *(III.6)*. Nevertheless, the play speaks of sins as having been committed by both of them.[7]

Hamlet too speaks of the King as adulterer (*Ehebrecher—I.7*). After

---

[7] Night in the Prologue says: "The King of this realm has been smitten with love for the wife of his brother, whom he has killed in order to take hold of her and the Kingdom. Now the hour has come when he holds his union *(Beilager)* with her; I want to cover them with my cloak so that both should not see their sins." [Denn es ist der König dieses Reiches in Liebe gegen seines Bruders Weibs entbrannt, welchen er um ihrenthalben ermordet um sie und das Königreich zu bekommen. Nun ist die Stunde vorhanden, dass er sein Beylager mit ihr Hält, ich will meinen Mantel über sie decken, dass sie beyde ihre Sünden nicht sehen sollen.]

the Queen's death, he says: "Nothing saddens me more than my mother. Yet because of her sins she too deserved this death." *(Nichts jammert mir mehr, als meine Frau Mutter. Doch sie hat diesen Tod wegen ihrer Sünden halben auch verdienet. V.6.)*

What were the Queen's sins, according to the text of the *Ur-Hamlet?* No sexual transgression is noted, nor any incestuous relationship, and yet she is reproached for sinning, and her violent death is called a just punishment.

In discussions of the Queen's second marriage, Henry VIII's marital adventures are usually cited. Recently, however, *The King's Great Matter* (de C. Parmiter, 1967) was admirably presented. In reading the record of the King's divorce from Catherine of Spain, one obtains a fairly different impression from what one might expect, considering the way in which it is usually handled in the literature on *Hamlet.*

On November 14, 1501, Catherine of Aragon (1485-1536), the youngest daughter of Ferdinand and Isabella of Spain, was married to Arthur (1486-1502), the oldest son of Henry VII. Yet Arthur died only four and half months later.

Politics made a lasting marriage tie with England advisable, however, and Ferdinand therefore tried to arrange a marriage between Catherine and Henry (1491-1547), the new prince of Wales. In June 1503, Catherine and Henry, who was 12 years old at that time, were solemnly betrothed, the marriage treaty stipulating that a papal dispensation was to be obtained because of the impediment of existing affinity between them, since Catherine had been married to the bridegroom's brother. (Whether this impediment actually existed is more than doubtful, for it is almost certain that the marriage between Arthur and Catherine was never consummated.) There were many reasons for the Pope's delay in granting the desired dispensation, yet it was finally granted; other reasons caused Henry to marry Catherine only after his father's death in April 1509.

Catherine was in all seven times pregnant (the last time in 1518), but only princess Mary (1516-1558), the later Queen, survived. When Henry realized that he would not obtain male issue from her, his plan for a divorce took on concrete forms. It is questionable whether it was his ardent love for Ann Boleyn that set in motion the whole affair. He had had an illegitimate son (Henry Fitzroy) by Elizabeth Blount in 1519, and Anne Boleyn's older sister had been his mistress between 1522 and 1525. It is not even known for certain when it was that Henry started to have relations with Anne. Circumstances favor the assumption that it happened in 1532, prior to her marriage with the King on 25 January 1533, at a time when her state of pregnancy had become undeniable.

What Henry now demanded from Clemens VII, but never succeeded in obtaining, was a judgment that the dispensation granted by Julius II with regard to his marriage with Catherine was invalid, inasmuch as marriage with a brother's wife was against divine law. Henry pretented that his conscience had become troubled upon his reading Leviticus XX, 21, which says: "And if a man shall take his brother's wife, it is an unclean thing, he hath uncovered his brother's nakedness; they shall be childless." How little Henry was concerned about the moral aspect of his marriage, and the fact that he used it as a mere pretense, can be learned from his earlier maneuvers; these had been designed to obtain a dispensation for a marriage to which there was the same impediment of an affinity of the first degree as the one he now asserted made his marriage with Catherine illegal (de C. Parmiter, 1967, pp. 21, 27-29). Indeed, since he had had intercourse with Anne's sister, while Catherine, as she had repeatedly stated, had not consorted with Arthur, this impediment might well have burdened his conscience less, particularly in view of his having a previous dispensation from the Pope.[8]

It is usually taken for granted that the marriage to a widowed sister-in-law is an offense unless a dispensation is granted. But a great Dominican theologian of the sixteenth century, Francisco de Vitoria, came to the conclusion that such marriage is not contrary to natural law, and at no time forbidden by divine law of the Old Testament, when the widow is childless; and that, in the absence of any human law, such a marriage is lawful, whether or not the widow is childless, and does not therefore require a papal dispensation.[9] A source that was even closer to Henry than de Vitoria saw no sound reason why such a marriage should be regarded as against divine law. It was John Fisher, bishop of Rochester, who later paid with his life for such opinions.

All this does not tell us, however, how Shakespeare and the average man of his times felt about such a marriage. Was it generally known that Henry's objection to Catherine was mere pretense and that his marriage to Anne was incompatible with the reasoning that he himself had applied to the former marriage?

---

[8] The impediment arising from a marriage ceremony that was not consummated was called *publica honesta* (de C. Parmiter, 1967, p. 16).

[9] It may be of interest that this is the present view on this matter.

Here one also has to consider the last of the five bills that Henry put before Parliament, after the royal supremacy over the Pope had been established. In it were defined the prohibited degrees of kindred within which marriage was prohibited by God's law. But how much of this really penetrated into the average Englishman's feelings, and how much of it was still alive around 1600?[10]

In the *Ur-Hamlet* the situation is clearly defined. The pope has granted a dispensation, yet the Queen laments that fact because her marriage has been the cause of Hamlet's mental imbalance. She believes that the reason why Hamlet resents this marriage is that it has made him lose Denmark's crown. Yet, as mentioned before, her guiltlessness is to no avail, and when she does not perceive the ghost in the closet-scene, Hamlet says: "You are no longer worthy of seeing his figure. Fie! Shame on you! I do not want to speak one more word with you," and departs (III.6.).[11]

[10] I am indebted to Mr. de C. Parmiter for having replied to my inquiry and having given me permission to quote from his letter:

"It is very difficult to make any reasonable statements about what was 'generally' known or understood in sixteenth century England, partly because a large proportion of the population was illiterate or almost so, and partly because of the slowness and badness of communications. It was a long time before Henry's matrimonial proceedings became the subject of widespread talk and comment, and even then it would seem that most of the popular feeling shown in favour of Catherine and against Anne Boleyn was due, not to an appreciation of the technicalities involved, but to a vague feeling that Catherine was a wronged woman, since she was considered to be Henry's lawful wife and he seemed to be concocting some scheme (not understood) to be rid of her.

". . . . I find it impossible to say with any sort of precision how far this rather technical matter [the impediment between Henry VIII and Anne Boleyn] was 'generally' known and understood in England; I should have thought that it was known and its implications understood only to a very small extent.

"You ask when Vitoria's opinion became the universal view: that is, the universal view among canonists and theologians, as their view was the only one that mattered. One cannot, of course, ever pinpoint the moment when any opinion becomes generally accepted; it is a gradual process. Accordingly, it is impossible to say more than that Vitoria's opinion was making headway during the sixteenth century. But it was making headway only among canonists and theologians; hardly anyone else would concern themselves with such very technical matters of theology and canon law. . . .

"I should have thought that most Englishmen in the sixteenth and seventeenth centuries would have reprobated incest out of a natural feelings of abhorrence, and would have thought of incest (if they thought about it at all) as arising only where the blood relationship was very close. I imagine that the 'average man' (if one can use such a term with any degree of reality) would not have bothered his head about the technicalities of the prohibited degrees; in so far as it was necessary to concern himself with such things, the clergy would probably keep him on the right lines."

I would therefore think that the critics may have been too quick in being so certain that a marriage between in-laws was considered a *prima facie* sin in Elizabethan times. The Old Testament was very much alive in the minds of the Elizabethans, and many a spectator of *Hamlet* might have thought of Onan's disobedience to Judah and his punishment (Genesis 38, 8-10), an episode that, to my surprise, does not seem to have played any part in Henry's extended wrangle. At least, I did not find any reference to it in Parmiter's historical presentation.

[11] Quite aside from the many problems that are met with in *Hamlet*, there is an historical question that is attached to its creation. Since the issue of marriage despite impediment of affinity plays

In Shakespeare's play the King and Queen are legally married. Their affinity is no secret nor is it in any way unknown. The churlish priest, if he symbolizes the institution of the Church, does not seem excessively submissive to kingly authority, even though he is quite ready to make compromises—which would be one further indication that the royal marriage was indeed regarded as legitimate and valid. Moreover, the danger that is described at the beginning of the play is one in which the *state* finds itself. It is clear from the talk between Horatio and Marcellus that the Ghost is assumed to be making his appearance in connection with *that* danger, and they suggest no connection between the Ghost's visits and any indignation he may feel about the incestuous marital relationship of his Queen and his brother.

The constellation is not unlike that in *King Oedipus*, where the question is also raised as to what crime has been committed, so to have aroused divine wrath. In that play, of course, it is a matter of a crime committed in secret and unbeknownst to the community. Yet if the royal marriage in *Hamlet* implies incest, it is difficult to understand why no remark is made about that fact during the conversations between the two soldiers and the scholar.

In the closet-scene, Hamlet's only reproach with regard to maternal misconduct has to do with Gertrude's choice of an unworthy object for her second marriage; his discourse there contains no reference to incest.

---

such a leading role in the play, and since that question must also (one would expect) have infringed on Elizabeth's sensibilities, one wonders why Shakespeare should have chosen such a subject for his tragedy. While one can surmise that a number of personal interests and motives drew him to this subject, one can scarcely conceive of any other topic that would have been likely to arouse greater indignation at court.

Shakespeare was intensely linked with the historical events of his time, as the many topical references in his plays prove, and one may rightly raise the question of whether he did have any political implication in mind. One might find the link, if *Hamlet* had been written after James's accession, and, indeed, there are voices that find in James I the historical source of Hamlet (Winstanley, 1921; Schmitt, 1956). Schmitt believes that Shakespeare and his promotors were expecting and wishing James to be successor to the Queen. However, if Shakespeare had had James in mind when he was creating Hamlet, that would have been politically immensely risky, since it was James's mother who had actually brought about his father's murder. Schmitt therefore adds: "I do not contend that Shakespeare's Hamlet is a copy of King James. Such a copy would not only have been inartistic [*unkünstlerisch*], it would also have been politically impossible" (p. 25).

This observation alone greatly reduces the probability of Schmitt's hypothesis. Nevertheless, ignoring Shakespeare's consistent creation of ambiguity throughout *Hamlet*, Schmitt suggests that it was the fact that Mary Stuart was involved in the murder of James' father that induced Shakespeare to leave it unclear whether or not Gertrude knew that her first husband had been murdered. Yet Plumptre (1796) suggested that some details in *Hamlet* served the purpose of flattering Elizabeth by adding "calumny" of Mary Stuart. Indeed, one would expect a performance of *Hamlet* to have aroused unpleasant political undertones, or even to have offended the Court outright, whether it took place under Elizabeth's reign or under that of James I.

When the Queen, under Hamlet's relentless hammering at her conscience, suddenly perceives in herself "such black and grainèd spots as will not leave their tinct" *(III-4-90f)*, this cannot refer to any crime so grave as adultery or incest, for that would have already been known to her and would not have needed Hamlet's homily in order to bring it to her attention. It is true, however, that an unworthy choice of object, a loss of dignity because of the relative mediocrity or inferiority of the object, may pass without notice on the part of the subject, and it would be quite in keeping with clinical experience for denial to have made the Queen unaware of the aggression against the deceased King that is implicit in her marriage with his brother.

The deep impression that the dialogue with her son leaves on her, the fact that from that point on she drops her spouse as a true partner with whom to share her life—this turning point in her relationship to her son requires that the son should have brought to her consciousness something new and hitherto unknown to her. Hamlet's own purposes may have been quite different. He has found himself in a state of extraordinary excitement, which requires discharge, and it is significant that, despite this inner upheaval, he does not resort to any graver accusation than misdirected object choice. At one time he comes close to betraying the secret of his father's violent death, and this has been interpreted as an attempt to sound out his mother's knowledge of the crimes that have taken place in Denmark. I am inclined instead to see in that remark solely the outcome of the intensity that his excitement has reached.

The grossness of his assault, however, makes the spectator overlook the relative lightness of the actual content of the accusation; error with regard to the *quality* of the chosen object can hardly be regarded as an excessive offense. To be sure, the Queen's more or less sudden recognition of her spouse's grievous inferiority to her late husband cannot help but have grave consequences for her relationship with Claudius. On the other hand, the fact that this recognition has come about under the son's tutelage must have resulted in an incomparable increase of the latter's stature in her eyes, and this leads to Hamlet's interdiction of intercourse with the father-substitute—the fulfillment of every boy's ardent wish, at the peak of the positive Oedipus complex. Yet, the question remains: why is it that Hamlet does not reproach his mother at this point for any greater offense than having chosen an unworthy object?

Consideration toward his mother, or the father's command "nor let thy soul contrive against thy mother aught" *(I-5-86)*, have been suggested as potent motives in the conduct of this dialogue with his mother. I do not see why either of these should have ruled out the reproach of incest. If it was true, she must have known so and understood that her son would surely feel deeply hurt by it. My own thinking is that the fact that Hamlet does not reproach the mother with incest when he confronts her reveals that incest is in the end Hamlet's *fantasy*. When he is with his mother, he verbalizes only what is justifiable in reality terms. On other occasions, such as during the soliloquies or in conversation with Horatio, the reality factor is sufficiently reduced for Hamlet to be able to indulge freely in the expression of his fantasies.

This is, by the way, in accordance with the real life of the mind. The soliloquies can be regarded as the equivalent of free associations; when Hamlet is speaking with Horatio, by contrast, he exchanges thoughts and fantasies in something like the fashion of exchanges between two adolescent boys. (It is significant, for example, that he does not let Horatio know of his grave self-reproaches and self-doubts, nor does he raise any accusation of incest on such occasions.)

Yet, at one point, even though in a very roundabout way, which makes it hardly recognizable to others, he seems to raise the reproach of incest directly. I have in mind the passage *(IV-3-51 to 54),* in which Hamlet addresses Claudius as dear mother, and justifies it by: "father and mother is man and wife, man and wife is one flesh, and so, my mother."

Now the concept of *una caro* was decisive in the Church's justification of matrimonial impediments. The theory was that the impediment of affinity—that is to say, an impediment brought about by close relationship to a former spouse—arose as a result of physical union. When man and woman become one flesh, the relatives of the one became the relatives of the other; in this view affinity and consanguinity became practically identical.[12]

If Hamlet's reference to "one flesh" is connected with the *una caro* theory, then it definitely contains the reproach of incest, for it implies that cohabiting with a deceased husband's brother is tantamount to consorting with blood relatives of one's own brother. The context suggests, however, that the King does not perceive the accusation and, indeed, it is

[12] This, of course, was important in cases of extramarital intercourse, which resulted in the same kind of impediment of affinity as marriage produced. Thus, when a man committed adultery with a relative of his wife's, and then resumed conjugal relations without dispensation, he committed incest (de C. Parmiter, 1967, p. 127 n5).

raised by intimation only. In the matter of murder, however, Hamlet proceeded differently. There he let Claudius unmistakably know not only what he suspects, but also what he knows.

There is a subtle point here. In terms of the plot, the murder of Hamlet's father did occur in reality, but the idea of incest is Hamlet's fantasy, and it is therefore not shared by others. As with most fantasies, however, it contains a grain of truth. When a brother marries his brother's widow, it is an incestuous impulse that he is motivated by. Claudius' crimes are, after all, essentially oedipal. The manifest content of the crime, however, is directed against a brother, and Gertrude stands for the mother only in the unconscious. Thus, Hamlet's roundabout and seemingly enigmatic *una caro* statement very subtly adumbrates the sort of psychological situation in which a subject is aware of having been taken possession of by a fantasy to which he nevertheless attributes only a limited degree of reality value.

I have presented all these details in order to demonstrate that the bad repute that the Queen has experienced among most literary critics should not be taken as the only conceivable one. An entirely different reading is possible. Oddly enough, her love and devotion to Hamlet are not often considered. This is one point about which the text does not admit any doubt: Hamlet's welfare is uppermost in her mind. Moreover, Claudius is aware of this, and respects it, as if he knew that any show of ambivalence toward Hamlet would deprive him of Gertrude's affection. Here one must say that a mother who feels unambivalently toward her son (and Gertrude is definitely depicted as such a mother) would never commit adultery. A second marriage, however—even a hasty one—is, to my way of feeling, quite compatible with this situation.

There is, moreover, another motive for that second marriage that is conceivable. I gladly admit that this motive is far-fetched and its assumption improbable, since no reference is made to it. The succession to the throne in Hamlet's Denmark was based on a combination of election and close relationship to the last King. The parliament (or whatever the institution may have been) was expected to elect the dead King's closest blood relative; as Claudius' election proves, however, it was not compelled to do so. Is it possible that Hamlet's absence at the time of the King's sudden death, his youth, and perhaps also some doubt about his capabilities as a sovereign endangered his election in favor of Fortinbras? The Queen's quick marriage, if there is any credibility to this assumption, would then have served also the purpose of averting that danger by making certain that the crown at least remained in the family. Hamlet's stay in Denmark during Claudius' reign and Claudius' speech from the throne, in which Hamlet is officially acknowledged as crown prince, would assure his succession. In that light, the Queen's marriage could also have been a wise political step, in favor of Hamlet's succession.

All this, however, is mere speculation. One is on safer grounds when the outline is drawn from interpretations that Shakespeare made possible. The range comprises two extremes: a passionate, unscrupulous woman who was incapable of mastering her appetites, and who therefore gave in to her husband's brother's blandishments, committed adultery, and perhaps even favored her husband's violent death; or a woman who was devoted and faithful to her husband, primarily concerned about her only son, well adjusted and well disciplined, and of considerable intelligence and skill (her way of handling Laertes and Claudius after the closet-scene, etc.). The only possible reproach one could make to Gertrude, if this latter version were accepted, would be her lack of discretion or dignity in her entering too quickly into a second marriage.

I owe to Dr. Ruth S. Eissler a different character picture of the Queen, which is more sophisticated and actually reflects a personality type not infrequently met with in clinical practice. Gertrude is the type of mother who, even though she is perhaps well-meaning, is too narcissistic to empathize with her son. She simply does not consider the hurt it must cause her son when she remarries a short time after his father's death and, in addition, makes herself instrumental in obtaining for Claudius the crown that would have gone to her son. She is insensitive—to a certain extent, simple-minded and naive, almost indeed fatuous—and acts as if the son has not grown up and matured, but is still a child. Her capacity to deny reality and its complexity is extensive. Even after the mousetrap play, which contains an open challenge, almost an offense directed at her, she acts as if she were altogether oblivious of this implication.

Indeed, this interpretation of the Queen's character may serve particularly well to explain her response to the mouse-trap. Yet the part of the subplay up to the end contains what are mainly slurs at her. The fact that the Player-King and Player-Queen have been married for 30 years, as is stated in the first line of the play, makes the reference to Gertrude inescapable. And yet she appears unruffled by what ought to have hurt her deeply. When openly challenged by Hamlet,[13] she gives the oft-quoted reply: "The lady doth protest too much methinks" *(III.2.234)*, which may easily be interpreted as a sign of her superficiality, as if for her the most important thing was that women should above all beware of giving away their secret desires by denying them.

Of course, this line permits many different interpretations. One such interpretation might be that, since she is so much concerned with Hamlet's welfare, she must avoid any open break with him. If she castigates him for his rudeness, she contributes to his further isolation at court. By not losing her poise and disregarding the slur, one could then say, she proved anew her presence of mind and superiority of wit. Her answer is neutral enough to leave it open whether she is on the side of or against the Player-Queen. Yet what in one interpretation may appear as poise may be regarded in another as denial, as if she were childishly narcissistic enough not to notice that in the Player-Queen she herself is represented.

Furthermore, the fact that she suspects, with seeming astuteness, "His father's death, and our o'erhasty marriage" *(II.2.57)* of being the principal causes of Hamlet's strange behavior may also be cited as an indication of denial. For in view of such awareness, one might have expected an entirely different course of action from her. Such knowledge without reverberation in action or feeling is a sign of inner emptiness. The son's masculinity is denied up to the moment in the closet scene, when Hamlet, by killing Polonius and violently upbraiding her, brings concretely and undeniably to her attention the fact of his virility. In line with this somewhat pejorative view of her character, one would then conclude that in her opportunism she is wont to side with the party that proves itself stronger.[14]

Yet, to return to the two extremes I have outlined roughly before— those of the "good" and the "bad" mother—I want to add that a psychological synthesis of these two extremes would take into consideration the fantasies that a boy forms about his mother. Even when she is beyond reproach in her actual conduct, such things as a second pregnancy, more or less overt suggestions of intercourse with the father, or her preference for her spouse as against her progeny, are likely to cause the son to form a disparaging image of her. Almost regularly one encounters among sons

[13] For a different interpretation of this episode see Holmes (1964, p. 122).

[14] Helene Deutsch (1944-1945) has given an exhaustive presentation of the variations and complexities with which female psychology abounds, and I do not doubt that her book contains character pictures that could be projected into the framework provided by Shakespeare.

the reproach of unfaithfulness, inconsistency, lack of love, and sexual impurity. Acts that are dictated by reality needs are often appraised as being immoral and unethical.

These fantasies may remain unconscious, yet even under optimal circumstances they are potent forces and produce far-reaching effects. Gertrude would then be at one and the same time the good mother, as she is in reality, and the bad mother, as the boy imagines her. That both extremes can be projected at the same time onto a screen, without causing confusion and without detriment to artistic perfection, but instead leaving it to the spectator's bent to determine which version will become relevant to him, is an accomplishment that will remain the secret of Shakespeare's genius.

Internalization and Appersonation.

Others (Hartmann, 1960, Hartmann and Loewenstein, 1962, Lampl-de Groot, 1947, 1962 and 1966) have also said, and with greater precision and scientific accuracy, what has been said here about the superego. I should like to make some additional remarks, however, because of the terminology that I have used.

What I have called appersonation of the superego has been, of course, observed and commented on by many others. Yet the tendency seems widespread to believe that it is as the consequence of a lack of *internalization* that the content of the superego preserves a representation in the outer world. When I suggest that the process of appersonation is central to Hamlet's development, this presupposes that Ophelia's despairing words about Hamlet's earlier personality *(III.1.153-163),* rather than being an example of momentary idealization by a loving young woman, put together in a moment of great frustration, constitute instead an accurate description of what Hamlet's social phenotype was prior to the play's beginning.

What makes that description so significant is that it suggests a man who is not at all opportunistic, but instead believes sincerely in the values of his time and his society and is ready as well as able to live up to them. This is someone who has formed his ideals and developed his superego in conformity with the standards of his cultural setting. He has not been at all ungenerous and narrow in so doing, but has instead branched out into all the different facets of cultural life (courtier, soldier, scholar), and has integrated those ideals maximally, so that they have affected all his functions ("eye," "tongue," "sword," "reason"). All this has apparently been synthesized and compounded into a conflict-free structure. Yet the harmony of his personality has rested on the assumption that the society whose ideals he has integrated has its foundations in an ethical base.

Hamlet is here in the situation of the truly religious person who has been leading a spotless life in conformity with the demands of the Sacred Texts. If it were now to be proved that these Sacred Texts are fraudulent or forged or otherwise invalid, such a faithful person would be thrown into a crisis comparable to the one that we witness in Hamlet. There is, however, one important difference between Hamlet and the religious person: there is no power and no argument that could in fact disprove for the latter the validity of the Sacred Texts. Since any doubt about their validity is in itself a sin the ideally religious person is quite well protected. Everything that happens in reality is renewed proof of the existence of the Divinity, as presented in the Scriptures.

It is evident that such psychological structures are highly internalized, even though responsibility has been surrendered to an outside force. Personal responsibility is in effect limited to unquestioning obedience to an external lawgiver. And this does not at all have to mean the debasement of the self to an unthinking, mechanical, shadow-like submissiveness. There are degrees of internalization, and "mechanical, shadow-like submissiveness" characterizes only one extreme among these. Degrees of internalization can be measured in terms of "rootedness." A firmly internalized superego, even though it has not been appersonated, still cannot be replaced by any other; on the other hand, the "when-in-Rome" type "adjusts" to the accidental demands of particular environments.[15]

In instances of maximal rootedness—that is, where there has been successful internalization—the entire personality reverberates with the ideal and rejoices in serving it. Ophelia uses words about Hamlet that convey the fervent and buoyant atmosphere that surrounds such persons: "noble," "rose," "sovereign," "sweet bells," "unmatched," "blown [in full blossom]." Internalization and appersonation must, however, be kept distinct: an appersonated superego feels responsible only to itself. Thus the mere fact of internalization per se does not tell us anything about the concomitant presence or absence of appersonation, which is a quite different condition of the superego.

Here a genetic factor has to be taken into consideration. The general trend of psychoanalysis is toward regarding the superego as

---

[15] What is recommended as "flexibility" in mental hygiene often amounts to a safeguard against the evolvement of a superego that is firmly rooted in the personality.

an essentially adscititious structure—that is to say, as one that has been wholly adopted from without. The discovery that there is nothing "innate" in man to give direction to his ethical feelings, that the evolvement of morality and ethics, of conscience, depends rather on the "accident" of environmental factors—this discovery has brought psychoanalysis into sharp conflict with other psychologies and philosophies, and particularly those that are religiously directed.

Once the basic fabric of a superego has become established, of course, the question of choice enters: the self has the potential endowment to select among the ideals that are offered to it in a free community. Yet psychoanalysis has found again and again that this choice is directed by unconscious forces, that the self is rarely capable of a purely autonomous selection of ideals and prohibitions.

Once established, the superego does not necessarily grow solely by way of new identifications. Its further growth may become relatively independent of those adscititious factors that still have great bearing on it during the individual's adolescence. Yet, in my opinion, the growth of the superego, during adulthood, in complete independence of external factors is rather rare. Spontaneous reorganization—that is, nonadscititious growth—of the superego can be observed, at least insofar as it is reflected in their writings, in such giants as Nietzsche, who are of incomparable importance to mankind, in that their works then become the sources for the essentially adscititious superego contents of subsequent generations.

Hamlet's pretraumatic superego is characterized—if we can trust Ophelia, and I do not see any reason why we should not, in this context —by the fact that it still carries the earmarks of its adscititious origin. I must add here that we would not know this solely from Ophelia's description of how Hamlet behaved before the great change came over him, but also through examining that description against Hamlet's appearance of grave doubt about the very values that had previously directed his ethical behavior.

A person may integrate ideal societal standards and even fulfill their requirements in practice (which Hamlet did); he may also appersonate them (which Hamlet did not do). In the latter instance, the superego is irreversible; in the former, it may collapse. The degree of appersonation thus cannot be appraised from without. Only during the course of a psychoanalytic investigation can degrees of internalization be ascertained, along with the fact and the degree of appersonation. An internalized but not appersonated superego and one that is appersonated may lead under optimal conditions to the same behavior; they may thus be externally indistinguishable, even though they are psychologically quite different. Yet what is here presented as two distinct functions is, in clinical reality, an intermixture. In practice, the two functions constitute a complementary series: we can observe in the same individual some superego contents that have been internalized yet remain inappersonated, alongside other contents that are indeed appersonated.

We can, then, speculate about the following possible sequence in the vicissitudes of Hamlet's superego. As a child, he must have evolved an intense Oedipus complex, with a strong idealization of the father. After being sublimated, this then became transformed into an adoption of the highest ideals current in the society in which he lived, a mode of existence that seemed to be independent of the childhood model.

It is only in this diffusion and extension of ideals, which included many more societal dimensions than were represented in Old Hamlet—who was first and foremost, and perhaps solely, warrior and faithful husband *(not* courtier and *not* scholar, and possibly more warrior than soldier)—it is only here that one can discover the first foreshadowings of later crisis. Clinically, one often finds such extension in the filial superego, and it is regularly a sign of intense conflict with the father.[16]

When Hamlet's father dies, a regression sets in, such as is unavoidable in true mourning.[17] This regression is in the service of the ego since, once accomplished, it sets the ego free for a new object choice. It is still within the bounds of what is called "normality," if, during the process of mourning for a deceased father, the paternal childhood ideal arises once again in its full glory and glamour; for any memory that ties a subject to the lost object is reawakened, in order to be worked through, with the goal of being decathected. This process of (healthy) mourning is apparently disturbed (or impeded), in Hamlet's instance, by the mother's behavior.

It may be that the fact that Gertrude's nuptials so speedily follow the loss of her husband arouses in Hamlet not only recriminations against the mother but also doubts about the father's greatness—doubts

[16] In one clinical instance, it became evident that the son's extension of superego coincided with an intensive wish in the father that the father had himself been prevented from carrying out by force of external necessities. Here one recalls Freud's proposition that the child's superego often stems from the parental superego.

[17] Heller and Heller (1960) stress the regression in Hamlet. Yet a temporary regression, provoked by mourning, should not, under optimal conditions, necessitate a reorganization of the superego. The authors challenge the ambivalence-arousing effect of Hamlet's conversation with the Ghost.

that necessitate, for defensive purposes, an excessive idealization of the father (cf. the first soliloquy). On this question, the text is moot; but the observation is frequently made that the death of a father heightens the son's critical evaluation of the mother, so as to reduce the oedipal wish, which is obviously incited by the freedom from external prohibitions that has resulted from the father's death. [18]

Paternal and maternal imagery are, after all, associated and have effects upon each other. At any rate, the Ghost's demand that Hamlet act on his behalf draws the latter back into the phase when the childhood ideal was not yet sublimated so as to include societal ideals. At that moment, the danger arose for Hamlet that the superego might become reduced to a single function—namely, that of carrying out a command given directly to him by his father. More importantly, what the Ghost has to report is undeniably incompatible with Hamlet's Herculean childhood ideal. With this violation of the childhood ideal, its later derivative —the sublimated, societal ideals—also goes, because these ideals were only internalized and not appersonated.

The reason why this decisive change in quality of Hamlet's superego has been overlooked may be that, in the end, Hamlet acknowledges a Divinity and it is in this acknowledgment that the critics have found a principal new point. They forget, however, that Hamlet had already acknowledged a Divinity in the first soliloquy. Acknowledgment of a force, moreover, does not necessarily mean submitting to it. In the first soliloquy, Hamlet submits to the Divinity passively and without questioning; at the end he acknowledges its ubiquitous presence, just as we acknowledge the force of gravity, which we nevertheless bend to our own purposes in just the way Hamlet does with the Divinity, in his dealings with Rosencrantz and Guildenstern and with Claudius.

One objection to my theory may be that it is too subtle and sophisticated to be able to account by itself for the noise, excitement, and bloodshed of the tragedy. That may be so, but the point is still far from being settled. Even now the theory still appears to be tenable that more human blood has been shed in the struggle for the enforcement of superego demands than for the sake of the fulfillment of wishes dictated by the carnal passions, the "id-wishes," as psychoanalysis calls them.

The Protopope Avvakum lived for two or three years in a prison at Bratsk, somewhere in the middle Siberian highlands. There he was exposed to terrible sufferings, being left without straw, light, or heating.

---

[18] One patient reported the appearance of nocturnal emissions after his father's death.

Even during the winter, the windows were kept open. At the end, he could no longer lie on his back, because it was festering and his body was ravaged by lice. And what was it for which poor Protopope Avvakum suffered all this from 1656 to 1658? His insistence on crossing himself with more or fewer fingers than the Orthodox Church prescribed or permitted!

What an irony of history that 300 years later hardly anyone at that place cared the slightest about making the sign of the cross [and I wonder whether even those few who still might do so would not argue about the number of fingers to be used]. One has to bow in awe before the power of the superego that can enforce the enduring of such terrible torments, and for what? for trifles? Or was there concealed behind the number of fingers a devilish question of essence?[19]

I should have liked to analyze Protopope Avvakum. Was there a masturbatory conflict behind his insistence on the number of fingers? I do not believe so. Then what was in the mind of a man who felt compelled to regard it as a question of life and death whether he crossed himself with any particular number of fingers between one and five? If man goes berserk because he faces starvation, or because the lives of his children and his wife are endangered, we can understand him by empathy; yet apparently the demands of the superego are as serious and uncompromising as the demands of the flesh and the heart. In the light of this all-embracing power of the superego, we may be all the more inclined to recognize the greatness of that moment when the superego changes from mere internalization to appersonation. No scientific discovery of modern times would have been possible without this momentous evolutionary change.

In general, it seems to me, the complexity of the superego, the drama of involvement in its tragic aspect, has not yet been sufficiently acknowledged. We are all too quickly given to pronouncing the judgment of "disease," and thereby to denying the objective validity of the tragic aspect that is inherent in the superego. Take the problem of span, which has two aspects. A superego should be integrated—that is, it should color all functions of the personality. Indeed, the civilized person eats, walks,

[19] Avvakum (1630(?)-1681), most famous of all nonconformist priests and author of an autobiography that has been one of the most popular books with schismatics, was an uncompromising archenemy of Nikon (1605-1681), patriarch of Moscow, who strove toward a realignment of the Russian church with the contemporary Greek branch of the Orthodox Church. The new ceremonial details that were closely connected with Church dogma had to do, among other things, with whether one should make the sign of the cross with three fingers or with two. Avvakum urged martyrdom on his followers, and he himself was burned at the stake.

thinks, feels, perceives, senses, dresses, speaks and loves in ways that are different from those of uncivilized man. Nevertheless, when observation is possible, one finds that one or another function does escape the civilizing process and lives its own life, untamed by superego demands.

If, however, the escaping function also escapes public recognition, and if it does not result in actual damage to the outside world, that fact remains a purely personal matter, which may pass unnoticed, even by the subject himself. The other aspect of span, however, which concerns the external world, is far more consequential. The superego should, after all, embrace the entire world with which we are in contact and, even beyond that, include the entire human universe.

Werther's problem—that he was killing life when he took a simple walk through a radiant landscape—will hardly find a sympathetic ear or any understanding among our contemporaries; it will quickly be dismissed as a problem of moral masochism. Yet it is, after all, a valid problem. It is, indeed, a horror-laden conflict, a basic ethical inconsistency, that individual human life is possible only at the cost of continuous destruction. If, at the Last Judgment, we were brought face to face with the enormous amount of organic substance that had been destroyed in individual forms by each single individual, it would be devastating indeed.

If Werther was little more, as some claim, than an oversensitive neurotic, Leonardo da Vinci, whom everyone admires as one of the greatest minds, expressed himself (although in a different context) in a quite similar vein, when he addressed himself to Man as follows: "King of the animals . . . I should rather say King of the beasts, thou being the greatest—because thou doest only help them, in order that they may give thee their children for the benefit of the gullet, of which thou hast attempted to make a sepulchre for all animals; and I would say still more, if I were allowed to speak the entire truth" (Richter, Vol. II, p. 103f., No. 844).

In cases of delinquency, the analyst is wont to speak of "lacunae" in the patient's superego and quite rightly so; at the same time, it should be recognized that lacunae are in fact typical of superego formation. The external span it embraces is frighteningly narrow. Leonardo and Werther are both appalled at the destruction man visits upon other species, even while they rejoice in so doing.

Yet man is no more charitable with his fellow-man. One may turn the whole problem upside down, and ask how it is possible for man not only to be able to endure the knowledge of his brethren's suffering, but even purposely to cause it—especially since a substantial portion of the Western élite have accepted the ethical demand of love of one's neighbors. The real problem of superego psychology is really the problem of wealth and poverty, of warfare, of a Pope who remonstrated against the Westphalian Peace after the population of Central Europe had already been reduced by two-thirds following the Thirty-Years War, and of many more such events.

Hamlet's outburst: "I could accuse me of such things that it were better my mother had not borne me" *(III.1.123)* is not necessarily the complaint of a melancholic or of a moral masochist; it may be no more than the expression of the sensitive awareness of ethical man, as he strives toward closing the wide gaps left by the narrow span of the superego. In some few instances, mankind has produced saints who have extended the span of their superegos by breaking through the denials, isolations and rigidities that keep the average man alive. Curiously enough, however, in studying their lives, one cannot escape the impression, in quite a few instances, that they were mentally unbalanced to the point of having to be called psychotic. The importance of these saints for the development of mankind is not brought into question by this observation nor is the greatness of their ethical achievement diminished. But why does so much psychopathology have to be brought into play in order for man to become serious about the actualization of ethical standards to which everyone else pays lip service?

A superego may be internalized and appersonated, and still condone or remain blind to an infringement of some ethical principles. In that case, the degree of what the theologians call "synteresis" is poor. The ethical demands may be high, yet one's conscience functions poorly as a guide to one's actual behavior; one is then able to sleep well while one's neighbors are destitute.[20] Man is more likely to evolve what the theologians call "syneidesis." He is given to passing refined judgments on his past actions, and gaining narcissistic pleasure from his ethical subtlety in evaluating the ethical shortcomings to which he long ago fell prey.

In melancholia, the contrast between synteresis and syneidesis takes on almost ludicrous forms: these show that what we are dealing with here is two distinct functions, which may work not only apart from, but in contradiction to one another: the melancholic becomes overaware of and overresponsive to his past irresponsibilities, yet he is totally incapa-

[20] Freud had already referred to this problem in 1914.

ble of carrying out acts of ethical value in the present. Hamlet's superego apparently had a high degree of synteresis before a series of traumata forced him to reorganize it.

During the pre-traumatic period of Hamlet's existence, society and superego were fused; more correctly, there was no conflict between internalized and societal demands. With the emergence of his awareness of the fact that realization of society's ideals would in fact amount to his countenancing and even sanctioning hypocrisy and crime, it became clearly necessary for him to repudiate those ideals.

Aggression against the forces in power became a necessity in the service of a now dawning, appersonated superego and ego ideal. The external span of reference of the appersonated superego became wider than that of the adscititious superego, for it went deeper in its thrust beneath the surface of society and thus responded to invisible, destructive forces at the root of society. It is noteworthy that, with this reorganization of the superego, the previously static conception of society changes into a dynamic one.

Alexander (1955, pp. 100-104) tried to demonstrate that Sophocles' writings about Oedipus contain a new and higher morality and are, by no means, merely a presentation of man's *hamartia*. By including *Oedipus at Colonus* and comparing it with the Book of Job, he arrives at the conclusion that the Oedipus plays are "an affirmation of a faith in righteousness, whatever the event." Alexander's commentary must be read in full, in order to grasp his analysis of the ethics of the two Oedipus plays. I must admit that I had some difficulty in following him, yet I myself feel the same way as he does about *The Brothers Karamazov*. Alyosha seems to be the bearer of a new superego, and it is most deplorable that Dostoevski's death prevented him from writing his Alyosha novel, as he had planned to.

All this, together with the foregoing, may prove that *Hamlet* is as much an oedipal tragedy as it is a tragedy of superego.

9. Difficulties in the Symbolic Interpretation of Literary Works (Dying Together)

Some criticism may be found about the interpretation of dying together as a consummation of love—an interpretation that I have used broadly in my discussion of the last scene in *Hamlet*. As a matter of fact, a good many characters die together at the end of *Hamlet*, and one could easily suspect the presence of a psychoanalytic bias in my singling out of Hamlet and Gertrude's dying together as a special case.[1] As far as this particular interpretation is concerned, however, I am, as a psychoanalyst, in a none too favorable situation. While my main proposition with regard to Hamlet's personality development stands on firmer grounds, and can be followed up, so to speak, clinically, this interpretation has to do with a symbolic act and, as is well known, symbolic interpretations, even in our clinical work, do sometimes contain some degree of risk.

The symbolic interpretation in question cannot in fact be confirmed by way of other data derived from the tragedy itself. The analyst finds himself here in a situation comparable to, if not quite the same as, the one he faces in the interpretation of dream symbols. There too it is not always altogether clear which dream is symbolic, in the narrower sense

[1] That death has a different meaning to each person has become a truism by now and does not need any further elaboration. For a recent study, which demonstrates this with regard to the two sexes, see McClellan (1966); for a comprehensive presentation of the topic, see Feifel (1959).

What I have in mind here is that the presentation of the deaths of different characters on the stage can evoke quite different sets of imagery in the spectator, depending on the personality and vicissitudes of the particular character involved. If this is so, then certainly the meaning of dying together must also vary from case to case.

of the word; and even when it is apparent that a dream is symbolic, its interpretation often has to be based on less solid grounds than those to which the analyst is accustomed, when he is dealing with the nonsymbolic dream.

As Freud observed, the patient's associations often fail to provide any clarification of the symbolic dream: either he does not produce any associations, or else those he does produce do not make any contribution to the understanding of the dream.[2] Be that as it may, it is possible, although not probable, that every dream is a symbolic dream, even if it is not at first recognizable as such, inasmuch as the symbols are buried in the overgrowth of the purely subjective elements. There are episodes in Shakespeare's tragedies—such as the appearance of an armed head, a bloody child, or a child crowned, as in *Macbeth (IV.1)*—that can be understood only as symbols, difficult as it may be to decipher their meaning.

Literary critics tend to look down upon symbolic interpretations, unless the symbols are clear-cut, as in the instance just referred to in *Macbeth*. Symbolic interpretations of the psychoanalytic sort tend to evoke outright scorn, yet those of the symbolist school of criticism often arouse indignation as well. It may be worthwhile to compare, on a tentative basis, the symbolic interpretations of psychoanalysis with those of the symbolist school of criticism.

Masefield (1924, p. 30), who is regarded as having started the latter school, wrote: "All things are in the mind of the great poet in the moment of his power, because he touches energy, the source of all things, the reality behind all appearance. In the moment of his power he is made one with Nature: his being is completed and his work perfected by the force of life itself." The school of symbolism makes it its task to unearth "the reality behind all appearance," on the ground that a literary work per se is an appearance, which contains a reality that is not directly visible but can be reached only by interpretation. It is in the symbol that reality makes its appearance, in a condensed form. Symbolism, as Knight (1966, p. 837) writes, is not a matter of conventional signs but of "some effect, person, object or descriptive passage which automatically radiates significance flowering from that effect's intrinsic nature." Since *all* things are

---

[2] It is noteworthy that it is precisely the most "vulnerable" topic in Freud's theory of dreams, the one in which the claims of psychoanalysis most offended common sense, that has been confirmed by experimental research (Hartmann and Betlheim, 1924).

purportedly in the poet's mind in the bursting creative moment, all things, I suppose, can also be found in the products of such moments.[3]

It is not clear to me, however, whether or not the act of symbolizing that psychoanalysis tries to uncover is the same as that which is dealt with by the school of symbolism. It is evident that the contents of the symbols in these two approaches are quite different. The symbolistic scholar derives highly comprehensive metaphysical interpretations from contexts in which others may find only plot action or psychological processes. While psychoanalytic symbolic interpretations seem to have decreased in frequency with the extension of ego psychology, curiously enough symbolic interpretations of the symbolistic school have referred extensively to ego processes.

Knight (1948, p. 128) rightly turns against disparaging views of *The Winter's Tale* as "a rambling, perhaps an untidy play." For him the play is "throughout deeply concerned" with "all those indefinables and irrationalities of free will and guilt, of unconditional and therefore appallingly responsible action; as in Leontes' unmotivated sin for which he is nevertheless in some sense responsible; with his following loss of free-will, selling himself in bondage to dark powers, and a consequent enduring and infliction of tyranny" (p. 126).

The analyst, of course, would not find Leontes' sin to be so completely unmotivated as the symbolist does. He will think of Leontes' unmistakably homosexual tie to Polyxenes, as well as of Hermione's pregnancy, which is always a time of strain for the paranoid type.[4] But Knight is, of course, even more interested in the message the play promulgates of freedom and creation, "the reverential wonder at Knowledge of Life where Death was throned." When Knight emphasizes the "death-reversal" in *The Winter's Tale,* he comes close to the psychoanalytic preoccupation with the problem of rebirth, which also plays a clinically eminent role (Nunberg, 1920).

Knight finds the source of resistance against his interpretations in "the ingrained academic reluctance to face the supernatural." The academic interpretation places undue emphasis "on intellectual and imagistic detail; and also on moral doctrine." The course of moralizing, Knight implies, is easier; besides, symbolic interpretation is, after all,

[3]A very concise criticism of Knight's work, particularly with regard to its methodology and its use of historical evidence, can be found in Frye (1963, pp. 4-6, 19).

[4]For psychoanalytic literature on *The Winter's Tale,* see Holland (1964, pp. 279-282). The effect of Hermione's pregnancy was already noted by Sachs (1919).

concerned with metaphysics. As he puts it, the keynote of symbolic interpretation is "the replacing of the moral by the metaphysical" (1966, p. 840). There are, of course, parallels between psychoanalysis and the symbolistic school: both encounter resistance; both are against moralizing; and both require intuition as a tool.

The results of Knight's interpretive work (1930, 1931, 1948, 1962) have often struck me as being giant projections of superego contents. I do not think that he has really escaped moralizing, after all. Since the term "moralizing" contains a somewhat pejorative coloration, Knight attempts to escape this implication by attempting to etherealize the day-to-day struggles of man with himself.

The penchant of the symbolistic school for the supernatural, the occult and the spiritualistic rules out any hope of ever getting its propositions into a verifiable frame; psychoanalysis, by contrast, is seriously concerned with the replacement of intuitively gained insights by explanatory and empirically provable propositions. By way of an approximation, we may say that the analyst is concerned with symbols that point below, whereas Knight is interested in symbols that point upward. Symbols of death-reversals or rebirth may function as a meeting ground, but there are also other areas in which the two touch surprisingly.

If the school of symbolism did not go beyond the area that is delimited and indirectly outlined by Murry's (1936, pp. 311-321) sensitive essay "Desdemona's Handkerchief," it would arouse, in general, less objection. In that essay, the psychoanalyst can feel thoroughly at home, despite the range of differences that he may also have with what he finds there. What is most significant is that the symbolic meanings there revealed do not rest on intuition alone, but rather find a solid foundation, small as the actual textual evidence may be. It is not unusual for trivia or for something that is hardly noticed to serve as the carrier of far-reaching symbols. Murry even comes close to converting Iago into the carrier of a psychological process that is rooted in the lovers, but he does so in a way that is methodologically unobjectionable.[5] However, when it is asserted, as Knight does, that these symbolic interpretations are sufficient to explain the drama as a whole, this may be questioned.

"The intuition of a third reality or dimension," Knight says, reveals

[5] When Knight (1966, p. 838) writes that Murry "was not generally at ease with symbolism as such," I surmise that it was really the other way around—that Knight was rendered uneasy by Murry's cleanness of method and the consequent simplicity of his presentation, both of which are so sorely lacking in most of Knight's own writings.

the essence of drama, which is found in "the knotting together" of philosophic overlay and human story (1966, p. 839). Without this, supposedly, drama would remain chaotic. How far does psychoanalysis go in that respect? It is difficult to decide. Freud's symbolic interpretation (1913c, p. 301) of Cordelia as a Death-goddess is a feat of extraordinary synthetic power; it could be regarded as, if not encompassing the entire play, nevertheless giving direction to it. Likewise, his discovery of a well-defined vicissitude of the oedipal triangle in *Hamlet* (in this instance not on a symbolic level) provides a developmental line that reaches from the beginning to the fifth act, yet does need an addition, since the so far inhibited deed is in the end consummated.

The psychoanalytic use of symbols has one clear advantage over that of the school of symbolism, to which Knight's proud claim that its laws "are rigid, and its analysis a severely disciplined study" (1966, p. 837) can least be applied.[6] The former can be checked, mainly by the investigations of dreams and by the observation of children. It is not very likely that metaphysical concern is really the mover of the dream, particularly in view of the fact that the physiological dream mechanism is already rooted in the newborn. The dreams of children are structured in essentially the same way as those of the adult are. The day-residues are, of course, quite different in the two, and a metaphysical problem may therefore penetrate an adult's dream, but not a child's. Yet in the study of dream symbols psychoanalytic theory stands on firm empirical grounds.

The existence of metaphysical symbols in Shakespeare's plays is, however, by no means precluded by psychoanalytic findings. Although the study of dreams is an important adjunct to the understanding of tragedy, it would be a grave error to believe that tragedy does not far surpass the limitations of the dream. A metaphysical view is, after all, part and parcel of human existence. Speculation about a world outside ourselves, even if we cannot ever hope to perceive it, is, I am inclined to say, unavoidable; a metaphysical element can be discovered in a myth, or a fairy tale. Hence it would not be surprising to find in Shakespeare's plays a world that is rich in metaphysical elements. I do not think that this is in contradiction to any basic psychoanalytic propositions.

Freud's aversion to metaphysics (in this respect, most psychoana-

---

[6] When Knight (1966, p. 840) asserts that Berry's (1965) delightful inquiry has to do with an "element of Shakespeare's symbolic activity," I cannot follow him. Berry discovered a formal, well-defined literary element and analyzed its implications convincingly. If the "inset" is to be understood as a symbol, it would certainly be a symbol, if at all, of an entirely different dimension from that in which the school of symbolism is rooted.

lysts have followed him) made him turn against its claims to explanation and its realistic assumptions. For the analyst, I would assume, metaphysics is primarily a psychological problem. He sees in it the projections of unconscious contents, and it is therefore to be expected that he will seek to find the chain that anchors the high-flung metaphysical symbol firmly in human life. Yet, for Knight and for many a metaphysician, human life is the realization of metaphysical forces.

Curiously enough, in Freud's work rudiments of an equivalent view are to be found. When Freud asserted that he regarded the biological, psychological, historical and cultural processes as revealing, in common, the manifestations of a gigantic struggle between Eros and Thanatos, he laid the foundations for something like a psychoanalytic metaphysics; but this was a metaphysics that, notwithstanding its high degree of abstraction, is not based solely on speculation or on deduction, but is rather rooted at one end, so to speak, in solid empiricism.

Freud has been sufficiently chided for this venture into metaphysics, yet he may have set forth a profounder truth in this respect than the present is ready to acknowledge. Philosophers of great stature, such as Georg Simmel, have contended that life flows through all human beings, who are only its transient receptacles. It is quite possible that science will one day look at man in this way, and man will then lose one more aspect of his autonomy. It has been difficult enough for man to assimilate his insights into the impacts that have been made on him by society and his own biological substructure. He may yet have to face the fact that he is *in toto* nothing but a battlefield upon which cosmic forces carry out their combats or collisions—in which case the historians may find themselves able to assert that the medieval epoch, during which some theologians insisted that in every man God and the Devil are fighting a struggle over a soul, did after all anticipate, even though in animistic language, a profound truth.

I do not know whether I am altogether wrong in saying that Knight is not very far from such a demonologic view. In reading some of his writings, one may (perhaps erroneously) obtain the impression that it is man's chief function to show evil or goodness or creativity. That the flair for metaphysics *can* clarify some disputed passage he has demonstrated, in at least two instances (1947b). It is also quite remarkable to observe how the symbolist draws far-reaching meanings out of passages that may appear to some critics to be rather neutral. Although there may be reason to disagree with Knight's interpretation (1949, p. 310) of the lesson that

Hamlet gives to the Players, the interpretation is nevertheless notable. Likewise, the author's comment (1947a, p. 319) on the significance of Claudius' conversation with Laertes *(IV.7)* about Lamond's horsemanship is a *tour de force,* made possible only by symbolistic interpretation.

I have the feeling that the symbolist method is particularly well suited for enlivening passages that seem to the ordinary reader to be neutral (and therefore do not elicit any emotional response to speak of), and for endowing these passages with depth—better suited, at least, than that method is to contribute valid interpretations to the crucial problem of a play. When Knight calls his first essay on Hamlet "The Embassy of Death" (1930, pp. 17-46), one has to say that for the most part he is on the wrong track.[7] "Embassy of death"—that is the impression that the average audience will carry away, the message that the text, when taken literally, may very well contain. But a commentary, if it is to deserve to be called an interpretation, must go beyond the visible—that is to say, beyond what is directly accessible to any intelligent audience that is capable of remaining awake and alert during a performance.

The psychoanalytic interpretation has been severely criticized for going beyond these bounds, but the criticism has been put forth by many who seem to have forgotten that the transcending per se of actions and words as they are put on the stage is a prerequisite of any form of interpretation. Thus, if we were to find that a commentary merely repeated, even though in general terms, what the playwright had realized on the stage, we would have to question the actual *interpretive* value of such an effort.

When the author describes Hamlet's soul as "sick," in the sense that "the symptoms are horror at the fact of death and an equal detestation of life, a sense of uncleanliness and evil in the things of nature" (1930, p. 23) his view may be challenged; but this is merely expressing, after all, only one among the many characterizations that have been made, and it is difficult to see the need for any specific interpretive method in order to reach this particular conclusion—if it can truly be called a conclusion.

Knight is really not so far from Madariaga's quite limited view, when he says: "Remembering only the Ghost's command to remember, he is paralysed, he lives in death, in pity of hideous death . . . he murders all the wrong people, exults in cruelty, grows more and more dangerous.

[7] See also Boklund (1965, p. 136) for a warning against looking upon it as "an agent of death."

At the end, fate steps in, forces him to perform the act of creative assassination he has been, by reason of his inner disintegration, unable to perform. Not Hamlet, but a greater principle than he or the surly Ghost, puts an end to his continual slaughter" (1930, p. 45). Knight's actual conception of Hamlet is probably more complicated at this point, but the statement quoted should prove once again that, even in this generalized view of Hamlet's character, no particular insight is arrived at that is not accessible to commonsense thinking.

In 1947(a), perhaps, Knight goes a little further.[8] Hamlet's alleged failure is now put into a wider frame: he "cannot act creatively"; "in the manner of the neurotic, he expends great energy without directing it wisely"; "he looks back, is critical, shows little love"; "he is left divided, all but insane, spasmodic . . . he is ill-mannered which . . . is perhaps worse"; "Hamlet is a symbol of man, with his highest idealism and best art, in our era, yet trammelled still in concepts of the Law, justice and death. The result is a multiplicity of murders" (1947a, p. 314f); "we must surely see guilt in Hamlet's behaviour, a guilt directly related to the inadequacy of his good. He cannot take the final step" (p. 316). The last statement is particularly baffling, but we may recall that Knight disputes Hamlet's final action, while allowing "circumstances" to be the executor of the deed.

Further: "Hamlet is or has been in relation to his society, thoroughly abnormal and dangerous" (p. 321). Nevertheless, after this very dark picture, Knight admits that, following "a subtle change," "Hamlet has somehow reached love, which is humility before not God's ideal for the race but God's human race as it is, in one's own time and place" (p. 322). Yet nowhere have I been able to find any reference in Knight as to how and why this highly significant change came about.

There is one particularly thought-provoking passage, which indicates that the metaphysician measures Hamlet in terms of Christian ethics and may therefore misinterpret as negative those steps by which Hamlet succeeds in transcending the Christian ethic. Hamlet "does not attain" writes Knight (1947a, p. 315) ". . . to the New Testament freedom from the Law. That is why he cannot move through society with the assurance of a Christ, or a St. Francis, and nothing else, it might seem, would serve his turn." True enough, Hamlet is not a Christ figure. But it is equally wrong to speculate that Christ's assurance would have been of

---

[8] The Author's essay (1931): "Rose of May: An Essay on Life-themes" does not go significantly beyond the 1930 statement.

any help to him. There are quite unique features in Christ's life. He was born free of original sin; his mother had been immaculately conceived and his father had created Purgatory yet was never in it. And yet, although exceptional measures were taken to spare him an Oedipus complex (those who are particularly touchy have denied that he ever had brothers and sisters), there are two records (Mark 3: 33 and Luke 11: 29) of his rejecting his mother or coming quite close to it, or, at least, being strangely unaffectionate to her. We do not know any too well, therefore, how Christ would have behaved if he had been in Hamlet's place, any more than we know how Hamlet would have behaved in Christ's position.

When Frye (1963, p. 19) reproaches Knight and his school for the lack of evidence in their "theologizing analyses," he is perfectly right in doing so; but his insistence that theologizing analyses can be accepted as correct only insofar as they conform to Elizabethan beliefs seems to me to go too far. One may discover in an old play a "theological phantasy" that is not consonant with those beliefs but grew out of the author's own deliberation. Frye rightly speaks (p. 5) against the fashion of discovering "some new Christ-figure or Christ-allusion in the plays," when such a discovery is made with regard to "the center of the tragedies" (Siegel, 1957, p. 231). But the Christ-figure is so pervasive in Western civilization, the child is exposed so frequently, even in modern society, to the sight of the suffering Savior, that the issue of identifying or not identifying with the Son of Man inescapably confronts the unconscious. I would expect on principle that in every major creation traces of the Christ-theme show up—openly or in a distorted form—and that the question can be only what relevance these traces have to the work itself.

I would not hesitate to assume that there is some sort of association between the wound that Hamlet sustains at the hands of Laertes and the wound that Christ receives in his side; but what is the relevance of that association? Is it possible that in the Elizabethan age a man could hear of a piercing wound without any such association being aroused? Yet when Hamlet is seen to respond with rage to his injury, one cannot help recognizing that the Christ association has had no power of diffusion or only little.

Symbols change their significance from age to age; in that observation Knight (1962, p. 29) is right. But then that is true of all cultural products. Hadas (1950, p. v) rightly stated that each generation requires "its own version of the classics, and similarly each generation requires its own interpretation of them"; but he also knew that "to say new or different things about Greek literature is neither easy nor safe." That was an observation that the school of symbolism did not apparently take to heart when it tried to say "new and different things" about Shakespeare's tragedies.

If the question of the correctness or incorrectness of particular symbolistic interpretations is put aside for a moment, it may be said, as a matter of principle, that despite the vast difference between psychoanalytic and symbolistic interpretations, both may be correct. It is conceivable that the tremendous tension that *Hamlet* in particular evokes in the audience rests on a synthesis of two different frames of reference into one single play. I must add that I am not here expressing an impression that I have actually gained but rather suggesting a theoretical possibility.[9] We do not need to expect any person, or, for that matter, life in general, to be consistent, and it may well be precisely a play's basic inconsistency that reflects the decisive quality in the cosmos within which life and human destiny take place.

Be that as it may, my excursus into the interpretations of the symbolistic school will show the considerable difficulty that lies in the making of any symbolic interpretation. And because of that very difficulty, the interpreter must avoid acting like the physician who, in disregard of empirical science, bases his diagnosis of the presence of an infectious disease upon olfactory impressions that he has received at the patient's bedside. It was to him that Freud (1900, p. 351) likened the analyst who relies in his symbolic interpretations solely on his intuition.

My thesis is that Hamlet proves in the end to be victorious on all fronts. He frees himself of all inappersonated remnants of paternal imagery (the killing of Polonius and Claudius, and the absence of reference to the dread command at the end); he is accepted by the younger brother as the new authority (Laertes' request for forgiveness); he takes possession of the mother (dying together); and he is resurrected or, as one may say, reborn in the form of Fortinbras.

Psychoanalysis has accumulated a rather impressive array of observations, sufficient to make it highly probable that the young male, in order to become a psychological adult, must solve in his unconscious two rather difficult tasks. He must free himself of his fear of his father, and dissolve his castration anxiety—which leads to the achievement of mental

---

[9] The two contradictory drifts that I believe were actually synthesized into the play will be set forth presently.

independence from the childhood ideal embodied by his father; and he must reorganize the childhood superego and integrate a new structure that squares with his *persona*. All this goes parallel with his unconscious acceptance of the mother as a permitted love object and his recovery of her in the form of an egosyntonic, ideal spouse.

In psychic reality all this is far more complicated, but a summary description will have to do.[10] When I find these processes embodied at the end of *Hamlet*, one could easily repeat the objection that, as in so many other instances, here too the investigator is merely projecting onto the play his favorite thesis.

The significance of my hypothesis would be that it makes a distinctive contribution to the explanation of *Hamlet*'s universal appeal. If, according to this thesis, the play embodies general, unconscious processes that are universally necessary for maturation, then it would be understandable why it may stir all generations of all nationalities. Nevertheless, a reservation has to be introduced at this point. The necessity (external or internal) for forming a personal superego is not universal. In medieval times, for example, man was by no means supposed to evolve his own philosophy (superego), but rather to accept as binding not only Christian revealed religion, but also its specific interpretation, as set forth by the Catholic Church. The implicit demand for the freedom to form a personal superego that I perceive in *Hamlet* may be the reason why *Hamlet* seems to have greater popularity in Protestant than in Catholic countries. Yet the play's ambiguity is broad enough to make it acceptable to *any* brand of the Christian faith.

Similarly, emphasis may be placed either on a politically conservative aspect (usurped power is defeated) or on a revolutionary one (the hypocritical forces at the helm are defeated), and it is this breadth that makes the play acceptable to a broad spectrum of political institutions. Yet all these different aspects would be held together by processes of human universality. That a human destiny is presented in Hamlet, no one will doubt; disagreement, however, remains about the meaning of specific details.

Freud's interpretation of Hamlet was not a symbolic one. Most critics have agreed that Hamlet delayed taking the revenge to which he was committed, but they have disagreed about the reasons for this; clearly, the playwright must have left something ambiguous or unspoken. Freud

---

[10] The fact that many investigators do not accept these psychoanalytic propositions will be ignored at this point and the theory will be assumed to be empirically correct.

sought to fill that gap by the assumption of a specific quality in Hamlet's relationship to his father and mother. He was in all probability right when he surmised that one has to look for the "missing link" in that area, in view of the tragical implications of man's relationship to his parents that have found undisguised representation in other literary works, such as Sophocles' *Oedipus Rex*, and Dostoevski's *The Brothers Karamazov*, which have stirred up an interest as intense as the interest evoked by *Hamlet*.

My own interpretation, however, goes beyond this. My belief is that the "latent playthoughts" contain a *consummation* of the oedipal wish.

The psychoanalytic approach to a literary work calls for the same sort of discrimination as is applied in the interpretation of dreams. The play's manifest content is straightforward: Hamlet's actions lead to the downfall of two families—that is, two families perish without leaving any posterity and as a result the country will be ruled by a foreigner. The progeny of the opponent of Hamlet's father have won out: Hamlet has thus undone his father's lifework.

The image of Hamlet as the bungler, the ambassador not only of death but also of destruction and annihilation, is widespread; but it is based not on interpretation but rather on a literal acceptance of the manifest content. It makes Horatio's words about "a noble heart," "sweet prince," "flights of angels" almost incomprehensible, unless we interpret them as being nothing more than *falsifications* and *denials* on the part of a loving friend, and there is no reason whatsoever for doing that.

One may object that the charge of "bungling" is too harsh, since Hamlet's failure is the failure of a naïve, pure and innocent man; and the fact that he was ready to bear the burden of grave conflict, without surrendering, would not be sufficient to justify Horatio's convincing eulogy.

Here is a flagrant example of the way in which reliance on the manifest content of the play brings one into loggerheads with the way in which the play affects the spectator. For Shakespeare's intention would not be fulfilled if he were to invite the spectator all along to identify with Horatio, and then to expect us to set aside the summation that he has Horatio give us of Hamlet's character in the end. For that reason, one is justified in asking what could be the latent, yet relevant images of Hamlet that make Horatio's encomium acceptable.

My thesis of the victorious Hamlet contains, I admit, a serious danger. Psychoanalysis' continual search for the forces *behind* observable phenomena sometimes leads to results that have the effect of converting what is plainly observable into its very opposite. Dr. Reik's (1940) book on masochism has always struck me as a classical example of this. The reader cannot help closing the book with the feeling that masochists must be the worst sadists. I do not want to deny that, in many masochists, and particularly in those who are excessively so, there is often considerable sadism lurking; nor do I disagree that, in general, masochism *also* contains a defense against sadism. Nevertheless, the fact remains that they are *masochists* and *not* sadists, however much suffering they may cause to others by their perversion.

In the same way, my thesis that Hamlet is in the end victorious on all fronts threatens to convert the manifest content of the play into its very opposite, to make it, if I may use a pejorative term, a "success story." In dream interpretation such conversions actually do occur and Freud produced substantial evidence to that effect. But the dream, the perversion, the neurotic symptom, and the literary work must not ever be regarded as being identical, despite their relatedness when they are looked at solely as psychological structures.

In the formation of dreams concealment and, if necessary, conversion into the opposite are legitimate, even appropriate goals, since under all circumstances sleep should be safeguarded and anxiety prevented. If the preservation of sleep is accepted as the dream's proximate function, one may conclude that emotional barrenness is the proper dream state, for even pleasant emotions or sensations may wake the dreamer, as can be observed in those dreams that lead to nocturnal emissions.

The legitimate emotional response to drama, however, has never been established, despite Aristotle. With regard to comedy, it is obvious that it should be laughter; but in tragedy, the ultimate response would be, I suppose, tears; outright anxiety (not to speak of panic or rage) does not seem to be compatible with the aesthetic experience, whatever may be meant by that somewhat vague expression (cf. Richards, 1925). All manner of emotions may properly appear in us—but in diluted form, never with sufficient intensity to take hold of the will and lead to immediate action, as was the case when an enraged French audience, following a performance of *L'Aiglon*,[11] tried to drown the actor who played Metternich.

[11] The drama's primary function is not concealment, as the dream's is; if it is worth anything, it arouses a wide gamut of feelings. When I say that this occurs in intensities and qualities that do not disturb the aesthetic experience, I am obviously disregarding examples to the contrary. Drama has been the signal to social action; it has set in motion important social movements. Religious drama

The manifest content of the dream is important as a starting point; but with the accumulation of free associations, it becomes dispensable. Its exact recording is unnecessary; what is necessary is only the exact description of what the subject recalls. With the symptom, it is different. Here exact knowledge of all the relevant objective details is decisive.

In a literary work, of course, everything depends on the text (Bowers, 1959) and we owe a great debt of gratitude to those who have taken upon themselves the arduous task of restoring the original text, at least as far as it can be restored. In dream interpretation, the free associations will rectify the misrepresented detail (more often than not, a misrepresentation will even enrich the record, since it belongs in the realm of the sought-for free associations); by contrast, any flaw in the text of the literary work may misdirect the critic's associations and lead to wrong interpretations. No matter how far the interpretation of a text may take us from its manifest content, it must never take precedence over the play itself. An interpretation that turns *Hamlet* into a success story is patently wrong.

Yet a gap does exist between Horatio's encomium and Hamlet's behavior, at least when it is taken literally. Whether it is right or wrong, my suggested interpretation would explain why, in the face of the evidence, the spectator finds no difficulty agreeing with Horatio. Overwhelmed by the spirit of tragedy that pervades the play, he feels pity for Hamlet; he would not mind being Hamlet himself, for Hamlet is a hero in his eyes and, as all critics seem to agree, everyone finds in the character something of himself. But why? One could hardly assert that Hamlet's vicissitudes or any of the specific details of the play are likely to have much similarity with the experiences of those who behold the play or make it the subject of study. Yet the interpretation I suggest would provide a frame of reference that would encompass human destiny in its singularity. What Hamlet accomplishes symbolically, in my opinion, at the

---

has affected spectators in a way that goes far beyond the aesthetic experience. In 1322, the *Landgraf Friedrich der Freidige* witnessed a play about the 10 virgins. When the five foolish virgins were condemned, he exclaimed: "What is the faith of Christians if God does not take pity on us for the sake of Mary and all the saints?" Thereupon, he was stricken, and he spent the rest of his life in melancholia and sickness (Holstein, 1886, p. 10). Nowadays, this play would be attended by hardly any Christians. Perhaps it is the very play that has had such stupendous effect outside the aesthetic sphere on its contemporaries that is less likely to be able to arouse interest in subsequent generations. Since *Hamlet* has proven its power to arouse interest and attention throughout the centuries from the time of its first performance, I feel entitled to use the ill-defined term, "aesthetic experience," here to suggest that common denominator that underlies the variety of responses the play has evoked in the majority of instances.

end of the play, every man faces in one form or another, as the content of a wish or a fear or a dream.

If this is so, then we are dealing here with a well-circumscribed and realistically presented manifest content, some of whose elements, when they are interpreted as symbols, unite to produce the very opposite of what is stated by the manifest content. Man's unconscious responds to symbols in a way that goes beyond the limits of disciplined and reality-adjusted ideation. The playwright can rely on man's unconscious disposition to experience as symbols those reality events that he puts on the stage—so long as he does not give a warning and thus arouse defenses in the spectator. Only when he is aiming at a metaphysical interpretation of symbols, must he apply explicit techniques, as Shakespeare did in *Macbeth*. The symbols that come from the psychobiological sphere, and are formed under the pressure of the repressed, work automatically.

The particularly intense effect of the closing scene in *Hamlet* may be precisely the effect of the intertwining of two disparate chains of events: one, realistically presented, appeals to consciousness and rational thinking *in unisono* with reality; the other proceeds subterraneously, and without the spectator's awareness, by means of symbols that are implicitly attached to the realistic stage event. Viewed in this light, details that the rational mind is likely to regard as mere accidents lose that quality; they are instead converted into necessary and highly determined events, inherently enclosed within the scope of the protagonist's destiny. In psychoanalytic parlance, this means that reality events are converted into direct excrescences of the unconscious. It would be strange, indeed, if we found at the base of the universe that Shakespeare created, at a decisive *locus*, the factor of accident.

Thus I have not converted the tragic into its opposite; all I have done is to assert that, on the symbolic level, the stage action carries within its vitals, so to speak, its opposite. Only together do they make *Hamlet* what it is. I cannot stress sufficiently by how much the artistic effect is reduced when this technique is used explicitly—as, for example, by Ibsen, who tried to accomplish it in *Peer Gynt*.

Yet I would venture to suggest that there may always be two different plots in great drama, or perhaps only in those of post-medieval origin in the West. It is quite possible that the great dramatic effect, the intense tension from which the spectator is released, can be traced back in the end to the opposition that exists between the effects a play has on his conscious mind and those it has on his unconscious mind.[12] It would not be surprising if it turned out that the message that great comedy delivers to the unconscious is a very sad one. In the case of Aristophanes and of Molière, I would say, this is almost obvious; but I may be indulging all too liberally here in unwarranted generalizations.

To give one example: The two texts that the author constructs from the extant text of *Romeo and Juliet* lead to conclusions that are quite unique, I believe, in the Shakespeare literature. Starting from the seeming contradiction in Lady Capulet's speaking of herself as an old woman (*V.3.207*) (*Urtext*) and as a young woman (*I.3.71-73*) (interpolated addendum), Laqueur arrives at the conclusion that in the second plot Romeo was in love with Lady Capulet and Juliet in love with Tybalt. These conclusions can be refuted on the basis of their own premises. If no more than a common-sense psychology is used, the statements about Lady Capulet's age lose their supposedly contradictory character. When a young mother urges her young daughter to marry, she feels young; when she faces the dead body of her daughter, however, she feels wretchedly old. In *Hamlet*, according to Laqueur, the plot of the *Urtext* had a young Hamlet whose mother had premarital relations and conspired in the assassination of her husband, whereas in the new plot the Queen is free of any premarital guilt, does not marry Claudius but becomes his mistress, etc.

If a play actually consisted of two mutually contradictory additive plots, and the author was so compulsive, to boot, that he could not rectify a line once he had written it —such a play could lead only to dramatic disaster. By contrast, a play that has been written with such skill that a message that is almost the opposite of the concrete and realistic event on the stage is subliminally conveyed to the unconscious by the symbolic medium—such a play may succeed in arousing aesthetic tension of the highest intensity.

I have not yet come to the heart of the matter: I have not discussed the probability that the dying together of the Queen and her son actually symbolizes an act of union between them. Because the problem of dying together seems to be quite visible in *Romeo and Juliet,* I feel it necessary to make a few comments on that play as well. Romeo's character has been a considerable plague to the critics. Since they have been searching forever for *hamartia* in some shape or form, it has even been doubted that *Romeo and Juliet* is a tragedy at all (Alexander, 1955, p. 136).

[12] I am here coming, even if in different form, close to Laqueur's (1955) abstruse theory, which compels me to make a special point. According to this author, in 32 of Shakespeare's 36 plays there existed an *Urtext* which was not written by another author but by Shakespeare himself; the latter changed, so to speak in midstream, the whole drift of the plot, and therefore had to interpolate a huge number of addenda. It was, as the author claims, a personal element in Shakespeare's creative style never to eliminate or to adjust the lines of the *Urtext* that stood in contradiction to the new plot. The result is that the text, as we now know it, is not a synthesis, but an agglomerate of two—albeit quite different—plots.

Yet Hegel found the tragic element in Romeo's "complete identification of himself with the power that moves him," in his not being a son or a citizen as well as a lover, but rather that his love is "the whole of him" (Alexander, 1955, p. 137). This view makes a little better sense than did Grebanier's previously mentioned finding of over-weeningness in Romeo which, as the author admits, is in contradiction to Shakespeare's "pair of star-crossed lovers." Other critics have found fault with the construction of the play.[13]

When Shakespeare has us believe that the family feud is "the only obstacle in the way of the lovers' happiness," he is allegedly forgetting that Romeo's love of Rosaline (who was also a Capulet) was frustrated not by the family rift, but by "her ideal of celibacy." Here, purportedly, is "a blot on the play," since either there is inconsistency or the feud cannot be taken seriously (p. xxviif). On the other hand, Shakespeare is reproached for the fact that he "blurs the focus and never makes up his mind entirely as to who is being punished, and for what reason," since the protagonists' "conduct is infantile" and "both of them are lacking, at certain points, in mature poise and balance" (p. xxixf).

Alexander (1955, pp. 139-142) has restored, and with a great deal of success, Romeo's character; he has shown him to be "a whole man." I should like to add a few remarks in order to demonstrate that the defense "that Shakespeare's plays are liable to be only partly naturalistic" (p. xxviii) is essentially inadequate, as is the *deus-ex-machina*-like apologia that it is in poetry that he achieved his successes and therefore the other failures do not count against him (p. xxxiii).

In *Romeo and Juliet,* in my opinion, Shakespeare offered a panoramic view of love. In the foreground is a spectrum that runs from crude sexual urge to its very opposite. I would guess that there has never been another play in which there is, at one and the same time, so much obscenity and so much of the grandest love poetry. But the panorama of love is not limited to love between the sexes, or the love of parents and particularly of mothers for their children; homosexuality in the shape of friendship (references to manifest homosexuality are not missing), and the sublimated love of God, also find their place.[14]

[13] The references in Roman figures that follow refer to G. I. Duthie's "Introduction" to the Cambridge edition of *Romeo and Juliet.*

[14] For a comment on Shakespeare's bawdy in *Romeo and Juliet,* which I find favorable to my view, see Stewart (1949, p. 18f).

Now the remarkable thing about the tragedy is that, of all the forms of love, it is only the one containing the synthesis of the two poles of love that leads to death. The relationship between Romeo and Juliet is characterized by perfect balance, by an ideal synthesis between sheer physical craving and the most affectionate tenderness. The temptation to put forward as the opposite of sexual appetite or passion, some form of chaste, pure, nonsexual affection may well have been close at hand, in view of the ancient tradition to that effect. I regard it as a cardinal point that Shakespeare chose, as the ideal love in this case, a sexually fulfilled love. In a modern play, this would have taken place outside the marriage vows; in Shakespeare's play, however, sexual fulfillment follows so closely after first sight that we can be quite sure that nothing would have stopped these two lovers.

As to their being united as well by something that lies at the opposite pole from the sexual urge, the poet makes that certain and beyond any doubt. The life, well-being and bliss of the other have become, for each of them, more important than their own. Romeo does not hesitate to give away, for the sake of the beloved, his own name, which symbolizes self, status, tradition, prestige. The two lovers evolve cosmic phantasies about each other, the universe being meaningful to each only as a projection of the other. Gratification of the sexual urge does not alter the fact that one is the center of the other. The self, in psychoanalytic parlance, is depleted of cathexis, which has instead flowed into the self of the beloved. And Shakespeare's message is that such love leads to death. Why?

I have tried to show how at various nodal points in *Hamlet,* the overwhelming effect of the play is brought about by a device through which deep, repressed psychological truths are shunted into occurrences on stage, which are then presented in such a way that they thrust themselves upon the spectator, as if they were more real than reality itself. These latter occurrences are so closely knit together and propelled with so much force and pressure that, at first sight, no covert or referential specifically psychological motivation is needed for purposes of explanation—the single exception, of course, being Hamlet's delay. Yet these apparently simple and clearly determined reality events are actually the carriers of a vast scope of psychological truths or insights. I find the same style in *Romeo and Juliet.*

The reality events there unfold with similar pressure and forcefulness. The interfamilial feud may appear to be "rather trivial, rather silly" (p. xxix); nevertheless it is forcefully and quite adequately presented as a formidable obstacle to the union of the two lovers—a union that they have no hope of solemnizing while still remaining in harmony with their own families. When Grebanier suggests that Romeo "has had but to inform old Capulet that he is now his son-in-law, and. . . Juliet's father would have welcomed him" (1960, p. 184), he has not considered *III.5. 126-195.*

What is more important, he apparently has no feeling for poetry, or for the shy chasteness of a young woman (a very young woman, at that), who could never confess to her progenitor the fact of her intercourse, and would surely never permit her lover to act as an interlocutor on her behalf. We may not look at this secret marriage with the "rational" eyes of the middle class. Even so, Grebanier will perhaps understand some of the problems in *Romeo and Juliet* better, if he puts himself three decades back from his own day, preferably below the Mason-Dixon line, and sees Romeo's cheeks as a shade darker than those of Juliet.

I regard it as a very meaningful point that Romeo's first love was also a Capulet. If she were not, the whole tragedy would move slightly out of focus. The logic of naturalism is in no way offended by that fact, as one critic has asserted. As actually observed on the stage, the Montague-Capulet enmity does not make nuptials as such impossible. But first things come first. If Rosaline had indeed responded to Romeo's flirtation, he might have had to worry about a marriage contract. Since the whole affair, however, never reached the state of marriage (assuming that Romeo would have wanted to marry Rosaline at all), it would have taken a rather obsessional young man to become excited about anticipated obstacles to a marriage bond at a time when the pursued is enforcing aloofness.

In my view, however, Shakespeare conveyed very subtly the idea that, under identical environmental circumstances, such love as that which Romeo harbored for Rosaline does not necessarily lead to tragic involvements—a fine point by means of which he suggests that it may not be only the family feud that drives the lovers to their bitter end. What is it then? Family feud, fate, the stars, misfortune, the lovers' heedlessness —and a long series of pure accidents.

There is an interesting crescendo in the rhythms of hurdles and countermeasures. The family feud is overcome by a secret marriage. This accomplished, the murder of Mercutio, which makes Romeo's revenge compelling, raises a larger obstacle in the shape of banishment. The Friar's plan to undo the unhappy consequences of the banishment is obstructed by Capulet's insistence upon Juliet's early wedding with Paris. This new and most threatening obstacle is ingeniously removed by the Friar's arrangement of Juliet's sham death. In turn, the messenger to Romeo is detained in a plague-infected house. This the Friar counteracts by going himself to the churchyard. All in vain! Romeo arrives a few minutes too early and his ill fate is sealed. Perhaps there might even then have been a happy ending—if only Romeo had arrived at the moment of Juliet's awakening. And yet the slain Paris would surely have plunged the lovers into everlasting unhappiness.

As in *Hamlet*, a compelling chain of reality events, covering a broad area drawn from all strata of life (political institutions, family structure, male rivalry, disease), has conspired to make two lovers tragically unhappy. It almost looks, not as if the lovers themselves unskillfully undid favorable chances, but rather as if events outside them were maliciously directed against their being able to achieve the fulfillment of their cherished wishes. And we agree: fight as they may, they will never find happiness. The vagueness of which the critics have spoken, which pervades the play with regard to the causes for the lovers' ill fate, this "blurring of the focus," is precisely what constitutes the greatness of the play.

It is my feeling that in itself *Romeo and Juliet* is a flawless masterpiece, and thus comes close to *Hamlet:* the latter is greater because its universe of discourse is larger, almost all-encompassing, whereas *Romeo and Juliet's* message is limited to saying that, among all the forms of love, there is one that is not viable—which is a much smaller universe of discourse.

The love of Romeo and Juliet is the most intense that man can experience and feel. The passionate drives, in their inexhaustibility and in the intensity of youth, create a psychic resonance of an amplitude that no later period in human life will ever match. The faith and incomparable idealism of youth casts this spell: that the loved object is absolutely irreplaceable. One or two more years and the "mature" ego will recognize this as an illusion, indeed the most charming illusion of all. But once the self has become hardened and is no longer under the spell of the illusion, the first step—small as it may be—has been taken toward that frightful end-product with which we become acquainted in the old Montagues and Capulets, who are unable to love any longer. If they had been able to survive, Romeo and Juliet would one day be just like their progenitors, whose repelling squabbles we are forced to witness.

It is this synthesis of inordinate physical passions with inordinate faith, idealism, trust, and tenderness that makes Romeo and Juliet the perfect lovers; indeed, they are no longer brothers or sisters, sons or daughters, citizens or believers, they are one-dimensional lovers. No canon, no prospect of hell-fire can hold *them* back; without a second's hesitation, they carry out their suicide when it has become unalterably certain to them that the last embrace has faded. And despite all the preaching of the Churches, the ideas that Romeo and Juliet do not go to Heaven would be almost unimaginable; I cannot believe that any spectator left the Elizabethan theater with pity for the damnation they would, theologically speaking, have to suffer because they died in sin.[15]

This perfect relationship is, even under optimal conditions, doomed by two sets of factors. One is, in a sense, extraneous to the relationship and has already been mentioned. The maturation of the personality, knowledge of the world "as it is," often results in rigidities. The ability to surrender oneself entirely to the love object becomes limited; the self's own—if you wish, selfish—demands make themselves felt and, if they do not make an end of this type of love, at the least they severely limit it.

What is more important is that such relationships as are exemplified in *Romeo and Juliet* are also *inherently ill-fated*, as can often be clinically observed. I would say that the disproportion between the stir of the event and the strength of the vessel is too great. Such relationships have a better prognosis in a youth who is less differentiated, less sophisticated or, one could say, culturally more primitive. Yet, with such primitivization of personality, the whole relationship takes on a different shape, and for that reason it cannot possibly be regarded as belonging to the Romeo-and-Juliet type of experience.

In its unsophisticated form the elation may be as great; yet there is less surprise to it, it is taken almost for granted. The love of Florizel and Perdita is viable, even though there, too, family and politics and status interfere; yet that love is also separated by miles from that of Romeo and Juliet. Here, too, the genius may have tried to undo an "early wound"; but, in order to make the love of youth compatible with life, he had to control his passion, so that the possibility of the two lovers living apart, even though it is not acceptable to them, is at least potentially conceiva-

---

[15] So little does the catechism count for when it comes face to face with true art: in terms of Christian moral theology, *Romeo and Juliet* is an unchristian play! It is interesting to view the suicide of Romeo and Juliet in the light of the discussion about Hamlet and the moral problem of suicide. Frye (1963, pp. 24-31) uses their suicide successfully to show up the inappropriateness of most critical efforts that try to arrive at an understanding of Shakespeare's plays by way of an application of theology.

ble. Neither Perdita nor Florizel would attempt to commit suicide if they were cut off from each other; a period of deep melancholia would suffice.

Clearly this is essentially different from the situation with regard to Romeo and Juliet. Not only are their passions so inordinate that any postponement of gratification, waiting, so-called "adjustment to reality" is out of the question; their mutual empathy, their experiencing of each other's emotions—each becoming the sounding board for the other, while maintaining personal identity, and even reaching full identity through total surrender to the other—these thin out their vital capacity to such an extent that they are *bound to perish.* [16]

In clinical reality, a tragic ending of that sort is usually replaced by an abrupt ending of the love relationship and, as if to deny the greatness of the experience, we call it, pejoratively, an "infatuation." Be that as it may, in the case of Romeo and Juliet, it is not infatuation, inasmuch as an unbreakable and, for that very reason, a nonviable state has evolved. A modern playwright would have elaborated on all this, but Shakespeare's technique of presenting conscious and even preferably unconscious processes by means of reality events limited him to expressing only the exquisite feelings that pervade the two lovers. [17]

If he had focused exclusively on the family feud or on the stars, he could never have created the truly tragic atmosphere that pervades the play—namely, that such love goes beyond the human capacity for endurance and through *inherent necessity* must lead to the disintegration of those who, by the very nature and intensity of their attraction, are prevented from freeing themselves of it. There is no tragic flaw either in Romeo or in Juliet, they are the perfect lovers; [18] and those who have un-

---

[16] It has been noted by critics that there are great stylistic differences in the play: passages of high conceit give way to profound ones; some passages express the deepest feelings of the human heart, others are highly ornate, conventional, artificial, full of verbal ingenuities (pp. xiv, xxxiv). These discrepancies have been explained in various ways. To me they constitute a reflection of that inner disproportion between strength of passion and fragility of the vessel, which could not have been conveyed, on the formal level, better than by having two antithetical styles pervade the lovers' speeches.

[17] To my delight I found in an author who is surely above any suspicion of psychoanalytic bias a similar procedure of dissolving stage events into psychic processes. Murry (1936, p. 318) says of *Othello* that Iago "is to be understood as a mere source of motive power whose function it is to bring the seed of death that is in the love of Othello and Desdemona to maturity within the compass of a play. What would be, in ordinary human life, *a process lasting many years*, with no violent outcome: ending merely in the death of love, and perhaps in its re-birth, has to be turned into 'sensation.' And Iago is the means by which it is achieved" (my italics)

[18] The meaning of Shakespeare's perfect plays can never be put into one simple formula, and I am well aware that a different reading is conceivable. In terms of the external events, it is Romeo's killing of Tybalt that places a very serious obstacle before the two lovers, and the translation into

covered all kinds of psychopathology in their relationship have uncovered, if it is really to be found there, only that from which the true love of youth can grow.

Gottfried Keller (1819-1890), the great Swiss novelist, wrote a short story *Romeo and Juliet in the Village (Romeo und Julia auf dem Dorfe)*. In it, two peasant neighbors fall into a discord that ruins both families. Their children are in love, but marriage is out of the question for them, as the result of a variety of external circumstances. The story ends with the two lovers sneaking at night onto a boat that is anchored on the shore and sailing it down a river. "When the boat approached the town, two pale figures, holding each other in a firm embrace, glided from the dark mass into the cold surf in the frost of the autumn morning."

The structure of the problem is quite different here from what it is in Shakespeare's tragedy. The reader is left with the belief that the two young people, who would otherwise have been quite capable of living happily together and making a successful marriage, were forced into suicide by their parents, who ruined each other's prosperous station by a chain of evil acts. Here the dying together is definitely a love symbol, for we can be certain that the two did not enter Heaven as virgins, even though the act was not actually comsummated before they boarded the boat for their last journey.

Dying together stands here for union and is conspicuously emphasized as a major contrast to Shakespeare's play, in which the tragic aura is heightened by the fact that each lover dies within sight of the dead or seemingly dead body of the other.

The fear of dying alone is a particular fear. Many people report that, if they knew for certain that they would die in the arms of their beloved spouse, they would have no fear of death at all. There may be a

---

psychology of the circumstances under which this happens yields a result that is of interest to the depth psychologist. When Romeo is challenged by Tybalt, he masters himself, since he has, after all, become one of the Capulets. In trying to separate Mercutio and Tybalt, however, he becomes an accessory to the former's death and from then on nothing can hold him back from revenging his friend. It was, in the last analysis, his love of Juliet that caused Mercutio's death, just as it was his love of Mercutio that made him kill Tybalt. In all this there is, on the one hand, the insinuation of a reproach against Juliet and on the other the implication of the effect of a homosexual tie.

Thus it may be said that it was homosexuality that in the end caused the defeat of Romeo's love for Juliet, and, indeed, the acute infatuations of late adolescence often come about under the pressure and necessity of the defense against homosexuality, since that so often constitutes a threat to heterosexuality in general. If this strand is regarded as a principal element, then one is entitled to conclude that the relationship of the two lovers was brought down by Romeo's homosexuality. I shall not discuss here whether or not the two interpretations I have suggested can be rendered accordant. For psychoanalytic interpretations of *Romeo and Juliet* see Menninger (1938, p. 320f), Reik (1945, p. 88f), Fliess (1957, pp. 263f, 274).

defense in this attitude: yet, depending on the particular instance, there may also be much truth (cf. McClelland, 1966). There is a passage in a German novel, whose title escapes me, in which the old pastor regards it as an act of Divine grace that he was privileged to carry out the charitable act of closing his beloved wife's eyes. What he meant was that he was permitted to spare her the cross of having to live in solitude. Such attitudes presuppose a strong, viable object relationship. The way in which Romeo and Juliet die is the very antithesis of dying together; this I link with the meaning of the play—namely, that their relationship was destined, for inherent reasons, to break apart. When Romeo says: "Well, Juliet, I will lie with thee tonight" *(V.1.34),* his statement does not conjure up the image of a permanent reunion.[19]

The tragedy of Antony and Cleopatra strikes me as being a desperate struggle for the achievement of that very dying together that becomes openly the consummation of the greatest closeness. Cleopatra knows that, as long as Antony is engaged in the pursuits of a statesman or a warrior, she will never possess him or, at least, she will not possess him as much as she needs, wants, and, is perhaps even entitled to, since she is, after all, the embodiment of womanly passionate love. My idea of Cleopatra may sound somewhat strange. Her intense narcissism notwithstanding, she is the ideal type of a certain female character, feminine to the highest degree. Thus, when her 60 ships turn about at Actium and flee, I do not see this as proof of aggressive or destructive impulses on her part, but rather as evidence of her great love, for it must have been clear to her that Antony's political defeat would also be hers, and for a woman with her ambition, that was no small matter.

This was the beginning of a process that deprived Antony step by step of any opportunity to channelize his energy and interest into a nonamorous activity. Antony is for her the ideal, the most masculine of men, as she states distinctly in the cosmic dream that she conveys to Dolabella *(V.2.79 -92),* and there is even a hint that, had she wanted to, she would have been able to ensnare Octavius Caesar as well. Her suicide, it seems

---

[19] In a relationship as mutually destructive and ferocious as that of Macbeth and his Lady, it is significant that in their dying they are separated by distances of both time and space. About Othello's and Desdemona's "dying together" not much needs to be said; here their dying in close sequence stands for brutal rejection and eternal separation. Frye (1963, p. 31) quotes J. A. Bryant's interpretation of *Othello,* which is quite different. See Eliot (1932) for an interpretation of Othello's last speech, which supports the view that Othello's suicide is the very antithesis of dying together. By equating himself with "the circumcised dog" at the moment of his death, Othello undoubtedly separates himself for all eternity from the love-object.

to me, is not enforced by the absence of any prospect of another victory over Caesar, which is hinted at by the fact that, upon looking at her dead body, he marvels that there is no swelling and says:

> but she looks like sleep,
> As she would catch another Antony
> In her strong toil of grace.

(V.2.345-347)

Be that as it may, it seems certain that Cleopatra would never have loved another man. Yet what did happen to Antony while he lived? "The lovers," writes Berry (1965, p. 49), "never enjoy a moment's peace together and when they are divided in space . . . they are no happier either." With great sensitivity, he pictures the external and internal forces of division that are at work. But how different this is from what happened to Romeo and Juliet! Had Antony and Cleopatra been permitted the kind of existence we are wont to ascribe to oriental sovereigns— strolling through gardens, unmolested by vulgar concern about the welfare of their people—they might well have lived out their lives in the all-consuming task of mutually gratifying their transported passions. This is quite by contrast with Romeo and Juliet, as I conceive of them.

In *Antony and Cleopatra* one gets the impression that the vessel was, indeed, solid and strong enough to bear the enormous agitation produced by the paroxysmal carnality of the chief characters, strong enough to uphold in the midst of this agitation their subtlest distinguishing qualities, the passions, so that even agitation could not flatten out their finely chiseled profiles. It is the world that again and again interferes with the grand love drama—not necessarily out of hostility to them but merely by way of the givens of existence. Thus the *persona amans* and the *persona laborans* must remain separate.

Cleopatra, the arch-female, who is so incredibly wise and magnanimous in the world of passions, knows this, for apparently Antony was the first and only man she loved so much that she found him worthy of being destroyed by her, in order that she might be undividedly loved by him. Rightly she assumes that she can engineer this state of undivided love only by making Antony believe that she is dead. He responds thus to the false information: "I will o'ertake thee, Cleopatra"; "we'll . . . make the ghosts gaze . . . and all the haunt be ours"; "I will be a bridegroom in my death, and run into't as to a lover's bed."

One could object that Antony's last thoughts before his death are not directed toward Cleopatra, and that a great deal has intervened between his death and hers. There is no doubt that the idea of dying together as a consummation of love is not stated explicitly at the end of the play; yet some of what Antony says, when he is apprised of her alleged death, points strongly in that direction. His supreme effort to die while looking at her might be taken as a confirmation of this view.

As far as Cleopatra is concerned, following Antony's departure, her remaining hours become for the most part a hurrying after him. "The stroke of death" becomes "a lover's pinch." Iras' death is to be regretted because on her Antony will "spend that kiss which is my heaven to have." The asp at her breast becomes a baby, and she dies with her lover's name on her lips and the question of why she should stay.

My guess is that in *The Winter's Tale,* too, there lies hidden the quest to die together, but I shall leave that possibility unexamined.

Once can distinguish between two kinds of symbolic interpretation in the psychoanalysis of literary works. One of these has to do with the symbolic meaning of speech, about which there will probably be little dispute. In *Romeo and Juliet,* or in Hamlet's discourse with Ophelia in the mousetrap scene, there is much talk that has to be understood as symbolic of gross sexual matters ("country matters"). A large part of it consists of allusions and therefore does not fall within the orbit of symbols, as psychoanalysis understands them; but aside from these direct references to physical processes, there is plenty that may still contain symbols, in the narrower sense of the word.

The second sort of symbol, however, is far more refractory to proof and explanation.

Symons (1928, p. 116), in a psychoanalytic inquiry into the graveyard scene that is of unquestionable merit—although I disagree with its general drift—interprets the two skulls that are thrown out of the graves by the first gravediggers as testicles. He proceeds on the principle that every detail of a literary work is psychically determined—I assume he means in the way the single element of dreams supposedly is—and, since these organs customarily appear in pairs, his interpretation would at least have the advantage of explaining that detail, although it is precisely here that esthetic (nonmotivational) factors may have their say. Symons does not, of course, introduce the interpretation solely because of the number two; that is only a welcome side-effect, with regard to a detail that might otherwise appear to be "psychologically" neutral. The idea of discovering this symbol in the skull seems to have come to him as the result of the profusion of references to the castration theme in the graveyard scene.

Since the theme of death is generally connected with castration in psychoanalytic theory, it is understandable that in the graveyard scene a score of details can be brought into connection with it. Yet one would still prefer to see more evidence before accepting the identity of the interpreted element with the symbolized content. The skull is also, after all, an iconographic element in the presentation of the crucifixion, in which it traditionally means Adam's skull, or refers to Golgotha; yet the crucifixion very probably has in the unconscious the meaning of castration. Be that as it may, I do not find any significant enlargement of our insight into the meaning of the graveyard scene as the result of this particular interpretation, which I have selected quite arbitrarily for the sake of making a general point.

Yet I can readily assume (I could even be convinced) that elements in such literary pieces as the graveyard scene are able to evoke in an audience, by way of the very itensity of their impact, unconscious imagery of the sort that Symons has suggested. The extent and the depth to which the unconscious is stimulated—perhaps one might even say irritated—in a sensitive spectator by the contents of literary masterpieces probably goes far beyond what is generally recognized. The bulk of this imagery is, one has to conjecture, of a personal nature: it consists mainly of associative links that are meaningful only in terms of accidental combinations particular to the individual spectator. Yet some of these associations would probably be found to be statistically preponderant.

If the unconscious associations to the elements of a play's manifest content were known, the psychoanalytic exploration of symbols could then be placed on an experimental basis, and some safeguards might thereby be established against the danger of arbitrariness. I do not think, however, that a psychoanalytic symbolic interpretation of any one element in a literary work necessarily presupposes that an equivalent process is actually taking place inside the mind's penetralia of any one of the spectators. I would regard such an interpretation as having to do with a content that is concealed in the play objectively—that is to say, independently of the question of whether or not the author or the audience does actually respond to it in their unconscious.

It is well known that the meaning of religious symbols changes during the course of time, that later generations may be completely unaware of the meaning that the symbol had at the time it was born. The psychoanalytic interpretation of symbols is sometimes helped by historical research, for the language of the unconscious is often less concealed during earlier phases; but when I suggest that the dying together of Hamlet and Gertrude is a symbolic act of union, I do not expect historical research to unearth a solid proof, or any kind of proof at all, although I might find a somewhat remote implication to that effect in Livy's story.

One does not really have to go quite as far back as some have, and maintain that the original Hamlet story was merely a Northern transformation of the Roman tale of Brutus, in order to become aware of a surprising reverse parallel: Tarquin, having been frightened by an apparition, sends his two sons Titus and Arnus to Delphi, in the company of his nephew Junius Brutus; when the young men ask to which of them the kingdom will belong, the answer is: "Whichever of you shall first kiss his mother, shall possess Rome," whereupon Brutus acts as if he has stumbled and touches the earth with his lips, the earth being the mother of all mankind.

The fact that the ancestors of Rosencrantz and Guildenstern were pretenders to the throne, with even a better claim to it than that of Hamlet's Roman ancestor, and the fact that Hamlet's ancestor was the companion in this instance, not the accompanied, should not concern us, as much as the enigmatic oracle with its statement about kissing the mother. Here the analyst would not hesitate to establish a connection with the oedipal myth, by maintaining that the oracle is promising the kingdom to that hero who has the courage to take possession of the mother. The subtle point in the saga would be that Brutus *understands* the true meaning of the oracle (equivalent to Oedipus' solving of the riddle) —which indicates that, while internally he is free enough to take possession of the mother, he restrains himself and performs the act only on the symbolic level. But this brings us quite close to what I have in mind.[20]

Symbolic interpretations of the sort I am suggesting here call for a scrupulous consideration of each detail. In so doing, one discovers that more than one interpretive possibility exists. The queen's affectionate turn toward her son is undisputed: there are no longer harsh words nor any recriminations; the relationship has become, in effect, conflict-free. Even though there were earlier signs of her siding with the son against

---

[20] My reference to Livy should by no means be understood as an effort to prove my point. With it, I cannot hope to do more than demonstrate that the interpretation fits the texture of the play. This "textual fitness," of course, will be accepted by only a few.

the husband, she now exhibits open preference for Hamlet. Physical contact is stressed by the Queen's wiping her son's face, an act that may evoke the legend of St. Veronica. The fact that the Queen "carouses" to Hamlet's fortune and thus inadvertently brings about her own death, rather than Hamlet's, which was Claudius's intention, constitutes the strongest possible symbol of her self-sacrifice for the son and her defection from her husband. The whole segment then culminates in her apprising him of the King's act of murder and thereby becoming the proximate cause of Claudius's own undoing. The ancestry of this element goes back almost to prehistoric times, since Gaia (or Rhea) twice encourages the youngest son to kill his father.

All these elements, taken together, strongly support the imagery of a symbolic consummation of the oedipal situation. So too Hamlet's addressing Claudius with the ironic question "Is thy union here?"; this is reminiscent of Hamlet's "Now get you to my lady's chamber," when he beholds Yorick's skull. In both instances death appears as a force separating the parents. But then a turn takes place, and Hamlet dismisses the dying King with "Follow my mother." This may continue the irony; but it may also mean, "I dismiss both of you. I am freed of parental imagery." I do not know which of these two alternatives is in fact to be preferred. The latter is of interest, in that many an analyst disagrees with the proposition that the male has to accept the mother in his unconscious as a libidinal object, in order to evolve his virility, but rather insists that this is attained only when the other sex has been freed of all oedipal taint. The ending of *Hamlet* may favor this view.

A decision upon this question, however, is of subordinate relevance since it has no bearing on the symbolic drift that I attribute to the last scene. Either way Hamlet emerges as the victor. He has regained the status of the ideal man: he is now an infinitely better person than he was at the beginning of the play, having been freed from whatever was involved in his having been the "mirror of society."

In short he is now autonomous, the ideal-type of individuality, and he is capable of action. The divergence between stage action and symbolic meaning is thus seen to be extreme. The two are in fact opposites, contradictory to each other, as they are perhaps in no other drama. Shakespeare had in effect created a new type of tragedy. The time was ripe for it, after all, since almost two millennia had already passed since Aristotle wrote his *Poetics*.

10. Fortinbras and Hamlet
(With a Note on the Effect of Elizabethan Stage Performances)

I

It may not be repetitive to stress here once again the interconnections between the main plot and the subplots:[1] Hamlet is a young man whose father, the King, has been murdered by his uncle, who thereupon married Hamlet's mother and succeeded to the throne; Laertes is a young man whose father was murdered by Hamlet; Fortinbras is a young man whose father was slain in a duel by Hamlet's father, and whose uncle thereupon succeeded to the throne thus left vacant; Gertrude is a woman whose husband was killed by her brother-in-law, whom she then married; Ophelia is a young woman whose father is killed by her lover, and who then "goes to pieces" under the impact of that event.

In short, all the chief characters except Fortinbras and Horatio die violent deaths. The idea that all this is set forth by Shakespeare solely out of adherence to a tradition, however, and that there is no meaning in it beyond what appears in the manifest action—that idea is so alien to my way of thinking that I am reluctant even to discuss such a possibility. There must have been, I feel certain, some other intention or purpose to it all. The Fortinbras story, for example, does not appear in the *Ur-Hamlet*, except for the dying Hamlet's request that Horatio "bring the

[1] For double and multiple plot in Elizabethan drama see Fergusson (1949, p. 114f), Salinger (1955, p. 58). For remarks on subplots in other Elizabethan plays, see Eliot (1931, p. 154f); see also Empson (1960).

crown to Norway for my cousin Duke Fortinbras so the kingdom will not fall into other hands" *(V.6)*[2]. One might consider the story in the *Ur-Hamlet* as having been tailored to a German audience, which was not familiar with the tradition, so that the Fortinbras aspect of it could easily have been deleted, if only in order to give the play a suitable length.

On the other hand, the *Ur-Hamlet* is richer by one character than either the Quartos or the Folio. This is the court fool Phantasmo, who plays a leading role in the earlier version, in that Ophelia, following her rejection by Hamlet, falls in love with Phantasmo in her madness. He is stabbed to death by Hamlet after he confesses that it was he who brought the goblet from which the Queen drank, this being the proximate cause of her death. In the *Ur-Hamlet*, parts that are later given in Shakespeare's text to Polonius and Osric are assigned to Phantasmo.

It is not at all likely that the Fortinbras subplot was so integral to the tradition that it could not have been deleted from what was, to boot, Shakespeare's longest play. It may be true that the Ghost, Hamlet's delay in carrying out the revenge (whatever his reason for it), the violent deaths of the mother and the King in the end—that all these were so deeply ingrained in the audience's expectations and associations with regard to the imagery surrounding Hamlet, that a later playwright would have hesitated to omit or to change them. By contrast Fortinbras remains a highly peripheral figure in the mechanics of the play; actually he is often omitted in modern performances (Berry, 1947, p. 94).[3]

The comparison of the *Ur-Hamlet* with Shakespeare's tragedy demonstrates the freedom from tradition with which Shakespeare allowed himself to go about shaping his own plot construction—except for an inner core that he evidently regarded as inviolable. Apparently, he felt no need or desire to reorganize or change that inner core, since—at least it seems reasonable to assume this—it was chiefly this that aroused his interest or attracted him, to such an extent that he chose to make it the raw stuff of his great tragedy.

[2] For a discussion of the development of the historical antecedents of the Fortinbras element, see Lawrence, 1946.

[3] The fact that contemporary audiences do not feel they are missing anything essential when they see the play without Fortinbras does not warrant any conclusion with regard to the expectations of an Elizabethan audience. It is noteworthy to report what happens to this role when a great actor takes it under his wing. Holmes (1964, p. 45) reports that Basil Gill, when playing the Ghost in 1936, "reappeared under a false name as an incredibly young and handsome Fortinbras. . . . Those who remember that magnificent and barbaric figure, with its golden locks and winged helmet glittering in the evening sunlight, will not easily forget the tremendous effect gained by the employment of a major actor to dominate the last moments of the tragedy."

The leading feature of that inner core was—and remained, in Shakespeare's hands—a son's reaction to his father's violent death. There are altogether four fathers (including one father substitute) in the play who suffer that fate, and three sons and one younger brother have to grapple with the ensuing conflicts. The cross-relationship to the female subplots is also quite evident: two men, who are beloved by two women, are killed by two men who are likewise beloved by them. While the sons know the full history of their fathers' vicissitudes, there is doubt in at least one instance whether the woman knows that she is in love with her husband's murderer. Yet it is a cardinal fact that in the life of each of the characters a violent death takes place. One is inclined to add that, according to the Hamlet-play, it looks as if suffering the violent death of a beloved person were part and parcel of human fate. There is also a sort of chain reaction among the males: Old Fortinbras is slain by Old Hamlet, who is slain by Claudius, who is slain by Hamlet, who is slain by Laertes, who is slain in turn by Hamlet (Polonius' death being perhaps an asymmetrical side branch, which may offend the purist's sense of order).

There are also other descending series. We know most about Hamlet's relationship to his two fathers, less but still quite a bit about Laertes' relationship to his father, and very little about Fortinbras' relationship to his. The same decrease in information exists with regard to the mothers: Laertes' mother is mentioned only once, Fortinbras' not at all.

It is interesting to measure the relative amounts of information supplied by the play itself with regard to the past of the parental figures. About the Queen's early past, nothing more is revealed with certainty than what a son is able to observe—for example, how she responded to the child's father. Among the father figures, it is really Polonius who talks the most about his past; we get from him some inkling of his youthful conduct.

In their old age, parents often do start to reveal things about themselves that, up to that time, they had kept secret even from their adult children. Hamlet's father lets his son know that he had maintained strict faithfulness in his marriage, and apparently he does not do so for the purpose of sharing knowledge with him, but rather in order to build up by moralizing his son's determination for the task of revenge. It is noteworthy that Polonius, by contrast, refers to his past sexual transgressions.

Yet the lacunae with regard to the past of some parental figures, as well as of some of the chief characters, are in themselves no source of vagueness, since such gaps may often be filled in by contrast with what is known; I suggest that, in this case, the relative absence of information stands as an index of the absence of conflict. If Fortinbras' mother is not mentioned at all, this may be understood as an indication that no conflict existed between Fortinbras and his mother. The one reference that Laertes makes to his mother is sufficient to reconstruct feelings of guilt, and oversensitivity on his part about her chastity—feelings of a kind, however, that apparently do not lead to conflict but rather serve as a spur to action.

It appears evident, to me at least, that the center of the play lies in such questions as: "what creates conflict?" "what is the structure of conflict?" "what are the reactions to conflict?" "what are the solutions to it?" rather than in "what keeps a subject conflict-free?" (although this last question may find an answer, too).

Fortinbras is not the sort of personality about whom one could write great tragedy. He might possibly be the proper subject of an epos; one could perhaps write a beautiful paean about him. Be that as it may, in terms of the tragedy's meaning, he is an integral part thereof, even though in stage reality he takes a somewhat distant and peripheral place.[4] I even have the impression that some aestheticians would regard him as something of an unfortunate by-product, like the unwanted side-effects of an otherwise wholesome drug. Aesthetically he may appear to the modern reader as a negligible curlicue, loading the entire structure by just enough to create confusion, or else to break the unity of action through the unnecessary intrusion of a foreign body. Indeed, if one judges *Hamlet* in terms of modern drama, with its aim of making a deep impression on the audience even if at the expense of artistic integrity, one may view the Fortinbras episode skeptically.

Hamlet is more than a play that leaves a deep impression on the audience. I feel inclined to speculate that, at that stage of his career, Shakespeare was able to take this effect for granted. Just as Mozart must have assumed at times that he could compose better than any of his con-

---

[4] Berry (1947, p. 94) admits to Fortinbras only the function of serving "as a foil to Prince Hamlet." This function seems to have been suggested earlier by J. Q. Adams, in 1929 (quoted by Lawrence 1946, p. 687).

temporaries, so must Shakespeare have taken it for granted, by the time he came to the writing of *Hamlet,* that nothing could come from his pen that would not be great theater. He therefore aimed at something quite different—namely, the creation of life (cf. Alexander, 1955, p. 154). That such creation would probably also mean prestige, admiration, success was perhaps a welcome side effect; but is there any reason to believe that he would have written different plays, if his audience had been narrow enough not to respond favorably to his literary products?[5]

I can scarcely imagine such consequences. A play such as *Hamlet* is more than just a play; it can be looked at as something like the *Divine Comedy,* in that it presents a cosmos, a kind of universe, and not merely one narrow section of existence. To be sure, the span of the cosmos is narrower in *Hamlet* than it is in Dante's epos. *Hamlet* may appear to be more like a cross-section than a longitudinal study. It is the Fortinbras element, however, that enlarges the circumference of the tragic circle.

Without that element, its circle would still be broad enough to raise the mental metabolism of an audience to a high pitch; but it is only the Fortinbras episode that brings the play close to what may be called "the tragedy of man." This may sound like an overvaluation of a detail, even if one does concede that that detail possesses its own beauty, meaning and dramatic necessity. It would indeed be an overvaluation, if its importance were assigned to it at the expense of the other strands of action. I think of it rather as the final touch, elevating the play beyond the bounds of a tragic hero's vicissitudes.

Main plot and subplots are interwoven, submerge, and then reappear, intertwining with such mellowness and mellifluence that the worn-

---

[5] Was Shakespeare actually the most successful playwright of his times? Members of the Western elite seem to have accorded him the honor of unmatched greatness, and his plays have indeed been successful with audiences at large. But are we certain that the number of performances and the monetary intake would not have been greater if he had bowed to the transient tastes of his Elizabethan audience? I do not doubt that, had he chosen to center his interest on achieving success with the audience, he possessed the technical skills to compose the most "successful" play of his times—provided he had been able to bring himself to shelve the depth of his perception. Mozart, after all, was not the most frequently performed composer of his times; it was Salieri. When Gabriel Harvey, at the beginning of the 17th century, annotated his Chaucer edition with the remark that Shakespeare's "Lucrece, his tragedie of Hamlet, Prince of Denmark, have it in them to please the wiser sort," one gets some inkling of how Shakespeare's contemporaries responded to the play. The highest number of performances of a play Rothe (1961, p. 84) could find from the study of Elizabethan records was 32, and this was not a play by Shakespeare. Rothe also gives full weight to Shakespeare's partial failure as a playwright even in the eyes of his own company. Cf. also Ornstein (1960, p. 8): "Although Elizabethans loved *Hamlet* on the stage, they preferred by far to read the somewhat banal *Mucedorus,* which, by the standard of printed editions, was the most popular literature of its period."

out comparison with a musical masterpiece, a symphony, can hardly be avoided. The relative importance of the Fortinbras theme is already adumbrated by its early appearance. The first reference to it is found in *I.1.61*, with Horatio's remark that the Ghost's armor is the same as the King's, "When he the ambitious Norway combated." It moves into the very center when Horatio explicates the "strange eruption to our state" *(I.1.69)* that the Ghost's appearance allegedly forbodes. The motive is almost overemphasized, in fact, by the dramatic irony that lies embedded in Horatio's conjecture. Not only will the eruption be found in an internal canker, rather than in a threat from the outside; it will appear in Claudius and not in Fortinbras, who is, after all, the only healthy force, and one whose hands will remain to the end free of murder.

In Horatio's historical report, however, there seems to me to be a flaw. His story tells how Old Fortinbras challenged Hamlet's father to a duel. The stakes of the contest are, on one side, Old Fortinbras' legal possessions ("Which he stood seiz'd of," *(I.1.89)*), on the other the King's "moiety competent," which some understand as "sufficient portion" (Lawrence, 1946, p. 677), but which really means a sufficient or suitable half, or a half that fulfills the requirements of the case. This may be interpreted in various ways. The challenger was throwing in his whole territory against the adversary's half. If the two areas were equal in their extent, then it was a fair deal. But it may also mean that the half offered by one was accepted against the whole offered by the other, which may make Old Hamlet appear to be a shrewd bargainer and Old Fortinbras a particularly reckless man. Be that as it may, in the Council scene we hear of another old Fortinbras, evidently the slain King's brother, who is now King of Norway but impotent and bedridden *(I.2.29)*, and who is ignorant of the fact that his nephew is levying troops from among Norway's subjects, in order to seize hold of what he considers to be his lost patrimony.

This is somewhat confusing. If Norway had lost his legal possessions to Old Hamlet, which would result in effect in Norway's becoming part of Denmark, how could the impotent and bedridden Fortinbras still possess a kingdom (unless we are to assume that Norway was divided between two brother Kings, for which there is neither any evidence nor the remotest probability)?

With Horatio's speech, information has already been conveyed about Fortinbras that is factually richer than what is yet known about Hamlet. After 812 more lines, we receive still new information. The ambassadors, upon returning from Norway, confirm that young Fortin-bras' levies were indeed intended for use against Claudius, but add that the martial youth had sworn to his uncle, who had assumed that the military preparations were aimed against the Poles, that he would never again raise arms against Denmark's King. Old Norway, "overcome with joy," had then stipulated a large annual grant for his nephew and commissioned him to use the levied troops against the Poles, after which he had begged Claudius to grant his nephew free passage through Danish soil for that purpose. It should be noted that this new information reaches us at a point when we know that Hamlet has already started on his course of "madness," and when Polonius is trying to convince the King and Queen that it is Hamlet's love for Ophelia that is the source of his disturbance.

In the present arrangement of the play, it takes 1583 lines (only 41 lines less than twice the former number) before Fortinbras is once more brought to the spectators' attention. This time he himself appears, while marching with his troops through Denmark. In the seven lines he speaks, he expresses his willingness to pay his respects to Claudius, if the latter so desires. Fortinbras casts a shadow, of course, over Hamlet's final monologue. After 1100 lines or so (a little more than 2/3 of the final distance),[6] his arrival in Elsinore is announced by Osric. The 19 additional lines assigned to him do not convey to the audience anything that is factually new. He asserts "some rights of memory in this Kingdom" *(V.11. 394),* thus indicating that he had never fully renounced his old claim, which opportunity now "invites" him to settle. Under Horatio's guidance, he makes all the immediately necessary preparations.

The parallels between Hamlet and Fortinbras are striking. Both have lost their thrones through the violent deaths of their fathers; both are tangled in a struggle, the center of which is restoration of one sort or another. In that struggle, both have to deal with their fathers' brothers. Despite these parallels, however, there are significant differences. Fortinbras lost his father through legal or legalized violence. Moreover, the perpetrator—if he can be called that, since Old Fortinbras was, after all, the challenger—has been reached by his Nemesis, so that young Fortinbras' "revenge" is at a level that is psychologically less dangerous than Hamlet's commitments, since it aims only at the reacquisition of land. Fortinbras is dealing with a weakened uncle, who has no authority to

---

[6] Somewhere around the midpoint falls the gravediggers' reference to Old Fortinbras.

speak of, and can therefore deal with his restless nephew only in terms of addressing appeals to him. By contrast, Claudius is a dangerous opponent, although he is restrained in his dealing with Hamlet by his profound attachment to Gertrude, who lives almost by Hamlet's looks.

Fortinbras has raised an army against Claudius—which is really what Hamlet ought to have done. Fortinbras is, so to speak, a free-floating crown prince, without any official role to fulfill; if *he* is able to raise armed bands under pretenses, should not Hamlet have been capable of doing the same thing? Fortinbras is dealing, however, only with external obstacles, being himself free of internal ones. He is flexible: since what he plans neither grows out of, nor is intertwined with neurotic conflicts, he is easily able to accept substitutes. When his thwarted aggressive impulse is displaced upon the war against the Poles, he again does what could well have been Hamlet's concern, had *he* identified with *his* father.[7]

When Horatio at the beginning interprets the Ghost's appearance as an omen of danger to the state, and perceives this danger in Fortinbras' warlike preparations, despite the dramatic irony, he does establish a silent identity between the two crown princes. By uncovering Claudius' misdeeds and bringing about the downfall of official authority, Hamlet will shake the foundations of a state that would actually have been in danger of falling to pieces, if Fortinbras did not step in on time and take over where Hamlet left off.

I wish also to call attention to the points in Hamlet's career at which Fortinbras is brought forth in the play. The first and second time this happens, it is before we have obtained any substantial notion about Hamlet. The third time that we are informed about the effects of Fortinbras' flexibility and closeness to action comes at just the time when we are observing the effects of Hamlet's puzzling conflictual madness.

---

[7] However, for a different reading of that passage in Shakespeare's text, see Holmes (1964, p. 60). A subtle similarity (by contrast) was discovered by Lawrence (1946, p. 687) in two lines of Hamlet's fourth act soliloquy. When he speaks of himself, he says: "Of thinking too precisely on the event" *(IV.4.41)* and 9 lines later, when he speaks of Fortinbras: "Makes mouths at the invisible event." "The antithesis is too sharp to be accidental; it must be due to deliberate design," says Lawrence. This subtle observation suggests a supplement to my interpretation of Hamlet's soliloquies in 1953, for the identity of the word "event" permits the interpretation that Hamlet has formed a new ego-ideal (Hartmann and Loewenstein, 1962, Lampl-de Groot, 1962), patterned after Fortinbras, which brings him all the closer to the point of acting. A comparison with the Hecuba soliloquy then leads to the conclusion that at that point the ego-ideal was shared with the actor. As a matter of fact, Hamlet's subsequent step was his attack in the form of the Mousetrap. The progress from one soliloquy to the other may then be summarized as the development of an ego-ideal that was highly autoplastically colored to one that was alloplastically directed.

The fourth time we hear of Fortinbras, it is in terms of his military action. This takes place while Hamlet is on his way to England, his potential for action seemingly reduced to zero, since he has been made the captive of Rosencrantz and Guildenstern, and is moreover destined for early execution. Hamlet's ensuing overactivity can conceivably be interpreted as his response to beholding Fortinbras' progress toward victory. It is with particular subtlety that Shakespeare makes their ways cross just at this point. Fortinbras, surrounded by an army, is invited to enter Denmark at the very place at which Hamlet will soon appear, uninvited and stealthily, shipwrecked on his way back to his father's hearth. Opposites are often taken for identities in the unconscious, and Fortinbras' appearance on Denmark's border in glory and power may be taken as a harbinger of Hamlet's return in prostration (an old mythical theme, reminiscent of the *Odyssey*).

I have already suggested that Fortinbras is Hamlet *redivivus*. Yet this must not be understood as saying that Hamlet could ever have become a one-dimensional character, as Fortinbras was. Even after his "recovery," he would have preserved his depth, his ability to find meaning and to be puzzled. As critics suggest: "Hamlet has ten times the brains and sensitivity of Fortinbras" (Berry, 1947, p. 102). Yet the same author says of Fortinbras: "He is now the hero of the play, and it is *he*, we are sure, who will prove 'most royally'!" (*ibid.*, author's italics).

It is this switch, this replacing of the dead hero with the new hero, that suggests in the latter the outline of the former. I myself would even go so far as to surmise that on that day when Old Hamlet and Old Fortinbras were locked in combat and Hamlet was born, Young Fortinbras too was born. Hamlet was about 20 at the beginning of the play; Fortinbras, at the time when he entered Elsinore, cannot have been older.[8]

I must admit that the idea that Hamlet and Fortinbras were born on the same night is close to my heart. I am in a quandary at this point, however, for I do not know whether I should rely on my imagination and follow up the thread, or drop the matter because of the lack of evidence. If they were born on the same night, this would suggest the twin theme (cf. Walker, 1948, p. 117). The fact that one of the twins takes over the

---

[8] The objection may be raised that Hamlet appears at the end of the play as if he were much older than Fortinbras. However, it must be considered that grave conflicts make a man age more quickly, and Fortinbras mirrors, if we disregard their difference in depth, a simplified Hamlet from whom the consequences—indeed the very fact—of conflict have been magically wiped away, just as the anguish of the evening may have vanished from the brow when one awakens refreshed, reborn from a single night's deep sleep.

active role and the other twin the passive role (Hartmann, 1934-35) could then rightly be adduced as an explanatory hypothesis, although emphasis on passivity in Hamlet's case would be slightly misleading, since it is the degree of differentiation that is the distinctive mark, as with Jacob and Esau, and not the presence or absence of activity.

On closer inspection, however, it becomes clear that the assumption that the two princes were born on the same night, although that detail would add its poetical, fairy-tale kind of beauty, is not decisive. The age difference between the two princes is not at any rate substantial, since the youth of Fortinbras is stressed repeatedly *(I.1.95* and *2.17, V.2.354)*. When Hamlet speaks of him, for example, as delicate and tender *(IV.4.48)*, he conjures up the image of youth. Fortinbras cannot in any case be older than Hamlet, which may suggest that he was posthumously born, an eventuality that I shall follow up later.

I want first to point out that the Gravedigger's tale about Hamlet's birth having taken place on the day of Old Hamlet's victory over Old Fortinbras may suggest the myth of the birth of the Hero.[9] Rank (1909) examined in psychoanalytic terms this frequent, if not regular, element in accounts of the birth of the Hero. One may therefore feel tempted to regard Old Hamlet's victory at the time when his son was born as a harbinger of the offspring's greatness. This, however, would be quite unusual, as I shall later show. The arrival of Prince Hamlet brought good luck to his father.

A psychological truth is contained in this episode. Males often become more productive during their wives' pregnancies, particularly during the first one; homosexuality is also stimulated at that time. I know of one instance in which a man had his only adult homosexual experience on the night his wife gave birth to their first child. Since the kings' wives were both pregnant at the time of the combat, it is understandable that male rivalry and competition were stimulated in the two Kings. Conceivably the combatants were stimulated by ambitions for the crown princes to reign over kingdoms far larger than those their fathers had inherited. But Prince Fortinbras' arrival or impending arrival did not indeed bode well for his father.

A frequent theme in the myth is a prophecy of disaster. "In the standard saga . . . during or before the pregnancy, there is a prophecy, in the form of a dream or oracle, cautioning against his [the hero's] birth,

---

[9] That Shakespeare's Hamlet follows roughly the vicissitudes of the mythological hero can be seen from Campbell (1949). Cf. also Slochower (1950), Poser (1965, p. 99f).

and usually threatening danger to his father (or his representative)" (Rank, 1909, p. 65). All this remains unspoken in *Hamlet,* but the mythological or legendary core is discernible. Hamlet brings his father good luck, Fortinbras ill luck. The former turn of events is apparently atypical, sons being in the habit of endangering their fathers. Yet this reversal is correlated with the same upturn in the son's fate, Hamlet being an unsuccessful "hero," if the play is taken literally. Shakespeare seems to extend the traditional pattern when he makes what is a good omen for the father bring disaster to the son. Consequently, from the mythological point of view, Hamlet and Fortinbras may be compared to object and its inverted mirror picture.[10]

As I mentioned earlier, the analysis of details hints at the possibility of Fortinbras' posthumous birth. In reconstructing Fortinbras' life history, one may further conjecture (always keeping an eye on the contrast with Hamlet) that his mother died in giving birth to him. Being born posthumously and losing the mother at birth are the most far-reaching events by which the physical (literal) prerequisites of the oedipal situation are eradicated. [11]

In clinical reality one observes that the mother's death in childbirth generally constitutes a devastating trauma, the consequences of which one can hardly hope to be able to cure therapeutically; the child usually has to face the father's unspoken reproach of having caused the end of his spouse's life. Assuming that my reconstruction merits discussion, I am tempted to place this question before the reader: by removing both parents from any contact with the child—in Fortinbras' instance, this is done in a way essentially different from the myth of the hero, in which the parents live far away from the son, who is exposed after birth and raised by substitute parents—did Shakespeare construct a situation that would offer the opportunity for the child to be immunized against the inroads of the oedipal "poison"?

Fortinbras and Hamlet both have bachelor uncles. In the case of the former, it is a confirmed bachelor, sickly and withdrawn, who is even oblivious to the true aim of his nephew's leadership of a gang. Fortinbras, we can be certain, was permitted to grow up without proper supervision and guidance. No identification with a masculine ideal was possi-

---

[10] I do hope that this multiplicity of interpretations will not be held against me. The theme of rebirth and the comparison with a mirror picture may seem to exclude each other. A similar contrast will recur when the relationship between main plot and subplot is discussed.

[11] Oddly enough, Siegfried, at least in the Wagnerian version, is also a posthumous son, whose mother died in childbirth.

ble. This may explain the juvenile, almost unmanly traits so richly painted into his portrait.

Claudius is also a kind of bachelor. He marries only late in life, and
his fixation to the mother is plain. If he had not committed murder, his
personality type would not pose too much of a problem. The type of man
who lives with his mother until she dies and then gets married to an incestuous object is well known. But the contrast between Fortinbras' and
Hamlet's uncle is strongly brought to attention, even though the two do
have this pattern in common. Consequently, an interpretation more in
keeping with the actual events on the stage would see in Fortinbras not a
Hamlet *redivivus*, after all, but rather the exemplification of one type of
oedipal situation.

The man who has been spared growing up under the burden of an
authoritarian father (the impotent Fortinbras), who has escaped feelings
of guilt (Old Fortinbras' death occurred under circumstances that did not
create implications compromising the son), and who has not become involved in a guilt-arousing relationship with his mother (no mother is
mentioned)—such a man can act without conflicting hesitation or doubt.
He is flexible and reality-adjusted and is thus spared any inner conflict
about his own destructive acts.

He unhesitatingly fulfills what is demanded of him by the existing
value systems, without at all reflecting upon them (Fortinbras' senseless
war against the Poles). In other words, man's destiny depends on the
structure of his Oedipus complex; Fortinbras, being the equivalent of
Aliosha, is not the hero of a play, not to speak of a tragedy. Since he is
not essential to the mechanics of Hamlet's tragedy, there must be a reason other than dramatic or aesthetic for his presence: he adds a special
type to the principal oedipal vicissitudes.

This circle is completed only when Claudius' crime is acknowledged
as oedipal. It is he who symbolizes the patricide who marries the mother;
Hamlet is therefore psychologically correct when he accuses Claudius of
incest. But as a result of the wave of repression that swept over the West
following the downfall of Graeco-Roman culture, it was not to be tolerated (or perhaps even imagined) that such a man could be a hero; he can
only be a criminal. The next wave of repression will regard patricide as a
deed that can grow only out of a physically diseased brain (Smerdyakov).
Thus Fortinbras actually enlarges the frame of the play, which is called
"The Tragicall Historie of Hamlet, Prince of Denmark," to that of the

supra-individual plight that is inherent in man's relationship with his father.

And yet if the psychology of tragedy is carried to a further point than it has reached in the modern era, the tie between Hamlet and Fortinbras may prove to be a far closer one. We have seen that the latter was quite ready to defeat Claudius—that is to say, to do what Hamlet should have done; and when we learn that, in the *Ur-Hamlet,* Hamlet is given Norway by Claudius, in compensation for his being excluded from taking power in Denmark, that he *is* King of Norway, this may make more acceptable my suggestion that the Fortinbras of the end of the play is Hamlet restored to life. Fortinbras's arrival is, as a matter of fact, announced by Osric *(V.11.354),* the same Osric whom we saw previously as the messenger of doom and death.[12] Now, in accordance with the unconscious equation of death and rebirth, he is the harbinger of Hamlet's chrysalis.

This aspect, however, would distract from—if not actually contradict—the definitive meaning I have just ascribed to the play as containing a general statement about man's oedipal crisis and its chief variations. Rather, it would speak in favor of *Hamlet* as the tragedy of a man who goes through the throes of an acute oedipal phase and matures only after he has slain his father and taken possession of the mother. It would also imply the ancient right of that man who, by carrying out the oedipal impulses in reality, becomes a Hero-God. Since all such contents are offensive to the Christian mind, processes of that sort can, of course, be set forth only in such symbols as are sufficiently distant from the contents of the unconscious, and their unravelling could never be the consequence of discursive commonsense thinking.

The reference to the Hero-God requires further explication. The full effect of Fortinbras's function in the structure of the play can be realized when one discovers that his final appearance is in fact, almost equivalent to another play. It took Greek tragedy two separate plays in order to make an adequate representation of the life of any man who has realized his human potentialities maximally. *Oedipus Rex* deals with man's grief and pain; *Oedipus at Colonus,* his transition to a sacred, demonic being (Alexander, 1955, pp. 100-104).

Man's dignity is not necessarily invaded when he is subjected to such torment as befell Oedipus. Borne properly, even torment that may

---

[12] Flatter's interpretation has been confirmed by Ehrenzweig (1953, p. 129) and Kozintsev (1966).

appear to be humiliating could lead to a higher god-like stage. Such an interpretation of Sophocles' Oedipus tragedy may sound Christian. But I think, as a matter of fact, that Alexander (1955, pp. 101-103) went too far in equating the hidden meaning of Sophocles' two tragedies with that of the *Book of Job*.

There are essential differences, one of which Cleanth Brooks (1955, p. 5) brings forth indirectly, when he says that the acceptance of suffering by Oedipus (and Hamlet) "is not a weary submission: the tragic hero is possessed of a tremendous vitality. . . . Nor is the acceptance necessarily a joyful submission to what the hero recognizes to be the just order of things. . . . The acceptance springs from a desire for knowledge, for the deepest kind of self-knowledge, knowledge of the full meaning of one's ultimate commitments. It is the glory of Oedipus that he insists upon knowing *who* he is. But so does Rosmer and so does Hamlet and so do all the rest" (author's italics). This is not, I believe, true of Job.

If Hamlet had ended on Horatio's "flights-of-angels" conception, the play might easily have become a kind of *Everyman*. It is the secular ending, in the form of Fortinbras' final appearance—the dual aspect of Hamlet's being at one and the same time reincarnated in Fortinbras and carried by angels to Heaven—that makes it quite distinct from its predecessors. That part of the tragedy that was elaborately evolved in *Oedipus at Colonus* is here reduced almost to a curlicue—Horatio's closing reference to Hamlet's ascension. The fact that the play concludes with Fortinbras-Hamlet's appearance—even if the latter is regarded as an equivalent of the ancient *deus-ex-machina* device—provides a strong sign of the secularization of Western man's thinking, no less than of his society.

II

Before going further into the Fortinbras plot, I shall make a tentative suggestion with regard to the general effect Elizabethan stage productions might have had on the audience and what the reasons for such an effect might have been.

Evidently Elizabethan stage performances did not end in the way the official manuscript says they did. Thus we read in a German traveller's diary, about the performance of Shakespeare's *Julius Caesar*:

. . . I . . . saw the tragedy of the first Emperor Julius with at least fifteen characters very well acted. At the end of the comedy they danced according to their custom with extreme elegance. Two in men's clothes and two in women's gave this performance, in wonderful combination with each other. (Harrison, 1940, p. 196, quoted after Chambers' *Elizabethan Stage*, ii, 364f).

This brings up the question of the "jig," about which, unfortunately, only little is known with certainty (Baskervill, 1929; Sisson, 1936, 1966). I am not thinking here, of course, of the jig as a dance, or as music or song or ballad, but rather as the performance given at the end of the play. It was suppressed by some justices in 1612 because of its lewdness, and we hear that it was confined to theaters of lesser repute. But the above-quoted passage from the German diarist proves that something equivalent to a jig followed even performances in reputable theaters. My own ideas on the subject are based on the assumption that Elizabethan stage performances had a far deeper effect on the audience than their equivalents do in our own time. The tension that mounted during performances must have been excessive: they not only went on without any break,[13] but also aroused the deepest feelings in the audience.

I would like to add here a note as to why the effect on the Elizabethans of these performances might have been greater than it is on contemporary audiences. Not only was Elizabethan man more impressionable, quicker to respond emotionally and far freer in his emotional expressions and discharges than the man of the present age; theatrical performances must also have been, I would guess, emotionally far more expressive than those of our time.

The modern actor arouses feelings in the audience by means of emotional expression. He may cry or scream in terror, or he may make a gesture of great expressiveness and with it infect the spectator. In thinking back over my own theatrical experiences in that respect, I recall two theatrical incidents that have left the deepest impressions on me. I owe them both to the unmatched art of Helene Thimig, a German actress, who never gained the renown in the United States that her incomparable gifts should have won for her.

In one episode, playing the role of a lesbian engaged to a young man, she received a bouquet of violets from a lover whom she had promised to break with, although she was still deeply in love with her (*La Prisonnière*, by Edouard Bourdet, 1926). She held the bouquet with one hand against her breast and stroked it with the other in such a delicate and tender way that I could not curb the impulse to look away rather than commit the indiscretion of observing. My reaction apparently was

[13] See, however, Holmes (1964, p. 82).

that it would be indecent to watch someone at a moment when she was expressing something very personal and intimate, which was not really meant for the eyes of an onlooker.

The other was an indescribable sound of disgust, repulsion that—I cannot describe it otherwise—groaned its way out of her throat. This terrible sound, which I can still reproduce in my imagination, was elicited when she was playing the role of an actress who has suffered a professional decline and is finally advised by her maid to sell herself, in order to obtain money for the expensive wardrobe that she badly needs in order to continue her career as an actress (*Les Ratés*, by Henri René Lenormand, 1920).

In both instances, the relevant or effective perceptive stimuli were the raw substratum of immediate emotions.[14]

The profound emotional stir created in the spectator was caused by the impingement of a direct and intense emotional expression, originating in the actor's emotions, upon the spectator's emotional sphere, without the use of any other medium such as words.

But who among our actors could recite the lines

Sweets to the sweet: farewell!
I hop'd thou should'st have been my Hamlet's wife;
I thought this bride-bed to have deck'd, sweet maid,
And not have strew'd thy grave

in such a way as to bring tears to our eyes? These lines are, after all, magnificently poetic;[15] they are drenched in emotion and thus potentially

---

[14] A comparable situation occurred once in a performance by the Grand Guignol of a play that takes place during the Spanish Civil War. I do not now recall at which side it was aimed, but one of the combatants was suspected of being a spy and therefore subjected to torture. His expression of physical pain was so horrible that I had to remind myself repeatedly that this was happening only on the stage. Yet I am not certain that this still falls within the area of aesthetic experience. The same doubt holds true with regard to the following. In a mystery movie the protagonist, acted by Georges Simenon, is unjustly accused of having committed a crime. He takes flight and falls from the roof, but then catches himself at the roof's gutter, from which he dangles for a long time before falling to the ground. When I left the theater, I noticed to my astonishment that the muscles of my upper arm were hurting badly. Apparently, I had by reflex tensed my own muscles unduly, as if I were going through the same situation as the protagonist, who acted his role in such a way as to evoke empathy, if not indeed identification.

[15] But is it only poetry that makes such verses as these so heartbreakingly beautiful? I am reminded of Eliot's thought that the beauty of a phrase may be "the shadow of a greater beauty" (1927a, p. 54); that there is "poetry of the surface" in which "unconscious does not respond to unconscious" and "no swarms of inarticulate feelings are aroused" (1919, p. 128). In these verses there is no poetry of the surface. Aside from the poetical beauty of these four lines, in them seems to be condensed Gertrude's tragic fate, her endeavoring to do good yet being crushed by fate, her gradual

carriers of stimuli that might have effects comparable to what I have already described in terms of modern acting.[16]

Georg Simmel (1917) found the essence of Rembrandt's art of portraiture to be in his unique ability to present, in a likeness, not only the subject's present but his past and future as well. This illuminating interpretation can be applied to many of Shakespeare's verses: he had the ability to compress into a few lines the whole fate of a human being.

My contention is that the Elizabethan audience was struck by such lines far more profoundly than any present audience would be. Of the many factors involved in that difference of response, I shall select only two: words meant something different to the Elizabethans than they do to us, and/or words were spoken differently on the Elizabethan stage. I am not here forgetting the Elizabethan's greater emotional susceptibility.

One could easily believe that words held a different position in the thinking of Elizabethan man, as many a historian has pointed out (cf., e.g., Salinger, 1955; Bradbrook, 1935). Even though the explanation of this interest in words, and this responsiveness to them, falls within the historical and sociological orbit, it is a question that may also challenge

---

awakening to an awareness of her son's irremediable grief and the dawning of her regret for a life that has been ill spent. But it is not only Gertrude's life that is epitomized here. Ophelia's hope of bliss and her terrible destruction also add to the "shadow of a greater beauty."

[16] I have found an indirect confirmation of this very point in Alexander's (1955, p. 22f) book. He criticizes the film-makers of the English *Hamlet* for omitting Ophelia's famous lines about "the glass of fashion" after Hamlet leaves her, and instead letting the actress cast herself down, writhing and howling terribly—a device that "seems to have been in fashion about the time the film was in the making." Yet, in my opinion, this device conveyed Ophelia's mood more poignantly than any declamation of the omitted verses could ever have at the hands of a contemporary actress. When the author calls these verses "the music of her own loving comment" and believes that a woman whose brother described her in the following words: "thought and affliction, passion, hell itself/She turns to a favour and to prettiness" *(IV.5.187f)* would not have shown an outburst such as shown in the film, since if she were indeed capable of venting grief and love in such a simple physical form, she would not have later lost her reason—I would have to disagree. To my ear, Ophelia's verses sound like the shrill tones of the greatest despair. Ophelia was also a kind of glass of fashion, a glass that was in its own way as brittle as was Hamlet's. Here was the first instance when her compulsion to behave in the way society expected the ideal woman to conduct herself gave way to an enormous emotional upsurge, such as may find expression in a loss of control. The affecting of her reason set in when the reality situation pushed her into a dead end from which there was no escape. It may be impossible to speculate how an Elizabethan boy actor declaimed these verses, but it is difficult for me to believe that they sounded like music of a loving comment. I would rather guess that the inner despair was most formidably brought forth, already announcing the later catastrophe. I imagine that he did not cast himself down, nor did he go through the sort of bodily movements that a contemporary actress has to employ; instead he spoke the verses per se in such a way as to arouse the same feelings in the spectator as are now elicited instead by the sort of devices that the British film-makers probably rightly considered to be necessary, in view of the level of contemporary sensibilities and the present limits on producing versed or long speech that is heavily loaded with emotions. (For a psychoanalytic study of creative theater, see Weissmann, 1965.)

the psychoanalyst, who in this instance cannot do more than speculate.

If a patient invested too much interest and psychic energy in words, and started to form new words, we might suspect that he was suffering from a schizophrenic disorder of some sort. Freud thought that, during the course of such a disease, the emotional charge attached to external reality is gradually withdrawn and partially displaced upon the language systems. Something of that kind occurred, it seems to me, when the full cathexis of the Scriptures could no longer be maintained. With the beginning of doubt in the all-embracing validity of a text that had long formed a more reliable guide to man than his own sense data—without its guidance, man would have considered himself almost literally blind, deaf and paralyzed—a considerable amount of psychic energy must have been set free. It is likely that this previously unbound energy was intercepted by the word systems.

Although there can hardly be any doubt about the heightened interest of the Elizabethans in language, I would be inclined to attribute importance, in regard to the question at hand, not only to the recipients but also to the speakers of Shakespeare's verses. I imagine that the Elizabethan actor recited his lines in a way that was vastly different from the way that is characteristically employed in such a historical period as the present one (cf. Joseph, 1964). I would trace this difference to a fundamentally different attitude toward man's femininity. It has been asserted —and probably correctly so—that homosexuality became quite widespread during the Renaissance. This increase seems to be well documented, at least for Italy, but I do not see any reason to doubt that this was true as well of other countries that also fell under the sway of the Renaissance.

There is no indication, however, that society's attitude toward homosexuality had basically changed. It was still regarded as sinful or objectionable, even when it was left unprosecuted. Yet one should not equate male homosexuality with male femininity; the homosexual, after all, squanders his femininity in a rather unconstructive way.

There is one cultural element that makes me feel certain that male femininity was acceptable to the Elizabethan man: he could watch males perform female roles without laughing or snickering (Davies, 1939). As is well known, the Elizabethan age did not tolerate actresses, so that female parts were played by boy actors. In our own times, however, it is an outworn comedy trick for a man to impersonate a woman; it arouses laughter regularly and almost without exception. A woman's presentation of a male role is far more acceptable, and some famous actresses have dared successfully to carry it off, quite aside from such instances as the *Rosenkavalier*. Why it is tolerable to our present-day audiences to watch a woman in a male role, while nevertheless it smacks to them of the ridiculous or perverse for a man to imitate a woman, I shall not attempt to discuss here.

I assume that a typical career of an Elizabethan actor started in his boyhood, when he played female parts (cf. Davies, 1939). Whether or not this is true of the majority of actors who became renowned in Shakespeare's times, I do not know. If it were so, I would attribute to it singular importance. It would mean that the Elizabethan actor had gone through a phase during which he could unfold, enjoy, and experience his own femininity, to an extent that is not permitted to males of our own times, without their running grave risks. I would guess that such inner and outer freedom to act in a female way had a general effect on Elizabethan freedom and the ability to express emotions.

At present, whether or not a man is manifestly homosexual, his femininity is a danger to him and he is ashamed of it. The feeling of guilt about it is also observable in those who seem to be uninhibited, who discharge their homosexuality, either actively or passively. The crusts, rigidities and general inhibitions that are generally present in man's emotional expressiveness today have been caused, to a great extent, by defenses against and inhibitions of an urge that, after all, does demand fairly continuous gratification.

It is difficult to decide whether one has to trace separately the opprobrium in which passivity is held and that directed against actual homosexuality. I think that this differentiation is indicated, but it is a distinction that goes beyond my knowledge.[17] It is possible that masculinity can be portrayed more penetratingly when the actor has already, in his youth, gone through the delights of being loved by Romeo, in the role of Juliet, without incurring any feeling of guilt. How often do a woman and a man embrace in Shakespeare's script? How often is there the occasion for any kind of physical contact between them? The poet proceeded with the greatest delicacy; it might have been the caution necessitated by the danger of physical contact that enforced all the more the flow of the most beautiful words. Thus there was protection against homosexuality,

---

[17] It seems that male passivity and homosexuality are almost fused in contemporary thinking and feeling—which is as unjustified in that regard as is the current equation of activity and penis envy in the female.

at the same time as there was the greatest freedom for the expression of male femininity.[18]

The whole question leads to an evaluation of contemporary sexuality. As is well known, the modern mind is unduly preoccupied with sex and at the same time far more liberal and permissive toward the expression of its many variations. Yet parallel with this process, it appears that, as far as males are concerned, at least, a decline in the vigor and quality of the sex drive has occurred (cf. Elias, 1939).

The Elizabethan overemphasis on words and freedom of emotional expression resulted, in my opinion, in an ability to pour enormous quantities of emotion into the declamation of verses, probably to such an extent that, if a twentieth-century man were to witness Elizabethan stage performances, he would find them ridiculous. Actors such as Alleyn whom, as critics generally contend but without further proof, Shakespeare had in mind with part of his critical allocution to the players in *Hamlet (III.2.3 to 14)*, may have gone too far, although a deep meaning seems to be revealed in the legend surrounding his retirement from stage. When the company was performing *Dr. Faustus*, which it did between 1594 and 1597, an apparition of the devil became visible, which frightened both Alleyn, who was acting the title role, and the audience. He was so frightened, in fact, that he thereupon retired to private life.

So far the legend.[19] What is its message? Here is an actor who is not only possessed by the role he has to act, to such a degree that he hallucinates the world as essentially complementing the one he represents on the stage, but also holds his audience in such pre-hypnotic submission that it too shares in the hallucination he had produced under the impact of the role he is acting.

[18] This question has found varied treatment in the literature. Granville-Barker (1934, pp. 53-56) believes that Shakespeare avoided physical contact between the boy actor and the adult actor. Davies (1939, pp. 172-201) raises objections that seem quite convincing. It is noteworthy that Philip Stubbes' *Anatomy of Abuses* (1583) and William Prynne's *Histrio-mastix, The Player's Scourge or Actors Tragedie* (1632), stressed the homosexual seductions of boy actors. They both wrote as if it were something universal—which it surely was not. It would be of great importance to know the frequency of manifest homosexuality among Elizabethan actors, in order better to understand and evaluate the sexuality of the crucial decades around 1600. My guess would be that overt homosexuality appeared with far less frequency among Elizabethan actors than it does among their contemporary counterparts, just because it was a time in which the male was permitted to *act out* his femininity in a constructive way without incurring opprobrium. Davies has concisely analyzed the sexual atmosphere of Shakespeare's stage, as compared with that of the Restoration stage, when actresses made their appearance and the custom of employing boy actors for female parts came to an end.

[19] For an attempt at a psychoanalytic and historic evaluation of legends surrounding artists, see Kris and Kurz (1934). Erikson (1958c, p. 37) has discussed the function of a focal legend in psychological research on Luther's life.

Following Hanns Sachs, who coined the term "daydreams in common" (*gemeinsame Tagträume*), one can speak here of hallucinations in common, which I would prefer to call "shared hallucinations." This is a chapter of psychopathology that has scarcely been investigated and yet I am sure that it has played a major role in the history of mankind. We do know a little about shared illusions and delusions, which are constantly at work and may indeed be indispensable to the establishment and maintenance of community coherence.

It may be that special historical circumstances are necessary in order for illusions to switch to hallucinations; yet here the phenomenon, if it took place at all, had to do with the area of artistic experience. That the legend, if it was no more than that, could take shape at all indicates that the relationship between actor and audience was in this instance a particularly strong one. It is a matter of mutuality and reciprocity of acting intensity and audience receptivity. As to the latter, there is not much to be said, aside from what historians have presented about that fascinating period that we call the Renaissance. Whatever else it may have been, that was a period of transition from, despite its being also a partial continuation of, medieval civilization (Lovejoy, 1936; Tillyard, 1943). Any portion of that tradition that extended into the period of the Renaissance acquired new meaning thereby; at least, Elizabethan man responded differently to it from the way his predecessor did. If from no other source, this can surely be learned from Shakespeare's tragedies and comedies.

What I would like to stress here is only the area of contact between the form in which the playwright's creation was realized and the psychological surface of the recipients. As I commented earlier, if modern man were to witness an Elizabethan performance, he would probably find it altogether bizarre and ridiculous. Acting styles are very quickly superseded. I once saw a short film of Sarah Bernhardt, who was unquestionably the greatest tragedienne of our grandparents' generation, and her performance seemed irresistibly humorous to the audience—so much so that it would seem to have been altogether beyond the contemporary spectator's imagination that such a performance could, under any circumstances whatever, be regarded as admirable. Curiously enough, the performances by the ancient Greeks and Romans would not, I think, affect us in that way. I should expect a feeling of alienation or strangeness in regard to them, but not one of ridiculousness.

Be that as it may, the cardinal point of Elizabethan acting, I should guess, was its capacity for sustained passion, its ability to maintain a high level of emotional intensity through a large number of verses, its capacity "to give an impression of overwhelming passion by purely elocutionary means," as Davies (1939, p. 115) called it.[20]

When they are viewed by a modern audience, Shakespeare's tragedies no longer have this effect, although many may still feel it on reading the text. At that time their imagination may be able to realize the potential that can no longer be awakened by actors' voices and movements.

If there is agreement with my proposition that acceptance of man's femininity and its fulfillment in the acting of female roles enabled Elizabethan actors to express emotions more forcefully than contemporary actors can, then it may also be concluded that the audience was stunned by this forceful display and gradually fell into a hypnotic-like state. High emotional charges must have accumulated in the spectator, as the play went on relentlessly for hours, without any intervals during which the senses could recover. It is understandable then that the audience needed a period of transition, in order to be released from tragic reality, so that they might then find their way back to actual reality. Did the "jig," in which the audience could join in one way or another, serve that purpose? If so, then it would have constituted a sort of *rite de passage*, an institution that, in my opinion, has served the purpose of protecting the individual in those situations in which he is vulnerable.[21]

The passage from stage reality to actual reality was such a situation in miniature; there is at least one instance where Shakespeare apparently made a special effort to construct this sort of *rite de passage*. I find it in the closing of *A Midsummer Night's Dream*, in which Shakespeare was preoccupied with theatrical problems. When the play within the play is ended and the actors are on the verge of starting the epilogue, Theseus says: "No epilogue, I pray you—for your play needs no excuse. Never excuse; for when the players are all dead, there need none to be blamed" *(V.1.362)*. While this remark is facetious, the play itself does end with an epilogue.

After the squelching of the Epilogue by Theseus, the Bergomask takes place, after which Theseus withdraws with his group; this is the

---

[20] If we look for equivalents among contemporary experiences, I would suggest the experiential intensity that many reached while watching the telecast of President Kennedy's funeral or the Eichmann trial.

[21] It may be that the problem of releasing the energy that had been pent up during the beholding of tragedy was already present in antiquity, for it seems that the performance of a satyr-play may have regularly followed a tragedy, the subject of the two being in some manner related (cf. Arrowsmith, 1952, p. 226).

signal for the fairy world to arise, which in turn leaves in dance and song, and the play then concludes with Puck's Epilogue—a truly multilayered ending, the spectator being softly handed over from one layer of existence to the other, until he is finally released by Puck to his own. In so doing, Puck reminds the Spectator that he was slumbering and that the play was "no more yielding but a dream," thus anticipating Prospero's comment on a play within a play, in which play and life are not only equated with each other but both identified as the "stuff dreams are made on."

The frequent reference to dreams and sleep in such contexts suggests that the psychological root of the problem in question was the process of awakening, whether it be awakening from sleep or awakening from a dream. However, Shakespeare was well aware how horrible such an awakening might be and that, under some circumstances, the aroused subject "Could not believe but that I was in hell, Such terrible impression made my dream." At times Shakespeare brought the world's hell on his stage and he may have feared, and with some justice, "such terrible impression" as his play had made.

III

Fortinbras, to return to our initial subject, is the very person to reconcile the audience to the crushing impact that *Hamlet* must make on it, if the full emotional content that slumbers in it is to be brought forth. If Fortinbras were no more than a *deus ex machina*, this would, indeed, amount to a grave flaw in the play's structure. Yet we have already encountered him—at the beginning of the play, even before we meet Hamlet—and we have been reminded of him intermittently thereafter. Since we perceive in him traits that he shares with Hamlet sufficiently for the audience to be able to integrate him as an organic successor to the latter, it is he who takes us into a future in which we feel secure again. And this monumental gesture toward the future renders unnecessary jig, dance, masquerade or whatever might have followed otherwise; it has thus proven its mettle as a kind of dramatic *rite de passage,* all of which perhaps contain a seed of rebirth. [22]

One further point remains with regard to Shakespeare's masterful handling of plot construction. I tried earlier—by way of a cross section of the play—to show that its plot and subplots illustrate a variety of types of oedipal constellation in the male. I contrasted this aspect of the play with

[22] Francis Fergusson (1949, p. 127) referred to Fortinbras as a *resurrection.*

the results of a longitudinal section, which reveals the development brought about in man by the pressure of the oedipal conflict—a development that carries him from almost pure conformism to well-integrated, egosyntonic, autonomous conflict-free action. If one makes Fortinbras a Hamlet *redivivus*, a Hamlet reborn, however, that subplot becomes synthesized into the whole. Fortinbras is thus no longer a device, when he appears at the end, merely to bring the play to a close, by supplying some sort of answer, without any particular qualities. The subplot has lost its appearance of being a mere appendage, and thereby threatening to impose on the whole the character of an aggregate; instead, it now has an organic function, that of increasing the degree of structuralization of the whole.

One has also to consider the sequence in which the subplots shift from periphery to center. The Fortinbras subplot is introduced, although with some degree of casualness, in the form of an inset; only at the end does it emerge as an organic part of the play. The Laertes subplot is introduced next, in the Council chamber, but it remains peripheral, becoming focal only upon Laertes' return from Paris *(IV.5.112),* which takes place prior to Fortinbras's moving into the center. The introduction of the Ophelia subplot occurs after that of Laertes, but it has already been drawn into the main plot as early as in *II.1.75.* The sequence of the termination of the subplots is also significant: Ophelia's comes to an end before Laertes', and Laertes' before that of Fortinbras, which is not terminated at all within the scope of the play.

Thus the introduction, focalizing and termination of the subplots follow a rhythm; they might even be said to show an organic concatenation. That which enters earliest is terminated, if at all, latest; that which enters second is the next to the last to go; and so on. The same holds true of the sequence of focalization. The sequence of first appearance is the reverse of the sequence of those points at which the subplots are focalized —that is, join the main action. What we have then is a series of concentric circles of diminishing radius.

Shakespeare seems here to be adhering to patterns that are more typically found in the visual arts. In a painting, colors are tuned to each other; the point at which each color either appears or disappears, as well as the area that it fills, is determined by aesthetic laws. In *Hamlet,* the appearance and disappearance, as well as the extent of the subplots seem to abide by equivalent rules; they are "grown" into the main action, being structured in such a way that the whole takes on the character of an organism. Indeed, one could describe a tragedy like *Hamlet* as "organific"—that is to say, as having the inherent momentum to *generate its own subplots,* like an organism that evolves its own well-integrated organ apparatuses.

This act of synthesis—the compounding of the longitudinal section and the cross sections (which at bottom pursue different trends) into an indivisible, organic structure—is clearly an accomplishment of extraordinary greatness.

11. *Not Mad Nor Feigning Madness*

When a large number of people have devoted their thinking over a long period of time to the same subject, one might be tempted to feel certain that by that time all possible permutations and combinations of thought will have been made. The one permutation that had been left undisclosed in our times was that Hamlet was neither mad nor feigning madness, and I suppose it was unavoidable that one day even that idea would be put forward. Grebanier (1960) asserts that he is the only one who holds this theory, and I am quite ready to believe him.

Since I have taken it for granted all along that some of Hamlet's behavior can be dealt with only in terms of either real or feigned madness, or both, it is necessary to make some comment on Grebanier's ratiocination, in the hope that it may also be of interest in other respects.

There are in the first part of the play two lines in which, according to current interpretation, Hamlet himself speaks about his madness, feigned or real. The first is the one about his intention "to put an antic disposition on" *(I.5.172)*, the other, less famous, "I must be idle" *(III.2.91)*, is spoken as the court is appearing to witness the mouse-trap play and is directed to Horatio. According to Grebanier, Hamlet says this because he does not want to be caught conversing with Horatio. Grebanier then rejects the conventional interpretation of both "antic" (pp. 141-148) and "idle" (pp. 224-227) on linguistic grounds and adduces some circumstantial evidence in favor of his interpretation. In these two instances, I do not want to dispute him. He is, however, demonstrably wrong when he says that "Polonius starts a rumor that Hamlet is mad, but there is no warrant to take the cue from that old fool" (p. 147). And on the next page: "After Polonius comes to his absurd conclusion, some of the persons of the drama *do* speak of Hamlet as mad" (italics by the author)—in which statement lies the clear implication that, without Polonius as their source, the others would never have come to the idea of Hamlet's having been transformed.

Unfortunately for Grebanier's theory, the King, in talking to Rosencrantz and Guildenstern, already assumes that "Something you have heard/Of Hamlet's transformation" *(II.2.4f)*—which proves that at that time Hamlet's condition was a matter of general knowledge at Court. When Polonius, 44 lines later, bursts out with his good news, "I have found/The very causes of Hamlet's lunacy," the reactions of the King and Queen make it clear that until then no doubt had existed in their minds about the *fact* of Hamlet's mental disorder, but only about its causation. Grebanier, however, tries later to rescue his unwarranted hypothesis by asserting that the fact of Polonius' being the first one in the play to make any mention of Hamlet's madness suggests that it is he who is the source of the unwarranted rumor. To Polonius' question: "Mad for thy love?", which is directed at Ophelia, Grebanier adds the following footnote (p. 346): "This is the first time anyone speaks of Hamlet as mad. Polonius may very well be the author of that idea."

In his thesis about Polonius starting an unwarranted rumor, Grebanier ignores Ophelia's lamentations about Hamlet's disorder, after he has given her ample cause to draw the conclusion that his mind has become unbalanced ("O what a noble mind is here o'erthrown"). Furthermore, some of the answers Hamlet gives Rosencrantz and Guildenstern betray unmistakably his intention at least to confirm the impression that the Court had necessarily had to form, in view of his suddenly changed behavior. The gravedigger too speaks of Hamlet's madness as general knowledge. What really clinches the case in my mind is Hamlet's farewell speech, in which he himself speaks quite openly of his madness: "His madness is poor Hamlet's enemy" *(V.2.243)*.

One might think that in the light of that last statement, there cannot be any doubt left; but the way in which the author extricates himself from this last piece of irrefutable evidence is surely the "neatest trick of the week." In a footnote to Hamlet's speech—the speech in which Hamlet asserts that all that he did to offend Laertes was due to "sore distraction" with which he is being punished and to madness—the author states:

> He [Hamlet] knows that there would be no point in attempting to unwind the tangled web of the courtiers' misconceptions concerning him. Besides, he wishes to say not a word in the presence of Claudius more than is necessary to win Laertes' forgiveness. For in a little while they all will learn the whole truth from his lips, when he flashes out his documents and takes his vengeance on Claudius. After that Laertes will surely understand what has been the nature of the "sore distraction" with which Hamlet has been "punished" [p. 473].[1]

The reader may feel somewhat confused upon hearing of a document that Hamlet would have "flashed out," if only fate had spared him. As we know from his own account, during his trip to England Hamlet came into possession of Claudius' letter to the King of England, in which the former had given orders for Hamlet's immediate execution. This is the document, the author claims, that Hamlet is now carrying, ready to read it to the court as the final proof of Claudius' guilt. Indeed, we are told, it was only for this reason that he accepted the challenge of the fencing match, since with the whole court present he would have the best opportunity to unmask the King (p. 176).

Yet the entire atmosphere and meaning of the last two scenes is so basically antithetical to the idea that Hamlet had made a plan of the sort the author suggests (which might indeed find its proper place in a picaresque play, or as M. Hercule Poirot's brainchild) that I am reasonably sure that no spectator since the time *Hamlet* first reached the stage, and certainly none of the literary commentators, has ever before held any such idea.

If this had really been Shakespeare's intention, he would indeed have been a very negligent dramatist, for every spectator must surely have forgotten about the document since it was first mentioned. He would not, of course, have forgotten the *content* of that document, for he was well aware that Claudius had been and was still plotting Hamlet's death. In general, things per se take subordinate position in Shakespeare's plays. The unbaited rapier, the poisoned cup are demonstrated to the audience *ad oculos* and their import is made clear when they are shown. But if an object per se is to have far-reaching affects, as Desdemona's handkerchief is, the spectator is over and over again reminded of

---

[1] I would like to point out, before dealing with it fully, that all this was put down in all seriousness, even though later on the author will make the quite preposterous assertion that Laertes knew all along about Claudius' having killed Hamlet's father.

it. Shakespeare's audience had not yet been trained in Conan Doyle's modes of conjecture and inference.

In a modern play, of course, Hamlet would try to find out from his mother, or from some member of the court, where Claudius had been on the afternoon of the King's death, whether he had shown any interest in poison, and whether the phial in which the poison was kept could still be found. Nothing could be further from the spirit of Shakespeare's plays.[2] With all the many crimes that do occur in Shakespeare's plays, I cannot think of one instance in which the idea of circumstantial evidence, of the collecting of traces, could have been even considered by Shakespeare. Murder had become, in Shakespeare's hands, a *spiritual* event, and the total absence in his plays of any notion of collecting traces and evidences points as much as does anything else to the basic change that has taken place since his time in Western thinking and feeling about crime. Hamlet, for example, resorts to forcing the culprit into selfbetrayal by *emotional surprise:* since crime had taken on the meaning of something predominantly spiritual, only spiritual means could be used to bring it to light.

It may be of interest to quote here a short story published somewhat more than 200 years later. I have in mind *The Duel (Der Zweikampf)* by Heinrich von Kleist (1777-1811). The Duke of Breysach has been killed, and the chancellor, in order to establish the identity of the murderer, sends the fatal arrow to all the workshops in Germany, in order to obtain the name of the person for whom the decorated arrow had been prepared. When it turns out that the arrow had been delivered to the Duke's own brother, the chancellor then investigates whether the Duke's brother spent the night in his castle, when the crime was committed, etc. All this, despite the fact that the tale takes place in a medieval setting. Then a trial by ordeal is finally ordered, in which it is a duel rather than the assembling of evidence that is to decide whether or not the Duke's brother was indeed guilty. The story is of interest in this context, since it reflects the transitional period between full confidence in technical evidence and

---

[2] Objects used as tokens of recognition—a device so freely employed in Shakespeare's plays—may be regarded as being rudiments of the modern approach. Imogen erroneously identifies Cloten's corpse as that of her husband's because of the clothes he wears; there is also Pyramus' mistaken assumption of Thisbe's death upon finding her bloody mantle. The idea per se of circumstantial evidence, moreover, was not foreign to Shakespeare, for in *The Winter's Tale (III.2.18f)*, Hermione's indictment speaks of "the pretence whereof being by circumstances partly laid open," yet what the circumstantial evidence consisted of remains unspoken. But compare Caesar's conjecture that Cleopatra's death had been brought about by poison: "for her physician tells me/She hath pursued conclusions infinite/Of easy ways to die" *(Anthony and Cleopatra, V.2.353ff).*

in divine decision. In *Hamlet,* of course, there is no trace at all of that immersion in the techniques of crime detection that has been taken for granted in relation to murder, ever since science made its refined techniques of detection available.

But to return to Claudius' commission. Aside from the fact that the document per se, apart from its content, has been only passingly mentioned, there is evidence that Grebanier is utterly mistaken about even the possibility of its use in the fencing-match scene; for Hamlet has handed the document to Horatio, as is indisputably implied when he says to him: "Here's the commission, read it at more leisure" *(V.2.25).* Would he have done this, if he were planning to make it the chief weapon in the attack on Claudius? Would not Shakespeare have then made him request its return, if for no other reason than to call the audience's attention to it?

Grebanier's *lapsus calami* is interesting, precisely because it does not fall into the realm of those interpretations for which some basis can be found. Goethe's theory of the "too delicate vase" does, after all, contain some truth, as does Bradley's theory of shock and melancholia, or Coleridge's theory of a too sensitive or thoughtful Hamlet. While none of these interpretations is satisfactory, yet they are all worthy of consideration; in their own way, they enrich our outlook and, besides, there are elements in the play that do provide some semblance of justification for such an interpretation. The interpretation of Grebanier's, quoted above, however, rests not on misinterpretation but on fantasy; since there is nothing whatsoever to be found in the text that will provide support for it, it amounts to a travesty.

During the course of his discussion, however, it becomes more evident why Grebanier was unable to discover any signs of either real or feigned madness. Apparently he would admit madness only if the person's speech became senseless. "But it is surely inexcusable that the scholars, instead of deciphering what he says, should, like Polonius, interpret his flashing brilliance as madness, real or feigned" (p. 254). The author does an injustice, as usual, to Polonius, who makes the famous remark: "Though this be madness, yet there is method in't" *(2.2.206),* thus acknowledging, and quite correctly, that madness is not necessarily chaos. Grebanier is apparently not aware that, even though something is capable of being interpreted, it may still be madness.

True madness always has method in it. By "true madness" I mean madness that is caused by a derangement of the mind. When the brain has suffered decay, as in sensory aphasia, then verbal productions do seem uninterpretable, for truly chaotic nonsense is then produced. I agree with Dr. Greenacre wholeheartedly, when she writes that "communicating nonsense always requires considerable talent" (1966, p. 675). At heart, man cannot, under normal circumstances, deliberately produce true nonsense, even when he tried to do so. When Hamlet says: "I am but mad north-north-west" *(2.2.381),* he is ostensibly talking nonsense. The phrase has been interpreted in various ways. I do not know whether Grebanier's interpretation: "the smallest deviation possible from north on the compass; i.e., 'I'm just a little bit off!' " (p. 362) is correct; but it would be erroneous to insist that any one of the various interpretations that have been suggested by the critics is the *only* one that can possibly be correct.

Such wide-framed, seemingly nonsensical utterances permit a variety of interpretations, of course; but when a person talks like that, there can be no doubt that he is either mad or else wants others to believe that he is. For the speaker must be aware that he is forcing others to assume that he is deranged, and if he is not aware of that, then he certainly *is* mad. If Shakespeare had been capable of having Hamlet talk in a way that would be uninterpretable (the only indication that Grebanier seems to allow as proof of madness), he would either have lost his audience at that point or else have created a comic figure.

The art of creating a person who is feigning madness consists, of course, of having him speak in such a way as to make no sense to the other people on the stage, while making sense—dubious as it may be—to the audience. When Ophelia and Lear are suffering from manifest madness, they both speak in a way that has meaning, and that sometimes even reveals a profundity previously lacking in their normal condition. Lear certainly becomes a more interesting character when he is shaken by madness.[3] This is also true, by the way, in many clinical instances. By insisting that, as long as a character's speech can be interpreted and contains meaning, he is not mad and is not feigning madness, Grebanier has, in my opinion, hopelessly barred the road to any understanding of Hamlet.

When I now turn to a discussion of Grebanier's use of the concept of *hamartia,* I am no longer dealing with comments that should never have found their way into print, because of their bizarre character—such as the idea of Hamlet's intention of reading a document to the Court in the

---

[3] Hamlet's madness, whether it is feigned or real, takes place, of course, on a level quite different from that of Ophelia's or Lear's.

last scene. The concept of *hamartia*, of course, has occupied a large place in the thinking of many a serious scholar who has devoted himself to the elucidation of tragedy. But, as will be seen, it is handled by Grebanier with particular ineptness, amounting at times to the ridiculous. If Grebanier had read Peter Alexander's text (1955), which does not show up in his bibliography, he might perhaps have been more cautious in his formulations.

It is impressive to what a small sector of the human universe the mental outlook becomes limited, once one relies on *hamartia* in one's approach to tragedy. Oedipus's *hamartia* is, for Grebanier, his over-weeningness, heedlessness, willfulness (p. 34). Had he refrained from killing men older than himself or marrying a woman older than himself, he would have escaped the prediction of the oracle. The *hamartia* of Romeo and Juliet is again—heedlessness (p. 35). "Romeo, we feel, has had but to inform old Capulet that he is now his son-in-law and. . . Juliet's father would have welcomed him into the family" (p. 184). How simple life would be if only people were reasonable!

Yet an Oedipus who is phobic, who kills only men his age or younger (always inquiring into a man's age before slaying him), and who likewise asks for a birth certificate before he couches with a woman, would strike us as being utterly ridiculous. Hence, we could not regard the suggested absence of "rashness" in his case as any great improvement upon his alleged *hamartia*. I must also admit that I could hardly admire a spectator's acumen or his capacity to enjoy the literary arts, if, while he was viewing *Romeo and Juliet,* the thought ever crossed his mind: "What a fool Romeo is!" or "Why doesn't he run to his father-in-law and announce his secret visit to Juliet's chamber?"

If Grebanier had really discovered a central psychological factor common to both the tragedy of Oedipus and that of Hamlet, his discovery would certainly have to be welcomed. But it is highly questionable whether Oedipus or Hamlet, or Romeo for that matter, is overweening at all; and if these three truly were, I do not know whether this could really be regarded as a central element, or even as contributing very much to our interest in their tragedy. If an otherwise reasonable person does something stupid or forbidden in a moment of rashness, one may seriously doubt whether that could be a matter of great and lasting interest to mankind.

It is quite an achievement on Grebanier's part to overlook the fact that in both *Oedipus* and *Hamlet* the central problem is that of the violent death of the father. In *Romeo and Juliet,* it is a matter of a secret and forbidden love that is opposed by two fathers. If I seem to be intimating that conflicts about love and murder are the focal points of tragedy, there may be objections that these are also the focal points of detective stories, fairy tales, myths, movies and the cheapest literature. Yet the reason why love and murder are encountered in all these different forms of artistic endeavor is precisely that they are the eternal problems of man.

If one takes out of the myths of Saturn and Cronus, the *Iliad* and *Hamlet,* forbidden love and a variety of manifestations of hostility, then these works will surely lose their hold on us, even if their beauty of language and their poetry, their subtlety and mastery of characterization are preserved. It is man's terrible suffering and his fate that make for tragedy. This does not, of course, say anything about the formal aspect; it merely opposes the traditional idea that *hamartia* is a necessary and integral part of tragedy. To my mind, *hamartia* is the idealist's excuse, his sop to make life tolerable—a piece of consolation in the ocean of suffering that man wishes to negate by denial.

There is a statement in *Lear* that is almost too terrible to consider: "As flies to wanton boys are we to the gods; they kill us for their sport." Alexander (1955, p. 94) says about it: "Critics of any discernment have long ago given up treating this as the key to Shakespeare's intention." Yet a high degree of discernment may perhaps come into being only among those sensitive persons who are vulnerable to the terrible. Perhaps the excessively ghastly *is* the key to Shakespeare's tragedies.

Did Shakespeare need *hamartia* in order to make life tolerable? Did he believe in the child's tale that if only you are good, you will thereby be protected against trouble? For what the concept *hamartia* means is that trouble could have been avoided—if only man himself were not cankered by some defect. What the tragedy of *Hamlet,* however, means to me is that even if man strives to live up to his potentiality, strives to bring to full fruition the seed that the Divinity, as we are told, has put in him, he is still bound to live a dangerous life, filled with conflict and suffering and with a great chance of meeting with catastrophe. As I intimated earlier, my belief is that Shakespeare did offer some crumb of hope in that sea of troubles by permitting Hamlet to be reborn in the form of Fortinbras. Yet that would be an appeal to the unconscious, so that the spectator may not grasp, even at the end, what it was that released him with a ray of hope from the Tragedy of Man. Goethe, by contrast, was not able to let his *Faust* end under the shattering circumstances of Faust's demise on earth, but instead found it necessary, apparently, to leave off with the delights of a heavenly apotheosis.

The belief in *hamartia* is in the end an attempt to free the gods from guilt, and at the same time to find protection against inner despair. It is for that reason, I would surmise, that Grebanier had to find *hamartia* in Hamlet, too; according to him (as also to others), its chief reflection lay in Hamlet's rashness in killing Polonius. Up to that point, he had acted with admirable circumspection; but in that moment of rashness, as Grebanier sees it, he cancelled out all the gains he had made until then.

How does the author prove his point? He refers to the Ghost's indirect reproach of Hamlet, his justifying his "visitation" in Gertrude's chamber in terms of Hamlet's "almost blunted purpose." Now Grebanier reasons that knives become blunted, "As every housewife could tell," from overuse. What the Ghost is accusing Hamlet of, therefore, is not of having done too little but of having done far too much. He is referring not to his son's mental attitude in general, but specifically to the murder of Polonius—an act that, by virtue of Hamlet's excessively hasty use of the sword, has blunted the edge of his revenge (p. 233).

I have the greatest admiration for Shakespeare's art of creating ambiguities, but if he had really intended us to think of the housewife's use of knives when he spoke of "blunted purpose," I would have to regard this as a flaw on his part. I can only assume that Grebanier has been the first (and perhaps the last) person to introduce this sort of imagery; the rest of mankind has been to my knowledge sufficiently lacking in ingenuity and therefore took "blunted" in the sense that Hamlet had anticipated by calling himself "tardy" *(3.4.106)*. We may be assured, however, that the author is ingenious enough to bend even this self-accusation by Hamlet in the direction of his purposes. "We have seen no procrastination, no delay—and now that the play is much more than half over it is too late to look for it" (p. 232). That it was he who may have misread the rather ample evidence thus far for Hamlet's delaying never seems to have dawned on the author.

In order for it to have dramatic effects, *hamartia* must produce dire consequences. Thus Grebanier, even if he has to do some violence to the bare facts of the plot, has to supply such consequences. He claims arbitrarily that it was the killing of Polonius that made it possible for Claudius to order Hamlet to go to England. Claudius' plan, however, has already emerged as soon as his suspicions with regard to the true nature of Hamlet's alleged madness have become aroused *(3.1.168)*, while he is listening to Hamlet's outbursts against Ophelia. His plan makes refusal by Hamlet impossible, since Hamlet is being entrusted with an affair of state: "For the demand of our neglected tribute." Is it conceivable that, under such circumstances, the crown prince will say no? "We feel fairly certain that Hamlet would refuse to go" (Grebanier, 1960, p. 223).

After the mouse-trap play, the necessity of removing Hamlet from Elsinore becomes, of course, more urgent than ever, and Claudius makes final preparations for it by assigning Rosencrantz and Guildenstern as Hamlet's companions on the journey *(III.21.1)*. There can be no doubt in anyone's mind that Hamlet will have to carry out the royal orders. Yet Grebanier writes: "This time we are convinced that Hamlet will never agree to leave Denmark now that his line of action is taking direction" (p. 223). These are utterly unfounded claims, and serve only to rationalize the author's conclusion that it is Hamlet's killing of Polonius that makes it impossible for him to refuse the King's embassy.

Oddly enough, according to Grebanier's peculiar interpretations, as will be seen presently, Polonius' violent death is not at all a matter of Hamlet's *hamartia*. From Ophelia's words, while she is distributing flowers in her madness, the author tries to prove that she knows of "Claudius' treachery, his and Gertrude's adultery and the murder [of Old Hamlet] itself." Ophelia, we are made to believe, "would in Polonius' household be treated as though she were not there during the discussion of the world's affairs, her father and brother fully confident that what she heard was safe with her. She had heard talk of Gertrude's adultery; she had even overheard talk about the murder" (p. 238)! Further, Polonius "must have been somewhat a partner" in the crime—which, Grebanier believes, also explains why the King permits him to eavesdrop in Gertrude's closet (p. 412).

This preposterous construction would not only make Ophelia a veritable imbecile, but it would also make a fool of Hamlet. According to the author, Hamlet has been forced to postpone his revenge mainly out of the necessity of proving to the court that the killing of Claudius was an act of justice; now, however, it turns out that the *histoire scandaleuse* of the royal family was a matter of court gossip, in any case, so that Hamlet had no reason at all to worry about how he would be able to prove Claudius' misdeeds. Moreover, if Polonius was also guilty of sharing responsibility for Old Hamlet's death and was therefore even a worse monster than Richard III, how could it be *hamartia* for Hamlet to kill Polonius? In view of all these belated revelations, what appeared first as rashness is now proven to have been an act of wisdom, if not of divine justice.[4]

Grebanier's interpretation of Hamlet also fails as the result of his ignoring the significant development that Hamlet has undergone during the course of the play. When he writes: "It is, of course, the same Hamlet we have known throughout the play who has come back to Denmark" (p. 461), he is essentially wrong, just as he misses the meaning of Shakespeare's going out of his way to make Hamlet 30 years old in the gravedigger scene. It is inconceivable for Hamlet to have been able to talk at the beginning of the play in the same way as he does at the end. Grebanier may be right in disputing Johnson's (1952) particular interpretation of Hamlet's development, but that *a development of some kind* did take place cannot be disputed.

Of course, no change of identity has occurred; the Hamlet whom we see at the end is an individual whose potentiality has been realized to the fullest extent. The two concepts, Grebanier's and the one that I share with such critics as Johnson and Granville-Barker, reveal the difference between a static and a dynamic-genetic approach. The times are gone when the literary critic was permitted to devise his own psychology, in order to interpret those characters whom literary geniuses had created. If Grebanier had at least taken note of the fact that psychoanalytic interpretations refer to the unconscious and that, for this reason, their contents cannot possibly be expressed directly in the words and actions of the protagonist, he might, after all, have learned something from the psychoanalytic literature on Hamlet.

* * *

After completing my reading of Grebanier's interpretation, I then came across a Jungian interpretation of *Hamlet*, in *Shakespeare's Royal Self* by James Kirsch (1966). Since the author accepts, with only a few exceptions, Grebanier's explanations of the plot,[5] it is appropriate to place my critical review of Kirsch's work in this section.

I am not familiar with Jungian literature; a somewhat cursory checking of it has led to my finding in it only two references to *Hamlet*. One is a short remark that Jung (1944, p. 80) made about "the skull soliloquies of Faust and of Hamlet": they are, he says, "reminders of the

---

[4] Draper (1939) sees in Claudius' downfall the consequence of his having been deprived of his main councillor, an interpretation that is quite in keeping with the historical surface of the play.

[5] However, Kirsch adds a general reservation. He feels that Grebanier has "failed in his attempt at understanding the mystery because he feels that everything in the play can be explained" (p. 9).

appalling senselessness of human life." A more far-reaching remark is to be found in a book by Erich Neumann (1949, p. 168). In his comparison of the *Oedipus* tragedy and the *Oresteia*, he identifies in the latter a further stage in the son's liberation from the mother. "In the *Oresteia*, and again with variations in *Hamlet*, the spirit of the father is the impelling force that compasses the death of the sinful mother." As far as I have been able to observe, Kirsch, without quoting Neumann, nevertheless makes this idea the center of his Hamlet interpretation.

As a passing remark in a general survey, Neumann's comment might have its place; for an analysis of the play it is not sufficient. I must admit that I was taken by surprise when I observed that Kirsch put so much trust in Grebanier's interpretation, which is surely one of the most shallow among the many that have been offered during the last 350 years and throughout shows explicitly an antipsychological bias. I have commented above on how Grebanier skirted the problem of Hamlet's madness.

Apparently the essentially unShakespearean legerdemain of conjuring the Royal commission into Hamlet's breast pocket was too much even for Kirsch; yet he himself dismisses Hamlet's confession of madness by a no less "neat trick," quite unworthy of any student of the human mind: "I do not think," he says, "we can take this term 'madness' in the modern sense as a clinical term, but, generally, as a mental condition in which consciousness is profoundly affected by an unconscious content" (p. 175). I myself am unable to find the latter description so greatly in conflict with what is called madness "in the modern sense as a clinical term."

Kirsch even thinks that the words Hamlet addresses to Laertes "make it *very clear* that what Hamlet means here by madness is the state of consciousness, which we call possession. Hamlet was not himself but in the power of the Ghost complex" (p. 175) (my italics). If this were so, then Dr. Samuel Johnson would be almost right in wishing that "Hamlet had made some other defense" and finding it inappropriate to Hamlet's character for him "to shelter himself in falsehood." A tragedy is really brought down to the level of a valedictorian's speech if the hero is to say shortly before he comes to his tragic end: "You must really excuse my strange behavior; it was all my father's fault."

While Neumann was apparently willing to recognize a progressive drift in the play, Kirsch sees in *Hamlet* only a decline from bad to worse. He is certain that Shakespeare shared the contemporary belief in the reality of ghosts and "he evidently had personal experience of them also" (p. 24). As far as the author himself is concerned, he sees "no way of proving objectively the existence or nonexistence of ghosts" (p. 24f). Thus, with the cards heavily weighted in favor of ghosts, it is not surprising that, according to Kirsch, the tragedy is the account of a young man who, instead of becoming independent of his father's influence, is poisoned by him and thereby brings havoc on his family and himself.

"It is a psychological truth that one becomes what one fights" (p. 41)—is the author's guiding principle. (I hope, for his sake, that this does not happen to him in his fight against the Freud-Jones theory of *Hamlet*.) For that reason, according to Kirsch, "Hamlet's acceptance of the task of avenging his father's murder makes him immediately decide to attack Claudius"—which then causes him to assume "more and more of the characteristics of Claudius, especially in his attitude to murder" (p. 42). Kirsch here anticipates Prosser's theory of the evil (see above) Ghost by a full year, and turns away with a shudder from Hamlet's killing Rosencrantz and Guildenstern in cold blood.

Since Claudius lives by falsehood, being forced to conceal the secret of his crime, Hamlet puts himself into the same position, according to Kirsch, by the fact that he accepts his father's command and by his having to keep it a secret. Wittily, Kirsch compares Hamlet with doctors "who have to keep many secrets" and therefore "undergo characteristic psychological changes, because secrets function like complexes—they become repressed contents" (p. 43). Such changes have also been observed in members of the Secret Service, he tells us, and he goes on to assure us, happily for us, that this "does not mean that such people become insane." Yet the urge to reveal the secret will require a conscious effort "to subdue the urge" (p. 43f).

How Kirsch reconciles a conscious effort with the repression of contents he does not tell us, nor does he say why he left out of his account such people as lawyers, ministers and priests—or the President. It is safe to say that almost any professional person in our society has to keep secrets, but Hamlet's problem is certainly not that of keeping a secret, which should not be too difficult for anyone, if he is even halfway discreet and not too exhibitionistic.

Kirsch evidently wants Hamlet to solve conflicts in the way in which an adolescent is expected to resolve them in present-day industrialized, democratic society. In this setting, an adult is assumed to have no further manifest obligations toward his parents than to assist them in the event that they are plunged into misfortune. Otherwise, he is expected to make his own choices, in freedom and independence, with regard to such important decisions as his choice of spouse, profession or religion. Kirsch rightly says that "*Hamlet* is a *Seelendrama*"; but he is wrong when he continues: "Hamlet's soul dies by drowning in the unconscious" (p. 165).

Here one has to call a halt to all further references to Shakespeare's art of ambiguity and the broad stream of interpretations that it makes possible, for the author is now speaking as a psychologist and not as a literary critic. Hamlet's manifest development toward autonomy is wholly incompatible with the author's metaphor of his "drowning in the unconscious." The author avers, in introducing his essay, that "he will not attempt to explain the mystery in *Hamlet,* but rather circumambulate it and emphasize one feature, because it is psychic; increase the mystery rather than reduce it" (p. 9). No doubt we are surrounded by mysteries, which is as true of *Hamlet* as it is of the living mind; but it is difficult for me to see where Kirsch has succeeded in *increasing* the mystery of Hamlet.

If his proposition that Hamlet is choked to death by the Ghost's poison were correct, this would of course eliminate the "mystery." But at the end he somewhat abruptly states that *mysterium* is "the archetype of the *coniunctio* which is always experienced as incest, and therefore sinful" (p. 182). Then he continues: "In *Hamlet,* Shakespeare 'outwent' nature. The *mysterium* of the *coniunctio,* an innermost mystery of the soul, was projected and materialized in the sexual union of Claudius and Gertrude, and thus violated its true nature. The *coniunctio* . . . set up a tragic course of events. Projected, materialized, it became a poison which destroyed Ophelia, Hamlet's soul, and ultimately killed him" (p. 183).

Now that is certainly wrong. The mystery of *Hamlet* cannot possibly be boiled down to offensiveness of intercourse between uncle and mother. When Kirsch speaks in hyperbolic terms of Shakespeare, he is following the fashion rather than giving us a clue to the poet's merit. One must say again, however, that it is not necessary for a psychologist to point out that the Queen's second marriage had profound effects, if that is all Kirsch had in mind. A local reporter could state the tragic effects in those same terms. Kirsch cites, in his conclusions, Shakespeare's poem "The Phoenix and The Turtle," to which I, too, attribute great importance. But then one has to perceive that the relevant *coniunctio* takes place symbolically (Jungian interpretations almost always move on the symbolic level) in the last scene, and to acknowledge that Hamlet does in the end carry out his duty (which Kirsch denies, on the grounds that an adult should not kill, even symbolically, and certainly should never obey his father's demand that he do so). When Hamlet actually does kill Claudius, perhaps this too lowers him in Kirsch's eyes "to the lowest level of a bitterly hating villain" (p. 117)—a level on which Kirsch himself feels compelled to put Hamlet, in view of the un-Christian words he hurls during the prayer-soliloquy.

Of the many critical comments one could make about Kirsch, I want to make only one more. It is astonishing to hear, from a psychologist who treats patients, that Freud's interpretation of Hamlet is not valid, because there is no reference in the text to infantile fantasies. About the scene between the Queen and Hamlet he says: "Both are possessed by an unconscious complex, a devil . . . In the case of the Queen the effect of her complex has been a tremendous sexualization, in the case of Hamlet a thirst for blood . . . At this climactic point in the drama, both are equally unconscious" (p. 123). That latter picture, I must confess, does increase the "mystery," after all, for I have always seen the two of them moving around on the stage quite agitatedly. Be that as it may, pages later the author announces, to my surprise, his discovery of "an incest complex in Hamlet" and "that he is quite unconscious of it" (p. 134). Yet he asks, does Hamlet's incestuous relationship with his mother represent "a so-called Oedipus complex"?

In order to answer—and we may be certain the question is rhetorical—he suggests the application of "the rule that things which occur at the same time belong together psychologically," and infers "that this incestuous sexuality in Hamlet is due to the influence of the Ghost," since it makes itself noticeable immediately after "the apparent materialization of the Ghost." He refers to similar clinical observations in adults, in whom "an intensive sexualization" occurs after the death of a parent, but this can be observed "more often when a close relationship . . . had existed when the deceased was still alive" (p. 134). This does not mean, in *Hamlet,* however, "that childhood fantasies are revived, but rather that it belongs to the intense and frequently perverse psychology of the ghost."

The author seems to assume that no psychoanalyst knows of instances in which the oedipal tie was continued into adult years, or in which it was brought about by seductive behavior on the part of the parent. Yet in *Hamlet,* he appears to assert, it was the father who talked the son into incestuous fantasies about the mother—an assertion that Prosser also made later, indirectly, when she used the Ghost's sensual imagery as another sign of his devilishness. If Kirsch's argument with psychoanalysis centers about the infantile Oedipus complex, one would agree with him—if only one were able to observe angelic children, who never indulge in fantasies of a physical nature about their parents. But what Shakespeare actually thought and felt about that matter is unknown.

Biographical records in general indicate that there are phases when the repressed comes to the surface. In such phases the genius gains insights of a "psychoanalytic" nature into his own development, which he then again represses. But it is not known in what phase Shakespeare was at the time he created *Hamlet*. If it was after his father's death, or at a time when his father was very sick and marked by death, one would assume that the repressed acquired unusual buoyancy and, for obvious reasons, did not merely tap softly at the entrance to consciousness but rather came upon it with resounding knocks.

Tennessee Williams, it is certain, if he were to write a tragedy akin to *Hamlet,* would offer ample references to the protagonist's childhood, since he is working in a period when science has already lifted some of the mystery from human development and has thereby made the creative process infinitely more difficult for the artist. Shakespeare, of course, was able to present the Oedipus complex only insofar as it is visible in the adult, and his remarks about the past do not go any further back than the time of latency.[6] Freud and Jones, however, were perfectly correct when they added an insight that has been gained by hard work during the years that followed the writing of *Hamlet.*

When Kirsch "dares the hypothesis that by writing this play Shakespeare may have freed himself from an illness and was thus able to continue more than ever to be himself" (p. 181) he is, I am certain, quite unaware of the extent to which, if he were right, he would be confirming a psychoanalytic proposition. Yet I have my doubts even about this point. The psychologist is all too inclined to confuse talent with genius. While the talented person does rid himself of disease by way of his creative productions, the latter is strong enough to face the complications of human existence without having to escape into illness. His psychopathology is characteristic of the creative process and in that regard essentially different from illness. In creating he does not rid himself of

---

[6] Old Hamlet's absence when Hamlet was born, however, may be interpreted—as I have suggested—as a clue that Hamlet's ambivalence toward the father goes back to infantile times.

anything, he does not induce structural changes; it is only the talented person who does these things, utilizing creativity for therapeutic ends. Some say that they have observed an essential change in Shakespeare after *Hamlet*;[7] if this claim is correct (I myself doubt it), then I would not hesitate to ascribe the change to the loss of his father and by no means to the writing of *Hamlet*.

Finally, Kirsch's interpretation of *Hamlet* is so poor, at times even puerile, that I hesitate to lay its weaknesses at the doorstep of Jung's analytical psychology, but would rather ascribe it to the author's own idiosyncrasies.[8]

[7]Murry wrote: "After Hamlet, the Shakespeare man never appears again. With Hamlet's death, he also dies" (1936, p. 230). Should he have said instead that, in writing *Hamlet*, Shakespeare suffered an incurable wound? I am inclined almost to believe in the latter. But our "adjustment" and mental hygiene-minded age would probably never accept the idea of a mind achieving the extraordinary and in that process *injuring* itself! For a view that sees in *Hamlet* the prelude to *King Lear*, see Whitaker (1965, p. 183ff).

[8]I would like to refer briefly to another attempt to apply Jung's analytic psychology to Hamlet by "a doctor familiar with the theory and practice of psychological medicine" (Scott, 1962, p. 11) and a practitioner of general medicine. His specific aim was to demonstrate the importance of the basic attitudes of introversion and extraversion, as presented by Jung in his *Psychological Types* (1923), "for understanding both Shakespeare's characters themselves and his own relationship with them" (p. 13).

It would lead too far afield to submit Jung's typology to a critical analysis and to demonstrate its inadequacy (which might have been expected to show up when Jung's theory was applied to such complex problems as those involved in the analysis of *Hamlet*. Aside from this, however, Scott's inquiry suffers from another principal deficiency. He makes a serious mistake in attempting to identify circumscribed psychoses in Shakespeare's main characters—as when he diagnoses Hamlet as a manic-depressive who suffers from a constitutional, inborn disease (p. 101). Richard Flatter (1891-1960), the able Shakespeare translator, inquired of Freud, when he sent him his German translation of Lear, "whether one is justified in considering Lear a case of hysteria." "I should like to say," Freud (1873-1939, p. 395) answered, "that one is hardly entitled to expect from a poet a clinically correct description of a mental illness. It should be enough that our feelings are at no point offended and that our so-called popular psychiatry enables us to follow the person described as abnormal in all his deviations."

Until recently, psychiatrists have asserted (possibly rightly so, in terms of the historical moment) that empathy with the major psychoses is impossible for a healthy mind. It took modern depth psychology to produce a basic change in this respect—that is, to enlarge the area of empathic abilities. Shakespeare never goes beyond empathic sensibility in his presentation of aberration. It must be stated, as a generalization, that with him, one should refer to "the abnormal" cautiously. "Often one calls normal nerves sick," wrote F. T. Visscher (1807-1887), professor of aesthetics and novelist, "for the nerves of the majority are blunted [*stumpf*] and thus the correct appears to them to be a pathological exception," (1878, p. 403). I wonder to how many of Shakespeare's creations this profound observation is applicable.

A playwright may, of course, make what is objectively an inborn abnormality the nodal problem of a play, but only by presenting it as psychologically meaningful. The physician-critic, however, asserts in this instance that we do not need to seek the cause for Hamlet's manic-depressive disorder, since it is constitutional and the environment is only, he says, a precipitating factor (Scott, 1962, p. 101). The likelihood is that, if the father had not died and the mother had not remarried, Hamlet would probably have gone on to be the ideal type of his time and his society. This, at least, seems to be implied in view of what we are permitted to know about Hamlet. We may also infer that nothing but parental behavior beyond expectation, at least in

Hamlet's eyes, would have been able to evoke a response of the sort we observe in him when he meets his father's ghost. All such viewpoints become senseless, however, if the medical psychologist's views contain even a modicum of truth.

It sounds almost comical when the medical psychologist, presumably applying his clinical observation that a history of the suitor's mental illness is the only reason for parents objecting to a daughter's marriage with an otherwise eligible young man, on that basis asserts that the true reason for Polonius' and Laertes' opposition to Ophelia's marriage is that "Hamlet had shown signs of mental imbalance before the period of the play" (p. 176).

The complex psychological process that fills *Hamlet* is reduced to four phases, three of which are taken up by the evolvement of a cyclic disorder: 1. up to the meeting with the Ghost, simple depression; 2. up to the end of the nunnery scene, agitated depression; 3. up to the trip to England, hypomania; 4. the rest is mental normality (p. 100).

When Scott cites Jones' (1949, p. 68) diagnosis of "a severe case of hysteria on a cyclothymic basis," to a certain extent he does him injustice, because he keeps from the reader the fact that Jones was disinclined "to describe such a condition as Hamlet's in clinical terms," and did so only in order to correct the widespread view of a psychosis—more importantly, the fact that Jones considered such questions "of academic interest only. What we are essentially concerned with is the psychological understanding of the dramatic effect produced by Hamlet's personality and behavior. That effect would be quite other were the central figure in the play to represent merely 'a case of insanity' " (ibid.). Jones' diagnosis—if it ever was meant to be a diagnosis—is so broad that it becomes meaningless for all practical purposes.

In reality Hamlet's *humanity* is so broad and comprehensive that, if it were possible to find his equivalent in present-day clinical reality, each different psychiatrist would probably succeed in finding in it confirmation of his favored diagnosis from psychopathy to schizophrenia. It is even likely that some would raise the question of whether or not the patient had ever taken LSD, or was an addict, or perhaps had had cortisone prescribed, some time earlier. However, when Jones places Hamlet in contrast to Ophelia and says that "such a person passes beyond our ken, is in a sense no more human" (ibid.), I must take exception. I am certain that, between the extremes of the Divine and the Satanic-Beastly, Shakespeare never created anything that was not human. Ophelia's "insanity" is, to my feeling, one of his most human structures, and, despite the disagreements that are evoked about the interpretation of a goodly number of Ophelia's effusions, it is a generally valid example (300 years before Freud) that the human mind does have the capacity to empathize with a variety of psychoses, as long as these are not primarily the direct result of diseased brain substance.

Scott's book, despite some original observation of details, stands as an instructive warning of how medical psychology should not be used, how under the cloak of a misunderstood and misapplied "rigor" a literary work may be not only deprived of its meaning but actually wiped out as a piece of literature.

· 358 ·

12. The Myth in "Hamlet": Development to Action

In his published works Freud refers to *Hamlet* about 34 times.[1] Sometimes this is a matter of a brief citation; sometimes he uses the play for clinical purposes, mainly for the demonstration of the Oedipus complex, or else he uses the latter in explanation of Hamlet's strange behavior. Three times the passages devoted to *Hamlet* are somewhat longer elaborations. Whatever the form in which the reference may appear each time, however, no hesitation or doubt is noticeable in Freud's mode of citation.

Freud evidently took it for granted, as a matter of course, that the reader would know in detail what he was writing about, when he dealt with the play. *Hamlet* had apparently become part of a living universe, such as anyone who read the author's books and papers could readily be expected to share. Indeed, Freud could take the knowledge of *Hamlet* for granted with greater certainty than he could the reader's fluency in the language in which he himself wrote. He could assume on good grounds, I think, that even before his writings became translated, they might well have aroused the interest of some readers in foreign countries who would perhaps have to struggle with German. He could hardly anticipate, however, that any one of these readers would have any doubts about Hamlet and the vicissitudes to which Shakespeare subjects him.

Indeed, it is probable that every educated person within the West-

[1] I have used the Index of the *Standard Edition* as my source. For the sake of comparison, it might be noted that there are 41 references to *Faust*, 14 to *Macbeth*, and 4 to *King Lear*.

ern cultural orbit has an internal image of Hamlet that is as vivid as his image of some person he has met in reality. In many instances, he will probably be able to say more about Hamlet than he will about many an acquaintance or even a friend; he may even have the feeling of greater familiarity and indeed greater intimacy with Hamlet than with some of the people with whom he is in daily contact. Curiously enough, even though he may be able to imagine a world from which all the people with whom he is familiar will have disappeared, it will hardly be possible for him to imagine a world without Hamlet in it.

If one considers the matter-of-factness with which we all refer to this created character, the vividness of his representation in the mind of any educated reader, one could say that he has become, in effect, the equivalent of a myth.[2]

Ancient philosophers could cite verses that referred to Greek mythology and be quite sure that these verses would be understood by the reader, in whose mind the world of the ancient gods was as much alive as Hamlet is in the contemporary mind. A myth is a complex of ideas that have become emotionally highly charged; it refers to a reality that is shared by groups and it is of great relevance to their actions. It also stands quite close to the repressed: more often than not, it is a close derivative of primary-process configurations.

Yet a myth is at the same time a product of diversified secondary processes. It is myth that keeps the human mind in motion; it also has the power to set in motion great historical movements and to pervade all the diverse layers of personal and community life. It serves as a cohesive force, yet it also creates dissensions, wars and crimes. On the other hand, it may give rise to acts of the greatest devotion, love and sacrifice. Christ, in expiring on the cross, reenacted the myth of the hero: the Messiah and the God-son; yet the millions of Jews that were slaughtered during the second third of our century were also the victims of a myth.

The subjects of myths are practically infinite in number, since they are capable of enveloping everything that is of significance to the human mind. There are famous myths about the origin of the world, the planets and the stars, the oceans and the mountains, and there are also myths about what happened in early times. Modern nations, too, attempt to mythologize their histories. And the body, along with its organs and

[2] Slochower (1950) has analyzed the three layers of the Hamlet myth (universal, Renaissance and psychologic).

functions, is the subject of myths that even our scientific era has not been capable of destroying.

It makes no difference whether a fact of human existence is general, like the mother, or relatively rare, like the stepmother; in both instances, a variety of myths is formed, as is true of all other kinds of family relations. Such ancient professions as law and medicine form the subject of myths, as well as more recent ones—such as the psychoanalyst or the atomic physicist.

Whatever is different from the average or the expectable rarely escapes mythologization, whether it has to do with minorities, such as Negro, Jew or Catholic; a handicapped person, such as the hunchback or the blind person; those who have remained unmarried, such as the spinster and the bachelor. Those who are envied, such as the wealthy, and those who are scorned, such as the mentally ill, the prostitute and the criminal regularly give birth to myths. The stronger the emotional response to something, the greater is the probability that it will provide the occasion for the emergence of a myth. For that reason, love and death probably constitute the most frequent contents of myths.

It has been pointed out, sometimes with wonder, that inquiry into specific myths occasionally leads to the discovery of an objective truth that is represented in these same myths. In some instances, however, one must guard against misjudging the nature of the connection between myth and objective truth. That the myth of the Trojan War goes back to a war that actually did take place in the locale assigned to it in the epos, or that remnants of a settlement have been discovered in Ur—these things are not as surprising as they may sound at first hearing. When Freud says about the paranoiacs that "they do not project it [what they do not wish to recognize in themselves] into the blue, so to speak, where there is nothing of the sort already" (1922, p. 226), he is asserting, in effect, that the delusion has a reality core of truth. One may assume that this is also true of myth formation.

One inference seems to be reasonably valid—namely, that myths contain a psychological truth, sometimes more profound than the rational mind may be capable of finding. Yet it may also happen that, if science discovers an objective truth in a myth, this may be no more than coincidence. Often one hears that the Jewish taboo of pork anticipated a later scientific discovery, as if this particular taboo had actually been formed on the basis of observation, even though perhaps subliminally. The fact is that the food taboos in the Old Testament also refer to many another species whose detrimental effect has not been confirmed by science. More important, if one considers that trichinosis sometimes causes scarcely any symptoms and sometimes leads to death, that there is no uniformity of sequelae at all, it would seem to be utterly impossible that mere everyday observation could ever have discovered the correlation between the intake of pork and disease.

I do not intend, however, to dispute the existence of a core of truth in many myths. Important as these cores may be historically, they have no bearing on the beauty of the myths or on the great power that they are able to exert over man's feelings and actions. This power stems from their closeness to psychic reality, most of which is covered by the unconscious and also includes huge parts of the superego. It is this too that is of some significance when one discusses the mythical meaning of *Hamlet*.

For a long time, however, it was those points of myth content that could be verified by reference to reality that attracted attention. As I have already said, many myths crystallize around a cluster of reality perceptions. Mythologists were long able to discover in myths representations of such natural events as the seasons of lunar elements. "Man's observation of great astronomical regularities," Freud (1930, p. 93) wrote, "not only furnished him with a model for introducing order into his life, but gave him the first points of departure for doing so." But what was it that became attached to the representations of the great astronomical observations? The imagery through which correct reality observations are represented is the derivative of the deepest and most archaic layers; and what makes the myth such a fascinating entity is the fact that in the representation of contents stemming from archaic psychic reality are embedded correct observations.

The more science approaches truth, the more abstract it becomes— until, in the end, the most profound knowledge is caught in a mathematical equation, cold and inhuman, the very antithesis of myth. Nevertheless, the truly great scientists were also great myth-makers. It is the mythical part of their findings and discoveries that becomes socially relevant and thus penetrates into the thinking of groups. The truth value of science is understood by only a small group. While science makes its greatest effect on society as a whole through its application in the form of technology, the reflection of science in the thinking of the largest number of people remains mythical.

There are times that are most propitious for either the rise of new myths or the transformation of old ones. Usually these are times of crisis, when conflicts within a community approach such intensity as to threaten that community with disintegration. Then a number of competing myths arise. Why one rather than another takes hold and becomes dominant is often none too easy to explain.

The great Western crises at the end of antiquity led to the expansion of the myth of Christ, which has held the West in its grasp for the unbelievably long period of one and a half millennia. The myth of Christ was gradually crowded out by various scientific myths, among which that of Newton's is most notable, in that it proved to be particularly enduring: the myth of an infinite space that consists of equivalent points, along with the myth of a universe of forces setting masses into motion.

Our own time, it seems, stands under the shadow of three great mythmakers: Marx, Einstein and Freud. It will probably puzzle later historians that, at both the beginning and the end of the Christian era, the myths that were endowed with the greatest buoyancy and power of penetration were created by Jewish minds. The myth-creating power of the Jewish people seems to be quite extraordinary. It is also worth considering for a moment the geographical distribution of these three myths. The myth of class hierarchies and revolution has now divided the world. Where it is upheld, the myth created by Freud is taboo, and vice versa. Only Einstein's myth is privileged to be accepted wherever science serves as the foundation of civilization.

My reference to the myth-producing effect of science contains no pejorative implication, since I am not saying anything in this context about the truth value of science. In order to show how inescapably science leads to myth-formation, I shall present a recent example. It has to do with one of those many delightfully written, thought-provoking missiles by Prof. Ashley Montagu (1967) that are sometimes just a bull's-eye length off center. In 1967, he vigorously attacked recent writings in which scholars, like so many others before them, have reaffirmed their conviction that "man is an innately aggressive creature."

The arguments he presents against such views sound quite convincing. He also sets forth reasons why theories of the innateness of aggression have this strong appeal. "Such books," he writes, "are both congenial to the temper of the times and comforting to the reader who is seeking some sort of absolution for his sins." When responsibility is shifted to natural inheritance or inherited aggressiveness, he asserts, one feels relieved of a burdensome load of guilt.

He therefore describes as a myth the idea that early man was aggressive, and he does not hesitate to put this myth into the same class as "original sin." To this myth he attributes particular importance—or so it would seem, to judge from the title of the article: "Original Sin Revisited." This surprised me, for it was specifically the fall of man that was, according to that theory, not the effect of his nature but the result of his free and spontaneous choice of the wrong values. The theory of an innate aggressiveness, of its rootedness in man's biological structure, therefore, does not seem to me to be compatible with the theory of "original sin," although Prof. Montagu is certainly not the only one to put the two into the same class.

I myself think that he is also in error when he finds the "real sources of man's destructiveness" to lie in "the unsound values by which, in a highly competitive, overcrowded, threatening world . . . man so disoperatively attempts to live. It is not man's innate nature, but his external nurture that requires our attention." Much depends, of course, on what we describe as "destructiveness." It is quite enlightening to read the anthropologists on the subject; for example: "He [early man] did not hunt because he was a 'killer', any more than contemporary man is a 'killer' when he kills animals in abattoirs so that he and others may eat them. Early man was no more a 'killer' than we are 'killers' when we sit down at the table to consume a steak or a chicken." This is a rather elegant piece of side-stepping. If only we were able to ask the cattle and the chickens for their opinion!

I would rather formulate the matter this way: It is because man is a killer that early man was capable of hunting. The anthropologist asserts, in all earnestness, that killing is not killing when it is done for the sake of satisfying hunger, particularly when it is the hunger of our beloved ones that is involved. It is precisely because life is not possible without destruction that the psychologist with a biological bent is forced to state that destructiveness is innate.

When Prof. Montagu (1967) maintains that evidence is lacking as to early man's murdering his fellow-man, I am ready to believe him. But in what way does this disprove man's innate destructiveness? Do not inborn tendencies need proper conditions in order to manifest themselves? I could enumerate a long list of such tendencies in order to prove this point.

Prof. Montagu is correct, of course, when he views the theories that he castigates in their historical perspective, and links them with all the preceding "myths" about man's innate depravity. What he may perhaps be overlooking, however, is the possibility that, when he counters, with all his evidence, the "myth" of early man's destructiveness, he is following instead another myth, as widespread as the other—namely, that man was originally "good" and through his own fault turned "bad."

Does Prof. Montagu really know whether or not early man killed *more* animals than he needed for the sustenance of himself and his group? Does he know what early man's feelings and fantasies were, while he was pursuing his prey and what his sensations were while he was killing it? Was he hungry while doing so? Was he thinking of his beloved ones or was he howling a cry of triumph upon the defeat of an adversary? And when he was gathering his food, what were his fantasies then? Is the anthropologist sure that early man did not have the fantasy of breaking a limb when he severed the stem of a plant?

The anthropologist's image of the purely useful abattoirs, of the peaceful citizen chewing his necessary steaks, is psychologically most unsatisfactory; it is only tenable in the light of a lack of that sensitivity that Leonardo da Vinci apparently possessed. Thus Prof. Montagu, despite the acumen of his arguments, remains unavoidably within the orbit of myth-making.[3] It would be presumptuous for me to decide which of the two myths comes closer to the objective truth, but it may be permissible to report the imagery (mythical, to be sure) that I have formed about the subject, to my own satisfaction.

When Prof. Montagu tells us that there is no evidence that either intra- or intergroup hostilities "occurred in human populations before the development of agricultural-pastoral communities, not much more than 10,000 years ago," this comes close to what I fancied. It is psychologically probable that man was not able, from the beginning, to destroy his mirror-picture. I fancy that, in the beginning, man's self did not have as rigid borders between himself and the outer world as he has possessed for these past many millennia. It is not improbable that, when he lived in groups, the various selves formed a syncitium—that is, a tissue in which the cells are not separated by walls. In such a state, he may easily have been incapable of destructiveness, at least when it was directed toward a member of his own clan. Whether this "inhibition" worked as well when he met a person of different smell or size, or one who dressed or decorat-

---

[3] Prof. Erikson (1961a, p. 141) once made the apposite statement: "Myths do not lie, but they find new forms closer to observation." Yet there are myths that do seem to exclude each other. To be sure, their reappearance occurs in ever more precise and better documented forms, yet it is questionable whether this leads to a *rapprochement*.

ed himself differently, I do not, of course, know. It would be more favorable to my theory, to be sure, if he were incapable of killing, even under such conditions.

To my way of thinking, the first deliberate murder was actually an incredible cultural advance. Human civilization, as we now know it, is based on the evolvement of ego boundaries. It was only with the development of such a border, which separated the self from all surrounding objects, that murder became possible, and aggression could immediately take advantage of the newly opened channel. Since then, it has become part of man's heritage. According to this theory, man was incapable of killing man at the dawn of culture, not because of any lack of aggressivity or of destructiveness, but because of a deficit in ego structuralization. As soon as the neccessary degree of structuralization was achieved, however, his destructiveness also turned against his fellow-man, and it must be admitted that, since then, man has more than caught up with what his early forebears might have missed because of their archaic ego-formation.

It is not only in the humanities that science has failed to drive out myth. There it only becomes glaringly visible. To fully understand the works of Marx or of Freud calls for years, if not decades, of hard labor; to orient oneself sufficiently to be able to discover even in part where Freud was right or wrong, or the significance of this or that error, requires almost a lifetime. Nevertheless, people who have never read a word of Karl Marx rush to the barricades and sacrifice their lives; empires crumble under the impact of the imagery that he created. Imagery reflecting Freud's discoveries has also penetrated popular thinking; even though much of that imagery deviates from the actual content of his writings to a degree that permits one to speak of falsification, it does preserve a vitality and a spark that are inextinguishable.

Physics in the West for a long time went along with Aristotle's myth of "infinite space"; and now it has turned to the myth of space extending its borders with incredible speed, only to start shrinking once again at an indeterminate point of future time.

Finally, we cannot escape myth in the ultimate modes of viewing life, the world, the universe. For some of what has been happening is part of what seems to be an unending chain of repetitions. Nothing can ever occur that could surprise the wise man, for he perceives in all events the return of the past, the workings of the iron laws that hold in their clutches everything that moves. For others, repetition and constancy is unthinkable. Not only is the river not the same as it was the day before, but even the body around which the river moves is quite different from the body that entered the "same" water the day before. Everything is in process of change, and is, for that reason, unpredictable.

Thus we have to wait until the two myths—of eternal change and eternal repetition—are compounded, until we have perhaps come to discover that time is an illusion, and that what we experience as sequences is in reality a set of simultaneous occurrences.[4]

Whether science itself is a myth for those who create and further it by their own productions is not the question. Even if it were to be proven that some few do achieve unmythical—that is, truly scientific—thinking and are thus capable of viewing the world objectively for at least some moments of their lifetime, this would have no bearing on what I am stressing here—namely, that human communities are for the most part swayed by myths.

There are good myths and bad myths: those that further culture and those that destroy it; myths that lead to genocide and to other such terrible crimes and myths that stimulate masses of people to the greatest achievements of charitable love and sacrifice. Despite the damage that a myth may create, however, I believe that the reign of myth is to be welcomed. If science were really to replace myth in every aspect of human life, rigidity and petrifaction would become serious dangers. It seems to me that it is the myth that lies inconspicuously embedded in science that gives it its vitality, drives it on, does not let it ever come to rest.

Here is a peculiar paradox. Myths, when they are overt, as they are in religion, tend to be conservative. How long did it take before the illusory nature of the ancient Olympus of the Gods was fully recognized and accepted? It is only now that it has begun to dawn on the West that even the story of Christ, which was taken literally for many centuries, despite the warning of a good many advanced minds, is a myth. For a long time to come, there will still remain an appreciable, even though ever-dwindling number of people who will keep on insisting that Christ *was* the son of God.

Yet the myth that is silently embedded in science is, just because of

---

[4] In an essay wrongly ascribed to Goethe but certainly written under his direct influence, one finds a synthesis of the two myths: "She [Nature] is eternally forming new structures: what now exists has never before existed. What has been does not return—Everything is new and yet always [a repetition of] the Old. [*Sie (die Natur) schafft ewig neue Gestalten; was da ist, war noch nie, was war, kommt nicht wieder—alles ist neu und doch immer das Alte.*]

its closeness to the primary process, a kind of field of force, disturbing the seeming permanency that is contained in the presentation of scientific systems.[5] In religious systems, at least in those of the West, the appeal to reason is not sufficient to silence doubt, or to distract the believer from an awareness of contradictions among some elements and the utter implausibility of others.

Myth, like almost all other forms of mental production, is a synthesis of mental forces that stem from different parts of the personality. Here I want to refer only to its effect upon the superego and the action sphere. The doctrine that the structure of society is ultimately determined by economic conditions and the level of technology is well known, but it is outside my provenance. The observational sphere of the analyst does not provide the data that are necessary in order to be able to reach reliable conclusions in that matter.[6]

The effects of personal and collective myths, their blending and their influence on everyday decisions and actions, are all too well known. But this is also true of the myths that have been engendered by science. Shakespeare's age was one in which, just as in ours, a mythological vacuum had spread—that is to say, the traditional myths no longer satisfied the needs of collective man. New myths therefore arose.

There are ages of a high degree of mental and cultural stability, and there are ages marked by a profound and ceaseless intellectual restlessness, such as does not permit a substantial part of the elite, or even of the population at large, to indulge in the peaceful enjoyment of a monolithic orthodoxy. The fact that one is living in a heterodox age, an age that is in quest of a new orthodoxy such as will be able to bind the community once again into something that may be likened to a homeostatic organism, is indeed a great privilege; but it is a privilege for which a price has to be paid, in anguish and in tears.

There were, according to Spencer's (1942) penetrating historico-

---

[5] The effect of intellectual curiosity, of course, or of the discovery of new facts is not here denied. Despite the great explanatory value that is contained in scientific systems, it may be that the restless curiosity, the passionate search for new observation, is more closely linked with the mythological core of the scientific process.

[6] Some correlation between the subject's social and economic background and his specific psychopathology is suggested by clinical observation. When some adherents of the doctrine go so far, however, as to postulate a strict correlation between economic structure and cultural productions, the contemporary psychologist feels, in the light of the present level of American psychology, somewhat bewildered. The United States is indeed a country of the highest stage of capitalist development, yet behavioristic and conditioned-reflex psychology is no less flourishing here than it is in the Soviet Union—and this at a time when its very antithesis, psychoanalysis, stands at the center of attention.

cultural analysis, three minds that were responsible for the Renaissance conflict: Copernicus, Machiavelli and Montaigne. The first of these had no serious influence on the development of Shakespeare's thought. He was put on the index only in 1616. When his work was published in 1543, it brought at first a sort of relief. For the medieval theory of the world's position was not geocentric but "diabolocentric" (Lovejoy, 1936, p. 102); therefore, "to remove man from the centre of things was to raise him from his low estate" (p. 104). The narcissistic injury that Freud (1917a, p. 139f) ascribed to the impact of Copernicus' theory evidently set in only later.

If the new astronomy did not touch Shakespeare's Renaissance conflict, however, Machiavelli's new theories did have their effect on him, as they did on Elizabethan tragedy in general. He was put on the Index in 1557—as soon as that institution got under way—so deeply had he offended contemporary sensibilities. He seemed to be a formidable menace, indeed, since he had overturned traditional ideas of law and order and replaced them with new ones, adjusted to man's "real" nature—evil and viciousness.

Montaigne fared the best of the three. His *Essays* were put on the Index only in 1676—that is, 96 years after the first two books had been published—although he may well have offended tradition in the worst way possible, by proving animals to be superior to man. Man thus lost "his crucial position in the natural hierarchy" (Spencer, 1942, p. 38). The cosmological, the political and the natural order were thus questioned, and the doubts cast by these three questioning minds upon the monolithic medieval orthodoxy have never since been erased.

Oddly enough, in our times too three minds have disquieted the age: Einstein, the modern Copernicus; Marx, the modern Machiavelli; and Freud, the modern Montaigne.[7] These latter three minds were by far the "unruliest" in modern times among the many "unruly" ones, who were unable to go on looking at the world in the accustomed way. Their works were not put on the Index; yet like Copernicus, Machiavelli and Montaigne, they too had the privilege of setting the problems that subsequent generations would have to face.

If I apply the foregoing to literary works, then *Hamlet* is, for most people who have been in one way or another actively engaged in cultural life, a myth that has proven through the centuries to possess a stimu-

---

[7] Cf. Spencer (1942, p. 220f) for a different parallel between our age and the Elizabethan age.

lating, productive and constructive power that is truly unparalleled. Like all great myths, this too does not preserve an identity of meaning during the course of successive generations; it has indeed been interpreted and reinterpreted in many quite different ways.

Great myths are the products of long chains of images that extend in many different directions. Here that ambiguity that I have discussed chiefly as an artistic, aesthetic literary device proves to be the prerequisite for richness of meaning per se.[8] The multidimensionality of *Hamlet*, insofar as it is a true myth, makes it well-nigh impossible to make a definitive statement—once one attempts to step beyond the purely factual—about what that myth is all about.

This is true of other myths, too. The factualness of Christ's last words, as these are reported in St. Mark, cannot be disputed. But the famous "Eloi, Eloi lama sabachthani?" can be interpreted either as the desperate outcry of man in his agony, or as a statement produced by the necessity of fulfilling the prediction that is to be found in Psalms 22:1. In the one instance, the myth is humanized, made the epic of man's tragedy; in the other, the divine aspect comes into play, for Christ's role has been theologized: he is in this interpretation the fulfiller of a divine role that was foretold, his function being only to fulfil it in a predestined manner. Each of these interpretations gives the myth one particular direction and meaning. It would be wrong, I believe, to say that one interpretation is correct and the other wrong, even though one of them may come closer than the other to the spirit in which the testament was originally written.

Shakespeare's version of the Hamlet myth has also been interpreted in different ways: as Christ (Siegel, 1957, p. 97, 219 n 38); as a soul that, almost about to replace the law of the Old Testament by that of the New, is tempted and fails (Vyvyan, 1959); and even as "a ritual battle of Summer and Winter, of Life and Death" (Murray, 1914). Even the Christ myth too was interpreted in different ways—as a type of Joseph or Isaac myth, or as an Orphic one (Guthrie, 1966); yet, whatever the classification may be into which the myth is put, the Christ story stands by itself and has had its enormous effect in its own right. The same holds true of *Hamlet*—whatever its antecedents may be.

[8] One-dimensional meanings, such as those that science, when it is living up to its own strict code of rules, ought to deliver, give rise to far less inspiring myths. One might expect that, once the ideal level of abstraction has been reached—that is, when a scientific law has been reduced to a mathematical equation—then science loses its myth-forming power entirely. And yet, mindful of the course of history, the beholder of Einstein's famous equation may hear the sound of those trumpets that made the walls of Jericho fall.

When I here raise the question of what the myth is in *Hamlet,* I do not do so in the way in which that question is raised in mythic criticism (see Quinn, 1966, p. 578f); instead, I wonder what is the mythical feature in the play that makes it live so strikingly in our minds. It cannot be the myth of the good or bad mother, or that of the girl who dies because of a broken heart, or any of the many other themes that are woven into the play.

One may perhaps catch hold of this particular element by considering Bertrand Russell's (1955) lampoon on applied psychoanalysis. There he toys with the idea of what would have happened to six of Shakespeare's male protagonists if they had been analyzed before they met with the terrible fate that Shakespeare lets them suffer. All of them had become well-adjusted, untroubled, average people; Russell has each one give an account of himself after having been analyzed by Dr. Bombasticus.

I shall quote a few passages of what Hamlet had to divulge, omitting Russell's comment on the oedipal conflict (Russell, 1955, pp. 24-27).

I was quite exceptionally fortunate in meeting Dr. Bombasticus when I did, for I was certainly in a very bad way . . . I had had a quite absurd sense of self-importance, and had thought that the time was out of joint and I was born to set it right.

Dr. Bombasticus persuaded me that I was very young and had no understanding of statecraft. I saw that I have been wrong to oppose the established order, to which any well-adjusted person will conform. I apologized to my mother for any rude things I might have said. I established correct relations with my uncle—though I must confess that I still found him somewhat prosy. I married Ophelia, who made me a submissive wife. In due course I succeeded to the kingdom, and in disputes with Poland I upheld the honor of the country by successful battles. I died universally respected, and even my uncle was not more honored in the national memory than I was . . .

It was Horatio! Yes, he certainly was a bad influence . . . I threw over Horatio and took up with Rosencrantz and Guildenstern, who, as Dr. Bombasticus pointed out, were completely adjusted . . . There are times—I will not deny it—when I feel a certain respect for the old fire, for the golden words that flowed from my mouth, and for the sharp insight that was at once my torment and my joy. I can remember even now a fine piece of rhetoric that I manufactured, beginning, "What piece of work is a man!" I will not deny that in its own mad world it had a kind of merit. But I chose to live in the sane world, the world of earnest men who perform recognized duties without doubt and without question, who never look beneath the surface for fear of what they might see, who honor their father and their mother and repeat the crimes by which their father and their mother flourished, who uphold the State without asking whether it deserves to be upheld, and piously worship a God whom they have made in their own image, and who suscribe to no lie unless it furthers the interests of the strong. To this creed, following the teaching of Dr. Bombasticus, I subscribed. By this creed I lived. And in this creed I died . . . I'd rather smile and be a villain than weep and be a good man.[9]

By using the technique of reversals, Russell may have brought to light a truth—namely, that Hamlet contains the myth of adjustment. Adjustment to what? To society, of course. But to what kind of society is it that Hamlet is supposed to adjust? One that is rotten throughout, indeed; what is more, this rottenness encompasses the entire structure of Hamlet's particular community solely because an oedipal crime has been committed at the top. While Hamlet's own Oedipus complex remains a matter of interpretation or conjecture or reconstruction, the oedipal crime at the top, the consequences of which trickle down to the foundation, is beyond dispute; it is outspoken and, when viewed sociologically, it is the core problem of the play.

It is indeed a far-reaching and thought-provoking dynamic constellation that, in the tragedy, what is manifest on the social level is what is repressed in Hamlet himself (assuming that Freud's interpretation was correct). The play suggests a sort of mirroring between the social process and the psychological, subjective unconscious process in the repressed; or one could say that an inverted Janus head would serve well as a symbol of Hamlet's relationship to his community. What Shakespeare is conveying here—or so it seems to me, at least—is that every society, not just a particular one, may very well be rotten; therefore, the myth that underlies the tragedy asserts that, in every society, it is the oedipal crime and its denial that are at the core of the "imposthume."

While the second point as a generalization is difficult to prove, there is no such difficulty involved in attempting to prove the first. I should like to be able to read the chronicle of a historical period in which the vast

[9] What Russell alleges against psychoanalysis can also be raised against other fields of science. I will not enter into any polemics with Russell about his misunderstanding of the psychoanalytic process, but only indicate that he is right, in my opinion, when he says in his Introduction that "sanity may be defined as a synthesis of insanities." This idea was not too far from what Freud probably thought (Freud, 1924b, p. 185). In a previous paper (1960), I made an attempt (perhaps unsuccessful) to present sanity as the right melange of neurosis, psychosis and delinquency. Along the lines of Russell's satire, one could write an equivalent on modern medicine, letting Thomas Mann's Hans Castorp report that he was spared his follies with regard to the philosophy of time by virtue of having been cured of his tuberculosis. *Doctor Faustus* would not have been written, if its hero Johann had only accepted his doctor's advice and followed up the treatment of his syphilis. Be that as it may, with fine intuition Russell selects Hamlet as the only one of these six characters of Shakespeare's whose "treatment" fails and who therefore prefers to revert to what he has been previously.

majority did not suffer as the result of the structure of the society into which it was born. To posterity, certain periods may appear in a favorable light, yet closer scrutiny always reveals in them the same hidden and sometimes not-so-hidden "imposthume."

In view of the execrable conditions at present (1968), of which only a few need be enumerated—the ongoing war; the daily death by starvation of 10,000 human beings all over the world; the division of the world into two irreconcilable camps, each armed with resources capable of extinguishing life, once unleashed; the spreading anarchy in all sectors of our society—any reasonable person may be tempted to look back with longing to a time two decades or so before this holocaust started, with the outbreak of World War I.

But would such a person really wish to have been a member of the laboring class at that time—without the protections of a union or health insurance or an old age pension? Would he be happy with a work-day of 16 hours, and a constant threat of unemployment? This is not to speak of the life of a member of the lowest stratum in the colonies, the degree of whose exploitation has entailed living and psychological conditions that are beyond all description (cf. Fanon, 1961).

It is apparently not easy for man to accept the repugnant idea that, up to now, societal existence has meant—*always* and *regularly*—inhuman sufferings, injustice, exploitation, neglect and hypocrisy. Every state rests, in a sense, on the "imposthume." In saying this, I am not saying anything new. Greater minds than mine have set forth this conception of the state; a multitude of books have been written, unmasking the state and society, in theory and in practice, and revealing the execrable rottenness that pervades practically every body politic.

For this, they have been vigorously criticized, and the results of their inquiries have been supposedly "refuted." Where this has not been possible, they have been reproached for not having emphasized quite as vigorously the large number of benevolent actions and institutions which the reprovers believe to represent an equally important part of the story. Community life does not, after all, consist—or so this view goes—only of exploitation and torment; it also consists of a rich flow of acts of affection, care and responsibility.

Yet here one seems to see something strange indeed. If from one day to the next, around the turn of the century, all the social progress had been instituted that has been realized since then—that is to say, if, from one day to the next, the work-day had been reduced from 14 hours to seven, and unemployment, health insurance and old age pensions had been introduced, along with unions and the right to strike and the rest— then the working people would probably have been overjoyed. A Pharaoh would probably have given a way half his kingdom for the opportunity to fly around the world in a single day. Yet all this technical progress, as well as the furtherance it has made possible of social institutions, has apparently made no one particularly happy.

Even more, it was probably beyond Dickens' imagination to envision a state of welfare such as is shared, after all, by a large number of children in our present population, or the degree of understanding and psychological protection that a substantial percentage also obtain. The unhappiness to which children are subjected in Dickens' novels will hardly be found anywhere nowadays. Yet has the liberation of the child borne those fruits that any reasonable person would have predicted? What one generation might have regarded as the fulfilment of a dream may well appear to the next generation, or to the one after that, to be little more than a fraction of its own minimal demands.

Technical progress is quickly taken for granted. A delay of an hour in the arrival of a plane may arouse in the passenger almost the same feeling of indignation and discomfort as that which the delay of a boat for days created in his predecessor. There seems to be no objective yardstick for comfort, of the sort that can be employed with regard to the determination of a physiological optimum in the intake of nutrients and liquids. We know pretty exactly by now what the body needs in order to feel comfortable, but the mind has no such objective frame: what seems to one generation to be the envied luxury of one select group may be, for another group, a minimum standard.

Further, the necessity of fighting for social improvement seems to detract from its enjoyment, once it has been realized. The image of the state remains associated with the image of a harsh father, who showers plenitude on a few of his sons, yet to the majority gives grudgingly and reluctantly—always too little and too late. The fact that what is called "social progress" is brought about only as a consequence of aggression and struggle may leave a feeling of guilt that can destroy the feeling of true enjoyment.

Following Rilke, I have called that historic hour *eine Sternenstunde* when, under Freud's guidance, a father for the first time in the history of mankind listened to his little son's confession of oedipal wishes, without experiencing an angry and punitive reaction. It was an altogether improbable event, in view of the history of fears and anger that ever since the dawn of mankind had taken hold of adults when they became aware of oedipal manifestations in children.

Since that *Sternenstunde*, the oedipal conflict has become a matter almost of daily conversation. A patient may introduce his initial interview with the remark that he is suffering from it. Such public media as movies, television, radio discuss it without hesitation; the whole structure has lost much of its initial terribleness. In order to reexperience the full dimensions of this tragic conflict, one has to read Sophocles (*Oedipus Rex*) and Dostoevski (*The Brothers Karamazov*). In our time, however, it has become intellectualized and mechanized—that is to say, *denied* by means of the most insidious techniques.

When Freud created the psychoanalytic situation, he once again achieved the culturally improbable. One could hardly have believed it possible for one member of a community to verbalize and express to a fellow-man *everything* that crossed his mind, to reveal his cruelest and most vicious wishes and impulses, even when they were directed toward the listener himself, and yet to do so with a full guarantee of freedom from any critical judgment, but rather with a certainty of the sort of benevolent understanding that would result in the conversion of the seemingly irrational disorder of his psychic life into a rational order.

If one feels the full dimensions of the psychoanalytic situation, one should be really awe-struck; yet we know how few people make adequate use of the opportunity it provides, how many indeed ridicule it. We are only too well aware how few have grasped its extraordinary quality, and that, as a result, it has not become integrated into what Prof. Erikson has so felicitously described as the "metabolism of generations."

One aspect of *Hamlet* is indeed the metabolism of generations, but that metabolism is there presented in its full awesomeness, which goes far beyond what could be solved by even optimal child-rearing practices. If these were indeed feasible at all, they would undoubtedly, once established, become traditional, mechanical and inadequate.

What Shakespeare says about the metabolism of generations in *Hamlet* is that *each generation is forced to commit the oedipal crime* and that each generation is likewise forced to conceal from and deny to the next generation that it ever committed the crime. And, indeed, *here* is the root of the "imposthume" that undermines every state—the inevitability of the hypocrisy that pervades any aggregation of human beings, whatever may be the specific group structure into which a number of these beings organize themselves.

Wherever human beings meet, whether it is as family, parliament, professional organization, Church—with the possible exception of such relationships as are to be found in the first love of the young (for example, Romeo and Juliet)—there is hypocrisy. And woe to the reformer, if he seriously tries to eliminate the "imposthume!" If he were to succeed, anarchy would be the immediate consequence. Foolproof "solutions" of the dilemma are, of course, as cheap as beans; but unfortunately they do not work at all in practice, or if so, only for a short while.

The first solution that comes to mind is honesty. If it is indeed true that at the bottom of hypocrisy is the denial of the oedipal crime, then members of the older generation ought to admit frankly to the younger that they too made themselves guilty of it. Yet it would be impossible for the young ones to form a reliable superego, if they grew up under the shadow of that knowledge. Hamlet would never have evolved his sensitive and forthright conscience and superego, if he had known that his father too had once been in the throes of an acute oedipal conflict. Throughout many of the phases of human development, therefore, true honesty between parent and child is neither possible nor advisable; and it is an as yet unsolved problem at what point a child or youth becomes mature enough to bear the full truth with regard to the role of the oedipal conflict in the community and in his own parents' personal lives.

One may therefore say, with only a modicum of reservation, that true honesty in child-rearing will more often than not lead to a cynical, hedonistic generation, with only very tenuous ties to any value system whose realization requires self-restraint. This necessity on the part of the older generation to keep a secret from the young and vice versa (as Shakespeare presents it in *Hamlet*, of course, this necessity is adjusted to the requirements of the play) is the true crux of the metabolism of generations. Unsolvable and tragic, it constitutes the perennial misfortune of the older generation as it gradually yields place, and of the younger generation as it gradually moves ahead.[10] Why should it be otherwise? The animal is free of the oedipal conflict and is also ignorant of death. If man wants to be man, he must accept the oedipal conflict and knowledge of death as a privilege and he must look with pride at the suffering that follows.

[10] Ferenczi (1933) has described the psychological core of the conflict of generations.

It may be that I seem to be preaching an attitude of pessimism, of the acceptance of human evil, that I am repeating the famous question: "What is man that he should bewail his fate?",[11] or believing that this world, as it is, is the best possible of all worlds—a belief that aroused Voltaire's unending, scintillating sarcasms. Perhaps I do believe it; but I also believe that, in order to make this human world a full and fulfilling one, there must be those who believe in panaceas, who have their hopeful illusions, their convictions and those formidable schemes with which they lift the world off its hinges, as Jesus did and Karl Marx, in the name of whom substantial parts of the world changed their face, for better or worse.

In order to be what it is—namely, human—the world is in need of sharp debate and of the unflagging endeavors of the few to remodel society by word or deeds. It would be a terribly inhuman world, were all people to agree upon the unavoidability of the "imposthume," in the way in which we all agree upon the unavoidability of the neonate's vulnerability to small pox and the necessity that flows from that for his vaccination. No, I do not really have any objection to a man's raising his voice and announcing to the world that *he* has found a solution to the world's evil, even though I may be convinced that he is wrong; in the present context, all I object to is his asserting that his illusion was also shared by Shakespeare when he created *Hamlet*. Shakespeare remained faithful to his transporting pessimism. Even in the *Winter's Tale*, the crowning harmony of the end is conceivable only as the consequence of the protagonist's paranoiac spell, which had caused so much heartache to those who had loved him the most.

G. Wilson Knight has spoken of Hamlet's "creative murder." This aspect of the deed could barely be described in a more felicitous way. Indeed, man's creativity, about the psychology of which we know so terribly little, is one of the great hopes. There is a group of a select few, in whom the "imposthume" leads to the greatest achievements, which then become mankind's pride. If all, or at least the majority of human beings were to pour their excess energies into creative acts, instead of into neurotic symptoms or acts of delinquency—that is, into self-torture or the torture of others—this would (even though creative people are by no means happier than the uncreative; if anything, the opposite seems to be true) give the world a friendlier appearance.

---

[11] "O was ist der Mensch, dass er über sich klagen darf!" (Goethe, *Die Leiden des jungen Werther*.)

Two reservations have to be raised here. Knight is right: when Hamlet kills Claudius, he performs a "creative" act; yet this is an act that causes pain to others. And in this may be contained a general truth. It is the excessively creative person who often causes great pain to those he loves. The Sterbas (1954) have demonstrated this in the instance of Beethoven, and I have found the same thing, although in a more camouflaged form, even in the life of Goethe, who was far more disciplined, urbane and understanding of youth than Beethoven.

The metabolism of the generations will not be healed by excessive creativity. Moreover, there is something rather strange about creativity. True creativity is an improbable thing; it cannot be expected among people in general. There was a time when the sheer possession of literacy was in itself a sign of considerable creativity and a guarantee of a significant career. Today literacy is a basic necessity, even for unskilled labor. If everyone were capable of creating sculptures of an originality like those of Michelangelo, melodies of the beauty of those by Mozart, paintings of the deepest humaneness, like those of Rembrandt, we would no longer look upon such production as signs of considerable creativity. Instead we would gradually—always assuming that every member of the species showed such creativity—look at it as a species-specific characteristic; it would then probably lose all its effectiveness as a cultural device in the service of decreasing the tension that is inherent in the metabolism of generations.

Two myths confront each other here: the myth of hope, confidence, faith and the myth of hopelessness, pessimism,[12] despair. The major part of *Hamlet* is dominated by the latter. Only in the end is Hope admitted: Fortinbras will uphold the health of the State. Yet even this final ray of light may be an afterthought. The tragedy is one of despair and pessimism, not one of defeatism. There is a significant difference between pessimism and defeatism: pessimism does not exclude action; defeatism does. The pessimist is often castigated by the community, as if he were advising acceptance of defeat. Cassandra, however, warned only against reliance on hope; despite her pessimism, she was not averse to action.

In the other myth, hope is man's great deceiver, for it provides him with illusions. Pessimism, by contrast, forces man to face the whole truth of his wretchedness. Freud was one of the great constructive pessimists;

---

[12] I am using the term pessimism here in a broader sense than I did earlier when I was discussing Hamlet's "To be" soliloquy.

his work is pervaded by a flavor that may be compared with the atmosphere of *Hamlet*. At one point in his work, as in *Hamlet,* however, a ray of hope breaks through the heavy clouds: "The voice of the intellect is a soft one, but it does not rest till it has gained a hearing. Finally, after a countless succession of rebuffs, it succeeds" (1927, p. 53). He calls it "one of the few points on which one may be optimistic about the future of mankind." To be sure, "the primacy of the intellect" lies in a far distant future but not "in an *infinitely* distant one" (author's italics). Finally, Freud believed in the victory of reason and experience, which nothing can withstand (1927, p. 27).

A year earlier, Freud (1926b, p. 193) had raised the question: "Have you ever found that men do anything but confuse and distort what they get hold of?" This would speak strongly against the possibility of mankind's ever reaching that distant point at which the primacy of the intellect or reason and of experience prevails. Did Freud become at one point at least unfaithful to his pessimism? In the "Future of an Illusion," despite the flicker of optimism, he maintained his skepticism, admitting twice that he, too, may be the victim of illusion (1927, pp. 48, 53). Nevertheless, he ended on the note that "science is no illusion." Is not the extreme pessimist in danger of becoming a defeatist and therefore of withdrawing from activity and consequently even undermining the morale of the community? Was this ray of hope in Freud perhaps the minimum that was necessary in order to keep him going despite his strong pessimism?

Returning to *Hamlet,* one may infer then that the tragedy is the myth of man who—despite his being surrounded by vice, despite his full acknowledgment of death and of the consequent senselessness of human experience, despite even an inner taboo of some sort against action—acquires the capacity to *act* (cf. Proser, 1965).

At one point Hamlet reveals what in psychoanalytic parlance is called his "ego-ideal." This occurs shortly before the mouse-trap play is about to take place and Hamlet is to be irretrievably forced to action. It will be a kind of "divide" in his life, for Hamlet expects that, after Claudius' involuntary self-confession, the last conscious motive with which he himself may justify hesitation will have disappeared. Shortly before this consequential event, he turns to Horatio *(III.2.64-75)* and confesses what he has admired in him from the earliest years on, implying by this confession what he himself would have liked to become and yet did not ever succeed in becoming: immune to suffering, independent of the vacillations of fortune, free from the pull of the passions.

Nowadays, we would say Horatio has achieved ideal ego autonomy. He is not dominated by the pleasure principle; he is independent of his environment; and he has mastery over his drives. Hamlet's ego-ideal, as it is personified in Horatio, can be easily characterized by *tranquilitas,* "a quietistic yet alerted state of mind" and *apathia,* "the absence of the passions."[13] For long these had been admitted to be "the *sine qua non* of a virtuous and rational existence" (Heckscher, 1967, p. 96). Their opposites were *tempestas* and *affectus,* tempestuosity and passion; it is these two that generally stand in the way of man's achieving the *vita contemplativa,* which Horatio has integrated almost completely. I add "almost," for at the end even Horatio sways and nearly falls upon viewing his dying friend. Now it is Hamlet who returns all the gifts he has received from his friend, and leaves him a heritage that will be succor and bounty to the end of his days.

Horatio's desire to follow Hamlet—the philosopher ready to commit suicide—is not only a point of the greatest dramatic power but also one that is full of momentous psychological implications. Apparently even Horatio, "whose blood and judgement are so well co-mingled," is bound by limits of endurance. Tranquility, Prof. Heckscher (1967, p. 103) reminds us, "rather than being withdrawal or escape, was a proud achievement, the result of militant self-discipline."

Horatio is not the sort of man who, having been disappointed by the world and its turbulence, withdraws to a monastery and contemplates the world from within the protection of walls that are impenetrable by secular temptations. Instead, he stays in the midst of worldly affairs and their impingements upon him, but he does not take an active part in these affairs, even though he does reserve the right to put an end to his life, in accordance with his own insights.

Yet, because he has not withdrawn from life but rather participates in it fully, even if inactively, he is also vulnerable; the danger to him comes from the area of his most intense participation. It almost looks as if Horatio were an idealized mirror-picture of Hamlet, and Hamlet Horatio's flesh and blood. The philosopher has made himself capable of maintaining his *tranquilitas* and his *apathia* by relinquishing to his friend all

[13] I am here following a lead derived from Prof. Heckscher's (1967) penetrating study on *Sturm und Drang;* although it has to do with a period one and a half centuries later, it may profitably be applied to Hamlet's conflict between ego-ideal and reality.

urge actively to perform. As is so often true in life itself, renunciation is made possible by surrendering one part of the self and its aspirations to an *alter ego* (cf. Anna Freud, 1936).

It is eminently subtle, psychologically, that Horatio's temporary collapse is correlated with Hamlet's agony and that, from the moment of Hamlet's departing, it is Horatio who becomes Fortinbras' mentor—the carrier of tradition and the recorder of history—and thus the guarantor of historical continuity. In this way, he also fulfills the function of societal superego.

A crucial point in the Hamlet myth is the question of why Hamlet did not ever achieve the ego-ideal that, in his own words, was personified in Horatio. There is no suggestion in the play that *tempestas* and *affectus* might have troubled him, prior to his father's death; yet Ophelia's description of him does not imply the presence in him of *tranquilitas* and *apathia*. It is clearly *tempestas* and *affectus,* however, that characterize the Hamlet with whom we become acquainted at the start of the play.

In order to understand fully the difference between Hamlet and Horatio, one has to consider their environment. While Hamlet is destined to become King, Horatio's status allows for the degree of reserve that is the prerequisite of a *vita contemplativa.* Prof. Heckscher (1967, p. 103), to be sure, does say of Sublime Tranquillity that he who partook thereof "was capable of exercising science and wisdom in a frame of mind which made him—be he *ruler* or sage, or both—not unlike Gods" (italics added).

Old Hamlet was certainly not a ruler of that kind. Although "Tranquillus or Tranquillinus was considered a suitable name for sons of distinguished families—a custom that was revived once more in the course of the Renaissance" (p. 103), I do not think it would have been a fitting name for Hamlet, even at the time when he was free of *tempestas* and *affectus.* As happens so often, young people do choose an ego-ideal that their life situation makes it impossible for them to realize. Hamlet himself seems to have been closer to his ego-ideal than his father was (cf. Peter Alexander, 1955), but he was certainly still a great distance from the level Horatio achieved.

My knowledge of the ancient Stoa and its derivatives is not sufficient for me to be able to decide whether consequential social action was considered possible at all, once a personality had reached the height we see embodied in Horatio. Be that as it may, it is unthinkable that Horatio should ever have been able to carry out the deed that Hamlet achieves in the end. It is significant that he is totally uninvolved in the sexual sphere but is instead characterized by a high degree of sublimated homosexuality; his abstemiousness left him conflict-free, however.

There is no reason to assume, of course, that Hamlet was entirely free of sexual affect during that period of his life when he was the ideal "courtier, soldier and scholar." He must, I would think, have been quite active, and in a way that excluded *tranquillitas* and *apathia*. With the breakdown of his ideals, however, *tempestas* and *affectus* broke through into his life. If we look now at the tragedy from the mythical point of view, the problem may be redefined: how can social action of an aggressive sort be carried out without *tempestas* and *affectus*?

The final question that Hamlet puts to Horatio, after enumerating all of Claudius' crimes: "is't not perfect conscience to quit him with this arm?" *(V.2.67f)* may be understood as the ego's question to the superego: "Are you satisfied now? May I now carry out the deed without incurring your censure?" I am coming here somewhat closer to Miss Prosser's (1967) conception of Hamlet. In analyzing Hamlet's relationship to Horatio, however, one may surmise the existence of an intrasystemic conflict in his superego, yet not one of a religious nature. The problem was to kill, without being overwhelmed by *tempestas* and *affectus*, to keep the way open still toward the realization of *tranquillitas* and *apathia*.

Since Horatio (the superego) gives his blessing in the end, despite the terrible *affectus* that Hamlet has revealed while committing the deed, one may say that here a new myth arises. Man may be able, after all, to maintain his ethical standing despite strong passions; the sort of social action that requires violent impulses and agitation of the mind can be carried out without any violation of ethical principles. Indeed, even murder may become a constructive act, if certain psychological conditions have been fulfilled. What these conditions are I have tried to reconstruct from the text.

There is another myth to be found in *Hamlet*, a myth that has to do with the community, its cohesion and the relationship of each of its members to it. Most people, despite occasional protestations to the contrary, feel happier in a humdrum sort of existence, one that has relatively small oscillations of excitement; it helps them to fulfill their societal functions with a minimum of upset, and it also provides at least half-way protection against traumatic injury. Who is it, that at the beginning of his maturity, feels drawn toward the great adventure (which always contains the possibility of shattering defeat), toward that insatiable search for the truth that may in the end result in involuntary isolation from the community? Who, one may ask in a general way, wants to make *full* use of his liberty?

The problems that are involved in freedom and liberty have occupied thinkers unendingly. Here I want to turn my attention toward only one document, Dostoevski's famous episode of the Great Inquisitor (1881), which I regard as a deep sociological essay presented in the form of a literary piece.[14] Scarcely anyone who has ever pondered on the problem of freedom and liberty has taken a more pessimistic view with regard to man's inner capacity to endure freedom. There is no chance, of course, that any member of an industrialized republic that bases its official political structure on liberty will fully understand Dostoevski's formidable statement that "for man and the human community, never and nowhere has anything existed that is more unbearable than liberty" (p. 505).

Likewise, when he speaks of "the unsolvable historical contradictions of human nature" (p. 504), this can easily be brushed aside as the fancy of a mind that has been misled by an excess of religious sentiment and by the impact that his own environment has had on him, in the form of an excessively autocratic political structure, with a strong Christian flavor. Be that as it may, it often happens that when the human mind has been excessively tormented, it will draw out of its sufferings myths that contain the profoundest truths.[15]

When one studies scientific works about the structure of society, one may readily get the impression one gets from pre-Freudian psychology. What was recorded there was not necessarily wrong, yet one feels that it was not man who was truly the subject of that inquiry. Similarly, it does not seem to be the core of society that is the subject of contemporary sociological scrutiny but rather peripheral non-essential phenomena. In reading "The Great Inquisitor," however, one feels immediately that what the Inquisitor is debating is core patterns, core factors, the nuclear conflict of human community. Dostoevski asserts that three factors are essential to community: miracle, secret and authority (pp. 511, 513).

---

[14] The quotations are my translation from the German edition by Moeller van den Bruck, which I preferred to do in view of discrepancies between the English and German translations.

[15] Dostoevski was threatened by excessive dangers—internally (he suffered from epilepsy), as well as externally (he once faced a firing squad and only at the last moment was he sentenced instead to deportation).

All three are revealed in *Hamlet*: the miracle of the Ghost's appearance, the secret of the murder of the former King, and the authority of Hamlet to "set right" the time that is "out of joint." In the context of the play, it is the second factor, the secret, into possession of which Hamlet arrived by a miracle, that is of decisive importance.

The problem in question is the necessity of keeping secret the foundation on which the state rests. Who has the courage to face this truth? Who is willing to become aware of the hypocrisy that is rampant within himself and also at the very basis of society in which he lives, in the Church to which he belongs no less than in his profession? The follies of past societies and periods count for far less. At the time of our first becoming acquainted with Hamlet, he has already succeeded in establishing the foundations for healthy adulthood. External events have forced him to do what everyone of us has to do if the potential of man's mind is to be used to its fullest: he has discovered the difference between appearance and reality—and the conflict between them.

This conflict is undoubtedly a central issue in the play and it has been interpreted in various ways. But it seems to me that what has been overlooked is that this is a *general* conflict, one that exists in all societies. There is no society in which reality and appearance coincide; only in a state of anarchy is the difference appreciably reduced, in that hypocrisy becomes unfortunately needless and latent aggression manifests itself to its fullest extent. If Hamlet is obsessed by this discrepancy, this is not due to any psychopathology on his part; it is to be explained by the fact that he is in the unhappy state of knowing the truth, of having unveiled that secret on which the authority of the highest representative of the state basically rests.

Denying the actual discrepancy that exists between societal appearance and reality can have a grave effect on man's reality-testing: it blinds him to anticipation of the historical future, which should constitute the most important function of reality-testing. The constant probing into this discrepancy should therefore be a never-ending task of the adult mind. Yet the question arises whether the end-result of such probing would be compatible with continuing to live; Dostoevski may have been right when he said, in effect, that the human community is only possible when it is based on a secret.

There is a ballad by Schiller whose content is germane to this discourse. A youth who has been driven by his thirst of knowledge to Sais notices a veiled image there. He is told that truth is hidden behind the veil and he is warned against lifting it. But he overrides the warning and, when he is alone at midnight, lifts the veil. The next day, he is found pale and unconscious. "A deep grief tore him into an early grave" (*Ihn riss ein tiefer Gram zum frühen Grabe*). This is, in my opinion, to be taken not symbolically but literally. Once the man has lifted the veil from the veiled image of Sais, he will thereafter see the tortured eyes of the dying man when he looks at the infant's healthy face—he will see the future ruins of the city in which he lives.

It is hardly to be doubted that the early Christians would have been paralyzed in the propagation of their faith if they had known what their followers would do a few generations later—if they had known, for example, the future truth of the Inquisition and the Thirty Years War. Would the Pilgrims have come to this continent if they had known the future truth of the Indians' fate, of slavery and lynchings, of the Civil War and Vietnam? To know the truth means to know the future, and I agree with those philosophers who say that knowing this would lead to the annihilation of personal existence.

Hamlet is not the Faustian type of truth-seeker: he is not driven to decipher the riddles and mysteries of the world. When he does come to grips at the end with the problem of death, this is not the consequence of an initial unquenchable thirst of knowledge, but rather of the necessity of finding an emplacement, a point of rest from which human action becomes possible. That is to say, reality experience has forced him along the path to the problem of man's end.

Reality having opened his eyes, he is now unfortunately the sole holder of a truth about his society—namely, that the fabric of the community rests on the oedipal crime, not one that was fantasied but one that was indeed carried out. This is an insight that cannot be integrated, nor is it one to which any individual could be expected to "adjust." In order to grasp the formidable implications of this insight, to attain to some feeling about its consequences, one would do well to consider the consequences that would have followed in medieval times for any person who had obtained irrefutable proof that both the Old and the New Testaments were forgeries.[16]

---

[16] At this point I would like to raise one further objection to Prof. Erikson's interpretation of *Hamlet*. He writes: "Where others lead men and change the course of history, he [Hamlet] reflectively moves characters about on the stage (the play within the play); in brief, where others act, he play-acts" (1962b, p. 8). Erikson thus pejoratively reduces acting on the stage to "play-acting" and thereby intimates the existence of an identity crisis. Yet in reality, by staging his play, Hamlet is ask-

The truth to which Hamlet comes is one in which all mankind should be passionately interested—namely, the truth about society's foundation. As for Hamlet, however, obtaining this truth was as unfortunate as it is for most others who try to penetrate the matter deeply. For I do not believe that Shakespeare was driven here to say something about a specific society, but about society as he understood it in general. Society can exist, he says, only when the structure of its foundation is denied and woe to him who does not share in this collective denial.

Yet what should be really exciting to the analyst who is interested in sociological implications is Shakespeare's assertion, in effect, that the cause of hypocrisy, of society's rottenness, is the oedipal crime. Is it not surprising that Shakespeare's message coincides with that of Freud, as it is given in *Totem and Taboo*, and in his *Moses* book, both of which were vigorously rejected by the experts—not only, I assume, for objective reasons? It would likewise be not surprising if the millions of people who have been stirred and deeply moved by the tragedy—and thus, at least within the context of the play, seem to have accepted the oedipal crime as the basis of society—were nevertheless to react as the experts did to Freud's two books—namely, to decry that truth to which they themselves may well have responded when witnessing the play.[17]

Furthermore, by declaring the oedipal crime to be both the source and the essential nature of the social canker, Shakespeare converts the social issue into a psychological one. In *Hamlet* sociology and psychology become one, with psychology definitely favored. It will take a long time before we know for certain whether or not here too the literary genius was far ahead of the scientific specialists, most of whom are still certain that this is a matter of two quite separate disciplines.

Hamlet's discovery that it is the oedipal crime that lies at the very base of the State has made his world seem changed in some essential as-

---

ing the world a question that is answered in accordance with his hypothesis. The play-within-the-play may be compared with an experiment that is performed in the laboratory before the physician dispenses his medicine to the patient. Similarly, Hamlet's play leads to action and the purging of the State. Nevertheless, it is not that I think that a scrutiny of Hamlet's play-within-the-play under the aspect of play-acting is inherently wrong. What I am maintaining here is that, even if in one layer of his many-layered personality Hamlet should prove to be a play-actor, this does not cover more than one side aspect. Interesting as that aspect may be, it does not reveal anything more essential than when Prof. Erikson writes that Hamlet's most passionate pronouncements "make his madness but an adjunct to his greatness" (1962b, p. 9).

[17] It goes without saying that here is one of those countless examples of how the artistic medium succeeds in conveying almost without resistance such contents as immediately arouse defenses when they are presented by science explicitly and rationally.

pects. But Hamlet is not a victim of a projection, as does happen to some schizophrenics at the beginning of their psychoses. In German psychiatry an experience of this kind is called *Primärerlebnis*. While Hamlet does undergo an experience that carries the earmarks of just such a *Primärerlebnis*, it is not, however, the projection of an inner disintegration but rather the intrusion of a formidable truth, one that is altogether incompatible with any of the observations and experiences he had made until then.[18]

Mauss (1950) has described the basic identification of ego and societal position in primitive society. Something of this same kind, however, persists in all societies, and it may be at the basis of what Freud called "social anxiety." It is an area in which the ego is devoid of autonomy. Hamlet is the hero who refuses to deny social reality and therefore loses his place in the "mutual confirmation." His denial is limited solely to his own oedipal wishes, which he acknowledges in only a highly disguised form in Lucianus' seemingly enigmatic speech.[19]

Be that as it may, Hamlet exposes himself to a conflict—or, if the play is taken literally, a conflict is imposed on him—to which every member of society should have the courage to expose himself but which most human beings succeed in escaping by denial. And this, it seems to me, is another essential factor that makes *Hamlet* a universally understood and universally stirring tragedy.

But I fear that I may have exaggerated grossly. The discussion and bewailing of social ills is the parlor game of the elite during certain historical periods and in those societies in which substantial funds are indeed raised for the benefit of the poor. These facts do not in themselves speak however, against my previous assertions about the denial of

18 Prof. Erikson writes: "Ego strength emerges from the mutual confirmation of individual and community," and further that "The individual . . . recognizes society as a living process, which inspires loyalty" (1962b, p. 11) This description, I believe, covers quite well the range of Hamlet's development *up to the moment of his return* from Wittenberg. The "mutual confirmation of individual and community" of which Prof. Erikson speaks is exactly the point of vulnerability in man's armor. Once he looks beyond this mutual confirmation and has the courage to break through the *harmonia praestabilita*, by putting himself outside the bounds that hold the individual tied to the community, he inevitably finds himself in Hamlet's position.

19 As a matter of fact, Freud's acknowledgment of his own oedipus complex probably prevented him from becoming a Hamlet, despite the rudiments of a Hamlet identification such as I have tried to demonstrate. From some of his dreams it is known how much rebellion there was in him (cf. Erikson 1962b), but evidently this was kept well under control. If anything, he came close to realizing Hamlet's ego ideal, as represented in Horatio, and became the man who was "not a pipe for fortune's finger . . . nor passion's slave." Here the decisive question may be asked whether, if Hamlet had indeed recognized that he was essentially no better than Claudius, in that he too harbored an oedipal conflict, he would still have been capable of carrying out the final act of purifying the State.

society's rottenness. Lament and charitable action do not reveal that the bewailer, or even the donor, has been penetrated to the depth to which Hamlet was stirred. Quite the contrary, what they do, in essence, is to relieve feelings of guilt and reduce or even stop the momentum of inquiry.

The feeling that Hamlet expresses—namely, that in view of the social reality, life has become unbearable—is spared man in general. Hamlet is in the sort of state that may be compared with the demands of some modern political leaders, such as Trotsky and Mao, for a "permanent revolution." The combination of injustice and crime, as the seemingly *permanent* foundation of society, is constantly on his mind; since it is within his sphere of action to "restore justice," he is bound to remain suspended in an unending conflict as long as that restoration has not been fulfilled.

I believe that we are too much accustomed to viewing murder, or other ways of eliminating human life, by way of their replication on stage and screen, for us to be able to be fully aware of the terribleness of Hamlet's task. I have to return to an example of modern times. Looking back, it may strike the reader as "natural" that Friedrich Adler killed the Prime Minister of the Austrian government during World War I. That government had violated the country's Constitution; the country itself was subject to an excess of sufferings; to go on with the war was senseless, inasmuch as the defeat of the monarchy was clearly written on the wall.

Yet even victory was not desirable, since the fact that the monarchy was irrevocably tied to a hopelessly reactionary policy had become quite apparent. Still, Friedrich Adler went through a desperate internal conflict that finally eventuated in the political murder already referred to above. His own father—and this is of extraordinary importance—who was a progressive, enlightened socialist, the leader and unquestioned representative of a working class that had been deprived of rights and minimum living standards, was certain, when he was apprised of the son's deed, that it had been performed by an insane person.

If we look back, however, what strikes us is the question of why the deed did not occur earlier. Why did the murderer have to go through the throes of excessive conflictual upheaval, in a situation in which conscience would surely castigate the commitment of the deed less than it would the refraining from it? A clue to the inhibition that came from the personal and repressed may be found in the fact that, while Friedrich

Adler was seated at the adjoining table, waiting for the opportunity to carry out justice, he was held back by the fear lest he injure a woman who sat between him and his intended victim. However, it would be a one-sided and therefore limited view, if only hesitation and postponement of social action directed toward the root of societal evil were to be attributed to the revival of the oedipal conflict, for the oedipal conflict often has the opposite effect.

It was Hamlet's own oedipal conflict that made him keen, and enabled him to sense the latent evil surrounding his father's death. His ominous "O! my prophetic soul!" may be interpreted, on the sociological level, as a manifestation of his particular alertness. It was, further, his own oedipal conflict that forced him to dismiss all other thoughts but those that had to do with the restoration of justice. Thus another unconscious equation is implicitly contained in what Freud set forth—namely, the self's unconscious awareness that by *not* committing the deed the ego would be admitting its guilt about its own past and present oedipal strivings. Both doing and not doing are bound to precipitate conflict in oedipal man; no one who is fixated to the preoedipal father or mother relationship would ever respond in that way.

Quite aside, however, from the shadow (or the sparkle) that the individual's own past may throw upon social action, denial of social reality seems to be a minimum necessity, if we are to make life bearable. Just as repression of part of the inner self is a preparation of mental health, so denial (cf. Weisman and Hackett, 1967) of one part of social reality protects the self against the dissolution that would otherwise threaten it, vis-à-vis the immensity of the tasks imposed on it by the eternal cry of the superego for justice and the alleviation of social evils.

Dostoevski rightly postulated "the longing for universal fusion" in man (p. 516) as one of the great sources of man's anguish. This is not only a matter of the feeling of "belonging," which is so widely referred to at present. Hidden behind the frequently expressed wish to "belong" lies the far stronger wish to fuse with the universe, the equivalent of Freud's "oceanic feeling." The Jewish religion solved that problem by offering to its adherents closeness to an all-embracing God. If one was loved by Jehovah, one became fused with the universe—a kind of fusion that was, however, the privilege only of the select. Vertical intensification grew at the cost of horizontal expansion, and no serious attempt was made to proselytize or convert others.

But Dostoevski was apparently not altogether correct when he wrote: "They [men] created Gods and shouted to each other: 'Relinquish your Gods and come in order to worship ours, or else death and perdition to you and your Gods!' " (p. 508). This is correct for only a few religions. Buddhism and Shintoism, for example, thrived side by side for centuries in Japan, each supporting the other and not at all acting as rivals. Yet his assertion is true of Christianity, and particularly of Catholicism, in which horizontal extension grew at the cost of vertical intensification. There is a deep truth in the Great Inquisitor's wry comment to Christ: "Nothing but unrest, confusion and unhappiness fell to man's share after You suffered so much for his freedom." (p. 514).

Yet the freedom that man was given by Christ was that of extending his identifications horizontally without limits. I believe that no religion has raised an equal demand for empathy, compassion, forgiving and identification with all forms of suffering. In the face of that demand, the self is in danger, because such a vast diffusion of empathy and identification threatens to thin out the ego's fabric, a process that may easily lead to the ego's own dissolution.[20] Denial of social evils—which can be present, of course, even when those evils are acknowledged intellectually—is a prerequisite for maintaining the functions of the psychic apparatus. I want to set forth two examples of denial. I select them arbitrarily, but they have both left a deep impression on me.

In view of the turbulent situation in Europe, immigrants coming from Europe in 1938 were frequently asked for their political opinions and predictions. When the answer was that a war was imminent and that, since the Allies were evidently unprepared to cope with the situation, this might make America's entry into the war necessary, regularly the reply was: "It is utterly impossible for an American boy ever to cross the ocean again."

It is important to note that this objection came from responsible people, liberals as well as conservatives, both the wealthy and the middle classes. Yet, if my political acumen had been greater and not limited merely to recognizing the high probability of American participation, I might have said: "Don't be silly. The United States will also cross the Pacific. It will destroy two cities in the course of seconds and later will send an Army to Asia to fight an undeclared war because, etc."

The interesting thing is that if I had spoken in that way, I would

---

[20] This may have been the danger that forced Christ's most scrupulous adherents for centuries to become anchorites, a way of life in which the extension of identification shrinks again to the self's narrow limits and the bliss of one's soul becomes the principal matter of existence (Lecky, 1869).

never have been accepted as a psychiatric intern, because I would surely have incurred the stigma of being unbalanced or suffering from psychopathy. But what does it mean for a nation to be absolutely in the dark about even the superficial drift its history will take during the next three decades? Further, shortly after the two bombs were dropped over Japan, I had the opportunity to hear on a jukebox in Texas the jingle "God gave us the atom bomb."

The Mitscherlichs (1968) recently published a book in which they demonstrated the denial of guilt, the inability to mourn that they were able to observe in the German nation after World War II. Such denial of a nation's "black record," however, is well-nigh universal. In 1938 the legend was rampant in this country that war is a "European disease," that the way of the United States is to stick to negotiating and compromising. All the facts were ignored that prove the opposite: the disinheriting of the native Indian population and its dispossession by force of arms; the importation of slaves and the stigmatization of races; the periodic occurrence of wars, and the inability to make compromises, even with regard to *internal* dissension, as happened in the Civil War (which, according to some historians, was the bloodiest war of the entire century, a century by no means poor in warfare).

And so it goes on and on, all of it leading to a black record that is not essentially different from that of other great Christian nations, even though the initial conditions and intentions seemed particularly propitious for teaching the world what Christians can do for their fellow-men, when they start from scratch on the building of what is to become a free commonwealth on free soil.

The peak of denial, of course, has been reached in the present Vietnam crisis. On this, there are various forms of denial, ranging from dignity to vulgarity. The peak of the latter I find in the implication of a speech that the President gave in 1966: "You never had it so good, despite inflation and Vietnam war" (*The New York Times,* September 7, p. 37). Such an implication, of course, should not have been "fit to print," because it will turn out to be the ineradicable shame of this country, of the Occident, of the whole of Christianity. Members of other nations, will, of course, say that this cynical boast is "typically American," just as the world said about Hitler's atrocities that they were "typically German," and previously about English Opium wars and other such excesses, that they too were "typically English." This breaking up of the cruelty of Christians into a variety of national cruelties already contains a

· 391 ·

strong denial, not to speak of man's inability to see in this surfeit of outrage man's uncovered face.

Within the rest of the community that has been compromised by the vulgarity of its highest representative, however, the very same mechanism is observable. To be sure, the majority, or almost the majority, have objected strenuously to the war, but one portion of this majority wants to shift the responsibility almost entirely onto the "strange ways" of the Commander-in-Chief. Clearly, however, it is the entire community that is guilty and the shifting of responsibility is an expression of denial, in order to escape guilt, just as the Mitscherlichs described it.

Let us assume that it *could* be proven beyond any doubt that the war in Vietnam is a just war, and let us assume also that South Vietnam was actually threatened and attacked by North Vietnam. Still, there will probably be no voice heard before the court of history, pleading in favor of the United States' justification of the war. A nation that was quite capable of witnessing calmly the occupation of Austria, Poland, France, Greece, Yugoslavia, Denmark, Manchuria and half of China; that was able to tolerate, without undue distress, the defeat of the legally elected government in Spain by foreign invaders; that itself was able to press upon Japan ruinous treaties and a new form of government and civilization, quite alien to its tradition, and that even participated, for that purpose, in the bombardment of a city without declaration of war; a country, finally, that fomented a revolution in another country solely in order to be able thereafter to take possession of its land for the construction of a canal—such a country may be able to make its citizens believe in the morality of its ways, but it has lost forever the likelihood of its being believed by any other peoples or by any later generations.

Let me go one step further. In order to safeguard liberty, in one province alone of that area that it is the United States' alleged purpose to protect, 70 per cent of the villages have been destroyed, 40 per cent of the population are now uprooted and live as refugees, another 40 per cent live underground—and every year there take place 50,000 war casualties (Schell, 1968). It is my contention that the population of the United States itself would never have endured a fraction of such revolting sufferings, in order to maintain their own freedom, but would instead have surrendered a long time ago, preferring an "unjust" government to such a holocaust.

But if a nation—and this is said under the assumption that the war is just—*is* compelled to inflict such terrible destruction for the sake of establishing liberty, then this is indeed an unprecedented national disaster. If the official version as propounded by the government is not pretense, but *bona fide*, then the simplest consequence would be for us to go into mourning. Such a nation has no moral right to luxury, a stock exchange, the theater, music and dance. If it wants to earn a shade of respect from other nations or to preserve a minimum of self-respect, it must renounce—at least during the time it is *forced to destroy its friends*—its accustomed ways of pleasure and amusement, and behave as those do who are stricken by the deepest grief. Yet despite the vociferous objection to the war—from, it would seem, almost every part of the population—the nation is frantically pursuing its accustomed (more or less empty) pleasures. At least, national statistics strongly indicate that the number of those who have shown even the slightest disposition toward letting the national catastrophe disturb their personal lives must be insignificant.[21]

As is by now admitted in most quarters, this nation still owes the world a satisfactory explanation of the two atomic attacks on Japan. Why did one not wait to see what would be the full effect of Russia's declaration of war upon Japan's willingness to surrender? Why was the second bomb used before Japan was even able to respond to the first one? Why did the United States not react more vigorously to Japan's earlier offers, which amounted indeed practically to surrender?

Let us assume once again that the official versions and explanations —threadbare as they are—are honest and correct; then, as it has turned out, the intelligence the Government had received was wrong and Japan was in reality entirely defeated. In that case, the two atom bombs caused a destruction of hundreds of thousands of civilians that cannot be described as having been "militarily necessary."

If I were ever to kill some person out of an honest conviction that my self-defense demanded it, only to find out later that that person did not have any lethal weapon on him and furthermore had neither the opportunity nor any intention of doing me harm, I would surely feel deeply affected by remorse, repentance and guilt. The Christian spirit should have called for at least two days of national mourning to commemorate those two days in which the cities of Hiroshima and Nagasaki were turned into heaps of rubble.

If God did indeed give the Americans the atom bomb, as that Texan

---

[21] The few instances of auto-da-fés or attempted auto-da-fés that have been reported would require special study.

jukebox boasted, it was not a God of justice and mercy that did this, but rather the ancient wild Tor of the Teutonic past. Thus the magnificent fight for freedom and against tyranny that the United States entered upon after Pearl Harbor ended with an eternal blemish, which not even a proper manifestation of guilt and remorse, nor any apology to the world and to Japan, in particular, would have been able even partially to cleanse. But not the slightest trace of this has been forthcoming, and one wonders a little when contemporary American authors assert that Hamlet, by killing Claudius, infringed on a Divine rule of conduct and was therefore torn by conflict.

I have a fair idea what the objection will be to such inferences, but the same revealed text as was turned to in Shakespeare's times is today upheld officially as a guideline to conduct and moral principles. In all the years before and since, during which the religious philosophers have spread the message by print, and the priests have enunciated it from the pulpit, it has not changed essentially. It will probably be easy for the historian to "prove," 300 years from now, that, in accordance with the principles that prevailed in our times, all Americans felt guilty about the avoidable mass destruction of life for which the nation had made itself responsible. The fact that guilt was denied where objective reason for guilt was evident may also be ignored in the future, just as it is at present.

Yet it is here that we discern the inevitability of such denial. At one point, *Terre des Hommes* in Lausanne, more charitable than our country was, offered to treat Vietnamese children who were mutilated by the war, and therefore requested that American planes returning empty from the Far East transport these war victims to their hospitals. The President refused, if I am not mistaken on the grounds that no means of transportation were available for that purpose. Who can take full notice of such an act of deliberate cynicism and deliberate cruelty without an unbearable feeling of despair?

If we had indeed to confront a full representation, in emotion as well as in thought, of the terrible plight that lies quite close in the slums, the hospitals and the prisons (or on a national level with regard to the black race and the dispossessed native population), or of the exploitation of the poor and the anguish and hunger of children—if this were so, who could integrate this ocean of injustice and tears and still maintain his sanity, or even one full moment of contentment? It is plain that denial and hypocrisy are the very foundations of society. Some forward minds are constantly driving home the true state of the community; yet the resistance to change, the resistance even to taking cognizance of what is, is rigid and impenetrable by insight. It may be that only an appeal to archaic mechanisms has a chance to set society in motion. This can be exemplified by a single incident from modern American history.

The period of "muckraking" at the beginning of this century is well known. It was a brilliant period, filled with great social liveliness, social criticism and sound, promising social tension. Yet although the urgent necessity of social reform was generally acknowledged, the most appalling disclosures of unsuspected corruption and evil in all strata of American society did not succeed in leading to any change. The nation resorted to social and political action only after Upton Sinclair published *The Jungle* (1906). Its social effect, "greater than that of any American work of fiction since *Uncle Tom's Cabin* . . . was produced by a few pages, regarded by Sinclair as merely incidental. . . . He had furnished gruesome details about meat production: the casual grinding of rats, refuse and even employees into beef products" (Morris, 1947, p. 302f). Rationality, insight, debate—nothing availed. But when an American became uncertain whether or not he and his family were being served human flesh at the dinner table, at that moment the possibility of social change became transformed into a reality.

When Moses threatens the Children of Israel with curses for their disobedience, he says: "And thou shalt eat the fruit of thine own body, the flesh of thy son and of thy daughters" (*Deut.* 28:53). The threat of cannibalism is apparently among the worst of threats. The most archaic, most deeply repressed impulse becomes the most terrible punishment. I have been told of a man who committed suicide after his liberation from a concentration camp, in which he had been forced to eat feces.

By accident (or was it unconscious intuition?), Sinclair touched on a spot that went beyond the possibility of denial and thus was able to create an unbearable situation at the national level. At the same time, it was proved once again that, in matters of greatest social concern, *ratio* is powerless and Moses' magic curses are the only efficient tools. Archaic, cannibalistic imagery and the horror thereof had to be injected into the clamor for reform. In Hamlet, too, an archaic mechanism is applied to the "reform" of the State, the oldest technique of all: murder of the person in whom power is concentrated.

The socialist vision is, at bottom, the institution of *rational* mechanisms of social change. Yet it may take a long time before rationality has extended into this area of human endeavor as well. It seems that changes which touch upon the foundations of the political structure can still be induced only by revolution—a word that generally makes the majority of a community tremble. And yet when a community has lost its potential for revolution, it has indeed reached a dangerous degree of rigidity; the loss of adaptability that is thus revealed must in the long run lead it to disaster.

Hamlet is not a revolutionary play. It ends in what is sometimes called a *Palastrevolution* ("palace revolution"): a revolution in the smallest possible area, in which one king's family is replaced by another. Real revolutions, however, have their own beauty: in a seemingly regressive process, old structure is dissolved and new structure arises. Old biases and beliefs are torn to pieces; man's mind becomes suddenly very original and strong, and unknown talents sprout into great leaders. Man shows himself at his worst by his cruel extirpation of the old structure and at his best by his organization of a new one.

It is this polarization of man's drives—Thanatos and Eros working independently of each other, yet toward the same goal—that gives a revolution its specific and unique coloring. The revolution rejuvenates the nation: it constitutes a new beginning (such as Fortinbras was). Man's sweetest hopes are validated for a while—until new burdens crush the budding dawn of freedom and man is once again made into a social tool, destined to keep society's existing machinery grinding.

During a revolution, man may reach such an extension of awareness by horizontal identification as to encompass all the suffering that has pervaded the community. Denial, however, will still have to be activated against the sufferings and anguish of the carriers of traditional power, who have now had it torn from them.

Hamlet is the hero who is strong enough to keep on living, even though fate has made it impossible for him to maintain the denial that living demands. The secret of the basic crime that lies at the foundation of society is known to him. Concomitantly, he has become aware of all the suffering and anguish that exist in the world. Wherever he looks, he perceives the denial of the "imposthume"; he must therefore feel alienated from the community, which not only appears hypocritical to him, but *is* in fact hypocritical. He succeeds in extending his identification and empathy to include all of society, and thus fulfills, curiously enough, what was demanded by Christ and what man cannot truly attempt to fulfill if he wants to preserve his survival in society.

In letting Hamlet's repression of his own oedipal conflict be mirrored by that denial of social reality that is the central mechanism of group cohesion, Shakespeare has marked off indelibly that area in which individual and society overlap.[22]

---

[22]It may be worthwhile summarizing what a mind as penetrating as Nietzsche's had to say about Hamlet. In essential points, it is the opposite of what I have suggested. First, Nietzsche (1881-1882, p. 283) anticipated Eliot's judgment of failure: "[Hamlet] . . . is a work *that turned out badly*: its creator would laughingly admit it, if I said it to his face." [*ist ein* missrathenes *Werk: sein Urheber würde es mir wohl lachend eingestehen, wenn ich's ihm in's Gesicht sagte.*] (author's italics) Second, he vigorously objects to finding in Hamlet anything of a *modern* personality. After pondering on what the French Revolution "incited," he continues: "Thus I hope that . . . one will thoroughly emerge from the absurdities of the *New Testament* or from Hamlet and Faust, the two 'most modern people.' " [*So hoffe ich, dass . . . man gründlich über die Albernheiten des neuen Testaments oder über Hamlet und Faust, die beiden "modernsten Menschen," hinauskommt.*] (Nietzsche, 1882-1888, p. 378).

The most relevant passage, however, is the following (1888, p. 56): ". . . dionysiac Man has a similarity with Hamlet: both once took a real look into the essence of things; they have *come to know* and it disgusts them to act; for their action cannot change anything in the eternal essence of things; they find it laughable or insulting that they are expected to set the world, which is out of joint, right again. Knowledge kills acting; for to action belongs the veil of illusion—that is the lesson to be learned from Hamlet, not that cheap wisdom of Jack the dreamer, who as the result of too much reflection, as it were of an excess of possibilities, does not get to acting; [it is] not the reflecting, no!—[but] the true comprehension, the insight into the ghastly truth [that] outweigh any motive that would propel to action . . . [ellipsis in original] Now no comfort is any longer of use, the longing goes beyond a world after death, beyond the gods themselves; existence, together with its glittering reflection in the gods or in an immortal other world, is negated. In the awareness of the truth, once viewed, man now perceives nothing but the dreadfulness or the absurdity of being; now he comprehends what is symbolic in Ophelia's fate, now he recognizes the wisdom of the forest god Silenus: it nauseates him." [. . . *der dionysische Mensch* [hat] *Aehnlichkeit mit Hamlet: beide haben einmal einen wahren Blick in das Wesen der Dinge gethan, sie haben erkannt, und es ekelt sie zu handeln; denn ihre Handlung kann nichts am ewigen Wesen der Dinge ändern, sie empfinden es als lächerlich oder schmachvoll, dass ihnen zugemuthet wird, die Welt, die aus den Fugen ist, wieder einzurichten. Die Erkenntnis tödtet das Handeln, zum Handeln gehört das Umschleiert sein durch die Illusion—das ist die Hamletlehre, nicht jene wohlfeile Weisheit von Hans dem Träumer, der aus zu viel Reflexion, gleichsam aus einem Ueberschuss von Möglichkeiten, nicht zum Handeln kommt; nicht das Reflectieren, nein!—die wahre Erkenntnis, der Einblick in die grauenhafte Wahrheit uberwiegt jedes zum Handeln antreibende Motiv . . . Jetzt verfängt kein Trost mehr, die Sehnsucht geht über eine Welt nach dem Töde, über die Götter selbst hinaus, das Dasein wird, sammt seiner gleissenden Wiederspiegelung in den Göttern oder in einem unsterblichen Jenseits, verneint. In der Bewusstheit der einmal geschauten Wahrheit sieht jetzt der Mensch überall nur das Entsetzliche oder Absurde des Seins, jetzt versteht er das Symbolische im Schicksal der Ophelia, jetzt erkennt er die Weisheit des Waldgottes Silen: es ekelt ihn.*] (author's italics). Later, once again (1888, p. 200): "Does one *comprehend* Hamlet? [It is] not the doubt, [but] the *certainty* that makes mad" [Versteht *man Hamlet? Nicht der Zweifel,* die Gewissheit *ist Das, was wahnisinnig macht*] (author's italics).

Here the existential misery of the mid-twentieth century is already in full blossom, and thus this viewpoint too might still make Hamlet a "modern" man. But even if the respect in which I have sought to establish Hamlet's modernity may be regarded as far-fetched, Nietzsche's interpretation does not fit the details of the text. Ingenious as is his reversal of Coleridge's interpretation, one wonders whether a man who is rejecting action because he has reached those heights of wisdom from which all action appears illusive would accuse himself as mercilessly as Hamlet sometimes does. When he does reach the peak of insight, in the graveyard

One closing remark on Dostoevski's view on society may be useful. Dostoevski predicted that the building of the Tower of Babel, which he uses as a symbol of science, would in the end disappoint mankind, to such an extent that mankind would turn away from science and reinstitute the Churches with their miracles, secrets and authority. Yet curiously enough, science satisfies each of these three conditions in its own way.

The more man penetrates into the "undiscovered country," the more he becomes aware that he is surrounded by secrets. Yet the application of scientific discoveries leads to achievements that man often experiences as miraculous; and in science man has an authority that dwarfs the authority of revealed texts. There is no taskmaster more dictatorial than truth; the scientist is forced to travel one and only one way—a way that is not mapped out by him in full freedom but rather imposed upon him by a reality that exists in utter disregard of his wishes.

Yet, even though science does satisfy man's secret hankering for miracle, secret and authority, Dostoevski's prediction may still come true one day. The more science progresses, the more mankind suffers from its side effects. The most glaring example is modern medicine, which has brought about the population explosion that may, in turn, lead to world catastrophe. To be sure, science has also produced the tools with which disproportionate population growth can be avoided. But science does not have the power to make mankind use these tools, and in order to achieve their proper use, social and cultural reorganizations would be necessary that, under present cultural conditions, it seems, cannot be carried out.

---

scene, he then moves *closer* to the possibility of action. To be sure, in my opinion what he there obtains is a viewpoint that goes beyond the dichotomy of action and non-action; yet it is unmistakable that the effect of that mysterious force that had held him back before is now no longer observable.

And, as Nietzsche's scheme does not at all provide for, he does act in the end.

It is different with Nietzsche's brief comments on Hamlet's madness. There he is employing the deepest insight, anticipating what few psychoanalysts would ever be able to say as penetratingly. In 1888 Nietzsche (1895, p. 296) wrote: "There are free and bold spirits that would like to conceal and deny that at bottom they are irrecoverably broken hearts—this is Hamlet's case; and at such a time even clowning can be the mask for an accursed *all too certain* knowledge." [*Es giebt freie freche Geister, welche verbergen und verleugnen möchten, dass sie im Grunde zerbrochne unheilbare Herzen sind—es ist der Fall Hamlets: und dann kann die Narrheit selbst die Maske für ein unseliges* allzugewisses *Wissen sein*] (author's italics). And about misanthropy and love, he had this to say (1882, p. 176): "One speaks of being fed up with people only when one can no longer digest them, and yet has a stomach full of them. Misanthropy is the consequence of an all too greedy love of humanity and of 'cannibalism'—but who told you to gulp down people like oysters, Prince Hamlet?" [Man spricht nur dann davon, dass man der Menschen satt sei, wenn man sie nicht mehr verdauen kann und doch noch den Magen voll davon hat. Misanthropie ist die Folge einer allzu begehrlichen Menschenliebe und "Menschenfresserei"—aber wer hiess dich auch, Menschen zu verschlucken wie Austern, mein Prinz Hamlet?]

Mutatis mutandis, this is apparently also true of modern physics. Science is a process that leads to the development of insights with which almost all the tasks of daily practice could be solved—except one: the spread of science itself. This is a historical process, the control of which mankind is hardly likely to attain before it is too late.

It is depressing to observe such basically antithetical persons as Dostoevski, the religious mystic and adherent of autocratic government, and Max Born, Nobel Laureate in physics and a true democrat, reaching conclusions that are not too far apart. "Though I love science," writes the latter (1965), "I have the feeling that it is so much against history and tradition that it cannot be absorbed by our civilization. . . . Should the race not be extinguished by a nuclear war, it will degenerate into a flock of stupid, dumb creatures under the tyranny of dictators who rule them with the help of machines and electronic computers."

In *Hamlet,* the dictators try, and with some success, to make out of mankind a herd of such stupid creatures; perhaps they fail in their attempt because they lack machines and computers. If we go along with Shakespeare, then we should expect that there will always be found some Hamlet who *cannot* be defeated, even with the assistance of machines and computers.

13. Was Hamlet Mad?

Of all the puzzling and exciting problems evoked by *Hamlet,* the prince's madness is surely the most interesting and most challenging— and at the same time the most difficult to solve. The explanation by Robertson that Shakespeare had to retain this element, like so many others, primarily because it was present in the original play on which he drew is quite unsatisfactory. So too is his proposition that Shakespeare got himself into insuperable difficulties by eliminating the traditional justification for Hamlet's decision to pretend mental derangement.

According to Robertson, Shakespeare had to drop the guards that surrounded the King in the original because such protection was no longer customary at the Elizabethan court. It is not evident, however, why Shakespeare should have felt constrained to present the court at Elsinore as if it were a contemporary institution. That a sovereign who had arrogated power to himself by means of a crime might be fearful thereafter of retaliation from whatever source, and might therefore be eager to live in the shadow of a protective guard—such a sequence of events would have been quite acceptable, one should think, to any audience. Why then did Shakespeare burden himself—apparently without any compelling necessity to do so—with a problem that, as Robertson and after him Eliot asserted, was beyond solution?

Neither of these critics seems to doubt Shakespeare's genius, yet they both regard Shakespeare's undertaking to rewrite Kyd's *Hamlet* in much the same way as we would regard a physicist's undertaking to construct a *perpetuum mobile*. In their reasoning there is, of course, a contradiction. On the one hand, they rightly assert that Shakespeare was forced to abide by those traditional elements that were inescapably connected with the audience's image of Hamlet; on the other hand, however, they also insist that Shakespeare was in no position to maintain other traditional elements, such as guards protecting a sovereign. This seems to me to be an arbitrary and unwarranted distinction. In my view of the tragedy, preserving the guards would have destroyed—or at least falsified and counteracted—the essential meaning of *Hamlet*, which is first and foremost a *psychological* play.

Out of a traditional story, which by and large, in regard to its psychology, stays within the stimulus-reaction schema, Shakespeare created a play in which the main events are correlated with basic psychological processes. Such processes are always hidden, inaccessible to the naked eye; what is discernible may thus seem to the observer to be no more than a response to an external stimulus. Something of the simple stimulus-reaction pattern is indeed to be found as the core not only of most of the observable behavior of everyday life but also of Hamlet's behavior. Without the Queen's rash marriage and the shattering message of the ghost, the stimuli that elicited Hamlet's conflicts would be absent, and no occasion would have been provided for his soliloquies.

Yet the area that is covered by stimulus-reaction patterns is actually quite small and only a precipitating function can be assigned to them. By contrast, the area that rests on extensive processes, which are neither directly visible nor observable, is quite large. For that reason alone, a multiplicity of theories has arisen with regard to the play and its characters. If in addition one remembers that the events that Shakespeare did put on the stage can be understood in a variety of ways, one can easily see why no agreement is to be expected with regard to the critics' interpretations. Indeed, I regard the extreme magnitude of this critical diversity as a sign of the tragedy's excellence, in the same way as the fact that, even now, the philosophers cannot find agreement about the meaning and purpose of life stands as one measure of the profundity of that question.

The contradictions that have been pointed out in *Hamlet* are, after all, not necessarily evidences of weakness in plot construction; they may well be meaningful and interpretable derivatives of forces that oppose each other, intermingle, or cooperate, as the case may be, yet in any event form a basic pattern in the universe that Shakespeare created in *Hamlet*. Out of them flows a wealth of directly observable phenomena, just as is true in real life.

One would like, of course, to be able to define a yardstick that will enable us to differentiate weakness of plot construction from organic, meaningful contradictions. I doubt, however, that such definitions have yet been formulated, and it seems necessary, therefore, to examine a number of individual instances, particularly in the case of such a complex structure as Hamlet's madness.

The Graveyard Scene.

The graveyard scene may be the suitable starting point for an examination of the variety of aspects inherent in Hamlet's "madness."[1] To me, this scene is the peak point in the play, if not in all of Elizabethan tragedy. Theodore Spencer has written a superb book on the thanatology of Elizabethan tragedy; yet, curiously enough, he has comparatively little to say about this dramatic episode; it is in three of Chapman's plays instead that he finds the clear and definitive expression of the Renaissance viewpoint on death (Spencer, 1936, pp. 236, 242-253).[2]

What Shakespeare has to say about death in the graveyard scene—although there are many strands connecting it with the Western tradition—is, in my opinion, a highly personal and at the same time original, almost definitive declaration. The episode has a three-layered structure: the exchange between the two gravediggers; Hamlet's discourse with Horatio; and Ophelia's funeral. In these three successive contexts, three quite different worlds are introduced: the realistic or naturalistic approach to death; the metaphysical view of death; and the shattering actuality of death's presence.

The realistic portion is entrusted to the two gravediggers, for which Shakespeare has been harshly censured by some critics, on the grounds that it was cynical of him to do so. In tragedy, comical figures are sometimes the servants of death. As Flatter has noted, Osric is just such a messenger and, in *Antony and Cleopatra*, the clown (*V.2*) fulfills the same function. The reverse is sometimes true of comedy. In *Tartuffe*, the tragic figures are M. Loyal and the police officer, who are harbingers of news grievous to the protagonists.

---

[1] For a very good analysis of the graveyard scene see Ornstein (1960).

[2] See Farnham (1950) for an analysis of the difference between Chapman and Shakespeare's Jacobean period.

Representing the terrifying by the comical at the symbolic level has the effect of heightening the dramatic tension to an almost unbearable point. To be sure, it is only Osric who is a truly comical figure in this scene, and the role is usually acted in a laughable manner. The gravediggers, by contrast, occupy a middle ground between the tragic and the comical; they are truly naturalistic in character. Under the guise of ignorance or boorishness, the gravediggers represent the world as it is, despoiling it of the romantic illusions that we cherish about it. By their realistic approach, they succeed in reducing the world to the bare facts of harsh and dissonant reality. "We must speak by the card," says Hamlet; but he adds "or equivocation will undo us." Yet is it really equivocation that undoes him? By stripping from the words that we commonly use these meanings that we project onto them in order to form and maintain our cherished illusions, the first gravedigger cuts right to the bone of these words. In so doing, he bares their primordial core, which lies buried inside the husk that has developed around most of them.

When Hamlet asks such a seemingly simple question as: "Whose grave's this, sir?" and receives the answer "Mine, sir," a rent is torn in an illusion. The only thing a living person is in a position to say is: "This will one day be my grave." Once he is dead, he has lost the capacity for ownership; if Hamlet wished to be exact, what he should have asked is: "What was the name of the person for whose body this grave is prepared?" Yet his first formulation is a reflection of the inescapable feeling that the body that lies in a grave is its owner—an illusion that permits one to regard the deceased *persona* as still maintaining its essential capacities.

Funerals acquire by their marginal character a highly emotional cathexis: as long as the corpse has not been buried, the deceased is not yet altogether dead for us. The funeral is a last farewell, and it is only at the burial that the feeling arises of life having totally spent itself. Immediately thereafter, however, the grave becomes a resting place, so that any subsequent visit to the grave stands for reunion with the beloved. When illusions are peeled off from the complex chain of highly cathected imagery referring to life and death—which are explicitly experienced, but integrated almost like routines—then it becomes clear that the gravedigger is right: it *is* his grave and not Ophelia's. By this reductive process a revolutionary effect has been achieved.

Yet the gravediggers represent only a destructive force, which does not offer any new elements to take the place of what has heretofore been shown to be corrupt and false. What they expose is the extension of class discrimination even into matters of death, thereby anticipating by 300 years Rilke's (1903-1910) thoughts on the question. The poor man's body fares worse than those of gentlefolk in cases of suicide—which is one reason why the first gravedigger advises the "great folk" to make more use of the privilege extended to them by the Church. In declaring Adam to be the first gentleman, since he bore arms ("could he dig without arms?"), the gravedigger implies that all his descendants are equal.

And then there is the conundrum about the best builders. One answer is the gallows-maker, "for that frame outlives a thousand tenants"; but the correct answer is the grave-maker: "the houses that he makes last till doomsday." The theme on which Hamlet will later elaborate is thus introduced: the gallows are the symbol of man's power over his fellow man. The First Gravedigger's retort is that if this were indeed true, then the gallows would be stronger than the Church: in setting up the gravedigger, who serves here as a symbol of death, as the one who builds strongest, he is raising death above both secular and Church power.

A supreme attack against the fundamental bastions of societal structure is thus launched in this exchange, but without fanfare, without open rebellion, without either commiseration or accusation, but rather in the forms of apparent submission to the forces in power. Consolation is to be found (and this too is only adumbrated) in the transitoriness of all that is human. Let arrogance and privilege have their day; they are destined to fall. The forgotten man, of whom the record will not say a word, performs his silent duty of paving the way for Death's march by preparing the pit into which everything that lives will sink.

Essentially, the gravediggers are caught up in the *hic et nunc*. To be sure, the sameness of all men is established by reference to the distant past, to the common biological origins of all of mankind and to the fate that awaits them in the future and from which there is no escape. Both past and future, however, are compounded in the present moment in the symbol of the gravedigger, who "bears arms" and digs a grave.

With Hamlet's entry into the scene, the discourse on death rises to a new level. The sight of man's final remains, which have thus far withstood putrefaction, evokes thoughts about the live antecedents of which they had once been part: "That skull had a tongue in it, and could sing once." Even though this is a logical, well-nigh inescapable sequence of ideas, it is also a terrifying one in its simplicity and in the additive character of the sentence's structure.

In everyday practice, life is bearable only when the wholeness of present structure is preserved in the subjective experience. When the total past and the total future of structures become attached to their present appearance, however, the world falls apart and becomes psychologically unlivable. A child would then contain the image of its origin: St. Augustine's famous *inter faeces et urinam*, and beyond that the divided germplasma, even the entire phylogenetic ladder.

Yet this would be only one end of the spectrum. The image of the lively, healthy, growing child would also contain its end-state: the face of the person dying in his old age and its deterioration; the disintegration of these very parts that once had made up its beauty and their conversion into new disgust-arousing structures.

Hamlet first proceeds along these lines in retrograde fashion. Starting with the end-state, he evolves the image of the live organ once attached to the now lifeless bone, and then of that organ's function. Later, he proceeds in the opposite direction, introducing Alexander and Caesar, the two most myth-stimulating men on the Olympus of Western history —heroes who had become, after their death, mythical figures, which served as prototypes of the sort of greatness that Hercules possessed in Greek mythology. And what has become of them? A stopper for a beer barrel, a patch to mend a wall.

Here the most concentrated forms of vitality, of a hyperpotency that transformed whole civilizations and gave a new look to the surface of the world, serve as the starting point for a process that ends with transmogrification into the basest, vilest state. The particulars selected for this last state are significant. It is not a tree or a flower, or a stone in a cathedral, that is selected, but the ugly and the defective. The stopper and the patch are particularly degrading, insofar as they are, to begin with, involved in the undoing of a not terribly significant defect, and serve only passively, as diminutive resistances to the not greatly significant pressures that impinge upon them.[3]

The trans-human is thus converted into the sub-sub-human and the perceptive world, for all its seeming beauty and harmony, into an agglomeration of horrors. When you see a child, you see the cadaver at the same time, and when you shake the dust off your feet, your ancestors may be part of it. Such thoughts as these are no longer vagaries, impassioned but essentially fantastic interpretations of the world, nor are they mere meditations, profound as these may be, upon the vanity and tran-

---

[3] If they were to be interpreted as dream symbols, one could think of them as cut-off penises, used now for degraded purposes.

siency of everything human. In them are expressed the deepest truths of human existence; in the accidental combinations of present sense data, the totality of the past and the future are perceived accurately, with the same clarity and distinctness as if they were themselves sense data.

And all this is done without any scientific frame of reference. Although this was the time when the propositions of Copernicus were vaguely felt to contain some remote possibility of providing the truth, everything that Hamlet says in the graveyard scene has grown out of a fundamentally mythological, magic, unscientific mode of experiencing the world. What he says does not require erudition to be understood. Ignorance of the great ancient philosophers would not impede the understanding of it, any more than would ignorance of the Bible.

It is quite significant that there is no reference to God: no consolatory illusion is permitted to penetrate this world of repugnant realism—repugnant to us, perhaps, but apparently not so to Hamlet. He does make one reference to the Old Testament that is quite revealing of the heightened level to which he has raised the discourse. Like the gravedigger, Hamlet goes back for one moment to the distant and mythical past; but it is Cain's jawbone, the weapon of the first murderer, that comes to his mind. Indeed, it is strange that, after death had been ordained as the human race's punishment for Adam's transgression, the first human death to occur was not a natural one but rather one that was brought about by human violence—the first human death thus being a murderous one, and its victim being the first human being of whom it is recorded that he revered God in true religiosity.

As I see it, Hamlet's conjuring up of the image of Cain's jawbone at the beginning of the discourse opens up the subsequent imagery of death as a murderer, who robs man of all that has been beautiful and cherished in his life.[4] Yet the discourse ends in a vision in which death is no longer a force separate from the cosmos and only later added to it, or working—in some sense from outside it—against the purposes of life. Instead the cosmos is viewed as impregnated, even saturated with death, so that the mental edifice goes far beyond the Christian view of death as an alien element, thrust into a world of paradisiacal innocence, in which man had previously enjoyed a life of everlasting childhood.

[4] Shakespeare's allusion to Cain's jawbone is one example of his unexcelled mastery in giving lines a depth that makes them strike the reader as inexhaustible in meaning and therefore in interpretation. A meaning that may be regarded as mythical or metaphysical or transcendental is, as has been intimated, contained in the line about Cain. But there is also a concrete link to the principal

It is important to observe that Hamlet's thanatological exposition has since been confirmed; science has provided the proof for what Hamlet scooped out of the depths of his unconscious. As science views it, the world is devoid of God; and floating somewhere in the universe, at an utterly insignificant point in it, is man, left to his own wits, without protection, and certain of only one thing—that he will die and that everything around him will ultimately decay and fall apart.

His universe, which is now expanding, may at some time start shrinking—indeed may already be shrinking, since the sources of the data that indicate expansion are millions of light years away. No one yet knows either why the universe started to expand or why it will shrink, crushing everything in its pathway.

Man has accumulated an enormous mass of knowledge, far more than Hamlet ever dreamed of as possible, even though he was aware that the philosophy of his own times knew only an infinitesimal fraction of what there was to be known. Yet that cometlike acceleration of insight into reality, leading as it has almost to a "superabundance" of knowledge, has not made man happy. It has resulted in a gap, no less unbridgeable than it is painful, between his reason and his feelings, for the cognitive gains have not been able to be integrated at the emotional level.

It is unacceptable to our feelings that, in the universe of which it is a part, this planet is less than a single molecule would be in a glass of water, aside from its being utterly without distinction with regard to its

---

theme of the tragedy, for the line refers directly to fratricide—in this instance, of the younger by the older. But the punishment for this murder was not death. It was, to be sure, a cruel punishment—a sort of ostracism, involving endless starvation and wandering.

More importantly, Cain was protected by the Lord against being slain. It is curious, when seen within the context of Hamlet's task, that the Lord promised a graver punishment for the slayer of the slayer than for the slayer himself: "Whosoever slayeth Cain, vengeance shall be taken on him sevenfold." Yet Lamech, bearer of the fifth generation after Cain, already boasted: "If Cain shall be avenged sevenfold, truly Lamech seventy and sevenfold." That is to say, revenge increased in geometrical proportion. This entire sequence serves to reduce the irrevocable necessity of blood vengeance, to which Hamlet had initially assented.

But there is a distinctive feature that links the myth of Cain to still another dimension of the tragedy: "The Lord set a mark upon Cain." Cain tried initially to deny the deed—as, in a psychoanalytic sense, Claudius also did; later, however, unlike Claudius, he did not hide behind a mask of hypocrisy but was prepared to be known as a fratricide by everyone he met. We recall that it was Claudius' hypocrisy that contributed so greatly to Hamlet's fury.

Furthermore, when Hamlet, in his meditation on death, comes to Cain, this may be a way of expressing the idea that, since fratricide appeared right at mankind's beginning, it is part of the web of life; in that sense, it has become somewhat freed of what would otherwise be its taint. Thus Cain's testimony adds to the drift of the entire meditation, which is that one must make one's peace with a world that puts up with a father being murdered by his brother.

place and course; that it is altogether of no importance whether I, you, society, mankind, the whole planet exist or do not exist; finally, that all insight is relative, since no firm truth or relevance will ever be obtained by man.

What science has discovered about this totality is, further, a conglomeration of horrors, so that man isolates his knowledge, trying to use it—wisely or unwisely, whichever his constitution permits him—but without letting it penetrate into his core. If that should ever happen, it would drive him into madness. And thus we see man healing his sicknesses, travelling to the moon, moving faster than sound, and even creating new species and new substances, as well as machines that work better, more precisely, more efficiently than those that have been created by natural evolution, yet all the while dreaming in the same way as his ancestors did in the epoch of mythological darkness. Man has not changed: that at least is the atmosphere of the graveyard scene. Yet *can* he change?

There is one decisive difference, however, between Hamlet and modern man. He did not isolate, but rather integrated and accepted into the very core of his personality the conglomeration of horrors that modern man is forced to keep in his mind as an isolated mass, of primarily rational character. At the time of the graveyard scene, Hamlet has aged. He is now 30—an age at which, in Shakespeare's times, a man probably felt old[5]—yet Hamlet does not complain and he does not rebel.

I do not find a single shred of cynicism or melancholia in Hamlet's discourse on death. Everything he says is true; it comes from the innermost recesses of his mind, as well as from the highest layers of abstract thinking, and it is synthesized into a consistent and uncompromising reality-adequate world view. There is no element of denial or intellectualization. "My gorge rises at it" contains the fullness of his emotional response, put forward in a fashion entirely suitable to the occasion.

The intensity of the emotional output ebbs and flows in proportion

[5] Draper (1939, pp. 48, 194) discusses the question of age-values in the Elizabethan period. Old age began at 35. "Life was short in the early 17th century, Iago at twenty-eight seems to be middle-aged." One gets the full flavor of what it must have meant to be an "intellectual" of 30 around 1600 from a comment that Murry (1936, p. 57) makes about Shakespeare's age when he was 28: "Twenty-eight seems young enough, but in the strenuous conditions of those days it was approaching middle-age. Greene, six years older than Shakespeare, was dying of disease and debauchery, worn out at thirty-four. Peele lasted till thirty-nine, when he died 'of the pox'. Marlowe, Shakespeare's exact coeval, was to be stabbed next year in a tavern brawl. Nashe was with the dead men by thirty-four. It is not surprising that in two more years Shakespeare was speaking of himself as an old man, and thinking seriously of the possibility of death."

to the distance from the ego of the aspect being hit upon at the moment, but it never comes to a standstill. The peak is surely reached at that moment when Hamlet beholds Yorick's skull and there follow the enchanting recollections of an irreparably lost childhood; his comments on that situation inevitably imply that his own skull too may one day be gazed at in that same fashion by someone else.

While his discourse is not limited to death, for good reasons it centers on death. He takes note, when he speaks of the peasant's toe galling the courtier's kibe, of the inner tensions and gradual changes within his own society that will one day make his own class decline and yield place. He further notes that he is considered mad by everyone in the realm. This does not upset his balance, even though it touches on that point at which most of us are most highly vulnerable—the narcissistic self-image and the security of the group of which we are members.

He still continues to voice his searching questions, unperturbed by what the answer may be or may lead to. Yet it is by putting death into the center of his discourse that Hamlet rises to the zenith. Death is truly that certainty that it is most difficult to integrate, among the many certainties and uncertainties with which human life is so filled.

A variety of reasons may be considered, in attempting to account for the fact that Shakespeare reintroduced Hamlet, after his prolonged absence, in a graveyard.[6] One of these reasons might well have been that, against that background, Shakespeare could fully demonstrate to what heights Hamlet had developed. The Hamlet we meet here is different from the one we had known at the beginning of the play, or at the time when he left Denmark. The full extent of the inner change can be best demonstrated, it is clear, when Hamlet is brought face to face with the most formidable problem that man encounters—namely, death—even though the existence of that problem is, by and large, denied in some civilizations, among them our own.

Until the rise of science, death was one of the most discussed topics, if not in truth *the* most discussed of them all. That man *has to* die must certainly come as a shock to a "keep smiling" civilization; since the smile is obligatory for social survival, the denial of death is a necessary consequence. Yet behind this denial, of course, lurks a death imagery as stirring and awesome to contemporary man as it was to those who were born in earlier cultures.

[6] It was Shakespeare who introduced the graveyard to Elizabethan drama.

Even in this century, as happened with a patient of mine, a person may give a structure to her life that is based entirely on the certainty that death will one day knock at her chambers. When this does come to pass, however, it will come as no victory, no triumph, because all that death will find then will be an "empty bag," a person who had never once felt a flicker of joy. Thus, as the end-product of the enforcement of a lifelong self-inflicted maximal deprivation, what may have been intended by death as a celebration of conquest will instead have been converted into death's defeat and her victory, for she will scornfully hurl against him: "You thought you were going to take something from me, but there is nothing there for you to take."

If Hamlet were truly "melancholic" (as he is so often described),[7] he might have given voice to such a trend of thought. But he is just as far away from a "keep crying" ideology as he is from a "keep smiling" one. In supreme autonomy, he looks death in the eye without flinching. And since he is now capable of doing so without fear, denial, rebellion or self-pity, but rather out of charity and unending sadness, at this moment he has reached incomparable heights.

This highlights the vast distance he has traveled from the Hamlet who regretted earlier that "the everlasting had fixed his canon" against suicide; who felt distressed that what happened after death still remained unknown to man; or who was outraged by the fact that he had been born to a certain fate without at least having been given a choice of alternatives. Now at last he accepts existence as it is: "If it be now, 'tis not to come; if it be not to come, it will be now; if it be not now, yet it will come."

I have never read any commentary on the history or even the meaning of this tripartite prophecy. It could stand in the Bible; it might have been part of an orphic song; it could have been spoken by any parson of depth in his Sunday sermon. It is one of the most beautiful sentences in

---

[7]It would be necessary to discuss here the evolution that the concept of melancholia underwent in the 16th century, a development that is usually ignored when Hamlet is presented as typifying the melancholic temperament. Panofsky (1943, Vol. 1, pp. 156-171), in interpreting Dürer's *Melancholia I,* set forth the full implications of melancholia in its relation to Saturn. Marsilio Ficino brought Aristotle's question to new honor: "Why is it that all men who have become outstanding in philosophy, statesmanship, poetry or the arts are melancholic?" (Aristotle, Vol. 2, p. 155). *Furor melancholicus* was identified with *furor divinus* and became the privilege of genius. Finally, it was stated that all men are melancholics (Panofsky, 1943, Vol. 1, p. 166f).

It would be of interest to investigate whether Hamlet's outbreaks were not meant to be manifestations of *furor divinus.* Here one seems to come upon the birth of an insight, later so often neglected, that genius and its concomitants constitute a separate category of psychopathology, not to be confused with ordinary mental diseases.

the English language, overwhelming in terms of the imagery that it precipitates, an imagery that can neither be defined nor even wholly put into words. While it cannot be rationally explained, yet it conveys an unmistakable and irrefutable meaning—even though logical analysis would probably throw this meaning aside as an empty, useless shell.

A metaphysical, transcendental summary of what existence is, it is in that respect an expression of the contradictoriness that constitutes reality and man's relationship to it. By bowing to the chasm that stretches between man and his end, Hamlet has made himself an organic part of the universe, as he experiences it, and has overcome the isolation in which we found him at the beginning of the play.

The tripartite prophecy sounds like fatalism, and it would be, had Hamlet not added: "The readiness is all." Here the clarion sounds with an impetuous call for action and battle—but this is no longer a battle *imposed* on Hamlet, in which he is no more that a foot-soldier, carrying out commands, or a battle that he must himself enforce, being driven to it by his own conflicts. This is man in a state of freedom, who will give battle when the occasion is ripe, when fate presents him with the opportunity, and his own conscience and insight make him consent to take it. To all outward appearance, he may enter the arena of history like any gladiator chained to the *Morituri te salutamus,* but in reality he has become the master of his destiny, having recognized that what is inevitable is also thereby an organic part of human life: "Since no man has aught of what he leaves, what is't to leave betimes?" And then he ends by fusing dirge and clarion with his all-encompassing "Let be."

As is true of all great masterworks, the content and meaning of Hamlet's discourse cannot be made fully explicit. Thus my interpretation, if it is correct at all, would deal with but one aspect. Yet, even though it is less than the whole, this aspect should not be regarded as negligible, particularly in the light of trends that play such a significant role in contemporary society. One of the things that makes this discourse great is its flow toward the future, which culminates in the tripartite prophecy.

No matter what its hidden meaning may be said to be, one can characterize Hamlet's transformation as having been from a person who is driven to immediate action yet is at the same time inhibited from its performance, to a person whose experience of the present is embedded in a broad stream flowing toward the future. This transformation has its effect on all areas of Hamlet's life; yet there is a special affinity between thoughts of death and the mental representation of the future.

The ability to live "in the future" is one of the supreme achievements of the human mind. In the very young, it is quite undeveloped; in the very old, it has, for the most part, fallen into decline. There is a general resistance against one's comprehensive projection into the future. As one person has told me: "It is dangerous to think of goals that lie in the future. If one overshoots the mark, then he thinks of death."

Many a person today makes himself part of that resistance against the mental voyage into the future. Writes Dr. Bettelheim (1955), in chiding me for my interest in the problem of death (he even thought that only someone who was given to radical political opinions could have such an interest): "I have always considered it a good indicator of mental health if a person lived well in the present and met its exigencies, and an indication of emotional disturbance if the pressing needs of the present were continually overshadowed by the unknown, but always anticipated, exigencies of the future" (p. 8). He feels quite enthusiastic about "living a sane and relatively happy life with one's family and neighbors" and recommends trying "simply to make a good life for his own" (p. 12f).

Such a predilection for the present may well be the correct and necessary attitude in certain civilizations that are not yet too well developed and whose innate potential of movement is still low. For a differentiated culture, characterized by a relatively high speed of change, however, concentration on the present is a death knell and carries with it catastrophic consequences.

To be sure, the *petit bourgeois* as civilization's dead weight, protects his society against too rash oscillations and thus does serve a useful societal function. Yet in the long run he chokes a culture and hastens it toward its lasting fall by his addiction to the present and the fact that he finds his supreme consummation in the "good life." Hamlet is the anti-*petit bourgeois*—which is perhaps one of the reasons why he is regarded by so many as pathological personality *tout court*.

In his discourse with Horatio, we see him as a man who is free of neurotic doubts, no longer divided within himself, and with a mentality that makes him capable of acting directly on reality. Before this change took place, we had indeed seen him in action, but one instance was an apraxia (Polonius), and the other served to bring to an end his doubts and scruples (mouse-trap play). In the final scene of the play, we see

Hamlet engaged in reality-adequate and ego-syntonic action; it is in his discourse with Horatio that the mentality out of which such action grows is demonstrated.[8]

While Hamlet's discourse, in which one can find the last remnant of castration anxiety, sounds as if death were a fate to befall men only, one against which women are protected,[9] it is a woman's death that now presents itself as a concrete reality. In the third part of the graveyard scene, Ophelia's funeral takes place. The rhythm of the sequences—from the ordinary, vulgar, and trivial by way of the abstract and general, comprehending both past and future, and finally to the concrete, realistic, and visible—is a masterstroke of dramatic structure, building up relentless tension.

By starting the third part of this scene with the themes of the burial of suicides and of class preferences, Shakespeare compounds these sequences into an organic whole and thereby avoids the dangers of what would otherwise be an essentially additive structure. The actual funeral furnishes the concretization of a societal process that had previously been presented as a generality, in the speculations of the two gravediggers. One could compare the shift from general discourse to concrete visualization with the transformation of latent dream thoughts into the manifest dream. The actual interment would seem to be a compromise: Ophelia is granted burial in hallowed ground, but with truncated rites.

Sympathy and pity already being with the victim, this compromise arouses feelings of aversion against the churlish priest. His assertion that charitable prayers would be denied her altogether, if the law were applied strictly, once again emphasizes the pitiable state of this type of woman (by contrast with the Queen), who is persecuted and "maimed" even after she has crossed the threshold of death. The dramatic climax comes later, in the violent struggle that shortly thereafter breaks out in Ophelia's grave, between Laertes and Hamlet. It was indeed by being trampled down in the cruel fight among men that she lost her mental

---

[8] This change in Hamlet's personality, which I perceive so strongly, is denied by many. See Bradley (1904); Tillyard (1950), pp. 16, 144; Wilson (1936a), p. 236f. Knight (1947a, p. 320) writes: "Certainly he comes back a subtly changed man." Johnson (1952) very ably discusses the literature on the question of whether or not Hamlet appears a different man upon his return from England. He himself assumes an essential change to have taken place from "student prince" to the "ordained minister of Providence" (p. 206). Cf. Braddy (1964): "Hamlet, a civilized university student, has at last molded himself into a justified avenger, with a cynical outlook on life and ample motive for revenge" (p. 57); p. 63: "The hero of the first Acts transforms himself into his opposite in the closing ones." See also p. 69.

[9] This is intimated by Hamlet's questioning for what man the grave is being prepared; it becomes even clearer when only men are associated with the skulls he views.

balance, thus typifying the fate so many women have had to suffer, not only in Shakespeare's time but in our own.

Greek mythology had already presented the woman who seduces men into the making of war (Iris or Helen) and the large number of women who become its victims (Aeschylus's *Persians*). That point I shall deal with later; here I would like to stress only that the hidden meaning of the episode may be revealed by a reversal of sequence—namely, Ophelia's having been killed during the course of a fight between two men over possession of her. Since Hamlet and Laertes represent to my mind two brothers, I see the duel as the outcome of competition between the oldest and youngest brother as to who loves the sister more.

Yet, to return to an interpretation that limits itself to the events on the stage, it does become necessary to explain Hamlet's outburst upon hearing Laertes' terrible accusation and curse against him. This outburst is called madness not only by the King and Queen, but also by most critics, and it therefore lends itself well to coming closer to the meaning of Hamlet's madness, about which there has been so much controversy.[10]

The externals are well defined. Hamlet has just returned to his native country and is in a metaphysical mood. At the very moment when he is giving voice to his deepest reflections on the horrors of death and the essential vanity of all human existence, the dreadful accusation is hurled against him that he was the cause of Ophelia's death. On the heels of that accusation comes Laertes' magniloquence to the effect that no one loved Ophelia more than he. It is inevitable that this should lead to a grievous upsurge of feelings of guilt on Hamlet's part.

What possible reaction could a sensitive person experience in such a situation? He could either be overwhelmed by his feelings of guilt or he could deny them. He could also perhaps disclaim all responsibility, continuing his philosophical mood; this would amount to intellectualization in the face of a personal situation that is intensely charged with emotions. Other possible reactions can easily be constructed; but what we actually see is a mechanism that is equivalent to identification with the aggressor.

Hamlet starts to speak in Laertes' vein and does an even better job of it than Ophelia's brother. However, since he exclaims: "I have loved

---

[10] The collision between Hamlet and Laertes is dubious on textual grounds alone. Hamlet's leap into the grave is based exclusively on a stage direction that is present only in the bad Quarto, and some critics insist that Hamlet does not abandon himself to the towering passion that has been prompted by Laertes' provocative words (see Ribner, 1960 p.86, for pertinent literature). As far as I can judge, the interpretation that follows is independent of the question of which of the two may be correct.

Ophelia more than Laertes did," the fact of identification with the aggressor may be disputed. On the other hand, by using not only the style of Laertes' magniloquence but Laertes' simile of Pelion and Olympus as well, which he rounds out by adding Ossa, Hamlet's outburst does show the earmarks of identification. There is a still deeper occasion, however, for identification. Both he and Laertes have lost their fathers by violence and have come face to face with the question of vengeance. What Hamlet has had to suffer passively, he has himself visited actively upon Laertes. Thus the identification also means: "I know well how you are feeling."

Yet Hamlet's entire outburst presupposes a profound love of Ophelia, and that has been doubted by some critics, notably Madariaga. While a discussion of that question must be postponed until later, at this point I do want to indicate that I take that love for granted. Although we have heard much earlier about Hamlet's love of Ophelia, what has actually taken place on the stage does not sound like love at all, at least in its literal sense.

Yet now we hear from Hamlet himself: "I lov'd Ophelia," and one asks what psychological circumstances have now made it possible for him to let others know of his love, when earlier he has acted and spoken as if the opposite were true. Can it be that he was capable of averring this love openly only by dint of the detour he has taken through identification with Laertes—that is to say, by using the latter's language? If the King and Queen refer to Hamlet as mad, then Laertes must also be mad, for Hamlet does not do anything more than Laertes does.

In view of Hamlet's response of "What! the fair Ophelia?" upon his being apprised of her death, Wilson (1936a, p. 269) seems certain that while Hamlet's love of Ophelia has long been dead and buried, he is now reproaching himself for the fact "that love is absent." Bradley (1904, p. 145), however, calls this response "one terrible pang, from which he gains relief in frenzied words and frenzied action." To this Wilson, in turn, remarks that Shakespeare would have had to phrase it differently, if that was what he had intended (ibid.).

Here the accustomed situation arises once again: that the same element may on good grounds be interpreted in opposite ways. How is one to decide whether the utterance is "one terrible pang" or an expression of deficient love, since the two interpretations appear to be equally well justified? The transitory identification with Laertes, however, does stand on solid grounds and may perhaps help in the establishment of another interpretation.

If Bradley were correct in his interpretation that the Hamlet of the fifth act shows a kind of sad self-abandonment, as if he secretly despaired of ever being able to force himself to action, and was therefore ready to leave his duty to some other power than his own (ibid.), then such identification would be a sign of utter mental weakness. A completely discouraged and exhausted ego would no longer have the capacity to respond on its own terms, and would therefore feel forced to cling to an external model in order to find a channel for emotional discharge.

My conception of the Hamlet of the fifth act, as just presented, however, is quite different. I do not find regressive features in Hamlet at this point, as Bradley does; what I see is just the opposite, a step forward, going far beyond what would be possible to ordinary human power. Similarly, I do not find this to be evidence of indifference or of self-abandonment on Hamlet's part, but rather evidence of the deepest involvement in the world as it is, and a firm rooting in an individual stance. For that reason I hesitate to interpret Hamlet's transitory identification with Laertes as an indicator of defeat.

It should be recalled, at this point, that Hamlet's initial conflict had to do with the disparity between the emotional indices observable in the subject and the true structure of the subject's mind. Is not the identical problem unfolded here, shortly before the end of the tragedy? I would call particular attention to the verses in which the Queen has already expressed her grief over Ophelia's death, verses that stand in their simplicity and radiance among the most beautiful dirges ever written. These four lines might well be contrasted with the Queen's earlier "All that live must die, passing through nature to eternity." That was how the passage ended with which she was introduced at the beginning of the play; has she too undergone a change since then, in that she is now capable of true mourning?

Laertes is somewhat ostentatious in his expression of grief, almost mawkish and certainly indulging in false pathos. Yet Hamlet is not prompted by this display to withdrawal, disgust or alienation from the world, but instead hurls himself right into the center of the situation. Whereas at the beginning of the play, in an equivalent situation, what Hamlet sought was distance and isolation, what he now seeks is closeness. The freedom with which he picks up Laertes' style and then drops it again reveals a flexibility that can be correlated with the inner freedom he had already demonstrated in his discourse with Horatio, upon being confronted with the ultimate problem of life.

His behavior, to be sure, is offensive to Laertes, yet it is not at all intended as an attack, for in the end he avers: "I lov'd you ever," thereby converting fraternal rivalry and jealousy into homosexual attachment, a process so well studied by Freud (1921). Later he describes this episode to Horatio as a forgetting of himself. He acknowledges that Laertes is confronted with the same question as he is, and being thus brought face to face with his intention to kill Claudius, he remarks: "The bravery of his grief did put me into a towering passion" ("bravery" meaning in this context bravado).

The fact that Hamlet himself regards the perception of another's insincere emotional manifestations as the trigger of his own passion may lend credibility to my fundamental proposition. Yet Bradley (p. 421) warns us against regarding Hamlet's account as the whole truth, and he believes that Hamlet's raving over Ophelia's grave "is the best card that the believers in Hamlet's madness have to play." Kittredge (1939, p. 282), on the other hand, suggests that Hamlet "does not realize that his words to Laertes have seemed insane to the hearers." He had forgotten, according to Kittredge, "that madness is his cue." In his parting words, "Let Hercules himself do what he may, the cat will mew and dog will have his day," he "reverts to his habitual style when counterfeiting insanity" (ibid.).

It is pretty clear that literary critics have arrogated to themselves the authority to decide when Hamlet is mad and when he is feigning madness, without having at their disposal any reliable yardstick. Yet does the medical psychologist have even now—when the study of psychopathology has made significant progress—any reliable yardstick? The concept of legal responsibility is certainly not sufficient, aside from the fact that there is a strong trend in contemporary civilization not to hold man responsible for his acts, whatever they may be. Indeed, the genius assures us that he is unable to master his own creativity, that he has had to create the works that have earned our admiration. The good likewise assure us that they are inherently incapable of doing evil, just as wrongdoers promise to improve their ways but, after they have once again indulged in their habitual ways, aver that it was literally impossible for them to curb their evil impulses.

If we disregard those people whose peculiar ways are set from infancy or early childhood on, the term "madness" is customarily reserved for those whose unacceptable behavior stands in contrast to their usual competent mode of behavior. The old standard—namely, where empathy, that is, the ability to understand behavior by way of partial identification, comes to a stop, there madness starts—is no longer valid; as a result of psychoanalytic investigations, the scope of behavior that may be spoken of as "understandable" has been greatly enlarged and now encompasses even the major psychoses.

Still, the area of "competence" is ill-defined. That Ophelia became mad one cannot doubt; her disorientation is apparent in all dimensions. On the other hand, Hamlet's attack against Laertes is surely not a deviation of such magnitude as to constitute *prima facie* evidence of madness; yet it seems to have impressed some critics as being so. While the King and Queen seem to agree with the critics in this matter, for at least one reason their judgment is to be taken with a grain of salt. Since they want to soothe Laertes, the quickest way is to convince him that Hamlet is, at that moment, *non compos mentis*.

Aside from the possible desire to protect Hamlet—a desire that is sincere in his mother and pretended by Claudius—no other explanation would seem to hold up in the face of his impetuous interference with the funeral rites. Even though Laertes behaves not very differently from Hamlet, he at least can count on being understood as giving expression to a state of deep grief, which is, under the circumstances, quite natural. Hamlet, by contrast, scorns the aggrieved—which is at all time considered reprehensible. Far from empathizing, he appears to the others to be provocative where he ought to have been repentant.

From Hamlet's point of view, to be sure, there may be no reason to repent. Yet he may be aware that the mourners have clues that would justify Laertes' allegation of culpable deeds on his part. In his heart Hamlet bears no grudge against Laertes and Ophelia, even though he had berated the latter violently while she was alive. (I shall have more to say about this later.) Yet ostensibly Laertes has sufficient reason to arrogate to himself the role of "defender of family honor."

It is this that Hamlet challenges by mocking Laertes and asserting that he will do a thousandfold whatever Laertes may do. By his insistence that he will outdo Laertes, Hamlet conveys to the mourners the idea that he has more reason to mourn Ophelia's death than Laertes has, that he is at least as bereft as Laertes is, if not more so. If my proposition is correct that Hamlet and Laertes are brothers in the unconscious content of the tragedy,[11] all of this, of course, falls into place. This is a case of

---

[11] I want to add two more incidents in the play that may support my proposition. At one point *(IV.5.206-208)* Claudius tells Laertes that under certain (though hypothetical) circumstances h⸱

an older brother disputing the right of the younger to step into the place reserved for himself—that of maintaining the honor of the family. Yet this interpretation would seem to have no bearing on the actions presented in the play.

There the conflict between Hamlet and Laertes centers, not in themselves but in Ophelia. Now is it madness if a man who has suddenly been brought face to face with the terrible fact that, without intending to, he has driven a girl he loved into suicide, suffers an outburst of intense emotions and identifies with the girl's closest relative, who is ostentatiously demonstrating his grief? I do not believe that in this action there is even that dram of strangeness that may stand between the spectator and Lear at the moment when he breaks out into his mad spell.

Nor do I see any trace of feigned madness in Hamlet's parting words. After having discharged the acute emotion whose intensity was appropriate to the circumstances at hand, he reminds himself of the world that is waiting for his action, whatever may be his personal conflicts. It is learning of Ophelia's death, after all, that draws him back into the life of personal involvements that he had made great efforts to shut out; after his brief return to a phase of the past, he extricates himself from the entanglements of the present and states that, whatever may be the distractions of the accidental, the hour of decisive action is at hand.[12]

Hamlet's Relationship to Ophelia.

Hamlet's encounter with Laertes is the last incident in the play that is usually attributed to his "madness." It may be appropriate, therefore, to go back to an earlier incident of that sort. We know about it only from Ophelia's report to her father that Hamlet had more or less suddenly appeared in her closet in disheveled attire, taking her by the wrist, holding her hard, staring at her for a long time and then leaving, with his head still turned toward her.

This episode has been interpreted in a number of different ways:

(1) Hamlet was feigning madness, testing his ability to pretend in a plausible way and choosing, for that purpose, a situation in which the danger of arousing suspicion would be lessened. This was also the most

could succeed him as King, and Hamlet ends his speech of reconciliation with Laertes by averring that "I hurt my brother."

[12] It seems to me, furthermore, that the reference to Hercules is slightly mocking, and that this is all the more noteworthy in the light of the fact that Hercules was traditionally used as the symbol of "superman." This too would convey subliminally the idea of Hamlet's growth and of his independence from an ego ideal that had, earlier in the play, found inflated representation.

practical way to begin the spreading of a rumor of his derangement. To all this, Goddard (1946, p. 464) rightly says that "to use a young girl whom he loved or had loved as a mere instrument for his own ends would be . . . unforgivable."

(2) Hamlet was being sincere in presenting himself to Ophelia in this way, since he was in fact distraught over having been so deeply betrayed by his mother and was now extending his recognition of his mother's frailty to all women (Madariaga, 1948).

(3) He was presenting himself to Ophelia in the way in which a lover whose avowals of love had not been granted was supposed to behave.[13]

That the hasty marriage of his mother had aroused a conflict in Hamlet with regard to his general relationship to women, no analyst would doubt.[14] But did Hamlet ever love Ophelia? Madariaga believes him to be incapable of real love. Ophelia, he says, was a kind of plaything to Hamlet. I doubt that. If she had meant no more to him than that, his violent reaction to the revelation of his mother's behavior would make no sense. It is "daily bread" to the analyst that men form their image of the female sex in accordance with the image they have of their mothers—an image that is certainly decisive in their actual dealing with women, and usually goes back to their latency and puberty phases.

Behind the surface structure that is built out of the self's actual experience, there may rest a different image, which is shaped by biological needs and early archaic imagery. Many a "woman-hating" bachelor is, in his heart, deeply attached to some female person, perhaps the mother or sister, or a nursemaid of his early infant years. Such observations are made again and again in the analyses of homosexuals, who are the only men that are truly faithful to their mothers, even though they show the most radical rejection possible of the female sex. Hence it is quite possible that Hamlet was unconsciously most deeply in love with Ophelia, despite the fact that, in actuality, he rejected her.

[13] Goddard (1946) is, I believe, the only critic who has raised the possibility of Ophelia's account being the result of a hallucination on her part. While he sets forth good arguments in favor of that possibility, still one would have expected, if his hypothesis is correct, that Shakespeare would have slipped in somewhere a remark that would provide some concrete evidence to that effect—unless he wanted deliberately to mislead the spectator, something I find no reason to assume.

[14] That is why I was all the more surprised to find that Madariaga, who rejects psychoanalytic interpretations, nevertheless puts forward this explanation. Hamlet's dependency on his mother's behavior in his judgment of woman is, after all, a marked consequence of his Oedipus complex. It seems to me that Madariaga underestimates the subtlety and sophistication of psychoanalytic theory formation.

Still, Madariaga (1948) raises a point that has rarely been dealt with by the critics. The reconstruction of Hamlet's character as it was prior to the start of the play has aroused the curiosity of some critics, and there are quite a few remarks scattered through the tragedy that furnish a solid enough ground on which to base a half-way reliable construction. One of these is Hamlet's love poem to Ophelia, which her father reads to the King. It is a first-hand, concrete and therefore indubitable cue of some value—unless one follows the suggestion by Goddard (1955) that the love poem was forged by Polonius. Despite much cogent reasoning set forth by the author, I do not believe this to be true.[15]

Yet everyone seems to agree that the poem is stilted and not worthy of Hamlet, as we already know him to be by the time Polonius reads it aloud. "However, he is but following the fashion of Shakespeare's time" (Kittredge, 1939, p. 182), and it is this very circumstance that has been regarded as being incompatible with this enemy of all fashions, unless "Hamlet himself passed through an Osrician stage of which the letter is a relic," as Goddard (1955, p. 414) remarks. Nevertheless, it seems to me that the comparison with Osric goes too far, since Osric is at best a caricature of what Hamlet was up to the point when the trauma brought about by the revelation of his mother's behavior cruelly taught him that the world in which he believed did not exist. The love letter is, in my opinion, concrete proof that Hamlet had indeed been following the fashion of his time, even in the very personal approach to his beloved. When Goddard writes that "If once upon a time Hamlet was a creature of fashion, it must have been far in the past," I do not believe that this was necessarily or even probably so.

In order to prove that Hamlet, prior to his father's death, was "a disciple of naturalness and simplicity," Goddard refers to his having

[15] Goddard's surmise is highly sophisticated, as well as appealing for its originality. But Shakespeare generally brings falsifications of any consequence to the spectator's attention in a more definite way, as in *Othello* or *Lear*. Polonius is not a paragon of truth, as many a critic has perceived, but this is usually a matter of relatively inconsequential falsifications, fabricated for the sake of one or another petty narcissistic advantage. In this connection, Goddard makes much out of the Reynaldo scene, in which Polonius does not hesitate to teach the use of falsehoods. Yet this rather mild deviation from strict truth-telling has nothing to do with hostility or any form of evil intent, since Polonius's intrigue is designed solely on behalf of his concern for Laertes, whom he wishes to protect under all circumstances against the possible consequences of that mischievous behavior that is appropriate to youthful years. Polonius is not a Machiavellian type, despite his plan to use his daughter as a decoy. A plan of that sort does not go beyond the permissible bounds of court intrigue, nor does it grow out of a primarily evil or destructive impulse. Further, seeking to move Claudius by way of the outright falsification of a letter would constitute disloyalty by Polonius to his sovereign, and there is no element one can find in his character on which to base such assumption.

selected Horatio and "not some rich and influential court favorite" as his friend from early years on.[16] If clinical experience—which, after all, is the observation of live conflict—may be used as a measure in literary criticism, I would say that it is often the *difference* of personalities that creates friendships. Hamlet may have loved Horatio precisely because the latter possessed in large measure what he himself was sorely lacking. His early friendship with Horatio appears to me to be a sign of latent uneasiness about his own personality. He apparently accepted his being "the glass of fashion," as Ophelia calls him,[17] but regarded Horatio as an ideal that it was not given to him to fulfill. To be sure, he had other friends besides Horatio, but Horatio was the one friend, dear to his heart, through whom he could enjoy a world from which he was excluded by birth, personal ambition and accepted societal ideals.

There is one feature that could be used to complement my proposition, except that one hesitates to use it because the objection of overpsychologizing may seem to be admissible in this instance; and besides, the feature in question is not fully established. I refer to the one word in Hamlet's love letter that does not fully fit it as a document of fashion, and has therefore puzzled the critics. He addresses Ophelia in his allocution as "the most beautified," which sounds "vile" alongside "celestial" and "my soul's idol." Some editors have emended the obnoxious word to read "beatified," others have tried to equate it with beautiful (*Variorum Edition*, Vol. I, p. 138).[18]

Now let us assume that "beautified" is true to the original. Whatever meanings the word may have had in Shakespeare's time, they included the vile association. Can it be that, by the use of this one word, which appears quite unexpectedly in a letter by the expected "mould of form," a hint is given that the man who was the glass of fashion was not fulfilling his function completely, because he had to fight down an inner objection, which rose to the surface in this use of an ill-chosen word? I do not want to go so far as to call it an apraxia, but surely it is at least an infelicitous choice—yet a choice that is accessible to interpretation, particularly since later in the play the custom on the part of women to beau-

---

[16] However, he had also maintained friendships with Rosencrantz and Guildenstern, as was proper for "the mould of form."

[17] I shall later return to Ophelia's characterization of Hamlet, since it adds so much credibility to a theory of character transformation in Hamlet.

[18] Some have also tried to exonerate Hamlet's use of the term by referring to the other occasion on which Shakespeare uses it, in the *Two Gentlemen of Verona*. But a study of that passage makes the matter, if anything, even worse (Cf. Goddard, 1955, p. 411, fn. 4).

tify themselves provides Hamlet with so much occasion for scorn. It is as if in this love letter, which for the most part followed the fashionable form, at least one element serves as a signal that Hamlet's acceptance of the fashion of his day was not quite conflict-free, even before the revelations about his mother opened his eyes to the true way of this world.[19]

Yet if Hamlet entertained a relationship to Ophelia that was patterned by fashion, is Madariaga not right when he reproaches Hamlet for his incapacity for true love? It should not be forgotten that it is Hamlet as he may have been prior to the trauma who is under discussion here. Madariaga uses the love letter to prove that Hamlet was simply incapable of love, and nothing more. He goes one step further than Goddard, however, in saying that the letter "might do for Osric; but from Hamlet's pen it can only mean *fun*" (Madariaga, 1948, p. 39). Here I would object. If Hamlet had written such a letter during that phase in which one actually becomes acquainted with him—that is, after his father's death—then I might feel inclined to agree with Madariaga. But Madariaga himself proves that the love letter was written at a time when no cloud yet hung over Hamlet's relationship with Ophelia—which makes it all the more necessary to evaluate it in terms of what Hamlet was like before the trauma.

At that time he was still trying to live and act in conformity with the ideal standards of his society and his times. Whether such ideals of self are sought intentionally or are taken for granted and followed automatically, they necessarily muffle the intensity and differentiation of object relations. This is seen very definitely in the love letter; nevertheless, in that context it does not mean fun but rather the curtailment of the capacity to express personal feelings, in the name of adherence to the patterns given by society. What the true state of an object relationship is cannot be determined accurately, as long as the subject successfully reflects the ideals of contemporary society. At the moment of clash with that very society, however, and in the light of the ensuing insights, which burst asunder the frame of reference that had until then been maintained as valid, the true level of object relations becomes visible, at least in some areas.[20]

[19] This may also be true of the choice of the word "machine" toward the end. Since that word was used only rarely in Shakespeare's times (Goddard, 1955, p. 404), its presence in the letter could be regarded as an instance of individual choice, unless what it is intended to convey is affectation.

[20] The friendship between Hamlet and Horatio, for example, is not only not disturbed by the trauma, but gains in depth as a consequence of it. On the other hand, Hamlet's earlier friendship with Rosencrantz and Guildenstern is not merely shaken by the trauma, but, considering its previous character, was bound to be wrecked.

The interpretation of the closet scene is particularly difficult, since all we have to go on is Ophelia's report. So far as Hamlet is concerned, we are able to see only the consequences: outbreaks of violent rage against the girl. This episode has found, as noted earlier, mutually exclusive interpretations, which have also been woven into consistent character analyses (Huhner, Madariaga). An interpretation will be here suggested that is in conformity with the clinical findings of psychoanalytic depth psychology.

No single cause is to be looked for with regard to such an event. One has the right to suppose that in Hamlet the sexual drive is at least as strong and untamed as is generally true at that age. Whether or not he actually entertained sexual relations with Ophelia, as some critics have devoted themselves to speculating, is not as decisive a question as it may seem to be. She is the only female whom we know to have aroused Hamlet's carnal appetites, and whether or not their being together has led to physical gratification, her companionship, the presence of the beloved, has had a calming effect. It is Hamlet who, on his own, breaks off the relationship.

There can be little doubt that it is the revelations about his mother that have led to the deflation of his esteem for women. Nevertheless, the significance of that sequence of events should not be overestimated. Deflation of the maternal image may at times lead to taking refuge with an idealized woman. Implicit in this is the assumption that, by being different from the mother, the beloved will reinstitute a harmony that has been lost, and demonstrate all the more effectively how bad the mother really is. As Hamlet admits at the end—and I do not find any valid reason for assuming that he is deliberately falsifying the record—his love had persisted despite the traumata caused by his mother's conduct.

One has to conclude, therefore, that his break with Ophelia and his subsequent ranting against her serve as his defense against a still strong affection. In the absence of such attraction, indeed, of passionate longings for her (at least in his unconscious), he would have not given vent to such a passionate outburst. Had he succeeded in truly breaking the tie between them, cold scorn or indifference would have been the consequence instead.

One has to look for other reasons for interference with his earlier love of Ophelia. It is not too difficult to find at least one such reason. As soon as he is apprised by the Ghost of the events surrounding his father's death, he knows that he will one day carry out the deed of revenge. Much may interfere with and delay his performance of that act, yet one day it will come to pass—because it has to. The question can be only under what psychological conditions it will take place.

Inevitably, a subject of a different order has to be discussed at this point. When Hamlet learns of his father's violent death, this new knowledge not only leads to a new relationship with Claudius, but as a consequence of it the entire world suddenly becomes divided into two quite different camps. This sociohistorical factor has, perhaps, been neglected by such critics as Madariaga, who views Hamlet as basically unscrupulous, and cites his dealings with Rosencrantz and Guildenstern as examples of Hamlet's cruelty and selfishness. He is certain that Rosencrantz and Guildenstern, if they were informed of the historical truth, would have supported Hamlet and left the King's coterie. Nevertheless, Hamlet deliberately ("Not shriving-time allowed" [*V.2.46*]) dispatches them to hell.[21]

If Polonius, Rosencrantz and Guildenstern could ever have been won over to Hamlet's cause, then Madariaga might be right, after all, but I find nothing in the play to warrant such an expectation. These characters were not only meant to be, but were also impressively put on the stage as "stooges" of their society, compelled by their own inner bent to serve on the side of those who are in power. They cannot be thought of in terms of potential rebellion; we must assume that they would not even believe Hamlet's tale, but instead would regard him as demented if he ever let them know about his discourse with the ghost. They would certainly turn against him if the situation ever arose of their having to make a choice.

At least Polonius shows some individuality, in his choice of techniques of plotting and intriguing. He does have some concepts of his own about man and life and conduct, even if the span of the values that he embraces is quite narrow. As a young man, he intimates, he too had his adventures; but we can be certain that they did not go beyond the confines of the wildness a young man was expected to show. Rosencrantz and Guildenstern, on the other hand, are burned-out tools of society, as is quite subtly intimated when the King and Queen interchange identical epithets with either of them and rather strikingly reverse the sequence of

---

[21] "Genius could go no higher to represent the utter human callousness of a brilliant wit, for whom the very detail of not allowing time for confession, a truly terrible cruelty in those days, is reserved for an effect in the story" (Madariaga, p. 18).

names.[22] They are interchangeable, utterly devoid of any individuality;[23] at a lower level, they are what Hamlet had once been at the highest level.

Being placed at the top of the social hierarchy, Hamlet had to embody the sublimest ideals. And he had done this—at a time when the state appeared to him to be organized and administered from top to bottom by the reign of law and justice. Now he knows better: behind the surface of order and honesty rages a concealed battle between good and evil. At this point, evil has triumphed, and the future of the good has been entrusted to his hands alone. The mere possibility that evil may go unchallenged and unpunished is unbearable to Hamlet—even more, it is a nightmare. Now everything that may serve, even if only indirectly, the success and reign of evil becomes an enemy that has to be extirpated.

Madariaga sees Hamlet's cruelty and egoism as the earmarks of the Renaissance prince. Perhaps so, yet it is far more than that. Did not Hamlet earlier acquiesce in his exclusion from immediate succession to the thone? Has there been any word of plotting or of forming a conspiracy? Has there been even a gesture of remonstrance? I do not find Hamlet to be much of a Renaissance prince, prior to the dread command. In the latter, he was given a single and individual mission to perform; and yet it took quite a while before that uncompromising activity evolved for which Madariaga castigates him so severely. Is not Madariaga here overlooking a general feature of historical events? How many were the heads that fell in the service of Christianizing the Occident? Whoever refused baptism was destroyed.

When a new idea takes hold that has the potential for spreading, it is generally brute force that paves the way for it. Even in the gospel of love we read, "I come not to send peace, but a sword. For I am come to set a man at variance against his father." Hamlet, indeed, does not show at the start even a trace of Renaissance unscrupulousness. That can be imputed to him only when the killing of Rosencrantz and Guildenstern is seen out of context and in isolation. Within the context of the play, these

---

[22] Cf. Alexander (1955, p. 33): "Rosencrantz or Guildenstern appearing alone might give the impression that here was an individual with unique characteristics, *whereas Shakespeare wishes us to see that their sycophancy and outlook are common and abundant*" (my italics).

[23] Draper (1939, pp. 17-23) very ingeniously draws individual character pictures of the two courtiers in the sense that Rosencrantz "expresses more Hamlet's own merry youth"; and Guildenstern "the sinister purposes of Claudius." This may be correct and it would be in keeping with Shakespeare's uncanny ability to give character and individuality even to the smallest part. He succeeded, according to Draper, in doing so even with these two who, it seems to me, were meant to represent that part of society that has become reduced to its appendage.

two are no more than unavoidable victims of the supra-individual battles that are fought on the stage of history.

To be sure, the murderous impulse supposedly lurks in Hamlet, just as it does in every human. At the beginning of the play, we notice this impulse, in the form of Hamlet's turning against himself. Imagery of suicide is, after all, intimated twice. Furthermore, upon receiving his mission from the Ghost, Hamlet does not jump at once to the discharge of his aggression, but instead bemoans his fate. Yet once he has become readied for action—and he has gone through several crises before reaching that point—he throws himself into his task with gusto.

One man alone, against the whole of society, indeed the world: a gigantic struggle that calls for the tensing of every nerve. Now he is no longer burdened by the assignment that he has been called upon to fulfill, but instead almost enjoys every inch of it. How else could he be victorious? When he rejects the idea of the courtiers' death being a burden on his conscience *(V.2.58),* that act is not a rationalization; it is, instead, recognition of a new dimension to his acceptance of death in the graveyard scene. Now he accepts violent death, even indirect murder, as a necessary part of the history of the battle of good against evil.

After all, he was ignorant at that point of his impending rescue by way of his accidental encounter with the pirates and had instead to prepare for a dangerous landing.[24] Hence the courtiers had to be eliminated. The speed with which this was done was also dictated by reality aims. The combination of circumstances permitted the assumption on Hamlet's part that Rosencrantz and Guildenstern were cognizant of the content of the King's message—a possibility that Madariaga does not seem to consider at all. Hence once he had been apprised of what was awaiting him, to delay the courtiers' deaths would mean running the risk of the King's true intent being revealed in England.

There still remains, to be sure, the Christian's duty to bemoan the downfall of his enemies. This aspect, to be sure, is totally absent. Yet I notice its absence generally in human history, regardless of the historical stage. Psychologically, the situation is only slightly different from what it is customarily. The courtiers being taken as mere appendages to Claudius, their annihilation is equated with that of Claudius himself, as is in-

---

[24] Even before Hamlet had any proof of the King's plot, he had the intention of doing violence to the two courtiers *(III.4.206f).* He evidently anticipated, as indeed he now had every reason to believe, that their survival would result in his having to stay abroad for an undetermined length of time.

timated by Hamlet's repetition of one element from the imagery about the death of his own father, as well as about that of Claudius: dying without the benefit of the sacrament.

Hamlet's sadistic triumph over the elimination of the two courtiers is a foreshadowing of his joy over his impending undoing of his arch-enemy. His ability to enjoy this victory is actually a sign of the self's liberation through the appersonation of an externally given task. From the psychological point of view, independently of the details of circumstance, everyone who is allied with Claudius has to perish—except, of course, Gertrude and Laertes. And here too, just as in its own sociohistorical context, the formula is valid: "Who is not for me, is against me."

Returning to Hamlet's relationship with Ophelia, it now becomes understandable why he had to enforce a break between them and to act in such a way as to convince her of the fundamental change in his feelings. As soon as he received the dread command, the world's appearance suddenly changed: major aspects of accepted society were now destined to be destroyed by him. At that point, Hamlet must have anticipated a fight, not only at sword's point with Claudius, but also with Polonius. What is so eminently clear about Rosencrantz and Guildenstern is also true with regard to Polonius, the King's councillor and the principal agent of his being in power.

The near identity of Claudius-Polonius is forcefully stressed from the beginning:

> The head is not more native to the heart,
> The hand more instrumental to the mouth,
> Than is the throne of Denmark to [Polonius].

(I.2.47-49)

One does not by any means have to think of Renaissance princes and popes, of Renaissance violence in the pursuit of political goals, to understand that, where there is such closeness, the heart will fall with the head, the mouth with the hand. At all times, a servant who is that close to the throne will suffer injury when the throne topples; at all times, servants who allow themselves to be identified that closely with the throne and who derive benefits therefrom are themselves held responsible for excesses by the crown. *Mutatis mutandis*, this holds true in our own times as well. Thus for Hamlet, Polonius was as much an adversary as was Claudius and, leaving aside for the moment all psychological implications, the political structure of the State of Denmark alone warranted

Hamlet's contempt and hatred of the "most important person in the state of Denmark after the royal family" (Wilson in the Cambridge *Hamlet,* p. 141).

When Claudius, in his speech from the throne, compares himself and Polonius with related organs of the same body, he emphasizes their political identity so strongly that any further reference to this group of motives in Hamlet for acting against Polonius became thereafter superfluous. During the course of time, *Hamlet* has become a purely psychological tragedy for us, to such an extent that the outward forms in which the personal, subjective involvements are dressed have tended to become, in part, lost sight of.

As I have repeatedly stressed, the grandeur of the play lies to a great extent in the *dual structure of motivations* that is encountered throughout. Motivations that are derived from valid and reasonable reality aims are paralleled by motivations whose origins take us to deeply repressed archaic layers. Thus, Polonius is at one and the same time the aging father whose mental decline has made him incompetent to hold a power for which the son is now far better equipped, the jealous father who wants to keep his beloved daughter to himself and therefore intervenes in her wooing by a lover, and finally the dishonorable chancellor who has helped, albeit unwittingly, an unworthy King to ascend the throne.

If that last aspect of Polonius is lost sight of, the balance is unjustly weighted to the disadvantage of Hamlet, who then becomes little more than a rude and arrogant egotist, abusing his inherited position and unnecessarily humiliating a defenseless, meritorious servant of the state— an interpretation that Madariaga does indeed set forth. If, however, the political motivation is given its due and Hamlet's anticipation of deadly conflict with Polonius is acknowledged, his break with Ophelia must be seen as inevitable.[25]

Some critics have raised the question of why Hamlet does not confide in Ophelia, and a number of reasons have been suggested, based on Hamlet's personality, as well as that of Ophelia. What seems to have

[25] Kittredge (1939, p. 178) took the same view: "Hamlet decides that he must renounce Ophelia and give up all thought of marriage and happiness." Grebanier (1960, p. 199) tries to refute Kittredge's interpretation. Naively he asks: "Why need Hamlet have involved Ophelia in his pursuit of revenge? Claudius managed to kill his brother without involving Gertrude." Should Hamlet have secretly poured poison into Claudius' ear? Although Kittredge's interpretation is the one that convinces me, I still think that the episode is drawn with sufficient latitude to permit the more widely held view of Hamlet's appearing in Ophelia's closet as the distraught lover. Here is one of the many examples of Shakespeare's ability to enable the spectator to make interpretations that are in accordance with his own emotional bent.

been forgotten was the fact that Ophelia was, after all, Polonius's daughter. If Hamlet had told Ophelia of his father's murder by Claudius, he would have precipitated in her the very conflict that caused her undoing in the end, even though he was trying to spare her that conflict. She would then have had to decide between loyalty to her lover and to her father. The former required a secrecy that was incompatible with filial obedience, the way it is depicted in *Hamlet* between father and daughter; that latter would have involved an act of betrayal that would lead to Hamlet's exposure and to the dangers that would follow. Once she was apprised of the suspicion that her father was serving a murderous and usurping King—and particularly when it was from Hamlet that she learned this—it would then become her duty to call that fact to the attention of her father, who would then, in turn, become duty bound to warn the seemingly lawful King.

If we now try to reconstruct Hamlet's reasoning, it must lead to the following results: "The elimination of Claudius, which I am now at the point of being able to bring about, must lead also to the ruin of the Chief Counsellor, who stands and falls with the King. Only by discontinuing the love relationship can I spare Ophelia the ensuing conflict that would expose her to unending pain and anguish, since it is a kind of conflict that cannot be solved by a daughter, without doing violence to her relationship with one or another beloved person." Thus, one of the meanings that can be read into Hamlet's break with Ophelia is his care for her and his concern about her future welfare, which lead him to the greatest sacrifice he could make in her service. [26] The conflict of a woman who is in love with the murderer of someone beloved by her was not new to Shakespeare. But the times of "wild psychology" and Richard III had gone; the ridiculousness to which the great Corneille exposed his Chimene had no place in Shakespeare's world in general, and certainly not in *Hamlet* in particular, in which the fathomlessness of human tragedy was to find its lasting and most telling record.

---

[26] Wilson (1936a, pp. 106-108) suggested that Hamlet is aware of Polonius's spying in his stormy confrontation with Ophelia and most critics have followed him, since some lines sound as if they may be addressed to the eavesdropper. Yet they may be understood quite differently, and as referring to a far more profound issue. When he suddenly turns from "Go thy ways to a nunnery" (*III. 1. 130*) to "Where's your father?" and warns her that he should stay at home—an advice that, after all, is very similar to the one that he has just given to her—he would, according to my interpretation, be insinuating that his change from love to rejection has something to do with Ophelia's father. These lines sound to my ears like a camouflaged plea that both she and her father should speedily withdraw from the affairs of this world so that the upheaval that he anticipated as inevitable, yet could not disclose to her, would not include her destruction nor that of any person she loved.

And thus the great epic of woman's tragedy was given shape: the lover, on his side, determined to spare his beloved the worst; the woman, on her side, determined to fulfill her duty. Yet, despite so much concern on both sides, Ophelia is doomed to perish—not by force of circumstances, as was to be true of Rosencrantz and Guildenstern, but solely as the result of an unbearable conflict of inner forces. Once her beloved father has been killed by the man she loves, there is no place left for her in this world.

If one accepts this reasoning, it is possible thereby to understand how it is that, when Hamlet hears about Ophelia's suicide, his conscience remains clear. He really has loved her more than Laertes ever did; he has sacrificed for her more than Laertes would ever have been capable of. He has gone to extremes in order to make life bearable for her, being concerned not so much with the possible consequences of her father's death per se, but rather with the expected impact of that particular set of circumstances under which her father might otherwise die—that is to say, at the hands of her lover. By empathy we are able to understand her psychotic disintegration when her father's violent death is, in fact, brought about by the man whom she still loves, despite his having rejected her publicly and in the most humiliating manner.

The fact that Hamlet went to the extremes he did go to, in trying to break Ophelia's attachment to him, cannot be held against him if we view it in this way. His advice to her that she henceforth renounce her present social habitat, and either withdraw from the secular world altogether or else abandon herself to her passions, in abnegation of any superego demand—such advice now makes good sense and delineates the only possible ways in which she would be able to guarantee her survival.

The fact that neither of these alternatives would have brought any benefit to him, but would instead have guaranteed his losing her, frees him from the charge of selfishness. He might have used other excuses if all he wanted was to free himself from her attachment to him. He might, for example, have pretended love of another woman, or he could have spoken to her of the hopelessness of their relationship. But this would have hurt her even more and very likely without destroying her attachment to him. This is apart from the fact that Hamlet was able to tear himself away from her only when he had first worked himself into a state of frenzy.

For the magnitude of Hamlet's sacrifice should not be underestimated; if, as some believe, there had previously been intercourse between them, his sacrifice would have been all the greater. In any event, Ophelia stands—either realistically or symbolically; which of the two makes no difference—for sexual gratification; separating from her therefore has, within the context of the play, the meaning of a permanent renunciation of genital satisfaction, a decision that has to be measured against what we now feel to be a characteristic Elizabethan impassionedness.

In this light, the procedure that promised most was for Hamlet to pretend insanity, as well as a seemingly spontaneous disgust with women and a baseless contempt for them. If the difficulties one encounters in attempting to explain Hamlet's dealings with Ophelia were really resolved by the argument I have so far adduced, *Hamlet* might be a play still to admire but it certainly would not move us as deeply as it does. This reconstruction of motives can hold only secondary place, just as the secondary gain does in the etiology of neuroses. Behind such well calibrated aims and purposes on Hamlet's part, there lurk the wildest among those conflicts that have raged between the sexes since Adam's times, when the female first made herself hateful to man by talking him into tasting the forbidden fruit. In *Hamlet* too the fear becomes visible that the enjoyment of women may make the world too pleasant a place within which to attempt to carry out those harsh but necessary duties whose fulfilment might well put an end to all such pleasures.

The enjoyment of this woman in particular may have the effect of weakening firmness of intent, since she is, after all, the daughter of the usurping King's principal mainstay. Nevertheless, it is clear that women in general distract, perturb, and weaken him. In the *Ur-Hamlet* (II.4), castration fear is expressed with an almost crude directness, when Hamlet tells Ophelia the story of the chevalier of "Anion" and his love for a woman who was, to look at, as beautiful as Venus. But then in the bridal chamber she took out first one of her eyes and then her front teeth, after which she washed off her make-up. Upon seeing her thus, the bridegroom was startled and took her for a specter: "That's how you deceive bachelors!" *(Also betrügt ihr die Junggesellen.)*

In Hamlet's violent outbreak against Ophelia, the dual character of his madness comes out most clearly. On the one hand, it is feigned in the name of valid and reality-adequate purposes; on the other hand, it expresses the most deeply repressed archaic contents. It is the result at one and the same time of the self's mastery of reality goals and of its being overpowered by the deepest archaic fears. Like every male, Hamlet has his castration fears, his feeling of superiority toward women, his distrust of the organ that was created for his pleasure yet is so much unlike his own. Still, none of Hamlet's fury would have been unleashed against the beloved woman, had the door to it not been opened by realistic necessities, such as his plan and purpose, which were dictated and approved by that part of the self that cunningly strives for the fulfilment of its ambitions and duties. Despite the possibility that the words he spoke to her were contrived, the emotions they reflected were true; for Hamlet, it seems to me, could malinger with the tongue alone, but not with the heart.

Discussion of another possible motive for Hamlet's break with Ophelia requires, to begin with, a more general consideration. It makes no sense to try to measure Shakespeare's female characters in terms of conceptions that are characteristic of the imagery encountered in modern society, where a diluted Christian belief, "cut to order," is the officially accepted standard. If one thinks of Ophelia in terms of emancipation, of a woman's right and duty to build up her own career, style of life and what not, one should rather turn to other types of literature than Elizabethan drama. However, in analytic practice one observes the extent to which the modern conceptualization of womanhood remains only something of an encrustation upon imagery that probably goes far back in the history of mankind, if not indeed as far back as its very beginning, and apparently still continues to exist in modern man's mind, even though subterraneously.

This imagery about the female sex takes two tacks, one of which is represented in *Hamlet* by the Queen, the other by Ophelia; the castrating, aggressive and the castrated, passive. The former is shrewd, energetic, and level-headed; strong, active, and well equipped both to manipulate reality and to take care of the objects of her interest. The latter is weak and passive; incapable of self-assertion or of the pursuit of her personal goals; submissive, accepting of her inferiority, and finding self-fulfilment in obedience. At least, these are the traits she accepts as valid or tries to give surface expression to; deviations from them she would probably treat publicly as unvirtuous and unbecoming. Just as Hamlet had earlier reflected the societal ideal of manhood, to the disadvantage of his own individuality, similarly Ophelia had to sacrifice her individuality to the societal ideal of womanhood. Indeed, she continued to fulfill this role right up to the moment of her mental disintegration, as if the poet was trying to say to us that in those days a virtuous woman could express her individuality only when she was psychotic—at least up to the time when she gave birth to a child.[27]

One result is that we see Ophelia agreeing with her brother, with her father, and with the King. She expresses a willingness to do whatever they tell her to do. Even under the impact of Hamlet's attacks, her defense is meek and reduced to the minimum. Therefore, I believe it is a misjudgment or at least a judgment that is out of kilter, for critics to castigate Ophelia for promising her father without any remonstrance not "to give words or talk with the Lord Hamlet" *(I.3.134)*. For her ideal of womanhood permits her to say only: "I do not know, my lord, what I should think" *(I.3.104)* and "I shall obey, my lord" *(I.3.136)*. With infinite subtlety and finesse, Shakespeare intimates that, behind these "I do not know" and "I shall obey" attitudes, processes of an entirely different nature were taking place, which we will learn about only later, when the psychosis has removed any shadow of self-restraint.

Nowadays, the response that Ophelia offers in her exchange with her father would be taken, of course, to be a sign of gross psychopathology, but to expect Ophelia to behave in any other way shows, to my mind, profound misunderstanding of her position. It was very likely because of these attitudes that Hamlet fell in love with her when he did. The way she is portrayed she is, of course, wax in her elders' hands: whether or not she wants to, she has to play to perfection the role of a decoy. To regard her doing this as evidence of maliciousness on her part or of lack of character would be wrong, even though the raw data for such an interpretation would seem to be present.

Moreover, since the prince has been behaving strangely and those in authority assign to her the role of decoy under the pretense of its serving Hamlet's welfare, why then should she not obey? I doubt that Hamlet resents her surrender to Polonius and the King if he has noticed it at all, as Wilson and others seem to be certain. After all, he knows the way women behave and he must know therefore that he loved her, and still loves her, for that very sweetness and charm with which she fulfils what is expected of her—which, of course, includes obedience to her father in matters of her relationship to Hamlet himself.

Yet it is here that I find the very point that arouses conflict in Hamlet. Ophelia is permitted to do precisely what he is no longer capable of

---

[27] This is not the place to enter into a discussion of the very tempting subject of Shakespeare's psychology of women. Yet this much at least may be stated: that, corresponding to reality, in general mothers are endowed in his tragedies with a different psychology from that of childless women.

doing without conflict. She is not only permitted to act as she does, but in so doing even finds consummation of her superego demands. She demonstrates almost to excess a mode of living in which Hamlet has until recently himself indulged, and which he is at this moment forced to give up. He has not yet succeeded in freeing himself from his reliance on those past techniques that have until now stood him in such good stead, and he is still stalking along the new road somewhat insecurely, when it comes to his full awareness that for a woman such behavior is well-nigh taken for granted.

One might even imagine that it is Hamlet's profound envy of the pleasure that Ophelia is enjoying by her passive surrender that triggers off Hamlet's raging against her. In the "Hecuba" monologue Hamlet actually raises this accusation against himself, and in perhaps the vilest form that the passive urge can take in male life. An interpretation, however, that makes Hamlet disappointed in Ophelia for letting herself be abused to the extent of being made into a decoy is not thereby rendered invalid. The data are on hand that are needed to rationalize Hamlet's furious behavior.

Yet the fact is that Shakespeare changed sequences. Previously, this episode took place much earlier, but Shakespeare placed it in quick sequence to the "Hecuba" monologue. The self-accusation of acting like a sexually perverted passive male is thus followed by a declaration that male and female are forever divorced, and cannot harmonize, because woman believes in values that are unacceptable to men, and so forth—all of which is done with stress on the disgust that female sexual behavior arouses in him.

That arousal of this sort testifies to the speaker's envy and to the desire to be able to act in the very same way is well proven by clinical observation, the disgust being a potent force for the warding off of such desires. This last motive can be summarized as follows: "I despise Ophelia because she surrenders passively and I must protect myself against the wish to act the same way."

Thus, as was to be expected, a plurality of motives is discovered, each of them valid in its own way. They endow every step in the play's action with unmatched intensity, and strike the spectator, not as an imitation of life, but rather as a recreation of life, in that each single event in a life process is generally under pressure from innumerable forces.

But we have moved away from our primary reason for interest in Hamlet's madness. It is more complex than that of Ophelia, which is at the same time both one-dimensional and irreparable. Reality in her case has become intolerable; her father's murder by her lover has torn a rent in the fabric of her relationship to the world. It is probable that she also suspects herself of bearing a share in the guilt. Had not Hamlet in his "madness" advised her regarding Polonius:

> Let the doors be shut upon him, that he may play the fool nowhere but in's own house.
> *(III.1.133f)*

Thus he had given her a warning that had gone unheeded. And how can she be certain that Hamlet did not kill her father precisely because he was in love with her and held her father responsible for the behavior for which he had castigated her so severely?

The obscene portion of her symbolic talk when she has become psychotic has been variously interpreted; Madariaga (1948), for example, concludes that there had been previous unchaste behavior on Ophelia's part. Yet early in the Hamlet discussion an astute mind had already observed that, in such mental derangement, unfulfilled wishes may be referred to as though they were actions of the past. When Huhner (1950) finds evidence of a confession by Ophelia of pregnancy, he may be right; yet it is equally possible that she is laboring under the delusion of being pregnant since, despite her most chaste behavior, we can be certain that she passionately wished to become one day the mother of Hamlet's child. The more the grosser appetites have been repressed, the more lewdly will they appear on the surface, after the self has lost control and has been thrown into a state of psychotic regression. Once again the poet has left it altogether unclear whether the girl is laboring under the recollection of action or under the weight of unfulfilled wishes.

Hamlet's madness is quite differently structured. Neither he, the others on the stage, nor the spectator can say for certain whether he is mad in the clinical sense or pretending madness, or is merely temporarily thrown off balance by the impact of actual or impending emotional stresses. The only thing that is beyond doubt is that, whatever the etiology, the meaning or the extent of the damage, the self has not been irreparably injured, for by the time Hamlet dies he is once again free of any mental encumbrance. Yet the multiplicity of possible interpretations is clearly visible in every episode that has been noted as evidence of Hamlet's madness.

I cannot lay too much stress on my belief that this is not at all a sign of artistic weakness, that it cannot be characterized simply as "vagueness," for the character in question is put onto the stage with incomparable realism and concreteness. Life is here recreated in one of its fundamental aspects, in that the most that can be said with regard to another mind amounts to little more than a question that the observer then answers in accordance with his own personal bent and prejudice. In Ophelia's case—at least we can agree upon the fact that her mind has finally been deranged—what we have is a striking exception to the ambiguity that is so significant of the way in which the other major characters are presented.

The Madness Proper.

The earliest lines in which critics have been prone to discover evidence of Hamlet's madness are those that Horatio describes as "wild and whirling" *(I.5.133)*. These are spoken by Hamlet some 40-odd lines before he announces that he may put on "an antic disposition" *(I.5.172)*. Since Horatio, a kind of Greek chorus, is meant to be in full possession of clear judgment, some degree of trust must be placed in his description, even though these particular words of Hamlet's may not sound especially wild and whirling to all contemporary spectators. It is true, of course, that they take on that form somewhat later, when he is dealing with the ghost's persistent commands from below; yet at that point his words do not seem to strike Horatio and Marcellus as evidence of unsoundness of mind.

It may be that what Horatio notices is Hamlet's state of excitement as a consequence of the encounter, or that what he has in mind is the discrepancy between what Hamlet should have been expected to say following such a pregnant event and what he actually does say. Ostensibly, at least, his communication is in terms of commonplace sayings. If these were uttered with great intensity, then Horatio's comment "wild and whirling" would make sense. Yet "wild and whirling" does refer to unbalance, and it is not inconsequential that the first reference to "an antic disposition" is made by Horatio, who, in the *Ur-Hamlet*, actually plays a far more active role in the initiation of Hamlet's madness. There he is told of the murder immediately after Francisco's dismissal *(First act, Scene 6)* and subsequently pleads with Hamlet not to kill Claudius.[28]

---

[28] In the *Ur-Hamlet* Hamlet asks Horatio to provide him with an "honest" funeral if he is found dead, since Claudius is surrounded by guards and the attempt on his life, which Hamlet will dare on the first occasion that he finds, may misfire. It is then that Horatio says: "I beg, your excellency, you do not want to do such, perhaps the ghost has cheated you." Hamlet rejects that possibility; yet immediately thereafter, in the next scene, when he is apprised of the actors' arrival, he says that he

This encounter of Hamlet with his friends following the revelation by the Ghost may have the value of a paradigm. Even when he is in contact with people who are well-disposed toward him and in whose presence no need to feign exists, there seems to be a discordant note at times, insofar as his mind is already filled with an intensely cathected content, not even the faintest inkling of which may be shared with anyone. That Horatio is later made his confidant does not count for much in this regard, since psychologically Horatio is really a part of Hamlet, the external embodiment of his superego. That is why an observant-critical function, such as reference to the intemperateness of Hamlet's speech, is appropriately assigned to him. Yet if even in the company of friends, Hamlet's behavior arouses suspicion, how will it be when he is at Court, exposed to public view among persons who will be watching him with a critical eye, all the while that he is incessantly preoccupied with an imagery that must remain concealed, and is preparing, to boot, to perform a deed whose aim must not in the least be suspected by others?

Here are two potent psychological factors that go into determining Hamlet's choice of an antic disposition. That the first insinuation of unbalance in Hamlet is introduced by Horatio at a well-justified point should remove any doubt about the artistic legitimacy of Hamlet's antic disposition, and silence those who guess at extraneous reasons for its presence in the play.

Further, madness has long been believed to be a sort of guarantee against an adversary's evil intentions. The early Brutus was said to have feigned dullness, without any rationalized reference to guards and suchlike trappings, but merely on the grounds that it would provide protection against suspicions on the part of an evil tyrant. A madman is not, after all, to be feared as one fears a cunning enemy. That a man who has not recoiled from poisoning his own brother does not deserve trust and belief when he goes through the motions of advancing the future claim to the throne of that brother's son, and officially declaring him heir to the crown—all that goes almost without saying. The cloak of madness, then, may permit the name of the stricken son to be removed from the list of those who are to be killed next.

Yet at no point is it intimated that Claudius' murderous impulses went beyond fratricide, prior to the mouse-trap play. His character is

---

will test the Ghost's veracity by having a tragedy of fratricide performed before the Court (*Act 2, Scenes 5 and 6*).

unmistakably drawn quite differently from that of Richard III. To him the Queen is not just one step on the ladder to power, which he would kick aside after it had served his aims of aggrandizement. He is affectionately tied to her, it seems, and it is left undecided whether his love of her and his lust for power match each other in strength, or if either of them actually outbalances the other. When I discussed earlier a possible necessity for Hamlet's seeking protection against further acts of villainy on the part of Claudius, I was thinking rather of implications and ideas that may have come to Hamlet's mind, even though neither of these is spelled out in the play.[29]

When proof is forthcoming, however, that Claudius has indeed aimed at Hamlet's life, this is not acknowledged by the prince (nor by Horatio and probably not by the audience either) to be a direct consequence of his having let the King know that he possessed the secret of his crime; instead, it is regarded as new evidence of the King's villainy. On strictly logical grounds, it should have been a foregone conclusion that Claudius would be forced, after the mouse-trap, to plot against Hamlet's life, since the fact that Hamlet would turn to murderous revenge, was, in turn, a foregone conclusion, in accordance with the mores of the times.

Similarly, neither Hamlet nor the audience accepts the Queen's death as an unintended side effect, a kind of apraxia on Claudius's part; rather, each holds the King fully responsible for its coming to pass, almost as if he had actually planned it that way.[30] All this may appear in retrospect as if it had been "in the cards" from the beginning, and may thus lend rational justification retroactively to Hamlet's antic disposi-

[29] When a theory that purports to explain Hamlet's behavior is put forward, the question necessarily arises as to why Hamlet never verbalizes the motives assigned to him by the literary critic. Among the answers given, two are frequently found—namely, either that the motive is implied by the situation, or else that it was taken for granted by Shakespeare's audience and therefore did not need explicit verbalization. A certain partiality regarding such assumptions on the part of the critic is almost unavoidable.

When I suggest that Hamlet implicitly had to fear that he might be next on the tyrant's list—as Brutus, who also feigned madness, had to fear—this motive may be rejected since no reference to it is found in the text. It is here not a question of an unconscious motive, but of one that is admissible to consciousness, as the prelude to a man's planning to preserve his life. The acceptance or rejection of this motive is not consequential, since it is, after all, of a secondary nature.

It may be asked, however, why Hamlet does not show any concern regarding his mother's safety. I think it is permissible to raise that question. His aim is directed toward driving a wedge between his mother and Claudius and making her stop loving him—either of which, in view of Hamlet's impression of Claudius' evil character, he ought to regard as a serious danger to her life, once he has received the Ghost's account.

[30] Oddly enough, Hamlet is held by many critics to be responsible for the number of corpses that accumulate at the end of the play.

Thus, there are those who think he should have used the shortest possible way of killing Clau-

tion. As a secondary motive it may be added here that, having fathomed the magnitude of the task on hand, he needed the antic disposition also to make the necessary break with Ophelia understandable to his environment. How could he, "the mold of form," ever resort to such an unchivalric act as abandoning a woman for whom he had repeatedly confessed his love, unless he gave himself the appearance of a man whose mind is deranged?

Nevertheless, there are other episodes that present Hamlet in a strange light—for example, his gross dialogue with Ophelia immediately before the mouse-trap—a discourse that has shocked more than one critic.[31] It should be remembered, however, that this very combination of grossness with passages of the tenderest lyricism, delicacy and profundity is to be found, as Coleridge had already noticed, in many a masterwork.

A notable example is Goethe's *Faust,* in which, toward the end of part II, between the terribly shaking scene of Faust's death and the sublime finale of the apotheosis, with its many mysteries, there is a short episode in which Mephisto is diverted from taking possession of Faust's body and soul, by becoming infatuated with the behind of an attractive angel. This coarseness has also shocked those critics who are inclined to forget that literary greatness is often achieved by such a synthesis of the sublime and the coarsely gross (cf. Reik, 1952, p. 110).

What is it really that Hamlet attempts to impress upon Ophelia? He is evidently in an unusually aggressive mood, the consequence of his impatience to find out the results of the test he has devised to trap Claudius. His attention is drawn toward Ophelia when the Queen invites him to sit near her, which he refuses, saying that Ophelia is "metal more at-

---

dius. To this way of thinking, apparently, the Queen, Ophelia and Laertes, and possibly also Polonius, would then have survived, and Hamlet is, therefore, held responsible for their premature deaths. On the other hand, there are those critics who castigate Hamlet for having killed Claudius at all, because of the moral offensiveness of the deed as such. No doubt, whatever strategy he had followed, he would have had to suffer the vituperation of some critics.

Evidently, no one has succeeded as yet in finding the answer to what Hamlet's proper action should have been or, in other words, what kind of action or sequence of actions would have spared him posthumous condemnation by certain moralizers among the Western intellectual elite. It may be that Shakespeare was fascinated by the Hamlet-problem because he knew that his particular conflict was unsolvable by the moral teachings that Western culture customarily puts at the disposal of its participants. It seems, apparently, to be difficult for some critics to acknowledge the fact that Western civilization has taken on a degree of differentiation such as creates irreconcilable contradictions among its various parts, and that this, in turn, forces the individual member to grope, by trial and error, for his own pathway, since institutional solutions are, aside from their inherent contradictoriness, too remote from human reality and practicality to be able to serve as guidelines for realizable conduct.

[31] In order to grasp the full vulgarity of this dialogue, the reader is referred to Partridge (1948) and Pyles (1949).

tractive."￼This reference to his mother within the context of feminine attractiveness—the mere fact of his saying that another woman is more "attractive" than his mother—signals an acute libidinal meaning that he attaches to the mother, indicating either that the earlier directly libidinal tie was never sufficiently repressed, or that the repression has been temporarily weakened by an acute stress.[32]

It is with this that an episode is introduced whose like one will hardly find anywhere, for intensity. Hamlet turns toward Ophelia with truculent fierceness; his technique of punning and denying evokes the imagery of crude physical processes. He interrupts the mouse-trap play three times with thrusts of an openly sexual meaning. The first is a direct request for intercourse, "Shall I lie in your lap?" which is then immediately denied by his averring that he would never talk like a country bum, only to be reaffirmed by his reference to the "fairness" of the thought of lying between maid's legs. No more devilish term could have been chosen for this statement than "fair," with its—at least, at present—multiplicity of meanings: unbiased, proper, moderately good, promising, bright, or free from blemish.

When Ophelia counter-thrusts with her "You are merry," he reminds her of the cause of his grief and sarcasm: his mother's cheerfulness —a reference that establishes the connecting link with the beginning pantomime. Once that is done, the next thrust occurs, with its impudent play on the word "show" and its exhibitionistic imagery appealing to undress. The third and last thrust occurs shortly before the final explosion of confession of murderous intent by Lucianus-Hamlet.

It is Ophelia who challenges this by calling Hamlet, ironically, a good chorus. The meaning of his reply, "I could interpret between you and your love, if I could see the puppets dallying," still remains, I think, unclear. One possibility is that he is applying the chorus' interpretive function to Ophelia's life and intimating his preference for seeing her making love to her swain. (A reference to the primal scene at this point would make good sense from the psychoanalytic point of view.) The puppet imagery[33] may refer to Ophelia's lack of self-determination, the self-constraint she shows in filling the role that circumstances have im-

[32] In this comparison of the mother with Ophelia, even though it is ostensibly to the mother's disfavor, the matrix is made visible of the later outbreak, which culminates in the Nero simile.

[33] I have found only in Grebanier (1960, p. 403) a confirmation of my guess that puppets here stand for breasts. This would make it clear that Hamlet is going through the process of undressing Ophelia.

posed on her, but it may also anticipate his subsequent reference to genitals (when Hamlet lets Ophelia know about his erection), as well as his remark about her virginity, which she would have to sacrifice in order to relieve him of it. This remark is ambiguous in that it may mean either "it would cost you *(only)* a groaning" or "It would cost *you* a groaning."[34]

One may approach this substructure of the play in quite different ways. Earlier I suggested that the play within a play stands for a dream within a dream. Now I will try to extend the suggestion also to the sexual dialogue that interrupts the subplay.

On the assumption that theater affected the Elizabethan audience quite differently from the way in which stage performances affected the audience in subsequent periods, one may imagine that, by the time the mouse-trap play began, the spectator was in a sort of hypnotic trance. A pretty long course of pregnant action, without interruptions or intervals of repose such as later became customary, must have deprived the audience of all self-awareness. And then came this scene, a scene of unusual complexity and challenge to the spectator's imagination and empathy, providing an intensity of stimulation that, in effect, hardly permitted critical deliberation.

There is an audience within the audience and a play within the play; there is the supra-ordinated, inclusive plot on the part of the principal actor: a King has criminally arrogated power to himself, and it has to be taken away from him, and the subordinate part-plot of the mouse-trap play, with its subdivision into pantomime and dialogue. There is the implied connection between the main play and the subplay, a connection that has entirely different meanings to the Queen, the King, Hamlet, and the neutral portion of the court audience on the stage. And, in between, there is the sexual contest between Hamlet and Ophelia, with its direct description of intercourse, not in symbolic terms but quite realistically, and thus a possible source of sensual appeal to an audience that by this time must have arrived at a state of considerable tension.

The whole thing is a *tour de force* of incredible daring on the playwright's part. Merely to keep the whole thing together is an accomplishment in itself; no more than a slight decrease of organizing power, even if only momentary, would permit it to fall apart. Each of the protagonists has to be brought in from time to time, in order to keep alive and interrelated the multifarious strands. At first sight, therefore, it is incomprehen-

---

[34] The statement in either form speaks very strongly against the assumption of previous intercourse between the two.

sible why Shakespeare should have added to all of this Hamlet's harassment of Ophelia, which would seem to be utterly extraneous to the main function of the sub-play.

Is it possible that, in view of such a superabundance of demands on the audience's empathic capabilities, this whole substructure was experienced unidimensionally, as in a dream? I must add that Hamlet says *expressis verbis*, at the very beginning, that he will play the fool ("I must be idle," *[III.2.91]*);[35] anyone who remembers that may not feel certain subsequently about what is feigned and what is genuine in Hamlet's words during the rest of this scene—which might easily have added to an uncritical attitude such as is characteristic of a dreamlike experience.

Furthermore, there is a variety of media: the ordinary language of the royal court, which pervades the whole play; the purely visual medium of the pantomime; the somewhat archaic language of the mouse-trap play proper, with its mixture of stiltedness and concreteness; Hamlet's crude, realistic grossness of language. And all these media are by no means kept separate; instead they are intertwined in an apparently helter-skelter fashion. If under such stresses, the subtle relief of the superstructure is flattened out and the episode is experienced unidimensionally, as most dreams are, then, of course, the critic is not justified in drawing any conclusions from the scene with regard to either Hamlet's or Ophelia's character.

Earlier I suggested an interpretation of the play-within-the-play that omitted the Hamlet-Ophelia exchange. If this is included in the dream, however, one would have to add to its interpretation as the revelation of the true oedipal content, the aspect of a nocturnal emission in the making, or of a fight against it. The sequence of Hamlet's thrusts against Ophelia starts with a request for intercourse, shifts to undressing her and ends with deflowering her. All this leads to the explicit verbalization of a patricidal impulse in the play-within-the-play, in the form of Luciano's speech.[36]

[35] Grebanier (1960, pp. 224-227, 393) insists, however, contrary to most commentators, that "idle" does not mean crazy in this context, but "inactive" as it does on all other occasions when Shakespeare uses the term. This does not seem justified, for in the First Quarto, line 1535, Gertrude reassures Hamlet that he did not see a ghost, but "this is only fantasie/And for my love forget these idle fits" (see *Variorum Edition*, Vol. 1, p. 235 and Vol. 2, pp. 58, 72). It would seem that this evidence and the context speak against Grebanier's interpretation, particularly in this scene.

[36] One may speculate either that the sexual excitement has the function of working against the aggressive impulse manifestly directed at the Player King, thereby reducing it to a defense, or that the aggressive impulse intervenes in order to prevent the consummation of the libidinal impulse directed toward Ophelia. Ophelia, by her twice drawing Hamlet's attention to herself yet withdraw-

Analysis of this sort will be acceptable at best to the psychoanalyst. The suggestion that one look at the sub-play in isolation, without drawing any specific inferences as to the protagonist's character, cannot lay claim to essential validity, not being much more than a possibility, and we must now turn to examine Hamlet's behavior in more realistic terms. Madariaga (1948) sees in it another evidence of Hamlet's egocentricity and his inability to love. This is one of the many interpretive possibilities that are created by poetic ambiguity, but I must admit that this possibility strikes me as being the least interesting and least satisfactory among them all.

After all, we have already observed Hamlet in his struggle to break with Ophelia, and noted that he was quite successful at it. Here we see a renewed approach: an open admission of acute sexual excitement and a frank statement of man's need of the female. The spectator might, after all, have been in danger of taking Hamlet's misogyny all too literally; the point had already been reached at which his intemperate condemnation of feminine foibles might have conjured up in the audience the image of a puritan—which Hamlet definitely was not.

In this sense, Hamlet now appears as a full-blooded male, intemperate and only barely capable of postponing gratification, as befits a man when he is in intense sexual excitement. All his expressed inhibitions and scruples have not emasculated him, we now see; he is capable of letting the beast in him loudly raise its voice.

He has been severely criticized by some critics for humiliating Ophelia in front of the court. Does she actually feel humiliated? Was such discourse admissible at the Elizabethan court, or at one of its subsidiaries? Nowadays it would closely approach the limits of the tolerable, while still, I believe, remaining bearable. Our times are not exemplary, however, and the contemporary decline of mores should not serve as a yardstick. The discourse takes place in a group situation of a kind that may favor regressive behavior, and therefore has a coloring that is different from the one it would have à *deux* or à *trois*. Curiously enough, no critical comment is raised by anyone who is present; this may mean that such behavior was not considered unusual, or else that the dialogue took place unheard by the others, or finally that the prince's folly was

ing each time, would then symbolize the dreamer's surge of desires and their later ebbing under the defensive impact. I have not tried to give here anything like a complete analysis of the sub-play as a dream, for I have not considered the particular turns of the sub-play at which the Hamlet-Ophelia dialogue intervenes, or Hamlet and the King step in.

taken for granted and tactfully bypassed, so long as the royal couple did not seem to mind it.

When critics express their belief that this apparent disrespect for a woman precludes love of her, one has to disagree. For external reasons, Hamlet has had to bring his courtship to an end; now he is letting Ophelia know that he is craving for her as always. Her responses are drawn with masterly ambiguity. To be sure, the dialogue takes place under circumstances that make consummation impossible—which may make the prince bolder than he might otherwise have been. Either association, "barking dogs do not bite" and "where there is smoke, there is fire," is thus permissible here. That such discourse was not the rule between the two while they were still on good terms with each other is quite evident.

Various interpretations are possible with regard to Ophelia's behavior. Madariaga, for example, holds that her answers are incompatible with sweetness and innocence (p. 44). If Victorian measures are applied, they certainly were; but in terms of such measures, a woman, in order to deserve a man's respect, was supposed never to have an orgasm. Yet Ophelia, as she herself lets us know, is a woman endowed with strong sexual impulses (to the dismay of some critics), otherwise she could never speak of "the steep and thorny way to heaven" *(I.3.48)*. If innocence means ignorance, then Ophelia is truly most unsweet, for she is fully cognizant of the facts of life.

Still her behavior under Hamlet's lashing does not preclude a pattern of conduct that was *expected* from a girl of her times without her losing the standing of virtue. A Victorian girl was supposed to be poor in physical desires, an Elizabethan to be sexually strongly motivated but in complete mastery of her appetites, so that she remained untouched prior to the wedding night. The way Ophelia is presented, she impresses me as being a woman who possessed all the abilities necessary to satisfy a man sexually, yet would have had, if Hamlet had married her, nothing but trifles to confess to, if she were to be asked about previous transgressions.

When Madariaga (1948) says that Hamlet "treats her as a young Elizabethan courtier would a young Elizabethan flirt with no particular inhibitions about anything" (p. 43), he may be right; yet Hamlet's expressed intention to pretend derangement speaks strongly against this interpretation. Whatever the Elizabethan mores may have been, such conduct as Hamlet shows toward Ophelia during the mouse-trap play must have been unusual for him, for quite aside from his announcement of unusual behavior, there is no indication that Ophelia either was accustomed to or expected to be treated in that way.

To be sure, Madariaga seems to be correct when he discovers in Ophelia's behavior signs of her encouraging Hamlet. He is right in saying that Victorian morality would have required her to leave the room, or to move away from him, or not to address him any further. Her not doing anything of the sort proves, to my mind, that she is not a prude and that she loves Hamlet. Her indulgence in feminine masochism, however, does not go so far as to deprive her of a rightful claim to virtuousness. She does not surrender to him, after all, and her protestations have just the proper weight to preserve her dignity without making her either a nag or peevish.

But what about Hamlet's madness? In his previous attack, when he rejected Ophelia, he verbalized complaints that are not only heard by analysts almost regularly from patients, but are also found in one way or another in the writings of illustrious men. In the three obscene thrusts we have discussed here, he expresses nothing that is not usually on a man's mind when he feels excited and sensually attracted by a woman. He does not say anything that Ophelia, if she were honest, would not have suspected (or wished) that he was thinking. What is unusual is only that these things are stated publicly and directly, and that they have an aggressive coloring.

There is yet another factor to consider. In Ophelia's references to Hamlet, as he was and acted prior to the onset of crisis, there is no mention of his giving voice to direct and blunt communication of unsublimated, virile sexual aggression. Perhaps such talk was customary with Elizabethan flirts, but it was certainly not Hamlet's habit to deal in such a way with a woman, or else Ophelia would not have fallen in love with him or called him "mould of form." Yet, as to the fact that such impulses must have been present in him for quite some time, of that we can be certain without any further inquiry. In his sexual thrusts, therefore, he would have been belatedly expressing to her something he had held back for years, or had tried to suppress, or had perhaps really succeeded in repressing.

Further, this was Hamlet's last chance to let his sweetheart know that, for better or worse, he was still in love with her. He surely knew that the ghost was right, and that within a short time he would be losing the last reason for further delay. Then he would have to resort to action —perhaps even with Ophelia's father as his first victim. A tryst, as well as any show of affection, was out of the question; insofar as the persistence of his love for Ophelia, despite the external break that Hamlet had contrived, was a secret that even Horatio was not permitted to know, aggressive manifestations constituted the only path left open to it for expression.

Since Hamlet was correct in anticipating the possibility that this might well be the last time he would see Ophelia (as a matter of fact, the next time he sees her, it will be in her grave), the gross vulgarity of his speech has the psychological meaning of a farewell. Tender words—the protestation that, whatever has happened between them, she should never doubt the truthfulness of the stilted love letter, but should rather be certain that she has been and will be the only woman he would love; the profession that he was parting with a broken heart for not being permitted to enjoy the delights of her young body; the vow that it was by no means because of fickleness that he grievously wounded her tender heart, but that stern and irrevocable commitments had forced him against all his own desires and wishes into a cruel and bloody world—all such confessions and their like had been rendered impossible by the mission he had agreed to carry out and the limitations on his freedom of communicating with her that this mission had been imposed upon him.

What else was there for this young man, so tragically ruled against by fate, to do under such circumstances, when for the last time he saw this beautiful girl in her youthful bloom, than fall into the revery of a delightful sexual dream, which he then sought to share with her? It stood in lieu of a passionate farewell kiss. At the very moment when Hamlet announces that Lucianus-Hamlet will get "the love of Gonzalo's wife," it is Ophelia who interrupts the play with: "The King rises" (one of the few moments in the play, if not the only one, in which she asserts herself) and in a second the whole fantastic world has disappeared into thin air, as befits a dream from which one is suddenly awakened.

Is it meaningful that Claudius does not depart during the dumb show, when the Player-King is poisoned by the ear, but only after Hamlet has thrown in his claim to the incestuous object? or that it is Ophelia who gives the signal, as if she were jealous and could not well stand the rivalry with Hamlet's infantile love object? Such questions may be an outgrowth of the author's psychoanalytic bias and therefore should not be overemphasized, nor further explored. Whether or not Ophelia understood what was hidden behind Hamlet's obscenities, we do not know

for sure. But that those critics who have castigated Hamlet for his coarseness have not understood it—of this we may rest assured.

Looking back once again, we may now understand better why
Shakespeare introduced into the mouse-trap scene Hamlet's undisguised
sexual drive. It not only served to round out the full picture of Hamlet's
personality and to warn us against seeing in Hamlet something of a puritan or an ascetic, who has renounced (or is trying to renounce) the carnal
aspects of human existence. Despite his break with Ophelia, he is
acknowledging the full impact of bodily desires, their rightful claims to
and inner acceptance by a man who is at the same time willing to forego
their gratification in the service of fulfilling his duty toward the world.

Only a master craftsman could synthesize all this into a subplay that
in itself serves two functions: to test the world and to express a deeply
repressed secret in the hero. That the adult's genital craving, reality testing and the repressed oedipal wish actually belong together may not have
been Shakespeare's explicit insight but it will sound familiar enough to
the depth psychologist. Here, too, Hamlet's alleged madness is a mixture: he avers both truth and counterfeit, which thereby serve at the same
time purposeful manipulation of reality and loss of self-control.

Hamlet and Polonius.

Some further remarks are in order concerning Hamlet's relationship with Polonius. From the beginning, his anger and sarcasm have focused on the latter. In the realistic context, this is aroused by the fact that
he is Ophelia's father and Claudius' main support, who had arranged
the irregular succession to the throne. In the psychological context, Polonius is also Hamlet's father; thus his weakness and word-spinning are
what make it possible for the son to come to terms first with this father
image. The realistic act of killing stands for the psychological act of
freeing oneself from the impact of an *imago*.[37]

The realistic context on the stage does create some ambiguity about
Hamlet's conscious aim when he is thrusting through the arras. His
thrust may have been aimed either at Claudius or at Polonius, or indeed
any force that was threatening to intervene between himself and the
mother. Such intervening forces are generally associated with the father.
If Hamlet's killing Polonius was indeed an apraxia, then psychoanalytic
theory may suggest that Polonius was his unconscious aim. Yet with re-

---

[37] The details of that process are little studied. It can be observed in the psychoanalytic process, and it occurs also in everyday life, although there it usually does not extend to deeper layers of the unconscious.

gard to Polonius' death Hamlet expresses repentance (regret rather than remorse), by contrast with his being instrumental in the deaths of Rosencrantz and Guildenstern, about which he feels nothing but triumph.

About Polonius' death one must take note of the fact—as I pointed out earlier—that, even in modern history, he would be a marked man. When the crown is charged with crime, the prime minister who has given it support is (justly or unjustly) held equally responsible. The political angle is barely verbalized in *Hamlet,* yet it remains the ever-present background, increasing the momentum of the action. The mind is troubled when the state is troubled, and vice versa.

The oedipal meaning of Polonius is nowhere made explicit. But it is intimated, particularly when he says that he "did enact Julius Caesar" *(III.3.104),* incontrovertibly the image of an elevated father. Hamlet's conduct is here put into a nutshell. What this means in his unconscious is that even a father of Julius Caesar's grandeur will one day fall into a decline and become a dotard—an anticipation of the rather gruesome imagery of the graveyard scene. Rosencrantz and Guildenstern, being mere sponges *(IV.2.12),* do not warrant repentance on Hamlet's part. But with Polonius it is another matter. He too has to depart from this life, since "heaven hath pleas'd it so" *(III.4.33).* He had bet on a card against the voice of history, whose "scourge and minister" *(III.4.175)* Hamlet feels himself to be, even though, in keeping with his times, he understands this mission to have been entrusted to him by the Heavens.

Polonius is thus the *imago* of the aged father who becomes the son's ward and responsibility and against whom the adult son's ambivalence rages mercilessly. To accept the father as suffering from weaknesses and foibles like any other human being is one of the most difficult of tasks, and in general man fails to carry it through. In this sense, it may be said that Polonius' death symbolizes the only way in which man can rid himself of this particular *imago*, just as an Australian nomadic tribe will actually dig a hole when the parents become decrepit, and leave them there, with ample provisions but not without first bidding them a tearful farewell.

Hamlet proffers a particular disgusting imagery in conjunction with Polonius' body and he has often been castigated for it. He wants to let the corpse rot, to be eaten by worms, but his ruminations end, significantly enough, with the fate of Kings: "a King may go a progress through the guts of a beggar" *(IV.3.33).* The voice of the unconscious is harsh, unpleasant and even cruel, and it is the language of the unconscious that

Hamlet's madness employs here. At this point, reality calls for particular craftiness on his part, since the deed has betrayed his real aim—to kill Claudius.

One may say that therefore he has to offer to the court an image of a severely unbalanced mind, if he is not to be seriously endangered. The more deeply repressed is the content that rises to the surface, the more insane the person appears; consequently, Hamlet takes hold of the most far-removed archaism, stemming from the prehistoric dawn of mankind, when the murdered father was eaten by the sons (Freud, 1913d, pp. 141-155). The sons, in accordance with dream symbols, are in Hamlet's speech reduced to maggots.

But there is one detail that shows that here Hamlet is not only feigning, that the archaic imagery that reels from the deepest layers has indeed overcome him. For, as Madariaga rightly points out, after Hamlet *(III.4.187f)* has averred to his mother that he is only "mad in craft" and not "essentially" mad, he has no reality motive for feigning when he is alone with her. Still, even after this admission, he goes on raving against the dead Polonius and indulges in contemptuous outbreaks, such as: "I'll lug the guts into the neighbour room" *(III.4.212)*. The killing of Polonius and the excesses against his dead body, and possibly also the violent assault against Ophelia, addressed directly to her, I assume, are the moments that Hamlet has in mind when, in the last scene, he expresses regret about the consequences of what he himself calls his "madness."

Hamlet's Farewell.

In order to fathom the depth of this farewell speech, I first have to draw upon a curious clinical observation. It has come to my attention— and there are psychoanalysts who will agree with this—that when one has the good fortune to accomplish what is vaguely called a "really deep" analysis, regularly at some point in it a doubt arises as to whether the patient may be schizophrenic, or at least latently so, or whether he has previously gone through a schizophrenic phase. Such doubts occur even in instances in which the subject is free, and has all along been free, of such psychopathology. Yet the fact that this doubt occurs with near regularity during some phase of the psychoanalytic exploration may be significant. It also happens during the course of a deep analysis that, having gone through many hours of free associations, the subject will sometimes suspect, or receive the impression, that some of his past actions were the resultants of pure madness. Such incidents, of course, occur, if at all, only in the analyses of patients whose personality is highly differentiated.

Without wanting to go here into a further analysis of this, I only wish to state that Hamlet's personality has achieved, during the course of the play, a degree of differentiation that is altogether comparable to that observed in this type of patient, when he comes to clinical observation. Yet it is essential to take note of the fact that it is precisely the processes that have led to these high degrees of differentiation that are retrospectively appraised by the subject as madness. For events that later meet with such evaluations are neither peripheral nor incidental but nodal—high points of relevance, unavoidable and determined by the deepest forces that have shaped the patient's destiny. And the moments when events of that sort strike the patient as having been madness are similarly important.

At these moments, the patient is not trying to create a subterfuge or an excuse. He is acknowledging the intensely personal and irrational character of these events—the fact that they cannot be justified as proper responses to concerns that have been imposed by external reality, but are instead completely divorced from anything external, being direct manifestations of the irrepressible breakthrough of the most intensely subjective. They are inevitable, in terms of the way in which this particular *condition humain* has been shaped. The terrified question, "How was it possible for me ever to do this?" is an expression of regret that it did indeed come to pass, even though it is well understood that if life were to be lived all over again, the same thing would be repeated, so deeply is it ingrained in the very fabric of the subject's existence. This acknowledgment of madness is an acknowledgment of inevitability and irrationality, as well as an expression of humility and remorse, and of both the acceptance and the rejection of responsibility—all rolled together in one.

It is in this sense that Hamlet's speech of farewell to this world must be understood *(V.2.230-247)*.[38] It is a declaration that is valid for anyone with conscience and sensibility, when, having reached the end of the road, he looks back over what he has come through. Numberless are those whom we have hurt, either voluntarily or involuntarily; many a tear may have been shed because of us, and we not knowing; images, memories, dreams will be left in many minds after our departure, yet we have no way of knowing how many of them will prove to be sources of

---

[38]Johnson and others (*Variorum Edition*, Vol. 1, p. 440) have taken offense at parts of this speech. My belief is that it is not to be regarded as defensive in character, but rather as an attempt at confession and explanation, and therefore free of any attempt to proffer an excuse.

grief, anxiety, and scorn. The more closely we have lived to another human heart, the more affliction we are likely to have brought upon it: the parent hurts the child and the child hurts the parent, far more and more grievously than would be true if the psychic pain were limited only to the fact that the parents die, or that the child grows up and loves others, whom he has never known before, and who have neither nursed him nor spent nights of terror when he was sick.

Hamlet's language was often coarse before that farewell speech, not because he himself was coarse, but because he spoke so often the language of the unconscious, the language that penetrates into and is understood by the heart. (All other language usually remains in essence mathematics, and stops at the border that marks off the brain from the heart).

They are hypocrites who deny that their own paths of life are strewn with Poloniuses, Ophelias and Gertrudes. The ear that listens attentively to the pulse of human existence does not care whether these corpses are symbols, dreams or realities. The main thing is that they are part of the life of everyone who reaches out into the surrounding universe, who is not willing to wait for the world to approach him, but wants to know and understand and act. In *Hamlet* ecstasy often stands for what we would call madness. A deep truth may lie in this equation. Ecstasy is probably madness and madness ecstasy, and it is only the meek, the dispirited, the altogether spiritless who forgo ecstasy and madness in their lives, heartbreaking as may be the remorse that follows upon them.

I am quite certain that Ophelia was right when she portrayed the Hamlet she had known before as "a noble mind,"

> The courtier's, soldier's, scholar's, eye, tongue, sword;
> The expectancy, and rose of the fair state,
> The glass of fashion, and the mould of form,
> The observed of all observers.

Indeed, he was once "that unmatch'd form and feature of blown youth." But while he was all that and much more, he had never before been capable of ecstasy and madness, had never tasted of that which makes human life what it is. It had apparently been a one-dimensional existence, perfect in all that human society says it looks for and wants; had Hamlet continued to travel that path, he would have earned an A+ in conduct for himself—and a splendid epitaph.

When he says farewell and beholds all the grief he has brought upon others, he bows in humility:

> Hamlet is of the faction that is wrong'd,
> His madness is poor Hamlet's enemy.

Here he forgives himself, and in that act of self-tolerance forgives all others as well, for as long as man censures himself, he cannot forgive others. The New Testament was wrong: perceiving the beam or mote in his own eye forces a man to seek the same in his neighbor's eye. Flatter has suggested that this speech is directed not to the brother but to the mother—a very appealing thought. I would go one step further and suggest that it includes Claudius as well, although I may thereby be reading into the play a meaning that it does not contain.

It remains unclear how far Hamlet goes in his forgiveness. Nevertheless it is clear that, because of his so-called madness, he has lost all claim to a splendid epitaph, unless Horatio does a great deal of writing to clear his name. By the time he delivers his farewell speech, he has reached an important stage of his development, even though he has abandoned along the way each single element of Ophelia's eulogy. But who would prefer being what Hamlet had been before to being what he is now? A mirror existence is a slave existence; even though it is free of physical bondage, it is worse even than such enslavement, for it is spiritual bondage.

Before our very eyes, Hamlet has thrown off the shackles of his mirror existence, and, even though he did much during the course of his chrysalis stage that puzzled us and even made us shake our heads—at times we were worried, and rightly so, for his mental balance (a worry that is typically aroused in whoever observes the adolescence of a superbly gifted youth)—he has now grown into an individuality with real bas-relief and solidly engraved features. He has freed himself from the illusions that are inherent in a mirror existence, and he has taken cognizance of that hypocrisy that is an essential concomitant to any community.

Above all, he is now aware of death as both the prime mover and the consummation of life, as well as of the inevitability of the grief and injury that man has to suffer at the hands of others, and the fact that this inevitably causes him to make still others suffer in turn. He is ready, in short, to understand and to forgive. He is free of anxiety and, most of all, ready to act. Scruples and doubts have vanished, and he awaits with serenity the unfolding of the future.

There is nothing saintly about him. He will not ever, upon being smitten on one cheek, turn the other. But the past has lost the grip it had on him, and when he does act, it will not be out of resentment or driven by a paternal command, but solely because of that inner necessity that binds man to the reality that surrounds him. He has achieved the highest degree of synthesis of activity and passivity—the freedom that allows for self-chosen action, so long as it is in accordance with reality.

I find confirmation of this view in the fact that Hamlet does not say one word about his father when at last he does kill Claudius. Madariaga (p. 102f) finds in this same fact confirmation of the only motive that, in his view, explains Hamlet's tragedy: his egotism. "Hamlet could not pour himself into action because he was too egoistic for that. All action—even crime—requires freedom from egotism. Man can only act by, so to speak, mating with the outside world, by forgetting himself for an instant, and becoming the object of his action. Hamlet could not forget himself, and, far from pouring himself into the world outside, he forced the world to pour itself into him. Since all the world was made to become Hamlet, Hamlet could neither do nor become anything in the world" (p. 105).

He also notes the absence of any moment in which Hamlet says: " 'at last, oh father, I have avenged thee' " (p. 103).[39] If Hamlet had ever said that, then the play would have been a Catholic play, in which the son acknowledged the father's greatness and bowed to it in humility, consummating his life in acts of obedience. It would also have been no more than a typical Elizabethan revenge play, whereas in the creation of *Hamlet* all traditional literary patterns were broken (even Aristotle's famous definition of tragedy, as I shall attempt to show later). But the tragedy of Hamlet's inaction tends to obscure his evolvement of formidable action, of action until then unheard of.

When this happens, then wicked man raises his head in invincible truculence, and hurls this at his creator: "What you want me to do is reasonable, just and good; but I will never do it so long as I shall be doing it only because you told me so. I will do it because *I* want to do it,

---

[39] In a source that I can no longer trace, there is the assertion that Hamlet, in killing Claudius, did not take vengeance for his father's death but only for the victimization of his mother and himself at the hands of Claudius. There this interpretation was not put forward in a pejorative sense, as with Madariaga (1948). The fact that Hamlet, when he kills Claudius, does *not* refer to his father may thus be taken as a sign that he was still possessed by his old doubts; or that he was suffering from a character defect; or it may mean that he had reached a higher level of personality development.

and only when the reasonable, just and good are *my* reasonable, just and good. Only then will the reasonable, just and good be done."

Adam had raised his hand against his creator, knowing full well that he was disobedient, yet being moved to action out of curiosity, out of his desire to taste a passion forbidden to him. That was not at all Hamlet's problem. Even after he has forgone the satisfaction of his passions, and has been an obedient son, he still does not carry out his creator's command. A rebellion takes place at this point that is far more dangerous than Adam's—one that, as we now witness, may even destroy man. This is a rebellion that perhaps ought never to have taken place, yet it was just as inevitable as Adam's. It is one that millions of people have been desirous of witnessing on the stage, but which they would never have had the chance to see, had Hamlet said: "At last, oh father, I have avenged thee."

Beautiful as the medieval epoch may be, with its cathedrals, its epics, its belief in God, and its fight with the devil, it *is* history, gone never to return again. It is therefore reexperienced by us esthetically in the same way as we admiringly experience the Parthenon or the Pantheon. As for *Hamlet,* that is ourselves and our present lives, even though it was created three and a half centuries ago—the beginning of a hurricane that still sweeps the world and whose end no one can foresee. Thus, Hamlet's madness, the greatest structure ever to be put on the modern stage, was a spark that set the Western world ablaze—for better or for worse.[40]

---

[40]Cf. Elton (1922, p. 35): "It is but half-true to say that Hamlet speaks to all men so strongly, because he anticipates the temper of modern doubt or modern melancholy. Better say that the modern mind has been to some extent propelled towards that temper by the figure of Hamlet; or, better still, that the new free intellectual movement of the time, which happens to be so sharply mirrored in Hamlet, is the ancestral cause, and the first fully conscious expression, of the modern impulse towards untrammeled thought."

PART THREE: APPENDICES

A. Freud's Approach to the Analysis of Literary Works (Explaining and Understanding)

Psychoanalysis may make contributions to the explanation of works of literature in either of two ways, which are different in method, purpose and result. One of these I shall call exopoietic, the other endopoietic.[1]

In the former, all the explanatory factors are sought from outside the literary work itself. In exopoietic research the literary work is taken as an embodiment of the creative mind, and such research therefore aims primarily at the reconstruction of the mental processes or other significant characteristics of the author.[2]

[1] I owe these terms to Mr. Harold Collins and wish to thank him for them.

[2] Is exopoietic research possible at all? I think Spurgeon's (1931, 1935) research proves that it is, although it also raises questions about the actual value of such research. Her discovery of the prototype of an unusual simile that Shakespeare used in *Lucrece* (1667-1673) in a still observable eddy under the 18th arch of the old Clopton Bridge (1935, pp. 97-99) is extraordinarily convincing and may be compared with an experimental validation. Her assumption is sound that "a dramatic poet ... unconsciously 'gives himself away' in his images," and one cannot challenge her method of "collecting and classifying the images" on the grounds that "the poet unwittingly reveals his own innermost likes and dislikes, observations and interests, associations of thought, attitudes of mind and beliefs, in and through the images, the verbal pictures he draws to illuminate something quite different in the speech and thought of his characters" (1931, p. 173). She is also correct in her assertion that, by this method, we may learn "what in daily life thrilled him with pleasure, what offended and revolted him, what were his personal tastes" (1935, p. 201) and many other things that she enumerates.

It is true that, in order to unearth such data, we need a special method in Shakespeare's case, because his life is so poorly documented. There are, after all, data that we usually obtain from a poet's diaries and letters, along with the accounts of his contemporaries. When Spurgeon proves that Shakespeare had an aversion against dogs (1935, pp. 195-199), this does not tell us anything about

It is worthwhile discussing at this point the ideas of a great scholar who took a stand diametrically opposite to the basic tenets of exopoietic research. I am referring here to Friedrich Gundolf (1911b), who insists that one will never apprehend the full meaning of a literary work except by reading it as if one knew nothing about its creator. "The work can never be explained from the biography; it is only by way of the work that the biography makes sense and that is the only justification it has in the history of ideas." [*Darum lässt sich aus der Biographie nie das Werk erklären, erst vom Werk aus gewinnt die Biographie einen Sinn, und das ist das einzige Recht das ihr in der Geistesgeschichte überhaupt zukommt*] (p. 6). He who would seek to elucidate the total being [*Gesamtwesen*] of a writer should not refer to his *curriculum vitae* but rather to his creations, "to those formations that contain his world and his ego at their most distinct—that is to say, at their most structured" [*an sein Werk, an diejenigen Gebilde die seine Welt und sein Ich am deutlichsten, d.h. am geformtesten enthalten*].

This program sounds strange to the analyst, who is guided above all by the aim of translating objective content and value into biography. Yet Gundolf's methodological position does contain at bottom a truth that is frequently forgotten. The minds that we admire as truly creative produced values that are greater than themselves. Great works are greater than their creators. It is on this basic paradox that the entire psychology of creativity rests and no one has yet succeeded in resolving it. It may be recognition of the fact that the work is greater than its creator that induced Plato to assume the existence of a world of incorporeal "ideas" and that also compelled so many great minds to maintain that a divine or otherwise supernatural power had revealed itself through them, they being, so to speak, nothing more than mere appendages. The same thing happens even to the scientist; thus Freud (1873-1939) wrote in a letter to Jones (Dec. 30, 1925), speaking about psychoanalysis—which he had created—and saying that by comparison with its greatness, "all of us [he and his collaborators] are small."

To be sure, the discrepancy between superb creative achievement and the ethical inferiority of the person who had performed the creation

---

Shakespeare beyond the sentimental. What we have a right to expect from exopoietic research is the answer to why he had such an aversion: was it a phobia? what did the dog stand for as a symbol? and many more such questions. Only data with regard to the structure of the personality are decisive, and it is debatable whether or not such data can reliably be obtained by exopoietic research, unless there is unusually rich documentation. Some analysts doubt that it can be done even under such favorable conditions.

has already been noted in many instances (Muschg, 1948); but that is not what is meant here at all, even though that discovery did cause quite a sensation for a while, in the instance of Beethoven (see Sterba and Sterba, 1954). The paradox can best be demonstrated by reference to the question of perfection. The greatest achievements in any artistic medium whatsoever carry something of this quality: it is impossible for anyone to conceive of how they could be improved; as a matter of fact, any attempt to change them would unquestionably diminish their quality. It goes without saying that this is not true of the artist himself. He is never even close to perfection, but rather shares, even under optimal conditions, the foibles, weaknesses, uglinesses of his fellow-men.

Nevertheless, the fact remains that the artist is capable of creating what he himself can never be; perhaps what rests in him is a potentiality that cannot grow into something psychic and personal, but can be realized only through and within an objective medium. Freud (1916-1917, p. 258) wrote of the "puzzling leap" from the mental to the physical (meaning, of course, the somatic); but there is an equally puzzling leap from the mental to the physical in the sense of the external, concrete cultural achievement. While the physician is concerned with the psyche's leap into the somatic, what the humanities are basically concerned with is the psyche's leap into one or the other among the huge variety of cultural products.

Are these cultural products more than the sum of all those psychic processes that took place prior to their creation? Gundolf's warning is perhaps based on the expectation that the cultural product will come out diminished in value after having been subjected to psychological explanation; that once it has been shown to be the outcome of innumerable psychic processes, it has thereby become deprived of what is perhaps its supreme value, its contribution to the history of human thought. Indeed, individual man does tend to disappear behind his own formidable objective achievement, in exactly the way that Freud experienced with regard to himself and psychoanalysis, which had grown in his hands into a formidable structure that then started to live its own life, developing in ways he could never have foreseen, no less planned. The cultural product is, indeed, in the position of progeny that is always more than the two gametes that joined to produce it.

Gundolf's approach, even though it has proven to be of great productive value in literary research, remains to the analyst unacceptable.

But it may also be of value for the analyst at times to study the cultural product while bypassing all the implications that it may hold for the creator's psychology, precisely in order first to determine what is the truly unique feature of the creation under investigation. It is often far from easy to find that feature. Hamlet's hesitation to take action against Claudius is certainly one of the most puzzling elements of the play; anyone who deals with the tragedy is compelled to come to terms with it in one way or another. Yet *Hamlet* is considerably more than a play about a young man who finally overcomes procrastination in the fulfillment of an obligation. It is indeed a hard task to discover and to set forth explicitly what is the unique feature that constitutes the specific greatness of a particular cultural product; and it is not without interest to speculate about whether or not, once we have been able to ascertain that uniqueness, we would then be able to discover the links between that particular feature and the creative mind's life history and psychology.

It struck me, in considering Einstein's mass-energy equation—perhaps the greatest achievement of human ratiocination—that nothing, literally nothing (except the meaningless fact of an unusually high I.Q.) could be inferred with regard to its author's mind, even though we are here dealing with the most consequential combination of five signs ever devised by the human mind. And yet, with regard to this equation, we are quite capable of stating what makes it unique. Thus, even though Gundolf's methodology is the opposite of that of psychoanalysis, it may nevertheless harbor implications for investigation that are not by any means lacking in potential importance to psychoanalysis.

Endopoietic research does not go beyond the boundaries of the literary work; all explanatory factors remain within the givens of that work. The paradigm of psychoanalytic endopoietic research is to be found in Freud's explanation of an apraxia that the German playwright Friedrich von Schiller put on the stage *(Die Piccolomini, 1.5)* (Freud, 1916-1917, p. 37). The slip which the speaker attempts to conceal from the person with whom he is conversing was used deliberately by the playwright in order to let the audience know that the speaker had suddenly recognized a state of affairs previously unknown to him. However, circumstances forbade him to spell out his discovery in the situation in which he found himself at the moment.

Curiously enough, Freud's endopoietic explanation did not contain anything that would not have been readily accepted by any reader, since

Freud was explicating only what was clearly the playwright's purpose.[3] Yet this more or less trivial example can be taken as an "ideal-type" model of endopoietic explanation, along psychological lines, of one element of a literary work. The fact that this explanation coincides with commonsense thinking should not detract from its value as a model.

Exopoietic and endopoietic research are not always wholly isolated from each other. By way of the latter, for example, the unconscious meaning of a work can be established, and only after this has been done can the work be meaningfully connected with some particular element of the author's life. Hanns Sachs' (1919) endopoietic investigation of Shakespeare's *Tempest,* for instance, brought to light the focal position that a daughter's marriage holds in the play, which discovery was then brought into meaningful connection with Shakespeare's relationship to his own daughter Judith.

The most frequent methodological mistake to be observed in exopoietic research is the assumption that the genius follows in all essential respects the same psychological laws as those that are followed by the average person, whose mental apparatus is in general so familiar to the psychoanalyst. On the basis of this assumption, a large number of papers have been written, in which conclusions about the genius's personality have been drawn from an examination of his created works, without corresponding verifications of those conclusions from the biographical record.

When such investigations are limited to the assertion that the artist had formed an Oedipus complex or had disclosed aggression or such other universal emotions as envy or rivalry, little objection can be raised, since such formations are, after all, universal and they may be supposed to exist in one form or another in *every* human being. The question then can only be whether or not the specific artistic element or structure can be connected genetically with the specific psychological element or structure to which it is supposedly related.

When Freud wrote the first extensive essay (1910) in which he used the exopoietic method, he emphasized that his inquiry had to do only with that part of Leonardo's personality that the latter shared with others, and excluded what we would call Leonardo's genius. From Freud's letters we know that he had had a patient in analysis who "seemed to

---

[3] It is remarkable that such a simple item as the slip that Schiller had one of his characters make, and which could easily have been understood for what it was by any schoolboy, contained *in nuce* the central ingredient out of which Freud built psychoanalysis.

have the same constitution as Leonardo without his genius" (Strachey, 1957, p. 60). This may sound strange today, since it is difficult to conceive of Leonardo without his genius; the interest has now shifted to what it is that makes Leonardo *different* from the rest of mankind. Whether or not Freud was right in his explanation of those elements that the genius shared with the rest of mankind, he demonstrated something that has since been confirmed—namely, that the flowering of genius depends on the early relationship to the mother. This was demonstrated by Freud negatively, perhaps, in that he showed how the growing child was hurt in that relationship and for that reason evolved inhibitions.

The emphasis fell on those factors that stood in the artist's way and thus diminished the output of which he would otherwise have been innately capable. Such defects—if they were defects—were already well-known from Leonardo's life. Yet one should not forget that there is a difference in principle between trying to explain why an artist completed relatively few paintings, and concluding from the content of completed plays that the playwright must have gone through manic-depressive phases—especially when nothing is known about him during the period in which he wrote these plays.

The tacit assumption is, first, that there is a parallel between the prevailing mood in the playwright and the atmosphere conveyed in his plays.[4] Second, it is assumed that a genius' mind works, with regard to the production of his extraordinary achievements, in the same way as the minds that are known to us from the intimacy of clinical observation. This may or may not be correct. For a conclusion to be drawn from an artist's achievement as to the processes of his mental functioning, one would have to presuppose that we are as familiar with the psychic apparatus of the genius as we are with that of the average subject of psychoanalytic investigation.

Since the psychic apparatus of the genius has been investigated chiefly by way of an analysis of his achievements, it could be said that most of the psychoanalytic literature on genius is, methodologically speaking, circular. Because someone who is endowed with the capacities of genius does not generally need psychoanalysis, it is necessary to use the few instances for which documentation is available in abundance and to reconstruct the genius' personality from his biographical record.

The situation is quite different in the field of endopoietic research.

---

[4] Cf. Freud (1913, p. 187). Bühler (1929, p. 25) rightly warns against the assumption of a parallelism between a creative mind and its creations.

Here we have a fixed record, open to the inspection of anyone who is interested, and one does not have to go beyond what is given in order to establish links with an external frame of reference, such as the artist's personality or his society. Freud's first major contribution to the explanation of a literary work has to be assigned to endopoietic research, even though its original purpose was to inquire into the nature of the dreams that authors have their characters dream. The underlying idea was apparently only to check whether the artist's conception of dreams showed any similarity with Freud's findings on that question. For this, the novel *Gradiva* by Wilhelm Jensen (1837-1911), which had been published in 1903, seemed an appropriate choice, since it contained several dreams. In the hands of the master, however, the study (Freud, 1907) went beyond this initial aim and became instead a comprehensive treatise. It can be used instructively as a paradigm of endopoietic research.

Freud's attempt to realize the original purpose of the study led to a truly amazing result. The dreams that the novel's hero dreamed followed to an astonishing extent the theories that Freud had set forth in his *Interpretation* (1900). The interpretations of the hero's dreams that Freud presented were therefore by no means strained; one does not discover a single trace of Freud's doing violence to the givens of the novel in order to establish some sort of agreement between it and his clinical findings. Even such an empirical detail as that the words spoken in a dream follow words that have been actually spoken or heard could be "confirmed" by the record investigated.

Indeed, when one follows Freud as he takes apart the protagonist's two dreams, one can scarcely suppress the feeling that Jensen had studied Freud's book on dream interpretation and then applied his knowledge somewhat mechanically to a character that was allegedly born from his fantasy. Yet the fact of the matter is that Jensen had no knowledge of psychoanalysis (see Freud, 1873-1939, p. 252f).[5]

Jensen wrote Freud about the way in which his story had been born. It was written on a sudden impulse and within a short time; he wrote it without reflection and in a somnambulistic way. How then can one explain this strange coincidence: that, writing in that fashion, the author nevertheless has his characters act and dream in complete accordance with the scientist's detailed research into the vast orbit of the

---

[5] In order to explain the seeming coincidence, one could perhaps suggest a case of cryptamnesia, but that can be ruled out here.

unconscious? If Jensen had been applying acquired knowledge, he would not have been able to proceed with such speed and in such a somnambulant manner. Moreover, the parallel between an insight that was based on science and the content of an artistic creation was not limited to dreams; Freud had also discovered the same thing as Jensen presented, with regard to the appearance and disappearance of a delusion in the novel's chief character, as well as the effect of erotic experiences in early childhood on later psychopathology, and many more such phenomena.

Yet what may be even more surprising is the fact that Freud utilized, in his analysis of the novel, certain clinical findings that, so far as I know, he had never referred to previously. He stated very radically—if I may so describe it—in connection with the protagonist's vicissitudes that "when what has been repressed returns, it emerges from the repressing force itself"; in other words, that it is easily possible "for the repressed to emerge behind the repressing force and take effect by means of it" (Freud, 1907, p. 35f). Curiously enough, Shakespeare had already described this mechanism in detail some 300 years earlier, when he had Angelo say in *Measure for Measure:*

> O cunning enemy! that, to catch a saint,
> With saints dost bait thy hook. Most dangerous
> Is that temptation that doth goad us on
> To sin in loving virtue: never could the strumpet,
> With all her double vigour, art and nature,
> Once stir my temper, but this virtuous mind
> Subdues me quite.

> *(II.2.180-186)*

Later, Freud was to demonstrate something similar for certain diseases, but he would never again set up such a general rule. I do not know whether Freud was right in his general statement, or may perhaps have been carried too far by the enthusiasm that his inquiry into the literary work apparently aroused in him. At any rate, it is a far-reaching and in fact splendid idea.

He also affirmed in this essay, for the first time, that "there is a grain of truth concealed in every delusion, there is something in it that really deserves belief."[6] He further demonstrated in his literary paper

---

[6] Mr. Strachey (*Standard Edition*, 7, p. 80, fn. 1) claims, however, that Freud had already expressed this view in his *Psychopathology of Everyday Life* (1901, p. 256). But in 1901 Freud, it seems to me, was referring to a formal quality, while in his *Gradiva* essay he was making an assertion with regard to content that introduced a new aspect of the question.

that the dream may contain a correct estimate and perception of reality, such as is denied in the delusion from which the dreamer suffers during his wakeful hours. Only many years later was Freud to make the observation that the dreams of a delusional patient are free of delusions, that "paranoia does not penetrate into dreams" (1922, p. 227)—an insight that he had apparently arrived at one and a half decades earlier.

I wish to make a categorical statement here. Freud has often been accused of "finding" in literary creations a confirmation of his theories, only because he had projected them into the subjects of his inquiry.[7] Freud was to anticipate this objection as early as in 1907 (p. 91): "It may be that we have produced a complete caricature of an interpretation by introducing into an innocent work of art purposes of which its creator had no notion, and by so doing have shown once more how easy it is to find what one is looking for and what is occupying one's own mind." If someone should raise this objection nevertheless, it could be pointed out that it was while he was analyzing the literary work that Freud made discoveries for which he only later found clinical confirmation.[8]

I should now like to trace when and how Freud evolved his oedipal theory. His letter of 15 October 1897 to Wilhelm Fliess contains the theory for the first time as a universal proposition. In the same letter, he refers to the Greek tragedy *Oedipus Rex* and tries to explain why, among all tragedies of fate, this was the one that left such an indelible effect on the human mind. Then he continues: "Fleetingly it went through my head whether the same thing [the oedipal complex] might lie at the bottom of Hamlet." (Freud, 1887-1902, my own translation.) Some explanations then follow, in loose sequence, ending with a comparison between Hamlet's way of bringing about his self-destruction (to repeat his

[7] Kenneth Muir (1952) in a thoughtful paper, the major part of which I agree with, warns against accepting "without reserve" any interpretation of Shakespeare's characters, whether it comes from Freud, Jung or Adler, since they differ completely but "conform . . . to the general theories of their authors" (p. 51). Reserve may be necessary in all scientific questions; Freud himself seems not to have been "without reserve" toward his own theories in view of the fact that he changed them considerably and impressively. If I understand Muir's remark correctly as implying that literary works have been used by Freud merely as receptacles of cherished theories (which I would call an abuse), I would have to disagree, as what follows aims to demonstrate.

[8] So it seems to me, at least. It is very difficult—well-nigh impossible—to determine when a productive mind has taken in the seed of what will later become a cultural achievement, whether this be of a scientific or an artistic nature. I have the feeling that all consequential ideas are born "in their rough-hewn form" between adolescence and early manhood. While that may be an exaggeration, it is certain that the rudiments of great ideas move about more or less aimlessly in the unconscious for a long time before they are given definitive form.

father's fate and to be poisoned by the same rival) and the behavior of hysterical patients.

The clinical theory and its application coincide literally, and thus an amazingly short time would have been left in order to evolve the sort of projections that some critics of Freud's Hamlet theory are wont to insist had occurred. I wish to stress here Freud's description of "fleetingly it went, etc.," which indicates that, at this stage, it was not yet a matter of a strictly discursive procedure, but rather of a groping for instances that may belong to the same type of problem.

Here it seems quite relevant to take note of a letter that Freud had written to Fliess 24 days earlier (21 September 1897), in which he quoted within a significant context Hamlet's aphorism: "The readiness is all" *(V.2.224)*. He wrote: "I vary Hamlet's words 'to be in readiness' [the last four words written in English]—to be genial is all [*Heiter sein ist Alles.*][9] I could have every justification for feeling quite discontent" (Freud, 1887-1902, my own translation). Apparently Freud felt at this juncture as Hamlet did when he was approaching the most fateful moment of his life—namely, killing Claudius. Both were at that moment on the eve of completed maturation.

Hamlet was 30 years old when he was "ready"; Freud was 41 when he quoted the passage.[10] Hamlet's chances of accomplishing his life mission after weeks and months of groping, doubting and searching had been at that moment reduced practically to nil. Yet he did not feel disheartened; instead he had a feeling of inner conviction that he was being carried along by a fate that was on his side. Freud felt himself to be, at that moment—after years of groping, doubting and searching—in an almost identical position, as he let Fliess know in the same letter. He had returned later than usual from an extensive vacation trip (Hamlet's journey to England?), and had come to recognize that the chief theory on which he had previously built his etiology of neurosis was wrong. The neurosis was *not* the consequence of infantile trauma of seduction, as he had been certain only a short while before; with this seeming insight went the fruits of his long and laborious research.

From this new state of affairs he had also gained the conviction that hysteria cannot be cured by psychotherapy. He was on the verge of ac-

[9] Unfortunately, this sentence has been translated as: "I vary Hamlet's remark about ripeness— cheerfulness is all," which may sound as if Freud had confused King Lear with Hamlet.

[10] From previous discussions of age in Shakespeare's time it will have become clear that the two ages are really equivalent. Cf. also Jones (1953, p. 267): "Eighteen ninety-seven was the acme of Freud's life."

cepting hereditary disposition as the etiological determinant of hysteria, after having thought earlier that he had successfully eliminated it as the preponderant etiological factor. All this meant that the fulfillment of his wishes, to which he had previously felt himself to be so very close, had instead vanished. Longingly, he meditated: "The expectation of eternal posthumous glory [*Nachruhm*] was so beautiful, as well as that of certain wealth, full independence, travelling, the children's rising above the grave worries that deprived me of my youth. This all depended on whether or not [the problem of] hysteria is resolved."

To his surprise, however, he did not feel ashamed, which might have been the most appropriate response to this recognition of failure. On the contrary, he felt "hearty and genial" [*frisch und heiter*], as he assured his friend in the first sentence, and this despite the fact that, in addition to his intellectual setback, he had his lack of patients as something to worry about. Oddly enough—one might almost say, senselessly—he had "the feeling of victory rather than of defeat." Although psychoanalytic commonsense might explain this paradoxical feeling as the outcome of denial, I would still venture to explain it in the same way as I have interpreted Hamlet's equivalent reactions—namely, as the consequence of an unconscious anticipation or knowledge of the fact that he was standing at the threshold of momentous events.[11]

Thus one seems entitled to postulate, on the basis of this letter, an almost exact replica of Hamlet's conversation with Horatio. And how *did* Freud fare? A little more than three weeks later, he held the theory in his grasp that, even though it did not bring him riches, did enable him to cure hysteria, as he had wished to do, and was to give him posthumous glory as well. What the theory said was that the male, as a boy, wishes to kill the father and to possess the mother. With this insight, Freud not only dealt a blow to illusions that were held in high esteem by his culture, he also cut the rope that had kept his own neurosis attached to him. As I see it, he accomplished with this what Hamlet had accomplished, except that his intensive work on his inner processes did not leave behind it the trail of blood that washes around Hamlet's corpse.

As the last point of similarity, which it seems unecessary to characterize as perhaps the most important, Hamlet's father had died four or five months prior to his exchange of ideas with Horatio, and Freud's fa-

---

[11] As a matter of fact, Freud wrote in the same letter: "Can it be that this doubt merely represents an episode in advance towards further knowledge?" (*Standard Edition*, 1, p. 260).

ther had died, to be exact, eleven months and two days before Freud felt "ready."[12] If we consider that *Hamlet* was written by Shakespeare either shortly before or shortly after his father's death, we may then say that the circle is closed.

At this point one may ask whether Freud really "applied" his theory to *Hamlet*. Could it not have been the other way around—namely, that his identification with Hamlet[13] was one (and possibly not the least) among the many factors that made his great discovery possible, or, at any rate, facilitated it? He wrote Fliess with regard to the oedipal involvement in *Hamlet* that he had not had it in mind to say that Shakespeare was following a conscious intention, but rather that "the unconscious in him [Shakespeare] understood the unconscious in the hero." But did not the unconscious in Freud understand the unconscious in Hamlet, when he quoted, in a desperate situation, "the readiness is all"?

One might therefore go a step further and even speculate that Freud may have discovered the Oedipus complex from his study of Shakespeare's tragic hero, as much as from his observation of clinical cases. In view of this possibility, it could very well be historically incorrect to call Freud's interpretation of Hamlet's hesitancy an "application of psychoanalysis." It may have been that Hamlet's Oedipus complex, as it was brought to life in Shakespeare's tragedy, was *one of the sources from which Freud derived his insight.* This conclusion might be correct even if it were proved that Freud was not aware of this source.

In another instance, one is able almost to prove that literary figures were not used by Freud only to demonstrate psychoanalytic theories and interpretations that he had arrived at earlier, but rather that these figures became objects of clinical study, the results of which enforced profound changes in his theory. Indeed, the artist is always ahead of the psychologist,[14] and a genius who is a playwright may be able to perceive and to represent depths of the mind to which even sharpened clinical observa-

[12] As a matter of fact, the oedipal theory was conveyed to Fliess one week before the first anniversary of the death of Jacob Freud.

[13] Identifications with characters from Shakespeare's plays should not be underestimated in Freud's life. In an unpublished manuscript (1965), I tried to reconstruct the meaning of Freud's very puzzling identification with Macbeth, which I have found to be strongly suggested by two passages in his correspondence (Freud, 1873-1939, p. 6; Freud/Pfister 1909-1939, p. 35).

[14] This can be demonstrated by way of some of Arthur Schnitzler's (1892-1931) writings. It is amazing to observe that at times Schnitzler described or presented psychic events that, only a few years later, would take a prominent place in Freud's theory formation. In the first play of the Anatol cycle: *The Question to Fate (Die Frage an das Schicksal)* (1889), Schnitzler takes as his theme the inhibition that a hypnotist suffers about asking the subject a question the answer to which he himself

tion has not yet penetrated. That is to say, literary creations may bring to the surface phenomena of the human world that are so deeply submerged in actual life and therefore overlaid by so many layers that they cannot be extrapolated from data actually observed. Such creations make the arcane observable.

Thus Freud (1933, p. 105f), in introducing the concept of a drive toward death in his *New Lectures*, exclaimed: "A queer instinct, indeed, directed to the destruction of its own organic home! Poets, it is true, talk of such things; *but poets are irresponsible people and enjoy the privilege of poetic license*" (my own italics). What conclusion may be drawn from the fact that Freud refers so quickly to the poets (it is only in the next sentence that there is a reference to their pathophysiology), when he is searching for an ally in defense of his most improbable construct?[15]

When the history of Freud's theories about death is followed up (I shall not do so here), one can observe that the first paper of Freud's in which death is assigned a central place is the one on the theme of the three caskets (1913c), in which he presents his interpretation of Cordelia as a symbol of death.[16] I therefore believe that the poet "who talks of such things," and from whom Freud may have received the first impulse toward his theory of the drive toward death, might well have been Shakespeare.[17]

Enough has been said to demonstrate that, for Freud, literary works were by no means entities, to be used either for the purpose of proving the correctness of his views or as receptacles of projected theories. Many more instances could be enumerated of Freud's approaching literary works just as he did other objects he encountered—as *stimulants toward inquiry*. Just as an hour with a patient was an occasion for him to make a new observation, to find a new pattern of explanation, which did not necessarily fit in with the ones that were already part and parcel of psychoanalysis, so he was ever ready to learn from the creations of a literary

is afraid of. This was written much earlier than Freud's research into countertransference; it contains in a nutshell the problems of anxiety and resistance as impediments to psychological research. For a different interpretation, see Kupper and Rollman-Branch (1959).

[15] Cf. Freud (1907, p. 8): "Creative writers are valuable allies and their evidence is to be prized highly, for they are apt to know a whole host of things between heaven and earth of which our philosophy has not yet let us dream. In their knowledge of the mind they are far in advance of us everyday people, for they draw upon sources which we have not yet opened for our science."

[16] For Lacan's conception of the development of Freud's thanatology—a conception that is quite different from mine—see Wilden (1966).

[17] It is noteworthy that, in his earliest division of drives into love and hunger, Freud followed, according to his own account of the matter, Friedrich Schiller.

mind.[18] He thus approached literary works as organic, live, real (the latter is here meant in a different sense from the one usually employed when one speaks of the "reality" of art). Shakespeare's creations may have been experienced by him, not as figments of the mind, or as artistic illusions, but rather as sectors of a live world that has to be analyzed in the same way as one analyzes the minds of live and really existing people.

I shall now present another similar example, because it will bring us closer to the question of the function of explaining in psychology.

Freud tried to make certain (and this is a question of principal importance) which elements of literary works are due to so-called poetic license and which are actually representative of a human reality—a problem that can also be formulated as that of the limits of psychological interpretation. Freud found in Jensen's *Gradiva* two chief elements that, to his mind, fell outside the realm of interpretability: one was the identity of physical appearance between the woman who had been the protagonist's childhood sweetheart and the woman who was depicted in the antique Gradiva bas-relief; the other was that the protagonist and the woman both take, at the same time and without knowing about each other, a trip to Naples. Consequently, they meet at the place where, in the hero's imagination, Gradiva had lived 2,000 years ago. Both elements, improbable as they are, are necessary, of course, in order to be able to put together the framework of the story at all, and may therefore be dismissed as "non-motivational" elements. Indeed, they do seem to be improbable events, enforced solely by artistic necessities.

Freud acknowledged this, but he added a remark that may incur the criticism of his having overpsychologized the events of the novel. Since the protagonist "takes flight" to Pompeii from the woman who lived next door to him—a woman of whose presence he had been unconsciously aware—and since Freud emphasized at that time the proximity of defense and the return of what had been warded off, he regarded with favor the author's use of a chance event: "for this chance reflects the fatal truth . . . that flight is precisely an instrument that delivers one over to what one is fleeing from" (1907, p. 42).[19] Flight is not always such an instrument, of course, even though it cannot be denied that sometimes flight

---

[18] Freud was certain that the writings of the great poets contained the deepest psychological insights.

[19] The belief that flight delivers one to the danger from which one is fleeing has literary precursors. I want to quote only one. In Calderón's *La Vida es Sueño* Clarin, when fatally wounded while hiding from the turmoil of battle, says: "Fleeing from it [*death*], I came/upon it . . .

does lead to results of that sort. Freud was here applying a favorite theory, which, in this context, has scarcely any explanatory value.

In the other instance, the identity of physical appearance between a woman depicted on a bas-relief two thousand years ago and a contemporary woman, Freud's ever-active ingenuity appears. He thought it would have been "a more sober choice" to limit that rather far-reaching resemblance to one single feature, such as the way both women put their foot on the ground when walking. In following "the play of our own phantasy" (l.c. p. 42), he suggested "a link with reality."

The girl's name *Bertgang,* which means "bright gait," describes someone "who steps along brilliantly"; the same thing is signified also in the name Gradiva. The name of the woman living in the present, Freud suggests, "might point to the fact that the women of that family had already been distinguished in ancient days by the peculiarity of their graceful gait" (p. 42). The girl's Germanic ancestors, one could suppose, were descended from a Roman family, one member of which was perpetuated on the ancient bas-relief. Since variations of form are interdependent and ancient types reappear, as can be observed, "it would not be totally impossible" for a contemporary person to reproduce not only the gait but all other bodily features as well of her Roman ancestors (*ibid.*).

This train of thought may for many reasons be called typical of one aspect of Freud's thinking—namely, his ability to see *through the coincidental to the essential,* to reach that point of objective reality that is manifesting itself in what merely seems accidental. The "paradigm" (Kuhn, 1962) created in this instance then led to the awe-inspiring theory laid down in the *Moses* book.[20]

The parallel between the Moses theory (a primordial trauma leaves a permanent trace in a people's history after a latency period) and the Gradiva situation (a woman's fate is decided by the fact that she has the same physical appearance as an ancestor had two thousand years ago)

---

he who flees its impact,/is the one who attains its effect . . . among weapons and fire/there is greater security/than on the most guarded mountain." I do not know whether Freud was influenced by Calderon. No reference to the playwright is found in Freud's works, although Freud was greatly interested in Spanish literature, particularly in his younger years.

[20]Dr. Stengel (1966) questions my assertion that this work of Freud's is the greatest achievement of psychoanalytic mentation. I do not know how Dr. Stengel would measure the greatness of "mentation," but I had thought that the relation between the extent of one's premises and the extent of one's conclusions was a partially tolerable yardstick. The theory that Freud built upon one contradictory element in a legend was enormous. I think that there is no other work in which Freud built so much on so little, and with unsurpassable logic to boot; that is what permits one, I feel, to accord a special place to the extraordinary mentation involved.

may appear far-fetched; but the two have this one idea in common: that the past is ineluctable, even beyond the personal boundaries. The Gradiva theory brings forth—far more strongly than any of Freud's previous writings—the idea of a repetition compulsion, which will acquire a focal position in psychoanalytic theory and later stands at the center of the Moses book.

In *Gradiva* Freud seems to have followed a sudden fancy, because he quietly dropped the thought as mere speculation. The author, he felt, should be asked for the sources of this part of his creation; then, he suggested, we would be in a position to show that "what was ostensibly an arbitrary decision rested in fact upon law" (1907, p. 43). Yet Freud had done this independently of whatever the author's sources might have been, because "access to the sources in the author's mind is not open to us."

The explanation that he offered did precisely what he had suggested: it changed arbitrariness into lawfulness. It is not, of course, a question here of speculating as to whether or not Freud's explanation was correct, but rather of emphasizing that, while a very good explanation may have been proffered, it does not contribute in any way to our better understanding either the novel or the personality of Gradiva. Thus explaining and understanding are disjoined: one could say that, in this instance, Freud's suggested explanation did not have anything to do with any psychic process, but referred instead to an improbable coincidence of two physical events.

That, of course, is quite true. But it has to do with a coincidence whose psychological meaning cannot be denied. Had the physical appearance of the woman not been identical with that of Gradiva, she would never have regained the affection of her erstwhile childhood sweetheart—and under particularly propitious circumstances, in that it facilitated displacement of her attachment to her own father. Be that as it may, the example demonstrates that explanation and understanding may not always coincide.

The one difficulty that haunts epistemological inquiry into the functions of explaining and understanding is linguistic. Both terms have a place in everyday language, but that place is filled by a variety of meanings that are sometimes contradictory, and that may also deviate from the meaning assigned to them in the objective context of psychology and the theory of cognition. Contact between human beings—daily social life—is possible only because human beings understand each other. They have tools of communication, which consist of verbal language, gestures, facial expressions—that is, of signs expressed in a variety of media and possessing meanings that are shared by all group members and therefore understood.

In most daily contacts, the function of understanding does not need to be explicitly activated; instead, it does its beneficial work silently. We say that we "understand" a man's rage and craving for revenge when we are informed that he was insulted in public, or that we "understand" a parent's heart being filled with sadness and grief, when we hear of the loss of a child, even if it did occur a long time previously. There is thus a wide range of psychological connections that are "understood" by us without further inquiry or empirical study. In other instances, however, understanding is arrived at only after a process of ratiocination of varying length. In order to "understand" Newtonian physics, for example, one has to go through a chain of interconnected explanations.

Finally, there are such theorems as: When A equals B and B equals C, A equals C. These are understood with almost the same evidential certainty as the just cited emotional instances, even though the two stem from entirely different universes of discourse and therefore have nothing in common when they are investigated in epistemological terms. The distinction between explaining and understanding evidently constitutes no problem in everyday life. When we feel puzzled, we make inquiries or ask others for explanations; as soon as we have obtained them, we respond with understanding. Nowhere are explaining and understanding experienced as constituting an antinomy, as being opposite functions.

It is different, however, when we are dealing with a scientific approach toward the world. The problem—or, as it may be called the antinomy—of explaining and understanding is a crucial one in psychology. The basic work, *Verstehen und Erklären,* the detailed study of which is indispensable for a grasp of the issues at stake, was written by H. Hartmann in 1927 and published in English as "Understanding and Explanation" (1964). It is a problem to which too little attention has been paid in this country, even though psychoanalysis as a science stands or falls with its outcome.

The problem began when Dilthey published his famous paper *Ideen über eine beschreibende und zergliedernde Psychologie* (Ideas about a describing and analyzing psychology) in 1894, which brought out precisely his views on the theoretical antinomy between explaining and understanding. At this point, I shall have to discuss the issue briefly. Dilthey distinguishes between an explaining psychology and an understanding psychology; for linguistic reasons, I shall call one *psychologia explanans* and the other *psychologia comprendens*.[21]

By *psychologia explanans* Dilthey meant all psychologies that work with the formation of hypotheses—that is to say, those that, having been impressed by the natural sciences, use their methods. *Psychologia explanans* derives psychological phenomena from "a limited number of explicit explanatory elements of hypothetical character throughout" (p. 144). Yet, aside from deriving psychological phenomena from a few hypothetical, well-defined elements, *psychologia explanans* may ignore the psyche altogether and derive those same phenomena solely from physiological factors. Dilthey demonstrated the shortcomings of a *psychologia explanans* by discussing the pathological systems of the two Mills, Spencer, Herbart, Taine and Wundt, all of whom had tried to explain psychological phenomena by the effect of factors or elements that were not directly observable or were not of a psychological nature at all. Thus, for example, they explained perception in terms of the stimulation of sense organs—or, in some instances, inner states—whose concatenations were interpreted as being parallel to processes in the nervous system.

Psychologia comprendens, by contrast, works without hypotheses. Its starting point is the totality of psychic life, as it reveals itself to consciousness. The first step is the exact description of the total live structural concatenation *(Strukturzusammenhang)*, which is not inferred from but represented directly in the everchanging contents of consciousness. For the understanding of this structural concatenation is given immediately and directly in the subjective experience. Once the structural concatenation has been described in its totality, it can then be analyzed *(zergliedert*—literally, dismembered), and thus its basic elements can be found without any need to introduce hypothetical or nonpsychological elements. On the strength of these views, Dilthey launched a vigorous attack against *psychologia explanans*, the fruitlessness of which he tried to demonstrate in all its forms, and set forth instead the principles of *psychologia comprendens*, which he accepted as the only workable and scientifically justifiable psychology.

Psychologia comprendens, by starting out from the immediately given live structural concatenation, adjusted its method to the subject

---

[21] This is necessary in order to avoid the monstrosities that might easily occur otherwise, such as "Understanding psychology understands mental life better than explaining psychology does."

matter. Here then was the essential difference between psychology and natural science: external objects are not given to the direct subjective experience in the same way as the structural concatenation is. The psychic exterritoriality, so to speak, of all objects of science necessitates the formation of hypotheses; in matters of psychology, however, hypotheses are fruitless and even destroy a scientific psychology. Dilthey tried to show that the set of hypothetical elements that one school of *psychologia explanans* uses for the derivation of psychic phenomena is just as good as that of another school, and that the choice of hypotheses is only a matter of preference or bias, and without any real consequence, since no one can explain psychic life, after all—at any rate, by means of such hypothetical elements.

By starting with a reliable and complete description of the total live structural concatenation, and then working its way to the elements through taking apart the totality, *psychologia comprendens* is able to penetrate to the core of the personality. This Dilthey found to exist in the drives and feelings (p. 185)—thereby establishing what was, at least in outward appearance, a surprising similarity with psychoanalysis.[22]

But, to return to Dilthey's principal differentiation between the basic mechanism of science and that employed in psychology (and in the humanities in general), one has to regret his choice of terminology. When someone has explained the Pythagorean theorem to our satisfaction—or perhaps the laws of motion and gravitation—we not only feel, but are entitled to say, that we now *understand* that theorem or those laws. I assume that Dilthey would not have objected to this formulation, for if I understand him correctly what he wanted to do was to differentiate between two mechanisms, both of which are employed in order to arrive at knowledge.

"In the [subjective] experience, processes of the *entire psyche* act together. In it [the subjective experience], connection is a given, whereas the senses offer only a manifoldness of singlenesses. An individual process is carried experientially by the entire totality of psychic life, and the connection in which it [the individual process] stands with itself, as well as with the totality of psychic life, belongs with the immediate experience. This is determined by the nature of the *under-*

---

[22] I have simplified Dilthey's paper, which had such grave consequences for German psychiatry and psychopathology. No one can infer from my simple summary the subtlety and sophistication of his ratiocination and, of course, I do not refer here at all to his eminent position in the history of ideas. After all, he was the first, if I am not mistaken, to assert the indispensable and basic role of psychology in the humanities.

· 477 ·

standing of ourselves and of others. We explain by means of purely intellectual processes, but we understand by way of the acting together of all psychic forces in the act of apprehension. We proceed in under-standing from the connection of the whole that is given to us as a living thing, in order to make out of it the single [element] comprehensible to us." (Author's italics; translation mine.)

[*In dem Erlebnis wirken die Vorgänge des* ganzen Gemütes *zusammen. In ihm ist Zusammenhang gegeben, während die Sinne nur ein Mannigfaltiges von Einzelheiten darbieten. Der einzelne Vorgang ist von der ganzen Totalität des Seelenlebens im Erlebnis getragen, und der Zusammenhang, in welchem er in sich und mit dem Ganzen des Seelenlebens steht, gehört der unmittelbaren Erfahrung an. Dies bestimmt schon die Natur des* Verstehens *unserer selbst und anderer. Wir erklären durch rein intellektuelle Prozesse, aber wir verstehen durch das Zusammenwirken aller Gemütskräfte in der Auffassung. Und wir gehen im Verstehen vom Zusammenhang des Ganzen, der uns lebendig gegeben ist, aus, um aus diesem das einzelne uns fassbar zu machen.* (Author's italics) (p. 172)]

Thus objects per se cannot be understood. By observation, experimentation, induction, inference and reasoning we may succeed in explaining whatever there is to explain in the reality outside our psyche. Yet it is the psyche that is given directly by way of inner experience. All we have to do is to turn toward the totality of that inner experience, describe it and then take it apart; after that, we will find the elements and their interplay, their effects and their development. And anyone who follows Dilthey's reasoning closely will agree with his momentous statement: "Nature we explain; mental life we understand" [*Die Natur erklären wir, das Seelenleben verstehen wir.* (p. 144)].

The problem of *psychologia explanans* and *psychologia comprendens* has found a revival in two recent papers by Prof. Kuiper (1964, 1965) who, by contrast with Heinz Hartmann—who has demonstrated that psychoanalysis is a *psychologia explanans*—asserts that there is a close affiliation between Dilthey's psychology and psychoanalysis. Since psychoanalysis uncovers, according to Kuiper's reasoning, unconscious motives that make actions understandable, it is a *psychologia comprendens*. He therefore accepts as explanations only the propositions of psychoanalytic metapsychology. In agreement with Heinz Hartmann, I regard this conception of psychoanalysis as untenable, in that it takes out of analysis its very marrow and backbone. Historically, it is certainly not correct.

Dilthey himself did not take cognizance of the beginnings of psychoanalysis, even though he died 11 years after the publication of *The Interpretation of Dreams*. Perhaps it never came to his attention; but even if it had, he would very probably have rejected it, as he did with every *psychologia explanans*. And from his point of view he would have been correct in doing so, for in epistemological terms, it is all the same whether conscious psychic phenomena are derived from processes in the nervous system or from the unconscious. This does not deny, of course, the well known and generally accepted fact that, in dropping his original "Project for a scientific psychology" (which he had written during the fall of 1895, and which was essentially neurologically oriented) and replacing it with an investigation into the broad area of unconscious repressed motives, Freud rendered an eminent service to psychology.[23]

Hartmann has very correctly pointed out that it is in terms of a hypothesis that psychoanalysis finds the foundation of mental processes to lie in instinctual ones (1964, p. 396). One is entitled to say, I believe, that any interpretation, in the narrower sense, when it refers to the unconscious (whether this be the repressed, the superego or the unconscious parts of the ego), is a construct and therefore hypothetical. To be sure, this construct may sooner or later be confirmed to our satisfaction by the subject's associations, actions or dreams. That satisfaction, however, is deceptive, as we shall later see.

First we have to take a closer look at the vexing problem of explanation and understanding. In that regard, it appears to me that Dilthey has set forth a valid antinomy—even though the conclusions that he drew (despite their correctness at the time he drew them) were later

---

[23] In abandoning neurologizing psychology after having completed his *Project* (Freud, 1895), Freud was not altogether original but rather followed the French example, with which he was familiar. Cf. Kris (1947, p. 336); cf. also Freud (1892, p. 135): "The clinical observation of the French undoubtedly gains in self-sufficiency in that it relegates physiological considerations to a second place."

It has its own piquancy to consider the moves and countermoves in the history of ideas during those last few years before the ending of the century: Dilthey was reading the death sentence over *psychologia explanans* in 1894, while Freud, probably without knowing of Dilthey's *psychologia comprendens*, was plotting out, almost at the same time, precisely a *psychologia explanans*, and carrying it to its most extreme consequences. By doing exactly what Dilthey had warned most strongly against, Freud carried neurologizing psychology *ad absurdum*, only to drop it and turn to creating a new *psychologia explanans*, which was to fulfill Dilthey's specifications, through its extensive use of the function of understanding.

proved to be wrong—at least so far as psychology is concerned, as the history of psychoanalysis demonstrates.

Historically it can be shown that explaining and understanding have frequently been—and, as will be seen, from a certain point of view always are—at loggerheads. The scholastic world view of the Middle Ages provided a "full understanding" of the universe: there were no gaps, no dark areas that might have puzzled man's mind. Today we know that, despite its unrivaled character as a source of "unlimited understanding," that world view had no explanatory value at all. Yet the degree of understanding that it did provide was greater than that which the scientific approach will probably ever be capable of producing—at least if current epistemological thinking is correct, with its supposed proof that a consistent system covering the universe as a whole is impossible, not only for practical but also for theoretical reasons.

The consequence of this view is that science must be expected always to have some areas unexplained. At this point one is forced to refer explanations to something objective, by contrast with understanding, which reflects solely a subjective state. The difficulty, of course, is that, in the common or literal sense, the understanding mind always has the feeling that it has been or is explaining.

The antinomy between understanding and explaining can be seen with particular sharpness if one considers Copernicus' heliocentric theory. It served one fuction brilliantly—namely, to explain the retrograde motions of the planets. But this advantage was almost trivial alongside the new unsolved problems that the theory created—for example, the state of rest of terrestrial objects (which was incompatible with a planet in motion), as well as the fact that an object that has been thrown vertically returns to exactly the point from which it has been thrown (which obviously could not happen if, in moving around the sun, the earth has changed its position). Thus a theory whose explanatory value was considerable—at least for a rather long period of time—initially left more phenomena unexplained than it explained, and certainly set new limits on the understanding of the universe, which seemed to have been understood quite well before the advent of the new theory.

Here the antinomy of explanation and understanding becomes particularly clear: whether or not I *understand* something only I can decide, since understanding reflects a subjective state; whether or not an event has been *explained*, however, cannot be decided in this subjective fashion but only objectively.

When Newton devised his theory of gravitational forces, he thereby made it possible to explain a wide area of observable data, and in due time these phenomena were "understood." It made sense to say that masses attract each other and to speak of the gravitational force as drawing all things toward the center of the earth. Yet it is questionable how many physicists would today suggest the existence of a gravitational force.

Scientific progress depends on two seemingly contradictory processes, as many have observed. These have to do with the ability to discover disorder, where necessary to *create* it in states of seeming order, and, by contrast, to discover—that is to say, to create—order out of states of seeming disorder. The scientist turns to areas of disorder within which no one has yet perceived order and in his research he is able to make new observations, or engage in speculations, which then will enable him to formulate new hypotheses and, ultimately, new theories. On the other hand, the scientist also discovers disorder in areas of seeming order: in what appears to others to be well explained, he brings to light hitherto unnoted contradictory elements and, after he has proven the existence of this disorder, he aims at new explanations that will then reestablish a state of order—at a higher level.

Freud proved his greatness in both directions: in discovering disorder in order and in establishing order out of disorder. What is most remarkable is the fact that he did not allow himself to be seduced by the understanding he had obtained through his own research, but relatively quickly discovered and revealed the disorder in that very state of order that he had created not so long before. Sometimes what made new theory necessary was a contradiction (state of disorder) that covered an area as amazingly small as that which led to his *Moses* book; but when he had formulated that new theory, he then expanded its area of relevance as far as possible, pushing toward extremes of inference, only to acknowledge later that he had learned once again how right Nestroy (the Viennese writer of comedies) was when he said: "Every step forward is only half as big as it looks at first."

The explanations set forth in the *Studies on Hysteria*, whatever their explanatory value may have been, did provide sufficient understanding of hysterical psychopathology to serve one or two generations of psychiatrists. But only a few years later Freud produced, in *The Interpretation of Dreams*, a far superior set of paradigms, which this time furnished understanding for only two decades. *The Ego and the Id*, written some 20 years later, might have provided understanding for longer than that, yet *Analysis Terminable and Interminable*, written close to the end of Freud's life, definitely announced that his unquiet mind was preparing for a new thrust. The direction in which it might have gone may be conjectured by an imaginative mind, yet it will remain forever no more than a hypothesis.

The sequence of phases in the evolvement of scientific insight seems to be: an extraordinary mind formulates explanations that offend common sense; if the formulator is lucky, a small group of similarly restless minds then become convinced of the suitability of his formulations. The advances made possible by these new formulations in the power to predict events; the increment they provide in the ability to deal with processes that are taking place in the real world; and the inner state of harmony they bring into being, as a consequence of their potential for temporarily eliminating contradictions within a limited area of the universe—all these gradually convince ever larger groups, until the new formulations, at one time rejected, wind up being taught as absolute truths in the grade schools or high schools.

Thus the conversion of new explanations, earlier regarded as violating common sense, into commonsense understanding takes place at the very time when, at the top of the scientific hierarchy, these same formulations are beginning to be recognized as internally contradictory and to be replaced by new ones, which will offend common sense as much as those explanations that they will gradually replace did earlier.

What I have referred to, without any elaboration, as "explanations," and then again as "formulations," have, of course, been made the subject of special inquiries by those who have a very serious concern about the theory of cognition. But whether one sees the progress of science as taking place through the creation of new paradigms (Kuhn), or defines the change from Newtonian to modern physics as the evolvement of a new system of decoding the messages that Nature sends us—however different may be the theoretical outlook that underlies these approaches, this does not affect the line of thought pursued in this essay. For psychologically it is always around the function of explaining that the subtleties and sophistications of modern theories of cognition revolve.[24]

At this point it may be proper to refer briefly to a somewhat less

---

[24] One of the many remarkable features in Freud's scientific career is that in one lifetime his creative potential undertook and realized a series of tasks such as is usually spread over several generations.

important aspect of understanding. When a scientist discovers a new solution or a new explanation, and particularly when this has achieved the dignity of a paradigm, in Kuhn's sense, he is often stirred to a temporary feeling of triumph. He has suddenly understood something that, only a short time before, had been an enigma. At that moment he is fully aware of the explanatory value of his finding. When these same paradigms become popular, however, and are absorbed by a whole generation; when they have become routinized—that is to say, made part and parcel of common sense—then they become, at least psychologically, vehicles of understanding rather than of explaining.

This is, indeed, one characteristic of the present phase of psychoanalysis. When Professor Kuiper asserts that psychoanalysis is chiefly a *psychologia comprendens*—that, in analyzing a patient, we discover unconscious motives, which make it possible for both the analyst and the subject to understand better the latter's feelings, thoughts and actions—most analysts, I assume, would agree. It may therefore sound paradoxical for me to say, in agreement with Hartmann, that psychoanalysis is nevertheless a *psychologia explanans*.

Psychoanalysis is now in a phase comparable to the phase in which physics was after Newton. Despite considerable differences of opinion and some rather large gaps in our knowledge, one has the impression that man's mind is now by and large understood. We do not have a well-defined yardstick that would clearly demonstrate the lacunae of knowledge, as the physicist and the biologist have. Yet all this is a reflection of the atmosphere during the heyday of Newtonian physics in the 19th century, when physicists did not "explain" but rather followed along the lines of the common sense that had been created by Newton's "explanations." There is, by contrast, scarcely any analyst who, despite his basic agreement with Freud's work, does not disagree sharply with at least one of Freud's findings or theoretical positions.

If all these "proofs of error" were to be put together, hardly any part of Freud's work would retain its validity. For this, it is not necessary to go so far as to include the critique of the neo-Freudian schools: I believe that an adding up of the varieties of criticism that Freud's work has found among those who would unhesitatingly regard themselves as following him closely would in itself produce that result. Curiously enough, no one critic would agree with the criticisms made by other critics. By and large he would say that to the best of his knowledge, only that part with which he himself disagrees is wrong; criticism of the other parts is unwarranted.

No doubt, psychoanalysis finds itself, in this respect, in an odd position. Its disordered condition should not be equated with the divergence of opinions that is regularly to be found in all advancing fields of science. In my opinion, it is due rather to the decline that our science has suffered through its having been perverted to a common-sense scheme, thereby losing its explanatory value.

From the psychological points of view, it seems to me that understanding in science almost always makes out of the content of explanations empathetic[25] processes. I am almost inclined to say that it is only when an explanation has been made empathetic that we evolve the feeling of understanding. Adler's psychological theories, for example, are much better suited for empathy than are psychoanalytic theories. This explains, on the one hand, their popularity and, on the other, the tendency of many psychoanalysts to simplify psychoanalytic theories in such a way as to make them hardly distinguishable from Adler's.

Some areas of psychoanalytic theory do not lend themselves well to empathy; these include the correlation that has been found between anality and avarice or pedantry (Hartmann, 1964, p. 394). The explanatory value of such constructs is enormous, even though they are scarcely to be described as empathetic.[26] On the other hand, constructs may be empathetic and yet wrong, because they do not *explain* anything.

Psychoanalysis is therefore a science only insofar as it *explains*, even though the temper of the times tends to demand and expect from depth psychology empathetic statements. Prof. Kuiper (1964, p. 25) even goes so far as to defend psychoanalysis against the reproach of being a *psychologia explanans*—a reproach that has been raised in some quarters, in which Dilthey's axiomatic statement on the methodology and task of psychology has been accepted. Prof. Kuiper, as we have already noted, ascribes only to psychoanalytic metapsychology the dignity of providing explanations; he criticizes psychoanalysts who use empathetic and metapsychological statements side by side.

It may appear as if he were right, when the structure of Freud's book on *The Interpretation of Dreams* is checked along these lines. Up to the seventh chapter, Freud presented all the observations he had made in

[25] By empathetic I mean what Hartmann's translator called "empathizable," when he was translating the German word *einfühlbar*.

[26] It was precisely this construct that earned Freud the greatest ridicule. It would be interesting to investigate whether or not the area covered by resistance is fairly identical with the unempathetic.

his analyses of his patients' dreams and his own—such as the bearing of day residues, the differentiation of manifest and latent dream content, the variety of mechanisms involved in dreamwork, and many more—only to declare suddenly, in the seventh chapter, that all that does not really explain the dream. He then proceeded to reconstruct the structure that a system must possess in order for it to be able to produce dreams.

The reader was able to follow Freud, in the first six chapters of his book, without being aware that everything that he himself was grasping required, for its explanation, an elaborate metapsychology. Just as, in Newton's theories, forces (for us, perhaps, like animistic spirits) are "understood" to have effects on the movements of objects, so in the first six chapters of Freud's book the reader was able to visualize unpleasant memories as being cathected with energies that were then displaced onto other more neutral images, which fitted into other unpleasant contexts and thereby acquired at last sufficient energy to form a dream. In the seventh chapter, however, a different demand was put on the reader's "understanding." It was no longer a matter of understanding empathetic processes, but of grasping the structure of a system.

The break between the sixth and seventh chapters of *The Interpretation of Dreams* has particular bearing upon our subject matter. Freud (1900, p. 511) asserts: "To explain a thing means to trace it back to something already known." This strikes me as being particularly un-Freudian when I compare it with Nietzsche's (1869-1871, p. 253): "All enlargement of our knowledge originates from the making conscious of the unconscious" [*Alle Erweiterung unsrer Erkenntnis entsteht aus dem Bewusst-machen des Unbewussten*]. That was a most profound insight, which nevertheless did not prevent Nietzsche from writing later (1882-1888, p. 127)—exactly as Freud was to do in 1900—"*Explanation:* The expression of a new thing by means of signs of something already known" [*'Erklärung': das ist der Ausdruck eines neuen Dinges vermittels der Zeichen von schon bekannten Dingen*]. Yet Freud, as Hartmann has pointed out, did not always differentiate in his terminology between explaining and understanding, as can be observed when he uses the term "meaningful" where "causally determined" is what is actually meant (Hartmann, 1964, p. 400).[27]

---

[27] It seems that Nietzsche, too, did not (at least at one point) differentiate between explaining and understanding. Cf. Nietzsche's just quoted definition of explaining with the following: ' "to understand' means naively only: to be able to express something new in the language of something old and known" "*Verstehen" das heisst naiv bloss: etwas Neues ausdrücken können in der Sprache von etwas Altem, Bekanntem* (Nietzsche, 1884-1888, p. 11).

What strikes the reader as being a break between the sixth and seventh chapters of *The Interpretation of Dreams* was therefore only apparent and not real—if it is judged from Freud's vantage point. In his inquiry into or, better, in his original attempt to cure neurotic patients, Freud found explanations for the patients' symptoms. Some (or probably many) of these explanations were of a kind that permitted empathy—that is to say, they consisted of unconscious images, thoughts, wishes, all of which are empathetic and can be reexperienced directly by the observer as phenomena to which he himself could conceivably be subjected.

That, in so doing, Freud did not proceed in the way that Dilthey proposed, and that he probably did not gain his insights primarily by empathy but rather by observation and the search for causes—both these can be regarded as being almost proven by the fact that some of the "explanations" that he found are scarcely empathetic, in fact almost inaccessible to empathy. These include the just-mentioned transformation of the anal drive into a well-delineated character picture. Since he was apparently guided far less by the needs of understanding than by those of explaining, it is small wonder that, despite all the insights that he had reported in the first six chapters, he did not stop there, but rather announced that the real work now had to begin—at exactly the point at which "the merely understanding mind" would have stopped.

Metapsychology is not, as Prof. Kuiper asserts, an edifice built up on explanatory statements, by contrast with the interpretations given the patient, which, according to him, are part and parcel of a *psychologia comprendens*. In any interpretation that is given, a metapsychological statement is implicit. For obvious reasons, this built-in metapsychology is only infrequently—if at all—verbalized to the patient. But when a hostile intent, which is thus far still unconscious to the patient, is recognized by the analyst, and when subsequently the latter interprets it to the patient by way of reference to a series of symptoms, dreams and let us assume also apraxias, in all of which psychic formations this hostility is shown to be the common element—one consequence may be the patient's asking why he himself has not had any cognizance of that intent. If, at that point, we thought it technically advisable to answer the question, we would have to tell him that the intent has been repressed, that his consciousness is opposed not only to these impulses but to many more. Some of these statements would necessarily be metapsychological by nature.[28]

Metapsychology should be no more than an abstract formulation of the analyst's findings.[29] Large portions of current metapsychology are the products of speculation and in that regard open to question. It thus becomes questionable whether metapsychological statements are explanatory at all; if they are, however, it would be misleading to take this aspect as differentiating them from contents obtained by interpretations.[30] To be sure, there is some sort of similarity between the interpretation of sense perceptions that takes place when the bacteriologist observes a slide and the interpretation of free associations that is made by the analyst. But similar or dissimilar as these two forms of interpretation may be— and a vast literature has accumulated around this question—what is essential is that both set out to *explain* objective data.

If Freud had aimed at understanding, his mind would have come to rest much earlier; it was because he used the methods of natural science that he was unceasingly propelled from one explanation to another. For one peculiarity of explaining is that there is no end to it: no explanation is feasible that would be final. If science were approached from another vantage point, one would have to say that, if one single phenomenon were to be *fully* explained, the entire universe would be, too—and by that same process.[31]

The view that maintains that all parts of the universe, even the smallest ones, are interconnected, that a change in any one part of the universe has some effects upon the whole—that view is probably tenable and perhaps even a necessary assumption. If one takes into consideration, further, the fact that a full explanation of any one element in the universe requires knowledge of its entire history, both past and future— that is to say, that the "complete" explanation of a simple apraxia would

---

[28]Kuiper warns us against using technical language with the patient and I heartily agree. However, the problem of what to tell a patient and what not to tell him is a technical one; it has no place in an inquiry into the structure of various types of psychoanalytic propositions, that is to say, of psychoanalysis as a science.

[29] I am aware that some problems of metapsychology may be purely speculative and cannot therefore be regarded as abstractions from observations (or from assumptions necessitated by observations). But the bulk of Freud's metapsychology was an abstraction from the observable.

[30] See Gedo *et al.* 1964, for a structuring of types of psychoanalytic propositions according to levels of abstraction.

[31] Cf. Mill's (1843, p. 207f) generalization of the law of causation, which amounts to asserting that complete knowledge of the state of the whole universe at any instant includes knowledge of both its past and its future. Since all single elements of the universe are by their nature interconnected, the application of Mill's general formulation to single elements is entailed in the law itself.

require knowledge not only of the subject's psychological history, but also that of his ancestors, as well as his ancestors' organic substructure (which would take us back not only to the origin of man but also to the beginnings of life and indeed of the planet)—then one will readily recognize that science has never succeeded in "truly" or "fully" explaining anything.

What it has been able to do is to establish interconnections among some elements of the universe. Scientists are forced to cut out of the universe a certain section of it, and to look at that section as if it were indeed self-contained. When psychoanalysis explains an apraxia, it follows it through only a short portion of its history; the explanation that it offers is therefore of necessity only a partial one. In pointing out that a dream is overdetermined, Freud stated that one never knows whether or not a dream has been adequately explained. Yet it is not only dreams, symptoms and even apraxias that are overdetermined. If the method of psychoanalysis were that of understanding, as Dilthey recommended, we would indeed know when a phenomenon is "understood"; but there is no place in Dilthey's psychology for the concept of "overdetermination" that is essential to psychoanalysis.

Professor Kuiper sets forth a few clinical examples in order to demonstrate how the method of understanding works, and scarcely anyone who analyzes patients will differ with the examples he presents. Every analyst, of course, seeks to *understand* his patients' motives, and does so in a large number of instances, during almost every hour of his working day. If the term "to understand" is used as it is used in the vernacular of everyday life, Professor Kuiper may be right. But his two papers, if I understand them correctly, are meant to solve problems of the theory of science.

Moreover, one has to be aware that almost all psychoanalytic propositions are hypothetical—that is, except for an eventuality that I am not considering at this point. Freud was aware of such a possibility, as is known from his letters, in which he expressed doubt that very much of his work would prove to be lasting truths. Yet it is precisely in this that the greatness of his work lies—even though it is overlooked by his critics and perhaps as well by many of his followers. Findings established by *psychologia comprendens* of the kind that Dilthey postulated will remain valid forever, because they do not *explain* anything but are merely descriptions. We know that accurate descriptions are not superseded; only explanations are.

The fact that psychoanalysis is throughout a *psychologia explanans* makes it certain that it will be superseded by a new psychology. Understanding, however, finds an all too early satisfaction. When we experience understanding, we are admitting a limitation, a defect, because in so doing we are manifesting either indifference toward the contradictions in existing explanations or our belief that all the facts are now indeed known.

If I knew for certain that the bulk of the psychoanalytic system, as we know it today, would still be valid in let us say one or two centuries, instead of being superseded by vastly improved explanations, I would be strongly inclined to agree with Prof. Kuiper that there is little explanatory value in psychoanalytic propositions. Paradoxical as this may seem, it is an unwarranted underestimation of psychoanalysis if one believes that its truth is permanent; up to now only descriptive statements have shown that quality. We may be certain that our textbooks of anatomy, as far as their description of structures and their topography are concerned, will not change greatly in the future; yet what a textbook of physiology will contain 50 years from now is anybody's guess. Understanding is *au fond* the enemy of explaining: it says that a satisfactory explanation has been found, even though we should know that there are no satisfactory explanations.[32]

One might therefore postulate that the truly scientific mind would discover new explanations and, at one and the same time, the defects necessarily contained in them. Ideal as this may appear to be, such a mind would live in chaos; it would never be capable of explaining anything. What seems like a defect of the human mind, as revealed in the experience of understanding, is actually an indispensable tool, for it enables us to make right choices. One needs a steering wheel of some sort, in order to be able to navigate among a huge number of explanatory possibilities. The history of science shows that correct explanations are often found at two or more places at approximately the same time; but it also shows that a great variety of different explanations for the same problem are often offered simultaneously, just as a variety of explanations all come at once to a man's mind, when he is in search of the right answer to a puzzling problem.

---

[32] Nietzsche (1884-1888; p. 13) has put it in a nutshell: "In so far as the word 'recognition' has any sense at all, the world is unrecognizable; but it is *interpretable*; it has no sense behind itself, but [it does have] innumerable senses" [Soweit überhaupt das Wort "Erkenntnis" Sinn hat, ist die Welt unerkennbar; aber sie ist anders *deutbar*, sie hat keinen Sinn hinter sich, sondern unzählige Sinne.].

If man's mind had at its disposal only the function of explaining, it would wander helplessly among a network of feasible explanations. Understanding makes it possible for him to steer through the bewildering variety of possible explanations, by pulling out of a large number of possible choices the one that best fits a particular situation and thus setting the mind temporarily at rest. In the genius, that state of rest does not take long and the arrest is therefore of short duration. Sometimes, however, it takes generations before a mind cannot any longer *understand* what had previously seemed to be so well explained.

In the long run, of course, understanding does not endanger scientific progress. The differences that separate one generation from another stand in the way of any quiet settling down on found and fond solutions. Routinized explanations become boring, contradictions in the established theoretical edifice are discovered, and then new facts are searched for—and found. A period of waiting sets in for the emergence of some richly endowed mind that will produce a new set of explanations or, better, paradigms.

It is well known that the atom still poses a number of unsolved problems; in all probability, science will never reach the point at which atomic physics can be said to have been completed. Is it likely that we have really made profound advances in the explanation of human behavior, if, after centuries of experimental research in physics, the atom still poses so many profound problems?

Common sense would therefore say that many a generation of research will have to pass before psychology will have succeeded in creating anything that can be even approximately compared with contemporary physics, in terms of exactness and profundity of understanding. Yet there is a faint possibility that we may be profoundly mistaken. Is a structure necessarily more complicated than its parts? Let's take a weathercock. It is easy to know everything there is to know about a weathercock; it is a simple instrument whose function and working can be understood by a child; it can be easily produced, even by an unskilled person. Yet if it is made out of metal, its parts are scarcely understood.[33] One does not know for sure what a metal is; once again we find ourselves face to face with the problem of the atom. *Mutatis mutandis*, one may conclude that it is an incredibly complicated substructure, the brain, that leads to a relatively simple organ, the mind.

Needless to say, what I am about to suggest is highly improbable—

---

[33] Cf. Rothacker (1954, p. 276) who rightly says that the simple hammering in of a nail is "theoretically inexhaustible."

except that improbability is not always the hallmark of error. There is a possibility, faint as it may be, that Freud cannot be truly spoken of as the Newton of psychology because he will not be followed by an Einstein or a Planck. Much will depend on what is found out about the infant. Is the infant's mind a less complicated structure or a more complicated one than the adult's? Present-day common sense would say that, for many reasons, an infant is of course simpler than an adult. In general, I assume, the simple is better understood than the complex; yet I think there is agreement that psychology knows more about the adult mind than about the infant's. That could perhaps be explained by the adult's rich ability to communicate, whereas the infant (like the animal) can be observed only from the outside and not from the inside. While that may be correct, one has to remember that the infant's mind is structured in such a way that it may develop in any of a number of different directions, whereas a more mature mind can move in only one or a few directions.

It is conceivable that a mind that possesses an unrealized potentiality for a huge variety of developments is more complicated than a mind that has already realized one of these directions and has even exhausted its potential in it. It is also possible that the degree of complexity depends on the number of unrealized potentialities that a structure contains, rather than on its functional differentiation. If this were indeed so, the historical comparison I made earlier between physics and psychology would have been wrong from the start.

Be that as it may, the one conclusion that I would derive from the foregoing reasoning seems to me to be valid: one should describe as a true explanation only one that goes beyond the common sense of the historical period. The scientist whose explanations move within the framework of contemporary understanding follows common sense; he is probably not activating the function of explanation, or only to a moderate degree. At this point, he should already have become puzzled by the loopholes that must gradually have become apparent to him in the set of explanations that have been by this time reduced to the level of commonsense thinking. Yet it is his "understanding" that prevents him from becoming aware of precisely these areas of difficulty, and the correct description would therefore be that he is applying his understanding but not explaining.[34]

[34] In my opinion, this is one of the more characteristic features of present-day psychoanalytic research. The reproaches of rigidity, unoriginality, stagnation and the like, which have been raised against the school of analysis that follows Freud, are partly justified. A psychoanalytic common

* * *

This rather ponderous discussion of *psychologia explanans* and *psychologia comprendens* has not taken us as far from *Hamlet* as it may have seemed to, for there are critics who accept character analysis as a method of literary criticism only if it will lead to a better understanding. When Freud *explains* Hamlet's hesitation by reconstructing Hamlet's childhood Oedipus complex, has he helped us to understand Hamlet any better? He has undoubtedly explained Hamlet's hesitation. If it were not known from innumerable instances of people who have undergone psychoanalysis that children, during the process of growing up into psychological adulthood, regularly develop specific wishes and impulses of the sort that Claudius did carry out in reality, the analyst would never have arrived at the idea of finding in the defense against such impulses and wishes the key to Hamlet's hesitation.

If we regard the tragedy as a self-contained system, one has to admit that one cannot find any direct clue to this solution of the problem. It therefore becomes understandable that the reconstructed infantile Oedipus complex should seem to many critics to be as alien to the development of the tragedy, as the assumption that an encephalitic inflammation must have taken place in Hamlet when he was a child. An astute scholar of comparative literature, however, might well raise the question of whether the outspoken parent-child triangle that appears in *Oedipus Rex* and *The Brothers Karamazov* may not also lie at the root of *Hamlet*.

Yet he, too, would face the charge of carrying into the tragedy an observation that he had derived from outside it. The only difference would be that, if one put Hamlet's Oedipus complex in between two literary works and thus rested the proof of its existence on objects of the same class, the literary mind might have less trouble accepting an explanation that sounded annoying when it came from the medical profession, yet would sound aesthetically acceptable when limited to three literary works of world renown.

---

sense has evolved that now provides a sentiment of understanding, and, without intending to, impedes the search for new explanations. Yet this criticism should not induce anyone to accept the theories of those who want to break out of the stalemate, even at the price of false theories, only in order to evade the stigma of unoriginality. It is to be expected, of course, that the mind that will provide a new push to psychology will probably be misunderstood initially, just as Freud was.

The literary critics who rejected Freud's explanation were essentially correct in doing so, because it was an explanation that did not enlarge their understanding. For the analyst it is different: he has no doubt of the correctness of Freud's construct. Still, one facet of Freud's approach to literary works should be made clear. He did not—as he has been accused of doing—abuse these works by reducing them to agents through which to confirm pet theories of his. He approached them in the same spirit with which he approached everything else he encountered in life: as a possible source of new insights.

The new insights that he derived from literary works fell, of course, into a broad network of assumptions—or better, interpretations—that he had gradually formed about life and man's mind. But even in this area he aimed at explanations, despite the fact that these may appear to the superficial eye in the guise of understanding. That he did not bend the literary work so as to make it fall into his already established explanatory schemata, but rather responded readily to facets of the work that did not coincide with his accustomed explanations—this the reader may now be ready to accept with greater willingness than when he was reading the beginning of this essay, in which I presented the source material.

B. A Psychosociological View

The relations between sociology and psychology—some maintain that they are independent of each other; others that one can replace the other—have been debated so often and by so many that no comment on them should be expected in this context. Yet it may be useful to examine a psychoanalytic interpretation of *Hamlet* in which it is the sociological viewpoint that has actually prevailed.

A suitable example to start with, because its shortcomings are easily detectable, seems to me to be the essay by Friedman and Jones (1963), in which Erik Erikson's theories are applied to the play. The authors reproach "Psychological Man," by which they apparently mean psychoanalysts, particularly Ernest Jones, for yielding to the "temptation . . . to reinterpret alien geniuses as mere Freudian forerunners."

They would apparently prefer these "alien geniuses" to be reinterpreted as forerunners of Prof. Erikson—which is what they themselves do, as will be seen presently. While they try to demonstrate that "Shakespeare can be instrumental in broadening the psychoanalytic theory of the Oedipus complex itself," they overlook the fact that everything they derive from the tragedy is an aspect that has been frequently described before them. Like so many others, they use the play only to confirm their own views.

Their first objection to Jones is that he (why they do not extend this criticism to include Freud is not clear) did not see "Hamlet's behavior in an adaptive perspective." In order to accomplish that themselves, they "move from the psychodynamic to the psychosocial level of analysis." By contrast with Jones, who finds the play's chief focus to lie in Hamlet's conflicts, the authors approvingly quote Fergusson (1949, p. 113): "We see that the welfare of Denmark . . . is the matter of the play as a whole, rather than Hamlet's individual plight." If we look more closely at the particular context from which they choose their quotation, however, it will be evident that they are quoting Fergusson where he is at his weakest.

In his polemic against Robertson's untenable claim that the Polonius-Laertes-Reynaldo scenes cannot be justified, Fergusson quite rightly discovers in these scenes "a comic-pathetic subplot, with many ironic parallels to the story of Hamlet and his father's Ghost." And since Polonius, Laertes and Reynaldo do have a stake in the welfare of Denmark, ergo—or so reasons Fergusson—the welfare of Denmark is the matter of the play.

As I have tried to indicate previously, however, all these scenes are quite potent variations on the theme of oedipal involvement; the discourses that take place among the three characters really contain hardly anything about the particular stakes each has in the welfare of Denmark. Instead, one encounters in them outspokenly intense psychological involvements, such as worries about the well-being of the younger generation, which is constantly being exposed to dangers. It is these very scenes that tip the scales in favor of a psychological approach, by pushing the oedipal conflict into the center of dramatic tension. And I do not say this in order to cast doubt on Fergusson's general theory of social involvements.

Furthermore, there is really no problem about the welfare of the State, which is quite clearly presented. The audience is rather precisely informed about the danger to Denmark: the King has obtained his power through a criminal act, but the crime has been left unpunished. Without Hamlet's intercession, the manifest truth would have been established of what *is* true so far in this case and is most feared by society—namely, that crime *does* pay. The psychologist quite rightly, therefore, addresses himself to the question that Hamlet himself poses: "Why do I hesitate?" The fact that he has the task of restoring the welfare of the State would seem to add an important motive to the many *conscious* ones that speak in favor of his carrying out the deed of revenge and punishment.[1]

[1] Another avenue of sociological criticism with regard to the main point of the Freud-Jones theory of Hamlet is to be encountered in Elkins (1959, p. 124). He raises his argument within the con-

Freud and Jones were right, therefore, in focusing on the theme of Hamlet's *internal* reasons for hesitation, since that is obviously the primary center of psychological concern. The question of the welfare of the State finds its proper place in a psychological analysis, as soon as any doubt has been cast on the appropriateness of Hamlet's intent to kill. I am convinced that to be distracted in any way from the *subjective* nature of Hamlet's conflict, to doubt in any way his conviction that, since his father, the rightful head of the Senate, was killed by the man who now sits on Denmark's throne, it is his *duty* to remove that man from the earth's surface—to do this is to do less than justice to the full depth of the tragedy.

Friedman and Jones are clearly wrong, however, when they invoke Prof. Erikson's idea of a society that is in need of rejuvenation, a society in which rituals have lost their power. The hero-King Fortinbras will in fact follow the same rituals as Old Hamlet and Claudius did. There is no indication of any need for a restructuring of society; it is solely a question of an exchange of personalities, the casting off of a criminal representative of power and his replacement by a guiltless one. I cannot stress sufficiently the circumstances (never fully verbalized yet scarcely deniable) that surround this new and innocent hero-King Fortinbras—namely, that he has not known either his father or his mother, and that his hands have never been bloodied by killing (except where this was done for "professional" reasons).

There is something rotten in the State of Denmark, but it is that the oedipal crime has been perpetrated, not that rituals per se are ineffective. If they are ineffective, it is because they are being performed by bloody hands; indeed, if under such circumstances they were effective, they would be self-abrogating. The fact that rituals are ineffective when they

---

text of "role-playing,"—an approach that has always impressed me as being the most superficial view among the many employed at present for the purpose of "explaining" human conduct. Elkins criticizes Jones for not considering "the problem in terms of role-conflict (Hamlet as prince, son, nephew, lover, etc., has multiple roles which keep getting in the way of one another)." I do not want to go into the matter of whether or not Jones really did not consider such factors but would simply point out that in his criticism of Jones, Elkins has missed the point, inasmuch as, by themselves, the conflicts among this variety of functions are not at all sufficient to provide any significant explanation of Hamlet's hesitation.

Elkins' objection implies an almost total reduction of the weight of unconscious motives and causation. Furthermore, the difficulty arising from the multidimensionality of the social world in which Hamlet moves can lead only to intrasystemic, conscious conflicts; it does not explain Hamlet's violent self-accusations, or, more importantly, his quite patent bewilderment vis-à-vis an inhibition that he is unable either to trace or to understand, since it is, after all, a shadow that the *repressed* has cast upon the ego.

are performed by a criminal hand is actually proof of their vitality, their good health, their reliability. Fortinbras will invoke a council, just as Claudius did; there will be an oration from the throne, embassies will be sent out, the paraphernalia of government will go on just as they did under the last King; only this time they will work effectively (that, at least, is the illusion) because the dispenser of ritual is himself innocent. All that is not spelled out, of course, but it is certainly implied, just as it is a foregone conclusion that after the dénouement Cinderella and the prince will live in conflict-free marriage to the end of their days.

Jones and Friedman do not limit themselves, however, merely to calling attention to Fergusson's sociological interpretation. In my opinion, Fergusson's approach is in no way incompatible with the psychoanalytic approach, and does do justice to the tragic aspect of life and to *Hamlet*. Yet Friedman and Jones, in their attempt to complement Fergusson's theory of the Welfare State (according to them, he has noted only "phenotypical signs of societal decay"), proceed to set forth "the genotypical source" of Denmark's rottenness. The latter they find in the child-rearing practices to which the children of Denmark (as the authors reconstruct it) must have been exposed!

With one stroke of the pen, the authors thus reduce the tragic fabric of Western culture, perhaps of culture in general, to little more than a farce. We are apparently to believe that, if only old Laius had employed the right child-rearing methods, he could have counteracted the oracle; not to speak of Karamazov, who would have profited so greatly if only he had had the benefit of a child guidance clinic! The mental hygiene movement seems intent on snuffing out the eternal truths to which Sophocles, Shakespeare and Dostoevski have given voice.

To be sure, in Shakespeare's *Hamlet*, the Oedipus complex is hidden like the figure in a *Vexierbild* ("find-the-figure") (Freud, 1942, p. 309; 1928, p. 188f) (which is also one of the reasons why the play has given rise to so much more thinking about it than either *Oedipus Rex* or *The Brothers Karamazov*). Yet once one discovers that Fortinbras grew up without having laid eyes on either father or mother, one recognizes that Shakespeare's design far transcends any range of problems such as might have been solved by the institution of proper child-rearing techniques.

The authors infer from the theme of spying that appears so regularly, in one or another form, throughout the tragedy, that spying by adults on children and youths was the preferred technique of bringing up children in Denmark. The conclusion they then arrive at, however, is not in any way entailed by their premise. The reason why as adults some people get into trouble may very well be the discrepancy between the child-rearing practices by which they were brought up and the techniques of the adult world.

Moreover, it is my impression that, if the spying theme in *Hamlet* is to be brought into connection at all with child-rearing practices, it has to be viewed in the context of the Almighty, about whom the child learns that He is all-seeing, so that every good Christian *ought* to feel himself to be constantly observed. It is quite possible that Shakespeare may be indirectly referring here to a sentiment that is essentially divorced from any element of the child-rearing that is characteristic of a particular locale, and may be one "existential" aspect of Christian pessimism or optimism, whichever one chooses.

Even if the authors' reconstruction of Danish child-rearing practices were correct, they would still be guilty of drawing untenable conclusions. *Hamlet* is the tragedy of life, and it is one of the cheaper illusions to believe that, if only children were raised in the way in which the academician has it all mapped out that they should be, life would become beautiful, pleasant, devoid of tragedy.

Once a pregnant woman, in great alarm because she had heard so often that it is the mothers who are the cause of their progeny's later ill-fate, came to August Aichhorn's Child Guidance Clinic in Vienna, and asked him to tell her how she ought to raise her baby, in order to keep such dire consequences from happening. "Give birth to the baby," Aichhorn told her, "and come back again six months later. I will tell you then what you have done wrong." He faced the issue squarely and honestly, never encouraging anyone to build false hopes on what would prove to be no more than quicksand.

Freud's insights, when they are applied to child-rearing, offer the hope that, under propitious conditions, neurotic solutions of the oedipal conflict may be, in individual instances, averted. Analytic experience and theory have broadened since Freud, and the range of psychopathology that it is possible to keep from occurring has been enlarged. But what the tragic characters have to suffer in *Hamlet* is formidable, to an extent that no human being is prepared to bear. When the authors speak of "the ease with which Laertes, Ophelia, Rosencrantz and Guildenstern become mere extensions of their elders' intrigues," they focus on one aspect of the tragedy that has come to the attention of many and which I have also stressed. (But I do hope that I too have not stopped at that.)

There is a very touching portrait of Ophelia in one of those pre-depth psychology studies (Bucknill, 1859), which is worthwhile reading (even though it does not contain a single psychological discovery), for it does present a richness of character traits and breadth of problems, united in this one character. When Ophelia is cast down into madness, a century that is addicted to "mental hygiene" may castigate such a deplorable downfall by calling it "maladjustment," "ego weakness," or "identity crisis." (The authors mentioned at the start of this essay "would expect the young of this society to grow up with weakened will and blunted purpose.") But are there child-rearing practices that could release the young into the adult world strong enough to be able to bear a conflict that centers in the father's murder by the lover?

There are mental torments so formidable that anyone who has gone through them without retaining a deep psychic scar can truly be regarded as severely pathological, even non-human. We are here face to face with almost the same folly that one encounters in Prof. Bettelheim's (1960) book on concentration camps. There is *no* preparation possible for psychic survival in concentration camps.

A strong man could perhaps survive without taint many years of solitary confinement and repeated physical torture; perhaps, when optimal psychological conditions are given, man should be capable of overcoming even the memory of the most atrocious sufferings on his own part. But once a man has been forced to witness unspeakable sufferings in *others* and to stand by passively, without any chance of raising a protecting or revenging hand, he has indeed lost the right to smile again, to be "normal." If he is normal, then he is sicker than the person whose sleep is beset with nightmares, or who is incapacitated for earning his livelihood. In some places, both *Hamlet* and *Lear* come close to a concentration-camp atmosphere (Kettle, 1964).

It speaks in favor of Ophelia's sensitivity, her understanding of life and its values, her affection for her father and her passionate love of Hamlet that, when her father has been murdered by her lover, she breaks off her ties to the world and takes flight into her archaic, although no less tragic dream world. She is right; she does not have any valid reason to remain in a world in which what she has been subjected to can possibly come to pass. Her insanity can thus be appraised as a sign of ego strength (cf. Nunberg, 1939; Hartmann, 1952, p. 177); with it she flings the gauntlet right into the face of a cruel world and a cruel society.

I may be reproached here with cheaply romanticizing mental sickness. What comes to mind is a story I was once told. When a physician who was in analysis with Freud, and whose character Freud apparently did not esteem highly because of his insincerity, once complained about having been impotent with his wife, Freud is said to have replied: "*Herr Kollege*, this is the first thing you have told me about yourself that is a manifestation of sincerity." If this story is not "legend" (it rings true to me, and was related to me by a person for whose reliability I feel inclined to vouch), I regret that Freud never published it, for it covers a chapter of psychopathology that is generally ignored.

Of course, the dimension to which Freud referred in his remark is present, even though infinitesimally, in most manifestations of psychopathology. The basic structure of adult psychopathology—I apologize here for what may be an almost unforgivable simplification—is that of a compromise between a basic repressed wish and a basic superego prohibition. With these primary dimensions of the symptom are linked certain secondary gains, one of which is well-known to the psychoanalyst in the form of a pleasure gain derived from external reality—for example, when a neurotic patient obtains a pension in compensation for a neurotic symptom. I would here add a secondary *moral* gain in addition to the success of the primary superego interdict.

Just as, in some cases, the secondary gain is highly inflated and the primary gain is to be discovered only after a long search, so too the secondary moral gain may be, in rare instances, enormous. This is, perhaps, the case with Ophelia's insanity. Under more propitious (or is it under more unpropitious?) psychological circumstances, another subject would have retired to a convent. It would probably have been a great lie, if Ophelia had maintained that mimimum of positive relationship to the world that is a prerequisite for even minimal normal functioning of the psychic apparatus.

The structure of the world, as it was unfolding under her eyes, was unacceptable; to go on living, therefore, would imply on her part, a "yes" to the world, however faint that "yes" might be. Had Ophelia been more aggressive, she would have fallen into melancholia. Her final disease still carries the sweetness of her love and the yearning for the fulfillment of finest womanhood. Her insanity thus also embodies an act of supreme morality.

What the sociologically-minded authors seem to overlook is that Ophelia, Hamlet and Laertes, having all developed into fine specimens of their society, were suddenly thrown into unendurable states of conflict. The sociologically-oriented psychoanalyst thereupon exclaims. "What kind of society is it that involves young people in such conflicts?" I shall take this up later, when I try to show that the authors have misunderstood the sociological "message" that *Hamlet* contains.

Jones and Friedman believe that the "mutuality" of the Oedipus complex, which they regard as Prof. Erikson's significant enrichment of the oedipal theory, can also be derived from *Hamlet*. I will not trace here the history of this concept in psychoanalytic theory, but instead sketch briefly what is, in detail, the most complete presentation of which I am aware.

August Aichhorn regarded the family as a dynamic field in which a variety of forces act both with each other and against each other. Stronger forces act along the pathways of least resistance; since children are the weaker members of the family, those parental forces that have not been neutralized almost always victimize the child.

Aichhorn's conceptualization was the key to his superb technique. It was formulated in such a way as to facilitate the description of the total family situation, in conceptions of the topographic, dynamic and economic aspects of psychoanalytic metapsychology. It is wide enough to include both the use and the abuse of traditional child-rearing practices, parental psychopathology as well as that of the child. Jekels (1917, p. 116) expressed years ago the "mutuality" of the Oedipus complex, in this terse statement: "A bad son will make a bad father" (it sounds somewhat more friendly if it is worded as follows: only a good son will make a good father).[2]

Friedman and Jones agree with Prof. Erikson's (1962a) *Hamlet* interpretation, according to which "Hamlet's single-minded and tragically doomed search for Fidelity" is the play's central theme. In order to un-

---

[2] The authors try to strengthen their psychosocial argument against Jones by asserting that their interpretation coincides with the way in which Shakespeare's audience understood *Hamlet*. In raising this argument, which I believe to be spurious, as I have indicated earlier, they set up that audience as arbiter. Despite this, they speak with sarcasm of Jones' positive evaluation of Polonius ("Finally, witness the untenable extreme to which Jones' single-minded psychiatry draws him in his view of Polonius, the prize specimen in Shakespeare's retinue of pretentious old prattlers"). Yet, according to Draper's (1939) reconstruction, Shakespeare's audience might have sided with Jones' view rather than with theirs. When they see in Polonius nothing but a "pretentious old prattler" and fail to show any understanding of Jones' interpretation, which is certainly warranted, the authors betray a psychological nearsightedness that may stem from the same prejudices as are reflected in their etiological schemata.

derstand this interpretation, one must be cognizant of Professor Erikson's "virtuology." Indeed, here is an area that is wide open for psychoanalytic research, since little is known about it psychoanalytically.[3]

When Professor Erikson tries to equate virtue and ego strength, this is already a dubious beginning:[4] " 'Virtue'," he writes, ". . . has always meant *pervading strength* and *strength of efficacy*" (author's italics) (1962b, p. 175). This is not meant to be taken as only a historical comment; it is one with which Professor Erikson agrees and which he utilizes as the cornerstone of his virtuology.

Much of Professor Erikson's work is based on a principle that is highly reminiscent of Leibniz's *harmonia praestabilita*. Thus one learns that virtue implies that "a tendency toward *optimum mutual activation* exists in the ego and in society" (1962b, p. 175), author's italics). One must surely agree with the author, however, when he adds that such an implication may be "brash." Here Professor Erikson finds a tendency exactly the opposite of what Freud called "the tendency toward conflict." Although the latter was limited by Freud to psychopathology, one can find it in creativity as well. Indeed, one must attribute to this tendency toward conflict a large share in the evolvement of culture and civilization.[5]

To be sure, Professor Erikson does not neglect pathology. His clinical vignettes are among the best clinical material in the psychoanalytic literature. Yet it seems to me that there has been a break, in fact a widening gap, between his clinical knowledge and his theoretical edifice. Virtue, of course, may sap ego strength, and faithful service to an ideal may turn into a menace to the ego's adequate functioning. The theoretician will say that, if that happens, it was not "true" virtue. Perhaps; yet it was still virtue.

In Professor Erikson's virtuology, the virtues appear in phase-ade-

[3] When the psychoanalyst is asked about man's assets, he finds himself in a situation similar to the one in which I found myself after many months of military work as a neuropsychiatrist in an Infantry Training Camp. I had learned a great deal about what makes a poor soldier—his anxieties, homesickness, back pain, flat feet—but I was still totally ignorant of what makes a good soldier. Driven by curiosity to obtain at least an inkling of what these were, I finally discovered (1960) a particular personality type whose psychopathology could dimly be recognized. My findings were surprisingly confirmed later by Grinker and Timberlake's (1962) elaborate inquiry into a certain type of student, whom they called *homoclites*.

[4] I may at this point have to make a digression into Prof. Erikson's theories before finding my way back to *Hamlet*.

[5] I would not be surprised if a truly psychoanalytic investigation of virtue were to find that the tendency toward conflict has contributed more to the evolvement of virtue than has Professor Erikson's supposed *harmonia praestabilita*.

quate sequences, as the life cycle requires them (1961a, b). He postulates an evolutionary schema (1961b, p. 161), the objections to which he himself foresees taking the form of the reproach: fetish of norms, negligence of diversity and undermining of individuality (1961b, p. 162). To these objections, I now wish to add: denial of the intrinsic tragedy of life, and distancing from clinical investigation.

The basic virtue of infancy, according to Prof. Erikson (1961, p. 115 sequ.) is hope, which, once it has been correctly established, will accompany the little citizen throughout his further career. Even at this point one can observe how the terminology alone betrays a singular "nonpsychology." Hope in the infant reminds me of Siegfried Bernfeld's delightful model of "the praying suckling," which he once designed in a lecture for the purpose of demonstrating what is *not possible* in psychology. But a "hopeful infant" is not far removed from a praying suckling. The virtue of Hope (if we are to call it a virtue at all) presupposes the awareness of a possibility, faint as it may be, that some wish may not be fulfilled. For that reason, I believe, it is a *virtue* that is rarely found in a patient who is suffering from schizophrenia: for him either an event will take place or it will not. The virtue of hoping that "it will" while knowing that "it may not" usually goes far beyond his functional potential. It is altogether out of the question for a neonate to be able to experience anything like hope.

It is the *absence* of hope that makes the infant so vulnerable to trauma; there is no representation in its psychic apparatus of that grave "it may not." That is why it is a spurious argument for Prof. Erikson to refer to Dr. Spitz's studies on anaclitic depression in infants, in order to justify the reference that hope is the basic virtue of the (ideally?) healthy infant. The fact that withdrawal of all affection may make the infant wretchedly hopeless, cannot be converted, by any syllogism, into the inference that its healthy counterpart is hopeful.

Yet Hamlet's problems do not center in the absence of hope, but according to Professor Erikson, in the absence of Fidelity, which is "the adolescent virtue" (1961a, p. 115), "the particular ego-quality which emerges, with and from adolescence . . . . the ability to sustain loyalties freely pledged in spite of the inevitable contradictions of value systems" (1961a, p. 125). Hamlet's tragedy, according to Professor Erikson, is that his "world . . . is one of diffuse realities and fidelities. Only through the play-within-the-play and through the madness within the insanity does Hamlet, the actor within the play-actor, reveal the identity within the pretended identities—and the superior fidelity in the fatal pretense" (1962a, p. 9).

I must admit that it is difficult for me to make head or tail of that last sentence. If I were to find it in an essay of literary criticism, I would let myself be happily guided by the author's fancy, and freely project the images of my own fancy into its beauty. About the mythological meaning of science I shall have to say something later, but the myth should be discovered behind sentences that convey ideas with some clarity. I miss clarity in the sentence I have quoted and in many other such sentences; I must make the best out of what is available.

What does it mean to say that Hamlet's world is one of "diffuse realities and fidelities"? Before Hamlet suffered his well-known tragic shocks, he seems to have been fairly conflict-free, as well as ideally competent to handle the various dimensions of the value system into which he was born. In the end, he is found to have attained a higher level, inasmuch as his new value system is no longer bound to the "accident" of his particular cultural habitat, but has evolved instead into one that has become supremely broadened in depth and extension. In between these two poles, we find a process of gradual change taking place. Nowhere, certainly, do we find his reality or his actuality (Erikson, 1962b) vaguely defined. At times he is presented as groping, but the alternatives between which he is attempting to choose are pretty clearly presented.

And fidelity? Why was Hamlet's fidelity "diffuse?" According to Prof. Erikson's own definition, fidelity is an ability that has to do with two different areas: freely to pledge loyalties and then freely to sustain them. I will have more to say later about this functional definition; I want only to point out here that, at least in terms of what Shakespeare let us know, Hamlet did indeed possess this ability. He also made use of it: he pledged himself and he sustained the highest ideals of his society in word and deed. Then came the "eye-opener": his society was not what it seemed to be. His ignorance was not his fault, however; neither Old Hamlet nor any other person in the kingdom knew of the "imposthume."

Yet Prof. Erikson has added to his definition that fidelity is given only when making the pledge and sustaining it occur "in spite of the inevitable contradiction of value systems." I would assume that he does not mean to say that, if mankind ever succeeded in harmonizing value-systems, fidelity would no longer be possible. I do not understand Prof. Erikson's addition. I had always thought that a certain type of youth—the sort whom I would most readily associate with Fidelity—strives unyield-ingly toward the elimination of contradictions, and therefore refuses to pledge loyalty to a value system that contains unresolved contradictions. This is a youth who is unwilling to make compromises. He has not yet learned to "be wise and to adjust"; instead, he still harbors the sort of idealism that flatly overrules the "necessities" of reality. I cannot regard such youth as without fidelity.

In Prof. Erikson's definition, it should be noted, there is one word that may demonstrate the degree of his distance from psychoanalysis. Fidelity is given, he writes, when loyalties are "freely" pledged. The suggestion that loyalties could ever be *freely* pledged is altogether out of keeping with all that psychoanalysis stands for.

The fact that so much in man's psyche is covered by unconscious-ness should prove to be an embarrassing one, in this context; it speaks strongly against Prof. Erikson's "virtuology." Freedom of choice of value systems, a "free" pledging of loyalties—all this may have its proper place in academic psychology (and increasingly, even there, to a reduced de-gree only) but *not* in treatises that are close to psychoanalysis. How can one say of impetuous youth, in whom the contribution of the unconscious is so enormous, that it can "freely pledge"? A psychoanalytic inquiry into a person's loyalties, if they are pledged with any degree of earnest-ness, invariably leads to revelations of the deepest conflicts.

As is well known, the concept of identity plays a large role in Prof. Erikson's work. Indeed, it is difficult to find a problem that has not found its place in his conceptualization of "identity crisis." This is real-ly not so astonishing. Since Prof. Erikson seems to identify identity with ego, and since all the psychopathology that the clinician has to deal with must necessarily show up in one way or another in the ego, an identity crisis is obviously to be found wherever one turns.

It is true that new conceptualizations have a way of developing a life of their own; in time they unfold an extension of applications that could not have been foreseen at the start. This "insatiability," as I would like to call it, is a general feature of those concepts that are productive and usable. One could perhaps think that something similar has happened with the concepts of "identity" and "identity crisis." I doubt it, chiefly because I do not think that a new level of abstraction has been reached with the introduction of this concept. The great appeal it has should not necessarily be taken as an index of its usefulness, or as a sign of its ex-planatory value. Its popularity may easily be based on a temporary swing of what is called "fashion." I myself do not see in *Hamlet* a problem of identity.

Eliot (1860, p. 440) writes about the protagonist:

> But you have known Maggie a long while, and need to be told, not her characteristics, but her history, which is a thing hardly to be predicted even from the completest knowledge of characteristics. For the tragedy of our lives is not created entirely from within. "Character," says Novalis, in one of his questionable aphorisms, "character is destiny." But not the whole of our destiny. Hamlet, Prince of Denmark, was speculative and irresolute, and we have a great tragedy in consequence. But if his father had lived to a good old age, and his uncle had died an early death, we can conceive of Hamlet's having married Ophelia and got through life with a reputation of sanity, notwithstanding many soliloquies and some moody sarcasms towards the fair daughter of Polonius, to say nothing of the frankest incivility to his father-in-law.

There is a deep truth, no doubt, in this comment; it points to a problem of major import. According to my view of Hamlet, he was not originally speculative and irresolute; or, at least, if he was, it was repressed and thus had no bearing on his phenotype. If his harmonious developmental drift up to the time of his mother's precipitate marriage had not been broken by a series of traumata, Ophelia would never have had to listen to "moody sarcasms," and Polonius' dotage would have found sympathetic ears, however conducive to boredom his garrulousness might have been.

By and large, Eliot seems to me to be right: a certain character had to be exposed to a certain "insult" or complication from without, in order to lead to a certain "destiny." This external complication, however, does not seem to find an adequate place in Prof. Erikson's analysis. Yet the study of man, when he appears most extraordinary, does seem to reveal that man himself is the prime mover of his own destiny. He impresses us as going out to meet his destiny; he *seeks* it. The tragic does not at such times intrude by accident; what may appear as though it were decreed by fate or Divinity may have been, in actuality, secretly contrived and sought after.

Character and destiny may be, after all, not quite divorced from each other, as Eliot thinks. Some of those who have cast a deeper glance into the human world have asserted that a man's future is written over his face. The Starevitch in *The Brothers Karamazov* bows deep before

Dimitri; he has suddenly recognized that this man is to encounter a great destiny. Georg Simmel asserts that Rembrandt's portraits of young people contain the whole of their future, of that which has not yet been lived.

Somewhat related to this problem is the question of whether or not a whole can be reconstructed from a detail, or of how many details need to be known in order to make a whole reconstructable. Such wholes, of course, contain both the past and the future.[6]

One may therefore tentatively suggest that character and destiny could also be looked at as a unit (cf. H. Deutsch, 1930), that only certain characters are capable of having certain destinies, and that the seemingly accidental environmental event is already part and parcel of the character. As applied to *Hamlet*, this would mean that the Ghost's supposed freedom to appear to a person of his own choice might conceivably have led just as well to his selecting Polonius or even Laertes as his potential avenger. He might even have communicated with Claudius, with the intention of driving him to madness by importuning him at odd hours, in the same way as other Ghosts chose to deal with Macbeth or Brutus, or Richard III. Yet the Ghost's visitation to Hamlet has to be regarded as part of Hamlet's character, without an assertion to that effect implying, however, any hallucination on Hamlet's part.

Whether such speculations are rejected as mysterious and arcane or are accepted, the fact remains that Eliot's remark has its validity. Yet if the inquiry into the play were to stop at this point, and one were to view the main action merely as the resultant of the coming together of *a* character and *a* tragic event, such a view, despite its partial correctness, would do injustice to the full depth of the play. Some authors have asserted that *Hamlet* represents "man's tragedy," (e.g. Davis, 1964) or at least that it contains some universal within the human orbit. If this is indeed so, then there must be some secret link between the character and the event that produced such dire consequences. The two cannot be in a relationship as alien as that between Ibsen's Oswald and his congenital infection.

[6] I recall Helene Deutsch's clinical seminar in Vienna, in which she was able, after the first few hours of a patient's analysis had been reported, to make extraordinary—later verified—predictions concerning the course his analysis would take and what unconscious contents would be brought to light. Aichhorn also possessed the ability to make incredibly far-reaching inferences from a small number of clues, which sometimes seemed almost trivial. At the root of Anna Freud's (1965) work on "profiles," and her systematization of the diagnostic interview, lies the same endeavor: to predict the spatial-temporal whole from the limited number of clues at hand.

When Prof. Erikson writes that Hamlet becomes "a mad revenger," that "what he accomplishes at the end is what he tried to avoid," that "his words are his better deeds" (1962b, p. 11) (it will be noted how opposite this is to my interpretation), then we can be sure of one thing—namely, that he has not put his finger on the secret link that connects character and event, thus endowing a specific sequence of events with a universal meaning. The story of a mad avenger has no universal meaning per se; it could hardly have had such a deep influence on Western mentality as *Hamlet* had had.

The same thing can be said about Prof. Erikson's assertion that "Hamlet may well stand, historically speaking, for an abortive leader, a still-born rebel" (1962b, p. 8). One could also say this about Christ, whose birth caused the massacre of the infants in Bethlehem, and who became a leader only as the result of His history—which included dying a miserable death.

Prof. Erikson points to the difference between Hamlet and Fortinbras, who gets his "dying voice." It is not quite clear what conclusion he draws from the fact that, in the end, it is a person quite different from Hamlet who steps into the place of real power. This conclusion seems to be connected somehow with the "denial of positive identity"; but again one may point to Peter's succession to Christ. Why "a mad revenger," "an abortive leader," "a still-born rebel" is called a man of superior conscience (1962b, p. 8), or "a special person, intensely human" (1962b, p. 11), Prof. Erikson does not make clear.

But then again, Prof. Erikson regards Hamlet as representing the conflicts and processes that are chiefly significant of adolescence or postadolescence. Here, indeed, one does come somewhat closer to the universal human, which may be able to stir man's heart throughout the ages. Nevertheless, although most critics, I assume, will agree that Hamlet does have the flavor of something adolescent, a note of warning is in order, which may have some validity for large parts of Prof. Erikson's work.

It was Siegfried Bernfeld (1929) who introduced the factor of societal *locus* in his research into psychopathology, a concept of primary importance for the understanding of puberty. The form and structure of a given adolescence depends on the societal place at which the particular youth finds itself. Prof. Erikson would surely be the last one to deny this or even to doubt it. Yet he does not seem to have drawn the full consequences of his acceptance of that sociological fact, in that what he devises as ideal canvases, with regard to the various phases through which man goes on his way toward death. What actually happens in clinical reality is then measured in terms of deviations from these ideal standards, whose derivations remain obscure, although their beauty, harmony and pleasing effect cannot be doubted.

Such a method must, of course, find itself at loggerheads with psychoanalysis. When Prof. Erikson speaks of psychoanalysis' "originology" and puts the term into italics besides, the pejorative implication is self-evident, just as it is when I speak of his *"virtuology."* Freud's "originology," his near addiction to the search for origins and the way in which he carried out that search—all this was a great accomplishment. In that sense, the search for origins remains the backbone of psychological explanation. Heinz Hartmann's (1939, 1950) remark that the genesis of a function does not necessarily determine its meaning and later purpose introduced a sufficient caution to protect us—at least methodologically—against those abuses of psychoanalytic originology that had, of course, inevitably occurred.

There are areas in human development on which the societal *locus* has no bearing and to which, therefore, rigid standards can be applied. I select one at random: thing constancy. In whatever culture, at whatever societal *locus,* and in whatever historical or prehistorical period man has lived, his perceptive apparatus has had to develop into one that was able to translate sense perceptions into object qualities. Every man acquires the ability to perceive an object's color, whether the light is bright or dim, or an object's true size, whether it is close or far away.

The errors that the perceptive apparatus may make, the limitations to which it is subject, the individual differences in efficiency it may reveal —all these have been examined in great detail. Yet the fact remains that at one time or another the perceptive apparatus must undergo this "process of objectification," this wresting itself away from recording merely its own reverberations, without any regard to the meaning that these stimuli may have in the outer world.

This is one of the most important steps in man's development, and it constitutes the very basis of the reality principle. So deeply rooted is it in biological processes, however, that it can be safely taken for granted; because it is in general totally conflict-free, it holds little interest for psychoanalysis. When this process is absent, of course, then one is justified in speaking, without any further inquiry, of psychopathology.

If we now switch to adolescence, however, we meet with a totally different state of affairs. Adolescence shares with the example just re-

ferred to only one element—namely, the evolvement of a biological function: the maturation of the genital apparatus and its proper function in
intercourse. This cannot, however, be taken for granted, as thing constancy is. It is a function that evolves rather late and is vulnerable, in
terms of its "efficiency." All other problems of adolescence vary with
specific cultural habitats. In ancient Egypt, the Pharaoh's genital apparatus had to function with his sister; in ancient Greece it had to function
with young boys. In some cultural habitats, it is expected to function
shortly after it has reached physical maturity; in such instances as Leonardo da Vinci, Michelangelo, and Beethoven, it may never have been
used in contact with another human being of either sex, and this may
have been the prerequsite for their unique accomplishments.

This breadth of choice, which is already noticeable in the biology of
adolescence, finds a counterpart in its psychology. There are puberties
and adolescences in which there is no trace of anything that could be
called an "identity crisis," and there are others in which processes of
heartbreaking tragedy occur. I doubt that any valid multidimensional
model of adolescence can be established, although I would admit that
there is hardly any one of us who escapes the temptation to try to do so.
Yet the danger of measuring the clinical reality against an arbitrarily designed model or ideal can be averted by adhering to psychoanalytic originology. It therefore seems to me that Prof. Erikson's inferences and theories concerning adolescence are to be refuted at the level of the very methodology that he himself employs.

Is Hamlet then the prototype of adolescent or post-adolescent crisis,
at least of a type (or of the singular variation of a type) that is significant
of post-medieval history in the West, and within a specific social *locus*?
Perhaps; but the same thing can be said of Don Quixote, Werther, or
Faust, to name only a few.[7]

---

[7] I think that in general we are too quick to establish "universals"; we are far too inclined to declare that elements of the highest degree of differentiation and of the subtlest individuality are "universals of mankind." If we were truly capable of scientific thinking—that is to say, if we were real-
ists—then we would probably regard such instances as deviations, exceptions, atypical (albeit welcome) mutations, as some scholars have actually done. But it is well-nigh impossible to get rid of our
own traces of that primary narcissism that pervades organic life. It is indeed a property of our species
and forces us to regard the highest achievement as if it were also a "species property."

In order to grasp what has made *Hamlet* understandable throughout the generations—has
preserved its appeal, despite the profound changes of culture that have taken place since Shakespeare's time—one could refer to one of Freud's early statements on drama (1942, p. 308f), in which
he indicates under what conditions the presentation of suffering may actually become a source of
pleasure (see later). It is certainly not in the rarefied atmosphere of Fidelity.

Prof. Erikson goes through a whole series of Hamlet's "estrangements," and, indeed, Hamlet is estranged throughout most of the play from most of the important dimensions of life. Yet is Hamlet's estrangement a pathological phenomenon, in the narrower sense? Is it not rather the inescapable consequence of the turn his life took and the consequent impossibility of denial on his part? I must repeat that those who have survived the concentration camps have the right and perhaps even the duty to feel estranged toward life, as anyone would have to do who is sensitive enough truly to reexperience in himself the avoidable destruction and death that stalk the community in which he lives, as well as the world surrounding it.

It may be argued that all this ought not to affect a man's feeling for the opposite sex. Is Hamlet's estrangement from women the consequence of "identity diffusion?" In order to evaluate it properly, one has to consider as well the general drift of Western man's feeling with regard to the opposite sex. From the early inscriptions on the rocks of the island of Thera,[8] to Tertullian's shattering pronouncement that women are the gate of Hell and the first deserters of the divine law, there is a chain of accusation, suspicion and derogation that has been continued into our own times, despite enlightenment and emancipation in our society.

Even Erasmus, that most humane and cultivated spirit, who died only one generation before Shakespeare was born, wrote (1503, p. 39): "Keep in mind that 'woman' is man's sensual part: she is our Eve, through whom that wiliest of serpents lures our passions into deadly pleasures." He quotes approvingly from Ecclesiasticus (42:14) that portion which makes a woman something to be held in abomination: "The iniquity of the man is preferable to the goodness of the woman" (p. 75).[9]

---

[8] It is generally overlooked that the first crest of Western civilization, in ancient Greece, on which our entire civilization rests, had already been preceded by encomia of love of boys. The little known inscriptions on the island of Thera, dating back to the seventh century, testify that the attraction of homoerotic love was at that time not a matter of poets and philosophers but a social reality, probably having a sacral meaning. One of these inscriptions announced that "Krimon has carried out his union with the son of Bathekles at a sacred district with an invocation of Apollon Delphinios" (Licht, 1928, p. 206). Certainly Hamlet's outbreaks against Ophelia would never have found a place in an ancient Greek tragedy; they presuppose the intervening victory of Christianity. But, although it is not known what really was the full meaning of the preference for homoerotic love at the dawn of Western civilization, one should never—if one wishes completely to understand Hamlet's relationship to Ophelia—limit oneself to an inquiry alone into Hamlet's individual givens but view that relationship in a broad historical context of Western man's relationship to both the female and the male sex.

[9] However, in Ecclesiasticus this sentence has a meaning that is different from the one that is implied when it is quoted out of context.

Woman's ability to be a moral being is disputed, and any ethical behavior of which she might be capable is cast aside as irrelevant.

One has to admit that Hamlet's aspersion, which, as I have tried to show, was partly in the service of protecting the woman he loved, is only a fraction of Ecclesiasticus' abomination. I am aware that every quotation that can be found in Western literature as expressive of an aspersion against woman can be matched with one that glorifies her. The cult of Mary, if nothing else, documents the trend toward the glorification and idealization of the female. However, Marilogy or Mariolatry developed out of the assumption that Mary did not indulge in the one physical function that Goethe had in mind when he wrote that priceless verse in which he called Adam and Eve "God's two most enchanting thoughts" [*Gottes zwei lieblichste Gedanken*] (*West-ostlicher Divan*). Christianity has long refused, however, to regard Eve as one of God's "enchanting thoughts."

The idea that anthropogenesis occurred in two phases seems widespread. The Greeks, to be sure, looked with contempt on brutish, coarse, primordial man, who was created by Mother Earth, by contrast with the man who developed out of him later, after Demeter had civilized him by the introduction of agriculture and the mysteries (Kerenyi, 1947). Judeo-Christian mythology has also insisted on a two-phase anthropogenesis—except that in it the direction has been just the reverse of what the Greeks regarded it as being. The male element created the first two human beings, who were perfect. It was in the second phase, however, that they became corrupted and contemptible—and Eve was the cause of it all. Just as Abraham's sacrifice of Isaac did not compensate in God's eyes for Adam's trespassings, so Mary did not purify women in the eyes of Occidental man. He continued long after to find the center of evil in lust and in that which arouses it.

When Wagner, the realist, asks Mephisto in Goethe's *Faust* for an explanation of why the psyche and the body, which fit so splendidly together and hold to each other so firmly, nevertheless continuously make the day miserable for each other, Mephisto replies:

Hold on! I would rather ask
Why man and woman get along so badly?
[*Halt ein! ich wollte lieber fragen:*
Warum sich Mann und Frau so schlecht vertragen?

(*Faust*, verse 6897f)

· 512 ·

Indeed, no one has yet found an adequate explanation of why God's "two most enchanting thoughts" are, more frequently than not, at loggerheads with each other, or even worse.

Hamlet has been in love with Ophelia. It was a more or less conflict-free, "normal" relationship. He is now shown in process of establishing himself as a male, as Romeo is.[10] His difficulty with Ophelia cannot possibly be seen as an adolescent or post-adolescent crisis. The crisis that Shakespeare has put on the stage is conceivable only in a man who has established a strong and firm relationship to women, who has strong passions and desires for them.

While he has established his "sexual identity," nevertheless these passions are in conflict with other aspirations of the self. Love of Ophelia has become incompatible with duties and responsibilities that the self has accepted as paramount. Only under these circumstances does Hamlet join the broad current of misogyny in Western thinking and make statements with which most illustrious minds would have been in agreement.

It may sound strange that, at this point, after I have discussed some of the psychic processes that led to Hamlet's rejection of Ophelia, and indicated that I regard it as the end-product of subterranean processes which are well known to the analyst, even though they are invisible to the naked eye, I now place a historical objective problem at the center.

To be sure, the correlation between the series of microscopic, subterranean processes, which are in the main unconscious, and the meaning of the end-product to which they lead, is still an unsolved problem, as are so many other problems of psychology. In psychoanalytic research, two tendencies can be observed: one is the tendency to equate subjective inner processes that are similar, despite the fact that they lead to essentially different end-products; the other is to assume or search for identical inner processes in order to explain what seem to be identical end-products.

The former tendency leads to such consequences as equating a creative mind with one that suffers from paranoid psychosis, because one

[10] Here I must raise a question, however, that should perhaps have been raised sooner. Did Hamlet's courtship of Ophelia start after his return from Wittenberg, or had it begun earlier? I can hardly believe that the love letter that Polonius discloses was written by Hamlet after his father's death. If the text were to make this assumption truly inescapable, then a good deal of my interpretation would become of quite doubtful value. As a matter of fact, most critics, as far as I can see, do date the courtship from an earlier moment, although external evidence is not clear on that point. When Ophelia tells her father that Hamlet has "of late" made "many tenders" *(I.3.99)*, this may be due either to evasiveness with regard to a true confession of the beginning of his courtship—or it may be the truth. The textual evidence does not preclude the possibility that Hamlet's courtship had started some time prior to his going to Wittenberg, yet had been noticed at court only "of late."

finds in both cases projective mechanisms and unconscious homosexual tendencies, as well as many other similarities; the latter leads to a theory of "depersonalization," even though depersonalization is a characteristic of a vast array of subjective experiences. In one instance, these may constitute the harbingers or symptoms of a grave psychosis; in others, they may be the result of fatigue or of some inconsequential and temporary emergency measure, adopted in an acute situation of conflictual stress. Whenever life took a turn for one of my patients that was all too threatening to her, the entire situation became depersonalized, and this changed appearance of reality was experienced by her as pleasurable. [11]

Just as the problem of the choice of neurosis (Freud, 1911, 1913b) is still unsolved, so it also remains unknown why the same conflict will lead, in one instance, to grave psychopathology, in another to the greatest achievement.

Freud (1925) calls Hamlet "this neurotic created by the author" [*dieser vom Dichter erschaffene Neurotiker*]; later (1928, p. 189), he says that Hamlet is paralyzed by his sense of guilt "in a manner entirely in keeping with neurotic processes." He focusses on that area in Hamlet's psyche in which the ego's freedom has been curtailed because of a repressed content potent enough to paralyze an ego function. When Freud (1916-1917, p. 335) says that the neurotic is an Oedipus turned Hamlet, he uses this aspect of Hamlet's character as a generally valid clinical example. [12]

I am reminded here of the different meanings that the figure of Cinderella evokes in Europe and in this country. In Europe, Cinderella evokes the picture of a girl who is being discriminated against and thus suffering permanent frustration; in this country, she is a girl who accomplishes a fabulous "rise" from low status to high. Likewise, we may think of Hamlet either as one who was held back from acting by internal conflict or as one who in the end resorted to "creative murder," as Knight has so felicitously called it.

The various comments about Hamlet that we find in Freud's work

[11] It is highly improbable that all the elements of the vast clinical spectrum of depersonalization phenomena have anything in common except the final pathway (a useful metapsychological concept introduced by Schilder, 1921). It is doubtful, therefore, whether inquiries into depersonalization, such as are reported by Stewart (1964), have any usefulness and validity (cf. Arlow in Stewart, 1964, p. 172).

[12] I cannot, however, follow Freud (1917b, p. 246f), when he says that, under all circumstances, a person is ill if he holds himself and his fellowmen in such low esteem as Hamlet does at times, independently of "whether he is speaking in truth or whether he is being more or less unfair to himself."

do not really pertain to the figure as a whole but to only one aspect at each time. It is understandable that Freud was chiefly interested in that phase of Hamlet's development in which he was struggling with his inhibition; yet he was, of course, aware that there was more to *Hamlet* than the one dimension for which he used the character in his published papers. (This can be seen in his letter to Fliess on the subject.)

In an early paper, published only posthumously (1942), Freud tells us more about his thinking on Hamlet than he does on any other occasion. He asserts that Hamlet, who "has so far been normal, becomes neurotic owing to the peculiar nature of the task by which he is faced" (p. 309) and that it is only insofar as a spectator is neurotic himself that he can derive pleasure from the tragedy (308f). That is to say, Hamlet's "neurosis" is the universal neurosis of modern civilized man, a theme to which I will return later. Yet Hamlet is definitely more than a neurotic. His inhibition is temporary; for the neurotic, however, dysfunction or paralysis is generally continuous. In Freud's work one does not find any comment on that development in the tragedy that finally leads to Hamlet's overcoming of his inhibition.[13]

Against my doubt in the correctness not only of Prof. Erikson's conception of Hamlet, but also in that of his methodology, one may refer to Max Weber's method of constructing "ideal-types." However, Professor Erikson does not give us ideal types, constructed after Weber's fruitful methods—against these there would be, of course, no objection—but rather types of ideal that, when presented within a psychoanalytic context, are highly misleading. Nevertheless, it may be that I should apologize for my critical remarks about Prof. Erikson's work. If one of his essays had not been devoted to an explication of Hamlet, and if two scholars had not reapproached the *Hamlet* problem by using (or abusing?) his method and findings, the reader would not have found any reference to him in this work. Yet rather than stop the discussion at the borders of the *Hamlet* problem I have considered the general direction of his work, without however doing justice to those areas of his broad research that are of great merit, and without going sufficiently into depth in what I did deal with. This cross between too little and too much must be excused, however.

[13] This is all the more surprising in the light of the fact, as I shall try to demonstrate later, that Freud expressed his identification with Hamlet at just the moment when he was himself on the verge of overcoming an intellectual inhibition. When Prof. Erikson writes (1962a, p. 145), however, that "Science, morality, and himself Freud took for granted," he is making a statement that is hardly worthy of rebuttal, in the light of Freud's historic self-analysis (cf. Erikson, 1958b) and the significant portion of his writings that he devoted to morality and science.

On the other hand, it was difficult to escape the temptation to bring up a series of problems that warrant some warning, particularly in view of Prof. Erikson's great influence on academic youth in their search for Fidelity. It would probably be more to their advantage if such youth were released to the community in a rather pessimistic frame of mind, aware of the inherent insolubility of the problem of man. It is better for such youth to be reminded that the life cycle in Shakespeare's universe does not go from the newborn's Hope to the Wisdom of old age, but rather from the first agonized cry (which anyone who has ever witnessed the first second of life will recognize) to the shattering unwisdom of King Lear (even though he does reach wisdom in the end).[14]

One may also observe with some misgiving that the high critical standards that Prof. Erikson upholds in general give way at a crucial point of psychoanalytic relevance. When he was demonstrating "The Nature of Clinical Evidence" (1958a) by the use of a model hour, Prof. Erikson included in his report his own emotional response to the patient's behavior. During the previous hour, the patient had shown promising signs of improvement; now he was in a state of excitement that might well have been ominous, brought about by a most disturbing dream. Prof. Erikson reviewed the interpretations that he was able to derive from the patient's associations, and then went on to comment, "I also told him, without anger but not without some honest indignation, that my response to his account had included a feeling of being attacked" (1958a, p. 72).

The reader may wonder what lay at the bottom of Prof. Erikson's all too subtle differentiation between anger and "honest" indignation. According to the dictionary, the latter term covers an entire gamut, from disdain to wrath. Furthermore, the reader may find confirmation of Freud's theory of "Negation" (1925b) when he reads shortly thereafter (p. 75), about the same incident, "By relating the fact that his underlying anger *aroused mine . . .*" (italics added).

---

[14] When one takes psychoanalytic stock of the much heralded wisdom of old age, one discovers that it rests on the foundation of a marked decrease of the passionate appetites. Now, when the drives impinge only weakly on the ego, it is easy to be wise. Were the drives to rise to adolescent levels, the old sage would act just as much "out of his head" as the youth, whom he tries to convince, but in vain, to accept a rationalized synopsis of his own life's experience. In this light, however, it becomes quite questionable where sagacity lies: in the aged man's wisdom *sans amour* or in the illusions of the impetuous adolescent. Not even wisdom is absolute and its location depends on the visual angle of the one who searches for it. The 69-year-old Goethe knew this. In looking back to youthful years while rereading a letter he had written in his younger years to a woman he had loved immensely, he commented: "How engaging one really is when we are young!" [*Was man doch artig ist, wenn wir jung sind*]

Whatever the reaction may actually have been—anger or indignation—the reason for my citing this episode is not that emotional derailments of this kind are rare among analysts. No one is, of course, immune to them; my concern is that Prof. Erikson justifies his anger, takes it as a constructive response and informs the patient about it, as if such responses were indeed legitimate and had to be tolerated by the patient. In truth, there is no justification for an analyst's anger, not to speak of his indignation, when he feels disappointed or accused by a patient. If such derailments occur, it is high time for the analyst to aim at some enlightenment with regard to what his own unconscious relationship to the patient may be.

I wonder about the meaning of the fact that a psychoanalyst's work is pervaded by ethical demands and sentiments far above those the human being can attain and yet he uses psychoanalysis for the purpose of rationalizing what is, quite apparently, a defect in himself. The latter move is evidently a compromise, designed to help him escape a situation in which another analyst would perhaps feel regret, or even guilt, for having failed to maintain professional standards; as for the former, however, I have no explanation to offer for it.

I cannot forgo the opportunity to close with a general remark about the variety of depth-psychologies that have sprung from psychoanalysis. Much has been written about Freud's relationship with his pupils and collaborators, who have stood "in his shadow" (Freud, 1914b, p. 51) for a while, and have then gone their own ways and founded their own schools. Most of these comments have been fundamentally wrong; in them Freud was generally pictured as being intolerant and authoritarian.

How little this is true can be seen from two of his letters, one written to Jung on April 16, 1909 (Jung, 1961, pp. 361-363) and the other to Rank, written on August 25, 1924 (Freud, 1873-1939, pp. 352-354). What is almost always overlooked (I think this is also true of Roazen's [1968] recent study) is the fact that so many side branches have grown out of psychoanalysis proper. How could a really authoritarian mind have had so many disciples who, despite their initial submission to his greatness, were nevertheless able to preserve sufficient independence— who were indeed stimulated by him to evolve their own theories and techniques, which generally deviated in certain essential respects from the master's? If we consider further that these new theories did not in turn become the mainsprings of new schools, it may well be that it was

Freud's followers who were authoritarian, after all; they did not stimulate their own followers to evolve original theories, either right or wrong!

The fact is that Prof. Erikson has built a theoretical system which, despite the marks of its psychoanalytic origin, deviates from accepted psychoanalytic theories—so much so, indeed, that a future historian will probably hesitate to call him a psychoanalyst (he usually calls himself, in his writings, a "psychotherapist"). This is in itself testimony to the fact that psychoanalysis did *not* lose its vitality after the death of its founder.

C. Relevance of Positive Audience Responses and the Doxaletheic Function

Proposition: The Artistic Genius and Psychosis.

> Shakespeare had his visions, which were nothing to those around him. Most men neither saw what he saw nor imagined what he imagined and his labour was to bring to birth in others something of his own awareness. If he could not do so he might well doubt his own sanity, for to see what no one else sees—is not that to be nothing else but mad? [Walker, 1948, p. 70].

In my opinion this statement, written by a literary historian who has no connection with depth psychology, introduces a viewpoint that calls for far-reaching assumptions with regard to the psychic apparatus of the artistic genius and its functioning. What it says, more or less, is that the genius has a primary need to evoke certain responses of a positive nature in his social environment, in order to be protected thereby against a breakdown of his mental functioning.

And, indeed, in searching for instances that may confirm Roy Walker's proposition, one may think of such geniuses as van Gogh, who suffered from a psychosis and committed suicide, Hölderlin (1770-1843), one of the great lyric German poets, who spent the last 37 years of his life (or almost half of it) in complete mental darkness, and Heinrich von Kleist (1777-1811), one of the great German playwrights, who ended his life at the age of 34—all of whom were denied sufficient positive environmental responses. If one were to accept Roy Walker's proposition, one would have to postulate an etiological relationship between environmental rejection and defeating psychopathology in the genius.

In what follows I shall try to set forth some of the implications that seem to me to be contained in the belief that the greater the artistic genius, the more he is in danger of psychosis and the greater will be his need for special safeguards, as compared with those that may be required by a person whose life is not anchored in the creation of unique cultural values.

Primary and Secondary Gain.

Psychoanalytic investigation has demonstrated that from the formation of neurotic symptoms the subject derives two kinds of pleasure gain. The primary gain consists of the solution of an inner conflict, insofar as the symptom itself is a compromise between two irreconcilably opposed inner forces, while the secondary advantage is brought about by alleviations in the patient's relationship to his environment. The primary gain is, in that sense, indispensable; without it, no neurosis can develop. The secondary gain, however, is conditional: whether or not it accrues depends on environmental accidents.

It would likewise seem that artistic creation is able to provide the solution of an inner conflict, no matter how short the time for which such a "solution" may last (primary gain), as well as secondary gains in the form of external rewards and fame. One may thus be seduced into using this distinction between gains as a basis for a typology of creativity, and so distinguish between those works of art that came into being almost exclusively under the impelling necessity of inner conflicts and those whose creators were motivated chiefly by ambition and the thirst for recognition and success. The tendency to seek consistency would then make us assume that, while creations in the service of primary gain are likely to be of lasting value, the quality of achievement will probably be inferior in instances where the search for secondary gains is the dominant motive. Such a proposition, however, is quite untenable.

In the majority of instances, the artistic creations of schizophrenics are born solely out of inner conflicts, and yet it is questionable whether one can attribute to them any objective artistic value (Kris, 1936). Even if the proposition stated above is limited to bona fide works of art, it appears questionable. Van Gogh continued his output of outstanding creative values, despite the fact that his own environment took little notice of him. Yet he was convinced that future generations would accord him full recognition; here the secondary gains, even though they were to be realized only after his death, seem to have been of great power to move the genius to creation.

Grillparzer, the great Austrian playwright, whose true artistic value is still a matter of debate, may be regarded as one of those geniuses who was devoted solely to creativity, and worked in complete disregard of secondary gains; in his later years, he objected even to the publication of his plays. Yet this aversion to public notice set in after one of his plays was ill-received by the critics. Thus, one may find, behind behavior that seems to be in the service of primary gain, and excessive sensitivity that betrays an all too great dependence on secondary gains.

In one bold stroke, Roy Walker's proposition puts an end to speculations about the psychological difference between primary and secondary gains in the genius' creativity;[1] his postulate is that environmental responses of a positive nature are just as important to the genius' maintenance of mental balance as is the creation of cultural values per se.

Although we are desperately ignorant of the details of Shakespeare's genius, we can be certain that he created under a kind of inner compulsion, which drove him relentlessly into the pouring out of one masterpiece after another. To such a mind, which one would suppose to be wholly passionately involved in the creative process, one would readily assume that audience responses were a matter of little concern. Whether the public at large received his plays with enthusiasm or coldly—what would such a question matter to one who wrote for eternity? This implies, of course, that society would provide an appropriate outlet for his creative impulse. After all, the playwright is realistically in a less favorable position than the writer of love poetry: the latter will always find, if he wants, an audience in the form of a maiden who cherishes his outpouring of passionate verses. But a playwright needs a stage, and a public audience, for the realization of his visions.

It would be hard to conceive of a Shakespeare who wrote tragedies and left the manuscripts in a drawer for posterity to read and admire (as a modern novelist may do); it would make no sense in the period in which Shakespeare actually lived and, further, such a situation would surely have stunted the process of growth that his output so vividly demonstrates, from *Titus Andronicus* to *The Tempest*. In order to learn his craft and to grow in depth, a playwright has to see his plays performed. A Shakespeare, on the other hand, who was concerned with success merely enough for him to be able to feel sure of having his next play performed, would still be compatible—at least, in part—with the image of a

---

[1] Katz (1963) has made the same suggestion for the psychopathology of neuroses. In my opinion, however, the differentiation retains its validity there.

genius who is predominantly and incessantly preoccupied with giving literary form to the characters that have taken hold of his mind.

What Walker does, however, is to ascribe the same psychological importance to success as he does to the genius' unique endowment: *both,* according to him, are prerequisites of undisturbed output. The audience must echo the playwright's vision: there must be some kind of harmony between the two; it must reflect, as it were in a mirror, the image that the playwright has devised. It must signal back to the playwright that his product has come to full reality in their minds, as it had already in his.

From this vantage point, to be sure, the concept of "success," which is usually associated in our minds with vanity, pride, pettiness, superficiality, and narcissism, appears to take on a new dimension. For if a playwright is successful, according to this conception, not only will he be loved, cherished and highly rewarded, but he will also have the added assurance that the characters he has created have been integrated, that they have become meaningful, have fully come to life in the minds of his audience—a factor that seems to be of primary importance for the maintenance of balance.

All this does not deny that there have been eminent talents, highly successful in their own times, to whom success has meant no more than personal advantage and the gratification of more or less narcissistic wishes. It means, however, that what is superficially and generally called "success" may also have a very profound and life-saving function in the career of the genius, in whose existence almost everything seems to have a meaning other than the one that it has in ordinary life. The plight of the genius is an extraordinary one, and it follows that success has a particular role to play in his existence.

On a Point of Method in Ego Psychology.

The future historian of psychoanalysis will probably regard Freud's scientific career as having been prematurely terminated by death, even though Freud would have hardly been able to find among scientists many rivals, in terms of the quantity and quality of creative output. Yet, if fate had granted him a few more years, he might well have put the *keystone* to his work by writing *Three Essays on the Theory of the Ego and its Function,* thereby creating the counterpart to his first book on clinical theory, which he wrote in 1905.

Prior to *that* work, psychologists were free to assume the existence of as many drives as they chose and felt themselves to be in need of. With the publication of that work, order was brought into the previous disorder of drive psychology. Not only was the concept of "drive" defined, and its structure and function determined; the possible number of drives was also made certain, and both their appearance and disappearance were brought into a meaningful—one is inclined to say, logical—system.

The writing of Freud's *Three Essays on the Theory of Sexuality* may be compared with Mendeleyev's formulation of the periodic system. Did chemistry become a science when Lavoisier introduced the rule of exact measurement and discovered the nature of oxidation, when the methodology of discovering chemical elements was established, when chemists were wont to "discover" any number of elements at any time? Or was it when Mendeleyev established the periodic table of elements, thereby determining the number of natural elements—which in turn led to the present "logic" of chemical elements, according to which the elements are so related to each other that even the properties of as yet undiscovered elements become predictable?

This was the nature of Freud's achievement in the area of drive psychology. He not only discovered a number of "elements," but also set up a kind of "periodic table" of elementary drives. Yet the future historian will note that the pre-Freudian disorder that had characterized drive psychology has still gone on reigning in ego psychology, inasmuch as any author may still "discover" at any time any number of ego functions, the equivalent of drives in the psychology of the ego.

Just as Moses was permitted to take cognizance of the Promised Land and to catch a glance of it from afar, but not to enter it, so Freud laid the foundations for ego psychology, yet did not live to determine its final form by the writing of the three essays in which he presumably would have defined the concept of function and described its structure, as well as determined the number and devised the "periodic table" of ego functions. The observational data that are requisite for the assumption of an ego function are not yet determined—which is one of the reasons why one may speak of the present state of "wild" ego psychology.

The most frequent methodological pitfall encountered at present is the conclusion that a process that *has* a function *is* the equivalent of a function—the necessary consequence of the absence of theoretical clarity. A thermometer *has* the function of indicating changes of temperature by way of the extension and contraction of a column of mercury. While it *has* a function, it *is* itself no more than an apparatus. The id *has* the function of replenishing the psychic apparatus with energy, but one cannot therefore say that it *is* a psychic function. Similarly, matter has memory (Hering, 1870) but not in the form of a function; it possesses memory only in the form of a property.

In psychology, however, we do not yet seem to be able to distinguish between function and the result of psychic functions.[2] We know that there exists a hierarchy of ego functions that are activated in patterns; that some are subordinated to others; that some reinforce one another, while others impede one another. Yet scrutiny of the literature will demonstrate more often than not that the concept of hierarchy is called in to cover ignorance. If one wants to take note of how Freud, at a time of dawning ego psychology, when it had not yet come into its rights, used rigorous exactness in dealing with ego function, and was extremely careful to describe an ego function precisely, to delimit one from the others, to make certain what its effects and achievements were, depending on whether it did its work alone or in conjunction with another, one should read his description of free association (1900, pp. 101-103). These few paragraphs may well serve as a paradigmatic approach toward the determination of an ego function.

Yet, as an added difficulty to the problem of establishing scientific ego psychology, ego functions are per se unconscious. This truth is generally accepted only with regard to defense. We are not aware of repressing and projecting; we notice only the results of these functions, what they *achieve* (Anna Freud, 1936).

Following Stumpf (1906), I believe that this is also true of perceiving, thinking and recalling. Man is aware of these functions only insofar as they produce perceptions, thoughts and memories. The function per se, however, escapes his awareness—which is very much in contrast with the drives, which, when they are not repressed, make themselves noticed directly: they impose a task on the psychic apparatus, as Freud set forth, and the ego has the ability to perceive that task. Ego functions, by contrast, are not tasks with which the ego has to grapple, but rather tools with which it solves tasks—tools of whose uses and consequences the self is well aware, but which remain per se invisible to introspection.

---

[2] An adequate discussion of Freud's use of the term function would lead far afield. This much may be said, however. In his earliest writings, Freud (1898, p. 296) writes of the function of memory in the sense that memory *is* a function. Later (e.g., 1925, p. 128; 1933, p. 16) the term is used rather in relation to the "question of whether dreams *have* a function . . . " (italics mine). In *Beyond the Pleasure Principle* (1920, p. 62) the term takes a middle place between activity and achievement, in the same way as Freud used it in his early *Project,* when he spoke of the primary and secondary functions of the nervous system.

I have purposely set forth here this small segment of ego psychology —which is probably one of lesser importance—because I myself shall postulate, in what follows, the existence of an ego function that I believe to be characteristic of the artistic genius. To my mind, it occurs only in him; or at least it is only in his existence that it acquires decisive importance.

Reality Testing and the Doxaletheic Function.

One of the most important ego functions is reality testing, which is based on the distinction between what takes place within the psychic apparatus and what occurs outside its borders. Any impairment of the efficacy of this particular ego function constitutes a serious threat to the overall functioning.

In this respect, an essential difference becomes evident between genius and talent (or the ordinary person). In a state of high inspiration, the fantasy life of the artistic genius assumes such intensity that the total response of the psychic apparatus becomes geared to the inner creative process and to the imagery that is involved. The outer world is, in effect, ignored and inner processes produce effects that are normally produced only by external events. The paradigm—whether it be historical truth or merely a legend—is Goethe's breaking out into tears when he reached the writing of the death of Mignon.

Indeed, the vicissitudes of heroes of the imagination may not only arouse greater interest in the genius' mind than the really existent people of his actual environment, they may even elicit far more passionate feelings. Apparently, such imagery is able to provide, under such conditions, a greater sense of reality than external reality itself. We may add: if the final artistic product is to compete successfully with existing reality in the minds of an audience, it must apparently have triumphed first over the representation of external reality in the mind of the genius. What would constitute a disease, therefore, in the noncreative or moderately creative mind is to be seen as a prerequisite of outstanding creations on the part of the genius.

But immersion in his inner fantasy life, to the exclusion of awareness of outer reality, and the consequent experience of inner reality as if it were "real" reality—this is only one of the many prerequisites of singular creativity. The genius' mind is—at least in its productive phases— bombarded by a huge variety of inner stimuli, many of which demand, with varying intensity, artistic realization. Even if it should turn out that, in creative states of particular high intensity, only that imagery makes its appearance that lends itself to artistic realization—or, in other words, that is required at that particular moment in the artistic task—so that no conscious act of choosing is necessary among rival images or sets of images, nevertheless, the assumption is almost inescapable that *preconsciously* a selection has already occurred among many possible avenues.

In states of high creativity, all layers of the personality are overcathected. The entire personality reverberates during the course of the artistic process, and the raw material that presses forward for artistic elaboration stems from a wide area, indeed. The genius' reality principle requires a choice within that inner universe, for among the vast area of possibilities, one and only one possibility is able to result in that artistic perfection that is characteristic of the relatively few artistic achievements of lasting power. I call this function of selection doxaletheic, in that it selects among the irrational, the unformed, the archaic, that which is artistically valid and true and is thus suited to lead to the production of artistic perfection.[3]

The average person too thrives on the irrational (which should be called in this context the nonrational) and the archaic, which forms the living background against which rational action takes its course. What it provides is that feeling of vitality without which "rational" action becomes machine action.[4] Yet the imagery that is derived from the all-embracing archaic matrix ought to remain reasonably separate from the ego functions that are engaged in grappling with external reality. Imagery of this sort is something of a hindrance to rational action; when it occurs— quite legitimately—in those intervals of freedom from dealing with external reality that are reserved for daydreaming, it is experienced by the subject passively.

He does not need to make decisions with regard to its artistic validity and value. Daydreaming is then in the service of discharge. Rational action, after all, presupposes the suppression of a good deal of energy that would, if not suppressed, steer the subject into rather irrational—

---

[3] I have constructed the terms doxaletheic by combining two terms that were used in Greek philosophy. By *doxa* was meant those delusional and ofttimes illusory representations of reality that are the product primarily of the lack of means to investigate, to know, to prove. The fact that such representations persist even after those means have become available is responsible for their being referred to in English as "(mere) opinions." By *aletheia*, in contrast, is meant what we now call "truth"—the sum and quintessence of those cognitions of being that can be known and defended on the grounds that they are the result of (scientific) inquiry into the facts.

[4] For the psychoanalytic metapsychology of action see Hartmann (1947); Waelder (1930).

that is, reality-inadequate—pathways. Daydreaming is then a useful safety valve, which relieves the psychic apparatus of accumulated energy that is unusable for reality-adequate action yet still demands discharge.

What is a burden for the ordinary man, however, constitutes the artistic genius' lifeline. In his creative phases, he is constantly facing a task that may be compared to a filtering process; it is accomplished by the function I have named, in a cumbersome phrase, "doxaletheic." The concept of "filtering" does not do justice to the process, however, because it insinuates passivity of the sort that is implied in the concept of the "protective barrier," whereas the doxaletheic function presupposes a high degree of activity, employed at one and the same time in an intensive vigilance against the intrusion of the raw and the unsuitable and in reaching out for the fitting and the suitable, such as will serve the occasion to perfection.

About a Hypothesis Regarding Pubescent Masturbation.

There are two different schools of thought with regard to those personalities who produce outstanding cultural contributions. One of these is inclined to regard the unusual features of these personalities as intensifications of properties that are also met with in the ordinary man; the other postulates differences in quality. Consequently, the assertion that the artistic genius has a special ego function at his disposal will meet with objection from many. The artist's grappling with the universe of his imagery will be compared with the situation in which the daydreamer finds himself. The genius poet and the daydreamer will thus be reduced to a difference in quantity of cathexis, with the poet being assumed to possess a far greater amount than the daydreamer. Further, Börne's essay (1823) on "The Art of Becoming an Original Writer in Three Days," which Freud read when he was a boy and which had such a significant effect on his evolvement of the technique of free association, will probably be cited in favor of this viewpoint.

Börne rightly advises any person who would like to become an ingenious author to write down consistently for three days everything that passes through his mind; he will then observe that the outcome has justified the effort, for he will have produced a remarkable document. The difference between daydreamer and author would perforce lie in the fact that the one does not find it worth his while to jot down his vagaries on paper, whereas the other does feel impelled to do so.

Yet it is not only in this that the qualitative difference, which is completely irreducible to quantification, will come forth. Freud once wrote to a former patient who had sent him a manuscript for evaluation that it showed promise but was still "too much of a symptom."[5] It is not easy to define what "symptomatic" productions are, yet the usefulness and validity of this category of literary criticism are certain. This is not the yardstick of value that is involved, for example, when we attribute greater literary value to Shakespeare's tragedies than to those by Marlowe. Both Shakespeare and Marlowe wrote plays of great literary value; and when one is preferred to the other, it is a matter of choice among members of the same class. But symptomatic productions belong to a separate class. As elsewhere, here too, of course, there is objectively an area of overlapping.

Nor is the difference between symptomatic and validly artistic productions of a kind that may be compared to the differences that we study when we compare productions in different media. Symptomatic productions are of greater interest to the mental scientist, the psychologist, than they are to the historian of literature. They may be valuable as personal documents, as conveyors of the author's peculiarities of mind and—far less, or even not at all—as objective cultural products, representative of those objective artistic values that are characteristic of works of art.[6]

Börne's advice would lead, with very few exceptions, to "symptomatic" productions, in which the psychopathology that is peculiar to the individual writer conspicuously manifests itself, yet which are likely to be almost totally lacking in literary value. The artist is constantly in danger of falling into symptomatic writing; it is the doxaletheic function that protects him against it. When he succeeds, the result is the creation of a structure that is severed from its author and becomes instead a value in its own right, meaningful and of interest to mankind, independently of what and who its author was. The symptomatic document, by contrast, makes sense only as a carrier of psychopathology—that is to say, we can learn something from the created work mainly about its creator.

Some great authors, before creating a masterpiece, first indulge in the writing of a "symptomatic" work, which sometimes sounds like a caricature of the later artistically valuable production. Apparently, they

---

[5] It was the recently deceased Austrian poet Arthur Fischer-Colbrie (1895-1968) whose early work Freud evaluated in such terms.

[6] Parenthetically, I should like to remark that one of the main disagreements between the literary critics and the psychoanalytic writers in their approach to literature centers in the fact that the psychoanalyst frequently takes the work of art as a "symptomatic" document, whereas the historian looks at it exclusively as the realization of an objective cultural value.

first have to get rid of the subjective dross, the discharge of which facilitates the creation of the artistically perfect. It must be emphasized that this is not only a matter of form but likewise one of content. To be sure, any archaic content potentially harbors the seeds of a work of art, but only specific contents fit specific constellations. It is one of the most important tasks of the doxaletheic function to select among the mass of images that come forward in states of inspiration only that set which will lend itself to the purpose of realizing the perfect; whereas Börne's advice, if followed, would result in the exclusion of the vestigial doxaletheic function, which some may assume to be present generally.

In considering which genetic factors are decisive in the development of the doxaletheic function, I am thinking especially of pubescent masturbation—particularly in its initial stages, when the phallic demand imposes itself upon the psychic apparatus with incomparable vigor and impetuosity. This is a phase when imagery acquires a vividness and exclusiveness that make it comparable (in this respect at least), to the artist's inspirational states, when representations of external reality recede into the background, having been overridden by the overcathected images of the inner world.

The pubescent subject is compelled to return incessantly to his sexual fantasies, which temporarily acquire a higher degree of reality than external reality itself. For a while, his entire life seems to be absorbed in the service of this imaginary world.[7] Almost all pubescents are unable to keep their genital urges in a state of suspension, and therefore succumb to the excessive demand. In the act of masturbation, then, the imaginary world finds biological realization. Real reality becomes boring, monotonous, humdrum; it pales in the light of the incomparable pleasures provided by the harmony between physical sensation and sexual visions.

I would surmise that the masturbatory record of those pubescents who later develop into outstandingly creative personalities is rather poor, and possibly entirely lacking: that from the start their fantasy world has been less devoted to the sexually raw and crude, but has carried instead the earmarks of sublimated contents (Greenacre, 1957). Once the adolescent has gone through the fires of puberty without letting himself be forced into a regressive form of autoplastic gratification, he has acquired the ability to keep huge amounts of libidinal energy in suspension without resorting to shortcut gratifications.

[7] I am dealing here, of course, only with a certain type of puberty, too well known clinically to require description.

I would venture to suggest the hypothesis that, when puberty has taken such a course in a highly endowed youngster, the final seal of creativity has been impressed upon the function of fantasying and imagining. While daydreams—the derivatives of repressed and therefore ungratified libidinal and aggressive wishes—impose themselves upon the average subject more often than not as masturbatory equivalents and serve thereby as camouflaged channels of discharge, the same material serves as signals to creative action in those whose main function in life is creativity; further, whereas most daydreams are attached to a masturbatory impulse, quite independently of the actual frequency of the masturbatory act in the adult, among the creative this impulse has been converted into the urge to create values.

In passing, I want to remind the reader that in most artistic media the hand is an integral executive organ (cf. Hermann, 1925, 1930). The creative person is apparently protected against the passive use of archaic derivatives for purposes of direct libidinal gratification (with or without masturbation), by activation of the doxaletheic function, thus making for the conversion of fitting derivatives into the pure gold of artistic values.

Since nothing is known about the pubertal genital life of subjects who later achieved cultural eminence, all this, of course, remains no more than speculation. However, I shall briefly report on some clinical observations I have made on an artistically endowed subject; although these observations do not prove my proposition, at least they do not contradict it and may even lend some probability to it.

A subject who started his analysis in late adolescence was incapable of performing an ejaculation, despite repeated attempts to do so. His manifest sexual life throughout puberty was restricted to infrequent spontaneous nocturnal emissions. There was no endocrine disturbance present. He was an excellent student, who achieved high grades without effort and participated with great enthusiasm in most cultural matters. From early childhood on, he had shown consistent and intensive interest in art and had become conversant with the handling of the relevant medium. Almost nothing he encountered "left him cold." Experiences both of nature and of art made deep marks on him and often elicited almost passionate outbursts. While his friendships with men and women were intense, he never fell in love.

Surprisingly, his inability to ejaculate did not lead to painful states of frustration, such as occur regularly in cases of *ejaculatio retardata*. He never expressed any inner need or desire for an orgasm or for relief of sexual tension, and he vigorously denied my suggestion that sexually he must feel enormously frustrated. He had asked for treatment solely because he was not able to do what other men were able to do. If he had lived during an earlier century, the same symptom would probably have given him a feeling of superiority over his contemporaries, and he would have been proud of going through life "without sin." Had he not entered analysis, his sexual life would have remained, in all probability, completely restricted to nocturnal emissions.

Here then was an adolescent of great artistic endowment whose life was eminently active and productive; who did not appear neurotic in his conduct; who was in no way curtailed in his intellectual development or in his ability to experience the world in both its aspects—natural as well as cultural—in a rich and meaningful way, and who enjoyed life with great zest—and all this despite the fact that he suffered from a symptom that is, under ordinary circumstances, clinically appraised as severe, even ominous. In the light of a totally impoverished genital life and a complete lack of conscious desire for sexual gratification, one might have expected a stunted personality, unable to experience the world in most of its dimensions meaningfully and productively.

As Heinz Hartmann so very correctly once said, in a clinical discussion, there are pubescents about whom one cannot determine the diagnosis of schizophrenia as long as they are still in puberty. Only after the conclusion of that developmental phase will it become clear whether their symptomatology belongs to this group of disorders or not. I would vary this observation and say that, during the puberty of an outstandingly endowed subject, one cannot predict whether or not he belongs in the class of geniuses. Only after puberty will this become clear.

Indeed, if Shakespeare had died after producing *Titus Andronicus*, a literary critic would have received nothing but scorn and ridicule if he had had the boldness to assert that its author had been the potential creator of *Hamlet* or a *Lear*. The same is true *mutatis mutandis* of predictions based on the tyro productions of Leonardo, Rembrandt and Goethe. Similarly, the late Quartets of Beethoven would be unpredictable if only his First Symphony had reached us. We may have an opportunity later to speculate on why initial achievements precisely of those who will later become geniuses are sometimes even less promising than the initial successes of those who will later develop into merely great talents.

Be that as it may, the patient I have sketched above, who succeeded in inducing masturbatory ejaculations after two years of psychoanalysis, impressed me as possessing the potential of geniushood; at least, his personality carried the earmarks of it. Of course, eminent achievements depend not only on personality but also on the possession of skills. He did possess unusual skills, but whether they were commensurate with the accomplishments of a genius could not ever be determined at the time I was acquainted with him. I doubt, however, that the cure of the symptom stood his development as an artist in good stead.

Looking back, I must admit that I made a mistake in his treatment. I should have concentrated—to the exclusion of the analysis of any other problem—solely on the question of why he was so urgently demanding to be made capable of performing an act that he did not desire to perform for its own sake but only for reasons of rivalry, envy and competition. Once this question had been answered, then the patient might have been satisfied with the way he was and perhaps his skills might have flowered later into outstanding achievements. As a matter of fact, when he left treatment he still impressed me as a person who was more richly endowed than the average person and most promising; yet the expectation of his later blossoming into a genius had already diminished.

In such rare instances, the analyst faces a dilemma he is not prepared to solve: should he or should he not free the patient from the obstacles that block the way toward a free phallic discharge? A delay in masturbation, not to speak of a total incapacity for it, is a warning signal and, to a certain extent, it appears to be the psychoanalyst's clinical duty to provide the patient as quickly as is feasible with a proper channel of discharge.

The overloading of the psychic apparatus with pent-up, excessive libidinal energy, divorced from any possible discharge may, if it lasts for a long enough period, damage the psychic apparatus, at a time when a subject has not yet become adult—which is to say, has not yet become sufficiently structured and solidified to bear without permanent damage enormous undischarged libidinal quantities.

Furthermore, an analyst should never play a godlike role. When a patient hankers after the ability to live a sexual life in keeping with the customs of his society, one may argue on good grounds that this is a reasonable demand and should be fulfilled, and that the patient's development should never become the subject of any analyst's speculation about the cultural potentialities dormant in him. On the other hand, the relevance of the problem may be denied and it may be said that the analyst ought not to overestimate the importance of his advice. If a person's "artistic impulse is stronger than the internal resistances, analysis will heighten, not diminish the capacity for achievement," as Freud said in answer to an inquiry on the subject (Jones, Vol. 3, p. 416). This statement may be true once a person has discovered himself as a talent, or perhaps once he has reached adulthood; but I am quite convinced that this assertion cannot be made with the same certitude about a potential genius who is seeking treatment during puberty.

My patient's sexual inhibition, if it was indeed a bona fide inhibition, was bound to give way one day under the impact of the psychoanalytic process or under biological pressure. Granted that outstandingly great artistic achievement is not necessarily compatible with normal sexual development,[8] then one has to face the possibility that, in this instance, psychoanalytic interference might well have blocked the way to unusual achievements.[9] In our times, when there is even a widespread belief in the *necessity* for youth to achieve full sexual gratification at the earliest possible time, the chance that the patient may produce values belonging to the class of genius could be greatly reduced by such interference, despite the relative frequency of talent.

The Fantasy of the Imaginary Companion and the Psychology of Creativity.

Dr. Ruth S. Eissler has called to my attention that in the search for model structures, occurring within the broad spectrum of normal development, that may be brought into meaningful connection with the psychology of creativity, the fantasy of the imaginary companion should not be omitted. In the creation of the imaginary companion the child's imagination takes a particularly creative turn, by means of which he makes himself independent of the frustrations imposed by reality. He finds an outlet for libidinal and aggressive impulses without having to come into conflict with his environment. Compliance with reality necessities is greatly eased, since the point of gravity of psychic life shifts to a relation-

[8] At least in certain personality types. It cannot be accidental that it is precisely the greatest artists—Michelangelo (Clements, 1965), Leonardo (Frey n.d.), Beethoven (Sterba and Sterba, 1954, p. 99), Newton (Manuel, 1968, p. 191), Kant (Herzberg, 1926)—who seem never to have had intercourse, so far as is known. In many others, a delay in heterosexual maturation can be observed. Goethe had intercourse for the first time at the age of 38 or 39 (Bode, 1921), and Mozart (1781) at 26.

[9] Of course, if an analyst were to object to my hypothesis about the libidinal economy of a certain type of genius, then my doubts and hesitations on this score would have no meaning for him.

ship in which all wishes are fulfilled. While other fantasies, such as those that relate to father or mother, may be shattered by the hard facts of reality, this configuration, which is constantly present and ever ready to serve the child's unconscious, fulfills the child's needs, whatever they may be. Feelings of guilt are aroused to a lesser extent by this fantasy figure than by those fantasies that show oedipal implications with less disguise.

In this light, it is interesting to regard the fantasy figures that the playwright derives as being equivalents of the child's imaginary companions. They, too, are constantly with him and behave and talk in a way that is subterraneously connected with the author's unconscious. Not only are they no longer connected directly with the creator of the imagery, they seem instead to have acquired an independent existence and therefore to constitute a significant step beyond the narcissistically bound "imaginary companion" of the child.

A comparison with the infant's transitory object becomes almost compelling. Just as the transitory object becomes a hardly avoidable stepping-stone toward the child's complete object relationship, so the imaginary companion may be viewed as a stepping-stone toward the evolvement of fantasy figures that have objective validity and are therefore usable for great artistic creations.

It is regrettable that nothing is known about the early fantasy life of the genius. One has to surmise that the imaginary companion makes his appearance there as an important early adjunct on the way toward the formation of artistically usable imagery. In clinical practice one often has the occasion to study the detrimental effect that the imaginary companion may produce, inasmuch as the child may become fixated to it, and refuse to tolerate the minimum of frustration and hardship that is involved in object relations even under optimal conditions. But the fantasy of the imaginary companion, in the potentially creative child, would be less in the service of an object-like relationship and tend more toward the creation of a world; it may therefore serve rather more constructive purposes that those one is wont to observe in patients who submit to the psychoanalytic treatment. Furthermore, as Dr. Ruth S. Eissler has stressed, the child often insists that his adult environment acknowledge his (imaginary) companion and regard it as real. In that sense this not so infrequent situation in the child's nursery may be the earliest instance of the search for "audience approval."

Wish Fulfillments in Cultural Values.

When Freud discovered that the subjectively unpleasant and even the painful—for example, a neurotic symptom—may harbor and serve a wish fulfillment, the way was then cleared for making the same discovery with regard to a number of cultural phenomena in which one would hardly have anticipated finding wish fulfillments. Freud was well aware of culture's quite opposite effect—the enormous frustrations with which it burdens man. Yet the tenacity with which some cultural phenomena maintain their roots in man's life can only be the result of wish fulfillments that mankind seems to find indispensable—if it is to endure the profound frustrations that are part and parcel of human existence in a civilized world.

Religion—the belief in a Deity who has created the universe and directs human destiny—is probably the supreme cultural reflection of mankind's needs; the existence of a Deity, however, or its equivalent is not the most probable among the great variety of constructions that man's ingenuity has had the potentiality to devise in the service of explaining the world, nor the one about which one could say that it harbored the greatest claim to probable correctness. Along with religion, art too contains the element of wish fulfillment. As easy as it may be to discover this element in aesthetic contexts, however, just so difficult is it sometimes to accept it so far as the *content* of artistic productions is considered. Such works as *Werther* or *Hamlet*, in which the tragedy of human life is so forcefully and penetratingly presented that the sensitive mind can respond only with grief and even despair, would seem to reduce the validity of any theory that attempts to link art with wish fulfillment.

What needs to be stressed first is that there is a decisive difference between art and religion with regard to the painful effect that both of them may possibly exert on the human mind. The preoccupation with the sufferings of the Savior that is central to the Christian religious experience arouses necessarily painful feelings, which are at least as intense as those evoked by some tragic literary works. The difference lies in the fact that the concentration of the devout upon the painful is in the service of a superego demand: powerful institutions, which demand such spiritual immersion, promise future rewards for submitting to it. But the turn toward the tragic in art takes place independently of any such motivations. No future rewards are offered to him who suffers the grief and the pain that are inextricably involved in certain artistic experiences

· 535 ·

Surprisingly enough, it is just those artistic creations in which the wish fulfillment is most camouflaged that seem to have the greatest effect upon audiences. This is a problem that has puzzled a great many illustrious minds, probably ever since art reached the level of tragedy. But I do not want to enter here into a discussion of the various theories that have been put forward as explanations of this curious phenomenon. By and large, I believe that most of these theories are of some value and that each of them does contain some truth; yet it seems to me that none of them has succeeded in explaining the phenomenon satisfactorily. Why is man eager to experience, by way of a performance on a stage, something that—if he met it in reality—would arouse in him terror and fright? Why does he stand in admiration before a painting that depicts events he would refuse even to look at, if they were presented to him in reality?

The emphasis that is generally placed upon the non-reality of artistically presented events has its merits; but it is not quite satisfactory, insofar as these terrifying events do acquire a kind of full reality, within the context that Freud called "psychic reality." From dreams and fantasies one learns that contents of artistic creations that have to do with painful subjects are as penetratingly represented in the psychic world as are those that actually do occur in external reality. When a person witnesses a street accident, he may turn his head away or close his eyes; his defenses against what may threaten to become a trauma set in automatically. If the horrible reality event takes on such proportions as to make momentary defenses of this sort impossible, and the person is forced to face it, one regularly observes a struggle, which sets in almost at once, to get rid of the memory and its effect by the instituting of defenses. (These vary, of course, from person to person.)

It is quite different with art. There a person will return over and over again to tragic contents. The more a person becomes impressed by Shakespeare's tragedies, the more he will be moved to spend time on their study and enjoyment. What would constitute a trauma if encountered within the context of reality, and is therefore to be shunned in whatever way possible, becomes a matter of unending attraction when it is presented in the form of a work of art. Thus it seems that the art work serves the function of overcoming trauma, of "taming" it—enabling the subject to integrate traumatic contents without having to suffer any injury in so doing.

Furthermore, at the core of many great artistic creations in the field of literature, one can observe a complex and contrived pattern that is equivalent to a psychosis. Whether one has to do with a poet's report of his travel through purgatory in the company of a colleague who has been deceased for centuries; or a prince who is made to believe by a ghost that his father was the victim of murder by his own brother; or a young man who cannot tolerate the idea of annihilating insects when he goes out walking, who falls in love with an unattainable woman and then commits suicide; or, finally, a knight who takes windmills for giants and kitchen maids for princesses—if one were to encounter any of these characters in reality, each of them would very likely evoke in a modern mind the sense that such a person must indeed be suffering from some severe mental disorder.

I believe that these two factors, the traumatic and the psychotic, are represented more strongly in Shakespeare's plays than in the creations of any other literary genius. But is it on the intense involvement of these two factors that Shakespeare's glory rests as the greatest psychologist in literature? Certainly not. Reports on the experiences to which the prisoners in concentration camps had to submit contain descriptions of traumata that make the traumatic experiences of Shakespeare's protagonists seem pale. Further, our textbooks of psychiatry contain histories of psychoses that demonstrate the structure of insanity explicitly.

Yet the former type of literature we either try to forget or else avoid reading altogether, while the latter is of interest only to a very small group of professionally interested readers. Among the large number of factors that make these types of writing quite different from Shakespeare's tragedies, I want to select only the one that seems to me to be of some importance in this particular context. In the literature on concentration-camp atrocities and in psychiatric literature there is an explicit presentation of traumata and psychoses as results of particular situations, as dealing with events that have nothing to do with the general characteristics of man but are rather exceptional, inherently avoidable, unnecessary or based solely on the coincidence of specific and rarely occurring factors—in brief, illustrations of what can *perhaps* occur, under *unusual* circumstances (when life goes astray).

The difference between Shakespeare's plays and these two groups of professional literature is not only a matter of form, although, of course, form is a prerequisite of the aesthetic experience. From the viewpoint I am pursuing here, it is decisive that the traumatic and the psychotic are presented in his plays as manifestations of life, interwoven into the fabric of an artistically created world in which we somehow find ourselves participating. They are part and parcel of Shakespeare's universe; one could perhaps even go so far as to say that, in Shakespeare's plays, life *is* trauma and psychosis. One of the great reasons for the attraction that Shakespeare's tragedies have held for people all over the world is his art of providing the mastery of anxiety, despite the presentation of what might arouse the peak of terror if it were to be experienced outside his universe. [10]

While what is presented on the stage may be that which we most fear, yet it is presented in such a way as not to lead in the beholder to an outbreak of anxiety. [11]

I have here viewed Shakespeare's tragedies from the general standpoint of man's relationship to anxiety with regard to external dangers (which leads to traumatization) and such internal dangers as disintegration of the mind (which leads to psychosis). Both are represented forcefully, and yet the spectator is able to take part in them without developing anxiety—all of which leads almost to a temporary state of immunity toward danger. It is as if these dangers did not exist qua danger, or were nothing one has to fear—which comes close to the area covered by the general term *denial*. Yet this is not the sort of denial that one encounters in clinical practice, for the dangerousness of the world is fully represented. If the element of danger were to be underplayed in a tragedy, it would most certainly lose its gripping effect. [12]

The denial I am referring to does not therefore have to do with the existence of danger and trauma. If anything, the anguish of life is presented in an exaggerated way. After all, the vast majority of people go

[10] The mastery of anxiety in the aesthetic experience is by no means a new discovery; it has long had its place in the psychoanalytic literature (see Freud and particularly Kris). Yet it deserves reemphasis here, in view of the fact that Shakespeare's tragedies are, like no other literary universe, an accumulation of naked terror. This makes it inordinately puzzling that the aesthetic experience is never weakened or interrupted by a sudden derailment into anxiety or disgust.

[11] As a biological model of man's ability to expose himself voluntarily to the unpleasant without feeling repelled, the behavior of dogs comes to mind. It is well known with what intensity male dogs sniff the smell of bitches in heat. But a like intensity of sniffing can be observed when what is involved is the smell of a rival that a dog has just attacked with utter ferocity and that has since been removed from sight. The psychoanalytic theory would make one expect a revulsion against traces of a hated object, just as Babylonian kings had the name of a hated competitor eradicated. To be sure, after long intensive sniffing the dog too "eradicates" the smell of his rival. In German one expresses a deep aversion against a person as "I cannot stand his smell" (*ich kann ihn nicht riechen*. Lit., "I cannot smell him"). Here the smell of a loved object and of a hated one evoke opposite reactions; but in a lower species differentiation depends on visual configuration, while the odoriferous part-object evokes identical responses whether it belongs to a loved object or a hated one.

[12] In an early paper, Freud (1908, p. 194 f.) pointed out "the feeling of security with which I follow the hero through his perilous adventures" in writings of "the less pretentious authors" of prose works.

through life without being exposed to anything like Hamlet's afflictions. Yet the fact that the great playwright has the power to force the spectator *mentally* to go through Hamlet's afflictions (by empathy and identification), and yet at the same time protects him against suffering their sequelae—this brings one aspect of tragedy close to the orbit of denial, as we know it analytically.

Be that as it may, a form of human creativity as complex as tragedy and a phenomenon as complex and paradoxical as man's ability to make the horrible and the painful enjoyable cannot be placed over the same denominator. Almost everything that is to be observed in human life is the outcome of opposing forces, and this must also be true of tragedy.

In order to develop what I have in mind, I have to digress once again to the subject of anxiety, as well as to that of masochism.

No one doubts a description of the *craving* of organisms for life and activity. Everything that is living seems to bear witness to an urge to continue to live; only in the final stages, perhaps, do some kinds of organisms seem to surrender to their end, without putting up any defense. As willingly as the concept of a desire for life is generally accepted, however, just so vigorously is the concept of a desire rejected that is perhaps of equal intensity—the desire to die. And yet the most illustrious minds have individually hinted at the existence of such a desire, or at a preference of death over life.

That preference has been stated explicitly, for example, by Sophocles: "Not to be born surpasses thought and speech. The second best is to have seen the light and then go back quickly whence we came"; and by Euripides: "One should lament the newborn with regard to the plentitude of woe that is awaiting him. But the dead who are liberated from all sufferings one should accompany on their last way with sacred sounds of joy."[13] And by Shakespeare: "Reason thus with life:/If I do lose thee, I do lose a thing/That none but fools would keep."

It would be incorrect, perhaps, to say that these excerpts prove that their authors held such gloomy views themselves, even though some philosophers have evolved systems of thought that are explicitly characterized by the rejection of life. Yet the mere fact that passages of such extreme pessimism have been put at all into outstanding plays, that great playwrights have assumed that they would be understood and tolerated by the audience, that many in the audience would probably even agree

---

[13] According to Licht (1925, p. 22). I have been unable to locate this passage in Euripides.

with such pronouncements—this seems to me to prove that there are many people in whom such an outlook must be quite alive, even if in most instances only latently. Moreover, it must be remembered that the spiritual foundation of entire historical phases—for example, the Christian Middle Ages—rested on the belief that life in this world is only a matter of a short moment, and that what really counts is the life after death.[14]

The profound pessimism of Greek tragedy stands in amazing contrast with Greece's renowned "joy of life." Yet it was more than a poetic necessity; it pervades the entire culture. Nor was it merely the belief of a people who were still confined within the shackles of a magical religion. The great mind of the Enlightenment, Gotthold Ephraim Lessing, praised the wisdom of his son, who did not want to leave the womb but had to be drawn out of it by force, and expired shortly thereafter.

I interpret such statements as philosophical and literary reflections of a biological desire for dissolution into nothingness, for return to the womb, for permanent release from the burden of life, for death. I am here following Freud's idea of a death instinct, leaving open the troublesome question of whether or not it is an instinct, and calling it instead a longing, a desire, for the most part unconscious and only at times surging up into consciousness. A human being who has never longed for death, never thought of suicide, never hoped not to awaken once he had fallen asleep would indeed be a rare exception. It may be that man must spend a third of his life sleeping as a tribute to his longing to die: he fulfills this wish in a wholesome (if partial) way, while the biological function of sleep may serve as a symbol of death. Man is the only species that is aware of death and, paradoxically enough, this awareness has made him the only species that possesses the capacity for committing suicide.

If the desire to die is in fact appreciable in man, it is evident, in view of the survival of the human species, that nature must have instituted a potent bulwark against man's falling victim to this longing. I postulate that anxiety is the mechanism—*sit venia verbo*—that vigorously counteracts man's longing for death. This is also, as I see it, the reason why anxiety plays such a greater role in man's life than it does in that of any other species. I am not ignoring here, of course, the infinitely complicating role of the superego, which makes man's life so much more complex than the

---

[14] From this, one would have to conclude that the death of a baptized child, before it had had any opportunity to sin, would be the most fortunate sequence of all.

animal's. I am here thinking primarily of a deeply buried biological necessity.

Freud correctly perceived the life-favoring, if not life-saving, role of anxiety in the process of birth. It is anxiety that by its innervation contributes to the activity of the lungs and the acceleration of the heartbeat, hereby protecting the organism against toxic substances (Freud, 1926a, p. 134), after it has been forced to relinquish the state of "lifeless life," as it were, in the womb. It is for that state that it will unconsciously crave throughout the rest of its existence—as is testified, if by nothing else, by the ubiquitous though not regular fetal position during sleep.

The moment of birth is critical; to speak somewhat adultomorphically (Spitz, 1965), the newborn does not wish to live. The beginning of life is painful and the adult world has to institute potent measures in order to counteract the neonate's desire to give up that life with which he has been endowed against his wish and desire. The adult world has to "bribe" the neonate to stay alive by providing the illusion, as well as it can, that the infant is still in the womb. If the newborn is not provided with a special pleasure premium of coddling and stroking, it may die even if it is given the needed amount of calories (Spitz, 1945, 1946)

The longing for death presupposes a desire to be injured and traumatized. Consequently it would be justified to presuppose in man not only a traumatophobia—a potent striving toward the avoidance of injury —but also a traumatophilia[15]—a desire to throw oneself into the pathway of injury, in order to be annihilated. Anxiety, in the proper proportion, increases man's keenness in perceiving dangers and thus often leads to adequate protection against those dangers. But this is, I think, a secondary gain; the primary gain is the countereffect against the desire to surrender to danger and to be traumatized.

If there were really no inherent desire to be traumatized, I do not think that nature would have had to institute such powerful means in man to make him avoid traumata. Clinically that can be seen best in patients who suffer from inordinate anxieties (I am not thinking primarily of phobic patients). I have never observed a patient whose principal symptom was anxiety who would not otherwise have suffered from inor-

---

[15] The term traumatophilia has been used by Ferenczi (1914, p. 305; 1916, p. 39). In modern psychiatric literature the term "accident proneness" has become popular. The subject of trauma and anxiety cannot be discussed adequately here. The reader may be referred to a recent publication (Furst, ed., 1967). A psychoanalytic discussion of traumatophilia would be beyond the scope of this study.

dinate masochism. One patient, who suffered anxiety that "every day was more severe than it had been on the preceding day," whose life was pervaded by intolerable anxiety, had already had as a child the wishful fantasy of being a speck on the mother's breast, an exquisitely masochistic wish.

It may be contended that it is difficult to decide whether anxiety makes a man masochistic or masochism causes anxiety. Yet this is a sham problem. The reason why anxiety is able to counteract man's desire to suffer and die as effectively as it does, is that through anxiety masochism is gratified in a nonnoxious way. As so often happens in the act of defense, part of what the defense is directed against is also gratified. Anxiety without displeasure is hardly conceivable, and the displeasure that forces man to abstain from masochistic gratifications constitutes at the same time a partial gratification of masochism.[16] Freud has delineated the development stages from the oral anxiety about being devoured to the phallic anxiety of castration. Yet the former is present when the child wishes to be devoured (Lewin, 1950), and the latter when the boy would like to be a girl and to give birth to children.

In tragedy man is able to enjoy the suffering of traumata without dire consequences. All those things in reality that he has to ward off by the evolvement of anxiety, he is able to enjoy without anxiety while beholding a tragedy.

Even if we were to meet in reality only a small fraction of the horrible things that occur in Shakespeare's tragedies, they would arouse in us repeated nightmares because they would have severely traumatized us. If anxiety were to set in while the spectator was following the events of a tragedy, that would force him to return to the pathway of ordinary life in which biological necessities make him avoid the enjoyment of traumatization. In viewing tragic events on the stage, however, he can permit himself "to be traumatized without being injured"—if such a paradoxical statement is permitted. He undergoes the full "enjoyment" of trauma —which is to say that the inner conflict between traumatophobia and traumatophilia has been temporarily reduced.

In my opinion, the existence of tragedy, even though it makes its appearance at the level of a highly differentiated culture, suggests that a traumatophilia exists in man on an archaic psychobiological level, such

---

[16] According to this viewpoint, Freud's early (but later discarded) theory (recently rejected with vigor once again by Rangell, 1968)—namely, that anxiety is in each instance a transformation of libido—would be proven to have contained a deep truth.

as is usually not observable clinically and only rearely reaches conscious-ness. Without biological traumatophilia, superego feelings of guilt, de-sire for punishment might not have been possible in the evolution of man's mind. Man's desire to re-experience the painful in art, his great admiration of tragedy—these presuppose traumatophilia. But all this should not make us forget that tragedy also serves as a sort of denial of trauma. It is the intricate blending of both that make tragedy what it is. If either of them dominates the whole, the artistic value is greatly reduced and may vanish entirely. When traumatophobia prevails and the world is represented as harmonious, contented, conflict-free, devoid of trauma, then the result is boredom; when traumatophilia prevails, as it does in trashy literature or "horror" movies, then disgust is the outcome, at least among the sophisticated.

Here it may be proper to make a few comments on subjective re-sponses to tragedy. Individual responses vary, of course, from person to person, but I must limit myself to a negative statement that may contain a significant generality. While the beholder is experiencing or re-experi-encing *Hamlet, Lear* or *Othello,* he is hardly likely to become afraid, in his own life, of being poisoned or approaching madness or of becoming the victim of a beloved person's jealousy. The more deeply the artistic experience has been felt, the less chance will there be that such reactions of fear are elicited in the beholder.

This is quite different from reading in the newspaper about just such happenings. Under the latter circumstances, we may respond in-stead with an increased awareness of how dangerous a place the world really is. Logically, one might expect that the sharing of such horrifying events as Shakespeare sometimes puts on the stage should release in us a state of fear. Events that would frighten us under ordinary circumstances should frighten us all the more, it would seem, when offered to us in the overwhelming, penetrating form devised by Shakespeare's genius.

To be sure, exquisiteness of form, according to Freud (1905, p. 137; 1908, p. 153), functions as a kind of "incentive bonus" (*Verlockungsprämie*), making the horrible palatable, acceptable, even enjoyable. Yet under the proper circumstances the performance of a Shakespearean tragedy may move the beholder so deeply that he breaks into tears—tears that are not the witness of a sentimental, melodramatic mood but rather the expression of a truly and profoundly tragic feeling.

As is well known, a child may respond to such situations with anxi-ety. I have often found, in the history of male patients, that they were severely traumatized, shortly after the onset of the latency period, by a film whose contents evidently confirmed for them the reality of castration. Even as late as during the final stages of delayed adolescence, artisic experiences may have traumatic effects. I am not as certain as some other investigators have been that the reproach raised against Goethe after the publication of *Werther*—that the novel was causing an increase in suicides among young men—may not have been justified.[17]

Be that as it may, having attained a certain point of development, the beholder's self becomes sufficiently solid not to be traumatized by contact with great art. If anything, after a stirring artistic experience, whatever the specific emotional response may be—and I wish to repeat that this holds true only if we exclude the feeling of anxiety—the subject feels *closer to life*. He is convinced that something extremely valuable has been added to his experience, something that he would not have wanted to miss. This sensation may also be described in other terms. To anyone who has taken part in a profound and stirring artistic experience, the details of everyday life become reduced in importance. The spectrum of what is important shifts then to contexts beyond the immediately urgent; the dangers of the present appear to have been shrunken. One may speak here of a "post-artistic" effect, just as one speaks of a post-traumatic one; but the two are antithetic in character.[18]

May I once again stress that it is only anxiety that is essentially incompatible with the experience of art. Aside from that, the response may be rage, despair, weeping, awe, etc. Even a direct sexual response may under circumstances be still compatible with the "aesthetic" experience.

[17] The theater (like most other artistic media) has been accused of corrupting man, but it has also been praised for making him rise to a higher level. As a matter of fact, the theater may have either effect. In terms of this context, it would depend on whether, by minimizing the danger of trauma, it makes man brazen, thereby causing him boldly to attempt to override the dangers of trauma (and of the forbidden); or reduces masochistic propensities and decreases traumatophilia (at least temporarily)—which in turn leads to loss of anxiety upon meeting with reality dangers. Man then lives in a world that in terms of his own daily life appears to be more secure, even though, taken as a whole, it is perhaps experienced as more tragic than before.

[18] Much has been written about the effect of art on the psyche, on morality, on human conduct in general. Here I want to quote only one passage from Nietzsche (1870-71, p. 56f), who called art (particularly in the sense of Greek tragedy) "a rescuing, healing sorceress" [*eine rettende, heilkundige Zauberin*]: "It [art] alone is able to deflect those nausea [ting] thoughts about the dreadfulness or the absurd [ity] of existence into ideas with which it is possible to live. These [ideas] are the *sublime* (as the artistic taming of the dreadful) and the *comic* (as the artistic defusing of the nausea of [aroused by] the absurd)." [*Sie allein vermag jene Ekelgedanken über das Entsetzliche oder Absurde des Daseins in Vorstellungen umzubiegen, mit denen sich leben lässt: diese sind das* Erhabene *als die kunstlerische Bändigung des Entsetzlichen und das* Komische *als die künstlerische Entladung vom Ekel des Absurden.*] (author's italics)

A patient of mine was once so overwhelmed during puberty by the beauty of a Rembrandt painting that he had to masturbate. The subject of the painting was not erotic; but, in accordance with the patient's developmental phase, excessive stimulation of any kind led to an effect on the genital sphere, in somewhat the way that Freud described in the *Three Essays*, with regard to the child. In my patient, "aesthetic" arousal had reached such an excessive degree that it brought about what Freud refers to, in a different context, as "the puzzling leap from the mental to the physical" (cf. Freud, 1916-1917, p. 258); and although he still had to travel a good distance in order to establish adequate sublimations, we would nevertheless not insist that his response was incommensurate, as we would have had to do if anxiety had set in.[19]

Yet, in making the absence of any arousal of anxiety in the spectator the pivotal point of the effect of tragedy, I seem to come into fundamental disagreement with Aristotle's *Poetics* and its central theme of catharsis through the arousal (and then the purging) of pity and terror. I cannot help making a few remarks on that difficult subject.

Aristotle's concept of "catharsis" has found different interpretations. Although it is extensively discussed in Butcher's (1894) classical text, I am not certain that the passage in Aristotle's text has yet found satisfactory explanation. Goethe's (1827) proposition—that Aristotle's intent was not to speak of psychic processes in the spectator but rather about the course that the action takes in the play itself—if true, would free the passage from its mystery; but that interpretation is generally rejected.[20]

Another question has to do with the sort of emotion of which the onlooker is to be purged. It may be asked whether Aristotle's concept of "terror" is identical with our term "anxiety."[21] Whichever way this question is answered (and indeed it has puzzled most commentators), there is a problem of more fundamental importance involved. Why would the arousal of terror in the onlooker reduce his terror? To be sure, Freud himself thought that his early technique—treatment by emotional

19 For anxiety as a disturbing factor in artistic experience, see Kohut and Levarie (1950); Kohut (1957).

20 The main objection raised against Goethe's interpretation is the fact that in the *Politics*, Aristotle uses the term "catharsis" quite clearly with regard to the effect of music on the psyche. While Goethe was well aware of the meaning of "catharsis" in the *Politics*, he rightly said that the two passages, even though they are "analogous," are not necessarily "identical."

21 For Aristotle's definition of fear (terror), see Butcher, 1894, p. 256. Anxiety may have held a different functional position in the ancient Greeks' personality (see Dodds, 1951).

discharge while the patient was in a hypnotic state—had a therapeutic effect. But to begin with, there it was a matter of the verbalization of repressed imagery, and the arousal and discharge of emotions most of which were being kept by the subject in a state of repression; second, the whole technique did not fulfill its promise and was therefore discarded by Freud.

Others who know more about ancient Greece than I do may be prepared to explain why, in the texts of Greek tragedy that have reached us, barbaric actions are apparently banished from the stage. As far as I know, no killing takes place in view of the audience. We hear the agonized cry of the victim, but the killing itself is hidden from sight. I wonder how the Greek audience would have responded to a Shakespearean tragedy, with its visual presentation of the most barbaric actions. Would they have found it intolerable? Would the ancient Greeks have been unable to bear the cruelties that were being visually presented? Would they have let out a great howl, or would a riot have broken out? or would they have run away in terror? Whatever their response, it is certain that their level of ego development was different from ours.

I am puzzled by the sort of patient who, in the emotional sphere, depends mainly on perception and to a far lesser degree on thought and knowledge. Such a patient will be able to report on certain facts with equanimity, yet respond with intense emotions upon perceiving the very same things about which he just had spoken so calmly. To a certain extent, this is a general property. All of us read with relative calmness about extraordinary catastrophes, yet become painfully affected upon witnessing even only a relatively minor street accident. Yet in the sort of patient I have mentioned, this discrepancy takes on a proportion far beyond that commonly met with.

Unless Greek tragedy had to bow to censorship, as Shakespeare also had to in religious or ecclesiastical matters, one may conclude that the Greeks in general suffered from perceptual fears. But since, according to Aristotle, the release of terror in the spectator was one of the functions of tragedy, one might expect that an intensification of terror by way of the presentation of a murder on the stage would have best served that purpose.

The discharge of pity is even more puzzling, since pity is, after all, a social asset: the cohesion of the community would seem to be greatly weakened by the fact that its members let that valuable emotion flow into fictitious situations and then returned to their daily tasks with less than they had had of it earlier. I refer the reader once again to Butcher's text, so that he may learn how the commentators have tried to bridge this and similar difficulties.[22]

After this digression into the dark problem of the psychological function of tragedy, let us return to the playwright. In the act of creating a great work of art, the artist places himself in a dangerous position, for he is exposing himself to an intrusion of the traumatic and the psychotic. For a while he must let what is usually denied, or made innocuous by other means, grow in himself until it becomes a truth of undeniable reality. Potentially, he may himself become traumatized or overwhelmed by the archaic-irrational, which he has been laboring to put into forms that will not traumatize or disgust his audience. In moments of high inspiration, the artist is in a state of excitement and reduced reality-testing; he is so immersed in the onrush of internal imagery as to be, in effect, immune to the reality that surrounds him—very much as though he were in the grip of an acute psychosis. Particularly in the initial stages of his career, but possibly as well throughout all his later creative phases, he is unable to foresee the end while the creative act is taking place, to be quite certain that he is indeed on the right path toward accomplishing the artistic goal that he has staked out in his imagination.

In many instances he may be—and more often than not will be—surprised by the voices that talk in and to him. A playwright of Shakespeare's stature is not, I believe, in the position in which a sculptor like Michelangelo finds himself, when he projects into the raw block of marble the figure that he will chisel out of it. The playwright may be altogether stunned by the world that opens up in him, perhaps closer to Dostoevski, who allegedly often did not know beforehand what turn the lives of his heroes would take.

It was just because Shakespeare had the ability to perceive a world that no one, either before or after him, was capable of experiencing spontaneously, that he had, as it were, of necessity to borrow his plots from chronicles or from other sources. His need to build the outgrowths of his imagination around narratives already contrived by others may be compared with needs of an organism that can take in only predigested food, since the "raw stuff," as found in nature, would provoke lethal reactions

---

[22] I must apologize for starting the discussion of an important problem and leaving it in such an unsatisfactory state. The audience response, however, is not germane to the main purpose of this book. I am not able to exclude it altogether and regret that I have to omit the even more important aspect of *conflict arousal* in the person who witnesses a tragedy. Slochower stresses this aspect.

in it. The fact that the plot had been preformed by others may have given him at least a minimum of reassurance that he need not worry about his own sanity.[23]

The Plight of the Artistic Genius.

When Freud, contrary to his own expectations, discovered a new world, whose existence had been surmised before him yet had never been presented in rational, scientific terms, and when his discoveries were rejected by his contemporaries, he found himself in a position comparable to that of the artistic genius who is far ahead of his own times and is therefore during his lifetime either ignored or condemned. However, in this period of doubt and struggle there was, as Freud himself reported, a fixed point that gave him the certainty of being on the right track—the interpretation of dreams—which he called "a solace and a support to me in those arduous first years of analysis" (1914b, p. 20). Here he was apparently able to obtain every day, by way of direct observation—one is almost inclined to say by sense perception—the conviction that his conclusions, even though they ran counter to most of the tradition of Western psychology and philosophy, nevertheless did contain an essential truth. They were not, he could see by way of living examples, the outcome of some misguided fantasy and projection, but instead set forth in scientific terms an objective reality.

The artistic genius is without any such reassurance. He creates, so to speak, in a vacuum—without a yardstick by which to measure the extent of his truth, his artistic validity; he is without any objective means of determining the viability of the universe he is in process of bringing into being. As I postulated before, there are functions, such as the one I have called doxaletheic, that exercise a kind of safeguard against the individual's slipping into the purely personal and unformed, which is without appreciable validity for the rest of mankind. But how is he to know whether or not he is treading the path of artistic validity; or, more basically, how is he to know whether or not the universe that fills him is a "mad world"—or an extraordinary and uniquely valid new cosmos?

It is almost necessary to assume that the artistic genius was already, as a child, evolving unusual imagery about the world. He may have become aware quite early that he is different from others. The child of aver-

---

[23] It would fit well with this conception if *The Tempest* had indeed been solely his invention, for in that final play almost all previous tragic motives reappear but are undone in a seemingly peaceful (the word "happy" would be objectionable) ending (see later).

age endowment also experiences himself as different, and he is indeed different, in the sense that every human being is an individual stamping of human life. In the life history of every socially adjusted adult, one comes across childhood experiences of considerable shame and embarrassment, when the child was reprimanded or ridiculed, in a situation in which he was only expressing his own individuality. The goal of "child-raising" is, after all, to lay the foundations for later adjustment; but the world at large does not care whether this will be adjustment or conformity (cf. Lampl-de Groot, 1966). By and large, parents wish their children to belong, when they become adults, to their own or a higher social class, to believe in the tenets of the church of which they themselves are members and to follow their party affiliations.

The more the young generation learns to conform, therefore, the more it will succeed in sparing itself conflict with the external world. Yet the genius can thrive only by discarding attitudes of conformity and cultivating in himself what is so very different from the ways that his environment pursues. Some geniuses are spared one part of conflicts of that kind by virtue of the fact that their unusual achievement consists not in smashing traditional patterns but in carrying them to a height not reached by their predecessors. This is true in part of Mozart's artistic career. Yet his "crazy" letters to his cousin (Mozart, 1777-1791) testify that he was in need of a channel to discharge the dross that he was evidently not able to sublimate into his musical compositions. There is a sector in which every genius is in opposition to his society, and that opposition, depending on its intensity, may be to him a source of the greatest doubt, conflict, and anxiety.

This may be one of the reasons why the early productions of what later proves to be an eminently creative personality are likely to be in keeping with contemporary tastes and even sometimes to appear less promising than the early artistic endeavors of a less talented person of the same age.[24] It may be the unusual character of his own imagery that terrifies the youngster who will later reveal himself as being strikingly original. He rightly feels initially frightened by the pull and drag of his wild imagination, and he therefore sticks close to traditional patterns as a de-

---

[24] The problem is more complex than I can present in this context. I came upon the problem by a comparison of Goethe with his contemporary J. M. R. Lenz (1751-1792), an extremely gifted German playwright who, after an initial meteoric phase of literary creativity, ended in a schizophrenic state. I was struck by Lenz's precocity, as compared with Goethe, yet this precocity may well have been the harbinger of the later grave disorder.

fense against this danger. When he does finally "get off the ground" and without inhibition produces what has been stirring in him, he is without any position from which to appraise the validity of the product of his artistic efforts. Only when an audience's response reveals that others have understood and appreciated the product does the playwright know that his unusual production does not reflect a deranged mind, but is instead part and parcel of a new valid universe, capable of being shared by others.

How far the fears and scruples (what the Greeks called *aporia)* of a young author may go can be learned from Goethe's impulse to throw the manuscripts of *Werther* into the flames, when his friend did not show sufficient signs of appreciation after having listened to his reading of the novel. Only later did Goethe learn that the listener had been so involved in brooding about his own wife's having been made pregnant by another man that he had not heard a single word.

With growing maturation and success, the truly outstanding artist may and generally does acquire sufficient self-assurance and self-criticism for his creativity to become audience-independent. Yet it is questionable whether the doxaletheic function ever acquires complete autonomy. Even in the final stages of his creative output, when the voice of the audience at large has lost its decisive power to resolve his fears, the genius maintains contact with a selected few, whose response he needs, if only as a faint guide-line among the unruly waves of his unconscious.

A compromise in this regard is often made at the start by producing a work as a gift for a beloved person. Goethe's first play of lasting value was written under his sister's encouragement and meant as a gift for her. It seems that, under such circumstances, responsibility for the end-product is regarded as being shared by the recipient of the gift; this functions as a trigger to the arousal of that minimal courage that is necessary in order for the tyro to surrender to the internal push, about which he does not yet know whether it will lead him to glory or to ostracism.

In this context, it is instructive to note that Goethe's readiness in old age to listen to suggestions by friends about his literary output, even when those suggestions were critical, stood in sharp contrast with his unbending hostility whenever his theory of colors was discussed critically. In the latter area, as is well known, he was mistaken; for reasons of his own psychopathology, he was unable to accept Newton's physical theory. In my opinion, a partial psychosis was involved in his relationship with Newton; he had, in effect, formed a delusional system about him. Concomitantly, freedom of discussion had vanished in all matters that had to do with the theory of colors. Yet it is remarkable that Goethe's flexibility and conciliatory empathy with critical remarks by friends seems to have remained intact in all other spheres of discussion.

Here, in one and the same personality, it is possible to observe side by side the stirrings both of eminent creativity and of a delusion. Even at the risk of repeating myself, I want to restate the similarity between delusion and the great work of art. Both are, so to speak, "corrections" of reality: the one a train of thought, a conviction, that denies an intolerable sector of reality or replaces such a sector with a more acceptable version; the other, the creation of a new universe that exists within or side by side with real reality and does not per se aim primarily at the denial of anything.[25]

A work of art is the result of selection: the genius is protected against delusion by the doxaletheic function, while the psychotic remains defenseless against the intrusion of the archaic. He has to accept it in the way in which it makes its appearance. Despite all the proofs to the contrary that the environment raises, to convince him that he is merely harboring delusions, the paranoid is unable to view the psychopathological contents from a distance and to evolve a critical attitude toward them.

The genius, in the inspirational state, is also overwhelmed: he responds with great irritability to anything coming from the outside that might interfere with his production. For short periods of time he may even totally reject external reality; yet, once the work of art has been created, it gradually loses its enormous cathexis and, after some time, he even may turn against it, ungratefully and unjustly criticizing it, and still later even regretting ever having created it. And yet despite such enormous differences between delusion and the work of art, it still remains difficult to be sure that, if for whatever reason the genius were prevented from creating, the difference between him and the paranoid would not be reduced to a negligible quantity.

Oddly enough, this takes us back to Roy Walker's statement, initially quoted. We find its confirmation in Shakespeare's writings themselves. Previously I raised and left unanswered the question of what may be the general meaning of the fact that the function of the Mousetrap play in *Hamlet* is not to be a message to the world but rather a

---

[25] Freud (1924b, p. 185) very rightly called it "the creation of a new reality," which is what Shakespeare's corpus also is.

question directed to the world, whose response will have a decisive effect upon the questioner's fate. In Elizabethan language the question was: "Was it a godly or a devilish ghost?" Translated into the modern jargon, it amounts to a sort of testing: "Was it a real ghost or a hallucination?"

It is the playwright's question: "Am I mad?"—a question that remains in general unasked, and yet may be latently inherent in the production of all great tragedy. If the universe created by the playwright is acclaimed by the audience—which, of course, means to the author that it has been shared and understood—he can rest assured that it is not esoteric or bizarre, some delusional excrescence of his unbalanced mind, but rather a valid universe with its own justified structure, in its own way as binding upon men's mind as is the real universe. That this idea found a symbolized representation in Shakespeare's corpus only in Hamlet's mouse-trap play should hardly serve to reduce its general validity.

In establishing an intimate and exclusive connection between genius and his achievement, am I overstraining the psychological factor? Rothe (1961, p. 185) seems to be quite certain that, if Michelangelo had not existed, the High Renaissance would have found another master for the realization of its inherent potential. "Also, if Shakespeare had never lived, his works would have been written," he asserts, inasmuch as Elizabethan theater was such a perfect form of art that it could not help finding someone to actualize all its possibilities.

That Shakespeare would not have been capable of creating his plays if there had not existed an Elizabethan theater; that all his work is deeply rooted in the historical momentum of his own time—who would or could doubt this? But to view the genius as merely the necessary transmitter and realizer of art forms that are inherent in the historical moment of his existence is a Platonic-Hegelian view, not warranted by observation.

It is the privilege of the genius to create values that others had not been able even to imagine, not to speak of creating them. If Shakespeare had not lived, no one, unless it were someone of equal genius, would ever have been capable of imagining his world, no less producing plays of the kind he has written. Prior to the genius' flowering, we are in a position comparable to that of the blind man, to whom one tries to explain colors; he cannot imagine what they are.

Without Shakespeare we would still go on believing that Marlowe was the fulfiller of Elizabethan tragedy, and without Michelangelo, Donatello would be regarded as the unsurpassable sculptor of the Renaissance. It is only *after* the genius has created values that we take cognizance of those art forms that were inherent in the historical moment. No human mind can determine the quantity and variety of art works that have never been realized, even though they were quite possible—*if* the unrealized possibilities of a historical moment had met a mind sufficiently endowed to make maximum use of existing potentialities. It would be equally brazen indeed to assert that the totality of those forms in which organic life has appeared up to now actually exhausts all possible mutations.

D. *"The Tempest"*
and the Christian Dogma

If I now turn to *The Tempest*, I do so because there seems to be agreement among critics that Shakespeare's final play is moved by a spirit of reconciliation. To what has the realistic pessimism come that so strongly pervaded *Hamlet* and his other tragedies? Did the author recant in the end and adopt a more conciliatory view of the world?

Furthermore, when James (1967, p. 1) calls *The Tempest* "one of the profoundest . . . of Shakespeare's creations," I am inclined to agree with him; yet I find its profundity in an area that is entirely different from the one in which James did. It is reasonable, therefore, to consider in what way Shakespeare could have been any profounder than he had already been in his tragedies.

In view of James' (1967) recent excellent study of *The Tempest*, I can dispense with any further introductory remarks and proceed at once to some comments on that play that may be pertinent from the psychoanalytic point of view.

Undoing of the Past and Reversals in "The Tempest."

It has been observed that in Verdi's last work, *Falstaff*, many themes from past works reappear, but in a different and more peaceful setting. While this trend is markedly present in *The Tempest*, it was already noticeable in earlier romances. Leontes, for example, unquestionably suffers from Othello's "disease" (cf. Empson, 1935).

What the critics have usually stressed is the spirit of reconciliation that pervades the later romances. In this, they are right. If one had to choose between repeating Othello's life or Leontes', it is not likely that one would hesitate—unless one were an incorrigible romantic, ready to assert that no torment, however infernal, could outweigh the delights Othello enjoyed with Desdemona prior to the tragic turn, while being at the same time doubtful of Hermione's sensual prowess.

Nevertheless, I must emphasize the existence of a hidden factor that could conceivably make the Leontes type of jealousy the more eerie and even the more gruesome of the two. Othello is *talked into* his tragedy—that is to say, he seems to be a victim of carefully contrived circumstances, if the play is taken literally. By contrast, Leontes' jealousy seems to come like a thunderbolt, unprovoked and unwarranted—whatever the psychoanalytic interpretation may add to this picture.[1]

Be that as it may, without aiming at completeness, I can readily point to some of the issues and questions in *The Tempest* upon which Shakespeare had elaborated previously and which now make their final appearance—sometimes dimly, sometimes with vigor, but always lacking in manifest tragedy. There is the theme of a brother's jealousy, of his impulse to kill for the sake of aggrandizing himself or of arrogating power to himself. But *Hamlet* is recalled in other aspects as well. Gonzalo is treated by Antonio and Sebastian as if he were Polonius and there is undoubtedly, despite all the differences between the two, some degree of psychological kinship between them. Prospero stands at the edge of a Lear-like conflict with Miranda when he goes through the motions of rejecting Ferdinand. Caliban, his appetites focused on Miranda, evokes the Moor's infatuation with his Venetian bride. The image of Sebastian and Antonio holding their swords over King and councillor, ready to stab, is almost a visualization of what we are informed of only by word of mouth in *Macbeth*. Antonio's boast of being untrammeled by feelings of guilt or repentance reminds one of Iago's expressed freedom from moral biases. Stephano's adorning himself with royal attire finds a counterpart in Hal's rehearsal of the (forbidden) wearing of the crown. Ferdinand and Miranda fall in love at first sight, just as Romeo and Juliet do. The father rejects the daughter's lover at once and, when Ferdinand draws his sword, Miranda might well have had to face Ophelia's tragic dilemma. But the Capulets and Montagues have here given up their vendetta and Milan woos for Naples' son despite a family feud (cf. Holland, 1964b, p. 305).

[1] Nuttall (1967, p. 156) also warns against looking at the late romances as a unit, without differentiating their individual shades of character.

Enough. The expert can surely find more and more corollaries.[2]

Another point of interest has to do with what may be called mechanical literalness of a formal quality. Prospero asks Ariel, shortly after the beginning of the play, what time it is *(I.2.239)* — a question that seems to me to be of no poetical or dramatic consequence at that point in the action. When Ariel answers that it is past noon, Prospero ["glancing at the sun"—why then did he have to ask?] says: "At least two glasses," which means "some time between 2 and 3 P.M." Shakespeare seems to have been a real stickler about time in this play, because on five other occasions *(III.1.21; V.1.114, 136, 186, 223)* he lets us know that the stage action of the play covers about three hours. Yet all these time notations coincided with the audience's physical time, since at the Globe a play started at two p.m. and ended at five.[3]

Much has been written, incidentally, about Shakespeare's handling of time. His ostensibly loose way with time relations has found different interpretations and explanations, which do not need to concern us here.

I wonder whether there has ever been another play in which "unity of time" has been taken so literally that every moment of the play's clock-time was designed to coincide with the audience's clock-time. The dynamic, human time that is characteristic of Shakespeare's plays has become literal, even mechanical in *The Tempest;* it is now the antithesis of what it once was. And indeed Shakespeare had been a great master in the creation of "human" time. He was far above the dreary regularity of Newtonian time, making full use instead of human time, in which seconds may last hours and hours seconds, in which time may even come to a standstill or go backward.[4]

All this magnificent panoply of time is now gone and time has been reduced to its dreariest—one is almost inclined to say, stupidest—form.[5] Is this not an act of undoing? If Shakespeare had been brought up under

[2] James (1967, p. 136f) points out the parallel between Prospero's comment on life, dreams and sleep and Hamlet's famous meditation on sleep and dreams. See also Slochower (1950), Plank (1968, p. 160). For the link between Prospero and Lear see Wilson (1936b, p. 14).

[3] Correct as this identity of stage time and audience time would have been at the Globe, I do not know whether it would have been true as well at the Black Friars and on the occasion of a performance at Court.

[4] For a splendid analysis of the concept of time, its changes, shades of meaning and variety of time experiences, see Glasser (1936).

[5] This did not keep Shakespeare from using his masterly way of handling human time even in *The Tempest.* Graves (1948, p. 354) refers to the "suspension of time" in Caliban's description of the effect of the island's music *(III.2.132 sequ.).* (Cf. James, 1967, p. III; Nuttall 1967, p. 144.) Yet this does not break down the general frame of physical time within which the play takes place.

the direct influence of Aristotle's classical unities, I would surmise that he was here expressing his regret for ever having jettisoned them.[6]

Shakespeare was probably not acquainted with Aristotle's *Poetics*, yet the unity of time must have meant something to him, since he was familiar with the ancient theatre. After all, he had begun in *The Comedy of Errors* with abiding by the tradition and it must have some meaning that he ended with that same tradition.

Thus I interpret Shakespeare's overconspicuous and literal adherence to the unity of time in *The Tempest* as a deliberate act of revocation: "I abjure the freedom I have taken and restore time to what it is. . . ." And so too with the rest: "I abjure murder and illicit love and dissension and revenge. If I had to rewrite my tragedies, Othello would discover in time the truth about Desdemona, Lear would not misjudge Cordelia, and Macbeth would be strong enough to resist Fate's enticing baits." I may perhaps be expressing all this in too extreme terms, but the tendency toward undoing is unmistakable in his last play. What could have been the reason for it?

Our period, in which mental hygiene is accepted almost as a panacea, is also one in which great art is viewed under auspices related to those of pragmatism and utilitarianism. Thus artistic creation is frequently seen as a process of restitution, adjustment, self-healing and what not. I can well imagine that such consequences as these may indeed hold true for many a talent and perhaps at times even for the genius. On the other hand, I can also imagine that a man who has gone through the nightmares of Hamlet, Othello, Lear and Macbeth has incurred psychic injuries. It goes without saying that whatever one asserts about the creative process in Shakespeare must needs be highly conjectural.

When Shakespeare became interested in a dramatic subject, I would imagine, the plot as he found it (or formed it) began to grow in him. I cannot see how this was possible without his undergoing deep-reaching identifications, although I am not asserting that such a mechanism is always and unavoidably at work. Whatever personal strands might have tied Boccaccio to his novelettes, brilliantly as they were written, I would not necessarily assume that he underwent any profound identification

---

[6] Indeed, I believe that the relinquishing of the classical unities was one of the most fateful steps in the development of European civilization. I should not be at all surprised if a cultural historian were some day to write an essay in which he proved that the state of anarchy in which Western culture and society now find themselves can be traced back to the pregnant moment at which a genius overthrew those basic rules that had had the function of keeping man's imagination, even when it was most excited, within a stable and clearly structured organizational framework.

with the men and women who people his tales. I would even venture the guess that they stood at the periphery of his self and were thus able to replace each other in quick succession and without any psychic wrench.

Yet human passions that were as penetratingly and unforgettably brought onto the stage as they were by Shakespeare must have shaken their creator with almost the same intensity as they did his characters. I do not know how many will accept this hypothesis. But if it is accepted, we ought to be ready to accept as well that, in going through the thousand deaths, the crimes, the shattering outbreaks of passion that he put on the stage, Shakespeare may himself have been traumatized.

Creating is not necessarily release, discharge, a salutary healing process. The truly great, who have the courage to plunge to the rock-bottom of human existence and its plight, to rivet their eyes upon depths "deeper than did ever plummet sound," may come up with deep injuries —if you wish, the same injuries (and more) as the average mortal suffers at the hands of fate. This is what *The Tempest* conveys to me. When he wrote it, Shakespeare was attempting to deny the tragic lives that he had created, like a mother who wishes to forget (and to have others forget) that she has given birth to idiots and criminals.[7]

Furthermore, I would suggest, as many have done, that to almost all great creative efforts there is attached a feeling of guilt.[8]

A good many reasons can be adduced in order to explain such feelings, particularly in Shakespeare, whose works are the most complete catalogue of human cruelty and folly. To be sure, the opposite aspects of human existence were not lost sight of, and found their way amply enough into the *oeuvre*; but at the author's peak, these latter aspects were greatly overshadowed by the darker side of human life. In *The Tempest* Prospero prevents crimes from taking place, and makes people

---

[7] The prevalence of undoing and denying may justify the claim that in this instance it was an impulse toward healing that was mainly responsible for Shakespeare's writing of *The Tempest*. It may be that something like a desire for deliverance or even salvation was in part responsible for the play. As I shall try to show later, however, in so doing the genius ran the risk of inflicting upon himself even worse injuries.

[8] In the case of Michelangelo, this is directly observable in his Sonnets (Clements, 1965). It is also possible that Freud's comment that he needed some mild physical discomfort in order to be able to write is connected with problems in this area. I am frequently told by subjects that, while engaged in a creative effort, they periodically feel the urge—sometimes amounting to a compulsion—to run to the refrigerator, in order to grab a bite before returning to their work. I am inclined to look at this as almost an essential part of the subject's creative effort, and I therefore believe it to be more than merely an attempt to find some form of discharge for pent-up energy. Yet, since these excursions to the kitchen are generally experienced as shameful, as well as guilt-arousing, I would surmise that they serve as substitute channels for those guilt feelings that have been aroused by the creative effort per se.

happy; he offers rewards to those who have deserved them and shames culprits by his consistent forgiveness.

Six times during the course of *The Tempest*, swords are drawn. Four characters are on the verge of being killed. The only female character in the play is fancied by two characters as a prospective victim of rape. Yet, while unleashed nature destroys a ship, in the entire play not a single human being is harmed. Evidently the machineries of destruction, as employed by both man and nature, even though they are set into motion as fully as they are in the tragedies, are miraculously brought to naught. Ostensibly the stage action teaches that, despite the dangers that surround him, man is after all able to survive. All of which may sound like the playwright's plea for forgiveness for having accused mankind of being evil-filled and chiefly destructive.

The theme of reversal is brought to our attention twice in direct form: during the tempest, the powerful of the earth, the kings and the princes and their counselors are shown, in their helplessness, to be dependent on "the rabble." If there was any hope of survival for that small community on the galley, it rested in the skills—and the orders—of the nameless, those whose voice is customarily overruled by kingly incantations. Here, then, the primary social relation is reversed and the Kings must obey those whom they were born to command. This sociological reversal is soon followed by an unusual verbalization of time sequence, which also amounts to a reversal.

When Prospero refers for the first time to clock time, in his conversation with Ariel, he continues: "The time 'twixt six and now/Must by us both be spent most preciously" *(I.2.240f)*. Unless compelling reasons are set forth to show that "twixt now and six" would have been offensive for aesthetic reasons, some psychological significance is to be ascribed to this reversal of time. As I have suggested, it is an open declaration that in this play time will be reversed and take a backward course, undoing the past in a sweep.

Though these two details are peripheral, they are welcome witnesses to what a number of important episodes seem to convey.

The Psychological Immobility of the Characters in "The Tempest."

The plot, in *The Tempest* is a quadruple one: one strand comprises Alonso and his entourage; a second, Prospero, Miranda, Ariel, Caliban; the third, Stephano, Trinculo, Caliban; and the last the love of Miranda and Ferdinand. The way in which these plots are interconnected is quite clear and does not need to be described here. Alonso's world is the stage of court, history, politics, with its concomitant intrigue, and even crime. Prospero's world is that of the life of the mind: art, intellect, morality, aesthetics, ethics and religion. Stephano's is that of the underworld of unleashed passions; the fourth is that of conflict-free love at its most beautiful.

From the psychoanalytic point of view, one could project into the four plots the various provinces of the personality: the King of Naples and his entourage would then symbolize the ego with its selfish wishes and its task of grappling with reality, while Prospero would represent the superego, Miranda and Ferdinand the friendly and loving aspect of the id, and the Caliban trinity that of the untamed and the aggressive (cf. Loewenthal, 1957, pp. 63-65). Yet closer scrutiny reveals so much overlapping that the value of such categorizing would appear to be highly questionable—which is also true of attempts to interpret some of the characters as symbolizations of separate ego-functions.[9]

I have earlier touched, however, upon an aspect that may be more promising to pursue. *The Tempest* is devoid of that at times overwhelming rush of dynamic psychological development that makes Shakespeare's great plays precisely what they are. We may call *The Tempest* a truly static play, in which there is almost no psychological development.

One way by which this is accomplished is evident: whenever the characters start acting in a manner that might lead to tragic complications, they are stopped—not by a change of mind in the person involved, but by magic—either Prospero's or that of Ariel, who is, after all, his master's arm prolonged. It is precisely this sudden effect of a quasi-mechanical force acting on the mind, used repeatedly on the stage, which creates the impression that the play contains no psychological developments, even though many of the characters do behave during its course in a way that is quite different from the way in which their dispositions would make them act.

Yet the changes that take place occur consistently by the *addition* of a charm, a spell, a magic infusion. One may compare this with pre-Freudian hypnotic treatment, in which the subject was ordered, during the hypnotic interlude, not to feel pain upon awakening, or else to do something he had previously felt incapable of doing. Many a critic would object to this proposition by referring to Prospero, who supposedly does undergo a development—from revenge to forgiving. His renunciatory

[9] Cf. Reik 1949, p. 336; Scott 1962, p. 181. Nuttall (1967, p. 159) warns against this kind of allegorizing.

farewell at the close is often regarded as the result of an insight or an experience or a revelation obtained during the course of the play.

Yet the critics seem to be mistaken in this respect. Early in the play *(I.2.16)* Prospero states that he had arranged the tempest for Miranda's sake, evidently having his subsequent matchmaking already in mind at this point—which in turn presupposes his readiness also to forgive Alonso. Everything that Prospero does is the unfolding of a plan that he had decided upon prior to the shipwreck at the beginning. One may therefore dispute, even in Prospero, the existence of a psychological development.[10]

Moreover, one should not overestimate, as some do, Prospero's development toward a Christian ethic. Prospero is at heart an angry man:[11] he has to fight off a good many outbreaks of rage, and he is not sparing in his employment of rough words, even toward Ariel *(I.2.294-296),* not to speak of Caliban. Even in speaking to Miranda—he is, of course, pretending—he says that he might hate her *(I.2.481).* The narcissistic component of Prospero's mercy *(V.1.20-31)* is revealed in his discourse with Ariel, who confesses his feelings of compassion toward Prospero's enemy. "And shall not myself . . . be kindlier moved than thou art?"[12] This narcissistic component is stressed once again when Prospero says: "the rarer action is in virtue than in vengeance."

Despite his good deeds, Prospero is far from being angelic. He has a disposition toward anger, and plainly it is not an easy thing for him to forgive his enemies. He is almost unable to part with his daughter, so much so that he tells Alonso that, just as the latter has lost a son, he has lost a daughter. In this he definitely equates loss by marriage with loss by death (cf. Sachs, 1919). Prospero's Epilogue ends with: "As you from crimes would pardoned be,/Let your indulgence set me free," thus insinuating that he has incurred even great guilt—one source being the strong aggressiveness that smoulders behind the gentleness that he displays on the surface.[13]

[10] Wilson (1936b, p. 17f) insists that Prospero's forgiveness is a sudden conversion, although he acknowledges earlier that the shipwreck was arranged with the purpose of getting Miranda and Ferdinand together. One cannot have it both ways. Their conflict-free love presupposes Prospero's act of forgiveness.

[11] Cf. Wilson (1936b, p. 16): "Real mercy is absent from his [Prospero's] thoughts." Cf. also Mannoni (1950) and Nuttall (1967, pp. 149, 156).

[12] Some critics interpret this line as if Ariel's remark induced Prospero to show himself to be merciful. I rather believe that he puts Ariel into his place and almost chides him for believing that *he* could have more mercy than his master.

[13] When the editors of the *New Cambridge Edition* see in this Epilogue "Possibly an apology to James I, author of *Daemonologie,* for dabbling in magic," they have looked at best at the surface. If I may deal once again with the biographical angle, it is far more probable that the ending adumbrates

Prospero is linked by some critics with guilt. Thus Kermode (1954, p. *l*) writes: "Prospero, like Adam, fell from his kingdom by an inordinate thirst for knowledge," and establishes a parallel between Prospero and Adam's Fall and Redemption.[14] If one takes Shakespeare's text literally, however, the existence of any such parallel is not confirmed. As far as reconstruction is possible, considering the sparseness of the data provided by Shakespeare, Prospero holds Antonio's vice solely responsible for his downfall and does not regret his own immersion in his studies. It is rather evident that Prospero still expects that an older brother should be able to withdraw to his study, without being cheated by the younger.

According to James (1967, p. 125ff), Prospero will return to Milan a changed man; he has learned his lesson and from now on will devote himself to governmental affairs. If this were so, indeed, then something of a developmental trend would be discoverable in Prospero, thereby disproving my proposition of a psychological immobility in *The Tempest*. It seems to me, however, that James does not prove his point.

Prospero is inclined to think of his existence in tripartite terms. Thus, when he gives Miranda to Ferdinand, he calls her "a third of my own life." From his initial presentation we know that the remaining two thirds were divided between his brother ("whom next thyself/Of all the world I loved") and his studies. What will be the distribution once he returns? "His every third thought when Duke again may be of his grave; but we must assume that every first and second will be of Milan and its affairs: he will hardly neglect them again" (James, 1967, p. 125). This is highly improbable, for at least one third will remain fixated to Miranda.

The idea that after the nuptials Miranda disappears from his life and stops filling out the third of his existence is hardly imaginable with regard to a daughter who has thus far filled her father's existence to such a depth. When he says that, after the nuptials, he will "retire" to Milan, the word "retire" does not mean the same as it does today, but probably

---

the depth of suffering to which great creators are exposed. These lines are, after all, the last two authenticated lines Shakespeare ever wrote. Why then the comparison with crimes, and why the plea to be set free?

Earlier Prospero says that his ending is despair, "unless I be reliev'd by prayer." Does all this point toward a man who is deeply burdened by guilt? After all, when viewed from a distance, Shakespeare's work does contain terrible accusations against mankind. And, if Prospero is the poetical vision of self-image, what *The Tempest* is saying is: "I could have prevented all the slaughter that goes through my tragedies, just as easily as Sebastian and Antonio were stopped in their tracks at a wink of Prospero's staff." Cf. Wilson (1936b, p. 21): "The Shakespeare we last catch sight of is ... a penitent on his knees."

[14] The connotation of Eden was an early reaction to *The Tempest* (cf. Nuttall, 1967, p. 135).

means instead "to return," as James correctly points out; yet the immediate juxtaposition of devoting a third of his thoughts to death conjures up the image of a man who is averse to the concrete and the practical and is inextricably tied to the spiritual and the trascendental. Prospero abjures rough magic but, "unregenerate" as he is, immediately meddles with climate and promises the party calm seas auspicious gales.[15] If Prospero had really overcome his ardent thirst for knowledge and his will to penetrate the arcane, one might expect a train of thought different from the one that leads in such short sequence to meditation on death.

James (1967) warns against viewing Prospero as an old man, but I do not see how else one can view him. After all, the Epilogue cannot be divorced from Prospero. It would have been incongruous to end the play on a note of Prospero's vigorous expectancy of a practical life, and then to follow it with an Epilogue, recited by the same character, that is full of resignation and appeals to be permitted to withdraw. The 12 years of Prospero's stay on the Island were not preparation for an active life, nor were they a kind of holiday prior to a period of fulfillment of duty. Those 12 years were Prospero's peak years, and in them he fulfilled his life's mission. We can see Prospero back in Milan, concentrating on his books, meditating on death and longing to be with Miranda, turning an unwilling ear toward those who request his decisions in matters of government. Indeed, it is even possible that he will reinstate Antonio, since he seems to believe in the latter's change of heart.

Prospero's expressed intention to break his staff may stand as a symbol of his willingness to forgo active white magic; but is it without significance that he says "I'll drown my book" and not "my books"? Until then, his books had always been referred to in the plural. My thought is that Prospero's intention is to turn away from *a* book—namely, that which contains the secrets of white and black magic—but to retain those that have to do with the liberal arts.

James (1967, p. 65) is, I think, the only critic who gives any thought to the question of the origin and timing of Prospero's use of magic. In Milan he was a scholar; it was only on the Island that he became a magician, and with his impending departure it is magic that he intends to abjure. It is both significant and ironic that his magical powers are based on Sycorax' black magic. Without Sycorax, Prospero would never have

---

[15] To be sure, he promises Ariel that this will be the last service requested from him. But has not Prospero talked in the same vein previously (*V.1.241*)? And will there not be over and over again a new "last service" requested?

acquired his power over Ariel, and we may suspect that he learned his tricks in part from Caliban.[16]

Here is an important source of Prospero's hidden feeling of guilt and of his desire to abandon magic, even though he had used it for commendable purposes. Yet Shakespeare found himself in quite the same situation as Prospero, at the end of his creative career. Had the world not been a place replete with evil, he would never have been able to write his great tragedies and acquire fame. He, too, had converted black magic into white and made out of the reprehensible and the horror-arousing something beautiful and profound. Was he, too, sensitive enough to feel guilty about it, as Prospero did, and was he therefore ready to put an end to his magic art?[17]

I shall have to turn back to Prospero, of course, more than once again, but I shall examine the other characters with regard to their immobility.

Gonzalo very conspicuously remains the same. In the end he feels the scent of Providence, just as he did at the beginning, and nothing will shake his belief in anointed Kings. It is often asserted that Sebastian and

---

[16] This conversion of the hostile and the destructive into the friendly and constructive is an ancient mythological theme. The great mythological heroes acquire their benevolent forces by seizing them from monsters or other evil creatures. One may see in this frequent conversion a mythical realization of an ubiquitous psychological process: the ego's absorption of id forces and their transformation into ego strength—that is to say, the taming of the less structured archaic, and its transformation and incorporation into the ego's organized framework.

In my opinion, it is this ubiquitous psychic process that made it possible for Colin Still (1921) to find a parallel between the action of *The Tempest* and the initiation ceremonies into the Eleusinian Mysteries. Still's book provides fascinating reading since it gives meaning to details of the play that otherwise appear accidental or arbitrary. His interpretation loses in significance, however, in view of its applicability (as Still himself asserts) to many other literary works. I would be inclined to go even a step further and say that, in great tragedy generally, initiation can be discovered. If it did not have the power to initiate, it would not be great tragedy. Initiation (here meaning the ascent to a "higher" form of existence) is principally correlated with the process of transformation alluded to above.

[17] I do not think that this view is incompatible with current explanations of Prospero's abandonment of magic. Kermode stresses that there was no task left for him to do: a state of harmony had been established by him "at the human and political levels" (1954, p. XLVIII), and he had acquired control over himself and nature. Later, I shall take up the problem of Prospero's failure, of which Kermode is not unaware, thus casting doubts on his own proposition. James (1967, p. 16ff) offers the very interesting theory that *"The Tempest* provides an ending to the history of magic and the occult in western Europe. Shakespeare's transcendent genius made him a maker and therefore a prophet of our modernity." It is "the farewell of the human imagination to magic." I am not certain that James is here guessing correctly. My guess would be that Shakespeare had the feeling (correctly, I believe) that the days of such great art as was his were over. As some writers have pointed out, he was no longer understood by his contemporaries, and Jacobean literature had taken a turn of which he did not approve. Art was on the verge of losing its magic charm and becoming a matter of rationality. It was high time for Prospero not only to "retire" (return) to Stratford, but really to retire from writing plays.

Antonio, on the other hand, have undergone a change. The critics seem to be in disagreement, however, as to which of the two really did change, and their doubt alone proves that the text leaves the question open. Both continue their banter and cynicism when the Caliban trinity makes its appearance in the last scene, and that is the last we hear of them. Sebastian's "A most high miracle" *(V.1.177)* upon perceiving Ferdinand and Miranda is a highly dubious remark, and his earlier, "The devil speaks in him" *(V.1.129),* when Prospero refers to his treachery, almost proves his adherence to his old ways.

Alonso, however, does seem to show regret and repentance. He resigns Prospero's dukedom *(V.1.118)* and asks for forgiveness; yet can one perceive here any psychological development? As soon as he thought that he had lost his son, he became depressed; now that he has found his son in the hands of his enemy, all that he offers is the restitution of what he had seized. What else was there really for him to do, especially since in the end his son is acquiring by marriage the realm that the father had earlier taken unjustly? His chief interest seems to be in obtaining from Prospero the story of how all this came about. It is true that he is responding to the change in his fortune, but it is highly questionable whether one should attribute to him a developmental change. In the beginning we observed him to be depressed, exhausted and disgusted; at the end he feels better, since he has found his son alive. Yet he is still the same more or less colorless Alonso, who has never measurably aroused either our pity or our anger.[18]

Ferdinand, who is pure and virtuous from the beginning, while still fulfilling the requirements of a courtier when he is drawing his sword against Prospero, will doubtless continue his style of life in Naples. He was no hero when he was "the first man that leaped" from the burning ship, deserting his father, and he will not be a hero in Naples, either. When he expresses his wish to live forever on the enchanted Island *(IV.1.122)* with his "wonder'd" and wise father (in-law), this may be a bad omen for his kingship. One can scarcely imagine Ferdinand anywhere else than in Miranda's arms. He no longer worries about his father's lot after meeting her and it would not be surprising if it were Sebastian who was in the end rewarded with Naples' throne. But even if this does not happen, Antonio will by this time either watch Prospero counting his days, or will, as the dispossessed former Duke, be a strong

---

[18] Strachey (1906, p. 66) speaks rightly of "the pale phantom Alonso."

political force in a community that is ruled by a monarch living far-off in Naples.

Miranda is and will remain the lovely, naïve girl, incapable of any lie or insincerity. Cressida's sort of falsehood is alien to her; she is free of Cordelia's inhibition, and Fate will protect her forever against Ophelia's misfortunes. She is one of Shakespeare's most charming creations; but precisely because she stands above all ambivalence, the idea of development is certainly in her instance altogether out of the question.[19]

Trinculo and Stephano have no past and no future. They are representatives of the people, the rabble, the anonymous crowd that serves as accessories to the powerful, like the "extras" in the motion pictures, who are hired to make the stars glitter all the more.

There thus remain Ariel and Caliban. Ariel is a nonhuman spirit, who has no inner conflicts. It is true that he suffers when Sycorax leaves him in a tormented condition and he craves full freedom. Yet these are problems that arise exclusively in his relationship to the external world. Once freed, he will go on living in whichever way his spirit moves him at the moment. He is not subject to processes of development.

There is more to say about Caliban, who is the enigma of the play. Caliban seems to share a structural factor with Ariel: he does not suffer from inner conflicts so much as from the way in which Prospero treats him, and chiefly from the loss of the island whose possession he rightly claims. When Prospero defends his rough handling of Caliban by asserting that "Thou didst seek to violate the honor of my child" *(I.2.348f)*, this is a mere rationalization (cf. Mannoni, 1950, p. 106), for Caliban had never asked to be civilized by the magician. Rightly he reminds Prospero that the latter had, in fact, learned a good many secrets from him that enabled Prospero to survive after landing on the island.

The topical implication of all this is clear at a time when colonization is beginning, but the general human and psychological implications involved should not be minimized or forgotten. I doubt that Shakespeare set out to deal with problems of colonial politics in *The Tempest*. That is why Caliban has not lost his powerful effect, even in a world of vanishing

---

[19] Interestingly enough, from the study of a character like Miranda's, one may draw the conclusion that ambivalence and evil are most potent factors in the *vis a tergo* that makes man's personal development a process without end. One should perhaps never let one's imagination play with the question of the future of the *dramatis personae* once the curtain has dropped, but the end of *The Tempest* offers a particular challenge. Shakespeare leaves us with the impression that despite the fact that Prospero has established order, the future may easily be a repetition of the disorders of the past.

colonial imperialism. He represents something eminently human, despite his ostensible subhuman origin. It is mere platitude to say that he represents a formation that is still alive in all of us.[20]

It would be worthwhile to go a little further into the matter of the universal meaning that is represented by Caliban.[21] His strong tie to his mother Sycorax, the witch, carries for the analyst the earmark of the preoedipal phase. The father is mentioned only as progenitor, and seems to have had no further contact with the son. The son was evidently Sycorax' favorite, and he still claims sole right of possession of the mother, as represented by the island. Prospero then is the father who tries to drive his son's preoedipal fixation out of him in order to teach him the modes of civilized behavior. He wants to raise him to the oedipal level and to all that is part of it, such as morality and ethics.[22] Yet the misbegotten son wants to accept only the pleasure-giving part of the Oedipus complex and to have intercourse with Miranda, who of course represents the oedipal mother in the disguise of virginal purity. The rivalry between father and son is rather obvious, since Prospero parts with Miranda with considerable inner difficulty.[23]

Contrary to many critics, I am able to find only in Caliban any evidence of development. If the text of *The Tempest* is taken literally, Caliban does reform, for his parting words are: "I'll be wise hereafter, and seek for grace." Yet Caliban is usually presented as unreformable.

It is true, of course, that he may be looked upon as being able only to obey the stronger party. When he abjures his erstwhile allegiance to Stephano and Trinculo by saying:

What a thrice-double ass
Was I, to take this drunkard for a God?
And worship this dull fool!

this must not be understood, it may be objected, as a decision based on insight, which has led to a real change of character, but rather as an act

---

[20] It will become important, during the course of my discussion, to decide whether or not Shakespeare was aware of this—if not explicitly, at least preconsciously.

[21] For a historical interpretation see Hankins (1947).

[22] One may think here of the father's struggle against the mother, which Neumann (1949) has discussed.

[23] The interpretation of Caliban as a preoedipally fixated creature does not seem to fit in with the mutual affection that reigned initially between him and Prospero. Caliban apparently continued his preoedipal mother fixation with Prospero. They have been able to get along as long as their relationship is symbiotic (Mahler, 1968)—Prospero nurturing Caliban without imposing demands that might afford displeasure and Caliban submitting passively to Prospero's wishes. The conflict between them breaks out as soon as this has become no longer possible.

of bowing to forces that have proven to be of superior strength to those he had previously followed. The lines of parting by Caliban may thus be judged to be merely perfunctory, to be serving only the purpose of bringing a rather complicated plot to a universally acceptable ending. When I attempt to conceive his parting words as having a deeper meaning, among the things that will likely be cited by way of refutation will be Stoll's (1933) adamant denial of the human factor in Shakespeare's world, and his consistent interpretation of the detail, as well as of the whole, as being the result of structure and convention, with a consequent total elimination of psychology in any form.

It is easy enough to minimize Caliban's conversion, to deprive it of psychological meaning. Indeed, when a character in the last four lines of his appearance on stage reverses his whole outlook of life, when someone who has been consistently brutish becomes at that point a grace-seeker, one may feel compelled, as Stoll recommends, to ignore any possible psychological implication. Stoll regarded Othello's transition from a state of the "want of any jealous, or sexually suspicious, nature" to uncontrollable jealousy as being "impossible as psychology" (Stoll, 1933, p. 6). He may be right that there is no resemblance here to the people whom we know and have met; nevertheless, it does contain a formidable truth, which there is no need to specify here. In *The Tempest,* however, a character like Caliban is almost consistently presented in a state that is incompatible with even the ability to grasp the meaning of "grace," and it may therefore appear psychologically unwarranted to present him as suddenly taking his leave of the audience as a seeker of grace.

I leave that question open at this point, but I believe that here too Shakespeare has implied a far-reaching psychological truth. Even the Calibans change. Indeed, it would seem that they are the only ones who do so in *The Tempest.*[24]

Montaigne and "The Tempest."

The Bermuda pamphlets and Montaigne are generally put forward as the two certain sources of *The Tempest.* The Bermuda episode of the *Sea Adventure* was unquestionably used by Shakespeare, but Kermode

---

[24] Hankins (1947, p. 800) insists that Caliban cannot change, although he does acknowledge "Caliban's recognition of his folly." He argues that the point needs no debate because Shakespeare "through Prospero's words" lets us know what he believes and thinks about Caliban. This, I believe, means begging the question. Much as I believe that Prospero is a projection of Shakespeare's self-image, it also contains his self-criticism. If one neglects the difference between the way in which Prospero conceives of Caliban and the way in which Caliban is presented, one loses an important avenue to the latent meaning of the play.

put it into the right proportion. He wrote: (p. xxv) "It is as well to be clear that there is nothing in *The Tempest*, fundamental to its structure of ideas, which could not have existed had America remained undiscovered, and the Bermuda voyage never taken place." I believe that, even though Kermode is right in warning against an overestimation of the Bermuda voyage, he goes too far. As I shall suggest later, the intelligence that Shakespeare obtained about the intercourse of Europeans with the aborigines became an important point of crystallization for him.

James (1967, pp. 72-123) puts new stress on the literature of travel and discovery and devotes much ingenious speculation to the question of the books that Shakespeare may have read. Thus he (1967, p. 120) believes that "we can make little of Caliban's speech" about the effect that the Island's music has on him *(III.2.132 sequ.,)* unless we bear in mind what Shakespeare had learned about Indian religion. Likewise, he derives Ariel's address to the three guilty men *(III.3.53):* "You are three men of sin" from a specific passage of a book about the New World that Shakespeare supposedly must have read. He may be right, although the specific examples do not sound convincing. Yet, be that as it may, it is my feeling that all this takes us away from the correct approach. It is in Montaigne that the key to *The Tempest* can be found.

Shakespeare's relationship to Montaigne has found various interpretations. Ornstein (1960, p. 40) believes that Shakespeare was one of the few who understood the implications of the *Apology for Raymond Sebond.* Lovejoy (see Kermode, 1954, p. xxxiv), on the other hand, argues that Shakespeare intended a satirical comment on Montaigne in *The Tempest.* Rothe (1961 passim) attirbutes to Montaigne a maximum effect upon Shakespeare.

If one acknowledges Montaigne's superior power of reasoning, the freshness and originality of his thought, the great scope of his ideas, the live presentation of his convictions, and if at the same time one considers that Shakespeare's mind must have been eminently penetrating and most avid to learn about the human world; if one further acknowledges that in the early 1600's Montaigne was the only philosopher who was commensurate with Shakespeare in breadth and depth of interest in the entire human cosmos, then one cannot, it seems to me, overestimate the effect that Shakespeare's acquaintance with the *Essays* must have had on him.

It is not to be expected, of course, that a mind as unbound by rules as Shakespeare's was would have submitted to Montaigne's genius. Yet Montaigne's *Essays* must have stimulated, challenged, and provoked

Shakespeare unceasingly. As is well known, it is Gonzalo's Commonwealth speech that proves beyond any doubt the existence of a direct link between *The Tempest* and Montaigne's essay *Of Cannibals* (Book I, 31). Here it becomes necessary to say a few words about Gonzalo, about whom I did not say very much in the previous section.

Gonzalo has been accepted as a just and lovable old man by those critics who have gone along with Prospero's grateful acknowledgment of his kindness. Yet Gonzalo is not really what he may sometimes seem to be: he is at times difficult to bear, and at bottom he is a bore. It is in a very flimsy way indeed that he tries to console the King who, to all appearances, has lost his son. He is something of a Pollyanna type, one who is most ready to discover Providence in all sorts of happenings—a question to be taken up later. Gonzalo's famous speech is meant in part to distract Alonso from his gloomy thoughts; the topic is certainly worthy of a King, but is it really adequate to the situation at hand? We sympathize with Alonso and understand him all too well when he finally says: "Prithee, no more: thou dost talk nothing to me." The side remarks by Antonio and Sebastian, ridiculing the councillor, are meant to characterize the speakers themselves as evil; but at the same time it should be noted that the wicked eye—as so often in reality—sees more realistically than the one that is given to virtue and to belief in ideals. [25]

There is also a moral blemish attached to Gonzalo, which is usually overlooked. He knew of Alonso's guile, the result of his conspiring with Antonio against Prospero, and he apparently disapproved of it, since he counteracted the conspiracy by protecting Prospero from the worst; yet he stayed in Alonso's service and continued to cater to him and to remain unruffled in his enjoyment of Court prerogatives. Here too psychological immobility is to be noted. The course he once took he will continue to take, and he will go on serving anointed power in his almost spineless way in the future as well.

The Commonwealth speech stands in the context like a foreign body. In no better way could Gonzalo's narrow understanding of the human world be presented than by his telling a King what kind of government he would set up if *he* were king, at the very moment when that same King is bemoaning the loss of his heir to the throne. The remarks by Sebastian and Antonio that accompany the councillor's speech and

---

[25] Cf. Nuttall (1967, p. 142) for the double aspect that surrounds Gonzalo: "Antonio and Sebastian are truly witty; Gonzalo really does talk like an old fool. But Antonio and Sebastian are themselves both foolish and wicked, while Gonzalo is not really a fool at all."

are, according to the general view, rude and cynical, are nevertheless not altogether uncalled for. I do not know whether it was Montaigne that Shakespeare wanted here to criticize, or those who misapplied Montaigne's teachings. Shakespeare apparently knew that, even though civilization may have spread evil in its wake, it was a process that could not be stopped—and probably should not.

In our times, there are also those who, observing the damaging effects of money, technology and science, would wish to remedy evil by discarding instruments that they attribute to the devil. Such reformers are not to be compared with the physician who severs limbs in order to preserve the body, but rather with the physician who would kill the body in order to end the disease.

Whatever Shakespeare's intent may have been in the Commonwealth speech, it draws only a fraction of what is contained in Montaigne's essay. Montaigne has often been presented as pursuing the line of thought that idealizes primitive man, by contrast with those who hold the opinion that man is a brute, if he is not improved by civilization. Indeed, he does seem at times to idealize primitivism; yet his essay *Of Cannibals* is complex and points in a variety of directions. Montaigne was certainly not given to simplifying matters. It is with profound regret that I abstain from discussing at full length his views on primitivism. He was fully aware of the relativism of what is called barbarous, of the narcissistic pride that each person takes in glorifying his own habitat. "Each man calls barbarism whatever is not his own practice; for indeed it seems we have no other test of truth and reason than the example and pattern of the opinions and customs of the country we live in" (Montaigne, 1580, p. 152).

How modern he was may be seen from his statements on the unreliability of those who report on other peoples and from his advice on how to protect oneself against misinformation; he even evolved a very clever psychological scheme as to what sort of personality would be best endowed to report objectively on foreign cultures. Montaigne reports all kinds of what we would call today "barbarism" about the cannibals, and he himself calls it just that: "I am not sorry that we notice the barbarous horror of such acts, but I am heartily sorry that, judging their faults rightly, we should be so blind to our own. I think there is more barbarity in eating a man alive than in eating him dead." And then he recites some of the execrable deeds he has witnessed some Christian perpetrating on another, in his own cultural habitat. He (1580, p. 155f) found cannibalism under certain conditions acceptable, but nothing could "excuse ordinary vices." What Montaigne maintains is that the values, particularly ethical values, of primitive man are in the long run superior to those of his own contemporaries.

It is rather evident, I believe, that Montaigne is far less interested in the ethics of faraway countries than he is in the meaning of all this to his own civilization and, indeed, he does not hesitate to castigate the latter mercilessly. Montaigne was a prophet who foresaw the irreparable wounds that the West would inflict on those primitive peoples who are "ignorant of the price they will pay some day, in loss of repose and happiness, for gaining knowledge of the corruption of this side of the ocean; ignorant also of the fact that of this intercourse will come their ruin" (p. 158).[26]

And in reporting the reply of one of the visitors who had come to France and was asked what he had found most amazing over here, Montaigne levels a deadly slap in the face of his own society, through his use of two arguments: the bias of social power and the bias of property. For what was most amazing to the visitors was the fact "that so many grown men, bearded, strong, and armed, obeyed a King who was a child,"[27] and "that there were among us men full and gorged with all sorts of good things, and that their other halves were beggars at their doors, emaciated with hunger and poverty, and they thought it strange that these needy halves could endure such an injustice, and did not take the others by the throat, or set fire to their houses."

This was the spirit to which Shakespeare was exposed in his reading of Montaigne, and since his mind was not torpid, the depth, reasonableness and striking power of Montaigne's argumentation, which in many instances might have coincided with or at least come close to what he may have vaguely sensed, must have left an indelible trace on his thinking.

Providence in "The Tempest."

Many a critic of *The Tempest* has centered his interpretation of the play upon the action of Providence, which teaches Prospero to master his

---

[26] In Book III, Chapter 6, Montaigne takes up the same topic. Before going into the details of the execrable atrocities committed against the innocent, he writes (Montaigne, 1580, p. 693): "I am much afraid that we shall have very greatly hastened the decline and ruin of this new world by our contagion, and that we will have sold it our opinions and our arts very dear."

[27] Montaigne was 26 when Francis II ascended the throne at the age of 15, only to be followed a year later by Charles IX, who was ten when he became King in 1560.

passions and leads "the princes into health again" (Kermode, 1954, p. xxx).

The reader may recall the earlier discussion about the meaning of Hamlet's taking up the theme of Providence toward the end of the trage-dy. In *The Tempest* Providence assumes an even larger place than it did in that play.

It is well known how human thinking deals, more often than not, with the concept of Providence. When success follows man's actions, he is ready to discover the hand of Providence at work on his behalf; when he fails, however, he prefers to hold the conniving of his enemies responsi-ble.[28]

Thus the thinking about Providence generally follows the line of the well-known saying: tails you lose, heads I win. It is a concept that, in the way in which it is customarily employed, cannot be disproved. Mon-taigne wrote an essay (strangely enough, the one that follows right after *Of Cannibals*)—"*We should meddle soberly with judging divine ordi-nances*" (Montaigne, 1580, pp. 159-161)—in which he warned against an abuse of thinking in connection with Providence. In it, he points out that it is precisely the things that are unknown that give cause for the strongest convictions, "nor are any people so confident as those who tell us fables." With some hesitation, he puts into the same group "a whole pile of people, interpreters and controllers-in-ordinary of God's designs, claiming to find the causes of every incident and to see in the secrets of the divine will the incomprehensible motives of his works."

Although events are discordant, "they do not stop . . . painting black and white with the same pencil. . . . It is enough for a Christian to believe that all things come from God," he continues, and it is bad prac-tice "trying to strengthen and support our religion by the good fortune and prosperity of our enterprises." He then gives historical examples of this bad practice. When the Protestants won a battle, they "used their good fortune as a sure approbation of their party" and excused their de-feats as "fatherly . . . , unless they have their following complete-ly at their mercy." The battle of Lepanto ended in victory over the Turks, "but it has certainly pleased God at other times to let us see oth-ers like it, at our expense." He enumerates several adversaries of the

---

[28] In modern times, Providence has been replaced by majorities. The majority in a vote decides where truth lies, and the elected candidate believes in all seriousness that the fact of his being elected proves his superiority over the loser, even though the historical record does not seem to confirm this at all. No one has yet explained just why mass opinion should be held to be superior to individual opinion.

Catholic Church who had died in a privy, "But what does this prove? Irenaeus happens to have suffered the same fate."

Indeed, almost four hundred years later one has to agree with Montaigne wholeheartedly, even though the number of those who see the hand of God in the misfortunes of their enemies as well as in the successes of their own enterprises is still notably large. How many people in Western civilization still believe in Providence it is difficult to guess, but with the decline of Church religion and the conspicuous curtailment of the power that is left to the Churches, it seems wiser for the devout to narrow down considerably the area in which Providence can be observed and instead to believe in the success of sin.

And how goes it now with "the action of providence" that Kermode discovers so extensively in Shakespeare's play? Actually, there is one event that could rightly be ascribed to Providence. When Prospero was cast out to sea in an utterly unseaworthy ship, which even the rats preferred to abandon, he was destined to perish.

Yet he reached the fabulous island that fulfilled his dearest wishes. This occurred contrary to all expectation, so that the spectator may well discover the hand of Providence in such unusual survival.

Rightly Prospero answers Miranda's question "How came we ashore?" with "By Providence divine" *(I.2.159)*. Had he already had magic at his command at that time, had he been able then to start storms and to stop them, he would never have referred to Providence. In this instance the reference to Providence is really in lieu of "I do not know," since what is called nowadays "the average expectable environment" made Prospero rightly expect certain death. Since this most probable—under such conditions, even certain—event did not take place, and no other explanation for that fact could be determined, it could have been effected only by Providence. My reconstruction makes me believe that Prospero reached his conclusion *per exclusionem.* It is in a different context that Ferdinand also invokes Providence. When his father believes Miranda to be a goddess who had separated father and son and united them once again, he says: "Sir, she is mortal;/ But by immortal Providence she's mine" *(V.1.188f)*.

I once had a patient who suffered from the idea that she had met her husband "by accident." "What would my life have been if I had not met him?" Indeed, it is a disquieting idea for lovers that they might never have met. The idea that their love was fated no doubt carries a soothing quality, allaying fears of separation. We shall agree by empathy with

Ferdinand's conviction that providential meddling arranged his encounter with Miranda, and will not scold Prospero in case he should smile while counting up in his mind all the labors that were necessary to bring the two together.

With Gonzalo it is quite different. Whatever may happen, he sees God's hand in the event, as long as it has a happy ending, and he finally sees even Prospero's loss of Milan as nothing but a stepping-stone "that his issue/Should become Kings of Naples." And so he goes on, including everything, from Claribel's voyage to Tunis down to the shipwreck in the tempest, as events arranged by Providence. Prospero, to whom one has to ascribe greater intelligence than one can to Gonzalo, is more cautious. The approach of the King and his entourage toward the Island he refers to as "accident most strange," "bountiful Fortune," "a most auspicious start" *(I.2.178 et sequ.).*

Shakespeare's audience may have listened to Gonzalo's speech in the same way as Kermode does 350 years later, and Shakespeare himself may have been quite happy about the audience's acceptance of reinstated Providence, after Prospero has indulged in a sorcery that could hardly have been to the liking of Shakespeare's monarch. Yet the literary critic who is no longer a subject of James I, and has studied Montaigne to boot, should not believe that Shakespeare had a mind less penetrating than Montaigne's, particularly after Prospero has emphasized that what accident, Fortune and the stars offered was an *opportunity*, of which conjuring man could make use in order to bring his enemies to bay and affiance his virgin daughter to a royal house. That Gonzalo's imperturbable propensity to perceive Providence has to be taken with a grain of salt, cannot be doubted. If Shakespeare really intended to disprove his giant contemporary, he would not have selected a "lightweight" like Gonzalo in order to do so.

Agreement between Shakespeare and Montaigne with regard to Providence may be postulated on good grounds. Yet it may seem as if their opinions about the nature of primitive man greatly differed. For Caliban, whose name was derived from Montaigne's essay and who is definitely the paradigm of primitive man, does not show anything in common with Montaigne's picture. On closer scrutiny, however, an *approchement* to Montaigne may become visible. One has to consider Kermode's remark (p. li) that "Caliban serves as a criterion, not of beauty and civility, but of the corruption of the nobly born"; or, further, that Caliban is used "to indicate how much baser the corruption of the civilized can be than the bestiality of the natural" (p. xxxviii). This function of Caliban in the play reflects Montaigne's assertion that while natural man may be barbarous, his vices are less than those of civilized man.

It is strange that the formulation "civilized man is more barbarous than natural man" is not the worst injury that can be inflicted upon civilized man's narcissistic pride. He is, after all, *civilized.* He is, according to his way of looking at it, not what he ought to be, but he does possess a potential superiority. It is regrettable that this potential may not be fully realized, but as an entity he remains—in his own eyes, at least—superior to natural man, even if he makes no use at all of this supposed potential.

When a father reprimands his highly intelligent son for his failure at school and points out that his brother, who is far less intelligent and gifted than he, nevertheless scores higher, the reprimanded youth may feel highly flattered. Indeed, if his scholastic achievements had been commensurate with his intelligence, he might never have received any comment at all on his superior intelligence. He might, on the other hand, have felt mortified if the father had declared that his failure at school was in effect a sign that the intelligence of both his sons was, after all, equally low. That is what I believe Shakespeare did—in a disguised way, of course. Caliban, I propose, is man—civilized or natural, it does not matter: when you look at man, you find Caliban.

Almost exactly in the middle of the play there is a sentence that contains a terrifying demand: "Be my god."[29] It is Caliban's request to Stephano. This is man grovelling at the feet of the God whom he himself has set up and begging it to serve that function. It therefore constitutes the most devastating attack against Christianity or, more precisely, against any religion as such, and seems to me to go far beyond what Montaigne was saying. There is, of course, hardly any likelihood that this view will be accepted, since most critics find in *The Tempest* a sublime allegory of Christianity.[30] Nevertheless, the line may contain *in nuce* a devastating attack against mankind's proudest invention, its religion. It is entirely possible for a great mind, upon discovering a truth

[29] If the lines are counted in accordance with the New Arden edition, the statement is preceded by 1042 and followed by 998 lines. The present text shows that there may have been two cuts in the first part, while the second lasted somewhat longer than is to be expected from the number of verses involved, since it contained masque and antimasque. If so, then this line may well have been spoken exactly at the midpoint of the play, if one measures by the time its performance took.

[30] Wagner (1933) carried this Christian allegorization of *The Tempest* to extremes. It would be easy to show that the extreme position she takes is untenable.

that is frightening as it is profound, to place it where he can feel certain its full meaning will not be apprehended.

If we agree that great comedy often contains a truth that would be unbearable if it had to be acknowledged without laughter,[31] then the Stephano-Trinculo-Caliban trinity will be recognized to contain a most profound truth. We are here facing a situation comparable to that one meets with in Freud's *Negation*. There Freud (1925b) spelled out a linguistic mechanism that functions in such a way as to bring the content per se (even though without its entire implications) to full awareness, without destroying the ego that has to face this brute truth. Laughter sometimes accomplishes the same thing (cf. Kris, 1939). Woe to the comedian who relaxes for a moment and thereby deprives a cue of its humorous coating. Take out of the unholy three that which produces laughter, and you are facing an abominable world—worse than that of *Hamlet* or *Lear*.

What is necessary—something that I am not able to do to my own satisfaction—is an exact determination of the rhythm of the main action and that of the subject of the unholy triad, their mutual dynamism and interlocking. The Caliban episodes seem to be merely limping after and they may sound to some like nothing more than a lingering resonance— and off key, at that. But are they to be understood as caricatures of their predecessors—leftovers, so to speak, like distorted after-images—or was it their function to set forth retroactively the true meaning of what has receded as an illusion?

Of the play's 2050-odd lines 315 have passed before we obtain Caliban's history, following that of the principal personages.[32]

When we next meet Caliban, it is in conjunction with Stephano and Trinculo. The action in this scene is future-directed, as have been the intervening scenes, in which Ferdinand and Miranda fall in love and Antonio and Sebastian form their plans for new crimes and efforts at political aggrandizement by force. Caliban finds God and King in the drunken sailor and hopes, with the help of his two new acquaintances, to escape Prospero's intolerable domination. This scene forms a unit together with the one in which Caliban and Stephano form the plot to murder Prospero, which is comparable to the plot in the King's entourage. The intervening short scene of Miranda's and Ferdinand's protestations of love and spiritual wedding could have been put as easily before or after. I assume that the brief interruption of the two sequences by the two Cali-

---

[31] After all, has anybody in literature ever sent a missile against the Gods as fierce as Aristophanes' *Birds*?

[32] The shipwreck scene is a prologue or prelude and does not therefore warrant inclusion in the present analysis.

ban-Stephano-Trinculo scenes was necessitated by reasons of theatrical technique—that is, of the need to take heed of the audience's rhythm of tension arousal and relaxation. The messages implicitly contained in the two triad scenes are perhaps too gruesome to be endured one on the heels of the other, without an interlude of sublime repose and beauty.

The scenes here mentioned have elements in common as well as contrasting ones. Antonio purposely casts an almost hypnotic spell over Sebastian, since his original crime is now to be repeated in an even more dastardly way—namely, usurpation of power by murder. Ferdinand and Miranda, through their mutual influence, are involuntarily also caught in an almost hypnotic spell—that of love. Caliban, on the other hand, is fascinated by Stephano—without the latter's *wanting* this to happen. His fascination thereupon recoils, by way of eliciting in Stephano impulses that would not have arisen had he not had the hypnotic effect that he did on Caliban. Thus, the spells cast by Antonio and Stephano both lead to preparation for the committing of murder. It seems that only such an interpersonal relationship as that of love between two young and beautiful people is free of crime and guilt; societal action leads instead to crime. Sebastian seeks illegal, usurped power; but was Prospero's power over Caliban legal?

With Act III, Scene 3 begins the phase of Prospero's efforts to convert Alonso, Antonio and Sebastian. In this scene, he does not get beyond raising feelings of guilt in them. The trend of Prospero's efforts is continued, however, by his setting Miranda free, and uniting the two lovers, not without an ethical injunction (he twice calls for premarital chastity on their part, a request that is repeated in the Masque). Caliban reappears in a new context when Stephano feels himself to be King because he is now wearing the external trappings of Kingship, which Ariel had laid out to deceive him. The triad is then chastised by Prospero in the anti-masque, when dogs and hounds are let loose upon them at the moment when they are trying to carry out their plot. Note the difference between Prospero's dealing with Antonio, Alonso and Sebastian, on the one hand, and Caliban on the other. (In the last act, it is once again Caliban who is the last to receive Prospero's pardon.)

While one is able without difficulty to visualize the future of most characters of the play, what will happen to Caliban is left open. Will he be reinstituted in possession of the Island? There is a surprising ambiguity toward the end of the play, which I have not found discussed anywhere. Prospero orders Caliban to his cell *(V.1.291),* yet ten lines later he invites "your highness and your train" to the same abode, which is scarcely feasible in realistic terms. Did Shakespeare purposely, or only by chance, indicate here that the Christians and "the salvage man" end in the same retreat?[33]

Be that as it may, it is surprising (and, I think, essential to the understanding of *The Tempest*) that Caliban, as a dramatic character, includes elements (however distorted they may be) of all the other *dramatis personae*. His resemblance to Stephano and Trinculo is self-evident; but he loves Miranda as Ferdinand does, and he too would like to people the island, as Ferdinand will do to Naples. He shares with Prospero the fact that for 12 years they were the only men Miranda knew. He was dispossessed of his inheritance, as Prospero was, and he had learned magic from his mother, as Prospero did from him (as well as, probably, from books). He tries to murder the present ruler of the island, as Sebastian intends to do with the ruler of Naples. He is councillor to a sham King, as Gonzalo is to a real one. He is even a King- and God-maker in his own right, and in this respect remotely resembles Prospero. In the end, he too is presented as renouncing, just as his master does. That he shares a hypnotic spell with Sebastian, Miranda and Ferdinand has already been mentioned. He is thirsting for freedom, as Ariel is, and shares the same master with him. Both had been close to Sycorax, and both had been removed from her influence by Prospero.[34] The elite of the Island is dependent on his menial services, as the court of Naples depends on the Boatswain; and just as the latter is cursed by Sebastian, so he is cursed by Prospero.

James (1967, pp. 130, 132) sets forth two additional points of resemblance that I myself had overlooked: (a) Ferdinand is subjected to "Caliban's indignity of log-bearing" and he too has to submit to Prospero's injunction of chastity; (b) Caliban surrenders the Island that by right is his to Stephano, just as "Antonio had in effect given the Kingship of Milan to Naples." Kermode (1954, pp. li, 82, fn. to 98) points to three similarities or parallelisms between Caliban and Miranda. Caliban has been only one woman aside from his mother and Miranda one man aside from her father; Caliban's mother practiced magic as Miranda's

---

[33] A mythological exploration of the entrance to Prospero's cell is necessary. Does it stand for entrance to the tomb, the maternal body or to Hell?

[34] James (1937, p. 240) even says: "Caliban and Ariel are one." Indeed, analytically one could suggest that Sycorax was the mother of both of them, the good son deserting to the father, the bad one remaining fixated to the infantile gratifications that the early mother provides.

father does; Miranda was taught and educated by Prospero, just as Caliban was.

Thus the circle is closed and there is no figure in the play whom we would not find reflected, in one way or another, in Caliban. There can be no doubt that Caliban is the principal character of the play: he is a synthesis of all other characters, a distorted resonance of the fate of the others—or are they his reflection?[35]

The Myth in "The Tempest."[36]

James (1937) has ingeniously set forth mythical strands that go through Shakespeare's last plays from *Pericles* to *The Tempest*, enumerating such themes as the finding of what is lost; the restoration of a state of peace and love after great suffering and acts of disloyalty; the loss and subsequent recovery of a royal position; the willingness to abandon royalty in the presence of eclipsing beauty; the exposure of children to terrible dangers and their rescue; and, finally, the return to life of the dead.

At times, James finds harsh words to say about this group of plays. He points out the absurdity and arbitrariness of some of their episodes (1937, p. 234): "We alternate throughout the plays between Shakespeare's high metaphysical symbolism and a sense of the silly." He even believes that Shakespeare conveyed what he set out to, but at the expense of his art, about which, as James sees it, he cared little in those plays (1937, p. 233). Shakespeare, he says, after he had discovered in his tragedies that life is fundamentally disjointed—torn asunder, so to speak—found a new mode of apprehending life, and resorted to myth in order to convey it. This myth he did not want to express in religious terms and, without ever surrendering to its traditional language, he tried to convey it by way of poetry.

I do not see any incompatibility between tragedy and myth, as James does. I myself do not understand how one can produce tragedy without being at the same time something of a mythmaker. But this may, after all, depend on one's definition of myth.

In trying to explain Shakespeare's switch from tragedy to symbolic plays or to whatever they should be called, one must also consider the

---

[35] Kermode calls Caliban "the ground of the play" (p. xxiv), "the core of the play" (p. xxiv), "the focus of the play's ideas" (p. lxxiv); but his introduction does not explicate Caliban's central position at all and it appears that Kermode did not draw any conclusions from his own pregnant judgment.

[36] Schmitt (1956, p. 69) says that Winstanley, who has devoted much effort to reconstructing the contemporary historical events that found their way into Shakespeare's tragedies (cf. e.g., Winstanley, 1921), has also written on *The Tempest*. I have been unable to find any reference to this study, and assume that it was never published.

exhaustibility of art forms. With his tragedies, and particularly with *King Lear,* Shakespeare had reached boundaries beyond which human art cannot reach, and which no other mind has indeed passed beyond since then. I feel almost inclined to say that no more tragedies could have been written. However, James (1967) may be right that, in writing these tragedies, Shakespeare might have had experiences or gained insights that needed, in order to be presented, a new art form. I am here disregarding the development of Jacobean literature which, of course, must have had its effect, and will try instead to guess what might have been some of the hidden problems with which Shakespeare was struggling during the last phase of his creativity.

It is a fact that Shakespeare had failed several times before he finally succeeded in producing one of his perfect plays, one in which he had at last succeeded in uniting the themes with which he had apparently wrestled previously. *The Tempest* does not contain the absurdities or any of the other weaknesses of its immediate predecessors. In *The Tempest* Shakespeare was again at his best and greatest, and one has to grant it the rare quality of perfection. But what was it that made him first fail and then succeed? The "myth" that is usually found in *The Tempest*— the myth of forgiveness and reconciliation and what not—is not really too original and should not have required for its production such strong inner qualms and conflicts as had apparently resulted in three previous failures. Besides which, are forgiveness and reconciliation really so strikingly pervasive in *The Tempest?*

When a king such as Lear has to undergo excruciating pain and conflict in order to arrive at length at a serene outlook, this may be quite impressive, in view of the great torment that one human being had to undergo, in order to come to a new outlook. To be sure, Prospero had suffered a grave injustice; but, after all, what he lost was a Dukedom about which he had not cared too greatly and which had indeed been nothing but a burden to him. ("My library/ Was dukedom large enough," "volumes that/ I prize above my dukedom . . . ") At the new abode forced upon him, he was able to pursue his real inclination far better than he ever would have been able to at the Court of Milan. Seven years before Shakespeare was born, the emperor of the largest territory that had ever until then been under one sovereign voluntarily resigned his throne at the age of 57 and retired to a monastery.[37]

[37] Plank (1968, pp. 163-165) discusses the possibility that the historical model of Prospero may have been Rudolph II of Hapsburg, who was Emperor from 1576 to 1606, when he was declared unfit to rule.

Thus, it would not have been unheard of, if Prospero had himself resigned his dukedom in order to immerse himself in his studies. And indeed, without the loss of Milan, he would never have met Ariel, nor acquired a power infinitely greater than that provided by his being a head of government. Nor was Miranda harmed in the bargain. Prospero himself admits that she received an education superior to that of her cognates and it may be doubted whether at a court she would have developed into a creature of such disarming innocence and naïveté.

Had Prospero sought to take his revenge, his progeny would surely not have obtained sovereignty over Naples. Forgiving amounted to dynastic succession, in Prospero's case, and it cannot therefore be regarded as an act of eminent Christian charity. There is even some negligence connected with it. Antonio unregenerate may easily start a new plot against the ruler of Milan, whether it be the one who returns to his former dukedom or that future one who will be unversed in the difficult business of government, his primary interest being in his almost unearthly love, the equivalent for him of Prospero's absorption in books. Yet there is no doubt enough left in the play—thin as the layer may be—to perceive an attitude of forgiveness that may seem to be related to Christian teaching.[38]

A different trend is brought to light when James writes (1937, p. 241): "*The Tempest* is the record of the final dissolution, the ultimate destruction of the world by the imagination. Shakespeare dissolved the world he had created; his interest was no longer in it; it was beyond it, and beyond the human." There may be some truth in the idea that creation always entails destruction, and James may be right that Shakespeare's farewell was the equivalent of a gesture of destruction, designed to annihilate his past creations. I myself have suggested that many an action in *The Tempest* sounds like an undoing of one or another evil that his chief characters had perpetrated in earlier plays. Yet undoing is not the same as destruction. Still it is noteworthy that James discovers a destructive component in the play, even though he does not state clearly why the playwright should have longed to do away with the eternal embodiments of his fantasy. That *The Tempest* as a whole does contain

---

[38] Prospero's all too pronounced readiness to break out into anger shows how little forgiveness has been integrated by him; it shows at the same time how little his forgiveness has to do with the Christian meaning of it. His forgiveness appears to be a pragmatic one, enforced by circumstances and going only so far as he considered it to be useful.

something of despair, dread, possibly horror of the future, however, seems to me quite clear.[39]

There is a strange thing about the masterpieces that geniuses create when they grow old. Some develop a new style, as if only now are they able to realize without shackles that with which they had been struggling since their earliest creative attempts. Others, like Goethe, show an extreme form of the Olympic, the Serene, the finally achieved conflict-free, which may strike one at first as particularly beautiful. On closer scrutiny, however, one is inclined to become suspicious of that very serenity. There is a paragraph in Goethe's last novel, *Wilhelm Meisters Wanderjahre,* which shows most surprisingly that Goethe knew all along of the impending usurpation of Western culture by technology; these few lines betray a dread of the threatening destruction of everything that he had considered to be of value in his world and had loved as tenderly as any Western mind had ever done.

But at 80 a man is tired. It was not that Goethe was withdrawn. He was even concerned with practical matters, as is proven by his eagerness to secure the welfare of his progeny after his death, as Shakespeare did. But the idea of a new civilization, which appears to be incompatible with truth and beauty as he saw and understood them and—perhaps even more important—as he had created them, is a dread-arousing one. Who would blame such a mind for denying at that stage of the game what he well knows and declaring the universe to be in harmony and well-balanced? He cannot, after all, change the course of history and a consistent denial, through the upholding of an Olympian serenity, may well facilitate the pathway toward a death without torment.

My belief is that the reason why Shakespeare failed in the three attempts that he made before *The Tempest* was that he had been struggling with a problem that he may not have dared even to state explicitly to himself (this would explain an ambivalent attitude toward the intended work), or for which, because of its enormity and dread, he had not ever succeeded in finding the right form. He did, however, succeed in creating something perfect with *The Tempest,* because he had discovered Caliban. It was Caliban who made that play not only effective, but even possible.

It is my impression that, with the figure of Caliban, Shakespeare

---

[39] Nuttall (1967, p. 156) brings this out when he says about *The Tempest:* "It is as if a second wave of scepticism has passed over the poet."

obtained the assurance that he would be able to utter what would otherwise have been a shattering truth, in a poetical form that would permit it to become acceptable to his society and probably to mankind. And he was right. The Christian gleam on the surface of the play has attracted enough attention to remove all suspicion that Caliban may, after all, be telling the truth, for the world surely stood in no need of Shakespeare to pronounce forgiveness as the ultimate conclusion of thought, since the Gospels and medieval literature had done all that before, and much better, to boot.

It is little more than a platitude to say that Shakespeare possessed a penetrating mind. But sometimes I wonder whether its depth of penetration is sufficiently recognized. There is a sense of the extreme that is evident in Shakespeare's tragedies (even as early as in *Titus Andronicus*) as well as in some of his comedies—a determination to go to the bitterest end, a refusal to compromise and an aversion against simplification, a readiness to meet the complex head on.

What happened when such a mind now came upon Montaigne's skepticism? Did it dawn on him that the two cornerstones of his society, without which, the belief was, it would be thrown into anarchy—the Kingship and Christianity—were based on an illusion; that the King was not God's vicar, to be regarded with a spiritual fear second only to that due to God, and that resistance to him was therefore not necessarily wicked; that Kingdom was not God-made and in that regard as real as a city or such kinship relations as a family, but in a sense merely accidental and therefore quite capable of being replaced by a different form of rule; that the Christian belief was not necessarily true, that it depended entirely on man's willingness to believe—in short, that man's religious faith has its roots not in metaphysical truths but in his own wishes? The Caliban scenes imply dangerous, rebellious beliefs.

After all, all those who are in power in the play hold it illegally—that is to say, by way of a crime or its equivalent. Antonia and Alonso are clearly guilty of such criminality, yet even Prospero's rights to sovereignty over the Island may be disputed. He did liberate Ariel and restore justice in that one area; but Caliban's accusation rested on good grounds, and Prospero's defense, even though it may have been in agreement with the biases of his times and was probably therefore accepted by Shakespeare's audience (cf. Kermode, 1954, p. xxxix), would not hold up in a court of law. It has certainly been shown to be hypocritical and arrogant, by the course that history has taken since then. Was Shakespeare's mind sufficiently penetrating for him to be aware that Prospero's rebuttal was nothing but a rationalization?[40]

It is a typical English sailor, brought up in Christian society, who is introduced in the form of Stephano: he is fascinated by the seemingly Royal attire, and believes himself to be King because he has put it round his shoulders. Does this not imply the same idea as lies at the base of the thinking of Montaigne's savage, who wondered that bearded men should obey a child? Has not the course of history since then convinced the Western world that hereditary power of government is based on bias, superstition, charisma, and that it is not necessary, not God-wanted, not in itself and by itself justified? Was Shakespeare's mind sufficiently penetrating to grasp that idea so far ahead of his time? And what does it mean that it is Caliban—who is described by the critics as unteachable, who can never accept civilization and culture—who, at the very moment when Stephano is tricked by sham, raises his voice in warning and says: "It is but trash"?

Here is the peak of poetic irony. Caliban, who has been befuddled by the drunken sailor and elevated him to Kingship and Godship, nevertheless acknowledges the transitoriness of the material realization of symbols, and in so doing exposes that pernicious disease of the human mind that makes it confuse reality and symbol, a magic belief no less rampant in our times than it was in Shakespeare's: he who possesses the symbols of power also possesses the power.

There is a sentence in one of the Caliban scenes that should make every member of the Western community howl. It contains the most savage condemnation that can possibly be poured into one brief statement, rejecting Christian society: "When they [in England] will not give a doit to relieve a lame beggar, they will lay out ten to see a dead Indian." I can well imagine the laughter this aroused in Shakespeare's audience. It is

[40] Caliban is at least 24 years old, if not more, at the inception of the stage action. It is not said at what age he did "seek to violate/The honour of my child." There is some indication that Prospero, Miranda and Caliban lived in the same cell. What Prospero apparently expects of Caliban is carnal abstention despite constant stimulation. Stephano responds to Caliban's description of Miranda in the same way as Caliban does to the live Miranda, and he intends to make her Queen of the island, yet he does not incur even a threat of punishment for the intent. Prospero apparently expects from "salvage man" more than he himself would be ready and able to accomplish—a question about which more will have to be said later. In having intimated that sexual gratification is one of the "inalienable rights," I may be reproached with carrying into Shakespeare's play ideas that properly belong to 20th-century mental hygiene. But the Elizabethan age seems to have been rather free in sexual matters, and Shakespeare himself may have been victimized by his own indiscreet appetites. The drive, its impetuosity and the difficulty of taming it are clearly acknowledged by Prospero's thrice expressed warning against prenuptial intercourse.

excellent theater and many a critic will insist that there is nothing more to it than that, plus a topical reference. Perhaps; but then one would have to say that Shakespeare was not a penetrating mind, after all. If the statement is bared of its comical implications, however, and the factual ones are set forth, one cannot help seeing that these declare Shakespeare's society to be a basically un-Christian one. Since the New Testament warns specifically against any interest in the dead, this statement of fact contains a particularly severe accusation. It describes wilful abstention from a charitable act, which it would be easy matter to perform, in favor of indulgence in a forbidden and useless pleasure of a perverse nature.

I have to digress here in order to deal with a strange dichotomy in man's life. Some psychiatrists have asserted that dreaming is a necessity for man's health and that insanity would be the lot of all of us if we were to be deprived of our dreaming. Modern research (cf. E. Hartmann, 1967) makes it highly probable that this is true. As is now known, dreaming is so essential and necessary to life that the dream mechanism is ready to be in full swing at the moment of birth and may even be at work in the womb. Yet it is also true that we would probably go "insane" if we were to recall all the dreams that our mind produces during the course of the night. Of all these, what we recall is in fact only a small fraction.

It thus seems warranted to say that both dreaming and forgetting dreams are among the necessities of life. If we were truly aware of all our dreams, the result would probably be a state of great pain, anguish and profound mental trouble. Aside from dreams that are forgotten in a "natural" way, there are thoughts, recollections, fantasies in every human mind that are not forgotten, even though they cause anguish and embarrassment and the subject would not want them to be revealed at any price.[41]

The artistically productive mind, with its great closeness to the unconscious and the dream, must harbor far more of such material than the ordinary person, who is already troubled aplenty by thoughts "unfit to print." Indeed, the creative mind—insofar as it is driven by a vigorous momentum of creation—tends to draw a wider and wider circle of its mental productions into the realm of its creative elaboration. It is sur-

---

[41] I doubt that the total literary output of a very productive mind has ever reached us, because many "forbidden" productions have been destroyed by the culprit-writer. I would even suspect this also of the artist who uses one of the visual media, but I doubt that comparable shame and guilt feelings are ever attached to musical compositions.

prising what finally comes to the surface. Nestroy was one of Vienna's great writers of comedy (he was subjected in *The Matchmaker* to a scandalous rewriting), and, indeed, reading his plays can even now be a source of delight and laughter. But in his last comedy (if it was a comedy) his "humor" takes a bitter oral-sadistic turn and the play is pervaded by the crudest sort of cannibalism, so nauseating that I have not been able to read it through to the end. Mark Twain, too, demonstrated at the end of his career his full bitterness and sorrow.[42] Shakespeare is one of the few dramatists who have produced both the greatest comedies and the greatest tragedies. Perhaps it was the fact that he had an outlet which provided him with the opportunity to express the tragic aspect of life that preserved him from ending his creative phase with a comedy à la Nestroy's last. Yet he comes close to it.

In general, I fear we are so taken by the beauty of Shakespeare's language and poetry and the sense of awe that surrounds his name that we are apt sometimes to overlook the implications of the contents of *The Tempest* (cf. Strachey, 1906). Caliban's quasi-physical reunion with Trinculo, when together they form a configuration that is taken by Stephano to be a four-legged monster, with a "forward voice" that speaks well and "a backward voice" that utters foul speeches; Caliban's "Do not torment me," with its ambiguous implications as to what Trinculo may do to him, when the latter seeks refuge under his gabardine—all this draws on archaic and frightening imagery, rivalling the products of Hieronymus Bosch's tormented imagination, and culminating in Stephano's image about Trinculo's being an excrement or the upshot of an abortion.

But then the phantasms turn to liquor that is "not earthly" and is equated with "the book," which Caliban is forced to kiss. It is at that moment that he begs Stephano to be his god and that he himself be permitted to kiss Stephano's foot—whereupon he is made to kiss Stephano's foot. Did not Shakespeare here go as far as he could without getting into serious trouble, in reducing to persiflage the question of the form in which the Christian should partake of Christ's body?[43]

If Shakespeare really did not have in mind here anything else but making fun of a sailor's dealing with an indigene, he certainly missed a

---

[42] One may, of course, regard such final productions, which often seem somewhat incongruous in the light of previous productions, as the result of weakened defenses, brought about by the aging process, but this, I think, would do an injustice to their real meaning.

[43] It may be of significance that Still (1921) failed to include this passage in his interpretation although he devoted much thought otherwise to the Caliban-Stephano scenes.

great chance. For Christian folly reached its peak when whole regions were depopulated over the question of whether a layman was to receive Christ only in solid or also in liquid form, the folly being equally divided between those who made the request and those who refused it. I am not denying or ignoring the pertinence and importance of the issue at the time when it did take up such an all-important interest, as well as resulting in such cruel effort; what I wish to stress is that it seems like exquisite folly 400 years later. I wish further to raise the question of whether Shakespeare's mind was sharp enough to grasp the essential folly of a mankind that is ready to kill man, who was "made in the image of God," in order to decide in what form he might partake of the body of his Creator's son. [44]

If my question should be answered in the negative, on the grounds that Shakespeare in all probability attended Church regularly—at least after his return to Stratford, and we may therefore be certain that his criticism of the Christian Church religion must have been a limited one —I would not accept this as sound reasoning. A man's behavior in his community should never be taken as a yardstick of what he is thinking, feeling and wishing. In Shakespeare's time it was a necessity to go to church and Shakespeare was no practical reformer, no theologian but a literary genius. Certainly he was no psychopath. From his Church attendance, I would not know whether he was an atheist or a fervent Christian, either Protestant or Catholic—as little as anyone could know from my paying taxes whether I am against or in favor of the war in Vietnam.

In reading Montaigne's essay "On Cannibals"—in case he had not received earlier intelligences and taken a position on the matter—he came upon a truly disturbing conundrum. A large group of humans was reported to have been discovered who had existed for as long a period as that part of mankind that had become Christian, and who were incontrovertibly also Adam's children. God had apparently wanted to preserve them in a natural state, which—even though it was far from ideal—may possibly have been (according to Montaigne, it certainly was) superior in its ethics to the Christians' state. This special group of God's creating did not molest the Christians, as many of the heathens living on the three continents of the Old World did; they kept apart. It was the Christians

---

[44] Murry (1936, p. 394) writes: "*The Tempest* implies a tremendous criticism of vulgar religion." Although his statement is not meant in the sense of my interpretation, it does seem worthwhile quoting at this point.

who penetrated into their "Island," which had evidently been reserved by God for them.

If Adam's children clung to ancient sin in the Old World, this was tragic and regrettable, yet it was still compatible with the broader concept of man's having jeopardized his state of innocence by the Fall. Though Christ's sacrifice did not visibly change anything in terms of the human plight on earth, still it might have broadened man's potential post-mortal vicissitudes and thus His incarnation might not have been in vain.

But now Christianity was prepared to penetrate new continents inhabited by natural man, and Montaigne predicted the ruin of these continents, precisely by way of their contacts with Christian civilization and culture. The strictly Christian view would have been a rejoicing (as some actually did) that new opportunities had been opened up to the spread of the Evangel, so that many more of Adam's children could be brought to see the light. Montaigne, however, did not rejoice. Today we know that his prediction was right, terribly right. Was Shakespeare less penetrating than Montaigne? Less prescient than Montaigne? It is scarcely imaginable, for he had looked deeper into man's mind, even though Montaigne may have been the greater philosopher.

Thus Shakespeare might have discovered the terrifying truth that the two pillars of his society were illusions unable to hold up the roof of the house in which he was living—a terrible insight at a time when one has become old and knows that his years are numbered.

What is comedy in one play may become the peak of tragedy in a later one.[45] The next step, therefore, would have been to dispense with the laughter that had provided such a convenient curtain in *The Tempest* for covering up terror, and now once again to resort to tragedy. Yet, in the light of such terrible and dangerous thoughts, might not this thought have arisen: "Is it, after all, worth the trouble? In doing so, I will not change one iota of the course of history, and yet it will lead to ostracism —or, even worse, death—once it is stated explicitly." Moreover, no actor would have dared to pronounce the words of Shakespeare's next tragedy, had he written one. For groups are in general unteachable, as groups. The narcissistic pride that they feel in what they have in common forms an impenetrable barrier: they would rather suffer destruction

---

[45] Does not Launcelot Gobbo, in a comic scene, say to Old Gobbo, his own father, who does not recognize him: "It is a wise father that knows his own child." Here it is hilarious farce; in a few years it will arise once again in *King Lear*, this time as the epitome of tragedy. What the highest internal injunction is directed against, however, must sometimes be searched for in comedy.

than change what they take pride in, however miserable that may actually be.

That is why Antonio is set above Caliban by the critics. Kermode (1954, p. lxii) says: "A world without Antonio is a world without freedom"—which also expresses Auden's (1945) view. Caliban, of course, being without grace, civility and art, is more readily relinquished—and without any sense of loss. Ugly, unlikely to yield to rule or nurture, he has no sense of right and wrong: he is less guilty than civilized men are of incontinence and malice, but he is more hopeless than they, since he cannot be improved. That is the way Kermode (1954, p. xlii) and others have seen Caliban, and it must have been the way in which Shakespeare's contemporaries, too, saw him.

Yet there is Caliban's strong, almost spiritual reaction to the kind of music that frightens Stephano and Trinculo. There is his superiority over Stephano and Trinculo, in that it is he who recognizes the royal wardrobe to be trash, whereas Stephano accepts it as valid.[46] There is his final determination to "seek for grace" and his seeming insight into his previous error. This last is all the more surprising, in that there is not the slightest indication of remorse in either Antonio or Sebastian.[47]

The idea may be that a Christian sinner, even one who is unrepentant, is better than a good heathen. But it was precisely this arrogance that had brought Christendom to its fall. Gone were the days of the early Christians when the narcissistic pride in knowing the truth had led to humility and martyrdom, to sublime acts of love and charity. Now the proud possessor of "ethical superiority" felt entitled to look down upon the non-Christian and torment him. If the narcissism of superiority does not succeed in leading to humility, it takes a terrible revenge by recoiling; indeed, it not only recoils, it ricochets, in fact, and kills the shooter. When feelings of superiority lead to arrogance, the consequence is a defi-

---

[46] This detail alone should be a warning against the interpretation of Still, who does not hesitate to identify Caliban with the Tempter. His speech about music is described (1921, p. 175) as "the most sensuous speech to be found in the entire Play." It "seems out of place in the mouth of Caliban until we realise . . . that he is deliberately using the sweet seductive tones of the Tempter." Caliban's final change is explained by the adage: "When the Devil is sick, the Devil a monk would be." Still (1921) consistently overlooks that Caliban was seduced by Stephano and tyrannized by Prospero and that he is the victim. A sociological analysis of Still's misunderstanding would probably reveal that inadvertently he was expressing some of those biases that has gradually succeeded in making integral parts of Western ideology and practice odious to large parts of the rest of the world.

[47] Kermode (1954, p. lxii) calls Antonio Prospero's failure, by contrast with Sebastian. On the other hand, James (1937, p. 229) does ascribe a change to Antonio. This difference in viewpoint is not the result of poetic ambiguity, however, but of misinterpretation. There is not a single statement in the play that would uphold in any way the belief that either Antonio or Sebastian has undergone a change for the better.

cit in the ego's structurization. A goal that needs to be arrived at by effort is taken as a matter of course by the ego, which then desists from striving for its achievement.

One can observe this in the cultural lag that the South has suffered in this country. The superior feeling of the whites toward the black man was experienced as being based on some innate complex of traits given by nature and by God, by no means as anything that had to be earned and accomplished with great effort. Since the self was so abundantly provided with effortless pleasure, since it had reached its goal before even having had to start on its way toward attaining it, the consequence was a general decline.

What took place in this country on a comparatively small scale was to become Christendom's fate throughout the world. Instead of practicing Christ's humility and charity, Christians annihilated whole realms, kidnapped the innocents and led them into slavery, exploited vast populations and held them in bondage—and all this with scarcely any feeling of guilt. Gone are the skies and the lakes and the virgin woods of the Indians. Those who once lived a free life on free soil are now corralled into reservations, forced to be content with one-third of their masters' schooling and one-third of their earnings, while only the length of their lifetime is permitted to be two-thirds of their masters'. White Christians have thought that with the Gospel in one hand and technology in the other they could make themselves masters of the entire world. Perhaps they might have been able to—if they had not betrayed the man whom they made their God, and caused mischief and disaster wherever they set foot.

This is part of the myth that I discover in *The Tempest*. If one looks behind the surface, one finds a world more terrible than the world one finds in *Lear*, so terrible indeed that it can be presented only in symbols and allegories. Caliban will seek grace, but where will he find it? He will be cheated over and over again, and no one will defend him, because the Stephanos, the Antonios and the Sebastians will laugh at him, and the Posperos will lose patience with him. Not one of them will be shaken by Caliban. Antonio will wait for his first opportunity, and Sebastian will plot, while Ferdinand lies in Miranda's arms or vice versa. Ariel will enjoy his freedom, unconcerned about the evil of the human world, and Prospero will count the days that still separate him from eternal sleep.

What a turn for the playwright! Hamlet was followed by Fortinbras, and Othello at the end said: "Had I only known!" Lear came out of disaster a changed man, and Macbeth's tyranny was followed, so far as we know, by benevolent government. But after *The Tempest,* what then? There was nothing left for Shakespeare to do but retire from the Globe, go to Church, administer his savings and wait—for death.

And why should he have gone on creating, after all? Did the world deserve it? He had indeed acquired incomparable fame: wherever there is culture, there his name is spoken with reverence. But has the world learned from him? It has indeed learned from him as little as it has from the Gospels. Perhaps in the end he had come to believe this too: that man cannot change, that he can only hope and wish and lament and reproach himself—and at the same time feel proud of the capacity that he ascribes to himself of adjustment, of love and of creativity. Every philosopher worth his name tells us in the end that, despite all, man is a superior being—whether it be Aristole's *zöon politicon,* or Rousseau's creature, who is good by nature and utterly corrupted by civilization. Shakespeare's myth in *The Tempest* is that the best that man can create is still not good enough, is basically bad. Caliban's magnificent riposte evokes the story of the Tower of Babel; indeed, it takes in the whole of civilization.

> You taught me language; and my profit on't
> Is, I know how to curse. The red plague rid you
> For learning me your language!

The only avenue apparently left is for two beautiful young beings, who have been protected by their elders, and prevented from falling into sin, to fall in love with each other and to be permitted to consummate it. There is a naïve passivity that is spread over the two of them: everything is prepared for them.[48] But Ferdinand and Miranda do not exist in reality; there it is only the Romeos and Juliets who exist. Man seems in this context to have no choice but to repeat the errors of his forefathers, to struggle and sin, and to be grateful if the pains remain bearable.

Prospero's Failure.

James (1937, 1967) has set forth a few structural factors in *The Tempest* that are in contrast to the three (relative) failures (*Pericles, Cymbeline, A Winter's Tale*). Since his analysis is concerned with literary structure, it does not fall within the scope of this essay—except for one statement. He alleges that "all that happens in it [*The Tempest*] is at Prospero's ordering: it is, in this sense, more something suffered or

---

[48] Ferdinand's log carrying we shall not overestimate here.

worked through . . . Prospero is . . . a presenter, as of a masque, that is, of a piece not embodying conflict and drama, but of something wholly prescribed and finished from its beginning" (1967, p. 157).[49]

Almost any reader will agree with James on this score and I could well imagine that it was Shakespeare's intention to produce exactly the impression that James reproduces. But a reader who studies the text carefully will also be shocked to find that, in a study as careful as James's, those lacunae are overlooked in which Prospero has no say, where indeed the action proceeds counter to his plans and outside his power. The shipwreck, the sleep-producing attacks that occur so often, the love between Miranda and Ferdinand, Alonso's remorse and much more—all these roll off in the way in which Prospero, the stage director planned and executed them. But he neither planned nor foresaw Caliban's meeting with Stephano and Trinculo, Caliban's deification of Stephano, or the triad's plot against him. Just as little did he foresee Caliban's conversion or have any inkling of the deep impression that the island music had made on him.

It is precisely James' oversight in this respect that has impelled me to look to the Caliban scenes for the key to the play, for in these scenes there is nothing that is even remotely comparable to a masque; here one finds instead real drama and conflict of an almost unbearable overtness. A sadistic quality appears here that is usually reserved for moments of high tragedy. Are there any other scenes in Shakespeare of such prostration as Caliban submits to? In it lies a deprivation of any dignity, a disparagement, almost a vilification, that reaches the embarrassing (to the onlooker) in: "I, thy Caliban,/ For aye thy foot-licker."[50]

I do not believe that this is meant primarily to characterize brutish "salvage man," for it is spoken in the service of revenge. Caliban's hatred of Prospero knows no limits at that moment, and no degree of degradation is to be turned away from if only it hold some promise of the elimination of the hated object.

True drama fills those islets of action that lie outside Prospero's agency. Two worlds are here facing each other. One is the world of the élite, with its corruption and its integrity, its crime and its virtue, its

---

[49] Wilson (1936b, p. 12) quotes approvingly Mackail who also claimed: "the action is throughout, down to its smallest detail, planned and ordered" by Prospero.

[50] Cf. Nuttall (1967, p. 143): "We feel a slight shiver when Caliban deifies the drunken butler. Long ago Schlegel and Hazlitt pointed out the vulgarity of the comedians and the utter absence of it in Caliban, who is without convention." And he refers to E. M. Forster's distinction between coarseness and vulgarity, "the first revealing something and the second concealing something."

beauty and its abysmal ugliness. This world reaches its acme in Prospero —chastened and ennobled, wise and resigned, so very attractive in that he stands above the superficial and the empty, deeply immersed in enduring values and in his striving for the supreme. James is right: sweetest beauty *is* spread all over Prospero's realm. Antonio and Sebastian could try for even worse than they do, and still they would not arouse disgust or revulsion, for they are, after all, well-mannered and know how to maintain appearances. Their crimes are not vulgar, but rather "educated" crimes; and, for better or worse, history will some day take notice of them and their portraits will land in due time in some museum.

Caliban and his consorts, by contrast, represent what is nowadays called "the forgotten man." Notice is taken of him only when he causes mischief; otherwise he is taken for granted, or else looked down upon. He stands outside "the masque," not even being admitted to it as an onlooker; the mere sight of him is an eyesore for the educated and the noble. It is one of the chief elements to give body and breath to this play that the world beyond Prospero's is presented. Were it not for the three Caliban scenes, *The Tempest* would be a beautiful but empty play, an utterly un-Shakespearean one. Benjamin (1928) speaks of "the devitalization and dismemberment that are inherent in allegorization" (*allegorische Entseelung und Zerstückelung*). Tentatively, I am suggesting that the late romances prior to *The Tempest* may be unsatisfactory because Shakespeare did not succeed sufficiently in eliminating these two elements. In *The Tempest*, at any rate, there is scarcely anything of devitalization and dismemberment to be observed. The fact that Shakespeare did finally succeed in steering clear of these two pitfalls constitutes the triumph of his dramatic power.[51] Whatever may be the allegorical meaning of *The Tempest,* the prologue is a masterpiece, in that it presents a catastrophe in an overrealistic form, the effect of which carries the beholder a long way.[52] Miranda's fearful preoccupation with the shipwreck, while Prospero is going into the recitation of the family history, may serve as an example of how lifeblood has been poured into a narrative that would otherwise have become lifeless. But the lifeblood of the entire play, that which banishes the danger of devitalization altogether, is to be found in

[51] For an opposite view see Charlton (1939, p. 268f): "The finding of Shakespeare in Prospero ... has deluded criticism. ... The dramatist is losing his intuitive sense of the essential stuff of drama, of the impact of man on men and of the things which in the mass make that experience which we call life."

[52] Even though it does not behoove the analyst to quarrel with the literary critic about such subtle questions as authenticity, I must say that it is rather difficult for me to follow Rothe (1961, p. 346) when he declares that this scene does not stem from Shakespeare's pen.

Caliban and his dealing with the sailors. These scenes make Prospero far more than a presenter of masques; they make him a tragic figure, tragically deceived, who has failed in his mission. It is chiefly through Caliban that he stands revealed as the epitome of poetic irony.

I have several times alluded to Prospero's mistakes with regard to persons in his own social group: his illusion with regard to Ferdinand and Miranda, who are utterly unprepared to meet the exigencies of real existence; his consistent ignoring of the fact that Antonio and Sebastian do not show any sign at all of a change of heart; in short, his basking in the mistaken belief that he has indeed attained his goals. Further, he shows true gentleness only to Alonso, "whose honour cannot/ Be measur'd or confin'd"; he even pleads with him not to "burthen our remembrance with/ A heaviness that's gone." Without the shadow of a reproach, Prospero offers full forgiveness and aims at the eradication even of any memory of a crime that could hardly have been erased by repentance.

Why should Alonso receive such preference? From the standpoint of Christian ethics, he deserves forgiveness as all malefactors do, yet, if anything, his age and his kingly status should have made him act more wisely than the young bloods. He is the only one in the play who never receives a single harsh word from Prospero, who even shows some signs of grovelling before him when he addresses him as "Your Highness." To my ear, it is arrogance when Alonso says, "Thy dukedom I resign,"—as if he had ever had or still possessed any rights to Milan.[53] Caliban's crime, if it was a crime at all, seems to me to be little more than a fraction of Alonso's.

All the failures that one can discover in Prospero are minor failures, however, when compared with his blindness regarding Caliban. Although his master mind has pretenses of penetrating into the recesses of the mind of others, and he plays on them as on a recorder (something that Hamlet so violently assailed), he has had no inkling of what has really been going on in Caliban's mind and heart. The play makes it clear beyond doubt that Caliban is not "this thing of darkness," "filth," "a born devil, on whose nature/ Nurture can never stick; on whom my pains,/ Humanely taken all, all lost, quite lost."

It is above all the last statement that shows how deeply Prospero had longed for Caliban's rehabilitation, humanization, Westernization— or whatever one ought to call it. His callousness and cruelty toward Cali-

---

[53] I am here ignoring the legalities of Shakespeare's times.

ban is a compensatory formation—a reversal into its opposite of an initially gentle, humanitarian impulse, the reversal having been brought about by his disappointment and by his supposed insight that no magic and no humaneness can hope to bring light into this abyss of darkness and inhumanity. Part of the poetic irony arises from the fact that, where Prospero thinks that he has been successful, he has been a failure (even with Ferdinand and Miranda, one may say), and where he is convinced of failure, there he has been successful.

Music plays a leading role in many a play by Shakespeare (cf. Sternfeld, 1963), and particularly in *The Tempest*, where it is introduced in a variety of situations and with a variety of effects. Challenging as it may be to investigate their structural differences and correlations, I must limit myself to that magnificent inset that conveys Caliban's depiction of the effect on him of the Island's music. The context is most touching. The offspring of witch and Satan, who has purportedly resisted all efforts at acculturation, is overwhelmed by repeated exposure to culture's most human medium of art; this is in marked contrast to his reaction to language, which he curses and rejects. Something of immense consequence, which I would never undertake to decipher, has happened: in his last play Shakespeare overrides his own medium, to declare categorically that man can be civilized by music.

Am I going too far, or on the wrong track, when I here find a concealed assault upon religion as well? It is not the word of the Bible ("In the beginning was the Word"), not teaching, not the intended, planned, rational approach, but the unplanned, so to speak, accidental contact with music that arouses the feeling of natural man. There is even a suggestion of his superiority over the uneducated man of a civilized society, such as Stephano and Trinculo, who becomes afraid while hearing the same sounds. Caliban has apprehended one essential aspect of aesthetic experience, which "give delight and hurt not"—something that is so eminently true of music, by contrast with words, which may leave ineffaceable wounds.

To be sure, Shakespeare's realism and his incomparable feeling of and for man protected him against idealization. The affinity between sleep and music in Caliban's aesthetic experience shows how far he still has to go before achieving true sublimation. The content of the dream provoked by sounds—clouds that open to show riches which are on the verge of falling on the dreamer, yet apparently never do—these carry the rudiments of sublimated oral-voyeuristic trends. That the riches do not ever come within the dreamer's reach reveals an ability to keep excitement in suspension, to postpone wish fulfillments. Emotional arousal per se becomes a source of pleasure, even though it does not lead to the direct gratification of drives.[54]

Pleasure is now gained without the need for physical discharge. Man has reached a stage out of which will grow such nonutilitarian values as beauty. Caliban has been won for culture; music as the primordial form of cultural sentiment—what an engaging thought! The anthropologists and Nietzsche might not agree, but that does not matter. And all this took place without Prospero's assistance, perhaps even counter to a secret wish of his. Sensitive souls sometimes feel offended by the ape's resemblance with man; if Caliban were indeed to become civilized, that might constitute an injury to Prospero's considerable narcissism.

Despite Caliban's favorable points, however, it remains open to question to what extent he has actually succeeded in integrating values. When he rejects the decoy with which Prospero and Ariel try to deceive the plotters—the royal garment that is "trash"—he proves himself superior to Stephano. Shortly thereafter, however, it is once again a garment that makes him veer toward Prospero and away from allegiance to his companions. For even before Prospero has intimated any pardon, Caliban referring to the ducal mantle explains "How fine my master is!" Does this mean that he has acquired the ability to discriminate between

[54] The interpretation of Caliban's dream that I am proposing is essentially different from that of Prof. Holland (1968), who stresses the pregenital wishes and the defenses against them—the wish for a good father and for freedom from slavery. This may be so, although I must confess that the present state of analysis makes it possible to find pregenital fixations in any dream—which fact alone arouses my skepticism on this score. But one wonders what is gained when the dream is used as a vehicle to convey contents that are shown openly on the stage.

Caliban is presented as being orally and anally fixated. His longing for a suitable father-substitute is also conspicuously exposed. It is not even probable for all these manifest traits to be the determinants of a dream. Is it not more essential that this dream is Caliban's response to music? Is not the function of this dream, then, to reveal an aspect of Caliban's personality that is *not* brought out when we observe him in the midst of the harassing pressures under which he labors throughout the play? Is not this dream expressing a mode of experience that a cruel environment does not permit the slave to have, through its constantly tormenting and humiliating him?

Every dream contains a secret. What Prof. Holland unearths is not a secret; it is already known to the onlooker by manifest, by no means covert events. But what the onlooker does not know, what Caliban himself does not show in his daily pursuits, so that he may not himself possess full awareness of it, is his capacity for sublimation. It is not always the more archaic that makes its appearance in the dream. Freud (1922, p. 277) has demonstrated that the correct perception of reality, at a time when the ego is victimized by delusion, may be banished to the dream.

Shakespeare here presents the man who is tied to a low level of existence by a harsh social reality, yet elevates himself to a higher level at those moments when he can escape the persecutor, just as an aesthete who has been sentenced to hard labor may hear heavenly music in his dream, without this necessarily testifying to an anal fixation, unless one equates sounds in dreams on principle with flatus.

pinchbeck and gold, or is it rather due to nothing more than the archaic propensity to accept that which glitters?

It is unnecessary to decide this question, however. In the end Caliban is admitted to Prospero's cell, from which he had been excluded since his attempt at rape. This probably does not mean that he is being admitted into the circle of Christian European society,[55] since the whole party is in process of leaving the island. Prospero gives his pardon peremptorily and brusquely[56] and ignores his slave's final turn: "And seek for grace."[57]

As one argument against my interpretation, it may be said that Caliban is not a member of the human race, since he is the offspring of a witch and a devil. Nevertheless, Miranda says that Ferdinand is the *third man (I.2. 448)* she ever saw, Prospero and Caliban necessarily being the other two; and Prospero too seems to include him in the species of man, when he reproaches his daughter:

> Thou think'st there is no more such shape as he,
> Having seen but him and Caliban.
>
> *(I.2.481f)*

Certainly he is here referring to the contrast between the two, yet his chiding implies *sameness of species.* Critics sometimes assert that Miranda's "nor have I seen/ More that I may call men than you, good friend,/ And my dear father" contradicts her just quoted "third man" statement. I do not see this. What she is here implying is that, after closer acquaintance with her lover, she does not any longer want to "call Caliban a man —*although he is one,"* and we are to understand this by empathy.

After having listened in the Army *ad nauseam* to what white officers born in the South had to say about Negroes, I feel entitled to say that all the words and phrases that are used in *The Tempest* about Caliban are still compatible with a creature who belongs to the species man. Furthermore, if there is a single clear-cut reference to Caliban as a human being, one is forced to give him that status and to regard all the nonhuman references, with which the play is more than full, as being no more than expressions of the aggressive feelings, projections and biases of the speakers who make them.

[55] Kermode (1954, p. lxii) speaks of "the circuit of noble virtue which excludes only Caliban."

[56] I have not yet found any interpretation of Prospero's: "as you look/To have my pardon, trim it handsomely."

[57] Luce (1902, p. 144) writes that this is "Not in keeping with Caliban's main character." Perhaps not with his *main* characteristics, but nevertheless, in my opinion, with his character.

Luce (1902, pp. xxxii-xxxviii) says that "Shakespeare tried to get too much into Caliban," that Caliban is not one character but three. He is, in this view, a compound of three typical ideas: the supernatural; the condition of slavery; and the "noble savage"—thereby fulfilling a threefold purpose, "embodiment of the supernatural, the social, and the political topics of the day . . . with a very doubtful consistence."

The idea of the supernatural can certainly be excluded with regard to Caliban. He is never shown engaging in a single supernatural act. All he can do is natural acts, on the strength of his superior knowledge of the island's natural condition. He wishes upon Prospero's head the evil effects of his deceased mother's black magic, yet in this regard he cannot do more than wish. He has lost the ability to exercise his mother's supernatural powers.

A profound truth is alluded to here. Caliban has been alienated from his own tradition, and made to submit to a new one, which remains foreign and cold to him—a new civilization into which he does not fit and which does not satisfy any basic needs of his. The loss of the power of ancient magic rites in the young, the Caliban generation, when it comes into contact with the West, thus symbolizes both the powerful effect of the new culture, as it combats an archaic tradition, and also the ambivalence of the indigene toward his own tradition, as well as his secret wish to become a member of the race he covertly admires as superior.

By excluding Caliban from magic power, Shakespeare conveyed one aspect of the social drama that is not limited to contact between an allegedly "superior" culture and an allegedly "inferior" one. After all, Caliban does form part of a well-integrated group with Stephano and Trinculo. There, having been accepted, he feels comfortable and at home. But Stephano and Trinculo represent the "lower depths" of the civilization that is officially represented by Prospero, Alonso and the latter's suite. My conjecture is that Shakespeare was not concerned primarily with the problems of colonial peoples. He used a political and social question that had grown in popular interest, in order to put the more general issue of social stratification on the stage.

The contemporary spectator does not in general associate Caliban with an Indian or any other aboriginal. For him, Caliban represents something generally human, which is meaningful independently of any specific historical situation: man as created by nature and unaffected by the civilization into which he has by chance been born. He does not represent solely the untamed id, since Caliban has a great deal of ego, and is far better adjusted to the physical-biological world than is Prospero, who can survive only if servants fulfill for him those ego functions that are geared to the primary necessities of physical survival (Weber, 1919, p. 139; Hartmann, 1956 passim). This theme was already introduced in the shipwreck scene, where the élite are shown as depending on the skills of the "uneducated."

Critics like Luce (1902), when they write that "Shakespeare attempted the impossible in making three characters into one" seem to doubt that Shakespeare accomplished in Caliban what he had set out to accomplish, which would have been not Prospero's but Shakespeare's failure. Stewart (1949, passim), however, has brought to our attention the fact that what may have appeared as inconsistency or artistic failure to an earlier generation of critics has been proven by modern psychology to be the consequence of man's basically conflictual matrix.

For me, Caliban is consistent in his inconsistency—that is to say, I do not see in the musical inset and the final plea for grace something either contrived or artificial. Both come as a surprise, it is true, and allow for ambiguity of interpretation. But these two characteristics are ineradicably inherent in life per se and conspicuously inherent to human life.[58] Nevertheless, one faces a danger here. Where earlier critics threw up their hands and exclaimed: "Inconsistency? That is irreconcilable with human nature!" the critic who is trained in depth psychology will rejoice at the discovery of inconsistency and exclaim: "What a wonderful presentation of human life!" The danger, of course, is that the more "inconsistent," "bizarre," "unexpected" the presentation of a character, the higher will be the value assigned to that presentation.

Some modern writers, it seems, speculate with success precisely on that formula; by so doing, they appear to have purchased stock that offers multiple capital gains. But how is one to distinguish between human and contrived inconsistency? Not all kinds of inconsistencies are admissible as marks of literary greatness.

Perhaps some of the characteristics that are true of Shakespeare's "inconsistent" creations can be used as a yardstick of literary greatness.

[58] In delimiting the area that is left ambiguous in Caliban, one perceives Shakespeare's greatness: what he does not tell us is the depth of Caliban's musical experience. Caliban possesses the capacity for experiencing a layer of existence beyond that which nature offers. He is moved by an artistic value; but will this experience take hold of him to such degree as to give his existence direction? He has the endowment to decide upon grace but how long will he seek it? Will not a person with a cloak more glittering than Prospero's divert him into some new direction that is incompatible with grace? The question is whether or not he has acquired some degree of autonomy or is stimulus-bound, and it is precisely this uncertainty that renders Caliban a viable figure.

To begin with, there is no noticeable slackening of interest on rereading —something that can be said of only a few authors. One does not ever reach the point at which one has the feeling of having arrived at complete understanding. Each renewed reading holds a new surprise, a new discovery, a new explanation, a new pathway worth traveling, because it holds the promise of a new dimension. It is impossible to make a definitive statement about Shakespeare's characters; they carry in themselves an infinity of depth, even more so than real persons do. They exist in an atmosphere that defies conclusive verbalization; in that respect they are like music, which also defies conclusive transposition into adequate descriptive terms.

Cressida is, for certain, one of the most enigmatic female characters ever created, and more ink has been spilled over her than blood over Helen. For whatever it may be worth, one may reach the tentative conclusion that she was, after all, truly in love with Troilus, and therefore right in acting as she did toward him. For there are indications that if Troilus had at last obtained his gratification, he would have abandoned her—and not because of any fault of hers that he might have detected, once the unavoidable sexual overvaluation of the passionately longed-for object (Freud, 1905, pp. 151-154) has worn off. In Romeo's case, this was out of the question. The memory of his honeymoon would have been so extraordinary that, even when juvenile love had "settled down," he would have remained faithful, if for no other reason than because of his gratitude for the extraordinary gift he had been privileged to experience. Troilus is, it is clear, no Romeo.

There are women about whose meeting with a beloved spouse one is inclined to feel regret. After spending years of real happiness with them, they are later exposed to unquenchable grief when they are abandoned by the beloved person. Analysts are prone to discover in such women symbiotic mechanisms, infantile dependencies and an assortment of pregenital fixations. All that may be true; yet their grief in the wake of deprivations—so at least one is forced to conclude—outweighs their preceding bliss and, in the final analysis, it might have been better for them, had they never met the spouse who gave them what has sometimes been decades of bliss. Cressida, I believe, was an eminently wise woman, although wisdom usually crumbles when passion takes hold. Why Cressida was able to maintain hers when she fell in love with Troilus, is a separate question; but I would not necessarily see in her ability to maintain her wisdom any proof that she had not truly been in love.

She may very well have been quite sensitive, sufficiently to know that Troilus would give her such pleasure as she would never be able to experience with any other man, yet also such pain as she would experience with no other. And she may very well have drawn the conclusion that it is better to enjoy only moderate pleasures, if one is thereby spared the worst of grief.[59] It is not a question, however, of whether or not I am right, in this context. I only wish to say that the understanding of the great characters created by Shakespeare is never really final. What seems at first like inconsistency, and may even appear to be utterly incredible, sometimes changes during the course of repeated readings. It may then take on the character of exceptional humanness, of serving to reveal something not necessarily as it is, but rather as it might have been, or will be, or ought to be. It has become something that finds a surpassing place in the order of disorder of humanity.

This may or may not be a reliable yardstick of literary greatness; yet it is surely true of Caliban. From an ostensibly subordinate character he turns out to be a giant figure, in whom all the woe and hope and tragedy of man is contained. He finally dwarfs even Prospero. Indeed, in immersing oneself in Caliban, one runs the risk of shrinking Prospero to a bore. Shakespeare's panorama of the human world is wide and rich; and it is not easy to maintain complete immersion in two of his protagonists at one and the same time, just as one cannot, after all, survey the entire panorama from a watchtower, without turning around, thereby losing the sight one had just enjoyed.

Prospero is now in disfavor with many critics, yet I think he has been done an injustice. He is a man of good will and his shortcomings are tragic. Who could have the certainty of being able to manage his affairs more efficiently than he? I would guess that his evaluation also depends on the vicissitudes of history. At present, when it has become so clearly evident that Christianity does not contain the answers to pressing problems of society's cultural and even its sheer physical survival, when one is living in a time of the disintegration of the Christian orbit of influence, then the critic is inclined toward harshness and oversensitivity with regard to Prospero's way of acting.

For Prospero's failure is rooted in his belief in absolute values, whereas Shakespeare, as I shall presently try to explain, demonstrates

---

[59] Perhaps I may be reproached with showing a bias in favor of woman, for earlier I tried to protect Cleopatra against calumny by calling her betrayal at Actium an act of love, and now I seem to be doing the same thing with Cressida's even more blatant betrayal.

the relativism of all values. One way he does it, I think, is in the way he uses the word "brave," which appears a full 14 times in the play. [60] Words too have their fashions. At present I hear, several times a day, "cop out," and "up tight"; "square" and "cool" seem, by contrast, to be in recession. I imagine that the word "brave" was popular around 1610. Prospero uses it twice *(III.3.83; I:2.106)* about Ariel, in reference to qualities that Ariel no doubt actually possesses. But abstract forms may also be "brave," as Miranda's reaction to Ferdinand shows *(I.2.414)*, and even what is ugly may be brave, as Prospero's praise of Ariel's performance as Harpy demonstrates *(V.1.241)*. Objects too may live up to that qualification: the Boatswain speaks of the "bravely rigg'd" ship *(V.1.224)*. The lecherous man will describe as "brave" that through which he hopes to gratify his appetites—for example, Stephano's "Is it so brave a lass?" *(III.2.101)*, about Miranda. This in turn evokes Caliban's response, in which he uses "brave" for that which does not yet exist, whose existence is anticipated or promised, namely, the "brave brood" that Miranda will "bring thee forth" *(III.2.103)*.

But then "brave" is also used for that which does not (and will not ever) exist at all, as in Ferdinand's "The Duke of Milan/ and his brave son being twain" *(I.2.441)*, [61] which elicits from Prospero his aside about the Duke's "more braver daughter." With Stephano's joyful anticipation of "a brave Kingdom" *(III.2.142)* that will be his and "where I shall have my music for nothing," begins a series of statements that set forth

---

[60] Prospero uses it four times; Caliban and Stephano three times each; Miranda twice; Ferdinand and the Boatswain, once each.

[61] This passage has understandably puzzled the critics, since it is the only reference in the play to a son of Antonio. It is unnecessary to review the various responses of the critics. Ferdinand has just referred to his permanent separation from the King, whom he believes to be dead, and he is now claiming the separation for the Duke of Milan and his fictitious son. In psychoanalytic thinking this would be called a slip of the tongue that could be interpreted in different ways.

Since, according to Ferdinand, not only the King but also his Lords (including Antonio) have perished, and Antonio, if Ferdinand's reference to a son was an error, would have died *sine stirpe*, it is Ferdinand who has become not only King of Naples but also Duke of Milan. Thus Ferdinand's error may express his secret satisfaction with the large realm he has now inherited. On the other hand, the error may be interpreted as a temporary disturbance of the sense of identity, as the result of traumatization.

Here is a good example of how the application of depth psychology can lead the critic astray, for one cannot rule out the possibility that the passage is "a howler," as one critic called it, or was the result of factors that are outside the realm of psychological interpretation. If it could be proven that it was not intended by Shakespeare, but was the inadvertent result of a slip on his part, one could still consider one of the interpretations suggested above. It would then constitute the interesting situation of a genius enunciating, by way of his own *lapsus calami*, a psychological truth of considerable depth. Of course, the whole matter may be one of textual corruption.

the perversion and corruption of values. Caliban has just ended his inset on the spiritual effect of music when Stephano describes as "brave" the quite antithetical value attached to the fact that this music can be heard free of charge. When Caliban calls the new god that he has found in Stephano "brave," *(II.2.118)* and Stephano later, in a kind of retort, exclaims: "A brave monster" *(II.2.118)*, then the corruption of values has indeed reached its peak.

The decisive appearance of "brave" occurs when Miranda and Caliban both use the term upon being confronted with the members of the court of Naples *(V.1.183,261)*, not one of whom deserves such an epithet. Here a strong point is being made in favor of a skeptical, even pessimistic view of values. In *Hamlet*, the conflict provoked by the discrepancies between appearance and reality is forcefully thrust forward, until it is finally dissolved in Hamlet's acceptance, as it is, of the structure of reality (in which this discrepancy is *inherent*). In *The Tempest*, there are innumerable allusions to this problem. Yet it is never explicitly stated. It is, in effect accepted without conflict, at times even converted into a virtue, or drowned in laughter, as when Stephano accepts trash for a Kingdom.

Miranda, for example, despite previous warnings by her father, once again falls for pure appearance, and squanders the term "brave" on a couple of crooks. Even Caliban, when he is finally drawn into the new civilization (which he has so "bravely" resisted until then), is tricked by appearances. By now, in short, all tragedy is gone, and instead the spirit of the masque is preserved and the audience dismissed under the illusion of a happy ending. It is as if the playwright were saying that the world is unteachable; if mankind insists, after all, on confusing surface with depth, let it enjoy its error while it may.

Consideration of the varied circumstances under which the term "brave" is employed in the play demonstrates that the intelligence that had reached England about the New World was of secondary importance to Shakespeare. Caliban is the lowest level of that stratum to which Stephano and Trinculo also belong. The latter make themselves the degraded tools of their masters and are somehow integrated into his society, whereas Caliban is an outcast, precariously shifting at the fringe of that society, and ostensibly moved solely by the force to which he is subjected. He is also ready to break any tie with the tyranny that has been imposed upon him. This is true, of course, only prior to his "conversion."

Since the ego must put up with forces that remain outside its power to tame, the influence of civilization, societal integration, does have its limits. Standing apart from this tendency of society to absorb all its members in its churning machinery are the eternal outsiders: perhaps the poet—chronically drunk, dishevelled and dirty—who will die in the gutter and whose poems will be read 200 years later in high school classes; perhaps a Caliban who persists in clinging to his archaic ways, which are so much more satisfying, since they provide discharge at a level so much closer to primary processes and ancient drives.

Here Shakespeare would seem to be putting in a strong plea in favor of those who drift along outside societal integration. Behind the glitter of the Court masque he is perhaps demonstrating the shakiness and the basic falsity of society's fabric. Open rebellion, protest, lamentation are over and done with; even a warning has proven to be futile. And so the Western world will dance to its destruction—ecstatically and with giddiness—just as did those superb aristocrats of the eighteenth century, with full awareness of what awaited them, indeed in full sight of the guillotine that was to decapitate them.

The Biographical Issue in "The Tempest."

There remains a biographical note. Luce was still devoting one section, in his Introduction to the Old Arden edition of *The Tempest*, to the play's autobiographical content. Kermode, by contrast, has omitted any biographical reference in his New Arden edition. He wrote (p. lxxxii): "Morton Luce . . . gave what may be the best account of autobiographical interpretation. I find his approach incompatible with my own." Here is a further example of the perniciousness of monolithic literary criticism. Kermode may be right in stressing "the conscious philosophic structure of his [Shakespeare's] plays, and particularly of his comedies," and in saying that *The Tempest* "is deeply concerned with difficult ideas and with the philosophic genres of masque and pastoral." Yet much as such problems may have contributed to the final form of Shakespeare's last play, when we view great art as a predominantly philosophical and intellectual structure, we remove it completely from life.

It is true that literary works have sometimes been produced primarily for intellectual, educational, didactic purposes; yet such works have in due time lost their hold on mankind. Every one of Shakespeare's great plays that has over and over again haunted mankind's imagination must have grown out of serious personal involvement. In most instances, the content of that involvement will likely forever remain a secret; in *The*

Tempest, even with the exercise of the greatest discretion and caution, the critic is entitled to recognize an autobiographical context in at least two matters: Prospero's resignation from the practice of magic and his demand for premarital abstention imposed on the lovers.

It is altogether impossible to assume that a playwright can present his central character in the situation of relinquishing a cherished and creative function, of retiring, without his expressing something personal —if at the very same time he is planning to go into retirement himself. If one is to deny such a connection as Kermode does, then literary criticism is indeed grown parched and utterly divorced from reality.

Shakespeare could not have brought out the question in a more conspicuous way. After a period of preparation in Milan, Prospero spent 12 years on the Island—his creative period—and now he is on the verge of returning to Milan, where he intends to live a contemplative existence, without pursuing his previous creativity. Shakespeare spent his first period in Stratford; from there he went to London, which is forever associated with his creative period, after which he retired to the place from which he had come and where his Muse was to become and remain silent.

White Magic is, of course, a very suitable symbol for the playwright's attempt to create new worlds.[62] While he does create new worlds, yet he does not change the physical structure of existing reality, any more than Prospero was able to do, even with the help of Ariel. At the level of psychic reality, however, the playwright experiences the effects of his creative effort in the very same way as Prospero boastfully puts it:

> I have bedimm'd
> The noontide sun, call'd forth the mutinous winds,
> And 'twixt the green sea and the azur'd vault
> Set roaring war . . . . graves at my command
> Have wak'd their sleepers, op'd, and let'em forth
> By my so potent Art.[63]

(V.1.40-50)

---

[62] Schücking (1919, p. 256f) rejects even the mere possibility of a biographical nexus because, as he asserts, there is contemporary parallel of this sort. This is a gross abuse of the historical method and a regrettable denial of a genius' ability to be more inventive than his contemporaries. Cf., however, Wilson (1936b, p. 4) for a precedent of this type.

[63] Campbell (1966, p. 858) uses precisely these verses to prove that autobiographical claims are absurd. He writes: "A playwright making so extravagant a boast of his own powers would have seemed to any audience . . . to have taken complete leave of his senses." But the autobiographical background of a play is none of the audience's business; awareness of it in the work of a contemporary playwright may even curtail the full aesthetic pleasure the play might otherwise evoke. Campbell's objection is, furthermore, somewhat insensitive, insofar as Shakespeare called forth more

Ariel symbolizes what some poets call their Muse. He stands for poetry, imagination and the gift for handling the artistic medium in a creative way. This is depersonalized in the play; it is not part and parcel of Prospero but rather something that he found and put into his own service. It has served him well, but now he will dismiss it. Many a great author has described his genius in like fashion. He feels grateful to his Muse, and asserts that by himself he accomplished little, that "it" forced him to create and "spoke out of" him.

Prospero, as a reflection of Shakespeare before his retirement to private life, shows a particularly high degree of self-awareness and self-criticism. Prospero's anger is Shakespeare's anger; it is a confession that even though he had combatted it bravely and replaced it with social attitudes, he had not been able really to convert it into love of his fellow-man. Anger (or better, rage) plays a leading role in the life of many a genius. Taming it is, of course, the task of practically every human being, yet the headstrong genius here encounters a special task.

The Sterbas (1956) have dealt with this problem, as it manifested itself in Michelangelo's life.[64] But Prospero is here presented as having failed through his having ignored the downtrodden and misjudged the humanly poorest, through having been un-Christian enough to forgive his (sometimes ignoble) peers with an almost ready heart, yet only perfunctorily to have extended his forgiveness to the dregs of mankind. (Shakespeare himself was a courtier and I assume that a certain degree of servility, of bowing to the powerful, was coupled with such a position.)

Prospero treats Alonso in a way that is conspicuously different from the way in which he treats any other person in the play. I must repeat that such treatment would have been far more appropriately addressed to Caliban. The image in the Gospels leaves no doubt that Christ would have turned His mercy above all toward Caliban; yet this evidently lies beyond Prospero's capacities.

What is so extraordinary is that Shakespeare—despite the fact that he made Prospero's surface glittering enough to deceive most critics—nevertheless also pictured his faults with sufficient distinction to be recog-

---

impressive things than mutinous winds in the terrible storm of *King Lear* or in the shipwrecking scene in *The Tempest*. He did open graves and wake their sleepers—something Prospero was unable to do, since the play makes it clear that Sycorax was the only being that had died on the Island. It is precisely Prospero's boastful verses that may well reveal a temporary fusion between the playwright and the projection of a self-image.

[64] Moses and his temper tantrums are of course always cited in connection with the task that the mastery of rage involves in the genius' life.

nized. He seems to be saying, by way of Prospero, "I, too, have not lived up to the demand of the Gospels; I too have not separated myself from the vices of my time and my society." An even harsher feeling of guilt on Shakespeare's part may be observed in connection with Prospero's magic —which is, after all, incompatible with Christ's teachings (as the writing of tragedy has also been asserted to be). Shakespeare was still close enough to that aspect of medieval thought that had warned against too great a preoccupation with secular matters and knowledge, and recommended instead immersion in prayer and concentration on God. In choosing magic here as the equivalent of artistic creation, Shakespeare may have been intimating the sense of guilt that he felt about his own past.[65]

I am well aware that this is in contradiction with the position taken by most critics (cf. Kermode, 1954, pp. xlvii-li), who cite that aspect of the Renaissance that favored magic and, in so doing, refer to its foremost representative during that period, Agrippa (1486-1535). However, Agrippa was a controversial philosopher and important voices in the Catholic Church regarded him as a heretic. My suggestion is based on the dramatic undertones of Prospero's speech of abjuration. This does not sound to me at all like the speech of a man who, having accomplished all his goals by way of magic, now has no further use for it. Such a viewpoint is insensitive to the psychology of magic, which is instead characterized by its boundless scope and depth (just as the primary process is, by contrast with the secondary process). Shakespeare intimates this at the very end of the play, when Prospero once again promptly invokes magic for the impending voyage.

Prospero was a tired man, as Shakespeare must have felt himself to be, when he prepared to return to Stratford "where/ Every third thought shall be my grave."[66]

[65]I am here bypassing the true depth of the feeling of guilt that lies dormant in the creative act per se. Of the many (cf. Muschg, 1948) who have grappled with the puzzling problem of creativity and guilt, I want to quote Thomas Mann (1946, p. 12) who asserts that "every creative originality, every artistic act" [*jede schöpferische Originalität, jedes Künstlertum*] is akin to "the form of existence of crime" [*der Existenzform des Verbrechens*] and he cites Degas' radical statement, quite unusual for someone in the visual arts, that an artist must approach his work in the same spirit as that with which the criminal commits his deed.

[66]Strachey (1906, p. 64) writes of Shakespeare's boredom at that time: "Bored with people, bored with real life, bored with drama, bored, in fact, with everything except poetry and poetical dreams . . ." In my opinion, Strachey was utterly mistaken. Shakespeare must have been not bored but completely exhausted. Although his total creative output was much less than that of other literary geniuses, it must have required of him an enormous expenditure of energy. When one thinks only of the creation of a single tragedy such as *Hamlet*, viewing it under the aspect of psychic economy, one has the impression that it must have taken more con-

But before Prospero could return to Milan, he had to forgive his brother, who had forced him out of Milan, and this raises the troublesome question of why Shakespeare had left Stratford, in the first place. Much speculation has been devoted to the question of Shakespeare's leaving his place of birth. There is only one factor, I believe, that can be conjectured with any degree of certainty. It was not a peaceful, harmonious departure or one that Shakespeare made under propitious conditions. It was not a step that was taken in conformity with expectation, like a student's departure for college or university. There is something irregular, puzzling, dramatic about this departure.

The little that is known does not evoke the image of a happy young man. Here it is necessary to deal with the other biographical allusion in *The Tempest,* the thrice-raised objection to premarital intercourse. Prospero does not mince his words and the evils that he predicts will be forthcoming when the "virgin-knot" is prematurely broken sound quite terrible: "barren hate," "sour-ey'd disdain," "discord," "weeds so loathly."

Although this should be sufficient to frighten even a couple that possessed less elevated standards, Prospero resumes the same theme 28 lines later, despite Ferdinand's most solemn pledges. This time he is not threatening but pleading with the young man, of whose steadfastness of character no one could really have any doubts. "The strongest oaths are straw/ To th' fire in' th' blood," says Prospero, and then adds something that seems quite dubious to me: "Be more abstemious, or else, good night your vow!" The subject is taken up again in the Masque. There it is foretold that the lovers will succeed in being temperate: Cupid "Swears he will shoot no more."

It may be too much to say that the topic is pursued compulsively by

---

centration and intensity than an ordinary person expends in a lifetime. One usually reads of the ease with which Shakespeare turned out his plays and, indeed, he must have poured out lines with incomparable rapidity, in view of the quick sequence of plays during the peak phase. I have read somewhere of the incredibly long time that it would take a copyist merely to copy the entire output of Mozart. The question of physical time is unresolvable when it is raised in connection with the lives of those giants who go through life unhurriedly, by contrast with the modern nervousness and its concomitant unceasing complaint of "shortage of time." But this apparent ease should not mislead. While Strachey thinks that Shakespeare was bored with everything but "poetry and poetical dreams," I would say that there were two areas in which Shakespeare was able to create without effort. Poems, I imagine, came to his mind like tunes. But a tune stands in the same relation to the *St. Matthew Passion*—or poetry to *Hamlet*, or a sketch to the Sistine Chapel—as a rifle shot does to a rocket. What is generally called ease of production, but is in reality rapidity or speed of output, probably makes a far greater demand on the psychic apparatus than does the laborious work of the compulsive person who, while creating, goes through long and tortuous periods of inner conflict.

Prospero, but I doubt that any aesthetic or structural reasons can be given for the introduction of the theme at all and even less for the frequency of its elaboration. It is scarcely possible not to be reminded of Shakespeare's own indiscretion in his younger years: as is known, his wife, who was eight years his senior, gave birth to their child 100 days before a full-term baby would have been born that had been conceived during their wedding night.[67]

The picture that is conjured up is that of a young man who for external reasons was forced to marry an older woman and, since the marriage had proven to be an unhappy one, left his native town after his wife became pregnant for the second time and gave birth to twins. This has been regarded by many biographers as a gratuitous construction. *The Tempest* and Prospero's relationship to Milan speak strongly in favor of this or a similar theory and make it more than probable that Shakespeare did feel compelled to leave Stratford for an Enchanted Island.

Since it is not conceivable that the great tragedies could ever have been written in Stratford, we should feel most grateful that Shakespeare felt greatly conflicted in his home environment. It is difficult to imagine a happily married Shakespeare, in well-ordered circumstances, leaving his

[67] Serious scholars, however, such as Peter Alexander (1961, p. 23f), say that to draw any conclusion from that fact would be "another instance of the danger of conjectural history." Marriage at that time, he maintains, "required neither church nor priest nor document of any kind, only the declaration of the contracting parties in the presence of witnesses." Chambers (1930, vol. 2, p. 51f), it must be noted, adduces some of the reasons for gainsaying this opinion. Alexander, to prove his point, refers to a contemporary instance, which Hotson (1938, pp. 132-140, 203-206) dug out from historical records and which concerned Shakespeare's good friend, Thomas Russel.

It is true that Russel and Anne Digges, the widow of the famous mathematician and astronomer Thomas Digges, "were mated, contracted, and assured" after "in the presence of witnesses, the couple [had] exchanged vows, and gimmal betrothal rings" (p. 138). Their marriage, thereafter, became extremely difficult, as the result of circumstances which it is unnecessary to set forth here. They lived in Alderminster, where evidently they were believed to be married. "Sensitive perhaps about standing up before the parishioners of Alderminster, they shipped off to their manor of Rushock, some twenty-five miles distant" to be married there when marriage became possible, without financial loss (in terms of Digges's will), three years later.

Sisson (1936) also describes two instances of such a declaration, but there too it is clear that the ceremony of contracting betrothal did not provide the right of "mating," but was an equivalent of marriage only in so far as both contracting parties thereby lost the right to choose another spouse. It seems beyond doubt that Anne Hathaway's child would have been regarded as illegitimate, if no marriage ceremony had been performed. But if a contracting betrothal (of which there is no evidence extant) had taken place, she would have been entitled to sue William, had he delayed marriage.

There is another riddle connected with Shakespeare's marriage: The license and the bond necessary for the ceremony carry two different names. Brown (1949, p. 49) suggests that Shakespeare had fallen in love with another girl, and gave in to the pressure of his later wife's family. Brown's theory does not sound unreasonable; it would make Prospero's harsh words even more understandable. It is of interest to observe that the idea of a premarital relationship on the part of the 18-year-old Shakespeare not only evokes embarrassment on the part of some critics but is automatically regarded by them as a detraction.

birthplace for an almost lifelong residence in London without at some point having his family follow him. Great works, however, are born in spiritual isolation. Living without one's family, in a metropolitan area that permitted one to choose at any point between companionship selected from among a large number and isolation, unencumbered by any imposed and unavoidable tie—that would seem to be a particularly auspicious mode of existence for the production of great works.[68]

Be that as it may, no one in *The Tempest* seems to have ever had a wife, and there are two—at least for the contemporary reader—peculiar remarks about bastardy that pass between Prospero and Miranda. When the latter, upon hearing that she is a Princess of Milan, asks in surprise whether it is not Prospero who is her father, Prospero, as if he has not understood the grounds on which the question is being raised, answers: "Thy mother was a piece of virtue." Sixty-three lines later, Miranda repays in kind Prospero's cynical remark by answering his question as to whether a brother could act as Antonio did, by saying that she can "think but nobly of my grandmother."

The salient point is that Prospero demands of the young lovers something that Shakespeare himself had been unable to accomplish. We may take notice here of an effort to undo; in this instance it is to be accomplished by the projection of avoidance onto the next generation. Prospero's technique is traditional and hardly eradicable: it is that which has been deeply ingrained in the intercourse of generations. Put in extreme terms, it amounts to each generation's trying to spare the succeeding one

[68] In view of the dire consequences that Prospero ascribes to premarital intercourse, one may assume that Shakespeare thought with regret and anguish of this transgression, and later wished it had never happened. However, as I have intimated, without this interlude, which Shakespeare himself and his family must have regarded as a most unhappy one, it may be that his later greatness would not have emerged. Thus we come again upon a paradox: what causes chagrin to a genius and is sometimes regretted by him for the rest of his life can to a certain extent form the necessary basis for his unusual achievement.

This paradox can be demonstrated succinctly in the case of Kafka. In his *Brief an den Vater* [*Letter to the Father*] (1919), he gave a full description of the sufferings and anguish that filled his relationship with his father. But only a genius who has maintained a relationship as deplorable and tragic as this one will be able to write *Metamorphosis*, a story that may one day be acknowledged as one of the very few truly great writings of our century. Objectively, Kafka ought to have been grateful to his father and rejoiced, since this kind of relationship was precisely the one his genius seems to have needed for his creativity. It is conceivable that with a mild, understanding, empathizing father, Kafka might never have written a single line of exceptional interest. But—and this is the second paradox—if Kafka had looked upon the relationship in such terms as these, he might never have been able to write the famous *Letter*, not to speak of *Metamorphosis*. A genius like Kafka is forced to experience the world as the neurotic does (or possibly the schizophrenic); but precisely what constitutes the undoing of the latter infuses greatness into the former. What they have in common is pathos.

those tribulations that it itself had to suffer, yet by so doing aggravating the young ones' fight for a place in the sun. The theme of demanding more from others than from oneself is not limited in *The Tempest* to the "metabolism of generations," to use Erikson's term once again.

The same theme forms a focus in Prospero's relationship to Caliban, inasmuch as he expects of his ward fulfillment of permanent abstention—a task much greater than the one he imposes on Ferdinand. But he also expects Caliban to bear the loss of his heritage although he himself, by contrast, is prepossessed by the desire to regain his own loss. And all this despite Caliban's far greater loss, brought about by his having been reduced to slavery. The question arises whether this perhaps unintentional stress on the imbalance between Prospero's readiness to sacrifice and the extent of frustration that he expected of others, should also be understood—aside from the autobiographical content—in terms of myth. If it should, then Shakespeare would be here referring to another canker of civilization—perhaps of all civilization, but certainly particularly of Christian civilization.

When the Romans occupied a territory, they demanded the fulfillment of only one condition: acceptance of their deified Emperor, whom they themselves held in reverence. Christian imperialism, however, expected from those it conquered a degree of morality that its own adherents were never ready to abide by. The present relationship of the West to China is a timely example. The West now reproaches the Far East for violence and lack of reasonableness; but when has China ever been treated by the Christians from the West without violence and with reason?

The same arrogance that is so conspicuous in the relation of the Christian conqueror to the non-Christian conquered, also manifests itself within the community in terms of race relations. Our nation raises a vituperative voice about the unreasonableness and the violence of Negroes; yet when has this race ever been treated by white Christians with reason and love? The mere possession of high ethical standards is apparently regarded as being sufficient to make their bearer proud, and to provide him with feelings of superiority, no matter how far short his own actions may fall of the inflated ideal. In the wings, however, stands Caliban, the nemesis of a deceitful civilization.

* * *

It would be tempting to end this essay on such a note. Yet to do so would be unfair to the play as such, for to conclude this way might leave the reader with the notion that Shakespeare was, in my opinion, driven above all by an impulse to accuse. That he was deeply distressed by man's plight, that he did look with sadness and grief into the future and the past, is more than likely. But who would doubt that he also had the sense of the beautiful and the exhilarating?

The fact that the latter became weakened as time went on would have been in keeping with the drift of historical events in his time, as well as with the process of aging. *The Tempest* does contain many lines that refer to the pleasing and the pleasure-giving—but they are embedded in tragedy. In no other play, I believe, is Shakespeare's humor quite as dissonant and harsh as it is here.

Nothing seems easier than to show up the defects of society. The fact that this is not done more often, and more consistently and radically, is probably the result of deep anxiety and of the taboos by which the child is frightened early. Yet every age does have its social critics. For these two reasons—the prominence of social corruption in his world view and the prefixed view of the future—the social critic tends to lose flexibility and his view of the world about him becomes hemmed in.

Nothing of this sort is met with in *The Tempest* or in the preceding plays, although some of Shakespeare's characters do express a great deal of social and "existential" criticism. From Shakespeare's plays and, in particular, from *The Tempest*, one gains the impression that he was able to step outside himself and his society, and to look critically at what he saw—probably not without grief, but surely without anxiety or trepidation.

The schizophrenic feels alone, ejected from society. It is a process to which he is unwillingly subjected and against which he usually fights desperately. In this state of being "expelled from" the world, he makes remarkable observations, which—although they are, as a rule, delusional—frequently contain reflections, however distorted, of essential aspects of existence that have escaped the awareness of the person who is living *in* the world.

A mind like Shakespeare's seems to me to have had the rare strength of being able to step outside himself and his society without feeling ejected from it. In order to experience the world in the extremely original and individual way that one encounters in his plays, one has to be able, I would imagine, to bear an unusual degree of aloneness. ("Aloneness" too has degrees and is not an absolute.)[69] One would suspect that in order to create and people the vastness that Shakespeare filled, an inordinate degree of loneliness is required, as well as an unusual degree of freedom, enabling one to bear that great loneliness.

This is the freedom of being unattached, throughout one's spells of highest creativity, to an object or belief or illusion—as the Lord must have been before He created His universe.[70] Yet at the same time, it is an aloneness quite different from that of the schizophrenic, who feels himself to have been expelled from the Enchanted Island and is trying in vain to find a path back to it. When the literary genius feels that he is floating in a vacuum, he has the strength to bear it, because it already carries within itself the potentiality of a world, still to be created, that will fill that same vacuum. The first step however, is to perceive—or better, to create—such a vacuum.[71]

The Tempest may well have symbolized this initial step, for Shakespeare first had to create in it a previously nonexistent Enchanted Island. While we know approximately those sources on which he drew for most of his plays, in this instance historical research has found nothing of relevance. A careful reading of the play will reveal that it was he himself who populated this Island with a complete society. It seems to me that in no other play did he succeed in shaping lines, almost all of which can be interpreted in two ways—namely, as referring to both a societal context and a psychological subjective one. I also wonder whether in any other play he has given so complete a cross-section of society.

As I have tried to demonstrate, in this play he also adumbrates the

---

[69] A person marooned on an island is physically alone, but he is not necessarily psychologically so. When he feels deserted, that alone would indicate his continuing attachment, for that by which he has been deserted is represented implicitly in his feeling.

[70] I am here referring to the type of ego-function for which Keats coined the excellent term *"negative capability"* (letter of December 21, 1817, to George and Thomas Keats). I have earlier (1963) suggested that, in order to create a new world, the artist has to tear himself away from representations of the world as it is. Weissmann (1968) has recently investigated those ego-functions involved in the creative process that could be characterized as "negative capabilities."

[71] I find this and much more reflected in Keats' verses:

> . . . the unimaginable lodge
> For solitary thinkings, such as dodge
> Conception to the very bourne of heaven,
> Then leave the naked brain. . . .

Here the poet-genius's vacuum and his aloneness have been eternalized.

past and the future of that society into which fate had flung him by accident. It is certain that the autobiographical context cannot be set forth in any other play as distinctly as it can be in this. It is therefore to be called a perfectly balanced play. In centering my comments upon the societal accusation that it seems to harbor, I have done so because literary criticism appears to have treated that aspect with dire neglect.

Thus, even into the process of allegorizing Shakespeare was able to carry his sublime objective realism, and so to add the projection of self with all the self's faults and defects. He was free, indeed, of illusions—at least, within the context of his plays; what his own personal illusions were, we do not know. I do not believe it is important to know these, however, for in the moment of creation, suspended in the vacuum that he was driven to create and then to fill, he was able to thrust them aside and shape his own world—not in the way he wished it to be or not to be, or in the way he feared it to be, or in the way he thought it ought to be, according to some higher principle. The ability to achieve all that presupposes a strong sense of self, of identity, or whatever we want to call it.

A crisis of identity, the struggle to achieve a sense of identity—these may play their part in a good many geniuses; but not in Shakespeare. I myself believe that "identity crises" are greatly overstressed in contemporary literature. It all goes back to Keats and his famous letter to Richard Woodhouse, in which he described "the poetical Character . . . of which, if I am anything, I am a Member" as "it is not itself—it has no self—it is everything and nothing"—a description that impressed Murry (1936) so deeply that he gave to the first chapter of his book on Shakespeare the title "Everything and Nothing," because "it is the best description of Shakespeare's character that has ever been given" (p. 28).

So far so good. In order to create the vacuum and to shed all illusions and preferences, one must be "everything and nothing." But Keats continues: "A Poet is the most unpoetical of anything in existence, because he has no Identity—he is continually in for . . . filling some other Body—the Sun, the Moon, the Sea and Men and Women who are creatures of impulse are poetical and have about them an unchangeable attribute—the poet has none; no identity—he is certainly the most unpoetical of all God's Creatures."

Keats' idea about the poet's lack of identity might well be valid with regard to his own personality and genius, which may be the reason why his genius has not had the power to quicken the pulse of mankind but only that of a selected few. Yet I believe very strongly that he was not correct in extending that same idea to Shakespeare.

To my way of thinking, it is wrong to characterize Shakespeare's creative potency as consisting of an ability "to fill bodies"; he *created* them, and the ability to create bodies presupposes an enormously solid feeling of identity. Only someone whose personality fabric is solid, whose sense of identity is assured, can let himself go, can pour his lifeblood into the bodies of his own creation. We observe in schizophrenics a similar mechanism of letting oneself flow into others, but there it arouses anxiety: the schizophrenic, as the result of his relatively weak sense of identity, does not know whether he will find his way back again, and he also doubts what may happen to him, once his soul has taken to abiding in another subject (Jacobson, 1964).

The man who created his self-picture in the likeness of Prospero had no such doubts about himself. He must have been altogether free of self-shrinking hesitation, and quite well aware that no psychic wear and tear could defeat—even though it might injure and exhaust—his indomitable self. That is why even allegory—that literary type that is so remote from life—was able to come aglow under the giant's blows.

Addendum A: A Note on "The Tempest" and the "Book of Judges."

When Caliban presses Stephano to kill Prospero, he suggests an unusual way of proceeding. "I'll yield him thee asleep,/ Where thou may'st knock a nail into his head" *(III.2.59f)*. Twenty-six lines later, Caliban adds an assortment of other methods ("brain," "batter his skull," "paunch with stake," "cut his wezard with thy knife") but knocking a nail into the head seemed unusual enough for commentators to find here to link to Jael, who is reported in the *Book of Judges* to have killed in exactly that fashion Sisera, King Sabin's captain, while he lay in sleep.

The technique of killing is, however, the only common element. Caliban is an unmarried man, Jael a married woman; Caliban wants to kill a person who is good and who should be and is protected, while Sisera serves a master who is by God's plan destined to perish and does perish. The reversals are obviously quite extensive. Is it without meaning that Shakespeare took over in *The Tempest* an unusual element of the *Book of Judges?*

One difference between the two works is conspicuous: the sparseness of the female element in *The Tempest* and its richness in *The Book of Judges*, which has become famous for antithetical types: Deborah, the hero-woman, the protectress of her nation, an ideal of vigorous action triumphant over the national enemy, and opposite her Delilah, the egregious symbol of treachery, the castrating woman, who defeats a national hero. In between there is Jael, who gives Sisera milk although he asks only for water, who covers the exhausted man with a mantle and inspires hope and confidence in him, yet kills him in his sleep (thus representing that most dreaded maternal type, that of the seductively loving mother who kills when she is trusted); in contrast to her stands Jephtha's daughter, most moving in her charming passivity, her unquestioning surrender to her father, and her joyful willingness to be sacrificed after having "bewailed her virginity" for two months.

Yet despite this difference, there are similarities that should not go unheeded.

(1) The *Book of Judges* describes events that take place when two civilizations clash: the children of Israel settling down in the Promised Land and the expelled peoples reacting to the occupation.

In *The Tempest*, Prospero's civilization clashes with the native population, as represented by Caliban.

(2) In *The Book of Judges*, the children of Israel are six times saved by national leaders and six times they regress to the religious ways of the heathens, which, being more archaic than the severe laws of the Lord, are closer to the primary process and therefore provide profounder emotional discharges. This regular regression is caused by the break between generations: the younger generation does not adhere to the higher standards of the older. *The Tempest* also has as its background a break between generations: Elizabethan tragedy being replaced by new literary forms. Shakespeare evidently did not feel at ease in the new cultural climate of James' reign, while the new generation no longer believed in or adhered to values that Shakespeare had created and which his generation had cherished. In *The Tempest*, Prospero and Alonso represent a departing generation.

(3) In *The Book of Judges*, the Lord assigns to the heathens a function of significant moral importance: they serve the purpose of testing the steadfastness of the children of Israel, who need to be exposed to the lure of polytheism and its simulacra. Contrary to His original promise, therefore, He did not annihilate all the enemies that threatened His chosen children.

Caliban, as has been stated, also fulfills an indirect moral function, inasmuch as he brings out the full extent of that sinful conduct of which a Christian may make himself guilty, without taking conscious leave of Christian dogma.

(4) In connection with the pagan conflict of the Israelites, intermarriage is mentioned. One passage in *The Book of Judges* insinuates that the seductive lure of exogamic love objects initiated the heresy of idolatry, as if only an endogamic choice of love object could preserve the purity of monotheism. Be that as it may, the break between Prospero and Caliban is precipitated and perhaps even caused by the sexual question. It is not only because Caliban tried to use force on Miranda that Prospero rejects him, yet it goes without saying that Miranda is forever and under all circumstances inaccessible to Caliban. It is most noteworthy that in *The Tempest* the clash between the two civilizations is established on the basis of sexual prejudices, a factor that, even though hidden, is still discernible in *The Book of Judges*.

The parallel is even more striking when Stephano permits Caliban to revere him as a god. Here the Christian is seduced, by the offer of a regressive and highly forbidden gratification, into transmuting himself into a structure more sinful than that which the children of Israel ever contrived.

(5) *The Book of Judges* constitutes, if one reads it without blinders, a shattering revelation. Whereas the reader may have expected until then that the Lord's promise to Abraham will, after all, be fulfilled once the haven of the Promised Land has been reached, he now becomes aware that this is not so, that the tribulations of the Jews will continue, and without any limit.

In *The Tempest* a "brave new world" is also promised. Does the resemblance to *The Book of Judges* perhaps indicate that this brave new world will fare no better than the one the children of Israel envisioned would be theirs, when they finally set foot on the Promised Land?

Addendum B: A Note on Shakespeare's Relationship to the Christian Mysteries.

I have speculated on various occasions about Shakespeare's attitude toward the Christian religion. Now that the manuscript has been finished, Henry D. von Witzleben has been kind enough to call to my attention Hugo Friedrich's (1949) outstanding book on Montaigne. Enriched by having obtained a deeper understanding of Montaigne's philosophy than the layman generally obtains upon reading his *Essays* separately, I am aware that I would have been better able to deal with Shakespeare's religious attitudes, had I been familiar with Friedrich's book earlier. What becomes evident is that in Shakespeare's plays one is struck by the same spirit with regard to religion that strikes one in Montaigne. When I spoke of atheism in Shakespeare or came close to doing so, I was probably wrong; but in reading Friedrich I came to understand why Shakespeare may perhaps strike the reader as being atheistic.

Montaigne was a fideist. This makes him part of a movement that has made its appearance sporadically and under a variety of different headings. By fideism is meant every Christian doctrine that rejects a rational manner of dealing with revealed truths (Friedrich, 1949, p. 134). In Montaigne the Christian truths of revelation are so far removed from the human world that they lose any meaning they might otherwise have had for it. What interests him exclusively is how man behaves, what he does with his religious teachings—never whether or not the truth that was allegedly revealed, is really true. Relativism is carried so far that the Christian religion finally winds up almost as *prima inter pares*.

"Christianity is to him a great spiritual [mental] potentiality of human existence [*Möglichkeit geistigen Menschseins*] but yet only one among many" (Friedrich, 1949, p. 141. My translation.). Religion thus becomes a purely human phenomenon, and it is considered solely under this aspect. If Montaigne had been an atheist, as may have happened to one or the other of his illustrious contemporaries, this might have limited the depth of his understanding of the human mind. His indifference toward any issue of orthodoxy served well his primary goal of grasping man. It gave him that flexibility that was necessary to accept the full spectrum of religious phenomena, and made it possible for him to focus on man without metaphysical impediments.[72]

---

[72] Friedrich's interpretation of Montaigne's religious concepts may be disputed, in view of some statements in the biography by Frame (1965, pp. 110, 137, 147), which may sound as if Montaigne's interest in Catholicism may have been, after all, dogmatic too. Yet a passage in the eighth essay of Book III, in which Montaigne (1580, p. 710) raises a specific argument against Protestantism, strongly suggests that he was concerned solely with elements of practicality. In the same Essay, one finds the description of a general attitude that one would guess to be very close to Shakespeare's. Montaigne wrote (1580, p. 704): "No propositions astonish me, no belief offends me, whatever contrast it offers with my own." It is precisely this freedom from axiomatic constraint that is at the bottom of the mental proximity of playwright and philosopher. Cf. also Frame (1965, p. 258): "It is surprising that such a stanch believer as Montaigne makes no use of the Gospel in his moral code; it seems possible that, without going against it at all, he is bypassing it as a moral force proven ineffective by the religious wars." Furthermore, about the puzzling refutation of Sebond in his *Apology*, there is agreement between Spencer (1942, p. 34) and Frame (1965, p. 170). The latter writes: "His

This, however, is also the impression that one receives from Shakespeare's plays. When Horatio speaks of the angels who carry Hamlet aloft, this was probably for Shakespeare an exclusively human event. Whether or not that event was compatible with some subtle or not so subtle point of Orthodoxy was probably a question that had no relevance to Shakespeare at all. It was a *humanly* most probably event for Horatio to be able to speak and feel and visualize in this manner (as is proven by its effect on the audience), and this was the only password that gave access to Shakespeare's world.

Important as the historical work may be, on the part of those who trace so many of the details of Shakespeare's plays to their sources—such as philosophers or theologians—most of them have not heeded a basic principle that Friedrich has stated concisely: "Unfortunately historical education leads us all too easily, when we discover a historical source for an author, to believe that when he drew on that source, the author's thoughts did not go beyond what was thought previously" (p. 7—my translation.). This should warn us against equating Shakespeare with Montaigne. Nevertheless the philosopher has to say a great deal explicitly that the playwright will only imply, and which in his case requires interpretation. Montaigne's work may be profitably used to become familiar with some general trends in Shakespeare's thinking.

In going to Montaigne, we may therefore spare ourselves the risks of interpretation and find instead direct contact with the mental atmosphere out of which Shakespeare's artistry grew; this we may do quite independently of knowing at what point Shakespeare actually became acquainted with Montaigne's *Essays*. That he rested so intensively under his influence after 1600 was possible, it seems to me, only because much of the philosopher's ideas and thoughts must already have been in him—at least latently—before that date.

Thus it is quite likely that the question of whether or not the content of Christian revelation is true had no relevance to Shakespeare in the composition of his plays, since he may well have perceived in it nothing but human beliefs, a conception that it was not without danger to state explicitly. Yet since it is Caliban who acts upon this principle (by arbitrarily assigning Godship to a human being), no one of Shakespeare's

---

[Montaigne's] skepticism is often a mockery of Sebond and apparently of Christianity itself; this must be conscious and intentional." Such mockery of Christianity as is found hidden in Montaigne's *Apology* may also lend some plausibility to my interpretation of one of the Caliban scenes as a satire on Christianity.

contemporaries would have been able to suspect the playwright of even sharing, no less advocating this view. And again I must raise the question of whether comedy—which does sometimes function as an antithesis to what a rational explicative statement could ever hope to set forth, if it were to deviate from average societal standards—may not in this instance have reached even deeper than the philosopher, who was, after all, bound to keep his expositions, as far as possible, within a rational frame, and whose conclusions were, so to speak, open to inspection.

Addendum C: "The Tempest"—A Dream?

James (1967, p. 149) has made the engaging suggestion that *The Tempest* may be looked at as a dream of Prospero's, "that Prospero in truth never left Milan, and that the island and all that we see happen on it was a dream of Prospero's only." One could indeed imagine Prospero falling asleep mildly worried that his brother has been absorbing all too many governmental functions and he himself becoming too much absorbed in his studies. The latent of dreamthoughts could have turned toward the possibilities of a successful plot by the brother.

In this situation, the dream would represent something of a wish-fulfillment, in the Freudian sense. The dreamer, having been miraculously rescued, can then live alone with his daughter on a remote island, where he acquires the art and the power of magic, and even makes certain that his progeny will come into possession of Milan and Naples. The dream would also make it clear to Prospero that he really does have to curtail his studies and participate, to a greater extent, in the administration of the state.

What is here suggested is a connection between play and dream, by means of which the play as a whole acquires in a simple fashion both consistency and logic. Curiously enough, we are able to reconstruct the conflict that might have been in Prospero's mind at the moment of his falling asleep in a convincing way, from the play itself. It may be of relevance that *Hamlet* too can be sensibly interpreted in that same way. Let us, for example, imagine the Prince in Wittenberg on an idle afternoon, feeling mildly homesick and longing for his sweetheart Ophelia, as well as being generally dissatisfied by the fact that, even in early manhood, he still has the status of a student and is daydreaming about how it would be at that moment if he were back home and a King.

If his father were to die, that would surely call for Hamlet's immediate return. For the father to die as a result of the son's wishes would, of course, necessarily arouse anxiety in the dreamer. But if the father is killed by his own brother, then the son is thereby freed of any guilt, and the aggression that was aimed at the father can be displaced—even taking on the form of a duty—upon a substitute object. Hamlet's doubts about the Ghost's message would then be due to a weakening of the displacement, which is threatened by the bitter truth that the King was, after all, the victim not of his brother but of his son.

In the Mousetrap play the dreamer is once again assured of his own innocence. At the same time, the longing for Ophelia, which had been at first warded off by devaluing her as a moral person, does obtain sexual gratification, albeit followed by a warning that it may lead to the girl's insanity and suicide. All this, taken together with the tragic end of the dream, reassures the dreamer that it is better, after all, to while away one's time in Wittenberg rather than to await a call to Elsinore. One could readily understand Hamlet, after such a dream, returning to his studies with greater zeal than he had felt prior to it.

Similarly, one could imagine an old and tired Lear wishing that he were rid of his royal duties and indulging in a daydream about dividing his realm among his three daughters. The subsequent dream (that is to say, tragedy) would likewise result in the light of the dire consequences that will follow from yielding to it.

Playwrights have made much of the affinity between life and dream, and of the fact that a dream may often have the effect of a warning, thus deterring a man from throwing himself into some adventure that would be fraught with great dangers. This does not exclude the possibility that sometimes a dream may have the opposite effect, and instead lure a man *into* adventure (as happened to Caesar when, as the story goes, he dreamed of incest with his mother before he crossed the Rubicon). Grillparzer gave one of his plays the title "The Dream, A Life" (*Der Traum, ein Leben*), the title itself conveying what the dream may be used for. In Calderon's play (*La Vida Es Sueño*), the problem takes on a still more complex form.

To look at *Hamlet* as if it were all a dream is not entirely original, since Glaz (1961) came close to doing just that some time ago. Yet Glaz did not proceed in the way James has suggested with regard to *The Tempest*. The results of Glaz's mode of interpreting the play could be the product only of "wild psychoanalysis" (if one is permitted to extend that term to applied psychoanalysis), but the method of looking at the play as dream material is legitimate. I cite this paper solely as a demonstration of what invariably happens when the psychoanalyst applies dream psychology to the content of myths and plays—namely, a colossal enlargement of the universe of discourse. The area under discussion becomes dilated—overdilated, as some critics have objected.

James's application of dream theory is quite different, and its results are correspondingly sober and plausible. All the events in the play—no matter how contradictory, ambiguous or mysterious they may otherwise appear to be—suddenly make sense when they are centered about the one point of the leading character's falling asleep with a wish, or a pattern of wishes, about whose fulfillment he is in doubt. One thereupon recognizes—with surprise, perhaps—that almost every element in any tragedy can be explained as serving, in that dream, either as wish-fulfillment or as warning.

This view would remain in keeping with Aristotle's theory of tragedy, insofar as a warning is the ego's counterpart to the discharge that occurs in catharsis. At the same time, it would also be in keeping with psychoanalytic theories: the warning can be subsumed under wish-fulfillment. In this instance, to be sure, we are not dealing with a repressed wish, but rather with the ego's aim of averting a danger that is being threatened either by a repressed wish that demands gratification or by a demand imposed on the ego by its rigidity and unwillingness to compromise.

Thus, in Hamlet's case, the desire to be in the father's place may generate a death wish; but the ego may then say that premature death can also be caused by political murder. Whereupon the superego will demand revenge, the carrying out of which may, however, lead to the death of the revenger, as well as that of members of his family, and following this the throne may be open to seizure by a rival family. *Ergo*, it is better for Hamlet not to wish to be King of Denmark at that particular time.

Furthermore, James' approach helps solve the problem of character ambiguity. Under such circumstances it does not make any essential difference whether Gertrude's character is read as that of the "good" or the "bad" mother; either way, it serves as wish-fulfillment or warning.

Nevertheless, appealing as James' approach is, and tempting as it may be precisely for the psychoanalyst, it is its infallible reliability that is its undoing: it is an instance of true "reductionism." The causative background is drawn so wide and so loosely that whatever takes place in the play can be interpreted in either of the two dimensions noted. Whether the hero succeeds or fails in his efforts, the outcome must necessarily be either wish-fulfillment or warning of the dreamer. In view of the fact that the results of this mode of interpretation cannot be refuted, it has lost its explanatory value.

Quite apart from this methodological obstacle, however, the basic proposition reduces the range of human experience to an almost unbearably small circle. It would amount in the long run to saying that life is not dangerous, for dreams will always protect us; the compass of human conflict is thus brought down to the scope of an afternoon snooze. If *Hamlet* were indeed no more than a prince's dream, occasioned by some transitory ambitious wish (which is cleared away when the dreamer awakens), then, by that same token, we could all repose in peace, and enjoy our sleep without the intrusion of nightmares—but, then, *Hamlet* would never have been written.

BIBLIOGRAPHY

Alexander, Franz (1933), A Note on Falstaff. *Psychoanal. Quart.*, 2:592-606.

Alexander, Peter (1955), *Hamlet: Father and Son.* Oxford: Clarendon Press.

—— (1961), *Shakespeare's Life and Art.* New York: New York University Press.

—— (1964), *Introductions to Shakespeare.* New York: W. W. Norton.

Alexander, Rose (1929), Hamlet, the Classical Malingerer. *Med. J. and Record,* 130:287-290.

Anderson, Ruth Leila (1927), *Elizabethan Psychology and Shakespeare's Plays.* New York: Russell and Russell, 1966.

Archer, William (1923), *The Old Drama and the New. An Essay in Re-Valuation.* London: Heinemann.

Aristotle, *Problems,* 2 Vols., tr. W. S. Hett. Cambridge, Mass.: Harvard University Press, 1953.

Arrowsmith, William (1952), Introduction to Cyclops. In: *The Complete Greek Tragedies,* 4 Vols., eds. D. Grene and R. Lattimore. Chicago: University of Chicago Press, 1959, Vol. 3, pp. 224-230.

Auden, W. H. (1945), The Sea and the Mirror. In: *Collected Poetry of W. H. Auden.* New York: Random House, pp. 351-404.

Bailey, Percival (1956), The Great Psychiatric Revolution. *Amer. J. Psychiat.,* 113:387-406.

Baskervill, Charles Read (1929), *The Elizabethan Jig.* New York: Dover.

Benjamin, Walter (1928), *Ursprung des deutschen Trauerspiels.* Frankfurt am Main: Suhrkamp Verlag, 1963.

Beres, David (1965), Psychoanalytic Notes on the History of Morality. *J. Amer. Psychoanal. Assn.,* 13:3-37.

Bernfeld, Siegfried (1929), Der soziale Ort und seine Bedeutung für Neurose, Verwahrlosung und Pädagogik. *Imago,* 15:299-312.

Berry, Francis (1947), Young Fortinbras. *Life and Letters.* Vol. 19, February, pp. 94-103.

—— (1965), *The Shakespeare Inset.* New York: Theatre Arts Books.

Bettelheim, Bruno (1955), Death, Life: Purpose? *Chicago Review,* 9:4-14.

—— (1960), *The Informed Heart.* Glencoe, Ill.: Free Press.

Bickerman, Elias (1967), *Four Strange Books of the Bible.* New York: Schocken Books.

Boas, George (1940), The Mona Lisa in the History of Taste. *J. Hist. Ideas,* 1:207-224.

Bode, Wilhelm (1921), *Neues über Goethes Liebe.* Berlin: Mittler.

Boklund, Gunnar (1965), Hamlet. In: *Essays on Shakespeare,* ed. G. W. Chapman. Princeton, N.J.: Princeton University Press, pp. 116-137.

Bonaparte, Marie (1933), *The Life and Works of Edgar Allan Poe, a Psychoanalytic Interpretation*. London: Imago, 1949.

Borges, Jorge Luis (1952), *Other Inquisitions 1937-1952*. New York: Simon and Schuster, 1964.

Boring, Edwin G. (1955), Dual Role of the Zeitgeist in Scientific Creativity. *Sci. Month.*, 80:101-106.

Born, Max (1965), Recollections of Max Born. III, Reflections. *Bull. Atom. Sci.*, 21.

Börne, Ludwig (1823), Die Kunst, in drei Tagen—ein originaler Schriftsteller zu werden. *Gesammelte Schriften*, 3 Vols. Leipzig: Reclam, Vol. 1, pp. 120-122.

Bowers, Fredson (1956), Hamlet's "Sullied" or "Solid" Flesh: A Biographical Case-History. *Shakespeare Survey*, IX:44-48.

—— (1959), *Textual and Literary Criticism*. Cambridge: Cambridge University Press, 1966.

Bradbrook, Muriel Clara (1935), *Themes and Conventions of Elizabethan Tragedy*. Cambridge: Cambridge University Press, 1960.

Braddy, Haldeen (1964), *Hamlet's Wounded Name*. El Paso: Texas Western Press.

Bradley, Andrew Cecil (1904), *Shakespearean Tragedy*. London: Macmillan, 1950.

Braunthal, Julius (1960), *Victor und Friedrich Adler*. Zwei Generationen der Arbeiterbewegung. Verlag der Wiener Volksbuchhandlung.

Breuer, Joseph and Freud, Sigmund (1893-95), Studies on Hysteria. *Standard Edition*, 2. London: Hogarth Press, 1955.

Bridges, Robert (1927), The Influence of the Audience on Shakespeare's Drama. In: *Collected Essays, Papers, etc.* London: Oxford University Press, Vol. 1, No. 1, p. 161.

Brooks, Cleanth (Ed.) (1955), *Tragic Themes in Western Literature*. New Haven: Yale University Press.

Brown, Ivor (1949), *Shakespeare*. New York: Time Incorporated.

Brunner, Otto (1956), Vom Gottesgnadentum zum monarchischen Prinzip. Der Weg der europäischen Monarchie seit dem hohen Mittelalter in das Königtum. Seine geistigen und rechtlichen Grundlagen. *Vorträge und Forschungen*, ed. Theodore Mayer. Lindau and Konstanz: Jan Thorbeck Verlag, pp. 279-305.

Bucknill, John Charles (1859), *The Psychology of Shakespeare*. London: Longmans, Brown.

Bühler, Karl (1929), *Die krise der Psychologie*. Jena: Gustav Fischer, sec. ed.

Burckhardt, Carl August Hugo (1870), ed. *Unterhaltungen mit dem Kanzler Friedrich von Müller*. Stuttgart, Berlin: Cotta, 1904.

Bush, Goeffrey (1956), *Shakespeare and the Natural Condition*. Cambridge, Mass.: Harvard University Press.

Butcher, Samuel H. (1894), *Aristotle's Theory of Poetry and Fine Art*. New York: Dover, 1951.

Cambridge Edition. (1948), See: Shakespeare, Wm. *Hamlet*, ed. J. D. Wilson, Cambridge Edition.

Campbell, Joseph (1949), *The Hero with a Thousand Faces*. The Bollingen Series, XVII. New York: Pantheon Books.

Campbell, Lily B. (1930), *Shakespeare's Tragic Heroes—Slaves of Passion*. New York: Barnes and Noble, 1960.

Campbell, Oscar James (1966), Comment on *The Tempest*. In: *The Reader's Encyclopedia of Shakespeare*, ed. O. J. Campbell. New York: Thomas Y. Crowell, pp. 856-858.

Chambers, Sir Edmund K. (1930), *William Shakespeare*, 2 Vols. London: Oxford University Press, Vol. 1, pp. 417-419.

Charlton, Henry Buckley (1939), *Shakespearean Comedy*. New York: Barnes and Noble.

Clements, Robert J. (1965), *The Poetry of Michelangelo*. New York: New York University Press.

Coleridge, Samuel T. (1836-1839), *Shakespearean Criticism*. Lectures and Notes on Shakespeare, 2 Vols. ed. T. M. Raysor. London: Dent; New York: Dutton, 1964, Vol. 1, p. 357.

Davies, W. R. (1939), *Shakespeare's Boy Actors*. New York: Russell and Russell, 1964.

Davis, Arthur G. (1964), *Hamlet and the Eternal Problem of Man*. New York: St. John's University Press.

Deutsch, Helene (1930), Hysterical Fate-Neurosis. In: *Psychoanalysis of the Neuroses*. London: The Hogarth Press and the Institute of Psycho-Analysis, 1932.

—— (1944-45), *The Psychology of Women*, 2 Vols. New York: Grune & Stratton.

Dilthey, Wilhelm (1887), Die Einbildungskraft des Dichters. Bausteine für eine Poetik. Wilhelm

Diltheys *Gesammelte Schriften,* 9 Vols. Leipzig and Berlin: B.G. Teubner, Vol. 6, pp. 128, 212.

—— (1894), Ideen über eine beschreibende und zergliedernde Psychologie. Wilhelm Diltheys *Gesammelte Schriften.* Leipzig and Berlin: B. G. Teubner, Vol. 5, pp. 139-240.

Dodds, Eric Robertson (1951), *The Greeks and the Irrational.* Boston: Beacon Press, 1957.

Doran, Madeleine (1940), On Elizabethan "Credulity" with Some Questions Concerning the Use of the "Marvelous" in Literature. *J. Hist. Ideas,* 1:151-176.

Dostoevski, Feodor M. (1881), Der Grossinquisitor in *Die Brüder Karamasoff,* 3 Vols. 1:492-532. Münich: Piper, 1922.

Draper, John W. (1939), The *"Hamlet"* of Shakespeare's Audience. New York: Octagon Books, 1966.

Dührssen, Annemarie (1956), Lebensprobleme und Daseinskrise bei Hamlet and Ophelia. Eine Studie zu Shakespeares psychologischer Konzeption. *Zeitschr. für Psycho-som. Med.,* 2:220-235, 295-311.

Edel, Leon (1957), *Literary Biography.* Toronto: University of Toronto Press.

Ehrenzweig, Anton (1953), *The Psycho-Analysis of Artistic Vision and Hearing.* New York: George Braziller, 1965.

Eissler, K. R. (1960), The Efficient Soldier. In *The Psychoanalytic Study of Society,* ed. W. Muensterberger and S. Axelrad. New York: International Universities Press, 1:39-97.

—— (1963), *Goethe. A Psychoanalytic Study, 1775-1786,* 2 Vols. Detroit: Wayne State University Press.

—— (1965), *Versuch einer Persönlichkeitsanalyse.* Unpublished manuscript.

Elias, Norbert (1939), *Über den Prozess der Zivilisation* 2 Vols. Basel: Haus zum Falken.

Eliot, George (1860), *The Mill on the Floss.* London and New York: Collier-Macmillan, 1962.

Eliot, T. S. (1919), Ben Jonson. In: *Selected Essays (1917-1932).* New York: Harcourt, Brace and Co., 1960, pp. 27-139.

—— (1920), Hamlet and His Problem. In: *The Sacred Wood,* ed. S. Wellman. New York: Barnes and Noble, 1966.

—— (1927a), Seneca in Elizabethan Translation. In: *Selected Essays (1917-1932).* New York: Harcourt, Brace and Co., 1960, pp. 51-88.

—— (1927b), Shakespeare and the Stoicism of Seneca. In: *Selected Essays (1917-1932).* New York: Harcourt, Brace and Co., 1960, pp. 107-120.

—— (1931), Thomas Heywood. In: *Selected Essays (1917-1932).* New York: Harcourt, Brace and Co., 1960, pp. 149-158.

Elkins, Stanley M. (1959), *Slavery, A Problem in American Institutional and Intellectual Life.* New York: Grosset and Dunlap, 1963.

Elton, Oliver (1922), *A Sheaf of Papers.* London: Hodder and Stoughton, Ltd.

Empson, William (1930), *Seven Types of Ambiguity.* London: Chatto and Windus, 1947.

—— (1935), Double Plots. In: *Some Versions of Pastoral.* Norfolk, Conn.: New Directions Paperback, 1960, pp. 25-84.

Erasmus (1503), *The Enchiridion of Erasmus,* tr. and ed. R. Himelick. Bloomington: Indiana University Press, 1963.

Erikson, Erik H. (1958a), The Nature of Clinical Evidence. In: *Insight and Responsibility.* New York: W. W. Norton, 1964, pp. 49-80.

—— (1958b), The First Psychoanalyst. In: *Insight and Responsibility.* New York: W. W. Norton, 1964, pp. 19-46.

—— (1958c), *Young Man Luther.* New York: W. W. Norton, 1962.

—— (1961a), Human Struggle and the Cycle of Generations. In: *Insight and Responsibility.* New York: W. W. Norton, 1964, pp. 111-159.

—— (1961b), The Roots of Virtue. In: *The Humanist Frame,* ed. J. Huxley. New York: Harper and Brothers, pp. 147-165.

—— (1962a), Youth: Fidelity and Diversity. *Daedalus,* 91:5-27.

—— (1962b), Psychological Reality and Historical Actuality. In: *Insight and Responsibility.* New York: W. W. Norton, 1964, pp. 161-215.

—— (1964), *Insight and Responsibility.* New York: W. W. Norton.

Fanon, Frantz (1961), *The Wretched of the Earth.* New York: Grove Press, 1966.

Farnham, Willard (1936), *The Medieval Heritage of Elizabethan Tragedy.* Oxford: Blackwell, 1963.

—— (1950), *Shakespeare's Tragic Frontier.* Berkeley and Los Angeles: University of California Press, 1963.

Feifel, Herman, ed. (1959), *The Meaning of Death.* New York-Toronto-London: McGraw Hill.

Feis, Jacob (1844), *Shakespeare and Montaigne.* London: Kegan Paul & Trench, p. 89.

Ferenczi, Sandor (1914), The Nosology of Male Homosexuality (Homoerotism). In: *Sex in Psychoanalysis.* New York: Basic Books, 1950, pp. 296-318.

—— (1916), Two Types of War Neurosis. In: *Further Contributions to the Theory and Technique of Psycho-Analysis.* London: Hogarth Press (The International Psycho-Analytical Library, No. 11), 1950, pp. 124-141.

—— (1933), Sprachverwirrung zwischen den Erwachsenen und dem Kind. *Int. Zeitschrift für Psychoanalyse,* 19:5-15.

Fergusson, Francis (1949), *The Idea of a Theatre.* Garden City, N. Y.: Doubleday Anchor Books, 1953.

Flatter, Richard (1949), *Hamlet's Father.* New Haven: Yale University Press.

Fliess, Robert (1957), *Erogeneity and Libido.* New York: International Universities Press.

Frame, Donald M. (1965), *Montaigne: A Biography.* New York: Harcourt, Brace and World.

France, Anatole (1888), Hamlet à la Comédie-Française. In: *La Vie Litteraire.* Paris and New York: Calmann-Levy, Vol. 1, pp. 1, 8.

Freud, Anna (1936), A Form of Altruism. In: *The Ego and the Mechanisms of Defense.* New York: International Universities Press, 1954, pp. 132-146.

—— (1965), *Normality and Pathology in Childhood: Assessments of Development.* New York: International Universities Press.

Freud, Sigmund (1873-1939), *Letters of Sigmund Freud.* Selected and edited by E. L. Freud. New York: Basic Books, 1960.

—— (1887-1902), *Aus den Anfängen der Psychoanalyse.* Briefe an Wilhelm Fliess. London: Imago, 1950. English: *The Origins of Psychoanalysis.* Letters to Wilhelm Fliess. New York: Basic Books, 1954.

—— (1892), Preface and Footnote to the Translation of Charcot's "Leçons du Mardi de la Salpêtrière," (1887-1888). *Standard Edition,* 1:132-143, London: Hogarth Press, 1966.

—— (1892-1893), A Case of Successful Treatment by Hypnotism. *Standard Edition,* 1:117-128, London: Hogarth Press, 1966.

—— (1895), Project for a Scientific Psychology. *Standard Edition,* 1:295-387, London: Hogarth Press, 1966.

—— (1898), The Psychical Mechanism of Forgetfulness. *Standard Edition,* 3:289-297. London: Hogarth Press, 1962.

—— (1900), The Interpretation of Dreams (Parts I and II). *Standard Edition,* 4, 5. London: Hogarth Press, 1953.

—— (1905), Jokes and Their Relation to the Unconscious. *Standard Edition,* 8. London: Hogarth Press, 1960.

—— (1907), Delusions and Dreams in Jensen's *Gradiva. Standard Edition,* 9:7-95. London: Hogarth Press, 1959.

—— (1908), Creative Writers and Day-Dreaming. *Standard Edition,* 9:143-153. London: Hogarth Press, 1959.

—— (1910), A Special Type of Choice of Object Made by Man. *Standard Edition,* 11:165-175. London: Hogarth Press, 1957.

—— (1911a), Formulations on the Two Principles of Mental Functioning. *Standard Edition,* 12: 218-226. London: Hogarth Press,

—— (1911b), Psychoanalytic Notes on an Autobiographical Account of a Case of Paranoia (Dementia Paranoides). *Standard Edition,* 12:9-82. London: Hogarth Press, 1958.

—— (1913a), The Claims of Psycho-Analysis to Scientific Interest. *Standard Edition,* 13:165-190. London: Hogarth Press, 1955.

—— (1913b), The Disposition to Obsessional Neurosis: A Contribution to the Problem of Choice of Neurosis. *Standard Edition,* 12:317-326. London: Hogarth Press, 1958.

—— (1913c), The Theme of the Three Caskets. *Standard Edition*, 12:291-301. London: Hogarth Press, 1958.

—— (1913d), Totem and Taboo. *Standard Edition*, 13. London: Hogarth Press, 1955.

—— (1914a), On Narcissism: An Introduction. *Standard Edition*, 14:73-102. London: Hogarth Press, 1957.

—— (1914b), On the History of the Psychoanalytic Movement. *Standard Edition*, 14:7-66. London: Hogarth Press, 1957.

—— (1916), Some Character Types Met with in Psychoanalytic Work. *Standard Edition*, 13:311-333. London: Hogarth Press, 1955.

—— (1916-1917), Introductory Lectures on Psycho-Analysis. *Standard Edition*, 16. London: Hogarth Press, 1963.

—— (1917a), A Childhood Recollection from *Dichtung und Wahrheit*. *Standard Edition*, 17:147-156. London: Hogarth Press, 1955.

—— (1917b), Mourning and Melancholia. *Standard Edition*, 14:243-258. London: Hogarth Press, 1957.

—— (1917c), A Difficulty in the Path of Psycho-Analysis. *Standard Edition*, 17:137-144. London: Hogarth Press, 1955.

—— (1917d), The Metapsychology of Dreams. *Standard Edition*, 14:222-235. London: Hogarth Press, 1957.

—— (1918), From the History of an Infantile Neurosis. *Standard Edition*, 17. London: Hogarth Press, 1955.

—— (1920), Beyond the Pleasure Principle. *Standard Edition*, 18:7-64. London: Hogarth Press, 1955.

—— (1921), Group Psychology and the Analysis of the Ego. *Standard Edition*, 18:65-143. London: Hogarth Press, 1955.

—— (1922), Some Neurotic Mechanisms in Jealousy, Paranoia, and Homosexuality. *Standard Edition*, 18:223-232. London: Hogarth Press, 1955.

—— (1923), The Ego and the Id. *Standard Edition*, 19:12-59. London: Hogarth Press, 1961.

—— (1924a), Neurosis and Psychosis. *Standard Edition*, 19:149-153. London: Hogarth Press, 1961.

—— (1924b), The Loss of Reality in Neurosis and Psychosis. *Standard Edition*, 19:183-187. London: Hogarth Press, 1961.

—— (1925a), An Autobiographical Study, *Standard Edition*, 20:7-74. London: Hogarth Press, 1959.

—— (1925b), Negation. *Standard Edition*, 19:235-239. London: Hogarth Press, 1961.

—— (1926a), Inhibition, Symptoms and Anxiety. *Standard Edition*, 20:87-172. London: Hogarth.

—— (1926b), The Question of Lay Analysis. *Standard Edition*, 20:183-258. London: Hogarth Press, 1959.

—— (1927), The Future of an Illusion. *Standard Edition*, 21:5-56. London: Hogarth Press, 1961.

—— (1928), Dostoevsky and Parricide. *Standard Edition*, 21:177-196. London: Hogarth Press, 1961.

—— (1930), Civilization and Its Discontents. *Standard Edition*, 21:64-145, 1961.

—— (1933), New Introductory Lectures on Psycho-Analysis. *Standard Edition*, 22:5-182. London: Hogarth Press, 1964.

—— (1939), Moses and Monotheism: Three Essays. *Standard Edition*, 23:7-137. London: Hogarth Press, 1964.

—— (1942 [1905 or 1906], Psychopathic Characters on the Stage. *Standard Edition*, 7:305-310. London: Hogarth Press, 1953.

—— and Pfister, Oskar (1909-1939), *Psychoanalysis and Faith*, eds. H. Meng and E. L. Freud. New York: Basic Books, 1963.

Freudenstein, Reinhold (1958), Der Bestrafte Brudermord: Shakespeares "Hamlet" auf der Wanderbühne des 17. Jahrhundert. *Britannica et Americana*. (Britannica, neue Folge), Vol. 3. Hamburg: Crain de Gruyer & Co.

Frey, Lina (1932), *Der Eros und die Kunst*. Leipzig: Huber.

Friedrich, Hugo (1949), *Montaigne*. Bern & München: Francke Verlag, Sec. ed., 1967.

Frye, Roland Mushat (1963), *Shakespeare and Christian Doctrine*. Princeton, N. J.: Princeton University Press.

Furness, Horace Howard (1877), *Hamlet. A New Variorum Edition of Shakespeare*, 2 Vols. Philadelphia: J. B. Lippincott.

Furst, Sidney S. (1967), ed. *Psychic Trauma*. New York: Basic Books.

Gedo, John E., Sabshin, Melvin, Sadow, Leo, and Schlessinger, Natham (1964), Studies on Hysteria. A Methodological Evaluation. *J. Amer. Psychoanal. Assn.*, 12:734-751.

Glasser, Richard (1936), Studien zur Geschichte des Französischen Zeitbegriffs. Eine Orientierung. *Münchner Romantische Arbeiten*, Heft V. Munich: Max Huber.

Goddard, Harold C. (1946), In Ophelia's Closet. *The Yale Review*, 35:462-474.

—— (1951), *The Meaning of Shakespeare*. 2 Vols. Chicago and London: University of Chicago Press, 1965.

—— (1955), Hamlet to Ophelia. *College English*, 16:403-415.

Goethe, Johann Wolfgang (1827), Nachlese zu Aristotles Poetik. In: *Goethes Sämtliche Werke*, 40 Vols. Stuttgart and Berlin: Cotta, 38, 81-85.

—— (1870), *Unterhaltungen mit dem Kanzler Friedrich von Müller*, 3rd ed., ed. C. A. H. Burkhardt. Stuttgart and Berlin: Cotta, 1904.

Gombrich, Ernst (1960). *Art and Illusion*. New York: Pantheon Books, 2nd rev. ed., 1965.

Graham, Clarence Henry (1951), Visual Perception. In: *Handbook of Experimental Psychology*, ed. S. S. Stevens. New York and London: John Wiley, 1960, pp. 868-920.

Granville-Barker, Harley (1934), Shakespeare's Dramatic Art. In: *A Companion to Shakespeare Studies*, eds. H. Granville-Barker and G. B. Harrison. Garden City, N. Y.: Doubleday and Co., 1960, pp. 44-87.

—— (1946), Hamlet. In: *Prefaces to Shakespeare*. Princeton, N.J.: Princeton University Press, 1965.

Graves, Robert (1948), *The White Goddess. A Historical Grammar of Poetic Myth*. New York: Creative Age Press.

Grebanier, Bernard (1960), *The Heart of Hamlet*. New York: Thomas Y. Crowell.

Greenacre, Phyllis (1957), The Childhood of the Artist. *The Psychoanalytic Study of the Child*, 12: 47-72. New York: International Universities Press.

—— (1966), On Nonsense. In: *Psychoanalysis—A General Psychology*, eds. R. M. Loewenstein, L. Newman, M. Schur, and A. J. Solnit. New York: International Universities Press.

Greg, Walter Wilson (1917), Hamlet's Hallucination. *Mod. Lang. Rev.*, 12:393-421.

Grinker, Roy Sr., Grinker, Roy Jr., and Timberlake, J. (1962), "Mentally Healthy" Young Males —(Homoclites). *Arch. Gen. Psychiat.*, 6:405-453.

Grinstein, Alexander (1956), The Dramatic Device: A Play within a Play. *J. Amer. Psychoanal. Assn.*, 4:49-53.

Gundolf, Friedrich (1911a), Hölderlins Archipelagus. In: *Dichter und Helden*. Heidelberg: Weiss'sche Universitätsbuchhandlung.

—— (1911b), *Shakespeare und der deutsche Geist*. Berlin: Bondi.

—— (1916), *Goethe*. Berlin: G. Bondi, 1917.

—— (1925), *Caesar, Geschlichte eines Ruhms*. Berlin: G. Bondi.

—— (1928), *Shakespeare: sein Wesen und Werk*, 2 Vols. Berlin: G. Bondi, 1949.

Guthrie, William K. C. (1966), *Orpheus and Greek Religion: A Study of the Orphic Movement*. New York: W. W. Norton.

Hadas, Moses (1950), *A History of Greek Literature*. New York: Columbia University Press.

Hale, Robert Beverly (1964), *Drawing Lessons from the Great Masters*. New York: Watson.

Halliday, Frank Ernest (1952), *A Shakespeare Companion 1564-1964*. Baltimore, Md.: Penguin Books, 1964.

Hamsun, Knut (1890-1891), *Psychologie und Dichtung*. Stuttgart: W. Kohlhammer Verlag, 1964.

Hankins, John E. (1947), Caliban the Bestial Man. PMLA, 62:793-801.

Harbage, Alfred (1941), *Shakespeare's Audience*. New York and London: Columbia University Press.

Harrison, George B. (1940), *Elizabethan Plays and Players*. Ann Arbor, Mich.: The University of Michigan Press, 1961.

Hartmann, Ernest (1967), *The Biology of Dreaming.* Springfield, Ill.: Charles C. Thomas.

Hartmann, Heinz, (1934-1935). Psychiatrische Zwillingsstudien Jahrbuch der Psychiatrie und Neurologie 50, 51.

——(1939), *Ego Psychology and the Problem of Adaptation.* New York: International Universities Press, 1958.

——(1947), Rational and Irrational Action. In: *Essays on Ego Psychology.* New York: International Universities Press, 1964, pp. 37-68.

——(1950), Comments on the Psychoanalytic Theory of the Ego. In: *The Psychoanalytic Study of the Child,* 5:74-96, p. 87f. New York: International Universities Press.

——(1952), The Mutual Influences on the Development of Ego and Id. In: *Essays on Ego Psychology.* New York: International Universities Press, 1964, pp. 155-181.

——(1956), Notes on the Reality Principle. In: *Essays on Ego Psychology.* New York: International Universities Press, 1964, pp. 241-267.

——(1960), *Psychoanalysis and Moral Values.* New York: International Universities Press.

——(1964), *Essays on Ego Psychology.* New York: International Universities Press.

—— and Betlheim, S. (1924), Über Fehlreaktionen bei der Korsakoffschen Psychose. *Archiv für Psychiatrie und Nervenkrankheiten,* 72:278-286. Published in part as: On Parapraxes in the Korsakow Psychosis, translated and edited by D. Rapaport. In: *Organization and Pathology of Thought.* New York: Columbia University Press, 1951, pp. 288-301.

—— and Loewenstein, Rudolph M. (1962), Notes on the Superego. *The Psychoanalytic Study of the Child,* 17:42-81. New York International Universities Press.

Heckscher, William S. (1967), Sturm und Drang. Conjectures on the Origin of a Phrase. *Simiolus,* 1:95-106.

Heilman, Robert B. (1965), The Role We Give Shakespeare. In: *Essays on Shakespeare,* ed. G. W. Chapman. Princeton, N.J.: Princeton University Press, pp. 3-34.

Heisenberg, Werner (1953), *Physics and Philosophy. The Revolution in Modern Science.* New York: Harper and Bros.

Heller, Lora and Heller, Abraham (1960), Hamlet's Parents: The Dynamic Formulation of a Tragedy. *Amer. Imago,* 17:413-421.

Hering, Karl Ewald (1870), *Über das Gedächtnis als eine allgemeine Funktion der organisierten Materie.* Akademie der Wissenschaften in Wien am XXX Mai, Wien, 1870.

Hermann, Imré (1925), Beiträge zur Psychogenese der zeichnerischen Begabung. *Imago,* 8:54-66.

——(1930), Begabtheit und Unbegabtheit. *Zeitschrift für psycholoanalytische Pädagogik,* 4:408-416.

Herzberg, Alexander (1926), Das Sexualleben der grossen Philosophen. *Verhandlungen d. I internationalen Kongresses f. Sexualforschung,* Vol. 3. pp. 68-73. Berlin & Köln: Marcus & Weber, 1928.

Holland, Norman N. (1963), Romeo's Dream and the Paradox of Literary Realism. *Lit. and Psychol.,* 13:97-104.

——(1964a), *Psychoanalysis and Shakespeare.* New York-Toronto-London: McGraw-Hill.

——(1964b), *The Shakespearean Imagination.* New York: The Macmillan Co.

——(1966), Shakespeare's Mercutio and Ours. *Michigan Q. Rev.,* 5:115-123.

——(1968), Realism and the Psychological Critic; or, How Many Complexes Had Lady Macbeth? *Lit. and Psychol.,* 10:5-8.

Holmes, Martin (1964), *The Guns of Elsinore.* London: Chatto and Windus.

Holstein, Hugo (1886), *Die Reformation im Spiegelbilde der dramatischen Litteratur.* Nieuw Koop: B. de Graff, 1967.

Hotson, Leslie (1938), *I, William Shakespeare.* New York: Oxford University Press.

Houben, Heinrich H. (1929), ed. and trans. *Frederic Soret, Zehn Jahre bei Goethe.* Leipzig: Brockhaus.

Huhner, Max (1950), *Shakespeare's Hamlet.* New York: Farrar, Straus.

Ichheiser, Gustav (1949), Misunderstandings in Human Relations. *Amer. J. Sociol.,* 55:2, pt. 2.

Jacobson, Edith (1964), *The Self and the Object World.* New York: International Universities Press.

James, David Gwilym (1937), *Skepticism and Poetry. An Essay on the Poetic Imagination.* New York: Barnes and Noble, 1960.

———(1967), *The Dream of Prospero*. Oxford: Clarendon Press.

Jekels, Ludwig (1917-1919), Shakespeare's "Macbeth." *Imago*, 5:170-195. English: The Riddle of Shakespeare's Macbeth. In: *Selected Papers by Ludwig Jekels*. New York: International Universities Press, 1952, pp. 105-130.

——— (1933), The Problem of the Duplicated Expression of Psychic Themes. *Int. J. Psycho-Anal.*, 14:300-309.

Jensen, Wilhelm (1903), *Gradiva: ein pompejanisches Phantasiestück*. Dresden and Leipzig: Carl Reiner Verlag, 1913; New York: Moffat, Yard, 1918 (English translation).

——— (1911), Drei unveröffentlichte Briefe. *Psychoanalytische Bewegung*, 1:207-211, 1929.

Johnson, S. F. (1952), The Regeneration of Hamlet. *Shakespeare Quart.*, 3:187-207.

Jones, Ernest (1911), On Dying Together. In: *Essays in Applied Psychoanalysis*. London: Hogarth Press, 1951, Vol. 1, pp. 9-15.

——— (1948), The Death of Hamlet's Father. In: *Essays in Applied Psychoanalysis*. London: Hogarth Press, 1951, Vol. 1, pp. 323-328.

——— (1949), *Hamlet and Oedipus*. London: S. Gollancz; New York: W. W. Norton, p. 19.

——— (1953), *The Life and Work of Sigmund Freud*, Vol. 1. New York: Basic Books.

Joseph, Bertram (1964), The Elizabethan Stage and Acting. In: *The Age of Shakespeare*, ed. B. Ford. Baltimore, Md.: Penguin Books, pp. 147-161.

Joyce, George Hayward (1933), *Christian Marriage: An Historical and Doctrinal Study*. London and New York: Sheed and Ward.

Jung, Carl G. (1923), *Psychological Types*. London: Kegan Paul, 1933.

——— (1944), *Psychology and Alchemy*. Bollingen Series XX. New York: Pantheon Books, 1953.

——— (1961), Memories, Dreams, Reflections. New York: Pantheon Books.

Kafka, Franz (1919), *Brief an den Vater*. München: R. Piper.

Kanzer, Mark (1948), The "Passing of the Oedipus Complex" in Greek Drama. *Int. J. Psycho-Anal.*, 29:131-134.

Kaplan, Abraham, and Kris, Ernst (1948), Esthetic Ambiguity. *Philos. and Phenomenolog. Rev.*, 8:415-485.

Katz, Jay (1963), On Primary Gain and Secondary Gain. *The Psychoanalytic Study of the Child*, 18:9-50. New York: International Universities Press.

Keller, Wolfgang (1919), Bücherschau. *Jahrbuch d. Deutschen Shakespeare Gesellschaft*, 55:143-180, p. 152.

Kerenyi, Karl (1947), Urmensch and Mysterium. In: *Niobe*. Zurich: Rhein Verlag, 1949, pp. 53-86.

Kermode, Frank (1954), ed. *The Tempest*. New Arden Edition.

Kernodle, George R. (1944), *From Art to Theatre*. Chicago and London: University of Chicago Press.

Kettle, Arnold (1964) ed. *Shakespeare in a Changing World*. New York: International Publishers.

Kirsch, James (1966), *Shakespeare's Royal Self*. New York: G. P. Putnam's Sons.

Kittredge, George Lyman (1939), ed. and annotator. *The Tragedy of Hamlet, Prince of Denmark*, by William Shakespeare. Boston-New York-Chicago-Altanta-Dallas-Palo Alto-Toronto: Ginn.

Klenze, Camillo von (1907), *The Interpretation of Italy During the Last Two Centuries*. University of Chicago: The Decennial Publications Lecture Series, Vol. XVII.

Knight, G. Wilson (1930), *The Wheel of Fire*. London: Methuen (4th edition, 1949; 5th edition, 1965).

——— (1931), *The Imperial Theme*. London: Methuen, 1951.

——— (1947a), Hamlet Reconsidered. In: *The Wheel of Fire*. London: Methuen, 1965, pp. 298-325.

——— (1947b), Two Notes on the Text of Hamlet. In: *The Wheel of Fire*. London: Methuen, 1965, pp. 325-343.

——— (1948), *The Crown of Life*. New York: Barnes and Noble, 1966.

——— (1962), *The Christian Renaissance*. New York: W. W. Norton.

——— (1966), Symbolism. In: *The Reader's Encyclopedia of Shakespeare*, ed. O. J. Campbell. New York: Thomas Y. Crowell.

Knights, Lionel Charles (1933), How Many Children Had Lady Macbeth? In: *Explorations*. New York: New York University Press, 1964, pp. 15-54.

Kohut, Heinz (1957), Observations on the Psychological Function of Music. *J. Amer. Psychoanal. Assn.,* 5:389-407.

—— (1960), Beyond the Bounds of the Basic Rule. Some Recent Contributions to Applied Psychoanalysis. *J. Amer. Psychoanal. Assn.,* 8:567-586.

—— and Levarie, Sigmund (1950), On the Enjoyment of Listening to Music. *Psychoanal. Quart.,* 19:64-87.

Kott, Jan (1964), *Shakespeare Heute*. München: Albert Langen; Wien: Georg Müller. English: *Shakespeare Our Contemporary*. Garden City: Doubleday, 1964.

Kozintsev, G. M. (1966), *Shakespeare: Time and Conscience*. New York: Hill and Wang.

Kraus, Wolfgang (n.d.), ed. *Symbole und Signale*. Birsfelden bei Basel: Schibili-Doppler.

Kris, Ernst (1936), Comments on Spontaneous Artistic Creations by Psychotics. In: *Psychoanalytic Explorations in Art*. New York: International Universities Press. 1952, pp. 87-117.

—— (1939), Laughter as an Expressive Process. In: *Psychoanalytic Explorations in Art*. New York: International Universities Press, 1952, pp. 217-239.

—— (1941), Approaches to Art. In: *Psychoanalytic Explorations in Art*. New York: International Universities Press, 1952, pp. 13-63.

—— (1947), The Nature of Psychoanalytic Propositions and Their Validation. In: *Psychological Theory*, ed. M. H. Marx. New York: The Macmillan Co., 1957, pp. 351-352.

—— (1948), Prince Hal's Conflict. In: *Psychoanalytic Explorations in Art*. New York: International Universities Press, 1952, pp. 273-288.

—— (1950), On Preconscious Mental Processes. In: *Psychoanalytic Explorations in Art*. New York: International Universities Press, 1952, pp. 303-318.

—— and Kurz, Otto (1934), *Die Legende vom Künstler, ein geschichtlicher Versuch*. Vienna: Krystall Verlag.

Kuhn, Thomas S. (1962), The Structure of Scientific Revolutions. *International Encyclopedia of Unified Science*. Chicago: University of Chicago Press.

Kuiper, Pieters Cornelius (1964), Verstehende Psychologie und Psychoanalyse. *Psyche*, 18:15-32.

—— (1965), Diltheys Psychologie und ihre Beziehung zur Psychoanalyse. *Psyche,* 19:242-249.

Kupper, Herbert I. and Rollman-Branch, Hilda S. (1959), Freud and Schnitzler—*(Doppelgänger)*. *J. Amer. Psychoanal. Assn.,* 7:109-126.

Lampl-de Groot, Jeanne (1947), On the Development of the Ego and Superego. *Int. J. Psycho-Anal.,* 28:7-11.

—— (1962), Ego Ideal and Superego. *The Psychoanalytic Study of the Child,* 17:94-106. New York: International Universities Press.

—— (1966), Some Thoughts on Adaptation and Conformism. In: *Psychoanalysis — A General Psychology*, eds. R. M. Loewenstein, L. Newman, M. Schur, and A. J. Solnit. New York: International Universities Press, pp. 338-348.

Laqueur, Richard (1955), *Shakespeares dramatische Konzeption*. Tübingen: Max Niemeyer Verlag.

Lavater, Lewis (1928), *Of Ghosts and Spirits Walking by Night*, ed. with introduction and appendix by J. D. Wilson and M. Yardley. London: Oxford University Press.

Lawrence, William Wibberle (1946), Hamlet and Fortinbras. *P.M.L.A.,* LXI:673-698.

Lecky, William Edward Hartpole (1869), *History of European Morals from Augustus to Charlemagne*, 2 Vols. New York and London: D. Appleton, 1919.

Lesser, Simon O. (1957), *Fiction and the Unconscious*. Beacon Hill, Boston: Beacon Press.

Levin, Harry (1959), *The Question of Hamlet*. New York: Viking Press.

Lewin, Bertram (1946), Sleep, the Mouth, and the Dream Screen. *Psychoanal. Quart.,* 15:419-434.

—— (1948), Inferences from the Dream Screen. *Int. J. Psycho-Anal.,* 29:224-231.

—— (1950), *The Psychoanalysis of Elation*. New York: W. W. Norton, pp. 103, 150f.

—— (1953), Reconsideration of the Dream Screen. *Psychoanal. Quart.,* 22:174-199.

Lewis, Clive Staples (1942), Hamlet: The Prince or the Poem. Annual Shakespeare Lecture of the British Academy. From the *Proceedings*, Vol. 30. Reprinted in: *Studies in Shakespeare*

(British Academy Lectures). Selected and introduced by P. Alexander. London-New York-Toronto: Oxford University Press, 1960, pp. 201-218.

Licht, Hans (1925), *Lebenskultur im alten Griechenland.* Wien and Berlin: Paul Aretz Verlag.

—— (1928), *Sittengeschichte Griechenlands,* 3 Vols., Zurich: Paul Aretz Verlag, 1925-1928.

Lincoln, Jackson Steward (1935), *The Dream in Primitive Cultures.* London: The Cresset Press, pp. 27-29.

Lings, Martin (1960), *Shakespeare in the Light of Sacred Art.* New York: Humanities Press.

Loening, Richard (1893), *Die Hamlet-Tragödie Shakespeares.* Stuttgart: Cotta.

Loewenthal, Leo (1957), *Literature and the Image of Man.* Boston: Beacon Press.

Lovejoy, Arthur O. (1936), *The Great Chain of Being. A Study of the History of an Idea.* New York: Harper and Row, 1965.

Luce, Morton (1902), ed. *The Tempest.* London: Methuen, 1919.

McClelland, David C. (1966), The Harlequin Complex. In: *The Study of Lives,* ed. R. W. White. New York: Atherton Press, pp. 95-119.

Madariaga, Salvador de (1948), *On Hamlet.* London: Hollis & Carter, 1964.

Mahler, Margaret S. (1968), *On Human Symbiosis and the Vicissitudes of Individuation.* New York: International Universities Press.

Malamud, William and Linder, P. B. (1931), Dreams and Their Relationship to Recent Impressions. *Arch. Neurol. Psychiat.,* 25:1081-1099.

Mann, Thomas (1929), Rede über Lessing. In: *Schriften und Reden zur Literatur, Kunst und Philosophie,* 8 Vols. 1:355-367. Frankfurt/M.: Fischer Bücherei, 1968.

—— (1946), Dostojewski - mit Massen. In: *Schriften und Reden zur Literatur, Kunst, und Philosophie,* ed. Hans Bürgin, 8 Vols. 3:7-20. Frankfurt/M—Hamburg: Fischer Bücherei, 1968.

Mannoni, Dominique O. (1950), *Prospero and Caliban. A Study of the Psychology of Colonization.* New York and Washington: Frederick A. Praeger.

Manuel, Frank E. (1968), *A Portrait of Isaac Newton.* Cambridge, Mass.: Harvard University Press.

Masefield, John (1924), *Shakespeare and Spiritual Life.* Oxford: Clarendon Press.

Mauss, Marcel (1950), Une Categorie de l'Esprit Humain: La Notion de Personne, celle de "Moi." In: *Sociologie et Anthropologie.* Paris: Bibliothèque de Sociologie Contemporain, Presses Universitaires.

Mendelson, Myer (1960), *Psychoanalytic Concept of Depression.* Springfield, Ill.: Charles C Thomas.

Menninger, Karl A. (1938), *Man Against Himself.* New York: Harcourt, Brace and Co.

Mill, John Stuart (1843), *A System of Logic.* New York: Harper and Bros., 1869.

Mitscherlich, Alexander, and Mitscherlich, Margarete (1968), *Die Unfähigkeit zu trauern. Grundlagen kollektiven Verhaltens.* München: R. Piper.

Moloney, James Clark, and Rockelein, Lawrence (1949), A New Interpretation of Hamlet. *Int. J. Psycho-Anal.,* 30:92-107.

Montagu, Ashley (1967), *Original Sin Revisited.* Rahway, N. J.: Merck & Co. Reprinted in *Reflections,* 3:2-10, 1968.

Montaigne, Michel de (1580), *Essays in the Complete Works of Montaigne,* tr. D. M. Frame. Stanford, Calif.: Stanford University Press, 1957.

—— (1580), *The Essays of Montaigne.* New York: Modern Library, 1946.

Morris, Lloyd (1947), *Postscript to Yesterday. America: The Last Fifty Years.* New York: Random House.

Mozart, Wolfgang Amadeus (1777-1791), *Liebesbriefe ans Basle, an Aloysia und Konstanze.* Mirabell Verlag, n.t. n.p.

—— (1781), Letter to his father of December 5th. In: *Mozart Briefe und Aufzeichnungen, Gesamtausgabe,* eds. Wilhelm A. Bauer and Otto Erich Deutsch, 4 Vols. Vol. 3:179-182. Kassel-Basel-Paris-London-New York: Bärenreiter, 1962-1963.

Muir, Kenneth (1952), Some Freudian Interpretations of Shakespeare. *Proceedings of the Leeds Philosophical Society,* 7:44-52.

—— (1963), *Shakespeare: Hamlet.* London: Edward Arnold Publishers, Ltd., 1963.

Murray, Gilbert (1914), *Hamlet and Orestes*. British Academy Annual Shakespeare Lecture. London: Milford.

Murry, John Middleton (1936), *Shakespeare*. London: Jonathan Cape.

Muschg, Walter (1948), *Tragische Literaturgeschichte*. Bern: Francke.

Neumann, Erich (1949), *The Origins and History of Consciousness*. Bollingen Series, XLII. New York: Pantheon Books.

Nietzsche, Friedrich (1869-1871), Aus dem Gedankenkreis der "Geburt der Tragödie." In: *Friedrich Nietzsche Gesammelte Werke*, 23 Vols. Munich: Musarion Verlag, 1920-1929, 3:169-392.

—— (1870-1871), Die Geburt der Tragödie. In: *Friedrich Nietzsche Gesammelte Werke*, 23 Vols. Munich: Musarion Verlag, 3:21-165.

—— (1875-1876), Aus den Vorarbeiten zu Richard Wagner in Bayreuth. In: *Friedrich Nietzsche Gesammelte Werke*, 23 Vols. Munich: Musarion Verlag, 7:359-377.

—— (1881-1882), Aus der Zeit der Fröhlichen Wissenschaft. In: *Friedrich Nietzsche Gesammelte Werke*, 23 Vols. Munich: Musarion Verlag, 11:129-317.

—— (1882), Die Fröhliche Wissenschaft ("La Gaya Scienza"). In: *Friedrich Nietzsche Gesammelte Werke*, 23 Vols. Munich: Musarion Verlag, 12.

—— (1882-1888), Aus dem Nachlass: Studien aus der Umwerthungszeit. In: *Friedrich Nietzsche Gesammelte Werke*, 23 Vols. Munich: Musarion Verlag, 1920-1929, 16.

—— (1884-1888), Der Wille zur Macht. In: *Friedrich Nietzsche Gesammelte Werke*, 23 Vols. Munich: Musarion Verlag, 1920-1929, 19.

—— (1886), Jenseits von Gut und Böse. In: *Friedrich Nietzsche Gesammelte Werke*, 23 Vols. Munich: Musarion Verlag, 1925, 15.

—— (1888), Ecce Homo. In: *Friedrich Nietzsche Gesammelte Werke*, 23 Vols. Munich: Musarion Verlag, 1920-1929, 21:167-286.

—— (1895), Nietzsche contra Wagner. In: *Friedrich Nietzsche Gesammelte Werke*, 23 Vols. Munich: Musarion Verlag, 1920-1929, 17:277-300.

Nunberg, Herman (1920), On the Catatonic Attack. In: *Practice and Theory of Psychoanalysis*, Vol. 1. New York: International Universities Press, pp. 3-23, 1948.

—— (1932), *Principles of Psychoanalysis*. New York: International Universities Press.

—— (1939), Ego Strength and Ego Weakness. *Amer. Imago*, 3:25-40, 1942.

Nuttall, Anthony David (1967), *Two Concepts of Allegory: A Study of Shakespeare's "The Tempest" and the Logic of Allegorical Expression*. New York: Barnes and Noble.

Ornstein, Robert (1960), *The Moral Vision of Jacobean Tragedy*. Madison and Milwaukee: University of Wisconsin Press.

Panofsky, Erwin (1943), *Albrecht Dürer*. Princeton: Princeton University Press.

Parker, Marion Hope (1955), *The Slave of Life*. London: Chatto and Windus.

Parmiter, Geoffrey de C. (1967), *The King's Great Matter*. London: Longmans, Green & Co. Ltd.

Partridge, Eric (1948), *Shakespeare's Bawdy*. New York: E. P. Dutton, 1960.

Pfister, Oskar (1913), Die Entstehung der Künstlerischen Inspiration. *Imago*, 2:481-512.

Piaget, Jean (1929), *The Child's Conception of the World*. New York: Harcourt, Brace and Co., p. 91.

Piers, Gerhart and Singer, Milton B. (1953), *Shame and Guilt. A Psychoanalytic and a Cultural Study*. Springfield, Ill.: Charles C Thomas.

Plank, Robert (1968), *The Emotional Significance of Imaginary Beings*. Springfield, Ill.: Charles C. Thomas.

Plumptre, James (1796), Observations on Hamlet. Being an attempt to prove that [Shakespeare] designed the [tragedy] as an indirect censure on Mary, Queen of Scots. *Variorum Edition*, Vol. 2, p. 236f.

Poetzl, Otto (1917), Experimentelle erregte Traumbilder in ihren Beziehungen zum indirekten Sehen. *Zeitschrift für die gesamte Neurologie und Psychiatrie*, 37.

Proser, Matthew N. (1965), Hamlet and the Name of Action. In: *Essays on Shakespeare*, ed. G. R. Smith. University Park, London: The Pennsylvania State University Press, pp. 84-114.

Prosser, Eleanor (1967), *Hamlet and Revenge*. Stanford, Calif.: Stanford University Press; London: Oxford University Press.

Pyles, Thomas (1949), Ophelia's "Nothing." *Mod Lang. Notes,* :322-323.

Quinn, Edward (1966), Mythic Criticism. In: *The Reader's Encyclopedia of Shakespeare,* ed. L. J. Campbell. New York: Thomas Y. Crowell, p. 578f.

Rangell, Leo (1968), A Further Attempt to Resolve the "Problem of Anxiety." *J. Amer. Psychoanal. Assn.,* 16:371-404.

Rank, Otto (1909), *The Myth of the Birth of the Hero.* New York: Robert Brunner, 1952.

—— (1910), Ein Traum, der sich selbst deutet. *Jahrbuch für psychoanalytische psychopathologische Forschungen,* 2:465-540.

—— (1912), *Das Inzest-Motiv in Dichtung und Sage.* Leipzip and Wien: Franz Deuticke.

—— (1915), Das "Schauspiel" in "Hamlet." *Imago,* 4:41-51.

Rapaport, David (1953), Some Metapsychological Considerations Concerning Activity and Passivity. *Collected Papers of David Rapaport,* ed. M. Gill. New York and London: Basic Books, 1967, pp. 530-568.

Reik, Theodore (1940), *Masochism in Modern Man.* New York: Farrar, Straus, 1949.

—— (1945), *Psychology of Sex Relations.* New York: Farrar and Rinehart.

—— (1949), *Fragment of a Great Confession.* New York: Farrar, Straus.

—— (1952), *The Secret Self.* New York: Farrar, Straus and Young.

Ribner, Irving (1960), *Patterns in Shakespearean Tragedy.* London: Methuen.

Richards, Ivor Armstrong (1925), *Principles of Literary Criticism.* New York: Harcourt, Brace & World.

Richards, Irving T. (1933), The Meaning of Hamlet's Soliloquy. *P. M. L. A.,* XLVIII:741-766.

Richter, Jean-Paul (1883), *The Literary Works of Leonardo da Vinci.* Revised ed. by I. A. Richter, 2 Vols. London-New York-Toronto: Oxford University Press, 1939.

Rickmann, John (1940), On the Nature of Ugliness and the Creative Impulse. *Int. J. Psycho-Anal.,* 21:294-313.

Rilke, Rainer Maria (1903-1910), *The Notebooks of Malte Laurids Brigge.* New York: W. W. Norton, 1964.

—— (1914), Letter to Marianne von Goldschmidt-Rothschild of 5 December, in *Briefe.* Wiesbaden: Insel Verlag, 1950.

Roazen, Paul (1968), *Freud: Political and Social Thought.* New York: Alfred A. Knopf.

Robertson, John McK. (1897), *Montaigne and Shakespeare.* London: A & C Black, 1909.

—— (1930), *The State of Shakespeare Study.* London: Routledge, 1931, pp. 35-39, 87.

Rothacker, Erich (1954), *Die dogmatische Denkform in den Geisteswissenschaften.* Mainz: Verlag der Akademie der Wissenschaften und der Literatur. Abhandlungen 6.

Rothe, Hans (1961), *Shakespeare als Provokation.* München: Albert Langen.

Russell, Bertrand (1955), *Nightmares of Eminent Persons and Other Stories.* New York: Simon and Schuster.

Sachs, Hanns (1919), The Unconscious in Shakespeare's *Tempest.* In: *The Creative Unconscious.* Cambridge, Mass.: Sci-Art Publishers, 1951, pp. 243-323.

—— (1924), *Gemeinsame Tagträume.* Leipzig: Internationaler Psychoanalytischer Verlag.

Sachs, Wulf (1947), *Black Hamlet.* Boston: Little Brown and Co.

Salinger, L. G. (1955), The Elizabethan Literary Renaissance. In: *The Age of Shakespeare,* ed. B. Ford. Baltimore, Md.: Penguin Books, 1964, pp. 51-116.

Sandler, Joseph (1960), On the Concept of Superego. *The Psychoanalytic Study of the Child,* 15: 128-162. New York: International Universities Press.

Sandler, Joseph et al. (1962), The Classification of Superego Material in the Hampstead Index. *The Psychoanalytic Study of the Child,* 17:107-127. New York: International Universities Press.

Sarton, George (1948), *The Life of Science.* New York: H. Schuman, 1948.

—— (1953), *The Appreciation of Ancient and Medieval Science During the Renaissance* (1450-1600). Philadelphia: University of Pennsylvania Press.

—— (1957), *Six Wings. Men of Science in the Renaissance.* Bloomington: Indiana University Press.

Saxo Grammaticus (fl. 1200), *The First Nine Books of the Danish History of Saxo Grammaticus,* trans. O. Elton. London: David Nutt, 1894.

Schell, Jonathan (1968), *The Military Half. An Account of Destruction in Quang Ngai and Quang Tin.* New York: Random House.

Schilder, Paul (1921), Über die kausale Bedeutung des durch Psychoanalyse gewonnenen Materiales. *Wiener klinische Wochenschrift,* 34:355-356.

Schmitt, Carl (1956), *Hamlet oder Hekuba. Der Einbruch der Zeit in das Spiel.* Düsseldorf and Köln: Eugen Diederichs Verlag.

Schnitzler, Arthur (1889), Die Frage an das Schicksal. *Die dramatischen Werke,* 2 Vols. Frankfurt am Main: S. Fischer Verlag, 1962, 1:30-41.

_____ (1938), The Baroque Character of the Elizabethan Tragic Hero. Annual Shakespeare Lecture of the British Academy, 1938. From the *Proceedings,* Vol. 24.

Schücking, Levin Ludwig (1919), *Character Problems in Shakespeare's Plays. A Guide to Better Understanding of the Dramatist.* Gloucester, Mass.: Peter Smith.

Scott, William I. D. (1962), *Shakespeare's Melancholics.* London: Mills and Boon, Ltd.

Seibel, George (1924), *The Religion of Shakespeare.* London: Watts and Co.

Shakespeare, William
    (a) *Hamlet,* ed. H. H. Furness. *A New Variorum Edition,* Vol. III, Part 1. Philadelphia: Lippincott, 1877.
    (b) *Hamlet,* ed. J. D. Wilson. Cambridge Edition, 1948.

Sharpe, Ella Freeman (1929), The Impatience of Hamlet. In: *Collected Papers on Psycho-Analysis.* London: Hogarth Press, 1950, pp. 203-213.

_____ (1946), An Unfinished Paper on Hamlet. In: *Collected Papers on Psycho-Analysis.* London: Hogarth Press, 1950, p. 254.

_____ (1950), *Collected Papers on Psycho-Analysis.* London: Hogarth Press.

Siegel, Paul N. (1957), *Shakespearean Tragedy and the Elizabethan Compromise.* New York: New York University Press.

Simmel, Georg (1917), *Rembrandt. Ein kunstphilosophischer Versuch.* Leipzig: Kurt Wolff Verlag.

Sisson, Charles Jasper (1936), *Lost Plays of Shakespeare's Age.* Cambridge: University Press.

_____ (1966), Jig. In: *The Reader's Encyclopedia of Shakespeare,* ed. O. J. Campbell. New York: Thomas Y. Crowell, p. 401f.

Slochower, Harry (1950), Shakespeare's Hamlet: The Myth of Modern Sensibility. *Amer. Imago,* 7:197-238.

Spencer, Theodore (1936), *Death and Elizabethan Tragedy.* Cambridge: Harvard University Press.

_____ (1942), *Shakespeare and the Nature of Man.* New York and London: Collier-Macmillan, 1966.

Spengler, Oswald (1918), *The Decline of the West,* 2 Vols. New York: Alfred A. Knopf, 1926, Vol. 1, p. 143.

Spitz, René A. (1945), Hospitalism: An Inquiry into the Genesis of Psychiatric Conditions in Early Childhood. *The Psychoanalytic Study of the Child,* 1:53-74. New York: International Universities Press.

_____ (1946), Anaclitic Depression. An Inquiry into the Genesis of Psychiatric Conditions in Early Childhood. 11. *The Psychoanalytic Study of the Child,* 2:313-341. New York: International Universities Press.

Spurgeon, Caroline F. E. (1931), Shakespeare's Iterative Imagery. In: *Studies in Shakespeare,* selected and with an introduction by P. Alexander. New York-London-Toronto: Oxford University Press, 1964, pp. 171-200.

_____ (1935), *Shakespeare's Imagery and What It Tells Us.* Cambridge: University Press, 1966.

Stedefeld, C. F. (1871), *Hamlet, ein Tendenzdrama Shakespeares gegen die skeptische und kosmopolitische Weltanschauung des Michel de Montaigne.* Berlin: Paetel.

Stengel, Erwin (1966), Review of "Medical Orthodoxy and the Future of Psychoanalysis," by K. R. Eissler. *Brit. J. Med. Psychol.,* 39:264-265.

Sterba, Editha and Sterba, Richard (1954), *Beethoven and His Nephew.* New York: Pantheon Books.

—— and —— (1956), The Anxieties of Michelangelo Buonarotti. *Int. J. Psycho-Anal.*, 37: 325-330.

Sternfeld, Fredrich William (1963), *Music in Shakespearean Tragedy.* London: Routledge and Kegan Paul.

Stevenson, Robert (1958), *Shakespeare's Religious Frontier.* The Hague: Martinus Nijhoff.

Stewart, John I. M. (1949), *Character and Motive in Shakespeare. Some Recent Appraisals Examined.* London: Longmans, 1966.

Stewart, Walter A. (1964), Depersonalization. *J. Amer. Psychoanal. Assn.*, 12:171-186.

Still, Colin (1921), Shakespeare's Mystery Play: A Study of "The Tempest." London: Cecil Palmer.

Stoll, Elmer Edgar (1919), *Hamlet: Historical and Comparative Study.* Minneapolis: University of Minnesota.

——(1933), *Art and Artifice in Shakespeare.* New York: Barnes and Noble, 1963.

Strachey, James (1957), Editorial Note: *Standard Edition of the Complete Psychological Works of Sigmund Freud,* Vol. 2. London: Hogarth Press.

Strachey, Lytton (1906), Shakespeare's Final Period. In: *Books and Characters.* London: Chatto and Windus, 1922, pp. 51-69.

Strong, Leonard A. G. (1954), Shakespeare and the Psychologists. In: *Talking of Shakespeare,* ed. J. Garrett, in association with M. Reinhardt. London: Hodder and Stoughton, pp. 187-208.

Stumpf, Carl (1906), *Erscheinungen und psychische Funktionen.* Abhl. preuss. Akad. Wiss. No. 4, Berlin.

Symons, Norman (1928), The Graveyard Scene in Hamlet. *Int. J. Psycho-Anal.*, 9:96-119.

Taylor, George C. (1925), *Shakespeare's Debt to Montaigne.* Cambridge, Mass: Harvard University Press.

Tillyard, Eustace M. W. (1943), *The Elizabethan World Picture.* New York: Vintage Books (Division of Random House).

—— (1950), *Shakespeare's Problem Plays.* Toronto: University of Toronto Press.

Tinbergen, Nicolaas (1951), *The Study of Instinct.* Oxford: Clarendon Press.

Trench, Wilbraham Fitzjohn (1913), *Shakespeare's Hamlet. A New Commentary.* London: Smith, Elder and Co.

Türck, Herman (1890), *Das psychologische Problem in der Hamlet-Tragödie.* Leipzig and Reudnitz: Hoffman.

Türck, Suzanne (1930), *Shakespeare und Montaigne. Ein Beitrag zur Hamletfrage.* Berlin: Junker und Dünnhaupt.

Ur-Hamlet (1781), Der bestrafte Brudermord oder: Prinz Hamlet aus Dänemark. *Olla Podrida,* 2: 18-68.

Van Dan. B.A.P. (1924), *The Text of Shakespeare's Hamlet.* London: Lane. *Variorum Edition* (New) (1877), See: Shakespeare, Wm. *Hamlet,* ed. H. H. Furness. Vol. III, Part 1. Philadelphia: Lippincott.

Verrall, Arthur W. (1895), *Euripides the Rationalist.* Cambridge: University Press.

Vischer, Friedrich Theodor (1878), *Auch Einer.* Stuttgart: Walter Hädecke.

Vyvyan, John (1959), *The Shakespearean Ethic.* New York: Barnes and Noble, 1968.

Waelder, Robert (1930), The Principle of Multiple Function. *Psychoanal. Quart.*, 5:45-62, 1936.

Wagner, Emma Brockway (1933), *Shakespeare's "The Tempest": An Allegorical Interpretation.* College Springs, Ohio: Antioch Press.

Waldock, Arthur J. A. (1931), *Hamlet. A Study in Critical Method.* Cambridge: University Press.

Walker, Roy (1948), *The Time Is Out of Joint.* London: Andrew Sakers, Ltd.

Weber, Max (1919), Science as Vocation. In: *Essays in Sociology,* edited and translated by H. H. Gerth and C. W. Mills. New York: Oxford University Press, pp. 129-156.

Webster, Peter Dow (1948), Arrested Individuation or the Problem of Joseph and Hamlet. *Amer. Imago,* 5:137, 225-245.

Weiner, Albert B., (1962), ed. *William Shakespeare's Hamlet.* The First Quarto, 1603. Great Neck, N. Y.: Barron's Educational Series, Inc.

Weisman, Avery D. and Hackett, Thomas P. (1967), Denial as a Social Act. In: *Psychodynamic Studies on Aging*, eds. S. Levin and R. J. Kahana. New York: International Universities Press, pp. 79-110.

Weissmann, Philip (1965). *Creativity in the Theater*. New York and London: Basic Books.

———(1968), Psychological Concomitants of Ego Functioning in Creativity. *Int. J. Psycho-Anal.*, 49:464-470.

Whitaker, Virgil K. (1964), *Shakespeare's Use of Learning. An Inquiry into the Growth of His Mind and Art*. San Marino, Calif.: The Huntington Library.

———(1965), *The Mirror Up to Nature. Technique of Shakespeare's Tragedies*. San Marino, Calif.: The Huntington Library.

Wilden, Anthony G. (1966), Freud, Signorelli and Lacan: The Repression of the Signifier. *Amer. Imago*, 23:332-366.

Williamson, Claude C. H. (1950), *Readings on the Character of Hamlet*. London: Allen and Unwin.

Wilson, J. Dover (1918), The Parallel Plots in "Hamlet." A Reply to Dr. W. W. Greg. *Mod. Lang. Rev.*, 23:129-154.

———(1936a), *What Happens in Hamlet*. New York: Macmillan; Cambridge: University Press.

——— (1936b), *The Meaning of "The Tempest."* The Literary and Philosophical Society of Newcastle-upon-Tyne.

Winstanley, Lillian (1921), *Hamlet and the Scottish Succession*. Cambridge: Cambridge University Press.

NAME INDEX

Abraham, 179, 512, 618
Adam, 313, 404, 406, 412, 432, 455
Adler, F., 388, 389, 467, 484
Adler, V., 158, 159, 160
Aeschylus, 210n
Alexander, P., 45n, 53n, 122, 142n, 151n,
    168, 175, 176, 243, 286, 302, 303,
    320, 328, 329, 332n, 347, 348, 381,
    405, 426, 610n
Aichhorn, A., 501, 507n
Aquinas, T., 182
Aristophanes, 302
Aristotle, 9n, 53n, 166-68, 170, 171, 299,
    315, 366, 410, 623
Arlow, J., 514
Augustine, 182, 223, 245
Avvakum, 282, 283

Beethoven, L. von, 378, 461, 510, 533
Benjamin, W., 594
Beres, D., 178
Bernfeld, S., 503, 508
Bernhardt, S., 336
Berry, W., 133n 213, 217n, 291n, 311,
    317, 324
Bettelheim, B., 412, 499
Bible, 207, 406, 410, 596
Bode, W., 152, 533n
Bonaparte, M., 55n
Borges, J., 35
Boring, E., 181
Born, M., 399
Borne, B., 527, 528, 529
Botticelli, 21
Bowers, F., 47n, 99n, 300
Bradley, A. C., 77n, 93n, 139 142, 242n,
    345, 413, 416, 417
Breuer, S., 56, 66
Buhler, K., 464
Burckhardt, J., 78n

Caesar, J., 405, 622
Calvin, J., 232, 245
Calderon, C., 472n, 473, 622
Campbell, L., 168, 183, 184, 185, 188,
    325n, 606
Chambers, E. K., 114n, 144, 145, 329,
    610n
Christ, 15, 165, 229, 234, 235, 294, 295,
    360, 363, 367, 370, 377, 390, 396,
    508, 607

Clements, R., 533
Coleridge, S. T., 19n, 142, 345, 397, 440
Collins, H., i, 6, 459
Copernicus, 21, 369, 406
Corneille, P., 430
Cusanus, N., 17

Danae, 12, 13
Dante, 29, 320
David, 29, 63
Davies, A. G., 125, 126, 127, 333, 334,
    335n, 337
DaVinci, L., 17, 21, 194, 196, 284, 365,
    463, 464, 510, 531, 533
Defoe, D., 29
Degas, E., 608
Delilah, 13, 617
Deutsch, H., 277n, 507, 507n
Dickens, C., 374
Dilthey, W., 120n, 475-479, 484, 486,
    488
Doyle, A. C., 344
Dostoevski, F., 5, 146n, 184n, 286, 298,
    375, 383, 384, 389, 398, 399, 497
Draper, J., 192, 193, 195, 196, 197, 198,
    199, 200, 203, 351n, 408, 426
Dührssen, A., 84n, 89n, 106n
Dürer, A., 410

Edel, L., 27, 75
Einstein, A., 363, 369, 370n, 462, 491
Eissler, R. S., 276, 533, 534
Eliot, T. S., 9, 17, 43, 132n, 150, 151,
    190, 310n, 316n, 331n, 397, 506, 507
Elton, O., 45, 77n, 230
Empson, W., 47n, 316n
Erasmus, D., 511
Erikson, E., 24, 335n, 365n, 385, 386n,
    387n, 494, 496, 501, 511, 515, 517,
    518
Euripides, 28, 29, 33, 237

Fanon, F., 373
Ferenczi, S., 376
Fergusson, F., 155, 156, 157, 160, 165,
    220, 316n, 338n, 495, 497
Flatter, R., 51, 64, 69n, 77, 86, 93n,
    113n, 119n, 124, 125n, 133, 196,
    257-262, 328n, 402, 453
Fliess, W., 163, 309n, 467, 468, 470, 515
France, A., 141, 141n

SUBJECT INDEX

Abstraction
  in inverse proportion to myth-forming
    power of science, 370
  key to New Criticism, 8
Achievement
  over- or underestimated by creator, 195
Accident
  and causation, in real world, 172
  and consummation, in *Hamlet*, 173
  and sequence, in *Hamlet*, 174
  in Aristotle and in *Hamlet*, 171
Act
  as end-product of chains of thought, 30
Adult
  tasks in unconscious, before becoming,
    296
Aesthetic experience
  not weakened by derailment into anxi-
    ety, 538
  literary and real reality in, 14
Ambiguity
  and laws of nature, 17
  and realistic presentation of uncon-
    scious processes, 132
  in plot construction of *Hamlet*, 77, 78,
    80, 86n, 87, 90
  in psychological interpretation, 22
  in Shakespeare's plays, not product of
    vagueness, 80
Ambivalence
  and classical logic, 84
  toward external demand, 102
Animals
  as ignorant of death, 376
Anxiety
  as countereffect against desire to be
    traumatized, 541
  life-saving role of, 541
  incompatible with experience of art,
    544
  mechanism counteracting man's longing
    for death, 540
Appersonation
  and enjoyment of revenge, 116
  as distinct from internalization, 279
  as one extreme of complementary se-
    ries, 281
  degree of, impossible to ascertain from
    outside, 280
  in Hamlet, and infantile aggressive
    drives against father, 179
  of ethical demand, 126

Apophasis
  function of, 119
Archaic heritage
  apparently unconquerable, 3
Art
  and external reality, 12
  as ahead of science, 31
  as contributing to science, 21
  as different from religion, in effects on
    human mind, 535
  as superior to life, 15
  form and content in, 13
  inspiration for, in philosophy, 121
Artist
  always ahead of psychologist, 470
  capable of creating what he cannot be,
    461
  potentiality of, realizable only through
    objective medium, 461
  self-assurance and independence from
    audience, 550
Artistic creation
  viewed in our time as process of self-
    healing, 557
Artistic genius
  capable of truth hidden from research-
    er, 161
Artistic production
  pattern equivalent to psychosis at core
    of, 536
  severed from author, and value in own
    right, 528
Artwork
  created in fugue state, 195
  dangers to artist, in creation of, 547
  growth of, in others' minds, 196
  inexhaustible depths of, 194, 254
  like delusion, a "correction" of reality,
    551
  not destroyed by repetition, 254
  overdetermined, like dream, 255
  separated from creator, 196
  serving function of "taming" trauma,
    536
Audience response
  and unconscious relevance, 18

Battle
  not imposed on Hamlet, but chosen by
    him, 411

Psyche
given directly through inner experience, 478
Psychic apparatus
damaged by overloading with libidinal energy, 532
Psychic resonance
in youth, 306
Psychoanalysis
Elizabethan concept of man not dissimilar to, 182
from insights to propositions, 290
now in phase like physics after Newton, 483
perverted to commonsense scheme, 484
Psychoanalytic situation
character of, 375
Psychologia comprendens
ability to penetrate to core of personality, 477
starts with totality of psychic life, 476
Psychologia explanans
derives phenomena from physiological factors, 476
uses methods of natural sciences, 476
Psychological
inquiry, favored by Elizabethan *Zeitgeist*, 181
processes, always hidden from naked eye, 401
realities
and ethical standards, 177
Psychology
abjured by New Critics, 8
conclusions verifiable, 22
essential to New Critics, 10
Psychopathology
essential to actualization of ethical standards, 285
individual and environmental, 71

Ratio
powerless in social matters, 395
Reality
and dream, in primitive societies, 57
in dreams and on stage, 55
real and created, 11
Reality events
necessary for unfolding of unconscious imagery, 267
Rebellion
of youth against fathers, 263
Reflection
blocks free access to motor system, 115
Regression
sets ego free for new object choice, 281

Reinterpretations
improvements or contradictions, 53
Religion
reflection of mankind's needs, 535
Remarriage
evidence to son of mother's carnal wishes, 267
interpreted by unconscious as adultery, 267
viewed as incompatible with chastity, 267
Reorganization
necessity for and cultural, 398
Repressed
as emerging from repressing force (Freud), 466
Revenge
in Fortinbras and Hamlet, 322
Revolution
as rejuvenating nation, 396
and extension of awareness, 396
loss of potential for, 396
Rosencrantz
interchangeable with Guildenstern, 426
victim of supraindividual battle, 427
Royalty
and neurosis, 75

Schizophrenics
observations by, and essential aspects of society, 613
Science
always leaves some areas unexplained, 480
myth-producing effect of, 363
progress of, and suffering from side-effects, 398
Scientific
findings
mythical aspects of, 362
process
curiosity, as core of, 368
progress
dependent on contradictory processes, 481
Self
early absence of borders between outside world and, 365
endangered by demands for empathy, 390
ideals of, as muffling object relations, 423
liberation of, through appersonation of task, 428
reorganization of, and ego-syntonic action, 169